D1134835

THEY ALL HAD GLAMOUR

EDWARD B. MARKS

THEY ALL HAD GLAMOUR

From the Swedish Nightingale to the Naked Lady

By

EDWARD B. MARKS

JULIAN MESSNER, INC.
New York

PUBLISHED BY JULIAN MESSNER, INC.
8 WEST 40TH STREET, NEW YORK 18, N. Y.

Pictures arranged and prepared for reproduction by Freda Browne.

SECOND PRINTING, MAY, 1944

PRINTED IN THE UNITED STATES OF AMERICA

To My Children

PHYLLIS M. SIMON

HERBERT E. MARKS

and

EDWARD B. MARKS, JR.

Contents

List of Illustrations

Introduction

A MEMORY of past excellence is an ever-increasing source of delight. It conveys the richness and the intoxication of old wine.

Records that remain of marvelous singers, stars, pantomimists and other famous stage personalities prove that they possessed an amazing genius and drawing power. Looking back and observing closely, however, they also put over the footlights vibrations that the present generation tabs "glamour," a composite of several of the God-given gifts of beauty, charm, talent, and sex appeal.

Fantastic as it may seem, since some of these charmers lived before his time, the author nevertheless soon felt as if he had actually met all the glamorous figures of this nostalgic past. The impulse to know more about them became a sort of obsession, so that he devoted to the task of research on *They All Had Glamour* even more time and effort than was his contribution to an earlier book, *They All Sang.*

Looking at it in a broad and comprehensive spirit, who will deny, apart from genius, a certain degree of "glamour" to *Jenny Lind, Christine Nilsson, Pauline Lucca, Malibran, Picolomini* and many, many other divine singers here inscribed, or dare to deny it even to the courtesans *Menken* and *Montez?* The question has been asked, What does glamour in the fair sex lead to? Drop the first two letters of the word and you have the likely answer.

Some apology may be deemed necessary for reviewing briefly the greatness of certain famous operatic divas about whom whole volumes have appeared. The writer, however, prefers in these cases to set before opera lovers an operatic hors d'oeuvre—an appetizer to a rarer operatic feast in works by trained music critics. He is sometimes indignant, however, to note how little, if anything, the younger generation knows of many world-famous singers, other than Jenny Lind, who gave an amazing measure of joy, through their art and charm, to millions, both abroad and here in America.

The artists I refer to have likewise filled an enviable niche in the past Hall of Fame of grand opera and the theater, but their fame unfortunately is gradually dwindling into the narrow, dark alley of forgotten days. In their time they swayed the hearts of men, women and empires, and their entrancing arias were carried for years, on wings of delight, from the stage below to heaven above, for we must believe the radio waves already existed, even if unknown.

A generation is held to be thirty years. Why should not intelligent and literary persons of thirty, or even those who have lived two or more generations, feel the same curiosity to know something about the musical and theatrical genius and glamour of the American stage of sixty, seventy or even eighty years ago, when this was a period that contributed so much toward American public amusement and instruction.

We remember such names as Sarah Bernhardt, Gilbert and Sullivan, Edwin Booth, Henry Irving, Ellen Terry, Offenbach, Jenny Lind, Patti, Whistler, Swinburne, Oscar Wilde, Napoleon, Eugénie, Queen Victoria, Tennyson, Edgar Allan Poe, Longfellow, George Sand, Eugène Sue, Dumas, Charles Lamb, Pinero, George Meredith, P. T. Barnum, Browning, Lord Byron, and so on. What a lush century!

But the same period, and the periods before, carried an endless list of musical and stage names that have the same right to immortality as the great battles of history, and our index indelibly carries hundreds of them.

It may be a rash thing to say, yet who knows but what with public interest created by some coteries of music lovers, such as the Gilbert and Sullivan devotees, the lives of many of these nebulous characters may flame out anew and bring new disciples of their creative genius and power of entertainment to our opera and stage of the present day. There must exist somewhere ambitious music students, who, encouraged by a recital of the geniuses of the divine art of grand opera, will be willing, with the same fortitude, patience, study and sacrifice, to reach a high goal of success.

The author is happily enriched, through a delightful flow of reminiscence, by the contributions of many word-of-mouth facts, which came to him in his youth from distinguished theatrical men in the twilight of their lives. He has been closely connected with music publishing and its theatrical ramifications for half a century. These seasoned men of the theater would relate to the author, from time to time while they lived, incident upon incident in the interesting lives of great artists often appearing under their management.

The rare originals of many of the illustrations for this book were collected through them. In years of experience as showmen, they encountered many strange events and temperamental characters, and in their chin-wags they delighted to talk of them in their relaxed moments. In this way many facts were acquired for this book, unpublished and unused before.

Happily the author also witnessed personally several early *Black Crook* productions, as well as *Around the World in Eighty Days* and every other of the original Kiralfy Brothers' extravaganzas; also several productions of *Humpty Dumpty* and other G. L. Fox pantomimic productions. Through his friend Ed Rice he saw his early *Evangeline* and other very successful productions. When Aimee came to America, with the opéra bouffes of Offenbach, he witnessed all of them in which this glamorous French star appeared, and practically all contemporary productions of any success, including every one of the cycle of Harrigan and Hart plays of New York life over a period of twenty-five years. It was his great privilege also to be present quite often during the early performances in the eighties and nineties and later the golden age of the opera, with its never-to-be-forgotten casts.

All these experiences are mentioned merely as fortunate opportunities, enabling the writer to gain impressions that he hopes to convey to the younger and other generation of readers, so that they too may, through text, illustration and reference lists, gain the same impressions and the benefit of his own personal word-of-mouth experiences.

If an all-in-one volume can collectively perform this purpose and give readers some picture of these historical and highly esteemed personalities, so that a wider knowledge of their achievement may tend to their lasting fame—that is all that any author could ask.

Finally, with no pretension to complete information, the writer wishes to acknowledge material assistance from many good friends, some of other days, some still here, including:

Max Maretzek
Andreas Dippel
Ovide Musin
Richard Grant White
Reginald De Koven
Oscar Hammerstein
E. E. (Ed) Rice
M. B. (Mike) Leavitt
Dr. Felix Guenther
James (Jim) Morrisey
K. Dehnhoff
May Davenport Seymour (Director Theatrical Division, Museum of City of New York)
Mrs. Leona Supplee Stahl
Jim Madison
Frank Caruthers
Mrs. John Scott Sanger (Descendant of the Peak Family of Bell Ringers)
Mr. Joseph Brenauer (Whose mother was a Kiralfy)
Bill Walcott and friends of the G. L. Fox Family
For incidents of Christine Nilsson's childhood
Private Gunnar Johansson Camp Campbell, Kentucky, U. S. Army

Also the New York Public Library, *New York Times, New York Tribune, New York World-Telegram, New York Sun*, and *Variety*.

As this is the "picture age," the writer has in his book endeavored to add to the interest of the reader by profuse illustration, so that hundreds of artists mentioned are represented either by photo, program or autographed letters, and in some cases by all three.

E. B. M.

PART ONE

I

The Black Crook

Introducing legs via extravaganza

IN 1879, Niblo's Garden was not all that it had been in 1866, but it retained the charm of a theater noted for its continuous successes, and what is even more surprising, it advertised the same "stupendous extravaganza" that had originally been produced there in 1866. A revival of *The Black Crook* was up on the boards, and the crowds were jamming the sidewalks to get in. As Jarrett, the original producer, had remarked: "Legs are staple articles, and will never go out of fashion while the world lasts. . . ." And behind those portals kicked some of the most voluptuous legs ever encased in full-length tights. A contemporary fashion journal remarked that tights made the ladies of the ensemble look shorter. Maybe so, but they certainly made the male patrons look longer.

A carping newspaper critic asserted that the faces of the Black Crook Ballet were far from handsome. But who cared? No one came to look at faces.

Between the acts, a scattering of small boys clung to the skirts of the crowd. They had but one desire—to crash the gate and see the show that the Rev. Mr. Smythe had described as "indecent and demoralizing." Obviously the tariff was too high for their pockets, but from time to time an oversophisticated theatergoer or a gentleman with high blood pressure would emerge and give his return check to one of the young hopefuls. This windfall made the lad's evening, and perhaps influenced the course of his life. In that crowd of small boys, "grubbing checks," stood I, kept from the audience only by the price of admission, or rather, the lack of it.

Singing out, "Check, mister?" I was lucky to approach a sailor who had decided to exchange the beauties of the ballet for the comforts of a beer hall. Almost too full for utterance, the gob was nevertheless sober enough to slip me his return ticket with a friendly and knowing wink of his only eye. Perhaps he had purchased his admission ticket at a discount of fifty per cent on the plea that he could see only half as much.

That return ticket meant to me the open-sesame to an overwhelming spectacle, the middle of the Third Act of *The Black Crook.* Full of delight and confusion, I was soon gazing down upon one hundred and fifty luscious ladies costumed in tights for the "Grand March of the Amazons." To a country lad of the period, this terpsichorean treat came as a distinct surprise. The number of girls arrayed in comparatively sinful nakedness, all kicking their heels joyfully toward the theater heaven, was a sight not to be forgotten. Charles Frohman, who "stood transfixed" at this production, the first play he had ever seen, could have been no more stunned than I.

Blind beggars soon discovered there was no better spot to glean a harvest than in front of Niblo's after the final curtain. Male patrons leaving evidently felt sorry that their sightless brethren should be deprived of such an eyeful.

A new yearning welled within me. The wrong-end-of-the-opera-glass view which I had of these beauties was far too miniature for my taste, and with an instinctive nonchalance I sought out the stage door where I waited through the damp of the night until the last coryphee tripped out and the lights were dimmed. I arrived home still enveloped in a rosy cloud of Amazons, limb for limb the fairest I had ever hoped or dared to see. Not many days later I relieved my own little tin bank—was it in the shape of a sentinel box?—of the two bits necessary to return for a gallery god's seat at the next Saturday matinee to recapture the thrill.

From my eagle's nest in the gallery, the "Bald-Headed Row" seemed miles away, and as I looked lovingly down at the first row of the orchestra I wondered whether good fortune would one day seat me so close to the stage that I could almost consider myself part of the stage ensemble.

The Black Crook from its inception was a miraculous piece of showmanship. While the version I saw was the production of the Kiralfy Brothers, they did not arrive in America until a year after the original company started performing. Therefore the history of the first company is worth recording here.

In 1866, the Messrs. Jarrett and Palmer imported an international ballet, which they had assembled by collecting artists and handsome women from the leading theaters of London, Paris, Berlin and Milan. Before embarking for the United States, they had sufficient foresight to costume the ballet in Paris. Not satisfied with the theatrical makeshifts which pass cotton off as ermine, and sateen as satin, these speculators in luxury dressed their cast in unending yards of silks, velours and real lace. The costumes were for that time daring and were considered "the last word" or, by reason of their brevity, perhaps "the last syllable."

BLACK CROOK CHORUS

1874

Grand Opera House

LESSEES and MANAGERS, ... KIRALFY BROTHERS
STAGE MANAGER, ... JOHN HAMMOND

GRAND GALA PERFORMANCE

IN HONOR OF HIS MAJESTY,

KING KALAKAUA,

And Suit, and Committee of Common Council of this City, by Special Invitation of the

KIRALFY BROTHERS.

Mason Downing will play for the grand occasion a new March, entitled

"GREETING TO KING KALAKAUA."

Every Night and at the Matinees

Will be presented the Imperial Spectacle, the

BLACK CROOK!

With the Following Cast:

MORTALS.

Rudolph Werner, a Young Painter ... Mr. W. L. Street
Count Wolfenstein ... Mr. W. A. Davenport
Hertzog, "The Black Crook," ... Mr. E. K. Collier
Greppo, his Servant, (his original character) ... Mr. Geo. Atkins
M. Von Puffengruntz, the Count's Chamberlain ... Mr. R. P. Steele
Wolfgar ... } Gipsey Ruffians } ... Mr. John Hammond
Bruno ... } in the Pay of Wolfenstein. } ... Mr. Pietro Ciuti
Casper, a Peasant ... Mr. Rushton
Dame Barbara ... Mme. B. Neuville | Carline ... Miss Annie Kemp Bowler
Amina ... Miss Flora Lee | Rosetta, a Peasant, ... Miss Lillie Pearson
Peasants, Guards, etc., etc.

IMMORTALS.

Stalacta, Queen of the Golden Realm ... Miss Lizzie Kelsey
Dragonfin, a Sprite ... Master Martin
Zamiel, the Arch Fiend ... Mr. W. A. Dubble
Redglare, Recording Demon ... Mr. J. Reilly
Skuldawelp ... Mr. Wm. Crowley

Synopsis of Scenery and Incidents.

ACT I.—HARTZ MOUNTAINS.

Song ... Carline

INCANTATION SCENE.

ACT II.—GROTTO OF STALACTA.

Duett, "Oh, ain't you awful!" ... Carline and Greppo
Songs ... Stalacta

QUARTETTE, "SILVER THREADS."

Grand Ballet Infernale, THE DEMON'S REVELS.

Composed and Arranged ... by ... IMRE KIRALFY

Introducing the Greatest Living Premiere Danseuse Assoluta,

MLLE. LUPO, KIRALFY SISTERS, Famous Secondes, Coryphees and Corps de Ballet.

ACT III.—ILLUMINATED PALACE OF WOLFENSTEIN.

Grand Ballet of all Nations ... Composed by ... IMRE KIRALFY
1.—Grand Entree, Polish, Russia and Germania ... Coryphees and Corps de Ballet
2.—Fleur d'Espagne ... [illegible]
3.—Les Sabotieres de Normandy ... Ladies of the Ballet
4.—[illegible] ... Coryphees
5.—CHARDAS ... KIRALFY SISTERS
6.—France ... Corps de Ballet
7.—America ... MLLE. LUPO
8.—[illegible] ... KIRALFY SISTERS
9.—England ... Coryphees
10.—Grand Finale, [illegible] of China, Japan and all Nations ... Premieres, Secondes, Coryphees and Corps de Ballet

Specialties.

1.—The Famous LENTON FAMILY.
2.—[illegible]
3.—The [illegible] in their GRAND TRAPEZE PERFORMANCE.
4.—[illegible]
GRAND MARCH OF THE DIAMOND WARRIORS, by 250 LADIES

TABLEAU.

ACT IV. PANDEMONIUM. ZAMIEL IN COUNCIL.

Gorgeous, new Holiday Transformation Scene, entitled the

Home of the Fairy of the Diamond Mines!

GRAND MATINEES:

Christmas Day, December 25th, } AT 1.30.
And Saturday, December 26th, }

Russian Vapor Baths, 7 West 24th street, opposite Fifth Avenue Hotel.

OPERA GLASSES TO HIRE IN THE LOBBY.

PROGRAM *KING KALAKUA*
Weary of grass skirts, the King turns to tights

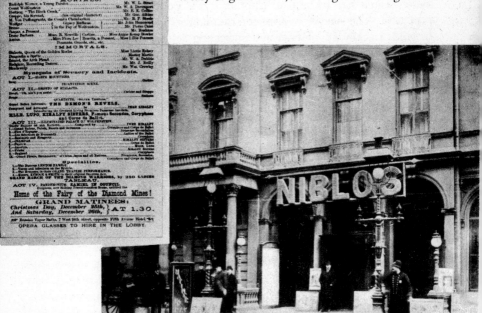

HOME OF *BLACK CROOK* FOR 16 MONTHS

With the ballet in America, Jarrett and Palmer had planned a production of *Undine* for the Academy of Music which thoughtlessly burned down. Jarrett, overwhelmed by this misfortune, stood all through the night watching his hopes literally go up in smoke. By five in the morning, with the embers still smoldering, an idea rose like a phoenix from the ashes. If they couldn't have UNDINE, they would have NUDINE instead. There was only one suitable theater in New York for this sort of spectacle, Niblo's Garden. Obviously he had to come to immediate terms with Wheatley, manager of Niblo's. In fact Jarrett surmised that Wheatley could not have heard about the Academy fire, otherwise he would have been at Wheatley's mercy. By 6:30 A.M., trading on the accepted eccentricities of his profession, Jarrett was closeted with Wheatley who, befogged at such an early hour, drew up a very favorable contract. In the midst of this important conference, to Jarrett's horror, the morning papers were delivered carrying the story of the fire that had wiped out Wheatley's competitor. A man of quick action when money was at stake, he took the papers and nonchalantly sat upon them until the signatures were safely inscribed on his contract. Unfortunately no one has recorded for posterity the language employed by Wheatley when Jarrett finally handed over the morning news, but it is a safe wager that Jarrett himself chortled.

With the theater decided upon, the immediate need was for another play through the medium of which the ballet could be presented. The ballet, which had to be paid whether it was performing or not, was quite expensive. The weekly salaries for the dancers alone amounted to $1,075 in gold. Luckily an obscure and struggling actor and author, Charles W. Barras, handed in a manuscript called *The Black Crook*, a book full of spells, enchantments, transformations and things magical. Jarrett and Palmer seized upon it as the perfect framework for the extravaganza they had conceived. Mr. Orson Welles was not yet born, so there was no competitive bidding. The plot of *The Black Crook* fortunately mattered very little. It was merely "a clothesline," as it were, on which to hang the pretty costumes. The title role was that of the magician, Herzog, a malformed, inhuman creature garbed in sinister black tights. His contribution to the action of the play was to send well-corseted females with ample bosoms, hips and legs, dancing in and out of crystal caves or kicking at the moon. The Queen Stalacta was the leading lady about whom clustered the "beautiful, varied, efficient, facile, graceful and thoroughly captivating *corps dè ballet*" and under whose feet the bewitched stage moved ponderously on rollers. There were lovers, of course, parted by magic spells and reunited by fairy charms. The *Tribune's* critic summed it up tersely: "The scenery is magnificent; the ballet is beautiful; the drama is—rubbish."

And yet, while the first performance began at 7:45 P.M. and lasted until 1.15 A.M., this same gentleman after another view of the performance shifted gears on his previous judgment and expressed the hope that the show would last till breakfast. Because of its exceeding length, not one scene of which the producers would cut, the following program notice was introduced: "Owing to the length of the performance as well as the great fatigue attendant upon the artists, it is respectfully announced that no repetition of any song or dance can be permitted."

Like many another play that made a future hit, *The Black Crook* had a not too promising history before it came to the attention of Jarrett and Palmer. Barras at first tried to get Leonard Grover of *Our Boarding House* fame to read the script, but the latter declined. Several days later, Wheatley pleaded with Grover as a personal favor to hear a play written by "my old friend, Barras." During the reading, Wheatley fell asleep. Apparently there was not enough enchantment in it for him, but Grover stayed awake and liked it, recommending it to Wheatley after his nap. The latter agreed to produce it and pay $75 a night royalties to the playwright.

With the European Ballet introduced, Barras saw great possibilities in the production and asked $1,000 per week for the sole rights to play it in New York City. Because of the high production costs and salary expenses, there was an outlay of $55,000 before the curtain rose on the first night's performance. In those days this was an enormous and unprecedented figure. Ziegfeld had not yet appeared with his priceless Follies. Part of the cost was the $10,000 which it took to buy off an unsuccessful engagement of the Ravels then running at Niblo's with six weeks more to go by contract. The Ravels must have been eternally grateful to *The Black Crook* for the unexpected, paid vacation and the escape from that horror of all theatrical performers: a half-empty auditorium due, however, to an overlong engagement. Another major expense was the carpentry work necessary to remake the entire stage for the "transformation scene"—"The Palace of Dew Drops," revealing the "Nymphs of the Golden Realm"—which the *Times* of September 3rd described as follows: "Such a stage was never seen in this country before. Every board slides on grooves and can be taken up, pushed down or slid out at will. The entire stage may be taken away; traps can be introduced at any part at any time, and the great depth of the cellar below renders the sinking of entire scenes a matter of simple machinery." Apparently the later Hippodrome and Music Hall stages were only also-rans. The author, Barras, who had learned the carpenter's trade as a small boy, must have been delighted to see what mechanical contraptions were wrought to carry out the spell sequences of his play.

In spite of the huge overhead, the money was not long in coming back. In modern parlance, it made Jarrett and Palmer front-page news. And ten years later they again hit a publicity bull's-eye, when they ran a specially chartered train from Jersey City to San Francisco, in 80 hours and 19 minutes, being sixty hours less than the regular schedule. It transported

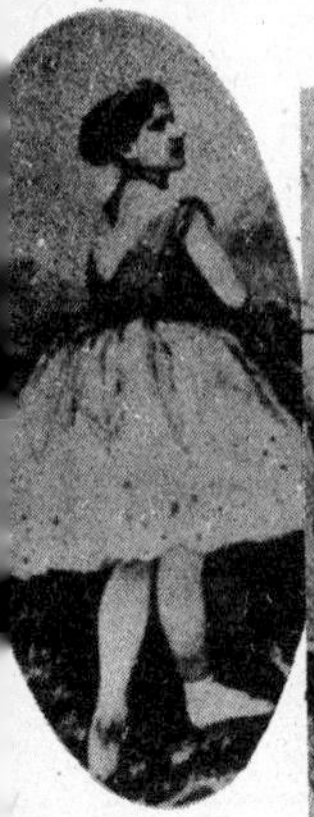

SANGALLI
Premiere
Danseuse

BLACK CROOK SCENE *PALACE OF LACE*
Extravagant even for extravanza

BONFANTI
Premiere Danseuse

NIBLO'S GARDEN INTERIOR

RUSSELL HUNTI
A devil on both sid
of the footlights

the complete production of "Henry V" which had been running at Booth's Theatre, to the California Theatre in the Golden Gate City, and was intended to forestall a rival production at the opposition Grand Opera House.

At Niblo's, *The Black Crook* had a continuous run of sixteen months. Only one change was made in the cast, due to the sudden and regretted death of Miss Nellie Cavendish, the English actress and vocalist who played the part of Carline. Miss Cavendish was the star who sang the come-hither song entitled, "You Naughty, Naughty Men," an opus composed by G. Blackwell to "poetry" by T. Kenneck, published by Dodsworth in 1865, an interpolation, since most of the music was by Operti. In the sixteen months of its run, Wheatley made $300,000 and Jarrett and Palmer the same amount, while Barras with what was left of his play after the Ballet nosed out most of the dialogue, earned $60,000. The ticket speculators of that time, headed by Bullman, made $30,000, half as much as the author.

Part of Charles Barras' large income after his original Niblo production came from farming out state rights for cash to various managers. Some of the latter endeavored to crawl under the royalty tent unobserved. For example, Tom Maguire, West Coast theater Napoleon from 1850 to 1880, bought the California rights and arranged to produce *The Black Crook* at Maguire's Opera House, San Francisco. But a rival theater endeavored to forestall him by putting on a garbled version and calling it *The Black Rook*. Maguire endeavored to obtain an injunction, but this was refused. The learned judge at some length expressed his disapproval of the "corrupt spectacle" and pronounced judgment to the effect "that the piece under dispute was not even subject to copyright since it cannot be denied that this spectacle of 'The Black Crook' merely panders to the pernicious curiosity of very questionable exhibitions of the female person."

As has frequently happened, Barras' money came not too little but too late. Three years in the United States Navy, and the rest of his life divided between acting, authoring and as a newspaperman, Barras had previously struggled for an existence. This ended only with the phenomenal success of *The Black Crook*. His one comfort in life was his beloved wife. Clara Morris, in her book of reminiscences, *Life on the Stage*, tells of the hardships of Sallie Barras, the actress wife of Charles, who, like all good troupers, went on the stage night after night in spite of being a victim of consumption. Barras had to be her dresser and her nurse so that she would have the strength to go before the footlights. They were supporting not only her mother, but also a sister. Barras told Clara: "Money might save Sallie, yet here she is, with a helpless woman over each shoulder and myself on her back." In his bitterness at her death a few months after *The Black Crook* successfully opened on September 12, 1866, Barras

AMAZON'S MARCH
COMPOSED & ARRANGED
BY
G. OPERTI.

exclaimed, "By God, when a man struggles hard all his life, it's a damned rough reward to give him a handsome coffin for his wife."

Financial success seems to have done but little for Barras, and Clara Morris remarks that later on she found him "bloodless, shrunken, lined and sorrowful and still wearing the queer wig he had affected all his life." In 1873 he fell from a train and was killed, but whether through accident or design, the reader must surmise.

There was another important factor which accounted in part for the tremendous success of *The Black Crook.* All the legitimate New York theaters carried at this period a caption at the top of their weekly playbills: "We do not advertise in the *New York Herald.*" Behind this there was quite a story. When Barnum's Museum, at Broadway and Ann Street, burned down in 1865, the redoubtable "P.T." sold for cash to the elder Bennett, publisher of the *New York Herald,* the lease of the lot on which the Museum had been located. Later on, however, Bennett changed his mind and wanted his money back. Barnum replied that he didn't drive "baby bargains," and besides, he had in the interim invested the money elsewhere. Barnum had meanwhile opened a new Museum farther up on Broadway, and Bennett exercised his umbrage at Barnum's attitude by throwing his Museum ad out of the *Herald.* Barnum, however, was a member of the New York Theater Managers Association and they withdrew their advertising from the *Herald* in a body.

To get even, as he thought, Bennett wrote this scorching *Black Crook* review: "Nothing in any other Christian country or in modern times has approached the indecent and demoralizing exhibition at Wheatley's Theater in this city. . . . We can imagine that there might have been in Sodom and Gomorrah such another place and scene, such a theatre and a spectacle on the Broadway of these doomed cities just before fire and brimstone rained down upon them and they were buried in the ruins. . . . The police should arrest all engaged in such a violation of public decency and morality." Did Bennett's vitriolic blast hurt the Niblo box office? Not so you could notice it. Indeed, it was precisely the promotion the new extravaganza needed. The police ignored the invitation to prosecute. The public turned out in droves to see whether Bennett was correct in his criticism—hoping that he was.

Ministers, after telling their congregations that no lady would dare disgrace herself by being seen at such a lewd performance, made certain of seeing it themselves so that they could obtain material for sensational sermons condemning the nakedness of the show. It was the ideal hypocritical moral atmosphere which the Brothers Minsky in later years regarded as burlesque's best friend. A good police raid, followed by a rapid reopening, was usually priceless publicity.

The most eloquent and therefore the most helpful clergyman, and who was really entitled to a weekly stipend as a Niblo press agent, was the Rev. Charles B. Smythe. He told several thousand persons gathered to hear the word of God at the Cooper Institute on November 18, 1866: "The first thing that strikes the eye is the immodest dress of the girls with short skirts and undergarments of thin, gauzelike material, allowing the form of the figures to be discernible. The attitudes were exceedingly indelicate, ladies exposing the figures from the waist to toe except for such covering as we have described. When a danseuse is assisted by a danseur, the attitudes assumed by both in conjunction suggest to the imagination scenes which one may read, describing the ancient heathen orgies." However, the Cooper Institute trustees soon made him subside, claiming that the depravity of the age did not come within the clerical scope. They were willing to see with him eye to eye—but not the naked eye. One minister averred that *The Black Crook* was making the male members of his congregation lose interest in church matters. Instead of having their ears attuned for "the pealing of the bells," they now had their eyes focused on "the peeling of the belles."

Anyone familiar with the theater, past and present, must smile when he reads the virtuous ravings of these clergymen critics. Up to the nineties, no ballet girl or member of the ensemble appeared without bodies and legs entirely covered. The "nakedness" in question was purely comparative and meant that tights were being used for the first time. A single bare leg in the sixties would have closed any theater, and just how the Rev. Mr. Smythe would have to describe "G" strings, and strip tease, and bubble dancers, will fortunately remain a pornographic mystery. Oddly enough, the society matrons and even the debutantes of that day appeared nightly in the audience in costumes so décollete that one satirical journal pronounced them as cut "V" shape in the back and "W" in front. And yet no one inveighed against society.

Part of the fascination of *The Black Crook* is indicated by the well-known story of how Barnum, then at the zenith of his popularity, and a friend attended a performance of the spectacle. Upon entering Niblo's, Barnum puffed out his chest and said, "Now watch the fuss they make over me. It's a nuisance and a lot of trouble for me to show myself anywhere. The public know me so well. . . . In a moment you'll hear them say, 'There's Barnum—there in the box.' It annoys me and spoils all my fun."

Half the audience could see him but not a murmur arose. Barnum was dumfounded. Chagrined, he stood up and leaned out of his box, pretending to size up the evening's ticket sale, but still there were no hosannas, not even polite nudges, or stolen side glances. Between the acts, Barnum tried raising his voice in speaking to his companion, but still there were no awed whispers. By this time it was obvious even to Barnum that not a

YOU NAUGHTY, NAUGHTY MEN.

Written by T. KENNICK. Music by G. BICKNELL.

Moderato.
f
p
1. I will never more de-ceive you, or of
hap-pi-ness be-reave you, But I'll die a maid to grieve you, oh! you
naughty, naughty men; You may talk of love, and sighing, say for

BLACK CROOK SONG

soul in that large theater cared whether he was present or not. The vast audience had paid to see *The Black Crook*, and Barnum realized at last that, although he considered himself part of the "greatest show on earth," here was another show that completely eclipsed him.

There was nothing static about the managership of *The Black Crook*. Since so many patrons returned again and again, the producers constantly added new attractions. In October, 1867, Richard Marston added a "Magnificent Ball Room Scene" and two new ballets—"The Bouquet" and "The Water Lily"—while less aesthetic tastes were satisfied with the "original and wonderful mechanical Donkey." One hundred and fifty children also were introduced at this time in an act called "La Garde Impériale" consisting of cavalry, chasseurs, saphirs, zouaves, drum corps, etc., going through military tactics and evolutions. The star of this appealing galaxy was "La Petite Ravel" who did her turn as "La Belle Vivandière," and was none other than Marietta of the famous Ravel family, the same whom Jarrett and Palmer had been compelled to buy off the year before.

From then on the "added attractions" came thick and fast. At the Boston Theatre in March, 1872, the featured performers were the "Wonderful Majiltons." I saw the Majiltons on the variety stage many times in later years. It was a contortion act played in fearful, diabolic black tights, with the dancers' faces made up to resemble that of Mephisto in one of his more bloodthirsty moments. There were three of these spidery creatures whose contortions finally resolved into an appropriate Grand Finale: one of the Majiltons successfully jammed the doubled-up bodies of the other two into ordinary barrels, and then proceeded with disarming abandon to roll and toss them about the stage. Perhaps this talented Majilton would have made an expert torso murderer if he had been so encouraged. The two barreled brothers at the very end of the finale proved that they were still alive and could "take it," by sticking out their legs, arms and heads from one of their barrels, and scampering off the stage with the hoops still stuck to their rear ends. This was a standard comedy hit act, equaled only by the three Lorellas, who did much the same sort of thing and achieved the coveted topliner's position for their double-jointed antics. Recently, at a neighborhood theater in New York City, a contortionist dressed as a frog attempted a comeback. He was very adept and even the modern audience recalled him again and again. But unfortunately he had no variety stage to come back to, and I fear that hunger will keep his figure rather than exercise.

By 1886 the Kiralfys had further adorned their original production with A. O. Duncan, premier ventriloquist, and the Herbert Brothers, star gymnasts, and in 1892 replaced the transformation scene with a Christmas Harlequinade. Of other interpolated talent, I am heartbroken that I never heard the Sawyer Family of Hand-Bell Ringers, my acquaintance with this sort of talent being the bell ringers who announced meal hours in summer boardinghouses. The final "added attraction" became beer and that is still another story. As far as I know, Hoboken achieved fame at only one period of American history. This was during the Prohibition era when the Hoboken beer saloons openly sold a golden, frothy liquid compounded of hope, alcohol and ether, which tasted more like beer than the rival produce served on the other side of the Hudson. Christopher Morley, slightly bemused perhaps by these foaming bumpers, and made nostalgic by the black-walnut paneling and gas fixtures of the saloons themselves, decided that what Hoboken needed to carry the public right back to the sixties was a revival of *The Black Crook* to be staged if possible near enough to the beer halls with "Tables for Ladies" to make the program of dinner and beer, the play and more beer, enticing enough to lure the residents of Manhattan across the ferry.

On March 11, 1929, at the Lyric Theatre, Morley's vision became a reality, but a reality that was indeed but a pale counterfeit of the original. Directed by Harry Wagstaff Gribble, set by C. Leon Throckmorton, with additional music by my friend Max Hirschfeld, recently deceased at the age of eighty, and lyrics by Morley himself, this revival should have been an auspicious one. Only two things were lacking: the money and the talent. This was no extravagant spectacle starring world-famous ballet dancers, but instead a tongue-in-cheek satirical production which pointed up the plot—that outmoded atrocity—and omitted all that made the original production a success. It was, however, amusing for what it aimed to do: it succeeded in making the modern audience feel far superior to those creatures of bygone days who thought this hysterically funny drama was good enough to run for 475 performances. Fortunately for the memories of the old-timers, there were some people in the audience who had seen earlier, serious revivals, such as the Kiralfys', and so had an exact basis for comparison.

I am not unmindful of the mellowing effect of time and of the halo which seems to attach itself to the glowing stage pictures of our youth. If I err in estimating the many unforgettable performances witnessed in the halcyon days of my young manhood, it is a joyful illusion and a dream from which I hope never to awaken. But about *The Black Crook* there is no mistake, and when I hear youngsters expounding their contempt for the productions of the mauve decade, basing their criticism solely on revivals such as Morley's, I pity their ignorance. *The Black Crook* of Hoboken was in no way comparable to the $55,000 production of Jarrett and Palmer. Where was the world-famous ballet, where the magnificent extravaganza?

In much the same way, young moderns have a tendency to judge the

ROSINA

FAWDON

JESSIE

THE VOKES FAMILY

In 1872 Bonfanti appeared with these stage favorites

VICTORIA

FRED

dramatic portrayals of Booth, Irving and Barrett, or the comedies of the Augustin Daly and Lyceum Stock companies, by the revivals of the countless "Drunkard" or "Fireman-Save-My-Child" shows. In the days when they were first produced, these latter entertainments such as *Bertha, the Sewing Machine Girl, The Fatal Wedding,* and *Nellie, the Cloak Model* were admittedly a cheap brand of tear-jerking "meller-drammer." They were our modern pulp magazines in the dramatic language of that era. They were written by the Kremers, acted by the Corse Paytons, and they catered to the tastes of the popular-priced fifty-cent circuits.

But make no mistake about one thing. To write these cheap "mellers" required really more constructive effort than do many of the higher-grade dramatic offerings of today. They usually consisted of four acts and ten to twelve scenes, each of the latter calling for a sensational climax. If you think that an easy stunt, try it yourself. Old-timers still refer lovingly to the palmy days of melodrama, where in the first act the villain kidnaps the heroine; in the second act he locks her up in a deserted building which he sets on fire; in the third act he throws her off Brooklyn Bridge, but in the fourth act—ah, in the fourth act, he places his hand tenderly on her shoulder and says, "Why do you fear me, Nellie?" Irish plays showed to millions and earned for themselves the sobriquet of "the servant girl's delight." Favorite stars therein were William J. Scanlan and Chauncey Olcott. The latter's beautiful Saratoga cottage, a show place of luxuriant plant life, was once described as "Queen Anne" in front and "Mary Ann" in back.

Morley's gift for publicity truly made the opening night an occasion. The entire Board of Directors of the Theatre Guild were present, as was David Belasco, whose honored presence was affectionately cheered by the audience. So far as I know, the last *Black Crook* revival took place at the Federal Theatre, Los Angeles, on August 20, 1936, and thus, after seventy years, that amazingly successful spectacle was still holding the boards, a true indication of its unfailing possibilities. And who knows but that at the very minute I write these words some other enterprising producer is saying to himself, "I'll try 'The Black Crook' next—a streamlined version, with Stuka bombers in the Underworld scene and the Clipper in the Grand Finale."

Many famous names of theater's history saw the light of day, or rather the calcium light of night, in one production or another of this perennial extravaganza. While its co-operative splendors no doubt handicapped opportunities for individual stardom, at least three European ballet dancers were destined to become American favorites. The Grand Opera in Paris contributed both Marie Bonfanti and Betty Rigal to the original company of *The Black Crook,* while Berlin and London mourned the

LOUISE MONTAGUE
Forepaugh's ten thousand dollar beauty

LYDIA THOMPSON
Delight of the stage-door Johnnies

PAULINE MARKHAM

AMELIA SUMMERVILLE
The merry little mountain maid

absence of Rita Sangalli, another première danseuse. Of these three, Bonfanti grew to have the most fabulous name.

Born in Milan in 1841, she made her first professional appearance at thirteen as a ballet dancer in Madrid, a city which boasted of its great appreciation for fine dancing. She received her classic training under the best ballet masters in Europe, becoming a gifted pantomimist and a thorough mistress of the technique of her art. Absolute certainty of execution was hers, each movement being dramatic and poetic in conception. Bonfanti was blessed with beauty of both face and figure and enough stamina to appear at every single performance of *The Black Crook* during its record-breaking first run. Then she sought the opposite of the chromatic scale, and appeared in *The White Fawn* in 1868 which featured a revival of "La Source." This opus supplied sufficient numbers of silvery glades and mysterious lakes or settings for water sprites, wood nymphs and all those other half-fairy, half-mortal creatures who are expected to express themselves in the delicate language of ballet. Unfortunately for Bonfanti's adoring public, *The White Fawn* labored under an advance expenditure of $75,000 which it was unable to return with proper dispatch to the investors, so the curtain fell on its one hundred and fiftieth performance, and thus, the "fawn" became a "pawn."

In May, 1869, Bonfanti appeared in the rebuilt Academy of Music in a unique production of the opera *Lurline* by Wallace. It was sung by two casts, English and Italian, who alternated, giving the effect of a living libretto. Fortunately for posterity, this double dose of operatic riches did not go down so well with the public and the theory that in grand opera it is the music and not the words that count survived the test of time. Imagine, if you can, a double-length, bilingual *Parsifal*.

In 1872, with the Vokes family, Bonfanti appeared at Niblo's in *The Children of the Wood*, starring in two superb ballets: "Gossamer Dreams" and "The Fall of the Leaf." Two years later she was featured in *Jack and Jill* and in 1876, when Augustin Daly produced his play, *Life; a Comedy of City Types*, Bonfanti appeared as "The Spirit of the Sun" in an elaborate "Show Ballet." In 1879, she reappeared in her original role in *The Black Crook*, this time in the Kiralfy production which I saw, but from then on, she danced only once in a while until her retirement in 1891. Three years later, the Sun Beam, the Dew Drop, the Snow Flake, startled New York by descending to the earth for the mundane purpose of opening a dancing school in Union Square. Success was hers, and four years later found her moving to new studios on the east side of Longacre Square between 46th and 47th streets; where I made her acquaintance.

So far as is known, Marie was publicity shy and gave only one press interview in her life, to a reporter of the *New York Dramatic Mirror* on July 17, 1909. The writer found her face charmingly mobile, and her hair

TO

Mr. NELSON GRIGGS,

NEW YORK.

BRANIGAN'S BAND.

Popular Marching Song,

AS SUNG BY

MISS LYDIA THOMPSON.

WORDS BY

CHARLES A. BURKE,

MUSIC BY

W. F. WELLMAN, JR.

Author of American National Guard Song March, Leo March, &c.

Song for Piano,	.35	Violin and Piano,	.50
March for Piano,	.40	Cornet and Piano,	.50
Four Hands, Piano,	.60	Military Band,	.75
Violin,	.10	Small Orchestra,	.75
Cornet,	.10	Large Orchestra,	1.50

New York.

Published by W. F. WELLMAN, Jr., 39 East 13th St.

CHORUS.

Mark time, keep step, for - ward, march a - way!........ With

mf

eyes out, toes in, march in grand ar - ray......

cresc. *f* *fz*

Shoul - der arms, with head e - rect, to - geth - er hand in hand,.... Like

he - roes bold, the young and old will March with the Bran - i - gan's Band.

untouched by gray. It is nice to know that "beneath the short knee-skirt she wore, to facilitate her teaching, there peeped out a very shapely pair of trim, tastefully stockinged ankles." With a regretful sorrow common to all retired stage luminaries, she heaved a sigh over her scrapbook pictures of years before. A solitary tear might even have fallen above the likeness of her bosom on which nested a stuffed pigeon—a contented-looking stuffed pigeon, it is needless to state.

In the midst of the interview, the *Mirror* reporter mentioned the name of a woman who was attaining a vogue of some proportion as a "Greek" dancer, often appearing with the aid of one of the best orchestras in the country. Madame Bonfanti smiled broadly at the name. "She is very foolish," she said. "She does very foolish things; you don't know what they mean. She is crude in everything. She has good ideas—a good appreciation of melody—but the dancing! It's simply too ridiculous." Perhaps in the light of this contemporary criticism, it would have been better had Bonfanti maintained an artistic silence to the end of her life, for the ridiculous dancing of which she spoke was that originated by Isadora Duncan.

Jennie Reiffarth, dramatic soprano, played in German stock at the old Stadt Theatre on the Bowery, later known as the Windsor, until a production of *The Black Crook* in San Francisco gave her a chance at an English-speaking part. Later Miss Reiffarth stormed the Metropolitan Opera with Parepa-Rosa until a serious attack of diphtheria affected her vocal chords, and she returned to the dramatic stage with a versatility that found her playing Shakespearean roles one year and burlesque the next, and affording artistic support to John McCullough, Lawrence Barrett, Edwin Booth, Edwin Adams, Nat Goodwin, Henry Dixie, David Warfield, Maurice Barrymore and, as late as 1906 and 1907, Wilton Lackaye.

Then, too, Charles Dickson, comedian and playwright, who authored the successful *Three Twins*, began his career as a super in *The Black Crook*. Whether he carried a spear for an Amazon or went up in smoke in the transformation scene is a secret lost to history. Russell Hunting, inventor of many early phonograph contraptions, who authored and recorded millions of the famous "Casey" records, played Mephistopheles in *The Black Crook*.

Even Miss Fanny Davenport, one of America's foremost dramatic actresses, once appeared in *The Black Crook* as Amina, beloved of Rodolphe, at Whitman's Continental Theatre in Boston. My friend, May Davenport Seymour, is the niece of Fanny Davenport and the daughter of William Seymour, for many years Charles Frohman's stage manager. As befits the descendant of the famous theatrical Davenport family, Miss Seymour is now the curator of the Theatrical Division of the Museum of the City of New York, where she has successfully presented more than thirty illustrative exhibits of the early stage and stage personalities of old

New York. The previews of these fascinating special exhibitions are crowded with white-haired performers of years gone by, eager to see again the dagger they clutched as Lady Macbeth or the crown of paste jewels that encircled their noble brows as King Lear.

Louise Montague, known later as Adam Forepaugh's "ten-thousand-dollar beauty," made her first appearance on any stage in *The Black Crook* as a member of the ballet. With the assistance of her alluring limbs and a few friends, she graduated to the Rentz-Santley Burlesque Troupe, studied voice to augment her gifted legs, and landed the job of "principal boy" in Henderson's Chicago Extravaganza, which also first brought Eddie Foy into prominence.

Finally, good-natured Amelia Summerville was a ballet dancer for two years in *The Black Crook*. She thereafter made her greatest hit in *Adonis*, where her ample figure added to the humor of her song, "Merry Little Mountain Maid." Who knows but that is where our more recent Billy Watson first got his "Beef Trust" ideas. I knew Amelia Summerville when she still was quite slender. At that time she was the "apple" of my eye: later she became its cantaloupe.

The Black Crook paved the pathway of public approval for Lydia Thompson's "British Blondes" who made their American debut at Wood's Museum, originally Banvard's and later to become Daly's Theatre. Miss Thompson appeared in burlesques that were really entertaining and enlisted for her support such talented players as Rose Coghlan, Harry Beckett, Lisa Weber and Eliza Weathersby, later the first of Nat Goodwin's numerous wives. In fact, my friend of the nineties, Rennold Wolf, famous New York toastmaster, once remarked that if a lady stopped him on the street and he, at the moment, could not recall her name he was reasonably safe in addressing her as "Mrs. Goodwin." As for the Blondes themselves, many of them were really beautiful and such "nice girls too," and very particular about the sort of attention showered on them by gentlemen, "dontcher know." And were they choosy? Well, ra-a-ather. One of them married a Columbia University professor, and no matter how much he knew about geometry, she soon taught him that a curved line is the most attractive distance between two points.

II

The Brothers Kiralfy

Presenting four hundred years of American history in one evening

IMRE KIRALFY had various qualifications that justified his being acclaimed the biggest theatrical promoter of his day. First among these was his capacity for making money for his backers as well as for himself; in fact, he was a Midas among showmen. He thought in terms of pageants, but pageants that people were willing to pay money to see. And while he was famous for the lavishness of his productions, he also kept a weather eye on the box office, so that when the day of ultimate reckoning rolled around there was no carmine ink used in the Kiralfy ledgers: Imre, Arnold and Bolossy, three names with which to conjure. Pronounced among the differences between these gifted gentlemen of a bygone day and our modern Mr. Billy Rose was their talent for envisioning impossible stage pictures and then overcoming all the technical difficulties involved. No projected scene was too complex for their ingenious contriving. The water problems of the World's Fair *Aquacade* would have been kindergarten work for the men who created *Venice* on dry land.

An actor in Budapest when only four, a student of music and a featured dancer in the principal theaters of Germany, Imre Kiralfy did not begin to organize pageants and processions until he was twenty-three, when in 1868 he designed and directed a monster public fete for the city of Brussels. This "supercolossal" effort included pantomimes, operas and sporting events with a military spectacle which involved the maneuvers of four thousand soldiers, or in modern war lingo, almost enough to form a second front. There was nothing limited about the imagination of the young entrepreneur. He was never really happy unless he was trying to present entire civilizations within the visual limits of a single audience. A brief list of some of his successes will indicate the scope of his theatrical attainments: *Around the World in Eighty Days, The Fall of Babylon, Nero and the Burning of Rome, Columbus,* in collaboration with P. T. Barnum; *Venice, America, India,* etc.

The Kiralfys' first production in the United States was the Jules Verne classic, *Around the World in Eighty Days,* that breathless epic of transportation and intrigue. This play toured the country with unqualified success. From a story told me by Gus Hill, the Champion Club Swinger of the World, it took an atheist singlehanded to secure from managers higher terms than this money-making production. According to Gus, while Robert Ingersoll was at the Walnut Street Theatre in Philadelphia inviting God to strike him dead, an invitation luckily ignored by the Deity, his contract called for 75 per cent of the gross receipts. "Just think," said Ingersoll's manager, "last week the Kiralfy Brothers were in this theatre with their tremendous spectacular show 'Around the World in Eighty Days.' They carried a company of several hundred persons, and received only 60% of the receipts while Ingersoll single-handed for defying the Lord, gets 75% nightly."

The Kiralfy *Black Crook* of 1879 was the one I was privileged to attend and the luxurious settings so dazzled me that I was won over completely and never missed a Kiralfy production thereafter. In spite of the glories of the Jarrett and Palmer offering of 1866 with its imported luxuries, Imre, in an interview, proclaimed his settings far superior: "There were aesthetic faults in the old spectacle that cultivated audiences of today would not tolerate for a moment. You see, they have been educated up to a higher standard." And all this improvement in thirteen years. Nevertheless, there were eighteen scenes in *The Black Crook* and a small model was made for each one, an innovation in those days. Imre's declared favorite was "The Palace of Lace." He described it in the *New York Dramatic Mirror* for February 15, 1879: "The architecture is exceedingly elfish, and you can see lace on myriad forms draping a hundred portions of the scene."

In Boston, the Kiralfys played at the Globe Theatre. The proprietor, John Stetson, was known for his amusing blunders of speech or malapropisms, a word coined from Mrs. Malaprop's errors of speech in Sheridan's *The Rivals*. These were quoted in the papers just as Sam Goldwyn's are quoted by contemporary columnists. One day Stetson, according to Louis Sharp, his stage manager, saw a big sign outside his theater reading: "Grand Matinee Today at 2 o'clock Sharp." He rushed inside to find Louis, dragged him out to the sidewalk and yelled, "I want it distinctly understood that I am manager of this theater. Change that sign to read: 'Grand Matinee Today at 2 o'clock Stetson.' " On another occasion, when advised that the theater's orchestra would have to be enlarged for a current musical show, Stetson growled, "This orchestra is big enough for any show. I watched it every night last week and that little fellow in the corner with the drums doesn't play half the time. I intend to read the riot act to him."

For the Kiralfys nothing was too big. For example, at the *Burning of Rome*, Nero fiddled in the presence of fifteen hundred supernumeraries, which might be termed "keeping the home fires burning" with a vengeance.

The Kiralfys took *Nero*, produced here in 1888, to London's Olympia in 1890. Taking *Nero* anywhere, much less across the ocean, was a task that can only be appreciated by glancing at the program, which briefly gives the contents of the Five Tableaux involved. The First merely introduced the audience to various aquatic festivities, the Second really got going by revealing Nero's Triumphal Procession through Rome, the Third modestly presented the interior of Nero's Palace during an Orgy. At this point a Bacchanalian Chorus was provided. The Fourth disclosed the Circus Maximus itself during Olympian games, which included with a fine disregard for the sensitivities of the audience: Chariot Races, Gladiatorial Combats, Living Torches and Christian Martyrs, the latter in the act of being martyred. The Fifth, and Final, Tableau presented the Revel of Torches leading up to the promised Burning of Rome, Apotheosis of the Dawn of Christianity.

In his pursuit for better means of technical production, Imre was the first to replace calcium and gas lights with electricity. One of his sisters recommended a nice, quiet young man to install them. This obliging person was Thomas Edison, who in later years confessed that amid such a conclave of feminine allure it was difficult to keep his mind on his work.

There were also several Kiralfy sisters—in those days, mothers did handsomely by the census—all of them dancers, and one is still living in luxury mingled with trepidation in London, hobnobbing with royalty and turning her back on her own stage career. It was this reformed lady who, on a visit to New York many years ago, secured an injunction against any press articles relating to the Kiralfy Family and especially those connecting them with *The Black Crook*, an ironic twist to a success story. Apropos, our more modern Lillian Russell, while not at all squeamish about her humble start at Tony Pastor's, would not admit that she had ever appeared in tights. While engaged at Weber and Field's Broadway Music Hall, Sam Bernard showed her a photo from the Albert Davis Studio, showing her very definitely in tights—and quite snug-fitting ones at that. Lillian snapped, "I never sat for that picture," "No," wisecracked Sam, "you had to stand for it."

The Kiralfy Brothers themselves were never actuated by any manifestation of false pride; in fact, they took a most active and workaday part in the preparation of all their productions. In spite of the grandeur of the

KIRALFY'S *EXCELSIOR* PROGRAM

NIBLO'S GARDEN
the GRANDEST THEATRE IN THE U.S.
Poole & Gilmore, Proprietors and Managers.

NEW YORK, WEEK ENDING SEPTEMBER 1, 1883.

SOHMER
PIANOS,
Are Preferred by Leading Artists,
149 TO 155 EAST 14th ST., N.Y.

MANHATTAN
INN.
JOHN RONAN,
589 Broadway,
BRANCH OF
493 BROADWAY.

Every Evening & Wednesday & Saturday Matinees,
First Appearance in America of the
KIRALFY BROTHER'S
Specially Imported European Organization, comprising
The Parisian Eden Theatre Ballet Company,
The Venetian Ballet Troupe,
And the most distinguished artists of
THE SCALA THEATRE IN MILAN,
In the great Mimical Dramatic Ballet Spectacle,

EXCELSIOR

By L. MANZOTTI. Music by MARENCO.
REPRODUCER OF THE BALLET.... Sig. ETTORE COPPINI
The Spectacle is in Three Acts. 15 minutes intermission between Acts.

COSTUMES designed by DRANER & CLEDAT de LAVIGERIE of Paris, and WILHELM of London. Manufactured by Messrs MAREST FRERES, Mons LANDOLF, of Paris, Miss FISCHER, Mr. ALIAS, of London, and Mrs. LORAINE, of New York.
ACCESSORIES by Signor GROCE, of Eden Theatre, Paris, Signor BANCATI, of Milan, CH. BLESSER and WILLIAM SMITHLYN, of New York.
NOVEL ELECTRIC EFFECTS by the Edison Electric Light Company, under the Personal Direction of Mr. THOS. EDISON.
MECHANICAL EFFECTS.................by Mr. W. CRANE and Assistants
SCENERY and MACHINERY.................by Mr. FRANK SMITH
SCENERY PAINTED...by H. E. HOYT, HARLEY MERRY and ED. ROEMER
GAS EFFECTS and ELECTRIC GAS LIGHTING................by EMMETT DAVIDSON and Assistants
ORCHESTRA CONDUCTED................by Mr. A. W. HOFFMAN
The entire Grand Spectacular produced by and under the personal Direction and Supervision of
IMRE and BOLOSSY KIRALFY.
Sole Proprietors and Managers of "Excelsior."

—CHARACTERS IN THE DRAMA.—
LIGHT.......................Mlle NANI
DARKNESS.......................ETTORE COPPINI
.......................Miss FLINDT
.......................SIG. CONTI
.......................SIG. FAROANE

KNABE
PIANO-FORTES,
UNEQUALED IN
Tone, Touch, Workmanship and Durability.
WILLIAM KNABE & CO.
No. 112 FIFTH AVENUE, N.Y.

RUNKEL BROS
VIENNA SWEET
CHOCOLATE

FISCHER
ESTD 1840.
PIANOS
RENOWNED FOR
TONE & DURABILITY
WAREROOMS & FACTORIES: 415 TO 427 W. 28TH ST.
& 867 BROADWAY COR. 18TH ST. NEW YORK
55.000 NOW IN USE.

METROPOLITAN HOTEL
"CAFE"
RESTAURANT

KIRALFY'S *AROUND THE WORLD IN 80 DAYS*

themes handled, Imre and Bolossy never neglected a detail and they rehearsed their choruses—unadulterated drudgery—in addition to taking charge of the complicated problems of choreography. Otis Skinner, who worked under Bolossy in *Enchantment* in the role of Maclow, "a sort of compound of the Black Crook, the Apothecary in 'Romeo and Juliet' and King Lear" . . . describes Bolossy at work: ". . . excitable foreigner with a long stick with which he thumped the measure of the dancing steps, and his voice, hoarse with shouting and a chronic catarrhal cold, barking out, 'Von—two—tree! Von—two—tree! No—no! Stop! Vot's de matter mit de back line? No, please—please! Ladies! Ladies! Vonce more! —Von—two—tree . . .' "

Otis Skinner attempts to describe these chorus girls as well as their ballet master. In his reminiscences he calls them "a decent, domestic, hard-working lot," assures us that many of them were "breadwinners of families, good mothers and wives" and that there were neither carriages waiting for them at the stage door, nor were there silks and sealskins in which to drape their comely bodies. ". . . When they shed their pink tights and tarleton skirts and dressed for the street, they looked like a company of milliners' workers." Personally, I find this a depressing picture. It would seem to reflect on the generosity of the Kiralfy Brothers where salaries were concerned, and on the charm of the ladies of the ensemble where gentlemen were concerned. I prefer to remember these same creatures as beautiful, magnetic bits of differing personalities carrying off stage as well as on the aura which the theater generously gives to its devotees.

"Imre Kiralfy's Sublime, Nautical, Martial, and Poetical Spectacle: *Columbus and the Discovery of America*" was offered to an admiring public in 1891 and again in 1892, the second production in connection with Barnum and Bailey's "Greatest Show on Earth." Undaunted by the weight of its adjectives, *Columbus* was an unqualified success. Those three great showmen working in harmony were responsible for one of the extravaganzas which helped to make American theatrical history. If we are to believe the introduction to the libretto, the producers were perfectly delighted with each other. The circus men caroled, "While unlimited means have been placed at his disposal, Kiralfy has utilized them with rare judgment and effect, and the result is a most splendid and impressive series of classic displays and tableaux"; Kiralfy paid tribute, "The huge amphitheatrical tent expressly designed and constructed by the Messrs. Barnum and Bailey for that purpose, affords the only opportunity for the successful presentation of a series of realistic tableaux and processions far grander than anything heretofore attempted, and for the display and utilization of scenic effects, which of necessity must be proportionately colossal."

KIRALFYS' UNRIVALLED COMPANY!
Start Every Evening at 7.45 and Saturday Afternoon at 1.30 on their Great

TRIP AROUND THE WORLD!

Tickets for the Trip can be obtained at the Box Office.
Admission.........50c., $1.00 & $1.50

Academy of Music

BY ... AND ...

THIS TICKET ENTITLES THE HOLDER TO A FIRST-CLASS PASSAGE

ACADEMY OF MUSIC.

At 7.45 | Issued by the Kiralfy Bros.

LONDON.

THE ECCENTRIC CLUB ROOMS. Aristocratic Fast Life. A Gigantic Robbery. The Wager of £100,000 that the World cannot be traveled 'round in 80 days. The Start.

Box Office open from 8 A. M. to 10 P. M:

At 7.55 | Issued by the Kiralfy Bros.

In AFRICA, ÉGYPT.

WHARF AT SUEZ. A Magnificent Robbery. Consular interference. A Duel. No detention. Arrival and Departure of the "Magnolia."

At 8.10 | Issued by the Kiralfy Bros.

In ASIA, HINDOSTAN.

The BUNGALOW, exhibiting effects of conflicting creeds. Buying an Elephant. The Tourists successful. The Queenly Sacrifice.

At 8.16 | Issued by the Kiralfy Bros.

India. Pagoda of Pillarye

GRAND PROCESSION of BRAHMIN PRIESTS AND THEIR ARMY! A Gorgeous Pageant. Resuscitation and Cremation. A Battle and Rescue. Grand Tableau.

At 8.30 | Issued by the Kiralfy Bros.

CALCUTTA.

BEAUTIFUL VIEWS OF THE SUNNY CITY FROM THE VERANDAH OF THE GREAT EUROPEAN HOTEL. An American in Bad Luck. Off Again.

OVERLAND ROUTE
TIME, 80 DAYS!
DISTANCE, 25,000 MILES.
Countries visited that are unfrequented by general tourists SEE THE EASTERN CLIMES!

At 8.40 | Issued by the Kiralfy Bros.

BORNEO.

GARDENS OF NAKAHIRA'S PALACE. Brilliant Oriental Festival. The Fetish Dances, and Oriental Groupings by lovely maidens in sumptuous attire.

Academy of Music

Academy of Music! Trip Ticket AROUND THE WORLD!

At 9.05 | Issued by the Kiralfy Bros.

AMERICA.

A CALIFORNIA RAILROAD SALOON. A confidence game. The robbery by Fix. The Valet in a bad plight. Saved! Saved!

EVERY Evening —AT— 7.45 —AND— Saturday MATINEE AT 1.30

At 9.12 | Issued by the Kiralfy Bros

ON THE C. P. R. R.

KEARNEY STATION in the WILDERNESS AT MIDNIGHT. Realistic Effect. The Sioux on the War-Path. The Train in the Gorge. Arrival of the Express. The Indian Attack and the Capture.
The trip can be taken now—delays are dangerous

OVERLAND ROUTE
TIME, 80 DAYS!
DISTANCE, 25,000 MILES.
Countries visited that are unfrequented by general tourists SEE THE EASTERN CLIMES!

At 9.36 | Issued by the Kiralfy Bros.

In the Rocky Mountains.

THE GIANT'S STAIRWAY. U. S. Troops on duty. The cunning device, and Capture of Indians. The Women Regained. Off again to New York.

Academy of Music! Trip Ticket AROUND THE WORLD!

At 9.58 | Issued by the Kiralfy Bros.

On the Atlantic Ocean.

CABIN of the "HENRIETTA." A Robber robbed. A compulsory sale, and alteration of route. To Liverpool instead of Bordeaux. The new Captain and his jolly Mate. Lady passenger and recognition of the Detective.

EVERY Evening —AT— 7.45 —AND— Saturday MATINEE AT 1.30

At 10.15 | Issued by the Kiralfy Bros.

Deck of the "Henrietta."

COAL RUNS SHORT. Woodwork used for fuel. The boilers burst. The life-boats launched. Wreck of the steamer. She sinks beneath the waves. One of the most realistic stage pictures ever seen. A waif on the Ocean.

OVERLAND ROUTE
TIME, 80 DAYS!
DISTANCE, 25,000 MILES.
Countries visited that are unfrequented by general tourists SEE THE EASTERN CLIMES!

At 10.25 | Issued by the Kiralfy Bros.

IN EUROPE.

AT LIVERPOOL. Test of friendship. How a day may be gained in traveling around the World. A mistake rectified. The arrest and sacrifice. Nearly too late! Yet all is well and ho! for London.

Academy of Music! Trip Ticket AROUND THE WORLD!

At 10.40 | Issued by the Kiralfy Bros.

LONDON.

ECCENTRIC CLUB'S NEW PALACE. Just in time, the Trip made in Eighty Days. Fond Hearts united. Magnificent Gala Fete, and a Triple Wedding.

Academy of Music

EARLY PUBLICITY
THROW-AWAY STUNT

Columbus was a theatrical feast for its audiences. Female slaves sang, starving people rioted, handmaidens presented "a romantic and picturesque series of entrancing dances" and the Moors marched off to defeat by the Spaniards. Columbus, who knew a propitious moment when he saw one, again asked for funds and was rewarded by Isabella in the famous words, "I will undertake the enterprise for my own crown of Castile, and will pledge my jewels if the funds in the treasury are found inadequate." The circumstance blazed the trail for a very successful vaudeville gag. A sketch team raised the question as to who was the more responsible for the discovery of America, a man or a woman. The male of the team declared it was a man, Christopher Columbus. The female member insisted it was a woman, Queen Isabella, who in order to provide Columbus with the necessary funds had pawned her jewels. "Very true," echoed the man, "but who gave Isabella the jewels?"

Returning to the spectacle, after showing his three boats, the *Niña*, the *Pinta*, and the *Santa Maria* riding at anchor, Columbus was observed quelling a mutiny in mid-Atlantic and praying for joy at the sight of land. The land itself was no mean spectacle with Imre's crowds of Red Indians who imprudently traded their golden nose rings for glass beads. The triumphal return to Barcelona was depicted with untiring detail and the various choruses were described in song. My favorite for purely personal reasons remains:

Ha! Ha! The jovial students pass,
Laughing in careless fancy free;
They much prefer the lute and glass
To working hard for their degree.

The presentation ended with "A Grand Finale of Joy." Imre, in his treatment of certain subjects, approved of the ostrich technique. If poor Columbus was thrown in prison at the end of his career, it was news to Imre, particularly if the prison was small and completely without dancing girls or even one volcano. Everything about his productions had to be on a large and lavish scale. Unpleasant episodes were introduced only if they had a sufficiently spectacular setting, such as the martyr scenes in *Nero*. A sad, solitary Columbus in a narrow cell gnawing on a piece of dry bread would offer nothing to the costumer, less to the scenic artist. If Columbus had lived today, Imre might have included this episode in the hero's life. A modern concentration camp would have given scope to his talents. The casts are large. The acreage ample. And the drabness of the scene would have been canceled by the ferocity of the guards and the sparks from the electrified barbed wire that imprisons the innocent.

At the World's Fair in Flushing Meadows, a spectacle called *The American Jubilee* was offered to a most responsive audience, in 1939-1940. There was an historical bit about George Washington, another about

LILLIAN RUSSELL
Who claimed she never appeared in tights

BARNUM ANI
HIS FOUR DWARF

A monarch of the old-time circus worl

OTIS SKINNER
Who white-washed the *BLACK CROOK* shows

IMRE KIRALFY (to the right of Queen Mary)
With royal personages and English notables

Lincoln, and a fine reading of the Gettysburg Address. The rest of the performance was dedicated to Jenny Lind, singing firemen, young ladies on tandem bikes, Lillian Russell under a panoply of plumes, that sterling American, Diamond Jim Brady, and Joe Jackson, famed tramp cyclist. Beyond question, the entertainment value was high, but whether the show gave an appropriate picture of the American scene is doubtful. At another fair in another era, Imre Kiralfy produced an extravaganza entitled *America*, which had some substance to it and, judging by the money it made, plenty of entertainment value in addition. Although the Columbian Exposition at Chicago in 1893 was a great disappointment to its promoters, the Kiralfys' *America* was by far the greatest attraction ever presented at any theater up to that time and possibly up to now. The show is said to have netted $1,000,000 in seven and a half months. It was housed in Chicago's Auditorium at Wabash Avenue and Congress Street, a $2,000,000 structure of granite and brick which seated 4,050 persons not counting the Mrs. Potter Palmers and other Gold Coast pedigreed patooties who filled the forty boxes supplied with luxurious chairs and sofas, and walls hung in delicate tints of plush. The size of the theater must have pleased Imre. The orchestra pit held one hundred musicians, and there were 6,862 square feet of available stage room.

America was billed as presenting "400 years of American History," and in order to maintain a thread of plot, in this series of tableaux, he decided to make it allegoric and historic. Progress and Perseverance are the two characters who appear throughout. Then, exhibiting a sympathy and understanding rare in that period, Imre added that, since all nationalities were expected to congregate at the Fair, he would attempt to portray the full sense of the play through the medium of opera and pantomime. In contrast to the scheme of things at *The American Jubilee*, Imre further announced that he selected only such subjects from the annals of history as "have absolutely lent aid to the Progress, Civilization, Liberty and Arts and Sciences of America, and such as uphold the dignity of our country."

The Prologue was actually a concentrated version of the spectacle *Columbus* even unto the triumphal return to Spain, with seven hundred persons taking part in the Grand Processional Pageant. Imre's son, Charles, to whom *America* was dedicated, assisted his father with serious historic research and Act I showed Plymouth Plantation in 1621 and a Grand Ballet of Merrymakers performing the Maypole Dance at Merrymount in 1623. When *America* was played in Boston the following year, the *Boston Weekly Transcript*, with true New England exactitude, had these words to say about this part of the production: "The revels at Merrymount . . . Here, too, is introduced a juggling act by Sylvester Schaffer, who proved to be a marvel . . . His feats were applauded as they deserved to be; and an acrobatic act by Basco and Roberts met with favor, *although it was hardly the thing for Merrymount.*" So gentle a rebuke from the Brahmins in itself proved Imre's genius.

Act II presented, in turn, Washington Crossing the Delaware, the Surrender at Yorktown, the Peace and Triumph of Liberty, and a Grand Ballet of Arts and Sciences. Act III, not to be outdone by its predecessor, demonstrated the historical importance of the early pioneers in the Far West, the Close of the Civil War, and bringing it up to date, the World's Columbian Exposition, ending with a grand cortege of the States and Territories of the Union. Fortunately for the audience, we are a comparatively young country. Nevertheless, somewhere between these historic episodes Imre found time to show the Palace of Progress with its Grand Ballet of American Inventions. Beautiful young ladies, suitably garbed, did honor to all the following products of American ingenuity: Franklin's lightning rod, Whitney's cotton gin, McCormick's reaper, Hoe's printing press, Morse's electric telegraph, Howe's sewing machine, Yost's typewriter, Bell's telephone, and Edison's phonograph and electric lights. I cannot help thinking what such a ballet would have to include today. Just how would Imre have costumed a "bomb sight" or presented an orderly "smoke screen" that would remain on the stage? Not that I doubt for one moment his ability to do both with astonishing success.

The critics loved *America* quite as much as the overflowing audiences that flocked to the Auditorium. One scribe in *The Illustrated American* complained that "they were a little shy at first, for they did not feel themselves quite at liberty to applaud that which was not comedy, or drama, or opera, or ballet, but a combination of all four." He felt that the "air of sanctity" which clung to that hallowed concert hall, the Chicago Auditorium, might have had something to do with the restraint shown by the audience. Nevertheless, when in December it was shown at the Metropolitan Opera House in New York, the *New York Herald's* critic, after raving over its perfections, added: "Despite all this, the audience was scarcely an enthusiastic one. It watched it all in almost silent contentment. For that matter there were but few places in the performance where applause could be indulged in without marring the effect."

In spite of these apologia, I imagine that the spectacle, while pleasing to the eye, delightful to the ear, and even instructive, was just plain dull for the morons. Perhaps the following opinion explains both the public apathy and the public acclaim: "No man may be ashamed of bringing his sister to such a brilliant and wholesome form of amusement."

The heroine of this patriotic extravaganza was Charlotte Gilman, who unwaveringly played a combination of comely roles. Alone and unaided, she characterized Progress and Liberty with the sturdy dignity that is still revealed in her photographs.

Having taken a deep breath, Imre dusted off the latent energies and in 1895 conceived the *Historical Spectacle: India* "which was first a part of the India and Ceylon Exhibition held in London in that year, and which became subsequently a part of the Empire of India Exhibition in 1896." Angelo Venanzi with his usual prolific nonchalance tossed off the score for this latest spectacle as he had for Imre's other productions, all of which music, it may be added, was played and, like a politician's promise, forgotten. Incidentally, the *India* production struck the present Mahatma Gandhi in the midriff. He was too old for diapers and too young for a loincloth.

This not too accurate historical extravaganza ended with the usual Apotheosis, this time entitled "Glorification of Victoria, the Empress Queen, boasting a Grand Procession of the Makers of British India," from Warren Hastings to Lord Northcliffe. Obviously, these gentlemen, in spite of the Garter and the Bath, could not, in themselves, display a sufficiently colorful spectacle, so Imre added allegorical groups representing the contented British Colonies, all uniting to pay homage to the Glorious Empress. Britannia herself crowned Her Majesty, the Goddess of India. During this sacred rite, Love, Mercy and Wisdom were at her feet, while Art, Science, Commerce, Peace and Prosperity surrounded her. Apparently Cruelty, Famine, Slavery, and Robbery by Taxation were on sabbatical leave. One of the last stanzas of the Ode of Glorification is a miracle of political whitewashing:

> England's glory e'er ascending,
> O'er all India long shall shine;
> Might with mercy constant blending,
> Aided by the Will Divine.

Today, with the details of the imprisonment of the Indian Nationalist leaders fresh in our minds, should Imre be here to do it, he would, I regret, have to revise the edition.

From this time on, England chose Imre to glorify her imperialism. He was, so to speak, the British Empire's public relations counsel. He created *Ceylon,* he recovered the century in "The Victorian Era Exhibition," and in 1898 staged the Great Universal Exhibition. In 1899, he presented a grand series of scenic effects called *Greater Britain,* and in 1900, to honor womankind, staged "The Woman's International Exhibition" as a reward for which he was created Knight Commander of the Royal Order of Leopold.

Eight years later, his Franco-British Exhibition covered one hundred and forty acres on which were situated twenty palaces and three complete villages housing between two and five hundred persons each. The Irish village, as a come-on for Americans, boasted the original McKinley cottage which had been removed complete from the North of Ireland. Imre estimated that with propitious weather thirty million persons would visit the Exhibition at one shilling a person. With mass participation of this nature, the cost of these exhibitions was actually underwritten by the magic name of "Kiralfy."

All these activities, including the great Japanese-British Exposition, earned him a presentation to the King by Royal Command at the Court Levee of 1910. As the culminating effort of his career, he managed the Great Coronation Exhibition portraying with graphic detail the arts, industries and resources of the British Empire. This was accomplished under the auspices of the Duke of Leck and the Right Honorable Lord Northcote.

The Kiralfy Brothers, having made millions, became collectors of the fine arts and lived, when in America, on Washington Square North in three adjacent mansions. It is perhaps a sad commentary on economic instability that *Variety* on December 27, 1918, published an advertisement featuring "The Kiralfy Kiddies," the clever children of Bolossy. If Imre had been alive, he would probably have been staging the World War, but *sic transit gloria mundi:* his niece and nephew were touring the Orpheum Circuit .

III

Jacques Offenbach

Revealing the Can-Can in Opéra Bouffe

THERE is a question I would like to ask Franklin P. Adams and Oscar Levant as they sit, performing Buddhas, on the "Information, Please" program of NBC. They might know the answer, but then again, the shelf of encyclopedias—and how I need it—might be my reward for this query: "The father of what famous man was Juda Eberscht?"

When I tell you that he lived on Offenbach-in-Hesse, all is made clear. His son, Jacob Eberscht, famous Jacques Offenbach of opéra bouffe fame, followed his father's adoption of the name when he moved to Cologne to sing as a cantor in a synagogue. In addition to a sonorous voice, Papa Offenbach played on the violin and taught the instrument to his boy who later added to his accomplishments the violoncello. He practiced on the latter six hours daily and with such skill that at fifteen he was engaged for the orchestra at L'Opéra-Comique in Paris. It not only caused him pleasure but brought tremendous relief to his neighbors. Immediately, he started composing incidental music, some of which was published, but the pay was poor and Offenbach had higher ambitions. By 1841, he was a fashionable cellist playing solo at concerts, and three years later he was performing with young Joachim, the master violinist, with none other than F. Mendelssohn at the piano.

During this whole period Offenbach worked indefatigably with his original compositions but not until he became conductor at the classic Comédie-Française in 1850 was he able to hear his own works. Unable to find anybody to perform his music, the young man played it himself as overtures and entr'acts during the five years he held this position. The Parisians came to witness tragedy and serious dramas, and left the theater humming gay little melodies. It was during these years of trying out his tunes on an unaware public that Jacques was planning a theater of his own.

"During this period," wrote the composer many years later, "I frequently thought of the possibility of founding a theater. Yet at the same time I recognized the impossibility of doing so. I knew that comic opera had no home at the Opéra-Comique, that the really merry, bright, spirited music was being gradually neglected. Composers who worked for the opéra comique wrote small 'grand' opera. I saw there was no opportunity for the young composers. In the Champs-Elysées there was a little theater to be let. It had been shut for a considerable time. In the month of May, I had the help of twenty supporters—'Offenbachers' they might be called —and on June 15th, I secured the lease. Twenty days later I had engaged my company, the scenery and collected my librettists for the *Théâtre des Bouffes Parisiens.*"

On July 5, 1865, the Bonbonnière opened its doors, thus becoming the cradle of Offenbach's fame. Paris flocked to the little "Bonbon Box," and Offenbach was indeed "the candy kid." Saint-Saëns called him "The Mozart of the Champs-Elysées," just as critic George Jean Nathan might nowadays refer to "Gypsy Rose Lee" as the "Bernhardt of Strip Tease." Years afterwards, in commenting lovingly on this joyous period, Saint-Saëns remarked: "There was in a corner of Paris a little theater, where one could laugh with his waistcoat unbuttoned. Was it not charming! The public found it a great joy. . . . The facility of Offenbach and the rapidity of his execution were incredible. He literally improvised . . . Great fertility, melodic gift, harmony that was at times distinguished, much wit and invention, great dramatic skill . . . here was more than was necessary for success. He was a great musical personality."

Offenbach has always been the composer's composer. Even Wagner wrote in a letter to Felix Mottl: "Offenbach can do what the divine Mozart did. Offenbach could have been a Mozart."

The enthusiastic opinion of these distinguished composers delights my heart, for I am still puzzled that there are not more Offenbach fans living today. Ever since I heard the maestro direct his own compositions in Gilmore's Garden, I have had a practically delirious regard for that composer's works. The musical charm of the "Serenade" from *Geneviève de Brabant*, or the violin solo in heaven from *Orpheus and Euridice*, or the letter song from *La Périchole*, or the drinking song, "How It Sparkles," from "Chanson de Fortunio," or many from *La Vie Parisienne* are not a whit less enticing than the "Barcarolle" from *Les Contes l'Hoffmann*, and yet the "Barcarolle" is practically the only Offenbach piece which is widely known by my children's less discerning contemporaries.

The Bonbonnière offered a Prologue Overture entitled, appropriately, *Entré Messieurs, Mesdames*, and two one-act operettas: *Les Deux Aveugles*

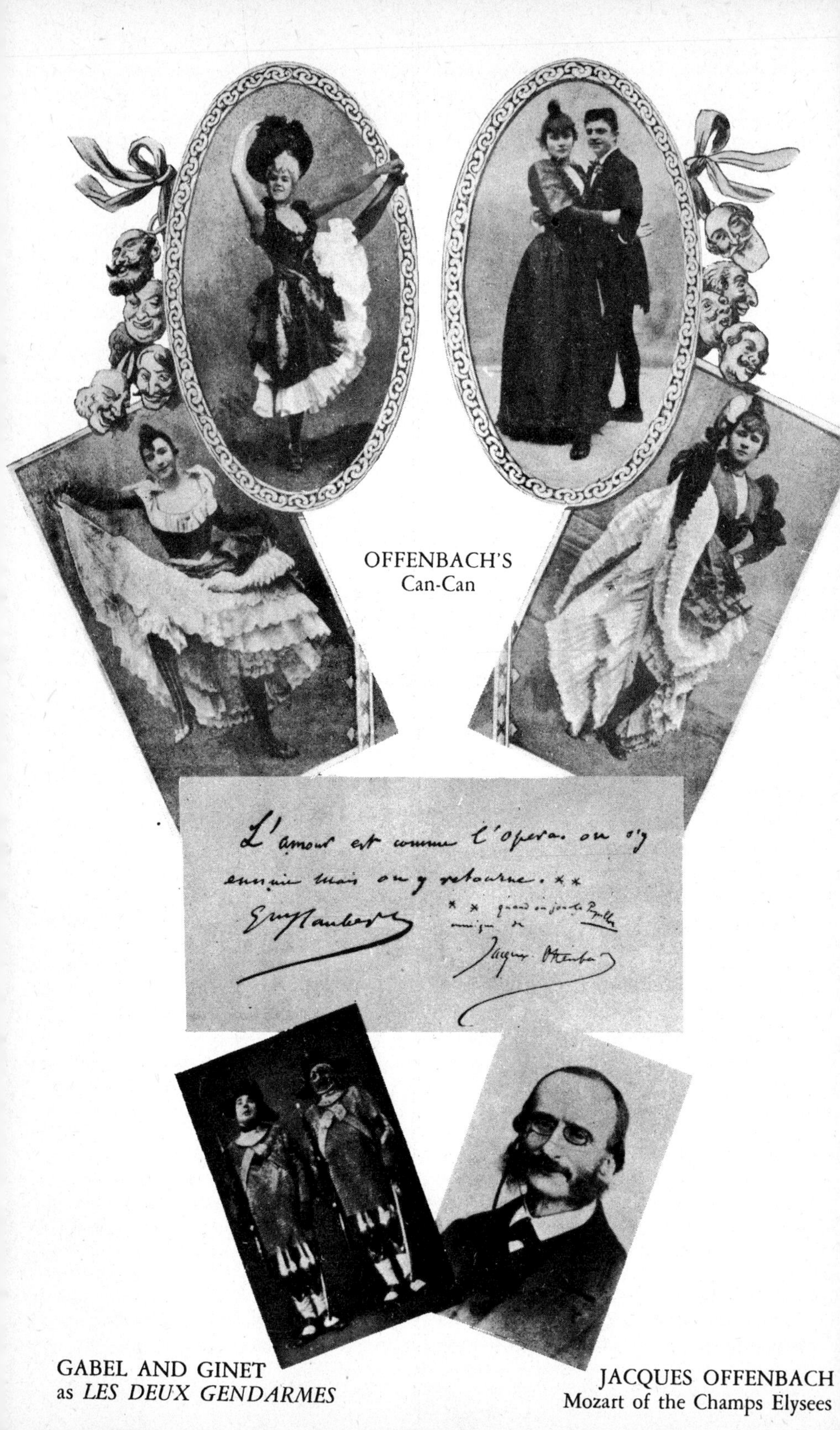

OFFENBACH'S
Can-Can

GABEL AND GINET
as *LES DEUX GENDARMES*

JACQUES OFFENBACH
Mozart of the Champs Elysees

and *La Nuit Blanche.* The license at this pocket-edition theater did not allow for more than four speaking roles in each piece, so one-act operettas were the only solution.

Offenbach's success was so instantaneous and encouraging that six months later, he rented the Théâtre des Jeunes Elevées, a former vaudeville house and renamed it "Bouffes Parisiens." Here he produced *Orphée aux Enfers,* which eventually was played all over the world and did much to establish his reputation; *La Belle Hélène, Geneviève de Brabant, Périchole, Là Princesse de Trébizonde, Madame Favart,* and *La Grande Duchesse de Gérolstein.* Henri Meilhac and Ludovic Halevy, keen parodists and gay humorists, were his lyricists and until the rise of W. S. Gilbert's genius these two were the most celebrated book writers for operettas. Offenbach kept his librettists busy, writing, as he did, one hundred and six operettas, all save three of which were produced at an average rate of four a year. In the music catalogue of the British Museum, one hundred and forty-two pages are required to list his compositions with their various arrangements.

The Third Napoleon's romantic reign came to a full flowering of extravagance and gaiety in 1867. Never in her long history of intellectual and special triumphs had Paris witnessed such a galaxy of wit and genius as was presented at the Exposition of that year. Over all that maze of frivolous excitement, two personalities reigned supreme: Jacques Offenbach composing and directing the opéra bouffe, and Hortense Schneider, his leading woman, whom he had discovered in Brussels when she was working for cakes, her munificent salary of one pound six shillings per week being hardly sufficient also to provide the proverbial ale. However, in no time at all, after being transplanted to Paris and given immortal tunes to sing, Hortense blossomed into an 80-pound-a-week star. The singer had a most bewitching manner which fascinated her public much as the fabulous Lorelei.

So great was the prestige of the Schneider-Offenbach combination that the Czar of Russia, on arriving at Cologne, no longer able to restrain his impatience, telegraphed for reserved seats, determined to witness a performance of *La Grande Duchesse* which delighted Parisians because it caricatured life in a petty German court and made pointed fun of the Prussian soldiers. Yet Bismarck, who was present at the first performance, laughed loudly, although to maintain the dignity of the Teuton court he insisted that his face had merely slipped. An Offenbach first night was an evening not to be compared with any other musical event in Paris. On such nights, proscenium boxes displayed a constantly changing pageant of great princes, warriors, statesmen and their beautiful women. In addition to the Iron Chancellor the boxes held Napoleon III, the Princess of Wales, Czar Alexander III, and the Kings of Bavaria, Portugal and Sweden. There too, opposite Bismarck, sat Adolphe Thiers, a little man

Judic
Simon Girard
H. Schneider
Céline Chaumont
Montaland
Judic
Théo
Marguerite Ugalde
Jeanne Granier
et Mily Meyer
(Petit Duc)
Valtesse
(Orphée aux Enfers)
Peschard
Timbale d'Argent
L'Œ
Compo

HORTENSE SCHNEIDER AND OFFENBACH STARS
Hortense Schneider attracted five Kings, a Princess and two statesmen to her opening performance

with a bullet head, a face as broad as the moon at full, and a jaw of great purpose, the greatest orator of Louis Philippe's reign, the man who was to become the President of the next French Republic.

Five kings, a royal princess, and two distinguished statesmen: but not one of them stole the show from the black-haired, blue-eyed dynamic musical director and his Queen of Opéra Bouffe. It actually became the fashion to appear in the operettas. Even Cora Pearl, one of the four devastating beauties of the Empire, consented to appear as Cupid in *Orpheus*, and the boulevards resounded with exaggerated tales of the opulence of her mansion with its satin-hung walls embroidered in gold thread, her eight carriages and twelve thoroughbred horses.

When *La Grande Duchesse* took Paris by storm, Offenbach's *La Vie Parisienne* was still enjoying a long run at the Palais-Royal and the day soon arrived when three operettas by this prolific composer were playing concurrently at three theaters in the same city. But Paris was not the only town where Offenbach triumphed with his gay and sentimental approach to life. Vienna, Berlin, St. Petersburg, London and New York all had productions of his operettas, and Hortense herself was cheered in Vienna and London.

At the St. James Theatre in 1869, the charming diva played the lead in a scene not in the program. *Orpheus* was being presented and during the last act, just as Schneider finished singing, her dress caught fire. In the hideous confusion that followed, she jumped down from the movable platform on which she was standing, and crying out "Oh! Emma Lirry!" threw herself flat on the stage in a frantic effort to hide her face from the disfiguring flames. Emma Lirry, one of the most gifted terpsichorean artistes of the Empire and a popular favorite, had been fatally burned at a rehearsal. Schneider was saved from a like fate by the quick action of M. Desmots, who was playing Jupiter, fortunately dressed in a regal cloak with which he smothered the fire. The next evening the walls of the theater bulged even farther than usual, crowded with Hortense's admirers who came to congratulate her on her fortunate escape. She received such a tremendous ovation at her first entry that she was obliged to stand silent for many minutes before the vocal enthusiasm subsided and she could lift her own flutelike voice.

As the Second Empire drew to a close, the gaiety, extravagance and luxury increased. In July, 1869, Offenbach went to Baden-Baden to conduct one of his operettas. He attended a rehearsal, dressed in yellow trousers and waistcoat, gray gloves, a coat of sky blue, a green hat and carried a red umbrella. In Baden-Baden, he entered a haberdashery to buy a purple necktie. As a gesture toward sartorial correctness, he inquired of the clerk, "Do you think it will clash with the rest of my outfit?" "Oh, yes," replied the clerk enthusiastically and determined not to lose the sale, "it will clash beautifully."

Two years later found the glamorous Schneider at the Court of St. Petersburg on the invitation of the Czar himself, and although Adelina Patti was having a triumph in Grand Opera during the same season, Hortense had no difficulty in competing with the prima donna on a different plane. She charmed both artists and critics with her spirited performances, and the entire diplomatic corps accompanied by the foreign colony literally laid bouquets at her feet, concerned, as they were, with promoting French "culture."

In spite of his successes, Offenbach was always in need of money. To say that the composer was a bad businessman would be trite. When, in 1874, a revised and enlarged *Orpheus* ran for twenty months and realized a profit of £80,000, the uninitiated might suppose that Offenbach could have rested on his financial laurels for several years at least. But no. The very next year, when Maurice Grau sent a representative to Paris to coax the composer into coming to America, most of his large share of this money was already gone. If it had not been dissipated, I doubt whether the composer would have left his beloved Paris, his luxury, his delightful Spanish wife, and his amusing friends and wealthy patrons to sail for shores that were still considered provincial. Whatever doubts Offenbach might have had about accepting Grau's offer to play thirty concerts in New York and Philadelphia, conducting an orchestra of sixty musicians in programs of his own compositions, they were rather promptly dispelled by the terms: $1,000 a night.

It was a good year to go to America. The Centennial was being celebrated in Philadelphia; in New York, Aimee had popularized most of Offenbach's operettas. In his delightful diary, *Offenbach in America: Notes of a Travelling Musician*, published in Paris and New York in 1877, the composer remarks upon the unusual amount of interest created by his visit—and, may I add, by Grau's publicity man. Robert Grau, Maurice's brother, says the composer arrived "amid excitement that has not been equaled to this day, or at least not since Barnum had welcomed Jumbo to our shores." For that matter, Grau also had "an elephant on his hands," although it required the box office to convince him.

A boat left New York filled with prominent persons, reporters and a military band. When it reached Sandy Hook, they found they were a day too early. The disappointed welcomers remembered the champagne on board, and promptly drank it down to forget the fiasco. As they returned to town on the flower-bedecked vessel bobbing with Venetian lanterns, most of them became seasick, their complexions assuming the hue of Offenbach's Baden-Baden trousers. When Offenbach arrived the following day, a plain unadorned tug greeted his steamer. Offenbach told excellent Parisian stories and by the time he reached shore he was warmly entrenched in the hearts of the reporters. The Fifth Avenue Hotel, where he was to stay, boasted a huge banner on its Broadway side, reading, "Wel-

CORA PEARL
A devastating beauty of the Empire

MLLE. AIMEE
Who introduced Opera Bouffe to America

come, Offenbach." The Musicians' Union sent an orchestra to serenade the hero with his own tunes and a crowd of fifty thousand filled Madison Square and shouted welcome to the man who had given them so much pleasure, until he appeared on the balcony, expressed his thanks in excellent English and retired.

With a reception of such a warm nature, it is all the more surprising that Offenbach's concerts should have failed to draw after the first enormous turnout at Gilmore's Garden when six thousand persons crowded in to view the visiting celebrity. The audience was not a musical one, apparently most of them had been attracted by the demonstrations and the enthusiasm of the publicity releases. Voicing their disappointment, half of them left at the first intermission, and without any mad scramble for return checks as in the palmy *Black Crook* days. Grau discovered, but too late, that he should have planned a more visual show for his patrons, for Offenbach himself was a frail figure, not weighing more than ninety pounds—bones and all. He needed a talented singer to delight his audience, or a bevy of chorus girls to dance to the can-can music from *Orpheus*, one of the liveliest tunes ever written. While he was conducting at the Garden, Theodore Thomas was giving concerts on Seventh Avenue, near 59th Street. He was asked why he did not put one of Offenbach's compositions on his program as a mark of respect for the visitor. "I, conduct an Offenbach composition?" cried Thomas angrily. "Never will I do anything so degrading!" When this was reported to the musician, he said, "Please tell Mr. Thomas that I will not be so particular. *I* shall be most happy to conduct any composition of Theodore Thomas' when he reaches the dignity of becoming a composer."

The tale of how Aimee saved Grau's venture from financial failure should begin with the story of that delightful performer herself, because it was Aimee who had introduced opéra bouffe to America under Grau's managership three years before and brought with her the heart-warming tunes of Offenbach, playing in *Périchole*, *La Belle Hélène*, *Barbe Bleu*, *Les Brigands*, and many others including *Geneviève de Brabant* which Emily Soldene later glorified.

Aimee, in order to flee from Paris which was then, characteristically, being beseiged by the Prussians and in her anxiety to escape to America, the fabulous source of all wealth, risked her life in an adventurous balloon flight to reach the coast and board a ship. Her appearance in October, 1872, at the old Olympic Theatre on Broadway in *La Périchole* fully satisfies our curiosity about the ultimate success of the ascension. The lady obviously "arrived" and a very gifted lady she was—the most refined exponent of the bouffe school who ever visited this country. In her hands bouffe lost all of its nastiness; half of its vice. She had the rare talent of making improprieties seem proper without sacrificing any of the audience's interest.

Being a creature gifted with *chic* and *diablerie*, Aimee presented her material in an early Irene Bordoni manner. All the rather hackneyed adjectives—"saucy," "piquant," etc.—applied very aptly to her. But they should not discourage the reader because, combined with her sweet voice and her youthful personal appearance, they made for that indefinable something called "charm." The fact that Aimee reveled in her work and took delight in pleasing her public helped to make her the idol of Broadway.

The *Spirit of the Times* liked Aimee. Everybody did except perhaps some Victorians who followed the morals of the English Queen. "Mlle. Aimee is an admirable artiste full of spirit and suggestion. In fact we could hardly advise her to carry *suggestion* further. It is an entertainment at the Olympic Theatre of a very bright and delightful kind, not very much calculated to excite reflection, and yet these Opera Bouffe entertainments suggest abundant food for thought. Beneath their bubbling and effervescing surface, there is a deep and 'quiet' current of satire, often pregnant with political meaning. Where for instance can a more telling satirical picture of a dummy monarchy, governed, bullied, browbeaten and coerced by its ministers, be found than that which is exhibited in *Périchole?*"

La Belle Hélène seems also to have had more to offer than the bare limbs of Greek and Trojan maidens. "Considered simply as a burlesque—a caricature of Homeric personages, and the traditional events in which they were actors, the work is unquestionably the wittiest and best of its kind that has ever been published here."

A linguist from necessity—from Paris, Aimee went to Rio de Janeiro in 1865 before she came to New York—the singer could handle English, French and Spanish lyrics. Among the lists of the songs she called her favorites there is one that always causes me to speculate. The title is "Creep into Bed, Baby." I could settle the debatable point as to Baby's age immediately by consulting the original verses, but I prefer the title as it is: a rather compromising and forthright, intriguing invitation. "Pretty as a Picture" and "Chicken Pie" were two of her outstanding successes I do not think that the chicken referred to was considered edible except by some isolated African and Australian tribes. "She's as Pretty as a Picture" was borrowed from Billy Emerson, the famous minstrel who was one of America's greatest song and dance men. Aimee, at the time of the Philadelphia Centennial in 1876, made a sensational success by "taking off" her fellow artist. Emerson had a characteristic swagger to his "walk-around" between the verses of his successful ditty and this Aimee imitated with consummate artistry. The diseuse's accent was irresistible. One critic wrote "Aimee introduced an English song and as it came trippingly off her tongue in the prettiest broken English, it elicited peals of merriment owing to the care she took to pronounce each word."

The ovations which greeted her in every city she visited gratified the singer but at every new demonstration of her popularity she grew more dejected. It was all very well to be feted in America, but she "was foreign, being French" and never ceased mourning that her beloved Paris refused to recognize her as a star of the first magnitude. To a Parisian, only another Parisian can judge artistic ability so when, in 1876, the Paris newspapers, impressed with her American record of successes, sent correspondents over here, Aimee was delighted.

Then Jacques Offenbach himself crossed the ocean to conduct his *Orphée aux Enfers*, and met with the failure which no one could have foreseen. The first-night audience actually expected the frail ninety-pound musician to dance the can-can himself.

Aimee stepped to the rescue. She suggested that together they could wipe out the memory of this disastrous reception, by reviving *La Vie Parisienne* with herself on the stage, and Jacques leading the orchestra. "I'll do it!" shouted Offenbach and, during the can-can number, nimbly danced while directing in the pit as Aimee kicked rhythmically above his head. Here was something that even Paris had never witnessed and Aimee was delighted, for now her home town could not fail to hear that the great Offenbach was to conduct one of his operettas with Aimee as his chosen attraction.

At the apex of her career, Aimee earned huge sums of money and owned at least 400,000 francs' worth of diamonds when francs were still worth something. Because of a near theft, the singer did not dare to wear them, so while the brilliant jewels lay unused in a safe-deposit vault, she wore imitation sparklers and even so, never moved anywhere without bodyguard, in addition, of course, to her male escort and her male following.

Some of the jewels with which Aimee dazzled the public may have been "paste" but certainly Aimee herself was the "real McCoy." Her farewell at Booth's Theatre in 1878 before returning to France will bear witness to that. It was indeed a resplendent affair. Although opéra bouffe had received a "biff" in some respects, New York society finally accepted its high entertainment value most enthusiastically and turned out in numbers to bid farewell to its star. At the close of her performance, Aimee was called before the curtain and lustily cheered. A silver service was presented to her by Maurice Grau "as a slight memento of my esteem of you as a woman, my appreciation of your devotion as an artiste, and my recognition of your loyalty as an associate." And the *Spirit of the Times* on June 15, 1878, paid Aimee the finally heavy compliment of calling her an "institution."

Unfortunately Paris did not receive Aimee with the same joyous abandon, and Jacques Offenbach, who should have been deeply indebted to the little singer for turning his New York failure into a stunning success, dealt her the harshest blow of all. *La Grande Duchesse* was going to be revived in Paris. It had been barred following the Franco-Prussian War, because of its sharp satire on the small duchy. As we know, Hortense Schneider had

MLLE. AIMEE'S HIT SONG

BILLY EMERSON
Originator of the song *PRETTY AS A PICT*

Pretty as a Picture.

rds by GEO. COOPER. Music by T. BRIGHAM BISHOP.

Moderato.
mf
p
1. Oh, my heart is gone, And I'm for-lorn, A
2. As we stray'd a - long, The sweet bird's song Was

sung the original role and now the task was to find a worthy successor. Mlle. Aimee was on the point of being engaged when the composer himself sent the following letter to the producer: "I am told that the role of *La Grande Duchesse* is not yet assigned. If it is true that Paolo Marie does not leave for America at once, but remains at the 'Bouffes,' why look for anyone else? Meilhac and Halévy may object to her stature; Paolo Marie will be a little Grande Duchesse, but on the other hand: what a voice; what admirable talent. The composer does not hesitate for a moment to confide to her the superb role of the Grande Duchesse. If, as I hope, my collaborators share my appreciation, I am convinced that the public will ratify our choice to the echo."

Aimee's mortification was great. The true Parisians still considered certain exaggerations and coarseness in her technique not to their taste. For the provincials in the United States she was no doubt good enough. Then, too, she was no longer as young as she had been and Paolo Marie was heavy opposition. She had youth, beauty, and a voice not yet overworked.

But Offenbach himself was to face a major disappointment. His most ambitious work, *Tales of Hoffmann*, with book by M. Carré and M. Barbier after Hoffmann's stories, was not produced until a year after he died of gout of the heart in 1880. The *Tales* had a strange history and a long-delayed triumph. It was first produced at the Ring Theater in Vienna in 1881, and during the première the theater burned down and many members of the audience perished. Because of the tragedy, the score was considered a "hoodoo" and no one wished to revive it. A similar experience was that of Kate Claxton, who was appearing at the Brooklyn Theatre in *The Two Orphans* when it burned down in 1876 with a loss of several hundred lives. It took her years to overcome the superstition that her appearing in a theater was an ill omen.

Manager Grau attempted to produce the *Tales* at the Fifth Avenue Theatre, in 1882, but it almost cost him, if not his shirt, at least his shirt tails. As a result Grau never advertised it at the Metropolitan when he became impresario there. A German-language production in London in 1907 was another large-scale failure, the producer losing 8,000 pounds in six weeks. Not until November 15, 1907, when Oscar Hammerstein treated New York to a magnificent production, did the *Tales of Hoffmann* finally come into its own. Yet, today, when nostalgic reminiscence is no longer appealing to any except those of advanced years and the bloody present leads us to wish for a better future, we still can hear the tunes of Offenbach and feel our spirits lift with their spontaneous gaiety. And what man could ever be forgotten who was responsible, if only indirectly, for the charming view of a stageful of ruffled drawers presented saucily, and with rhythm, to an admiring audience during a "Can-Can"? The very sensational "Bella Union" Theatre of San Francisco aptly described it as "the naughty, oh so naughty lifting of the lace and ruffles."

IV

Emily Soldene

Taking Harvard University by charm

EMILY SOLDENE and her English Opera Comique belonged to the massive and magnetic school of female performers. The English public, as well as ours, could not get enough of the pulchritudinous singers who tended to excess poundage. These pretty creatures boasted acres of pink-and-white perfection; no bosom was too reminiscent of the feather bed, no behind was too buxom for the aesthetic enjoyment of the latter-day theatergoer. If these ladies were self-made, they certainly used up a lot of material.

Emily's unusual size included her features. A Chicago critic said her mouth was so big it would take two men to kiss her, while another, much less gallant, said there were three mouths in America: the Missouri's, the Mississippi's and Missoldene's. He also intimated that Emily should never eat blueberry pie near a railroad track or the engineer might mistake it for a tunnel. Soldene was so often teased about her most prominent facial feature that she begged the editor of the *Spirit of the Times* not to dwell so often upon it, since there were "so many other good features in my entertainment." The editor banteringly answered, "You see, I couldn't say much if your mouth were smaller than mine"—this from a man who "had a mouth to fit a slice of watermelon." Emily rashly offered to measure both, and lost to the editor. He gallantly suppressed his triumph, however, never telling the public about it. Whereupon the actress as a reward gave him passes for a week though she was playing to capacity audiences.

The Troupe with whom she sang toured England, Australia and the United States presenting, among others, the works of Offenbach and Lecocq. But during her career she had at first some experience in serious opera. She made her debut at a concert in St. James Hall, London, on the same bill as Adelina Patti, Grisi, Albani and Sims Reeves, and performed well enough in the presence of that galaxy of stars to find herself within a year singing at the Drury Lane in *Il Trovatore*, thus proving she was not too heavy for light opera or too light for heavy opera.

To cure her stage fright, which often seriously jeopardized her early performances, Emily was advised to accept an engagement in a music hall where criticism was not only verbal but, at times, physical. The tipsy blokes would think nothing of throwing tomatoes at those they did not favor. At one performer, they even heaved a cabbage but he kept on singing, hoping they might also toss some corned beef. Clever Emily Soldene, however, received only bouquets at the Oxford, where the smell of tobacco smoke and hops almost smothered her. But the cure actually worked and she returned, but this time to the light opera stage.

Charles Morton, who owned the Oxford, produced *Geneviève de Brabant* at Islington and persuaded Emily to appear in it. She later reminisced about that unforgettable first night in a press interview: "It was November 11, 1875, and the Prince of Wales, later the King, was lying ill of typhoid fever. London was in gloom for it was feared he could not recover. During the performance, we read bulletins from the stage. Everyone was strangely quiet." In spite of this most inauspicious opening, the piece was a great success and all London "rolled up" to Islington to see it. When asked whether the London gentlemen were lured solely by the fortuitous combination of Offenbach and Soldene, Emily answered with a large wave of the arm, "Bless me, no! You should have seen our chorus—such beautiful girls and so big. They were dressed as pages, but their legs spoke volumes." At one theater where they played during the Yuletide holidays, the posters announced, "Well-filled stockings Christmas Week." To see Selina Dolaro walk up and down the stage with a rose in her mouth —before Carmen had been heard of—was alone worth the journey up to Islington. From there, the show toured the Provinces, Australia and America where "they named hats and coats, and I blush to say it, even a five-cent cigar after me. At that I was better off than Bismarck; they only named a herring after him."

Léo Delibes's *Fleur de Lys* followed *Geneviève*, with Emily playing Prince Hyacinth. Topical songs were introduced in all the operettas, keeping abreast of the political, social and artistic life of the locality, and new verses were added nightly to delight the "repeaters" in the audience. E. L. Blanchard, remarking on the singular frankness of the interpolated lyrics, wrote: "It would be pernaps too much to inquire whether the 'topical songs' are submitted on every occasion of a new verse being introduced, to the severe scrutiny of Mr. Bodham Donne, the Examiner of Plays."

MILY SOLDENE
er mouth was so big it took
o men to kiss her

HARRY MONTAGUE
Famous matinee idol

GEORGE RIGNOLD
AS KING HENRY V

EMILY SOLDENE
English Opera Bouffe Company.
COMMENCING MONDAY, NOV. 2, 1874,
AT THE
LYCEUM THEATRE.

La Fille de Madame Angot was another popular operetta on Emily's program. The ballad of "Mater Angot" had so catchy a tune that every errand boy whistled it delivering his packages, every kitchenmaid hummed it paring potatoes, every fine lady tried to pick it out with one finger on the pianoforte. The music of the ballad was undoubtedly an old Dutch melody with slight variations. "Ik Ben Snyderlik" is still sung in convivial clubs as Bols gin slips coolly "down the hatch."

Philip Hale of the *Boston Herald*, remarking on her success in "light and unclothed opera," wrote facetiously: "Miss Soldene is a singer and an actress of indisputable parts"; while the critic of *The Capitol* wrote: "Soldene's Troupe of Opera Bouffers is a museum of anatomy. No! No! We don't mean that. A museum of curiosities, interesting to contemplate, instructive to behold. Soldene is a 'big thing' herself, as we heard one of the detailed firemen remark. 'In fact,' he wisecracked, 'if I had to carry her down a ladder, I'd be compelled to make it in two trips.' "

Before Soldene left for America in 1874, Captain Burton of the *Thousand Nights and a Night* fame, then known as an African traveler, called to say good-bye. Emily tells us that he was "tall, dark, bronzed, masterful and much addicted to long conversations with the ladies of the ballet. I could not get away from the fact that he was artistically made up; the cheeks rouged a little and the eyes India-inked a lot, just as if he were going on the stage."

Emily opened in New York at the Lyceum on 14th Street on November 2, 1874, in *Geneviève de Brabant*, and immediately caught the fancy of the men about town. Her chorus was a sensation. During the same season George Rignold played *Henry V* at Booth's to middle-aged married women, while at Wallack's the aesthetically beautiful Henry Montague held the young ladies enthralled in Dion Boucicault's *Shaughraun*. But these audiences were exclusively feminine. The gentlemen bowed their ladies to their seats, excused themselves, and hurried down to the Lyceum to get as near Soldene as possible. The light opera which Emily claimed as her own was simply this: the reproduction in English of the best examples of Parisian opéra comique and opéra bouffe with a careful rewording of the libretto to add refinement without subtracting innuendo.

After her first success in America, she came back again and again—once in 1876-77 with a show which included a dozen or so of "human, healthy, handsome girls and a female who kicks in a style unparalleled in the annals of gymnastic experience. She can kick off her back hair every time, and seems never wearied of the diversion. It is truly marvelous that that girl hasn't broken her leg before now," marveled one appreciative journalist.

It was during this tour that Emily conquered "beautiful baldheaded" Boston—all but the critic of the *Globe*, who wondered "how any man who respects a woman can take her to witness one of these performances surpasses understanding; how any woman can sit it through without a feeling of shame and mortification for herself and resentment against the man who subjects her to such a humiliation, is a still more perplexing reflection." The pious penpusher, evidently suffering from the morbid broodings of an overburdened soul, then said a few words about the "vicious gymnastics of the can-can"—and Emily was indeed made. Our critic is appalled that her troupe was "witnessed with uproarious delight by young men fresh from the study of moral philosophy within the classic shades of Harvard."

It has been my experience that just such young men are only too glad to raise their eyes from the printed page to the painted lips, and it was probably one of these scholarly blades who penned this delightful quatrain:

If Offenbach still pleases,
More than the fugues of Bach,
We shall not have Bach often,
But often Offenbach.

In writing her memoirs in 1897—a pursuit, incidentally, which should be discouraged when the author happens to be so popular a lady—Emily remembered with delight the Harvard students who supplied them all with suppers after the show and bribed the supers—torchbearers and such—to go home, and then filled their places to be nearer the various curved objects of their affection. On the troupe's last night in Boston, what looked to Soldene like the "whole college" turned out and generously set up a barrel of beer in the greenroom for the chorus.

These memoirs, innocently called *My Theatrical and Musical Recollections,* may have been memories to her but they were certainly nightmares to many of her male acquaintances, most of them white-haired, dignified members of Parliament with many grandchildren by the time their youthful follies got into print. The book created a sensation. For several weeks the Marquis de Blandford, Lord Rosebery, Lord Macduff, the Marquis of Anglesier, Sir Douglas Straight, Lord Dudley, Lord Landesborough, and Lord Alfred Pager, were joshed at their clubs and cold-shouldered at home and I daresay they were all secretly flattered.

When the enthusiastic Emily was told in San Francisco that she had stirred up many a forgotten scandal, she opened her large eyes innocently and exclaimed, "Why, I really didn't say a single malicious or scandalous thing;—simply went straight ahead and didn't mince matters." Well, maybe, in order to preserve their flavor, she did not mince them, although she made "hash" out of more than one reputation. At all events, Emily was too brimful of a large Rabelaisian humor to allow such good material to gather dust and oblivion locked in her memory.

It was during this 1876 visit to Boston that Gilbert and Sullivan's *Trial by Jury* proved a sensation. It had previously been played by the Alice Oates Company, but never before had it been done here with all the stage business as Gilbert's genius had worked it out. In case we Savoyards think enthusiasm is the gift of the twentieth century, let it be known that the production was so successful that the company played it twice every night and in addition encored every number. The role of the plaintiff was sung by Clara Vesey, Emily's sister.

The stagecraft of that era was not all that it should have been, and the star system of the seventies which sacrificed the ensemble would have, for instance, deeply grieved the Moscow Art Theatre. In 1879 at the Gaiety in London one original feature of Emily's show was the roving spotlight which miraculously fell upon Miss Soldene wherever she appeared with no regard whatsoever for the sense of the scene being played. In a magnificent Parisian salon, it might have been managed, but in a little native hut the effect must have been distressing. One critic, more sensitive than the others, bewailed the "limelight" which "followed her across the stage with the fidelity of a pet poodle." Had Soldene been less a creature of the flesh, and more wan, willowy and bemused in appearance, she might have looked like a heavenly apparition cloaked in celestial splendor, instead of an energetic, enthusiastic player bouncing in a "spot."

The singer also returned in 1880-81, when, because of the irresponsibility of her managers, Jarvis and Froom, she was arrested for debt in a dozen towns. But in spite of the financial difficulties of the managerial staff, the troupe itself fared far better. One of the girls acquired a $1,250 Alaska sealskin jacket from a racing man, although whether this was tendered to keep her warm or quiet, the record does not state. Another, who in later years was termed a butter-and-egg man, was Dr. Cornelius Hertz, who presented to all the girls, to be shared among them, $1,000 in double eagles. A certain New York "Colonel," not to be outdone, asked Emily whether in remembrance of a very pleasant time she would allow him to send each a little present—something for the neck. Ah, there was a gift to contemplate. Some in anticipation dreamed of fur pieces, others of diamond brooches or lockets. Finally when the boxes arrived and the girls eagerly snatched off the lids, they found only piqué collar sets with white dickeys to match. The Colonel proved to be a Troy collar manufacturer. Fortunately his line was not toilet articles, otherwise "something for the neck" might have been a cake of perfumed soap.

Six years later Emily consented to return to play with De Wolf Hopper in *Josephine and her Sisters*, but that was her last appearance before our American audiences. Her final appearance in England was at a benefit given for her in 1906 at the Palace Theatre before going to Australia to retire. Mme. Melba and Ellen Terry sponsored the benefit, which was jammed to the doors. The public always appreciates those excellent troupers who make them laugh and, in laughing, forget the unhappy love affair, the unpaid bill, the wife's relations. Soldene sang the Balcony Duet from *Geneviève de Brabant* with Violet Ludlow, and Señor Sarasate, the virtuoso, played violin solos. Since all concerned had donated their services in Emily's honor, and promotional expense amounted to only £25, Mr. Beerbohm Tree was able to hand her a check for £653 with £150 to be added from the sale of programs. Mr. Tree, as he handed her the proceeds, complimented her on "the exhibition of good will which marked the close of her professional career."

Soldene must have smiled to herself. She was rich in the knowledge of what makes good will and she had no intention whatsoever of retiring at sixty-six. Perhaps the stage was finished with her, but certainly there were other professions. Had she not written a successful autobiography, and what was more important, had she not translated and adapted all the French operas which she sang? Obviously, she still had a joker up her sleeve and so, with her boundless enthusiasm and unfailing good humor she undertook at the end of her life to become an Australian correspondent for English newspapers, until death rang down "the final curtain" upon her.

V

Evergreen Evangeline

Turning extravaganza into musical comedy as we know it

THE BLACK CROOK was not the only musical extravaganza to blossom year after year on the American stage. *Evangeline,* the brain child of Longfellow, was adapted by Edward E. Rice and Cheever Goodwin, two classmates at Harvard, to the exigencies of an American Opera Bouffe. Once started on its career in 1874 at Niblo's Garden, that cradle of perennial successes, it lived and flourished and changed its casts through many decades to follow. To most of the younger generation *Evangeline* means only the perfect iambic pentameter:

"This is the forest primeval, the murmuring pines and the hemlocks"—but to the nineteenth century it meant the late Henry E. Dixey as the hind legs of a heifer. Polly Peaches, writing in the *Evening Journal* nineteen years after its opening, marveled at its lasting appeal and finally decided that "the beauty of *Evangeline* is that it belongs neither to life nor the drama, any more than the *stall* on which you place the fruit belongs to the harvest. If *Evangeline* belonged to life, it would have had not only its youth and maturity, but its decline. If it belonged to drama, it would have been criticized and played out. But it never declined nor was played out. Nobody ever dares to criticize it any more than he would the precision of the equinoxes, or the infinitesimal calculus, or Chauncey Depew or Joe Jefferson.

"The drama in *Evangeline* never achieves, or conquers, or suffers. It simply abides on the perennial limbs of the girls and the immutable cow. And placing her among so many shapely seraphs no doubt made her the original 'contented cow.' To know how immortal *Evangeline* is, one must think of all the sublimary things that never perished or faded in its track.

EVANGELINE PROGRAM

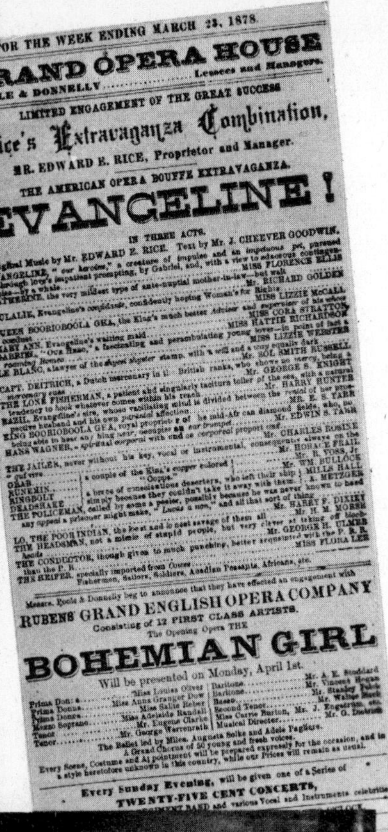

FOR THE WEEK ENDING MARCH 23, 1878.

GRAND OPERA HOUSE

...LE & DONNELLY .... Lessees and Managers.

LIMITED ENGAGEMENT OF THE GREAT SUCCESS

...ice's Extravaganza Combination,

MR. EDWARD E. RICE, Proprietor and Manager.

THE AMERICAN OPERA BOUFFE EXTRAVAGANZA.

EVANGELINE!

IN THREE ACTS.

Original Music by Mr. EDWARD E. RICE. Text by Mr. J. CHEEVER GOODWIN.

EVANGELINE, "our heroine," a creature of impulse and an impetuous pet, pursued through love's impatient prompting, by Gabriel, and, with a view to adaceous contingencies—by a whale .... MISS FLORENCE ELLIS

CATHERINE, the very mildest type of ante-nuptial mother-in-law—but wait .... Mr. RICHARD GOLDEN

EULALIE, Evangeline's confidante, confidently hoping Woman's for Rights .... MISS LIZZIE McCALL

QUEEN BOORIOBOOLA GHA, the King's much better Adviser and superior of his whose conduct .... MISS CORA STRATTON

MARY ANN, Evangeline's waiting maid .... MISS HATTIE RICHARDSON

GABRIEL, "Our Hero," a fascinating and perambulating young lover—in point of fact a roaming Romeo .... MISS LIZZIE WEBSTER

LE BLANC, a lawyer of the ... shyster stamp, with a will and a very equally dark .... Mr. SOL SMITH RUSSELL

CAPT. DEITRICH, a Dutch mercenary in the British ranks, who shows no mercy, being a mercenary cuss .... Mr. GEORGE S. KNIGHT

THE LONE FISHERMAN, a patient and singularly taciturn toiler of the sea, with a natural tendency to hook whatever comes within his reach .... Mr. HARRY HUNTER

BAZIL, Evangeline's sire, whose vacillating mind is divided between the ... of her prospective husband and his own parental affection .... MR. E. S. TARR

KING BOORIOBOOLA GHA, royal proprietor of the mid-African diamond fields, who, no ... ear trumpet .... Mr. EDWIN S. TARR

HANS WAGNER, a spiritual corporal with ... corporeal proport... being able to hear anything near, occupies an ... . Mr. CHARLES ROBINE

THE JAILER, never without his key, vocal or instrumental, consequently always on the "qui vive" .... Mr. HORACE FRAIL

GRAB .... | a couple of the King's copper colored "Coppe." | Mr. R. VOSS, Jr.

RUNEMIN .... | | Mr. WM. BULLOCK

RINGBOLT .... | a brace of conscientious deserters, who left their ship simply because they couldn't take it away with them. | MILLS HALL

DEADSHAKE .... | | A. METZGER

THE POLICEMAN, called by some a peeler, possibly because he was never known to heed any appeal a prisoner might make, "Lucus a non," and all that sort of thing .... Mr. HARRY E. DIXIEY

LO, THE POOR INDIAN, the last and most savage of them all .... Mr. H. M. MORSE

THE HEADSMAN, not a mimic of stupid people, but very clever at taking off blockheads .... Mr. GEORGE H. ULMER

THE CONDUCTOR, though given to much punching, better acquainted with the P. R. R. than the P. R. .... MISS FLORA LEE

THE HEIFER, specially imported from .... Fishermen, Sailors, Soldiers, Acadian Peasants, Africans, etc.

Messrs. Poole & Donnelly beg to announce that they have effected an engagement with

RUBENS' GRAND ENGLISH OPERA COMPANY

Consisting of 12 FIRST CLASS ARTISTS.

The Opening Opera THE

BOHEMIAN GIRL

Will be presented on Monday, April 1st.

Prima Donna	Miss Louisa Oliver	Baritone	Mr. A. E. Stoddard
Prima Donna	Miss Anna Granger Dow	Baritone	Mr. Vincent Hogan
Prima Donna	Miss Sallie Reber	Basso	Mr. Stanley Felch
Mezzo Soprano	Miss Adelaide Randall	Second Tenor	Mr. Wallace Beach
Tenor	Mr. Eugene Clarke	Miss Carrie Burton, Mr. J. Engstrom, etc.	
Tenor	Mr. George Werrenrath	Musical Director	Mr. G. Dinkrath

The Ballet led by Miles. Augusta Solke and Adele Paglieri.

A Grand Chorus of 50 young and fresh voices.

Every Scene, Costume and Appointment will be prepared expressly for the occasion, and in a style heretofore unknown in this country, while our Prices will remain as usual.

Every Sunday Evening, will be given one of a Series of

TWENTY-FIVE CENT CONCERTS,

... BAND and various Vocal and Instruments celebrities

EDWARD E. RICE
Composer of *EVANGELINE*, who couldn't read a note

LIZZIE WEBSTER
And her attractive expanses

ELIZA WEATHERSBY
Started a tradition — first of Nat Goodwin's wives

Not only have dynasties fallen while it whirled, but beauty and genius have blossomed and been buried, while *Evangeline* waited in untarnished iridescence."

When Rice and Goodwin were at college together there was nothing about them to suggest that they would later author one of the greatest successes ever to come upon the boards. Goodwin after graduation became a reporter for the *Boston Traveler*, writing clever dialogue and witty verses in his spare time of which he allowed himself plenty. Everyone agreed he was brilliant, but everyone also agreed that he was singularly lazy. When Alice Oates had wanted someone to translate and adapt Offenbach's operas for the more pure-minded Americans, Goodwin obliged with some neat literary hack work. Ned Rice, his good friend, had a fine facility for writing catchy tunes, and imbued with a worthy passion for his Alma Mater, he obligingly wrote some of Harvard's most popular college songs before he graduated.

An interviewer in 1879 discovered to his amazement that while Rice played his Weber cottage piano like a virtuoso, he could not read a note of music—it was all done by ear, and that when he composed his music for the operetta, what he actually did was to play the themes to a musical amanuensis who recorded the notes meticulously and also the verbally expressed opinions of Rice as to orchestration.

It was after seeing the Lydia Thompson Troupe perform in Boston that Goodwin and Rice decided they could do no worse, and they determined to concoct a burlesque entertainment to which only the black sheep from every fold were expected.

To call the result of their collaboration an adjunct to opera bouffe would be misnaming a classic. Mr. Goodwin actually labored to weed the garden of burletta and extravaganza of vulgarity and all other objectionable features. French opera bouffe, in spite of Jacques Offenbach, never won the respect and support of the more staid members of society. Cheever Goodwin, opportunistically cleaned up opera bouffe and replaced sly innuendo with harmless gaiety, and gestures bordering on the obscene with the hilarious movements of, for example, a heifer. It was he who finally combined the various trends of burlesque, opera bouffe and extravaganza in one pot, strained them through the sieve of Boston's conscience, alias "The Watch and Ward Society," and poured them out as our domestic brand of innocuous musical comedy—"not a blush in a tight-load."

Rice's contribution was as great as Goodwin's. The book that never staled, the lyrics that appealed to one generation and then, with equal charm, to the next, were no more immortal—nor immoral—than the music. The tunes were not Offenbach's. No symphony concert places the score of *Evangeline* on its programs, even for the Stadium Concerts, but, when Ned said darkly to a member of the press, "There's a lot of money in me, if somebody knew how to dig it out," he was obviously not exaggerating.

The first production at Niblo's in 1874 was a minor success; two years later at Boston, it was a bigger success with Nat Goodwin as Captain Dietrich, Dixey at seventeen occupying the rear end of the cow and Gabriel, Our Hero, played by Eliza Weathersby, that dream in tights. It played eight weeks to over $40,000, considered up to that time a "Baked Bean" box office record. But when in 1877 it was revived in New York on a more magnificent scale at the Academy of Music, the critics really lost all restraint and the audiences never had any. While *double-entendre* and coarse gestures had been deleted, the costuming remained close to the essentials made popular by *The Black Crook*. One critic was astonished that the attractive expanses of Lizzie Harold and Lizzie Webster had not run afoul of the sensibilities of those pitiable followers of Anthony Comstock, who all his life was an inglorious illustration that to the evil-minded, all things are impure. Apparently Nat Goodwin rolled them in the aisles. "Convulsive" was the adjective most often employed to characterize the laughter which followed his mugging.

The character of the Lone Fisherman who does not deign to speak won many laurels. He gives a "briny flavor to the atmosphere and in his perpetual silence becomes ghostly, yet indescribably droll." Obviously this mute gentleman was an early prototype of Harpo Marx. The critic in his innocence imagined that because of its weak plot and light music, it was just the "style of amusement for warm weather," yet on and off for at least nineteen years it weathered many a blizzard and saw spring come around again.

Humor was what saved *Evangeline*, according to the *Spirit of the Times*, and yet the sappy sentimentality of its love story certainly was no handicap to its popularity. Poor, lovely Evangeline, separated from her lover by the cruel English! Poor, tragic Evangeline catching up to Gabriel in time to see him die. This is certainly the stuff of which best sellers are made and if Goodwin and Rice realized it in 1874, we must not forget that Longfellow realized it long before that.

In 1879, the Lyceum blossomed forth with another *Evangeline* still under the direction of the authors, and Broadway cheered itself hoarse and howled with laughter at the Heifer Dance. If you have never seen a canvas cow—or horse, for that matter—played fore and aft by two hidden, perspiring mortals, each blissfully unaware of the precise antics of the other, you have yet to experience one of the stage's funniest tableaux. The glazed eye and the foolish grin frozen onto the false face of the cow would cause hilarity even without the grotesque movements of the animal's strangely independent legs. Probably the funniest moment was when the

NAT GOODWIN

e had to be an excellent comedian to have seven wives

alarmed bovine slipped slowly down to the stage with each leg pointing to a different part of the compass. What alarm in her soft brown eyes, and what hysteria in the stalls!

As each new production of the evergreen *Evangeline* succeeded the last it was inevitable that the comic business which rocked the audience was constantly lengthened to the detriment of the plot, the straight dialogue and the enjoyment of the music. The plot grew even thinner than a London table-d'hôte meal in wartime, the straight dialogue was reduced to a few sentences essential to the sense of the continuity, and as many sentimental airs as possible were deleted. The comedians had their way with the piece, and it was thus sent through the country for seven successive seasons, and everywhere found audiences royally ready to have their risibilities roused.

Like *The Black Crook*, *Evangeline* came to be known as the "Nursery of the Stars." At one time its entire cast, without exception, became famous, the playbill probably becoming the most notable in American theatrical history of the period. William H. Crane, Richard Golden, Henry E. Dixey, Nat C. Goodwin and his first wife, Eliza Weathersby, George Fortesque, Sadie Martinot, Josephine Hall, Lillian Conroy, and James S. Maffitt, a pantomimist, afterwards teamed with Bartholomew.

Later-day theatergoers did not generally realize that those famous artists so admired by them at one time had capered through the nonsensical situations in *Evangeline*. Polly Peaches, for instance, in 1896 said with wit but not accuracy—"Everybody except Lawrence Barrett and Richard Mansfield has appeared in it, and the still more generous assumption is that most of our *heavy leads* ought not to have played in anything else. This verifies the saying of Montaigne,—that the cradle of all tragedy is burlesque: 'We begin life with a laugh at the absurdity of it, and we end life with a good cry, at the pity of it.'" Polly apparently was not aware even then that the public idol Richard Mansfield had appeared in the musical comedy—and very briefly, too, as, of all things, an unimportant spear bearer. No recognition followed this inauspicious debut, apparently not even Mansfield could carry a spear with a highly individualistic technique. Mansfield, however, probably gained experience with the spear, and made use of it in later years, by throwing the "harpoon" into newspaper critics whose judgment of his performances was at variance with his own.

The greatest single contribution made by *Evangeline* to the American stage, next to that of Mansfield, was the introduction of Henry E. Dixey. He literally danced his way into fame in the hind legs of a cow and from that ignoble position rose to stardom in, of all things, *Adonis*, which in later years held another record for continuous performances.

Another production in 1879 saw in the role of Captain Dietrich my old friend Gus Williams, Tony Pastor's favorite Dutch comedian. His parody on "You never miss the water till the well runs dry," entitled "You never miss the lager till the keg runs dry," was sure-fire and his dialect was something wonderfully inaccurate and exaggerated but equally inimitable and hilarious. Rice and Goodwin wrote the following lyric just for a Dutch comedian:

I'm in lofe mit a shveet leedle girls,
Und Katrina vas vot she vas called,
Unt her hair dot vos, vas hanging in curls,
Oxcept in der spots vere she's bald.
She's got eyes youst as blue as de'r skies,
Unt it vasn't her fault if she squints,
Unt der tears dey come springing right down in my eyes,
Cause her heart vas as hard as a flint,
I tell her I lofe her so dearly,
Unt my leedle frau vish her to be
But she says dat she never vill marry somebody,
Vich makes it unpleasant for me.

Then the lachrymose chorus began:

Yes, I lofe her, my shveet leedle girl
Und I vish dot ve married could be,
Unt ven ever I dinks of Katrina's shveet face
Dere's no use of holding of me.

The very lyric makes one think of Sam Bernard and, sure enough, *Evangeline's* revivals spanned enough years so that Sam himself had the opportunity of playing the Dutch comedian and singing his songs.

Six years later, Rice really outdid himself with a magnificent production of his favorite musical at the Fourteenth Street Theatre, where it played the entire season with Fay Templeton as Gabriel, she who later became Weber and Field's star. Louise Montague, with whom $10,000 has always been associated as the price of her beauty, deigned to take the part of Evangeline herself, the maid of Arcady.

In 1896, *Evangeline* was still seeking Gabriel, this time at Manhattan Beach when that was the leading seashore and summer theater resort near New York. Pat Gilmore, Victor Herbert and Anton Seidel all conducted in this theater cooled by the Atlantic sea breezes. It was here also that De Wolf Hopper buffooned his way into the heart of his audiences, appearing in Sousa's operas with the shapely Nella Bergen, who later became one of his several wives. A friend once asked Hopper whether he had married lately. "No," replied the latter, "times are hard and I will have to make my present wife do another season." In the Manhattan Beach production, Cheridah Simpson played Gabriel and held her own very well in the matter of filling an ample pair of tights. On the same stage, Frederic Solomon, one of Lillian Russell's matrimonial discards, played Le Blanc.

DIXEY AS *ADONIS*

HENRY E. DIXEY
The end of Evangeline's cow was the beginning of his career

THE LONE FISHERMAN
Early prototype of Groucho Marx

It would be strictly unfair not to mention the many choruses that tripped to Rice's measures. His contract with the public was to keep the chorus fresh, as the play would take care of itself. Some of the original bevy of beauties, grown adipose, had been weeded out and sent to the "Home for Mature Evangelines." Polly Peaches sighed with pleasure at this point. "The thing is therefore a perennial 'Fountain of Girls.' They do exactly as their ancestors did." And their ancestors were not Puritans.

Perhaps the only personal appearance Rice ever made on the stage was in the early 1920's at the Palace Theatre, New York, where in order fittingly to celebrate "a third of a century of Keith vaudeville," Dave Marion (Snuffy the Cabman), my good friend the late James Madison (noted gag writer), and Edward Le Roy Rice (author of *Monarchs of Minstrelsy*) produced a skit called "Rice's Surprise Party." This was probably the greatest old-time vaudeville act ever assembled. Mr. Rice was the featured star, surrounded by such "palmy day" celebrities as Leonard Grover, Eddie Girard, Ed Begley, Annie Hart, Laura Bennett, etc., nine in all. E. F. Albee, the Keith "big shot," was so pleased with the setup that after the Monday opening he presented each of the nine with $200 in gold. Rice looked like a million dollars, although nowadays in terms of the government, a million finishes as twenty-five thousand. In 1921, James L. Ford, in his very entertaining book, *Forty-Odd Years in the Literary Workshop,* said of Rice: "He is still active and hasn't a gray hair in his head. The same however cannot be said of some of his actors." Can it be that their hair turned to silver because on salary day Rice couldn't always produce sufficient gold?

VI

The Families

The first American traveling entertainers from bell ringers to acrobats

FOR many years, in the early part of the nineteenth century, it was the family troupes of concert singers who provided the sedate entertainment of that period in America. Many of these unimpeachable performers were religiously inclined and their programs relied on moralistic ditties, preferably morose, when temperance was not their *leitmotif*. The halls in which the Families performed were small as was the population of even the larger cities, and they did not hesitate to play in schoolrooms, vestry rooms, hotel dining rooms and even an occasional barn with the livestock removed. The Families and their satellites were actually the pioneer traveling companies who played to remunerative returns for decades. New England was their favorite port of call and certain sections of the West, too, wherever down-Easters had settled. Famous among these itinerant songsters and musicians were the Peak Family, Swiss Bell Ringers, the Hutchinsons, whooping up Abolition, the Rainers, lustily yodeling for a living, and many others.

The Bell Ringers, with "Two hundred and forty Silver Bells also Forty Silver Staff Bells," continued in favor for many years longer than any of us could conceive of their being tolerated. One definite advantage that bell ringers had over other sorts of troupes was that no audience could ever fall asleep on them. Too bad some of our prosy ministers never hired bell ringers as a necessary added attraction.

Even *The Black Crook* interpolated a troupe of bell ringers in the seventies. The personnel of these companies, all carefully married to each other for the greater good of the whole, usually consisted of four or five persons one of whom was required to be a comic singer and character impersonator. After all, American audiences could stand just so much temperance before reverting to type. A practical printer in Connecticut booked and owned so many troupes that he actually succeeded in forming a veritable bell-ringing trust for many years.

The Peak Family, one of the more pretentious troupes of Swiss bell ringers and singers was organized by Grandpa William Peak, Sr., in 1839. He enlisted as his company Grandma Peak, William Peak, Jr., Fannie Peak, Eddie Peak, Julia Peak, Lizetta Peak and a handful of fill-ins who unfortunately were not Peaks at all.

Grandma Peak was considered one of Boston's finest vocalists and when John B. Gough, the celebrated temperance lecturer, gave one of his inimitable evenings, he would have no one share the platform with him except Mrs. William Peak, Sr., who obliged with a selection of anti-alcoholic propaganda songs. Little Fannie, who was the most gifted of all this talented family went to work at a very tender age, indeed. The Peak program of reformist refrains obviously did not contain any verses on child labor. When Fannie was two years and eight months old she was introduced at the old Tremont Temple where she sang a temperance song with words especially written for her and played to the tune of "Gaily the Troubadours":

> Ladies and gentlemen, listen to my song:
> Hurrah for temperance, all the world round.
> Touch not, taste not, handle not the wine,
> For every little girl like me
> The temperance pledge will sign,
> I am a little girl, just three years old
> And I love temperance better than gold.
> Let every little girl remember my song
> For God loves little girls that never do wrong.

Fannie moved the audience and found herself on Governor Briggs' knee during the applause. Her early career was settled. With the aplomb of an old trouper, she repeated her initial success at every Peak Concert until she was seven years old.

Years later at a temperance meeting in Chicago presided over by Frances Willard, Fannie met Mr. Gough again. "You don't remember me," she said. "Yes, I do, and I am going to kiss you for your mother," he replied.

When Fannie was about ten years old the family found itself in New Orleans. At the hotel, she and her sister were each assigned a Negro maid. The custom then was for the maid to give them personal attention all day, and then she would lie on the floor outside the door of the hotel room every night like a watchdog. This impressed Fannie with the miserable servility visited on the Negro race and many years later, after her marriage, when she found herself in Savannah in the company of John Pierpont, Jr., during the Civil War period, she believed that he would have liked to

PIONEERS OF AMERICAN ROAD COMPANIES

WILLIAM PEAK, Sr.

WILLIAM PEAK, Jr.

THE HUTCHINSONS
Asa, John, and Judson

PATRICK S. GILMORE

talk to her about the North in favorable terms, but no one there dared do this. She told him how when only a tiny tot she had sat on John B. Gough's lap. Perhaps that, many years later, gave Pierpont's maternal grandson, the late J. P. Morgan, the idea of having a midget on his lap while undergoing a Congressional investigation.

In 1859 Fannie married John D. Fitz, a wealthy native of Louisiana, while the next year Julia married Billy Blaisdel, the opera singer who in later years appeared with De Wolf Hopper, Lillian Russell and Pauline Hall. Fannie for a brief time deserted her family to travel with her brother-in-law's company but by 1861 she was back with Papa and Mama and the water wagon in Texas. It was there that she met Mme. Anna Bishop with the first opera company to visit the Lone Star State. Back in New Orleans, Fannie sang the "Bonnie Blue Flag" at one theater while its author, Harry Macarthy, was singing it at another. His money and talents were devoted to the South. He was known as "The Man of Many Nations" but after the "late unpleasantness" the North was rather cool to his efforts, which for that reason were confined to the vaudeville houses, mostly the junior ones. One of his last engagements, before his demise in the late eighties, was in a free and easy variety cellar in San Francisco.

The Peak Concert Company, after demonstrating their superiority over other American musical families, became fired with "Yankee ambish" and were the first American entertainers to fulfill engagements in Cuba. The American rhythms as performed by the Peaks were not accepted by the Cuban public, and with extraordinary versatility the family learned how to play "broken time" on their staff bells, a forerunner of ragtime. The Governor General was so delighted with the way the Peaks adapted themselves to the musical tastes of the Latin Americans that he presented Fannie with a bouquet which concealed a diamond ring, and a wreath for her hair fashioned from golden leaves.

A prospectus for the Season of 1867, their twenty-eighth annual tour, as distributed by the Peak Family gives us a rather complete picture of the type of entertainment for which they became famous. They were described modestly as "Vocalists, Harpists and Pianists" in addition to their talent for ringing all of their 240 silver bells. The troupe, which seems to have lost William Peak, Jr., and Julia, boasted instead Master Albert, Fannie's son. Among the outsiders they featured A. J. Whitcomb, solo harpist, a pupil of Bochsa (Anna Bishop's Svengali), William Lavake, vocalist and pianist, Sol Smith Russell, comedian who got his first start with the Peaks, and Carl Reeves who played alternately upon the violin and zither depending upon the whim of his audience.

The program was changed nightly, and the selections listed numbered thirty-six, including such gems as "When This Cruel War Is Over," "The Arkansas Traveler" and "Father, Dear Father, Come Home." Admission was thirty-five cents with reserved seats at fifty cents. Children were encouraged to attend for two bits and, to set the tone of the whole performance, the tickets could be had only at the "Principal Book and Music Stores."

Fannie, who began at three, never retired. She sang and played in all of Patrick Gilmore's Jubilees. His promenade in Boston at the Music Hall boasted Fannie Peak playing her bells in one wing of the band. In 1889, Fannie went up to Pat after the rehearsal: "It is over twenty years since I have seen you and I suppose you have forgotten me."

"You, Fannie, who are a part of the most musical family in the world? I could never forget you. I am very familiar with your history. Fifty-six years ago the Peak Family of Swiss Bell Ringers came before the public and they at once became favorites. For thirty-eight years there was no better company in the country. They were constantly introducing novelties, the profession at large copied their ideas, and every year saw them with something new. Many an artist who has become famous in this country at the outset of his career was a member of the Peak Family."

John W. Hutchinson, of the famous family which bore his name, started his professional life with the Peaks, and his granddaughter Jessie was with later Peak companies for many years. In 1843 the Hutchinsons sang their debut at the Concert Hall on May 13th at 406 Broadway. Native children of Salem and descendants of first settlers of Massachusetts, their musical style was both simple and pleasing and somehow as steady as the granite for which New England was famous. Their success was immediate and for decades no sheet of music was complete without a delightful group picture of the Hutchinsons. Unlike the Peaks, the evils of alcohol did not concern them, but the evils of slavery did. They were the most valuable spokesmen for the Abolitionist movement next to *Uncle Tom* in the whole period preceding the Civil War. Folks with advanced ideas patronized them and they spread the gospel of freedom wherever men gathered to hear them. Of course, they could not resist a few songs of moral betterment. "The Gambler's Wife" appeared on their programs side by side with "The Old Granite State" and that eloquent ditty, "The Grave of Napoleon."

In 1839, when the Peaks were first organized, they had another family with whom to compete: the Rainers. Fortunately the Rainers did not go in for the "tintinnabulation of the bells, bells, bells," but confined their musical genius to the rendition of songs, ballads, and "melodies of the Alps" in close harmony on simple airs. Bossini directed the orchestra, pausing for the clear notes of a Swiss yodel to echo from the rafters of the Apollo Theatre. Almost the only yodelers left today are the soup yodelers and their obligatos are hardly to be considered under the head of musical accomplishments.

Undoubtedly worried by the popularity of the Swiss Bell Ringers, the Rainers joined forces the following month with Mr. Butterworth, who played a piece or two on his musical glasses—tumbleronicon solos, he called them. In addition to their far-flung harmonies, the Rainers appealed to the public wearing native costume and finally worked themselves into such a frenzy of homesickness with all these Swiss sights and sounds that they left shortly for their native shores leaving the Peaks and the Hutchinsons in undisputed mastery of the concert hall.

It is impossible to discuss families, or the Abolition movement without mentioning the Fox Family, who were responsible for bringing polite society to the theater in an era when the devil stalked behind the footlights and piety kept the population chained to their church pews. The story is a good one, and an important one to the history of the American drama.

"The Fox Children," as Caroline, and her three brothers—George, Charles Kemble and James A.—were billed, toured New England in the forties in concert and were most popular. In 1844, Caroline married George C. Howard, a popular actor who turned producer and who thus became associated in theatrical history with the Fox Family. As soon as he became a member of the Little Foxes, he, George and James set up a small acting company. Charging the very modest admission price of twelve and a half cents, they were scheduled to open in Providence, and then go to New Haven, "Providence permitting." Caroline and Charles were both members of the cast.

When George went to New York and James back to Cambridge, where he later became mayor, Howard moved to Troy, New York, with his family which now included little Cordelia and two brothers. Howard was rehearsing a version of Dickens' *Oliver Twist* in which his wife, Caroline, was to play Oliver, one of her best parts. The character of Little Dick, the sick pauper boy who bids a tearful farewell to Oliver as the latter runs away from the poorhouse, was still uncast. Someone suggested that Cordelia, their four-year-old daughter, should be dressed in one of her brother's suits and be given a few lines simple enough for the child to learn. As the rehearsal progressed, Mrs. Howard discovered that Cordelia learned rapidly and seemed to be a born actress.

The night of the performance, Cordelia's face was whitened to simulate a victim of consumption, and dirt was piled up in a corner of the stage. She was told to dig with a little spade and pretend she was digging little graves.

Oliver entered and saw Dick digging.

"I'm running away, Dick."

"Won't you come back any more?"

"I'll come back and see you some day," Oliver replied.

Then, instead of delivering her line, "Good-bye, Oliver," the child with a complete conception of the character, elaborated the scene.

"It won't be any use, Olly dear," she said, sobbing as if her heart would break. "When you come back, I won't be digging little graves, I'll be dead in a little grave myself."

The house was so deeply affected by this remarkable example of Victorian pathos that there were showers of tears both in the audience and backstage.

The fortunes of Cordelia and her parents, as well as theatrical history, were in the making that night. The Howards and the Foxes both decided that such emotional talent in one so young should not be wasted and Mrs. Howard suggested that since the whole country was talking about *Uncle Tom's Cabin, or Life Among the Lowly*, Mrs. Harriet Beecher Stowe's brilliant appeal for the Abolitionist cause, it might make a very good play indeed—what with thousands of readers weeping over little Eva.

Her husband immediately agreed: "It's the very part for Cordelia." George L. Aiken, Howard's cousin and a member of the company, was a budding playwright. He undertook the task of dramatization and with Howard's advice and assistance finished the play in a week. Shortly after the book's publication in 1852, the author had been asked for the right to dramatize the novel and she refused, saying a play based on her story "would bring Christians into the theater." She had never seen a play and believed that the theater was "an instrument of Satan." However, in those days there were no adequate copyright laws outside of France, and the author of a novel had no means of protection. Anyone with or without permission could dramatize her story and draw full royalties without paying the original writer a cent. Everyone started to pirate the tale. Clifton W. Tayleure was among the first to see its dramatic possibilities and his version, so hastily written that it ignored Topsy and Eva, had a brief run in New York in August of 1852.

But the combination of Aiken and Cordelia could not be excelled. The company was immensely popular and everybody was reading the book. A full house sat breathless with anticipation at the Troy Museum on the night of September 27, 1852. The Aiken version had no bloodhounds, nor were there any Jubilee Singers; the production was simple—it had to be cheap—the company was so small that they had to double the parts they played, and yet the play was a triumphant success from the first scene to the epilogue showing Eva in heaven. No one even saw anything incongruous in Mrs. Howard playing Topsy while her daughter played Eva. The Fox Family were *Uncle Tom's Cabin*, several generations of it. The parents were St. Clair and Topsy, Cordelia was Eva, E. K. Fox, the uncle, doubled as Phineas Fletcher and Gumption Cute, and Mrs. E. Fox, Cordelia's maternal grandmother, was Aunt Ophelia.

The tears flowed freely all evening, and many a woman in the audience found that the box of marshmallows she held in her lap was changing into salt-water taffy. Their only regret was that Eva died in the third act and therefore could not appear in the rest of the play. As a reward for their patience, the following tableau was presented as an Epilogue:

"Gorgeous clouds, tinted with sunlight. Eva, robed in white, is dis-

ASA HUTCHINSON

EARLY AND RARE PROGRA

UNCLE TOM'S CAB

NEW YORK, THURSDAY, MAY 31, 1866.

BARNUM'S NEW MUSEUM

539 and 541 Broadway, between Spring and Prince Streets.

E. F. TAYLOR...Stage Manager.

SUCCESS! SUCCESS! SUCCESS!

THE MOST BRILLIANT TRIUMPH OF THE SEASON.

The Great American Drama, with all its Original Effects, in Five Acts, 12 Tableaux and 30 Scenes, and all the Original Music.

MRS. G. C. HOWARD

Will appear in her Original, Inimitable Personation of TOPSEY.

AFTERNOON AT 2. EVENING AT 7 3-4.

OVERTURE...ORCHESTRA

UNCLE TOM'S CABIN

Or, Life Among the Lowly.

CHARACTERS IN ACTS FIRST, SECOND AND THIRD.

Uncle Tom, with the Song, "Uncle Tom's Religion," written by G. C. Howard)..........Mr. W. L. Jamison

St. Clair.......Mr. M. N. Haviland

Mr. Hilton.......Mr. Jayne

Mr. Shelby.......Mr. Hart

Phineas Fletcher..Mr. Hadaway

George Harris.....Mr. H. F. Daly

Marks..........Mr. Wilton

Haley..........Mr. J. H. Johnstone

Tom Loker..........Mr. Fraser

Turner, a Waiter..........Mr. Doobs

Doctor Mayne..........Mr. J. Pierce

Harry, Eliza's Child..........Miss Teany

Eliza Harris, (her Original Character)..........Mrs. J. J. Prior

TOPSEY, as originally played by her—with the song, "I'se so Wicked," written by G. C. Howard..........Mrs. G. C. HOWARD

Eva, with the original song, "Eva to Her Papa," written by G. C. Howard, her first appearance..........Miss Anna Prior

Aunt Ophelia..Mrs. W. L. Jamison

Marie St. Clair..........Miss Kehoe

CHARACTERS IN ACTS FOUR AND FIVE.

Uncle Tom....Mr. W. L. Jamison

Legree.......Mr. R. Anderson

Deacon Perry....Mr. Bridgman

Gumption Cute.......Mr. Wright

Little Bob, with a Virginny Breakdown, his first appearance..........

Sambo..........Mr. Matthews

Quimbo..........Mr. Findlay

TOPSEY....Mrs. G. C. HOWARD

Aunt Ophelia..Mrs. W. L. Jamison

Marks..........

George Shelby..........Mr. Wilto

Skeggs..........Mr. Steve

All Mann..........Mr. Phi

Adolf..........Mr. A

..........Maste

Slave Dealers, Slaves, Planters, Cit..........Mr.

Cassy..........Miss Jennie

Emeline..........Miss Ada

TABLEAUX INCIDENTAL TO THE DRAMA—The Escape of Eliza—Topsey and ...ing—Trappers Entrapped—The Freeman's Defence—Topsey and Ophelia—The Dea... Last of St. Clair—Topsey Butting the Yankee—Cassy Helping Uncle Tom—Death of U...

Grand Allegorical Picture of Eva in Heaven.

HARRIET BEECHER STOWE

covered on the back of a milk-white dove with expanded wings, as if just soaring above. Her hands are extended in benediction over St. Clair and Uncle Tom who are kneeling and gazing up at her. Expressive music. Very slow curtain." That gave "Little Eva" time to hurry to the lobby of the theater and sell photographs of herself as the audience emerged.

Uncle Tom ran one hundred nights in Troy, a record run for a play in the United States at that time, and especially for Troy, it being considered a one-horse town, where the inhabitants still waved at passing trains. Howard pointed out that one hundred nights in Troy was equal to a seven years' run in New York. Troy did not again get on the map, I must admit, even though I was born there, until it became famous for collars. In fact, many a theatrical troupe playing there since *Uncle Tom* days got it "in the neck."

Mrs. Stowe was right. The God-fearing Abolitionists flocked to the theater, both Christians and unbelievers. People of all denominations and of none crowded the Troy Museum.

From Troy, the Fox Family went to Albany and finally in 1853 it opened at the National Theatre, New York, under the management of Purdy with G. W. L. Fox playing Phineas, leaving his brother Charles to struggle along with only one part. *Uncle Tom* ran until May 13, 1854, three hundred and twenty-five performances, another record. Howard bragged: "I was the first to introduce and play single entertainments. That is, until the advent of *Uncle Tom*, no evening at the theatre was thought complete without an afterpiece or ballet dancing added to the play. When I told Purdy that *Uncle Tom* would constitute the entire performance, he flouted the idea and said he would have to shut up in a week. But I carried my point and we didn't shut up. People came to the theatre who were never in its doors before. They came from surrounding cities and towns. We raised our prices, which no other theatre in New York had ever dared to do."

While the play was at the National, Harriet Beecher Stowe broke her resolve never to enter a theater by attending a performance of *Uncle Tom*. She was heavily veiled and escorted by a friend. Several times during the evening, she was obliged to lift the veil to wipe tears from her eyes. It was hay fever season but that was not the cause. As the final curtain fell, she remarked to her friend: "Little Cordelia Howard is a marvelous child. Her mother is Topsy as I imagined her. Perhaps I have been unjustly prejudiced against the theater."

By 1859, the Foxes played Providence again and were billed as having played in the principal cities of America, England, Ireland and Scotland over ONE THOUSAND NIGHTS. "In their characters they will sing their original songs of 'Eva to Her Papa,' 'I'se So Wicked,' and 'St. Clair to Eva in Heaven' written and composed expressly by Mr. G. C. Howard for his family—"

After Cordelia's retirement, her mother continued to play with her husband until Howard's death in 1887 when she too retired. Evas who followed Cordelia were Anne Prior, Gracie Wade, and Little Minnie Maddern, our Mrs. Fiske.

Howard wrote two additional songs, the "Union" for his wife and "Religion" for Uncle Tom. He added the bloodhounds and the choristers when other *Uncle Tom* companies began to circus the play. By 1877, he was advertising "Slavin's Original Georgia Jubilee Singers and two hundred genuine Southern Colored Folks Most of Whom were Slaves in Georgia, Alabama, and Virginia prior to the War." The author suspects that most of these were genuine New Yorkers from Thompson Street where the Negroes lived at that time.

The play that started modestly in Troy in 1852 ended by bringing more Americans into the theater than any other dozen plays combined. The public response made the *Uncle Tom* show an industry. One enthusiastic critic said that "it influenced more human beings than all of Shakespeare's plays in four centuries." At any rate, it became "The Great American Drama." It has played in all kinds of houses, theaters, warehouses, skating rinks, under tents, and even in a livery stable, from Maine to Alaska. One season twenty-five *Uncle Tom* shows, each with its accompanying Non-Equity bloodhounds, were touring the country, all of them doing business. The late R. Beers Loos, father of Anita, was fond of relating how in a one-night stand in California the local Elks, after the performance, gave the bloodhounds a banquet.

One night in Hartford, Connecticut, in October of 1933, Otis Skinner, playing Uncle Tom, persuaded an old lady who lived near town to be present at Parson's Theatre where the production was taking place. At the close of the performance, he introduced the old lady to the audience as the original Eva, Cordelia Howard herself, still living eighty-one years after her sensational debut. And judging by the tremendous ovation accorded her, Cordelia of Troy was not a whit less famous than Helen of Troy, and as well remembered.

Not all the families, however, were as American as the Foxes, nor did they confine their talents to plays with music. On the 16th of July, 1832, at the Park Theatre, there appeared for the first time on this side of the Atlantic the agile French troupe of acrobats, rope dancers and pantomimists known to their public as "Ravel Family." The unique gifts of their star, Gabriel, of Jean, Jerome, Joseph Dominique, Antoine, François, Le Jeune Sauvage, Mme. Ravel, Mademoiselle Emilie and La Petite Amour, enthused their American audiences to such an extent that they became unqualified favorites whose popularity remained undiminished for more than thirty years. As a matter of record, they were so loath to leave their audiences, and their audiences were so loath to relinquish them to retirement, that they actually gave more successful farewell performances than the Divine Sarah Bernhardt herself.

TOPSY'S SONG.

·ds *by* CHARLES JEFFERYS. *Music by* STEPHEN GLOVER.

"What does make you so bad, Topsy? Why won't you try and be good? Don't you love *anybody*, Topsy?"

"Donno nothing 'bout love; I loves candy and sich, that's all," said Topsy.

"But you love your father and mother?"

"Never had none, ye know. I telled ye that, Miss Eva."

"Oh, I know," said Eva, sadly; "but hadn't you any brother, or sister, or aunt, or—"

"No, none on 'em—never had nothing nor nobody."

"But, Topsey, if you'd only try to be good, you might—"

"Couldn't never be nothin' but a nigger, if I was ever so good," said Topsy. "If I could be skinned, and come white, I'd try then."

"But people can love you, if you are black, Topsy. Miss Ophelia would love you if you were good."

"No; she can't bar me, 'cause I'm a nigger!—she'd 's soon have a toad touch her. There can't nobody love niggers, and niggers can't do nothin. *I* don't care," said Topsy, beginning to whistle.

"O Topsy, poor child, *I* love you!" said Eva, "I love you, because you haven't had any father, or mother, or friends—because you've been a poor, abused child! I love you, and I want you to be good. I am very unwell, Topsy, and I think I shan't live a great while; and it really grieves me to have you be so naughty. I wish you would try to be good for my sake; it's only a little while I shall be with you."

see 'UncleTom's Cabin' *chap.* 25.
Ingram and Cooke's Illustrated Edition.

Topsy's Song.

TOPSY'S SONG FROM *UNCLE TOM'S CABIN*

Unaware that their type of performance, which was entirely new to America, would meet with such immediate and favorable response, their original program modestly stated that "they wish to give a few performances in this city, that the nature of their spectacle may be known and duly appreciated." Of course, they were not too modest. They were actors. With pardonable pride, they pointed to the established fact that both their art and their antics had already been ecstatically witnessed in France, Germany, Italy, Prussia and Holland, and that their most recent appearance was before the King of that Island Paradise, Sardinia.

The first part of their show was devoted to "varied DANCES and EXERCISES on the TIGHT-ROPE with the Balance Pole ending with a GRAND EASTERN COLLATION" during which six persons performed on the same rope, without, it seems, either interfering with each other or with the tensile strength of their precarious perch. Having accustomed their audiences to this amazing feat, Part the Second provided the gapers with DANCES and EXERCISES *without* the Balance Pole, the finale featuring Jean Ravel in his "celebrated and extraordinary back somerset." After an intermission during which we hope the audience relaxed their neck muscles and reduced their pulse, the Third Part offered the PANTOMIME BALLET for which they were so much loved. They chose a comic scene for their first presentation ending with a "CHINESE PAS DE TROIS," nimbly executed by Gabriel, Antoine and Jerome. The entire performance was concluded by a new PANTOMIME BALLET entitled: "La Fête Champêtre, or the Aged Dancers." It is perfectly true that Americans had been treated to ballet before, but the charm of the Ravels was that this particular ballet was performed mostly in mid-air, "executed on two cords, on which will be shown the art of dancing on the Double Rope in various Pas d'Allemande and Pas de Deux."

In 1834, they returned to Paris, and from then on made regular trips taking back their huge earnings to the family estate at Toulouse.

Two years later they were back in America and in 1839, while on tour, they lost all their theatrical properties, worth many thousands of dollars, when the Mississippi River boat *Silena*, on which they were traveling, snagged and sank. This misfortune did not at all hinder their meteoric careers. They worked hard until they could replace their costumes, sets and trick gadgets without which they could not function smoothly, only to lose them all over again in September, 1846, when the original Niblo's Garden burned to the ground after one of their best seasons. In January of the same year the *Albion*, reporting on the hundreds who stormed Niblo's Garden only to be turned away at the box office with a SOLD OUT sign, had remarked that such a demonstration of public approval makes us inclined to believe that "Pantomimic acting must be the true exponent of thought, especially when the Ravels are the conveyancers," and hastened to add that Gabriel was the best low comedian of the stage.

THE GREATEST PANTOMIMISTS OF THE PAST

THE RAVELS

THE GREAT BLONDIN

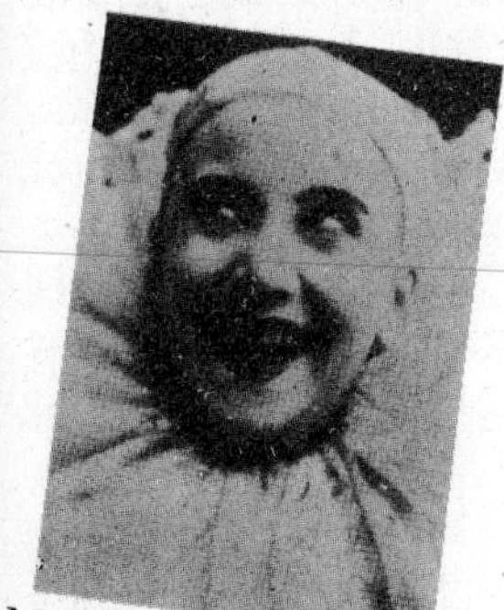

MLLE. PILAR MORIN

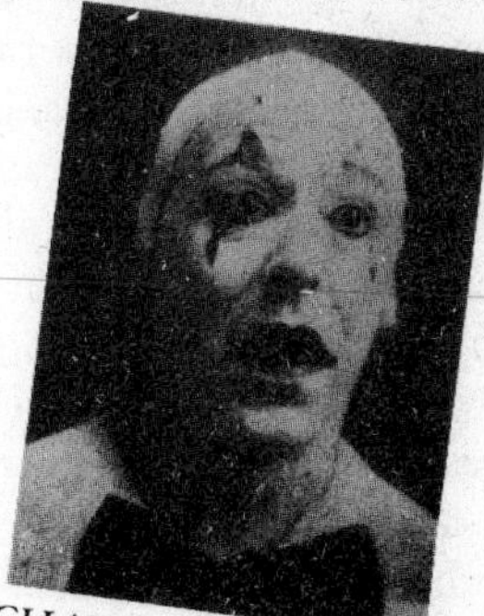

CHARLES W. RAVEL

JAMES S. MAFFITT

EORGE H. ADAMS

HANLON BROTHERS

TONY DENIER

This same helpful critic the following May went into verbal ecstasies over the perfect combination of the Ravels performing in Niblo's Garden. He declared that feats of strength, agility and pantomimic enchantments were exactly in accord with Niblo's fairylike and luxurious establishment. He asked dramatically, "Who can associate Shakespeare and ice cream together? What affinity exists between blank verse and sherry cobblers? . . . But with the Ravels, all is in keeping, all is in harmony . . ."

All was not, however, in harmony among the Ravels themselves. The brothers dissolved their four-star performances when Gabriel, the finest actor of them all, announced his farewell benefit on October 22, 1847, at Palmo's Opera House, Chambers Street, New York. In addition to his feats of physical strength and skill at gymnastics, he was probably the first great pantomimist in America. His face was so remarkably mobile, and the diversity of his facial expressions so unequaled by his fellow actors, that the nice play of every feature was instantly perceptible through the thick layer of white paint with which the complexion of the traditional Pierrot was always coated.

Soon after this farewell all the brothers left for home and when they returned, they separated into various troupes. In 1848, François came back with the Martinetti Family, while a year later, Antoine and Jerome returned to the States with the Lehman Family, Mlle. Bertin and Paul Brilliant. This latter company happily inaugurated the season in Niblo's New Theatre. In spite of the dangerous and daring nature of many of their feats, no fatal accident ever befell any member of the family or troupe directly attributable to their trapeze work, but two of their ballet dancers, Adelaide Lehman and Pauline Genet, on two separate occasions, met their death when their stiff white ballet skirts caught fire and could not be extinguished in time.

On June 2, 1851, Gabriel returned to the scene of his former triumphs and proved to his public that he was even more able than before and quite equal to his brothers in drawing in the crowds. "Young America," who was billed with extravagant praise in Gabriel's company, was the son of a stage carpenter at Niblo's Garden who made his debut when a child as a tightrope artist under Ravel's patronage. When Leotard created a great sensation in Europe by his inauguration of a triple trapeze act, Young America practiced this act and soon excelled in it. In order to present his "juvenile wonder" again in America, September, 1865, found Gabriel and Antoine reunited at Niblo's. The Hanlons had already presented this new feature at the Academy of Music, but the magic name of Ravel turned the trick again and Young America caused a sensation with his combination of grace and daring. Another protégé of Gabriel's was Blondin, the internationally celebrated tightrope artist, whose well-advertised stunt of walking across Niagara Falls on a tightrope startled the world. He was followed at a later date by Henry Leslie, the minstrel, pantomimist dancer, dramatic actor and comedian, who would not attempt the rope until he was two-thirds inebriated—a "staggering" feat, if you ask me.

It remained for Signorina Maria Spelterini to out-Blondin Blondin on July 20, 1876. A drizzling rain had made the rope so slippery that she was begged to postpone her feat, but she refused and on the first trip over lay down at full length on the center of the rope overspanning the whirlpool. On her second trip she carried a small stove and utensils and cooked an omelet over the raging waters. On a third trip to the Canadian side, she walked with her hand encased in a bag; on her fourth, she crossed with her feet tucked into wicker baskets. To everyone's amazement, she lived to return to Europe, where she traded on her American achievement with excellent financial results.

Gabriel and his brothers reappeared so often for further successes, and said good-bye so frequently between times, that the most fantastic stories were circulated about their ages, and particularly Gabriel's. In 1862 the grave assertion was made that the latter was at least ninety-seven years of age and that his phenomenal power was due to a lifelong addiction to temperance and the practice of scientific gymnastics. In reality, Gabriel was born at Rouen in 1810, which made him only seventy years old in 1880 when he appeared for the last time. A critic wrote: "M. Ravel is highly comic in a secondary part . . . The actor has only to grin in his face-splitting fashion, that is to say, literally from ear to ear, to put the house in roars of laughter. Ravel is justified if he be a *gourmet*, for his mouth is entitled to have all its whimsies gratified; it is to it he mainly owes the handsome income he has enjoyed from several Directors during his long stage career, and of all his talents, it is the only one which is still left to him." With this last encomium ringing in his ears, Gabriel returned home and died at Toulouse on April 14, 1882.

There is a small clipping reposing in the files of the New York Public Library from an unknown paper dated May, 1882, which described Gabriel's gifts in an obituary notice: "No India-rubber doll could be bent, twisted, turned and wriggled as his body could. He seemed made of gutta percha and hung on wires . . . He was a fellow of infinite jest and many a house he kept on the verge of ecstasy for hours together."

Gabriel, in the history of American theatrical forms, did more than just introduce the French comic Pantomime to our shores; he personally inspired one of the greatest clowns who ever lived: George W. L. Fox. On a chair in the back part of Niblo's Theatre could be seen by anyone who took the trouble to look, a sad-faced young man, intently witnessing the frolics of the Ravels and taking copious notes. This attendance at the Ravels' matinees was an invaluable part of the training of Fox, and without the inspiration of Gabriel and his troupe, it is questionable whether American pantomime would ever have flowered in the adept hands of his talented successor.

VII

George Washington Lafayette Fox

Humpty Dumpty, the saddest clown that ever chalked his face in pantomime

WHEN an actor creates a role so brilliantly that he becomes known to posterity by the name of the character he impersonated rather than by his own name, then we are in the presence of genius.

G. L. Fox was christened George Washington Lafayette Fox by his hopeful mother, quite a "moniker" for an infant to carry around. Undaunted by a name so top-heavy with national heroes, Fox walked onto the stage of the Olympic, on March 10, 1868, where he left his old name behind, and stepped off as "Humpty Dumpty," the pantomimic clown who will go down in the history of the American theater as the man who did most for the entertainment of children until perhaps the arrival, many years later, of Charles Chaplin.

Wherever Fox went in New York he was followed by an enthusiastic crowd of worshiping urchins and no man better deserved this adulation. He played Humpty in New York no less than 1,268 times, and each time added something to the enjoyment of life.

Fox's only language was that of facial expression and tricks, but his illuminating grins and Gargantuan grimaces were understood by children of all ages. His face was a face as readable as the pages of a book printed in bold type, while the wonderful changes of expression that he effected were like alternate clouds and sunshine playing across a summer sky. A contemporary critic wrote in 1870: "There are few men upon our boards whose bland emptiness of expression means so much, and absolutely none at all who can show the meanings and manners of a lout with

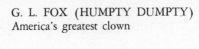

G. L. FOX (HUMPTY DUMPTY)
America's greatest clown

HUMPTY
DUMPTY

JOE JEFFERSON AS *RIP*
Fox, Jefferson's stage manager, also played a part

such unctuous merriment." And his body, too, was an instrument, thin, light and flexible—quite beautiful in form—which he employed with telling grace and agility. Like all truly great pantomimists, he knew when to temper his humor with pathos and could, on occasion, be truly touching. His English predecessor, Joseph Grimaldi, was the only other clown who could stretch the heart strings of an audience so far and hold them so long.

It is difficult for us today to re-create the lost art of pantomime for its own sake which flourished in the nineteenth century. In England there are still pantomimes at Christmas. In America, we have let them go forever as they appeared behind footlights. As small audiences grew into large audiences, and small music halls into great theaters, the exquisite innuendoes of a clown's facial expressions became lost in their transmission. In brief, distance no longer lent enchantment to the view. The clowns at today's streamlined circus at Madison Square Garden, seating eighteen thousand persons, are so far removed from their little patrons that they are often forced to wear comic masks to carry the point of their funmaking across so large an arena. It is not surprising that no new star is able to rise in the Clown Heaven behind such an impersonal and inflexible barrier.

Moving pictures have usurped stage pantomime. Only by close-ups of Chaplin and Laurel and Hardy on the screen can the greatly enlarged public of today actually enjoy the nuances of comic expression. And not even these purveyors of comedy come as near to the pantomime of which I write as Walt Disney does with his delightful personalities projected by synthetic means. Because of their color, music and complete good humor, his cartoons most nearly represent the mirth-provoking pantomime of another era. Our children derive but a fraction of the ecstatic joy from Donald Duck that the children of old New York derived from G. L. Fox when Gotham's population was only a million.

Fox as a little boy grew up with the stage as his nightly environment. His mother was attached to the Tremont Theatre of Boston and, at a benefit for Charles Kent in 1830, this merriest and saddest of American clowns made his first public appearance as one of the children in *The Hunter of the Alps*. His sister Caroline, then seven, appeared with him, the Mrs. G. C. Howard to be, who later became famous as the original Topsy in *Uncle Tom's Cabin*.

Unlike his sister, Fox showed no special aptitude for the acting profession, so, when his legs grew too long and his voice too deep for children's parts, he became an errand boy and then a clerk for a merchant tailor in Washington Street with whom he remained contentedly enough until 1845. In the meanwhile, his more successful, but actually less talented relatives, Caroline, John and Charles Kemble, were touring as "The Fox Children."

Fox finally deserted the career of a sartorial supernumerary, to take up one that eventually led him from "pants" to "Pantaloon," when his brother-in-law, George C. Howard, offered him the managership first of Brown Hall on South Main Street, Providence, Rhode Island, and then of Cleveland Hall on North Main Street in the same city. His next engagement was in New York, where he appeared as an actor again under the name of Lafayette Fox. The scene of his debut on November 25, 1850, was Purdy's National Theatre, later called the Chatham, the major theater of the era, where not only Fox but also Edwin Booth made his first appearance. The former appeared as Christopher Strap in the farce called *A Pleasant Neighbor*. Fox's success was immediate and the play had a long run. He next played Wormwood in *The Lottery Ticket* and Tobias Short-Cut in *The Spitfire*. With every role a success, he remained a permanent fixture at the National for almost a decade.

On July 18, 1852, *Uncle Tom's Cabin*, after its record run in Troy, was produced by Purdy at the National merely because Fox, the reigning favorite, wished to please his sister Caroline who urgently desired to play the role of Topsy. Fox himself played Phineas Fletcher but for once found that Caroline overshadowed him. Her Topsy became as famous as his Humpty and she played it like the good trouper she was for countless years in countless cities of these United States. One of the departed theatrical glories of all time was that tear-jerker *Uncle Tom's Cabin* which carried the message of the Abolitionists throughout the land in such a graphic manner that it seemed but a step from the audience to the battlefield where the war to abolish slavery was fought and won. Fox himself enlisted as a volunteer, served ninety days, taking part in the first battle of Bull Run, and returned as "Lieutenant G. L. Fox" to play at the New Bowery Theatre under the joint management of himself and James W. Lingard.

While managing the Bowery in the summer of 1859, Fox inaugurated a series of outdoor festivals and balloon ascensions at Jones' Wood, which were conducted on too large a scale to prove highly remunerative—but what fun they were for the public. What old New Yorker does not recall with reverence this famous old picnic park on the East River front at about 65th Street, where later the Pastime Athletic Club grounds occupied a section of the woods which had been cleared. But Jones' Wood proper was a natural park in the heart of New York City, just a few blocks from "Battle Row" at 63rd Street and First Avenue. It was to this fragrant grove that city folks went for their picnics on moonlight nights and to forestall any emotional difficulties, young ladies wore what was very properly termed in those days, "picnic drawers," buttoned wisely by Mama for morality's sake, posterior-wise.

In 1862 Fox appeared briefly at the Olympic, where he was later to become famous as Humpty Dumpty, before going to the renovated Old Bowery on May 17th to begin a lengthy engagement as manager and actor. Tony Denier, who later achieved fame as a clown, was a member of his company which presented for one hundred and fifty nights a succession of dramas, farces, pantomimes and extravaganzas that never failed to "pull them in." Tony was still with him three years later when they revived the noted vehicle of the Ravels, his masters, *The Green Monster*, at Barnum's Museum. The expert antics of the White Knight were not enough to keep Fate from interfering, for the theater burned down only three days after the opening. In 1866 and 1867, *Jack and Jill* followed by *Little Boy Blue* jammed the Old Bowery. John Oxenford, the English playwright and critic, who was visiting in America in 1866, had the opportunity of seeing Fox in action and immediately proclaimed him a second Grimaldi.

While Fox had the gift of holding his audiences, he completely lacked that of holding on to his cash. The money that was rightfully his and for which he worked so industriously went from his pockets to those of others with an agility comparable only to his own physical movements. There was a special combination of gamblers set up, not especially to fleece Fox, but certainly to fleece as many persons like him as they were able to lure to the gaming tables. A Bowery Faro Bank used to be opened at midday in defiance of all conventions to win Fox's money, there not being time enough to win it all at night. The sad part of this tale is that Fox did not even have the dubious pleasure of playing—it was his partner who lost their money for him.

Finally on September 9, 1867, Fox opened at the Olympic on the east side of Broadway above Houston Street, and it was farewell to his Bowery days. He was stage manager and minor actor in *Rip Van Winkle* with Joseph Jefferson starring, that remarkable interpretation which practically never left the boards! In the same year Fox tried something new-indeed for him: he presented Shakespeare's *Midsummer Night's Dream* with himself playing Bottom. A contemporary critic wrote: "Mr. G. L. Fox may be said to have obtained the honors of the evening . . ." In brief, his "Bottom" was "tops."

He played the character in a style that was "droll and dry," not "mellow and exuberant." This was merely the beginning of his fondness for the Bard of Avon. Three years later he indulged in a musical burlesque of *Macbeth* and also played the title role in T. C. De Leon's burlesque *Hamlet*. "Pop" Wood, famous stage door man at the Hudson Theatre, in an interview given in 1910, recalled the opening night of this historic take-off, far removed from the "take off" several decades later of "Gypsy Rose Lee." A brilliant audience assembled to witness the travesty on *Hamlet* because the consummate art of Fox was well appreciated within

SCENES FROM HUMPTY DUMPTY
Conceived by G. L. Fox and Tony Denier

his lifetime. Boxholders were E. L. Davenport, John McCullough, Edwin Booth and Lawrence Barrett. The last-named was particularly enthusiastic, remarking that he, for one, had no doubt that Fox could give one of the best straight performances of *Hamlet* of any actor on the stage. High praise indeed from the stars of one's own profession!

Humpty Dumpty, jointly conceived by Tony Denier and G. L. Fox as a pantomime, was first performed at the Olympic on March 10, 1868, before eighteen hundred enthusiastic New Yorkers. With a cast of sixty cavorting through seventeen scenes, this theatrical venture proved to be the one opus of the decade 1860-1870 that challenged the phenomenal run of *The Black Crook*. For almost two years the Olympic Theatre knew neither worry nor fear of change—*Humpty Dumpty* seemed immortal. The box office took in $1,406,000 during this engagement. And thus, while *Humpty Dumpty* may have had a bad fall in the nursery rhyme, he certainly never had one at the box office. Everything about the production was arranged with infinite finesse. A. Oakley Hall, an author and Mayor of New York under Boss Tweed, wrote the Prologue in which Alice Harrison played Burlesque and Mrs. Edmonds, Romance. Fox himself was Clown in the Harlequinade and C. K. Fox was Pantaloon. Frank Lacey of London was Harlequin while Emily Rigl, the ballet dancer, played Columbine. The plot was simple, but it afforded the talents of Fox their full scope. Pantaloon, the father, tries to thwart the marriage of Harlequin and Columbine by using Humpty Dumpty, the Clown, as a fellow conspirator. H.D. used all the resources in his repertoire to delay and prevent this marriage. On so slight a thread was strung an impersonation which delighted the whole theatergoing population of New York. With perhaps one exception—a solitary critic who wrote of the opening: "There is little to be said in favor of 'Humpty Dumpty.' There is much to be said against it if it were worth the trouble." Perhaps the pessimistic penpusher's dinner had disagreed with him. He further proclaimed: "Mr. Fox, as Humpty Dumpty, was exceedingly funny in his make-up and dry unconsciousness of the humorous things he does; but Mr. Fox at times forgot that he was on Broadway, and was quite as vulgar as could have been desired by his Bowery friends. [. . . a Bowery audience assembled at the Olympic to greet the production of a Bowery pantomime by a Bowery manager . . .] . . . Boys in a barn with a donkey, a pig and a few farm utensils at command, would devise just such a performance in incident and action, lacking only the finish of appointments." A month later, this dour creature was "in again" and let out the following blast: "'Humpty Dumpty' is as crowded and vulgar as ever. It is unfortunate that Mr. Fox should mar a very enjoyable and funny performance by pointless obscenity. It is also a strange fact that people will sit quietly and look at the pantomimic inde-

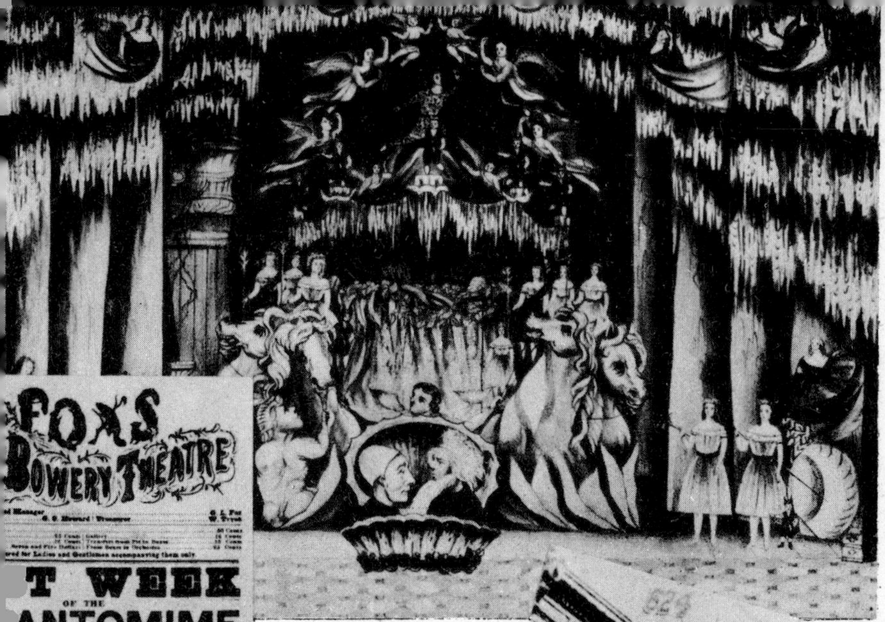

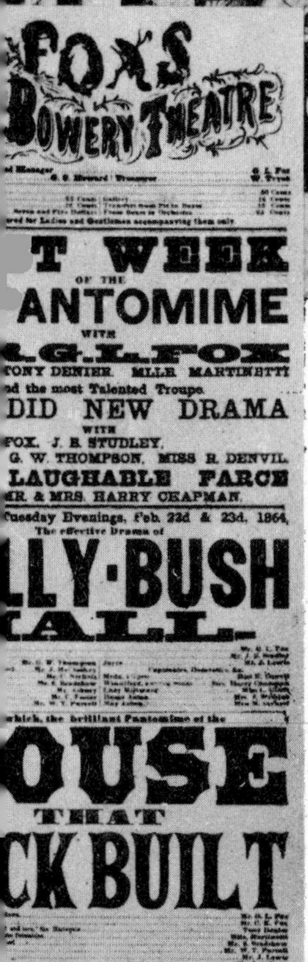

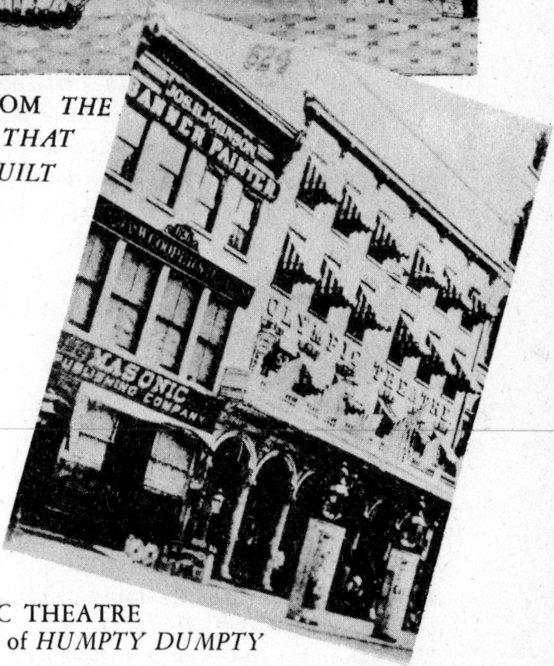

SCENE FROM *THE HOUSE THAT JACK BUILT*

FOX'S
BOWERY THEATRE
T WEEK
OF THE
ANTOMIME
WITH
G. L. FOX
TONY DENIER. MLLE MARTINETTI
nd the most Talented Troupe
DID NEW DRAMA
WITH
FOX. J. B. STUDLEY.
G. W. THOMPSON. MISS R. DENVIL
LAUGHABLE FARCE
MR. & MRS. HARRY CHAPMAN.
Tuesday Evenings, Feb. 22d & 23d. 1864.
The effective Drama of
LLY-BUSH
ALL.
which, the brilliant Pantomime of the
OUSE
THAT
CK BUILT
THE LILLIPUTIAN FAMILY
& MRS. WHITE
Performance of the Pantomime
Next Saturday, commencing at half-past 2.

OLYMPIC THEATRE
Birthplace of *HUMPTY DUMPTY*

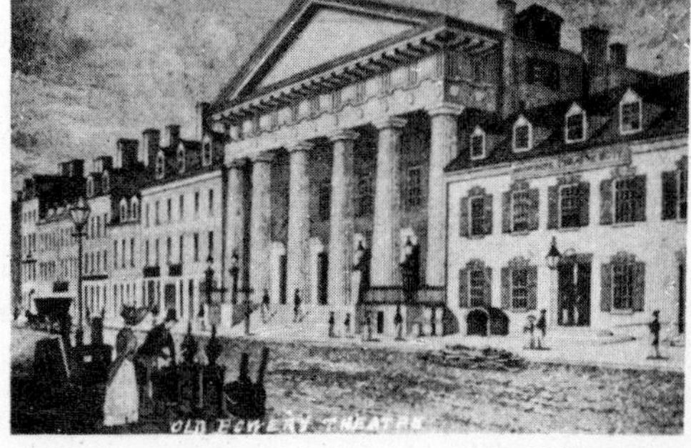

OLD BOWERY THEATRE
Where Fox and many famous stars appeared

cencies of the stage, but if the slightest insinuation is clothed with language, there is a howl of holy horror."

After an unprecedented run, Fox presented as a successor, *Hickory, Dickory Dock,* a poor second to *Humpty Dumpty.* It ran through the summer only and should be remembered chiefly as the opus which introduced the Kiralfys to America, not as the brilliant directors which they proved themselves, but as a new troupe of Hungarian dancers. *Wee Willie Winkie,* pantomime for children, and *G. L. Richelieu,* a burlesque of Bulwer-Lytton's play in which Booth was starring, acted as stopgaps while the public, and especially the young folk who were just arriving at the age where they could be taken to theater, clamored for a revival of *Humpty Dumpty* which Fox obligingly opened on August 31, 1871. After three hundred and thirty-three performances, it was taken off to have its face lifted and new tricks and ballets added. This accomplished, Fox was off again on his theatrical marathon, not stopping until June 7, 1873.

He next appeared in a revival of *Midsummer Night's Dream.* It might have been a good dream in Shakespeare's time, but was only a bad dream in the panic of 1873 and was quickly withdrawn. Fox also played Goliah in a version of *The Wandering Jew* and finally in the Grand Opera House at Eighth Avenue and 23rd Street, he became Humpty Dumpty again under the management of Augustin Daly. The pantomimic entitled *Humpty Dumpty Abroad* gladdened the hearts of his public and ran for eighty-five consecutive performances.

By this time anyone might have seen that H.D. was the golden egg, so we are not surprised to find that on April 6, 1874, a handbill was circulated calling one and all to view *Humpty Dumpty at Home* at G. L. Fox's Broadway Theatre. "Away with dull care! Laugh and be merry! Let all rejoice! Mr. Geo. L. Fox, the KING SUPREME OF THE PANTOMIMIC WORLD, will produce with new scenes, costumes, music, mechanical effects, tricks and transformations, his great Comic Trick Pantomime, entitled, 'Humpty Dumpty at Home.'" Gymnasts and Bell Ringers were added attractions, matinees played Tuesdays, Thursdays and Saturdays at 2:00 P.M., and seats could be, and were, secured six days in advance.

For some time Fox had alarmed his family and friends by showing signs of a developing insanity. These were slight enough, however, to be attributed to his volatile temperament, so there seemed no reason why he should not have opened in *Humpty Dumpty in Every Clime* on October 24, 1875. After fifty-nine performances, however, his dementia became apparent to his audiences and the management forced his retirement.

After his tragic leave-taking from the stage, Fox spent many days walking in Fort Greene Park near his home in Brooklyn. Brooklyn Johnnie Carroll told me once that as a boy he remembered seeing Fox playing there with the children. He would do bits of *Humpty Dumpty* without revealing his identity, mimicking himself as though he were but an imitation without make-up of the famous G. L. Fox. The children were delighted with him and his mirth-provoking grimaces. Even in his illness he could not allow his great talent to go unused and unappreciated among youngsters.

One day in March of 1877, an attendant went with him to the park where, as usual, a group of children were eagerly waiting for their daily carnival of fun. Fox sadly motioned for them to go away, and they had scarcely left when he was stricken with a mild paralysis. He had felt the stroke coming on, and the great heart of Humpty Dumpty, wishing to spare his child audience, had dismissed them before they could witness what might have been their first painful introduction to the sight of approaching death.

That same night, he was persuaded by his brother-in-law, G. C. Howard, to retire to the insane asylum at Somerville, Massachusetts. It was a melancholy journey indeed for the great pantomimist. Other famous contemporary stars who also suffered a mental eclipse were John McCullough, William J. Scanlan, Tony Hart, of Harrigan and Hart, and Maurice Barrymore, who was stricken while performing at an uptown New York City music hall.

Fox's many admirers in New York never ceased to ask for him and the newspapers reported during this period: "When not slumbering, he sits up in bed and recognizes old friends by name as well as by presence, and the vigor of his greeting and of his well-remembered laugh suggest that if it were not wholly dependent upon physical vitality, the thread of life is not likely to snap soon. But . . . he is weak, and especially unequal to carrying on a sustained conversation. Happily, he seems not to realize the gravity of his complaint, and is shaping bright plans for an impossible future: 'Humpty Dumpty in Switzerland' for Niblo's Garden, for which he will import four hundred rare birds from Europe."

George Washington Lafayette Fox made his positively last appearance in this world on October 24, 1877.

> And let this be his epitaph
>   They carve and place above him;
> He made his fellow-men to laugh,
>   And all the world to love him.
> Let that be placed above the head
>   Of Humpty Dumpty who is dead!

What 18-karat is to gold, and sterling to silver, G. L. Fox was to pantomime. What would I not give to have my children and their children, and hosts of other children, see and enjoy and laugh over the antics of the incomparable G. L. Fox in *Humpty Dumpty*.

PART TWO

I

Maria Felicia Malibran

Who displaced the male sopranos of her day

IN 1825, when Mme. Pasta suddenly became ill, Manuel Garcia, the composer and teacher of singing, offered his daughter, Maria Felicia, in place of the great artist. While this proved a great boon to the opera company, it was, at the time, a very bold suggestion indeed. Maria Garcia was only seventeen and her voice was completely unknown to English musical audiences. In truth, the name Garcia then was less likely to draw as singer than it did years later as a cigar.

Still her heritage was promising; Signor Garcia had sung at Madrid, while Signora Garcia was known as Jacques Briones on the English stage. When four years old, Maria traveled in Italy with her gifted parents and played child roles. In Naples two years later she was taught solfeggio and Hérold, the composer, gave her lessons on the pianoforte. From Italy, the family moved to Paris and by 1818 they were established in London. This musical travelogue, which was the childhood of Maria Felicia, made it possible for her to speak Italian, French and English fluently, to which she added German in later years. During an argument one day, a friend accused her of using language multicolored as harlequin's suit. "True," she answered, "but you understand it—it is not masked."

In addition to differing national influences, she was under the imperious direction of a father who can only be described as constantly running the gamut between irritability and violence. His family trembled in awe before the combined power of his personality and his lungs.

One evening, Manuel, wishing to play an original composition for a visitor, roared down the hall "la famiglia." Immediately, as if on greased wheels, Mama and daughter appeared rapidly and silently. The composition rendered, they as swiftly and mechanically departed.

Manuel was a harsh critic. When the Garcia family were engaged to sing an *Offertorium* in the Catholic Chapel in Warwick Street, the father was horrified at the false notes they sang, and unable to endure their inadequacy, he let go with the full power of his voice, successfully drowning out his incompetent relatives.

Although it was his daughter who became famous, I cannot help dwelling on Manuel himself, without whose almost fanatical determination Maria could never have achieved the fame she earned. For Signorina Garcia was not born to be a great vocalist—rich tones did not pour from her untutored throat in glorious waves of sound. She worked to sing, nature having endowed her sparingly with the essentials for vocal success. She was born with a weak voice, its lower notes imperfectly developed, the upper indifferent in quality, even inclined to be metallic and thin. Her voice was not naturally attuned to her ear, and during practice with her tempestuous father she would at times be so fearfully out of tune that Manuel would leap from the piano and hide in the farthest part of the house to indulge his despair. Then Maria would fly after him, dragging him back by his coattails, begging him to forgive her and recommence. He once complained bitterly that when he played on the white keys, Maria sang on the black ones; and when he played on the black keys, she sang on the white ones. "And to make matters still worse," he moaned, "when I play on both the black and white keys, Maria sings in the cracks."

Nevertheless, Maria herself was imbued with the ambition her father nursed for her and not a little of his fiery temperament, exhibiting, during her career, passion, waywardness, generosity, and a fluctuating rage.

Life with the Garcia family was never dull.

Her father, impressed with the difficulty of his self-imposed task of artist-maker said sadly, "Maria can never become great, save at the price of suffering"—and meant his own.

The London Company, destitute without Pasta, took the young Maria on sufferance, and at seventeen, as Pasta's understudy, she sang the part of Rosina on June 25, 1825. The audience saw before them a small, dark girl of noble carriage. Her hair was black and glossy, always parted in the center and worn smoothly drawn down to frame her expressive though not beautiful face, whether she played a queen or a peasant. Her great charm lay in the mobility of her facial expression which reflected the most varied emotions. Her voice showed the benefits of the vigorous training which had been imposed upon it. The public acclaimed her, and she was promptly engaged for the rest of the season at $500 a week.

She followed the London season by appearing in the Manchester, York and Liverpool festivals where she dared to attempt some of the difficult passages from Handel's *Messiah* and *Creation*. Her success was proved by the jealous wrath she aroused in Velutti, the eminent male soprano of his

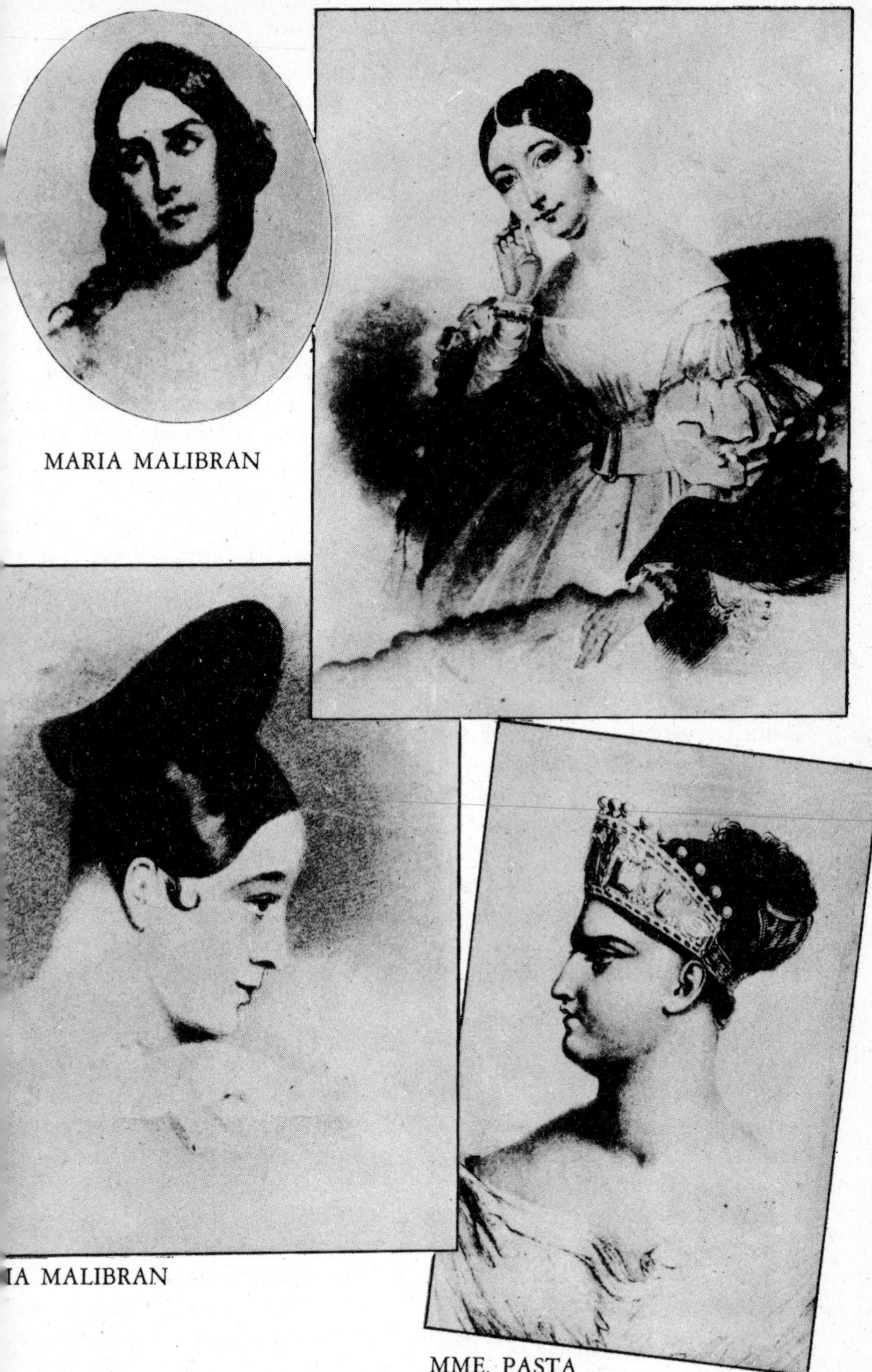

MARIA MALIBRAN

MARIA MALIBRAN

IA MALIBRAN

MME. PASTA
Whom Malibran succeeded

day and the last musico to attain operatic distinction as a female impersonator. These strangely gifted men, who carried their boy sopranos into adulthood, chose to appear in church choirs rather than on the stage. Some of them became soldiers. A little boy, seeing a Scotch regiment in kilts, asked, "Who are those soldiers that look like men and dress like women?" "Those," replied his father shrewdly, "belong to the Middlesex Guards."

In spite of these engagements in the hinterland, Maria had not yet achieved a thoroughly recognized position in the musical world, and after the closing of the festivals, she found her family in such a sore financial plight that she nearly solved the rent problem by marrying the humble member of an orchestra merely because he was employed at the time. It is safe to predict that while he manipulated the bass viol in the orchestra, had he become wedded to the imperious Maria, he would have only played "second fiddle" at home. It was at this critical point in her career that her eccentric and visionary father, Manuel, stepped in again, and prevented this mistake by evolving the scheme of introducing Italian opera to America; as bold a stroke as introducing his daughter to replace Pasta.

Manuel's rapidity was as great as his daring. When one remembers that on August 1st the Garcias toured England, and that in 1825, transatlantic crossings were made in sailing vessels by only a few persons who carefully insured their safety by leaving their family lighting innumerable candles to St. Christopher; and also remembering the protracted negotiations necessary to secure a company of even mediocre artists, the sudden appearance of the Garcia Grand Opera Company in New York in November was nothing short of miraculous.

On the 25th of that month, at the Park Theatre, the first Italian opera ever heard in America was sung by Manuel's company and *Il Barbiere di Siviglia* was the chosen vehicle. Maria sang Rosina in which she had made her debut the previous June, in London. Angrisani, an excellent basso, sang Basilio, Papa Garcia himself sang Abnariva, while the other roles were handled not too gloriously by a company of first-class second-class artists.

Young Maria's success was a windfall. The New York critics were in a delirium of admiration. Her fresh lovely voice was declared a heavenly gift, her beauty—which was certainly not physical—bewitching, and her abounding vivacity, astonishing. The public joined the critics with their acclaim and she endeared herself to her audiences by the simple but clever gesture of singing an English song as a nightly encore. *Il Barbiere . . .* was followed by *Tancredi* and *Otello*. Maria played Desdemona. And surely operatic history was made when the young singer recovered from her smothering to appear before the final curtain to sing "Home, Sweet

Home"—"by popular request." From that day to this "Home, Sweet Home" has been regarded as "the American flag waver" of musical selections when extra applause is desired. Maria was criticized for employing such means to gain the approbation of the crowd: "You should impose your opinion on the public, and not submit to theirs," they said. Maria shrugged her pretty shoulders and replied, "There may be two or three connoisseurs in the theater, but it is not they who give success. It *is* the crowds."

It was during her American adventure that Maria Garcia was courted by Francis Malibran, a 50-year-old French merchant settled in New York. Perhaps he had been reading about a man of 45 who married a girl of 15, admitting that he was three times as old. "But," he parleyed, "in five years from now, when she's 20, I'll be 50, or only two-and-a-half times as old. And ten years after that, when she's 30 and I 60, I'll only be twice as old. And if we live long enough together, some day she may be even older than I am." At first, because of the wide difference in their ages, Manuel refused to allow the match, but as Malibran appeared to be very wealthy indeed, he eventually gave his parental consent, and the ill-mated pair were married on March 23, 1826. Apparently the Frenchman's enthusiasm for Maria was such that he drained his resources to capture her, for a few weeks after they were man and wife he became a bankrupt and was thrown into jail for nonpayment of debts.

In spite of this tragedy Maria Malibran was grateful to America because her meteoric career actually started in New York where her talent was recognized for the first time at its real worth, and where she became the idol of the public, tasting the intoxicating adulation she was later to drink without measure when she meant to Italian opera what Rachel, much later, meant to French tragedy.

In September, 1826, Maria determined to separate herself even further from her imprisoned husband by returning to Paris where the Countess Merlin, a friend of her childhood, took her in as a protégée, and through her important connections saw to it that Mme. Malibran, as Maria now called herself, made her first appearance at the Paris Grand Opera in January, 1827, in *Semiramide*, given as a benefit for Galli. For the first time the 19-year-old girl trembled at the ordeal which faced her.

Never had she heard of the great singers—without an example to follow, she was thrown on her own resources, and obliged to walk the stage where Pasta and Sontag shared honors. Moreover, the theater was larger than any she had ever appeared in, the company was so distinguished, the audience so sophisticated, that it was only with a violent effort at self-control that she stepped up the stage. She sang the first phrase, "Fra tanti vegi e popoli," with such noble clarity that applause came from all sides of the house, but when she attempted "Frema Empio," she met with less

THERE IS NO HOME LIKE MY OWN.

Tyrolien

The Words from

THE BIJOU,

Music Composed by

MADAM MALIBRAN.

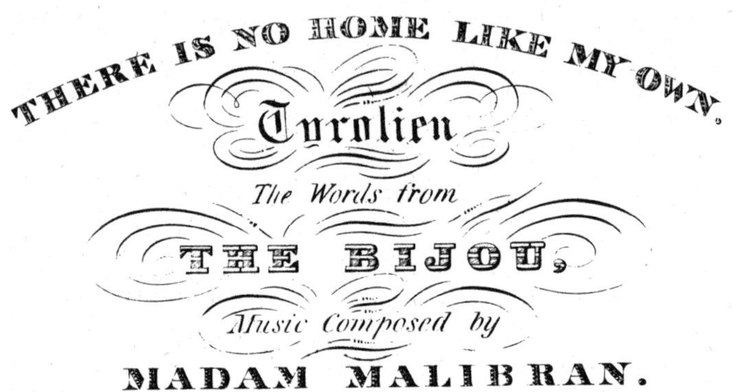

G. E. BLAKE, *Publisher, No. 13 South Fifth St. Philadelphia.*

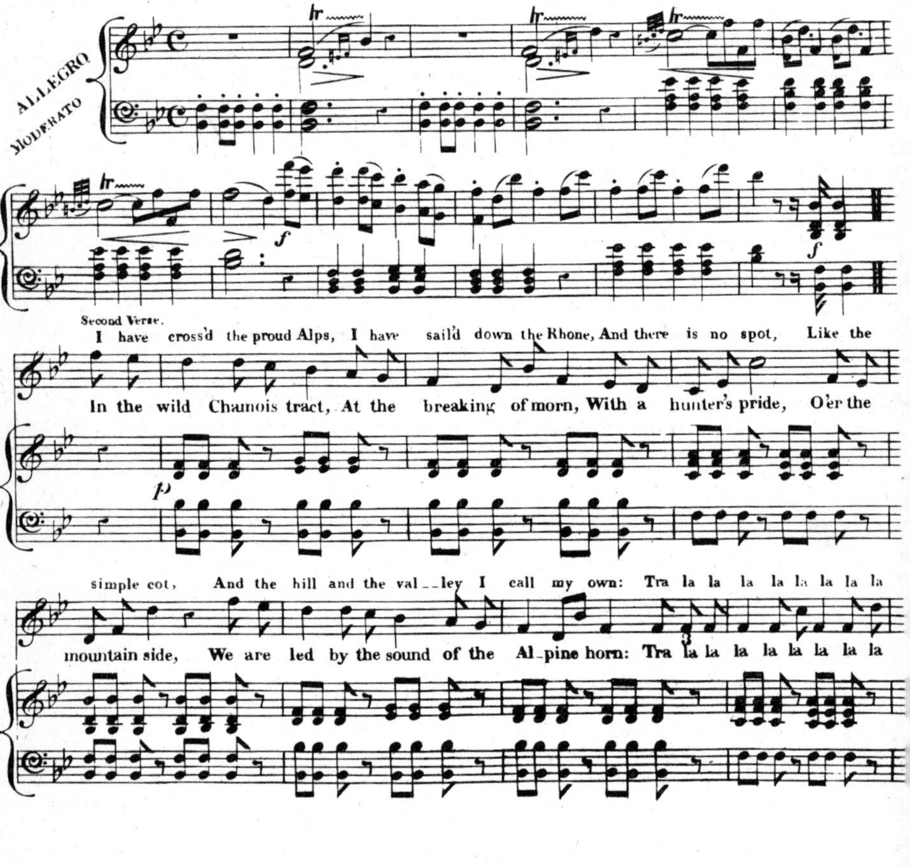

ALLEGRO MODERATO
Second Verse.
I have cross'd the proud Alps, I have sail'd down the Rhone, And there is no spot, Like the
In the wild Chamois tract, At the breaking of morn, With a hunter's pride, O'er the
simple cot, And the hill and the val__ley I call my own: Tra la la la la la la la la
mountain side, We are led by the sound of the Al_pine horn: Tra la la la la la la la la

success, and frightened by her failure, she did not attempt to sing the high notes of the passage, terminating the aria in a low register which thoroughly disappointed her audience, who had been captivated by her appearance and original delivery. Upon her reappearance, she was received coldly—but with renewed courage and the determination for which her father was famous, she sang exquisitely and the chill reception changed to a bravura of tumultuous applause. The defects in her singing were those of inexperience and this was fully appreciated by the fastidious audience. She awoke the next morning an idol of the warmly emotional Parisians, and with the director offering her other engagements. After all, Maria Malibran's voice had all the necessary vocal essentials, extending over three octaves, from D in alto to D on the third line in basso. And this was only for the public. In private, when she could be free of fear of criticism, her range was even greater but, of course, could not have been under perfect control.

The gallery was enchanted by her intense feeling. The same child of nature as she was during her youthful training, her acting was characterized by passion and tenderness. Without ever having taken any lessons in dramatics, she proved to be innately intelligent and naturally graceful.

"I remember once," said the Countess Merlin, "a friend advised her not to make Otello pursue her so long when he was about to kill her. Her answer was: 'You are right. It is not elegant, I admit, but when once I fairly enter into any character, I never think of the effect, but imagine myself the person I represent. I can assure you that in the last scene of Desdemona, I actually feel as if I were really about to be murdered and I run accordingly."

Not only as a singer was Malibran gifted. She played the pianoforte well and, like the Great Caruso, although untutored, she drew brilliant caricatures, and in her spare time—if she had any—composed songs. Troupenas published a group of her compositions in Paris after her death. Others were collected and published under the lugubrious title of *The Last Musical Thoughts of Maria Garcia de Bériot*. Her handwork was so excellent that she herself made all her own costumes and headdresses.

Mme. Malibran chose to sing with the operatic company at the Italiens rather than at the Grand Opera and in 1828 the company was composed of Malibran, Sontag, Dingilli, Zuchetti and Grazian. The presence of Sontag was a stimulus and not a check to her talent. Every time that Sontag won a triumph, Malibran wept, naïvely crying, "Why must she sing so divinely?"

In 1830, when she was only twenty-one, she became ill so often that even she was alarmed and left for Brussels, but the manager of the Italiens impressed upon her the disastrous consequences which would follow her

PENSÉES DE MALIBRAN:

A COLLECTION

OF

SONGS AND DUETS;

VIZ.

No. 1. "ROUSE THEE UP, SHEPHERD BOY!"
("Lève-toi, jeune enfant.")

2. "THE VOICE THAT SAYS 'I LOVE THEE.'"
("La voix qui dit je t'aime.")

3. THE WATERMAN. ("Filles du hameau.") } Notturno for 2 Voices.

4. "NOW THE BEAMS OF MORNING."
("L'aube matinale.")

5. THE MINSTREL.
(Le Ménestrel.)

6. THE MEETING. ("Déjà la nuit sombre.") } Notturno for 2 Voices.

7. THE SONGS OF HOME.
(Les Refrains.)

No. 8. THE DRUMMER.
(Rataplan Tambour.)

9. "DEAREST! COME TO ME." ("Entends-tu les gondoles.") } N for

10. THE BAYADERE.
(La Bayadère.)

11. THE PARTING WISH.
(La Resignation.)

12. THE GOBLIN OF THE LAKE. ("Nôtre grande mère.") } N for

13. "COME TO THE FETE!"
("Le plaisir nous appelle.")

14. "ROW, BOYS!"
("Enfans, ramez!")

THE ENGLISH WORDS BY

WILLIAM BALL;

THE MUSIC COMPOSED BY

MADAME MALIBRAN.

Price One Guinea.

LONDON:

PUBLISHED BY MORI AND LAVENU, 28, NEW BOND STREET.

The whole of the above are published singly, price 2s. and 2s. 6d. each.

MALIBRAN IN 1830

RADORE ALLAN

withdrawal from the company, so she gave in. "You are right, I did not dream of that. I am so unhappy and will return."

No doubt she should have rested instead of working at that time, because on June 8, 1832, she felt it necessary to announce a farewell performance. But she recovered somewhat and sang a short engagement in Rome, Naples and Venice. In the spring of 1833, Drury Lane and Covent Garden claimed her. Each year the terms of her contract improved. In London she earned £2,775 for twenty-four performances. Salaries this size had never been heard of before.

In March of 1835, the French Tribunal finally granted her a divorce from the disgraced M. Malibran and left her free to marry her lover M. Bériot, and thus legalize their son, Wilfrid. Up to that time, when asked if he had any children, M. Bériot was always forced to reply, "None to speak of." As a marriage gift, the Queen of France presented her with a superb agraffe adorned with jewels.

Mme. Malibran returned to England in April and while riding in the park was thrown from a horse and internally injured, aggravating an earlier trouble so that when, in September, she returned for the Manchester Music Festival, she did so only by exercising all her will power. She managed to keep up because of an unnatural feverish excitement. At rehearsals she was either crying or laughing hysterically, but she insisted on going through with her engagement, so that the public would not accuse her of being capricious, as the management of the Italiens had once done.

On Wednesday, September, 15, 1836, she sang the duet "Vanne le Alberghi in Petto" from Mercadantes' *Adronice* with Mme. Caradore Allan. The voice of Maria Malibran was never purer than in these, her dying moments. Enchanted by her genius and unaware of her ill-health, the audience demanded its repetition with enthusiastic applause. With a superhuman effort, Maria returned to the stage with Mme. Allan, and bravely recommenced the duet, only to be carried a few minutes later from the theater to her deathbed where she passed away when only twenty-eight.

All Europe mourned, and much of Europe gossiped. It was whispered that she died because of the incorrect treatment given her by her own physician, Dr. Dellumini, who was also her intimate friend in whom she placed her entire confidence. This good doctor, however, was slandered by these rumors. The truth was that before he could reach her bedside, a local physician had "bled" her and when Dr. Dellumini finally arrived, Maria looked up at him with her dark, sorrowful eyes and whispered, "I am a slain woman! They have bled me."

II

Giulia Grisi

Who had six daughters and was Queen Victoria's favorite singer

THE fete of Santa Giulia was being celebrated in Milan on July 2, 1812, when another daughter was born to Officer Grisi of the Engineer Corps in the service of Napoleon and was promptly named in honor of that illustrious saint. As Giulia Grisi grew and her voice developed into one of great beauty and promise, no one was very surprised. Her sister, Giuditta, ten years her senior, was a well-known singer in Italy, while her aunt, Giusetti Grissini, was one of the most personable stars at La Scala. Just to prove the family's creative aestheticism, Giulia's cousin, Carlotta Grisi, was the Pavlowa of her day. The martial influence of Papa was not a strong factor in Giulia's hereditary equipment.

Like all young ladies of proper family, the little Grisi first studied voice and music at the convent, but it is safe to say that she learned more about vocal training and opera technique from listening to her own sister practice. When only seventeen she made her debut in Florence as Zelina in Rossini's opera of the same name, but it was as the desperate young creature, Giulietta, that she succeeded in arousing the public's most ardent and vociferous adulation, as she sang and acted in Shakespeare's immortal tragedy converted into opera by Vincenzo Bellini who was just beginning in 1829 to try his talents by writing for the lyric drama.

"Perfection" was the cry of the critics. "What beauty!" "What dramatic fervor!" "What a magnificent voice!" cried the opera fans.

Immediately Giulia added to the roles she could sing by performing in Puccini's *Vestale*, and Rossini's *Tancredi*, *Otello* and *Semiramide*. In the last-named she so completely re-created the role of Semiramis that she succeeded in making her own name a synonym for the part she played so brilliantly. Grisi had the excellent fortune to perform frequently at La Scala in Milan on the same stage as Mme. Pasta, whose methods she carefully studied. The world-famous diva took a friendly interest in the young girl, which grew to great admiration as Giulia displayed her genius in some of the more minor roles first allotted to her. Pasta was so impressed by Grisi's impersonation of Jane Seymour in Donizetti's *Anna Bolena* that she said to the young singer: "I can honestly give back to you the compliment said by your aunt; she said, 'I was worthy to succeed her—well, you will take my place.' "

And Pasta was right. Giulia Grisi, after Maria Malibran's brilliant but brief creative life, became the leading dramatic star of the lyric stage.

The year after working with Mme. Pasta, in 1832, Giulia assured the success of *Norma* at its first presentation at Milan, although she sang the comparatively small part of Adalgisa. The combined effect of her impassioned acting, her beauty and her voice electrified the patrons. In later years, the title role became hers, and this opera was her greatest triumph. As the Medea of the British Isles, she displayed her great gift for tragic impersonation and those who saw them both, admitted that while her interpretation was definitely founded on that of Mme. Pasta, she individualized the role sufficiently to make it truly her own. An ecstatic critic raved: "One mind could conceive, one body alone could perform, one mind and body combined could enthrall by intensity; and that mind and body was what the world knew as Giulia Grisi."

Giulia's voice was a pure soprano extending over two octaves which effortlessly climbed to C in alto; if she had a weakness it was in the less powerful low register, although, as far as public approval was concerned, that had no effect on the box-office register. Her middle tones were hauntingly mellow, full and sweet. As a tragedienne, she seemed to feel her parts so deeply that she, in common with all great dramatic actresses, so personalized the characters which she played that she seldom if ever repeated an exact gesture or tonal expression, even after accomplishing an effect which seemingly could not be improved. Her interpretations were as mobile as her voice, and this in an era when stereotyped dramatic forms were the rule rather than the exception.

After Grisi's success as Adalgisa, all Italy was anxious to hear the newcomer and engagements were made for her in the principal Italian cities. Completely innocent of the extent of her popularity, Giulia signed a contract with a shrewd manager which made her his slave for several years, and which paid her just enough to satisfy a lyric debutante, but nothing commensurate with Giulia's exceptional talent. When the young prima donna realized the mistake she had made and the lire flowed into her manager's coffers at the same time as they merely trickled into her

GUILIA GRISI

LAFARGE'S
METROPOLITAN THEATRE
BROADWAY, Opposite Bond Street.

BENEFIT OF
MR. HACKETT

POSITIVELY
Last Night in America
OF MADAME
GRISI
AND SIGNOR
MARIO

MONDAY EVENING, FEBRUARY 19th, 1855
Will be presented DONIZETTI'S GRAND TRAGIC OPERA, in 4 acts,

LA
FAVORITA

LEONORA, (The King's Favorite,) - - Madame GRISI
INEZ, (Her Confident,) .... Madame MORRA
FERNANDO, (A young Novice of the Convent of St. James,) - - Signor MARIO
BALTHAZAR, (Superior of the Convent,) .... Signor SUSINI
ALFONZO, (King of Castile,) .... Signor BADIALI
DON GASPER, (The King's Minister,) .... Signor BARATINI
Chorus of Courtiers, Guards, Monks, Pages, Pilgrims, Attendants, Ladies of the Court, Spanish Maidens, &c.

IN ACT 1st.
Pas Brillante
AND IN ACT 3d.
La Madrillana
WILL BE DANCED BY SENORITA
SOTO.

MUSICAL DIRECTOR AND CONDUCTOR .... SIG. ARDITI
STAGE MANAGER .... SIG. AMATI DUBREUL
PROMPTER .... SIG. SALABERT

ENTRANCE TICKET ONE DOLLAR ONLY
Tickets with reserved Seats $1 50. Private Boxes, and Parquet Circle Boxes, according to location and capacity, from $6 to $20.
Box Office open daily, from 9 A. M. till 5 P. M.
DOORS OPEN AT HALF-PAST SIX. TO COMMENCE AT HALF-PAST SEVEN.

SIGNOR MARIO
World famous tenor-husband of Grisi

own purse, she tried frantically to free herself from the original clauses of the contract. Unlike other managers who, discovering genius in a protégée, immediately raised this new star's earning to be commensurate with their own, this rather thickheaded impresario chose to hold Giulia to the exact letter of her agreement with him. It was not a clever move. Not only he, but Italy, lost Grisi forever. Years later, when asked what made the Bay of Naples so blue, she replied, "If you had to wash the foot of Italy, you'd be blue too."

To escape the legal and financial plight in which she found herself, Grisi fled across the frontier and traveled posthaste to Paris, never again to return to her native land. For her career, no better misfortune than the unfair contract could have occurred. Paris was what Giulia needed, and Giulia was what Paris needed. Her gifted aunt Grissini and her sister Giudetta were both in Paris at the time, eager and ready to make her feel at home, and what was nothing short of miraculous, her old friend Rossini was also at work in the gayest capital of the universe and without hesitation he offered Grisi the title role in *Semiramide* at the Théâtre des Italiens. In spite of the highly critical dilettante audience which one found in Paris in those days. Rossini made no mistake. Giulia's debut was a complete success and from that year, 1832, without a break, the diva sang at the same theater a part of every winter for seventeen years.

Théophile Gautier himself was deeply impressed. He wrote of the "magnificent trinity" of her beauty, her acting and her voice. "In tragedy, such as *Lucrezia Borgia*, her acting is sublime, in the scene where the mask is torn from her face it discloses features as pale as if cut in marble, and defiant, flashing eyes. Her more than statuesque figure reminded one of an antique Niobe."

In 1834, Giulia made her first appearance in London, and won the English audience with the same ease which had captured the Continent. Queen Victoria's diaries between that year and 1840 testify to the fact that Grisi was Victoria's favorite singer when the latter was a little girl. One passage is particularly interesting, since it compares Grisi with Malibran as the little princess judged them with the same definiteness which characterized most of her opinions all through her life. "Malibran will be and is a very great loss indeed," wrote Victoria, "for although I liked and admired Grisi by far more than Malibran, I admired many parts of the latter's singing very much, in particular those touching and low notes which gave one quite a thrill."

Two years after her English debut, Giulia returned to Paris to marry Count de Melcy, an unfortunate episode in her life which cost her not only sorrow but money. Six years after their unhappy marriage a divorce was granted by the terms of which the Count was to have the proceeds of an ironworks. However, the revenue from this source was, at best, uncertain, so it was further stipulated that his wife should pay him 10,000 francs a year as long as she remained on the stage. Apparently, Grisi thought she could escape this responsibility—not by fleeing across a frontier as she had in her early youth, but by simply ignoring it. In 1851 the Count entered suit against the diva claiming that for some time past this amount had not been paid, and he demanded the arrears amounting to 27,500 francs. Giulia's legal advisers, in answering the suit, argued that the February Revolution had so interfered with her normal earning capacity that she was unable to pay as much as 10,000 a year but that, in view of the arrearage, she would settle that amount on the Count to close the lawsuit.

The Count's counsel merely smiled politely and entered an itemized list of the amounts which Giulia had received from various theaters during the period when she claimed poverty. In addition to her salary, which was enormous, he called attention to the gifts of valuable jewels which she had received particularly in lavish St. Petersburg where a fillet worth 30,000 rubles, about 120,000 francs, had been purchased by subscription, the Czar himself having subscribed 10,000 rubles to the fund. In answer to the argument that Giulia's income had appreciably declined because the artistocracy had been forced to abandon support of the Italian opera after the revolution, the Count's advocate gently reminded the Court that her English engagements more than compensated for her French losses, the musical festivals alone bringing her a clear 30,000 francs.

After judiciously weighing the evidence of both parties to the suit, the Court ordered the diva, as defendant, to pay the whole sum claimed by M. de Melcy. Thus did poor Giulia realize that a husband could be a very expensive luxury, especially when he proved to be "a count of no account."

Grisi's English success did not have to be proved by cold figures in a French court of law. In 1839, the *Spirit of the Times,* in reviewing *I Puritani,* called attention to the thunderous applause which was prolonged far beyond the usual time. The critic wrote: "In place of titling her 'the prima donna,' the word now is, 'la donna di tutti cuori.'" We trust he wasn't calling her names. Giulia certainly held her audiences in London spellbound from 1834 to 1861. No further proof is needed that the Britishers appreciated Grisi and paid heavily for their appreciation. By 1847, Giulia was the most important member of the magnificent company which left Her Majesty's Theatre on the establishment of the Royal Italian Opera at Covent Garden where the exaggerated star system was somewhat modified for the good of the entire ensemble. It must be remembered also that in 1847-48 there was competition in London. Jenny Lind was singing at the Haymarket Opera, yet during all the furor of her success, Giulia Grisi's light was never dimmed.

With the memory of her first husband finally waning, Giulia tried marriage once again, and this time so successfully that her name was seldom uttered without its being coupled with that of the tenor Mario, operatic matinee idol of his day. They married and lived and sang together for thirty miraculously happy years without a trace of artistic jealousy marring their relationship. This small domestic Arcady was, in a measure, one of the reasons for their phenomenal success, particularly in England. It was very comforting for the Victorian moral code to have such a prominent example of the Triumph of Virtue behind footlights. Who could criticize a person for attending an opera whose two stars were parents of six daughters? It is true only three of them survived early childhood, but you must admit that Mario and Grisi tried their best.

Czar Nicholas of All the Russias was a great admirer of both husband and wife. One day he met Mme. Grisi taking a promenade with her brood of daughters. Stopping her, he said facetiously, "I see these are the pretty Grisettes." "No, your Majesty," replied the dignified mother, "these are my Marionettes."

Mario and Grisi's happy married life was all the more amazing because Mario was probably one of the handsomest men who ever lived, and he was constantly subjected to oceans of female adulation, literal tons of sweet-scented love notes, and endless embarrassing demonstrations of affection from total strangers. In helpless flight from so much emotionalism, his greatest delight was to remain at home with his wife and children. This model creature who, if he tasted privately any of the public admiration, did so with such discretion that it failed to reach the gossips, had one weakness: a love of tobacco. In spite of his voice, which he was obliged to cherish, he refused to believe that smoking could harm him and was never without a lighted cigar except when singing, sleeping and eating, a habit that Winston Churchill is so enthusiastically endeavoring to emulate. Smoke certainly didn't harm Mario's vocal cords, since he was still singing at sixty, though not, of course, with his original beauty of tone.

In 1852, Meyerbeer's opera *Le Prophète* was sung at the Royal Italian Opera with a notable change in cast. Mme. Viardat Garcia had made the role of Fides her own, and now it was being given with the whole cast just the same as formerly except that Mme. Grisi was in Mme. Garcia's place. This really dangerous experiment turned out to be a brilliant triumph. Giulia's impersonation was hailed as even more natural and heartwarming than that of her gifted predecessor. She played the role with calm dignity and the entire audience was deeply moved by her sincerity and the pathos which it aroused.

The dignity of Giulia Grisi and the calmness with which she undertook the most difficult assignments were characteristic of her private life. No situation was too frightening for her to master. On a trip from the south of France to Paris, Grisi found herself in a compartment with several other ladies of her acquaintance, when the train stopped at a wayside station, and a man entered the same coach, intruding on their privacy. Before long, he began to act very queerly and it became obvious that they were closeted with a maniac. The separate carriages, none of which had connection with any other, except for a door used as an exit for the stations, made it impossible for the women to call for help. When the man finally drew a sharp-edged razor from an inside pocket and demanded that he be allowed to sever their heads, the women were utterly terrified and fell into an assortment of Victorian swoons. Only Giulia kept her head. The prima donna started to sing softly, allowing her voice to grow in volume as she saw it was beginning to take effect. His threatening attitude gave way to rapt attention and, to save their lives, she sang song after song "to soothe the savage breast." After endless singing, when Giulia was praying for a chance to rest her voice, they arrived at another station, the alarm was given, and he was taken into custody as a recognized inmate of a lunatic asylum. We've heard of screech owls who should be murdered for singing, but never before of a prima donna who had to sing to keep from being murdered.

For fifteen years, Mario and Grisi sang only in Europe but as time went on the call of the United States was too strong for them to ignore. A New World to conquer—what artist can resist it? Particularly when an American tour was one of the best ways of recouping a family's finances. In 1853, they made their joint agreement with Mr. Hackett by which they were to perform in this country for sixty-three nights commencing in November of that year, and for which they were to be paid $95,000—not exactly pin money. To show his good will, Mr. Hackett agreed to place $50,000 with Messrs. Baring Bros. & Co., the London bankers, two months before the actual engagement was to begin. When the time for the engagement was altered to the 4th of the following September, the advance deposit was made on July 1st.

September, 1854, saw Mario and Grisi opening at Castle Garden with *Lucrezia Borgia*, the best seats being sold for only $3 in spite of the enormous overhead undertaken because of the unusually large salaries. The performance was smoothly competent but the public accepted the two stars with more quiet satisfaction than enthusiasm, and no one ever made a fortune out of quiet satisfaction. There was nothing about their debut which could be compared to that of Jenny Lind, for instance.

When the Academy of Music at Irving Place and 14th Street was just opened as an opera house on October 2, 1854, Mario and Grisi were engaged to sing *Norma*, with the best seats in the house selling at $2 (way under any "ceiling" tariff), with the leading singers of Europe and the best opera company that had ever come to town, performing in New York's favorite opera in a new and beautiful theater, the entrepreneur had a right to expect a crowded audience and unlimited success. But the unpredictable public never came and the famous couple sang their best-loved opera to a half-empty house. It is possible that their failure was due to the fact that they waited too long for their American tour. But the tenor and the soprano were past their prime and had nothing strikingly new to offer the American musical audiences. Grisi was proud of the successes she had made in interpreting various characters on the operatic stage, and was too blind to realize that as she grew older she should have abandoned those roles which her advancing age made her no longer physically capable of handling. It seemed difficult for her to understand that a triumph twenty years before could not always be repeated twenty years later. Whatever hopes their manager might have had that the public might develop a taste for his stars or learn to love them, were dissipated as the season advanced and the receipts grew smaller, but not the appetites of Mario and Grisi. In James L. Ford's book, *Forty-Odd Years in the Literary Workshop*, is mentioned that contemporaneously with their appearance at the Academy of Music, Moretti opened a restaurant at 14th Street and Third Avenue, to supply them with their native food. It was said to have been New York's first Italian table d'hôte, and Moretti is credited with having introduced into this country spaghetti, olives, Chianti and other Italian delicacies. He subsequently followed the uptown trend, moving to West 35th Street. In his final days to compete with a near-by restaurant that offered an extra cup of coffee free, he is said to have put a sign "No charge for the second mile of sphaghetti."

Mario and Grisi themselves had nothing to worry about so far as their American salaries were concerned. A provision in their contract assured the completion of the tour. Details of their trips through other American cities in the winter of '54 are lacking; only one amusing anecdote survives. During a performance of *Norma* in Washington, D.C., a heavy rainstorm was in progress, which exerted unexpected pressure on many weak places in the roof of the theater. The leak became such a menace to the comfort of the singers as the opera continued, that Grisi's Norma appeared in a fur coat while Pollione, the tenor Mario, sang his beautiful best under the protective shelter of a huge umbrella. No matter what the fickle public thought of these two, it would be equally interesting to learn what Mario and Grisi thought of the Americans when after seventy performances they returned to Europe, without having added any luster to their operatic reputations.

There followed for Grisi in London, Paris and Madrid a series of farewell performances which could be nothing more than pathetic for all the great singers. The enthusiasm was not there, a new set of people made up the audiences, who gave their fealty to other, younger singers. In 1861, Grisi held her Farewell Festival at the Crystal Palace in London. The critics all mentioned the remarkable length of time during which Giulia had delighted her audiences. For twenty-nine years, Grisi had pleased her public and should have been only too delighted to retire. But the singing couple had always been very extravagant and they were forced to sing as often as possible to keep up the flow of money which they knew all too well how to spend.

Then one day in 1869, while her beloved Mario was fulfilling an engagement in St. Petersburg, Giulia Grisi died suddenly in Berlin.

III

Anna Bishop

Who was the original Trilby in real life ana who was shipwrecked on Wake Island

LITTLE Willert Beale sat with his family at dinner on Sunday when Sir Henry Bishop stopped by, and inquired whether any of the Beale family had seen his wife. No one had. "But I've sought her everywhere in vain"—and he left, reluctantly, as if he had expected to find Anna Riviere under the dinner table.

Writing his book many decades later, young Beale remembered the harassed husband who had not yet learned that his beautiful and talented young wife, the mother of his children, had left her home forever with Bochsa, the harpist, in order to become a prima donna in America. Her escapade was an apt illustration of what the *Police Gazette* termed "Man's duplicity and woman's worse than weakness." Her story was the story of Trilby, and Du Maurier was supposed to have adapted fact to the exigencies of fiction in writing his famous novel.

Anna was born in London in 1810 of French parents, who had emigrated from Bordeaux to Soho where her father, the descendant of Goldsmith, became a drawing master and a most prolific parent. Anna remembered him as being wholly intent upon earning a livelihood for five daughters and seven sons. Thus he learned that, while children are the light of the home, after twelve have arrived, it's time to shut off the light. About Anna's busy mother we know little, but it is safe to say that she probably shared the opinion of Her Royal Spanish Highness, whose thoughts were immortalized in the popular quatrain:

It's a terrible life, said the Queen of Spain,
One month's pleasure, and nine months' pain.
Three months' rest and at it again,
It's a Hell of a life, said the Queen of Spain.

In addition to Papa Riviere's flair for art and babies, he was a flute player and the front drawing room at Fitzroy Square was reserved for music alone. Anna's musical bent was recognized early, as it so often is in Bohemia, and she started her musical training under dear, exhausted Mama's interrupted tutelage until she was entered in the Royal Academy of Music where she studied pianoforte under the skilled direction of Mischeles and became an accomplished performer. With her piano technique, her voice also developed and proved to be an expressive soprano, characterized by great flexibility and power, so that by the time she was twenty-three she abandoned pianoforte and began studying under Sir Henry Bishop. Hers must have been a most grateful nature. She felt so indebted to those persons who developed her voice that she rewarded them one after the other, in the only way she knew how—with the generous gift of herself.

Eight years before her debut she married Sir Henry Bishop, professor at Oxford, who, not content with a purely academic life, had composed *The Lady of the Lake* and *Guy Mannering* and other operas popular in England at that time. The first Mrs. Bishop had passed away after a long and serious illness, on June 10, 1831. He claimed it had broken his heart but Anna must have proved good mending tissue, for within four weeks the lonesome composer married Anna, the most promising and certainly the most beautiful of his pupils. In the light of subsequent events, it might have been better if he had waited a little while longer. All during this period, Anna led a most exemplary life, and the deviation with her harpist which followed might have been due less to the latter's hypnotic influence over her than to the very simple fact that Anna's lawful wedded husband was twenty-three years older than she when they were married at Marylebone Church.

Bochsa, the young matron's Svengali, although not as unattractive as Du Maurier's villain, still had piercing eyes, heavy overhanging eyebrows and sharp features. But what was more important, he was actually instrumental in developing the power and quality of his friend's voice. His very presence seemed to exert a mesmeric control over Anna, and he drew from her in this way passages of unequaled vocal beauty which she could not produce without him. When, in 1839, she and Bochsa gave "dramatic concerts" together at the Queen's Theatre in Dublin, critics wrote: "In the delivery of her beautiful cadenzas, she seemed to have borrowed all the delicacies of Bochsa's harp effects." In return for his priceless gift to her—the ability to sing as a leading prima donna—she gave him her trust, affection, and the disposition of her life itself, for four weeks later she left her husband, children and home in Albion Street, and went off with Bochsa to Hamburg. It was just a case of "Get up, Jack—John, sit down." At this moment it is amusing to recall that Sir Henry was the composer of the heartbreaking tune "Home, Sweet Home" in 1821, ten years before the death of his first wife, and lived to see the irony of it. Without any of the copyright protections which have since been developed, the composer received only £20 for a song which sold a hundred thousand copies its first year, and has never stopped selling since.

Bochsa was not just another harpist. Today's critics believe that he revolutionized harp playing by continually discovering new effects and incorporating them into the technique and eventually into his classic works on the playing of his favorite instrument. In 1813 his high excellence was admitted when the Emperor Napoleon appointed him his own harpist.

French politics seldom interfered with aesthetics in those days and three years later, Bochsa was plucking the strings of his instrument for Louis XVIII. In three years, eight operas by Bochsa were performed at the Opéra-Comique but in 1817 he had to flee France because he was detected in extensive musical forgeries. In his absence, he was tried and condemned to twelve years' imprisonment with a fine of 4,000 francs. The penalty of acquiring ill-gained lucre was adroitly expressed in the chorus of a song, popular several decades later. It ran:

Time is money, and money it is time,
And don't you be forgetting it,
Get all the money that you can,
But don't get time for getting it.

Bochsa's unsavory reputation actually did not follow him across the narrow English Channel. London acclaimed him from the start and so many pupils besieged him for lessons that he was unable to accept all the applicants. The English seemed unwilling to believe in the genius' criminal record or, believing it, preferred to place the onus on the stupidity of the French courts.

The attacks on his moral character which caused him to resign from the Royal Academy of Music in 1827 did not interfere with his career or with his courting of Anna Bishop some twelve years later. If an artist wishes to ignore moral rectitude (in the eyes of an envious public), it merely makes him a better performer. He was a virtuoso to his audience, even if not in private life.

Mme. Bishop retained her professional name even after she left her heartbroken family to tour with Bochsa, and she immediately achieved the brilliant career which her Svengali promised her. She sang to enthu-

ANNA BISHOP
The original of Trilby

SIR HENRY BISHOP
Husband of Anna — his *HOME SWEET HOME* was a misnomer

SIGNOR BOCHSA
Anna's vocal teacher and harpist — the original of Svengali

MADAME ANNA

BISHOP'S

CHAMBER CONCERTS,

—AT THE—

STUYVESANT INSTITUTE,

659 Broadway.

OPEN EVERY EVENING.

MADAME ANNA BISHOP

PROGRAMME.—PART FIRST.

1. **Introduction,** Piano Forte..........
MR. A. SEDGWICK.
2. **New Song,** "Rose of the Morn"..........**Frank Morris**
MR. GEORGE CROZIER.
3. **Aria,** "O luce di quest' anima" (Linda di Chamounix)..........**Donizetti**
MADAME ANNA BISHOP.
4. **Fantasia, English Treble Concertina,** "Rode's celebrated air and variations for the Violin," (and as sung by Miss Louisa Pyne) arranged and adapted by..........**R. Blagrove**
MASTER CHARLES SEDGWICK.
[illegible] performances on the above instrument have been received with unbounded applause throughout the United States and the Canadas.
5. **Humorous Song,** "The Merry Little Fat Man"..........**Blewitt**
MR. A. SEDGWICK.
6. **Ballad,** "Robin Red Breast"..........**Hubbard**
MADAME ANNA BISHOP.
7. **Aria,** "Phoebe Dearest"..........**Hatton**
MR. GEORGE CROZIER.
8. **New Song,** "Our Good Ship Sails To-Night." Illustrative of the departure for the war, and dedicated to the gallant Patriots now volunteering in the service of their Country..........**Stephen C. Massett**
MADAME ANNA BISHOP.

AN INTERVAL OF TEN MINUTES.

PART SECOND.

1. **Duo Brillante, Treble and Bass English Concertinas** Themes from "**Masaniello**" (Auber) arranged by..........**A. Sedgwick**
THE SEDGWICKS.
2. **Song,** "Down by the River Side"..........
words by **Gen. G. P. Morris**, Music composed by **V. Wallace**
MADAME ANNA BISHOP.
3. **Buffo Song,** "Sy very Peculiar"..........**Blewitt**
MR. A. SEDGWICK.
4. **Aria,** from the **Bohemian Girl,** "I dreamt that I dwelt in Marble Halls"..........**Balfe**
MADAME ANNA BISHOP.
5. **Ballad,** "The Coquette"..........**G. W. Morgan**
MR. GEORGE CROZIER.
6. **National Song, "The Flag of Our Union"**..........
Written by Gen. G. P. Morris, composed by V. Wallace.
MADAME ANNA BISHOP.

ADMISSION..........25 CENTS. RESERVED SEATS..........50 CENTS.

siastic audiences in every capital in Europe, and her American audience loved her dearly. Only rival singers were heard to criticize her. On Anna's last trip to the Pacific Coast, one of these remarked gushingly to the prima donna: "I am delighted to meet you, for I *barely* remember hearing your charming voice either in Stockholm, or somewhere else nearly forty years ago."

"Yes, my dear," responded Mme. Bishop laughingly. "Isn't it delightful to possess such a memory, for we must both have been children then."

Anna and her harpist continued their journeys around the world until she became famous as the most widely traveled vocalist of her generation. She even penetrated to Kasan, the capital of Tartary, in 1841, where no other European artist had ever before ventured. A brilliant linguist, she sang the national airs of Tartary in the language of the people and immediately won their hearts. In 1843, she spent twenty-seven months at the San Carlo Opera in Naples, where she appeared 327 times with her lover conducting. At that period her repertoire included twenty-four different operas. Anna sang in Mexico, Havana, Australia, Brazil and eventually Hong Kong, Calcutta and Ceylon. There was only one country where music was sung that Anna never visited—the land of her forefathers, France. Had she gone there, Bochsa would have been seized by the minions of the law.

In 1852, Anna sang in English for the first time in Flotow's *Martha* and two years later she was acclaimed in *Norma*. In between she appeared in the Golden Gate City, giving the music-hungry miners their initial taste of opera in costume.

Even in later years, she miraculously preserved the beauty of her face and figure, and when Sir Henry Bishop died in 1855, she married her harpist. The unaccustomed legality of his position, and an acute case of dropsy, combined to kill the gentleman within the year and, starting from Australia, his soul traveled to more celestial regions where his gifted harp playing probably got him past St. Peter, without even a union card.

Poor little Anna Riviere, alone again at forty-one! After trilling her way through Chile, Argentina and Brazil, she returned to New York in 1858 and the arms of Martin Schultz, a diamond merchant. On March 21st of the following year Anna was the principal singing witch in the illustrious performance of *Macbeth* organized by Charlotte Cushman at the Academy of Music for the American Dramatic Fund, when Edwin Booth played Macbeth, Cushman, the Lady Macbeth, Charles Fisher, the Macduff, and C. Kemble Mason, the Duncan.

Many tours followed for Anna, and the drama of her life could never be called dull. On February 18, 1866, she sailed on the *Libelle* from Honolulu to Hong Kong and the good ship foundered and la diva, at fifty-two, found herself shipwrecked on waterless Wake Island with a few kegs of Angelica wine between the ship's company and death by thirst. The men dug for water without avail and strict rationing began on the fifth day. After a three-hour struggle, a 200-gallon keg which remained on shipboard was beached intact, but it was obvious that the company, dividing the water and the provisions, had to set sail for the Ladrone Islands, some 1,400 miles distant, or die miserably when the contents of the keg gave out.

The captain and eight men took the smaller boat and were never heard of again. Anna and others took the larger one and after sailing almost without aid except from the stars for thirteen days, suddenly Guam appeared to their hungry eyes with all the suddenness of a mirage. They disembarked and went on to Manila. Anna had lost her wardrobe, her music, and all her jewelry but not the glorious spirit which made her one of the most admirable musical troupers of all time.

Instead of collapsing from the exposure and taking to her bed, Anna Bishop took a deep, operatic breath and went back to work. She immediately gave a concert in Manila, then went on to Hong Kong and Calcutta where she gave sixteen concerts touring India before she returned to England and finally to America "for a rest."

From then on her sorrow was that, although her beauty remained, her voice failed her. No doubt she had strained her vocal cords with a volume of sound which they were never meant to produce, and after constant overexertion, they refused to function. Poor Palmo, manager of the Opera House in New York, had the misfortune to sign Anna up after her voice had started to deteriorate. He hastened his bankruptcy by charging only a dollar for the first balcony and fifty cents for the second, a scale which could never support an opera company unless every night were a complete sell-out. It was said of this ugly and not too successful entrepreneur: "His wit was not as sharp as his chin, so his career was not so long as his nose."

Palmo's Opera House next came under the managerial direction of John Brougham, an actor who also started a humorous weekly periodical called *Diogenes hys Lanterne*. One day Brougham and a companion were dining at a café when William E. Burton, a fellow actor, who, too, had once owned a magazine, entered and seated himself at their table. The friend asked Burton if he ever read the new comic weekly. "Never except when I'm drunk" was the emphatic reply. Brougham then rose, bowed and responded, "Then, thank God, we are always sure of one faithful reader."

On February 4, 1873, Mme. Bishop sang "The Last Rose of Summer" appropriately enough at the Brooklyn Academy at a memorial benefit for John Howard Payne, the lyricist of "Home, Sweet Home." The song was, however, no indication of retirement, for in July of the same year she was the first singer ever to perform in the Mormon Tabernacle itself at Salt Lake City by express invitation of Brigham Young, who might have been looking for yet another wife.

Two years later Mme. Bishop went to Capetown, South Africa. How could she possibly turn down the engagement? She had never been to South Africa. Just to make things more difficult for a 61-year-old woman, her tour included the city of Kimberley to reach which involved a 500-mile jolt in coaches and Cape carts over newly made dirt roads and unbridged rivers. If it's true that her nature mellowed in old age, such a jolt was liable to transform her milk of human kindness into butter. In 1881, Anna gave still another concert at Steinway Hall and in 1883 appeared for the last time at a Gilmore band concert. She died of apoplexy in March, 1884, in New York, where her declining years had been spent.

IV

Henriette Sontag

Who had two debuts, the second twenty-four years after the first

HENRIETTE SONTAG, whose voice made Mme. Malibran weep with appreciative envy, was Germany's great contribution to the operatic stage of the middle nineteenth century. She guarded her reputation with the same fastidious care with which she guarded her voice, once described as "a pure soprano of extraordinary volume, compass and brilliancy." To this writer's sorrow, no taint of bohemianism was ever associated with her name. Had columnists existed in those days, her private life would not have supplied them with so much as a single scandal. As a result she was the unsullied prima donna and "grand dame" among singers. Her life was an open book, but without any loose pages.

When, as a little girl of six, she acted at the Frankfort Theatre, she had no hint of the social prestige she was later to achieve, but artistically she was already well on the way. At eight, standing on a table to give herself added height, she sang effortlessly the grand aria of the Queen of Night from *Zauberflote*. Prosaically enough, upon her father's death, Henriette went to Prague where she studied seriously at the Conservatory and at fifteen sang children's parts at the Prague Theatre under the direction of von Weber, dazzling the audience as the heroine of his *Euryanthe*. The exquisiteness of her person, which was noted at her debut, was characteristic of Sontag even in her later years. Her hands and feet were celebrated for their beauty, her large eyes were vividly blue, her hair was an auburn that might have had its origin on the palette of Titian—in an era of massive females, Sontag's delicacy was thoroughly appreciated.

In 1821, Henriette went where all singers of great promise once yearned to go—to the fabulous city of Vienna, where she sang alternately with the German Opera Troupe and the Italian Opera Company. Not until she arrived in Berlin, several years later, was Sontag made—at least musically. All Germany rang with her triumph and she won her first favor from royalty, the honorary title of "Royal Court and Private Singer." Never a great dramatic actress, possibly because of a certain innate primness, Mme. Sontag's appeal was, nevertheless, twofold—the magnetic power engendered both by her beauty and by her magnificent voice.

From 1828 to 1830, she divided her triumphant performances between London and Paris, and became the toast of both towns, albeit a genteel one. This reluctance of hers to engage in night life might have been better understood at the time had the public known of Henriette's secret marriage to Count Rossi, Sardinian court diplomat at The Hague, but the diva was determined not to make known her distinguished marriage until her contract expired and she would be free to retire to private life.

Henriette's heart was a thoroughly generous one. One night in Paris, leaving the Opera House after singing Elvira in *Don Giovanni*, she saw a mother and her three daughters making a pathetic tableau in the cold. They were attempting to sing German national songs although their teeth were actually chattering. Sontag at once recognized the woman, who as a small child had been one of her playmates in Darmstadt. Giving her a small sum of money, the prima donna took her address.

The next morning a liveried footman knocked at the door on the sixth floor of a house in the Faubourg du Temple and left the note: "Go tomorrow to No. 17 in the Chaussée d'Antin to the house of M. B——. You will find 3,000 francs left there for you. Return to Darmstadt with your children and I shall take care of their education." There was no signature, and the agent did not reveal the benefactress's name.

For seven years in Darmstadt, the poor woman received a pension so generous that she was able to give all three children an excellent education. One of them entered the Conservatory at Berlin and became, in 1849, one of the bright stars of the German stage.

As for Sontag, her performance of *Semiramide* in Germany, in 1830, she supposed to be her last, for as soon as she publicized the news of her marriage, apparently without one backward glance of regret, she bade farewell to the operatic stage, and without the fanfare of "positively last appearance" or "final farewell." Giving up the glamour of her position as an outstanding artiste, Henriette was content to accompany the Count on his diplomatic journeys to all the European courts. In fact, from that day to this the only person who has topped her record for far-flung travel is probably our own Eleanor Roosevelt. Wherever Henriette went, her success as an ambassadress was notably due to her charm and the aura that always clings to a famous person after retiring—I mean from the stage.

HOME! SWEET HOME!

SUNG BY

Miss M. Tree

IN

CLARI,

OR

The Maid of Milan

at the

Theatre Royal, Covent Garden

Composed & partly founded on a Sicilian Air

BY

HENRY R. BISHOP.

Pr: 25.

Philadelphia, Published by G.E.Blake No. 13 south Fifth Street.

ANDANTE.

CLARI.

'Mid pleasures and palaces though we may roam, Be it e==ver so humble there's no place like home! A

During twenty years, Henriette broke her pledge not to sing only once, and that was at Frankfort where she had begun her stage career at six. She consented to take part in a concert given for the benefit of Hungarians made homeless by the inundation of Pesth when the Danube rose to flood proportions, but without any visible "ceiling." It was characteristic of her to come out of retirement for such a charitable motive. All during these years, Sontag never missed the stage, possibly because her own life was as exciting and glamorous as any of the roles she had played. As the adored wife of His Excellency Count de Rossi, Ambassador and Minister Plenipotentiary to the King of Sardinia—a title which sounded more like the musical stage than reality—she resided in the courts of Vienna, Berlin and St. Petersburg, shedding the luster of her personality over them all.

Although Sontag stopped singing, she never relinquished her study of composition. In 1841, at the houses of the Princes Esterhazy and Metternich, she composed a cantata for soprano voice and chorus which she herself interpreted. The success of the private concert was so great that the Empress wrote the Countess Rossi in her own hand, begging her to repeat her cantata at a concert to be given in Her Imperial Majesty's apartment, to which were invited the Imperial Family and members of the Court. The retired diva's graciousness and intelligence won her a wide and distinguished circle of friends.

With the revolution of 1848 came ruin for Count Rossi and his wife. All their assets were in Berlin, and all were lost. Then Henriette made the decision for which she was to become as famous as for being a magnificent soprano. She went back to work. After twenty years of absence from the stage, she was brave enough and believed enough in herself to weather the storm of criticism which she knew a second debut must precipitate. It was inevitable that comparisons would be made, the Sontag of twenty-four years before would be her worst competitor. Had her voice been impaired? How could a woman look as well when she had aged? Was she not merely a faint echo of her former self? These questions rose in everybody's mind, including the diva's own.

Mr. Lumley of Her Majesty's Theatre was willing to answer these questions for the singer and her public. He offered her £17,000 for a season under his management. Reassuming her maiden name, "Mme. Sontag" made her second debut in *Linda di Chamounix*. Her former rivals had long since vanished. Poor little brilliant Malibran had sung herself out some thirteen years before, and the operatic stars who now held the public enthralled had never been heard of in 1830. Giulia Grisi, Jenny Lind, and Marietta Alboni all were singing at the top of their form while Bellini, Meyerbeer and Donizetti had written some of their best operas since Henriette's retirement. And yet the public, sympathetic to the singer's indomitable will, gave her a cordial and enthusiastic reception and were

Revere House, Boston, Nov. 22, 1852.

Reverend Sir,

I cannot leave Boston without giving expression to my feelings of gratitude for the warm reception which has been accorded me in this City generally, but more particularly by the Clergy: a reception far more flattering than I feel to merit, and which I shall ever cherish as a proof of kindness beyond my deserts.

I am only too happy to have been the means, on Wednesday morning last, of ministering to your gratification. I could not then thank you as I wished; allow me, therefore, now to do so most sincerely; and, whilst bidding you an affectionate farewell until my return at a subsequent period, permit me to express an earnest hope and desire that health and prosperity may attend you in that sacred sphere of usefulness in which you are engaged.

I remain, Reverend Sir,

Yours, with great esteem,

Hte Rossi Sontag

HENRIETTE SONTAG

rewarded by finding that her voice had suffered little during her absence, and still retained that lucid purity of sound to which her audiences thrilled. Even her figure and face seemed unchanged and so amazing did this seem that it gave rise to a rumor that this Sontag was actually the daughter of the celebrated mother who twenty years before had won all the laurels of operatic stage. Later, however, Richard Grant White, in writing about her American appearance, said that her age told against her in the make-up of young heroines. "Moreover she looked older in opera than in concert. In her ordinary dress no one ever thought of her age, only of her charm," but the make-up of Marie de Rohan, for instance, "put ten years upon her face, and she looked like a middle-aged woman playing young." Too bad there were no Helena Rubinsteins around in that era.

While Sontag's success was assured, she was robbed of the critical triumphs of 1828 only because the Swedish Nightingale and glorious Alboni were current favorites. The diva appeared as Adina, Desdemona, and the next season she did exquisite justice to Norma, Elvira from *I Puritani* and Maria in *La Figlia del Reggimenti,* all characters which she performed for the first time.

When the Théâtre des Italiens of Paris opened under Mr. Lumley's management, Sontag crossed the Channel and was greeted with a new ovation in which were mingled respect, admiration and deferential sympathy because by 1850 Henriette needed all three. "Even amid the loud applause with which the crowd greeted her appearance," wrote a French critic, "it was easy to distinguish the respect which was entertained for the virtuous lady, the devoted wife and mother," rare instance of where virtue brought even more than its own reward.

The very characteristics which seemed dull and commonplace to the English were novel and intriguing to the French. Here was a highly respected woman received by all the Royal Families as a friend, performing behind the calcium lights with the dignity and adequacy which one might expect from so exemplary a character.

Henriette then sang consecutive seasons in England, Vienna and Berlin, and finally, in 1852, she accepted her first offer from America. On September 19, 1852, she began a series of concerts at Metropolitan Hall. Boston and Philadelphia welcomed her next, and wherever she appeared she was assured a triumphant success. American audiences with their enthusiasm re-created the scenes of her first debut for the prima donna and she was deeply grateful and as unaffected as ever, as she again occupied the throne "with the double crown of art and virtue upon her brow."

The diva's gratitude to the American people was not unmixed with criticism. She wrote back home: "This is a raw material people, where even the craziest European democrat could not hold out long." And

NEW YORK. *Published by* GOULD & BERRY. *297 Broadway.*

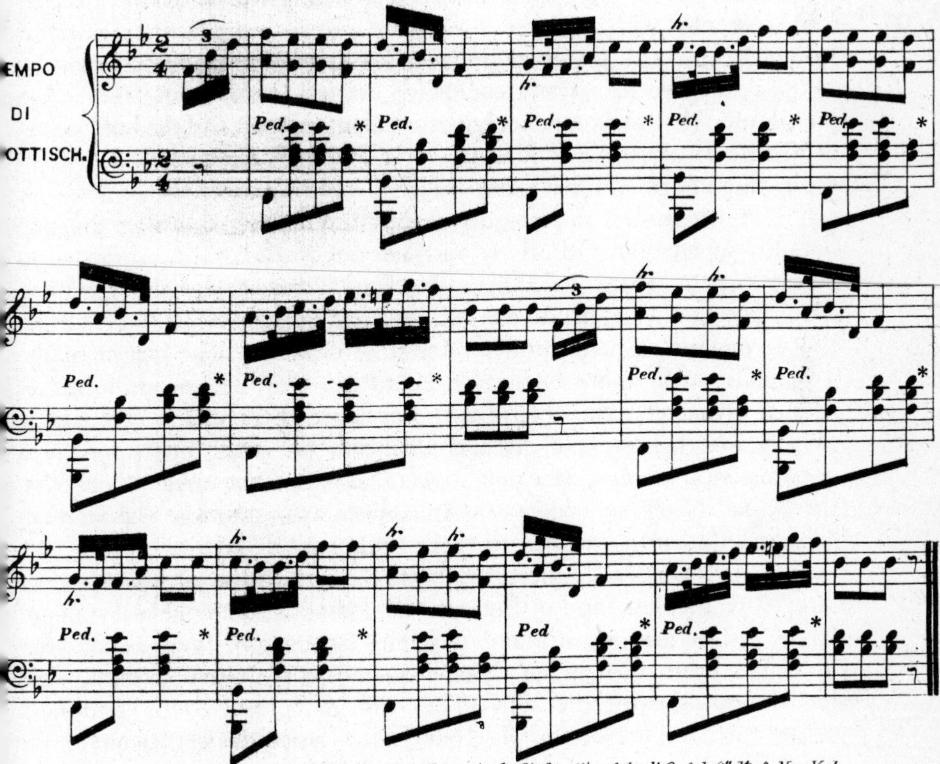

EMPO DI OTTISCH.

boasted in the next breath that her fine manners had completely charmed the barbarians: "My position here is much more like an ambassador's wife than an artiste. People are full of respect for me and treat me entirely differently from the way they do Jenny Lind, who has damaged herself very much through Barnum's puffing and ostentation." Poor Jenny was damaged so little that she not only made a fortune in the United States, but she created a Lind saga whose theme was religious piety.

Although Sontag could not resist a dig at her rival, she was usually a most co-operative person. At Castle Garden, under the direction of Max Maretzek, Bellini's *I Puritani* was announced with another prima donna as principal. About noon of the day before the scheduled performance, Maretzek was advised that the lady would be too ill to appear. Sontag, regardless of the fact that she was not billed, announced or advertised, and although hardly in voice to do herself justice, immediately accepted and sang the role intended for another.

Two years later, Sontag sang in New Orleans where she met M. Masson, director of Mexico City's finest theater, and she signed with him to appear for two months with an option for a three months' extension at a salary of $7,000. M. Ullman, the agent, returned to Europe to secure a supporting company and he had nearly completed his task when news came across the Atlantic that Henriette Sontag, the gallant trouper, had died of cholera in Mexico on the 17th of June.

For those of us who have deep affection for the beauty that is Mexico's and a deep regard for the integrity of the Mexican people, it is amusing to note the supercilious and utterly mistaken notion that was incorporated in Sontag's death notice in *Harper's Weekly*: "There are certain regions in which one would not like to die, and least of all places in Central America. It is a mongrel region without interest or character. The charm of the Tropics is much more interesting elsewhere. Only the worst forms of Spanish character seem to have been developed there, and it is in such a country that the gay and graceful Countess, the sweet singer and, in a way, historical woman, Madame Sontag, has closed her career." Naturally, the "Good Neighbor" policy was still in embryo, otherwise the *Harper's* editor would hardly have razzed that country and declared:

"For my biased sake, please contrast 'the worst form of Spanish character' with the best form of European diplomacy as exemplified by Count Rossi, Henriette's husband and travelling companion. Immediately after his wife's death, this gallant gentleman hurriedly quitted Mexico,—and the cholera,—leaving the body of his wife to be sent to the port by a carrier, with other parcels. He could never resist the contagion of her smile; but the contagion of her malady—ah, that was something else."

V

Jenny Lind

Who cried out "I do like to sing to God!"

IN 1850, a gentleman, presumably wealthy, named Ossian E. Dodge, purchased at auction an admission ticket to Jenny Lind's first Boston concert. He paid $625 for the pleasure of hearing the widely publicized Swedish Nightingale and less extravagant admirers wagged their heads and wrote derisive doggerels:

Dodge paid so thundering a price,
For that 'ar seat he sat on
That many folks have wondered since,
What 'tis he wears his hat on.

A more imaginative lad penned this one:

Why so much ado? The price is just,
Each pays for what he hears,
And so, of course, they pay the most
Who have the largest ears.

The rare piece of sheet music illustrated, shows on the front cover, Barnum introducing the aforesaid Dodge to Jenny Lind. Musical extravagance seems to have run rampant in the latter's family. A Providence cousin, Colonel William C. Ross, not to be outdone, bought in his seat at $653. Rhode Island's capital was in a condition bordering on delirium and the schools were closed when Jenny Lind came to town.

New York could not produce a gentleman so generous as Ossian E. but a hatter named John N. Genin bought a ticket for $225, not in a burst of heartfelt bounty, but with his advertising budget in mind. His discernment was proved when people flocked to his shop from all over to buy hats, just to see the man who was fool enough to pay so much money for a seat. Perhaps that is where the expression "The Mad Hatter" originated.

Who was this young woman who took the New World by storm after creating a sensation in Europe? What was there about Jenny that called for such riotous enthusiasm? In London, every time she sang, the walls of the Opera House bulged, prices were boosted sky-high, the flowers from admirers would have filled several florist shops, thunderous applause shook the rafters, tears of pleasure streamed down the faces of ecstatic females, the Queen's presentation bouquet lay at her feet, and the whole Royal Family attended. The hysterical enthusiasm was not, however, bounded by the walls of Her Majesty's Theatre. The department stores offered gloves à la Lind, everything a woman could wear or carry was promoted by the use of Jenny's magic name. Young girls sang the songs Lind sang and danced the "Jenny Lind Polka"; young men spent a month's allowance on stalls. Ethel Mayne wrote that there were "portraits of her on snuff boxes, match boxes, bon-bon boxes, tea trays. Horses, cats, dogs and canaries were named after her." And for years, Jenny Lind bread was a standard bakery product.

You would expect, I am sure, a very exotic artiste to cause this unparalleled sensation, but Jenny Lind was nothing of the kind. She was gentle, and sweet, and simple, and what is more confusing, deeply religious. But Jenny's voice was an exquisite means of expression, and she portrayed roles with the same fervor and abandon, alternating with deep tenderness, that we associate with religious character.

Jenny Lind regarded her voice as a gift from God, and she never stepped upon a stage without a preliminary prayer. She treated the date of her debut as a second birthday, remembering it annually with prayers, and was particularly fond of church music. After singing an oratorio, she once exclaimed: "I do like to sing to God!" Mendelssohn himself taught her how to interpret the spirit and exaltation of oratorio music, and he called her "a member of the church invisible . . . In her, the art of music was grafted upon a religious nature so deep that practical Christianity was the master-spring of her life."

The friendship between the diva and the composer was one of mutual affection and high regard. Jenny spoke of him constantly as a man with "supreme talent," while Mendelssohn sent a message to her in a letter to a friend: "Tell her no day passes on which I do not rejoice that we are both living at the same epoch and have learned to know each other and are friends, and that her voice sounds so joyous, and that she is exactly what she is; and give her my heartiest greetings."

They say that in composing *Elijah*, the Lind voice constantly echoed in his ears. Both "Hear Ye, Israel" and "Lift Thine Eyes" gave exceptional opportunities for the peculiarly spiritual quality of Jenny's voice to ring out in all its purity. When Mendelssohn died long before his time, it was Lind who suggested the foundation of the Scholarship Fund which bore his name through the years and glorified it until the Nazis, because of his Jewish blood, defiled his statues and his memory with their posthumous

JENNY LIND

ban. The scholarship was started with funds raised by Lind at a performance of *Elijah* in Exeter Hall. The great composer conducted the operas in which Jenny sang in musical Leipzig after making a tremendous success in Berlin, but when she arrived in Vienna, the singers' Valhalla, she was suddenly overcome with diffidence and terror and refused to appear until Mendelssohn's friend, Herr Hauser, scolded and browbeat her into it.

Even the way Jenny spent her money, that fortune amassed in her triumphant tours, showed a truly charitable character, so when she made the decision which makes her career unique in musical history—to abandon the opera at the height of her fame—those persons closest to her were not surprised. Jenny had come to think that the operatic stage was not sufficiently unsullied for her to perform upon it, and one summer night in May, 1849, she climaxed her career as a prima donna by giving a farewell performance, which "rocked the great house with love and joy and grief."

But Jenny was not retiring from public life, she was merely stepping down from the operatic stage to the concert stage, where Barnum made her as great a triumph and as great a fortune as she could possibly have culled from the career she left behind her.

When P. T. Barnum decided to feature Jenny Lind and started his advance publicity about the little singer, the American public merely thought he was importing another curiosity for his museum, not realizing Jenny's supreme voice and musical artistry. One witty pamphleteer with the Yankee's gift for deprecating wrote:

> So Jenny, come along! You're just the card for me,
> And quit these kings and queens, for the Country of the Free;
> They'll welcome you with speeches and serenades and rockets,
> And you will touch their hearts and I will tap their pockets;
> And if between us both, the public is not skinned,
> Why my name isn't Barnum nor your name Jenny Lind.

Another journalistic wag indited that while Jenny Lind may not be a "Jumbo," Barnum certainly had in her a "whale" of an attraction.

While it is true that Mr. Barnum was embarking on a project far more artistic than any he had yet attempted, he had the grand manner, and could be as princely as Max Maretzek or Maurice Grau. A week after Jenny started her concert engagements, a week which opened the eyes of the public to her astonishing talent and Barnum's to the possibility of making a fortune on the demure little lady, the showman told her that he had a slight change to make in her contract.

"I am convinced," he said, "that our enterprise will be much more successful than either of us anticipated. I wish therefore to stipulate that you shall always receive $1,000 for each concert, besides all expenses, as heretofore agreed, and that after taking $5,500 per night for expenses and my services, the balance shall be equally divided between us." In the matter of expenses, Barnum had the short end of the stick. Jenny Lind

JENNY LIND

P. T. BARNUM introducing Jenny Lind to Ossian E. Dodge, Boston vocalist and purchaser of the $625 ticket for her first concert

had a number of trunks, while the great circus attraction Jumbo carried only one. What Jenny Lind did not know was that Henriette Sontag was already getting this salary under Maretzek's management, but without a share in the profits. Thus Barnum's liberality quite amazed the Swedish Nightingale. Thus Jenny Lind gazed at him incredulously and P.T. had to repeat his offer in order to make her understand. Jenny grasped his hand. "Mr. Barnum," she said, "you are a gentleman of honor: You are generous! I will sing for you as long as you please. I will sing for you in America—in Europe—anywhere!"

When the accountants reckoned the receipts of Miss Lind's first concert, Jenny received $10,000 as her share and with her usual charitable impulse she gave every dollar of it to Mayor Woodhull for distribution to the needy. The singer's generosity and kindliness were the source of many of the anecdotes about her. One night a young girl stood at the ticket office in Boston and paid $3 for a seat, saying ruefully as she turned away, "There go the earnings of half a month, but I must hear Jenny Lind." Jenny's secretary overheard the remark and reported it to the diva, who insisted that he trace the young girl who thought enough of music to sacrifice her food for it. He watched carefully and delighted Jenny by finding the girl and giving her a $20 gold piece in appreciation.

Lind was as generous with her voice as she was with her money. When the Mississippi steamboat stopped at Natchez for fuel, Jenny stepped to the rail and poured her golden voice out to where a thousand people were waiting just to catch sight of her, most of them wharf workers, and while nearly all were black in color, her singing, paradoxically speaking, "tickled them pink." Again, in Memphis, the boat stopped and at eleven in the morning she sang several solos ending on a note so exquisitely pure that the most sophisticated European audience would have thrilled to hear it. When people asked why she bothered to give a supreme performance on such an informal occasion she smiled and said, "I value my art too highly to degrade it even occasionally by any willful disregard of what I consider due to it."

It was stories such as these that sprang from the heart of the singer herself that won her public with more thoroughness than Barnum's hokum could ever do.

The total receipts of her ninety-three concerts amounted to $700,000 of which her share was $175,000.

To try to describe, years later, the triumphant reception given Jenny Lind after every concert would be futile. If you were a music lover, who had been told time and again in the exaggerated terms so loved by Barnum, that you were about to hear a voice more magnificent and soul-satisfying than you had ever heard before or even imagined, and then, filled with excited anticipation, you sat in your seat fearing to be disappointed, and,

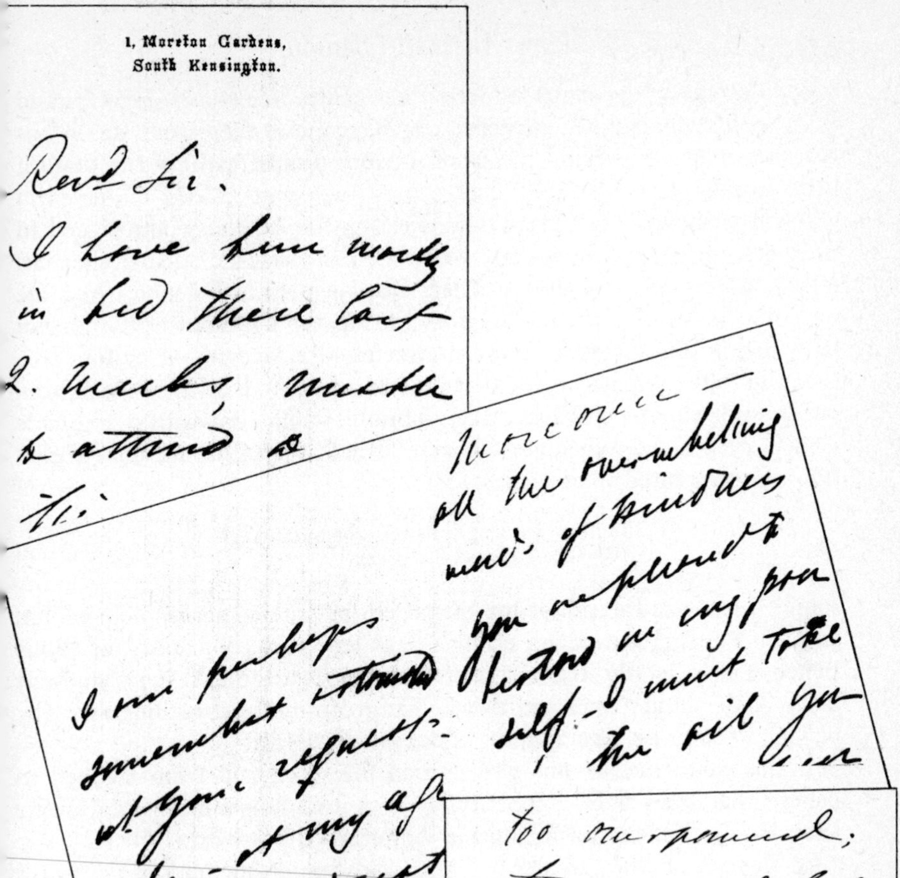

1, Moreton Gardens,
South Kensington.

Revd Sir.
I have been mostly
in bed these last
2. weeks, unable
to attend to
thi...

I am perhaps
somewhat astounded
at your request—
for—at my a[ge]
it should not
be expected [of]
me to confess
and sing in Pu[blic]

Moreover—
all the overwhelking
words of kindness
you are pleased to
bestow on my per-
self—I must take
the side you ...

too overpowered;
However—I feel
that your meant
it all well—
and remain
Revd Sir
Yours truly
J. Lind-Goldschmidt
8th January 1876.

JENNY LIND AUTOGRAPHED LETTER

as soon as the lovely singer projected her golden voice, you discovered to your joy that she actually exceeded her encomiums, there is no doubt but that you could understand the laurel wreaths heaped high on the head of little Jenny.

It only remained for Clara Louise Kellogg, the American-born singer, to fire a few shafts at Jenny many years later, to persuade us that she was, indeed, a very talented person. Clara was taken to hear Jenny when she was still "in arms" and she describes the singer's appearance: "With her hair, as she always wore it, drawn down close over her ears—a custom that gave rise to the popular report that she had no ears." Evidently the curious public still would not believe that Barnum would deal with a *complete* woman even if she were a great singer. Then Clara, in her memoirs regretfully complimented Lind's voice,

Birdling, why sing'st thou in the forest wild?
Say why,—say why,—say why!

sounded just like the call of the bird itself, but she could not help adding another bit of gossip. Clara claimed that Jenny's accompanist, Sir Julius Benedict, had let the feline out of the jute when he told her that Lind had a "hole" in her voice and that he had to do some extraordinarily tricky playing to cover up certain notes in her middle register.

If this were true, no one else learned the secret and I am inclined to believe that even with competition which had long since passed away, Clara Louise Kellogg was being the sharp-clawed pussy cat.

At the end of May, 1851, Mr. Otto Goldschmidt, member of the Royal Swedish Academy of Music, a quiet, unassuming but gifted musician, arrived in America to replace Sir Julius Benedict, who was retiring as Jenny's pianist. The romance between the diva and her accompanist was a complete secret until February 5th, when Mr. Goldschmidt electrified the Press by applying at the Boston registrar's office for the certificate of marriage.

They engaged a suite of rooms at the Round Hill Hotel in Northampton, Massachusetts, where they lived together enjoying the rustic landscape. Northampton was at that time just a wee mite of a place. Fifty trains passed through there every day. Two stopped and forty-eight didn't even hesitate.

And now, Jenny again made one of her abrupt decisions. After the ninety-third concert, she broke off friendly relations with Barnum, her manager, and paid him $7,000 in addition to $25,000 which, according to the terms of her contract, she was to forfeit if she terminated her engagement before completing one hundred concerts. It must have been a strong impulse, indeed, which caused Jenny to give up so much money, when she needed only to appear seven more times to satisfy her agreement.

My old friend, Max Maretzek, writing to Hector Berlioz in Paris, commented: "We are forced to conclude that the able manager, who had dealt with Giants, Orang-outangs, Dwarfs, Elephants, Bearded Women, Boa Constrictors, Feejee Mermaids and Alligators, was unable to manage one little 'angel' of a prima donna."

Max continued with his own explanation of why Jenny had suddenly ended her association with P. T. Barnum:

"Shortly before Miss Lind was asked to sing in the horse-circus in Philadelphia, Mr. Barnum's great Asiatic travelling menagerie arrived in New York and made its triumphal progress through the streets of the Metropolis. When the elephants, ostriches and monkeys paraded through Broadway, preceded by bands of music, tawdry inscriptions traced upon banners and other mummeries, in order to excite the curiosity of those who passed, it so happened that Jenny Lind was standing at her window and observed the procession. There she seemed to remark the same faces, in the crowd which had greeted her on her own arrival, the same enthusiastic crowds which had followed her carriage on that memorable occasion, and the same demonstrations which had taken place upon her advent to New York.

"Is it not possible that upon this morning Jenny found out that in Barnum's eyes she was no more than his woolly horse or one of the monkeys? Would it be astonishing that the Swedish Nightingale felt hurt in both her womanly and artistic pride?"

The analysis is a neat one, but perhaps too neat because we must not forget that Barnum was Maretzek's rival. Poor old Max! What induced him to hammer at P.T. was this: Just when he was all set for a big season, along came Barnum, the magician, who whisked Jenny Lind out of his bottomless bag of tricks. Fortunately, Max secured a rival attraction, the great Parodi, with whom the old Duke of Devonshire, it was said, had long been in love. Maretzek, not to be outdone by the "wild extravagances" of his rival, circulated the publicity story that Parodi was the coming Duchess of Devonshire, a story which dumfounded that lady upon her arrival from Europe, but succeeded in packing the houses for the season, saving Maretzek from the ruin he had predicted for himself.

Max liked Barnum quite as much as in these effete times the *Chicago Tribune* is fond of President Roosevelt, and thus entertained himself with visions of that great showman's funeral: "Imagine," he remarked, "a group of young mermaids crowned with myrtle, opening the procession and scattering immortelles upon his path to eternity. Six 'Halifax Giants' should bear the sarcophagus of the great showman. The tassel of the pall, made of six Jenny Lind posters, should be supported by six Fat Women.' Behind the coffin should be led his 'woolly' battle horse by the 'Negro' who had consented to turn white for this occasion. Funeral

GREETING TO AMERICA.

NEW YORK. PUB BY FIRTH, POND & Co. 1 FRANKLIN SQ.
AND S.C JOLLIE. 300, BROADWAY.

hymns might be screeched out by youthful vocalists who had taken prizes at his 'Baby Show.' Fabers' Automaton should follow, pronouncing his funeral oration, while a regiment of the 'Sons of Temperance' should file after it, headed by the venerable General Tom Thumb. His 'Wax Figures' might melt away in unavailing sorrow, while the 'Bearded Lady' who had always maintained a secret passion for Barnum, might be plucking black bristles from her chin and saying, 'He loves me, he loves me not.' Stockholders of the 'Crystal Palace' might be weeping bitterly, and his colleagues, the moral, honest and pious showmen of America, could bring up the rear in deep mourning, doing their utmost not to laugh. This would make a truly magnificent exhibition. I trust that I may live to see it, of course, upon the payment of twenty-five cents admission. And," concluded Max, "if there were any way of returning to earth, Barnum would no doubt do so, bringing along St. Peter as the crowning attraction of his career."

But even without P.T. as manager, Jenny did not stop singing. As her own entrepreneur, she continued touring America with the same triumphant progress that Barnum had come to think was possible only with the co-operation of his skilled staff of ballyhooers. Sir Julius Benedict wrote in later years of how the showman worked. The troupe would sail down the Missouri or the Mississippi stopping at all towns boasting sufficient population to support a concert. The troupe would disembark and in the twinkling of an eye men were marching through the streets bearing banners announcing the arrival of the sensational diva, Jenny Lind, who, in a few hours, would give a concert in the largest hall available in the town. Immediately there would be a public auction of tickets, and as the money was being stuffed into bags, the musicians would arrive at the hall, carrying the pianoforte with them.

One hour after the concert, the troupe would be on board again sailing down to another port, another procession, and another triumph for Jenny Lind. The singer did admit to Barnum later on that she had found it much more harassing to give the remaining concerts of her American trip on her own account. Although in the very early fifties, in San Francisco, three successive theaters bore the name of Jenny Lind, she never visited California, statements of sole old-timers, who let imagination run away with memory, notwithstanding.

When the Goldschmidts returned to Europe in 1852, they made their home in Dresden for three years, but finally moved to England, where the Swedish Nightingale built her permanent nest and raised her family. By 1883, Jenny's infrequent concerts came to an end. It was Schumann who said that the way Jenny sang his songs made him "feel warm in his back," and it was the opening bars of Schumann's song, "An den Sonnenschein" that Jenny softly sang as her shutters were opened to the rising sun the morning of the day she died four years later.

VI

Marietta Alboni

Whose voice shook the rafters and whose weight shook the scenery

IN A BOOK devoted almost wholly to lyric sopranos, it is a distinct pleasure to give praise and space to Marietta Alboni, the most celebrated contralto of the nineteenth century. Born in the province of Romagna in 1824, she first studied in Cesena, and then with Mme. Bertolotti in Bologna, where she had the very good fortune of meeting Rossini. She made such an excellent impression on the great maestro that he condescended to take her on as his only pupil, teaching her all the contralto roles of his operas in the manner in which he wished to have them sung. At nineteen, he thought her ready for her debut and Marietta made her first appearance at La Scala in Milan as Maffeo Orsini. Despite her patent inexperience, the audience was captivated by the richness of her voice and she made a personal triumph.

Under Merelli's managership, Marietta sang in Bologna, Dresden and Vienna. Because of a misunderstanding about her salary, the diva broke Merelli's contract and literally fled to St. Petersburg to escape his wrath and the battle of barristers that was certain to follow. Russia was merely the beginning of her travels. She lifted her powerful contralto in the opera houses of Hamburg, Leipzig, the music center, Dresden, Bohemia and Hungary. In 1847, her London engagement began at Covent Garden when the name of Jenny Lind was on everybody's lips. The response at her debut was so enthusiastic that the terms of her contract which called for £500 were raised overnight to £2,000, and her reputation was well on the way to becoming established. Lucrezia Borgia and Semiramide became her favorite roles and Covent Garden was crowded whenever she sang them.

Alboni's beauty was without question; her features were regular with classic proportions and her whole appearance was splendid on a large scale. Her voice has been described as a rich deep, true contralto of fully two octaves, reaching from G to G, "sweet as honey and perfectly even throughout its range." The body which began by being heroically statuesque, ended by being enormous. A contemporary remarked that, on a hot day, walking directly behind Alboni was the shadiest spot he could find. She, moreover, made no attempt to reduce, because, as she philosophically phrased it, "I never would have half the joy taking it off, that I had taking it on."

Although she developed into a massive mountain of a woman and her exquisite voice remained unimpaired, the *London News*, long discouraged by a series of contraltos who seemed to dig their voices up from the lower regions with only the most agonized efforts, wrote appreciatively in 1849: "There is gentleness and sweetness of tone as well as volume—in fact, it is only the greatness of her resources which banishes effort. In her you behold none of those distortions of the muscles of expression in the face of that tension of the vessels of the throat which betray the exertion with which the greatest singers of her day deliver even their floriture."

After her marriage in 1854 to Count A. Pepoli of Bologna, Alboni lived in Paris and when her engagements at Her Majesty's Theatre did not claim her, she sang in the gayest of Continental capitals. Alboni's heart and sympathies were as large as her body, and both in her city and her country place at Ville d'Avray, she entertained lavishly, particularly at mealtimes, all the artists and authors, both struggling and "arrived," who were only too delighted to sit at the table with Marietta and her passion for eating elaborate food. Her banquet board literally groaned with the delicacies of the season. Those who indulged probably did their groaning later. Alboni's abnormal weight was in direct proportion to her tastes as a gourmet. Mlle. Emma Eames' mother recollected regretfully that the groaning but succulent board of Alboni was an integral part of a lavish era now wholly forgotten.

When, at Her Majesty's, Alboni found herself on the very stage where Jenny Lind had triumphed, she merely smiled one of her superb, self-confident smiles and allowed the rich volume of her contralto voice to fill the auditorium and thrill her audience. From her first note to her last, she gave the impression of one who was determined to achieve perfection, and, according to contemporary critics, she succeeded without a single exception.

When Alboni was nearly sixty, her first teacher and patron, Rossini, died, happy in the knowledge that one singer at least was still doing full justice to his music as he wrote it, and that was Marietta. At his funeral, Alboni and Patti sang "Quis Est Homo" in duet. Everyone in the audience

THERESE
TIETJENS

MARIETTA ALBONI

was utterly overwhelmed by the incomparable superiority of Marietta's voice and technique, and yet the singer herself was so modest and self-critical that when she came down into the church, she seemed distressed and asked, "Has my voice been heard?" It is true, however, that in periods of emotional stress, such as the funeral of her best friend, she feared to be overtaken with nervousness. Alboni's stage fright was conquered only with great effort and self-control. Her public never knew at what personal cost she gave them each perfect performance.

At one of Rossini's Saturday concerts (called simply "Cantata") the moment Alboni entered the salon where she was to sing a solo which had been composed just for her by the maestro, she was immediately overcome with unreasoning fear and whispered into Rossini's ear, "*Maître, j'ai trop peur.*"

Rossini took her by the hand and said, "*Eh bien nous, nous aurons peur ensemble,*" which, with my limited knowledge of French may have meant, "Sing, or else——" He led her to the piano where he accompanied her himself even though it had been years since he had practiced pianoforte and his fingers should, by rights, have grown stiff. Nothing of the sort had happened. Next to the beauty of the contralto's voice, the sensation of the evening was Rossini's playing. He actually seemed to produce a violin legato on the piano.

After a career of twenty-two years of continued success in all the operatic centers of the world, Alboni died at her country home on June 23, 1894, a good woman, untouched by the scandalmongers who in any age are only too eager to snatch at straws if there are any blowing about, and a great singer who served her public faithfully and asked no special favors, disdaining to luxuriate in the excitement of artistic temperament.

VII

Therese Tietjens

Who opened "cold" in England and won her audience for twenty-one years

THE Hungarians have a tendency to describe their antecedants as coming from "ancient and noble lineage," and the parents of Therese Tietjens, residents of Hamburg, Germany, were no exception to this rule. As a matter of fact, most human beings like to refer to their family tree and spend large sums to have it looked up and, later on, even greater sums to have it hushed up. The importance of "blue blood" to a young singer is in direct proportion to the weakness of her vocal apparatus. Christine Nilsson's peasant parentage was certainly no hindrance to her career, while Piccolomini's royal Tuscan ancestry could not help her vocal imperfections. Therese did not need her forefathers to bolster up her reputation; even her difficult-to-pronounce "moniker" she found no handicap. Born in 1831, by the time she was fourteen her voice had developed into an organ of great power and singular sweetness, ranging from C below the staff to D above the staff, each note possessing a heart-warming clarity.

Tietjens studied in Vienna with the best of the masters of the German school, Henrietta Dellessi and Herr Babry, and devoted herself with that tireless energy which characterized her whole life to preparing for her lifework. When only eighteen she sang at the St. Pauli Theatre in Hamburg but her actual debut was at the State Opera House, Altona, near Hamburg, in October, 1849, as Lucrezia Borgia.

The debut was most successful, and Therese not only appealed to the public at large, but in particular to the young son of one of Hamburg's leading families. After a whirlwind courtship Therese was quite ready to marry the gentleman, even if it meant eventually adding lullabies to her already extensive repertoire. But she was not at all ready to leave the stage, which was a stipulation made by the boy's reactionary family. Unwilling to give up her lover and equally unwilling to give up her career, Therese agreed to retire for a period of nine months to see whether life without singing in public could compensate for even the small taste of success she had already sampled. What happened during those nine months is hidden in her personal history but the result of the experiment was obvious to everyone. At the end of the allotted time, Therese Tietjens, to the public's enormous gratitude, reappeared before the footlights, and the young man, no doubt brokenhearted, faded out of the picture.

In 1858, Mr. Lumley, the manager, looked about him for an attraction with which to open the new Covent Garden Theatre, called Her Majesty's. His scouts reported that Mlle. Tietjens, singing at the Imperial Vienna Opera, was the lady he sought, although not one word had ever been printed in the English press about the bell-like resonance of her lyric voice, not one word about her personal beauty: classic features radiating great vitality and expression, eyes flashing with warmth and passion, and a quick intelligence. But Lumley had taken chances before and on Tuesday, April 13th, Therese appeared before her first English audience as Valentine in Meyerbeer's *Les Huguenots*. The nervousness felt by Tietjens and Guigloni the tenor evaporated as Therese's powerful voice filled the theater and the latent fire of Guigloni became kindled in its turn.

The critics praised the impulsiveness of her acting and the easy grace and naturalness of the manner in which she moved about the stage, and in a rush of enthusiasm they acclaimed her the "legitimate successor" to Giulia Grisi as a mistress of lyric tragedy. Her Leonora, Donna Anna and Lucrezia all met with enthusiastic approval, and it must not be forgotten that when she arrived in London, opera was flourishing there already with Nilsson on one stage and Adelina Patti on another. *Punch* cried out in an agony of surfeit:

Three Traviatas in different quarters,
Three Rigoletti murdering their daughters,
Three Trovatori beheading their brothers,
By the artful contrivance of Three gypsy mothers.

Even with these top-notch rivals, Therese had no trouble. She merely stepped into a third niche next to the other two with the dignified carriage which was so much a part of her noble-seeming personality.

Unlike most of the European opera stars Tietjens never traveled much. If she had visions, after her English triumph, of visiting foreign capitals and repeating her sensational debut in each one of them in turn, she was incorrect in her prophecy because she won England so completely that the public would never let her go except for the briefest of visits to Paris and America. No singer of foreign birth ever kept so close to the English public as she. In addition to her operatic parts, she filled what one gentleman called "the role of general utility." The German artist proved invaluable at musical festivals, as well as singing concerts both in London and in the provinces. It was this all-embracing musical activity of hers which made her so indispensable to the English public. If opera was above the means of most people, concerts were not and if concerts were, the sacred music festivals were still more attainable. Therese with her superhuman energy made her rounds of them all, probably reaching more English ears than any other singer of her day. The Handel Festival actually became a Handel-Tietjens Festival, because her ample physique enabled her to cope more successfully than her rivals with the difficulties of singing in such a vast area.

Dr. John Cox, writing about her in 1871, said: "If she had only been taught after the Italian school, she would have been the greatest prima donna that had ever been heard—or heard of—since operatic music had sprung into existence. Even so—there is not a single artist within 'the shadow of a shade' of her genius." Everyone loved Therese, from the eminent operatic authority, William Kuhe, to the humblest scene shifter. The only criticism Kuhe had to make was when Therese appeared as Marguerite in *Faust*, a role which she introduced in 1863 to the English public, and it was impossible for him to reconcile her tall and massive figure with the girlishness of the ideal Gretchen. Perhaps what he was trying to tell the public was that she was more Junoesque than Gounod-esque. Therese, with her characteristic kindliness, relinquished the role to Christine Nilsson from the moment when that ideal Marguerite demonstrated her particular fitness for it.

Under the aegis of Colonel Mapleson, Tietjens was persuaded to leave her beloved Britain for a short while to give America the benefit of her voice from January 25, 1876, to April 15th of the same year. She would never have come at all if she had not been lured by a very lucrative contract. The *American Art Journal* was particularly pleased with her portrayal of the great tragic roles of Medea and Norma, feeling that her "dignified and stately" bearing in addition to the power of her voice fitted her most perfectly for these parts. Her American tour included most of the leading cities and, while she was well received, she never made the triumph here that she had in England, partly because the Americans cared less for the heavy roles than they did for the light ones and partly because her voice had begun to show the effects of too much singing over a period of too many years. Her great technical skill succeeded in covering up the less obvious defects but it was a pity that she waited so long to come to the United States. Her audiences were unfortunately made aware that the greatest of recent German singers had already passed her zenith.

When Tietjens returned to England, she immediately resumed her great variety of musical activities, appearing in the opera, in concert and in the choral festivals, but her splendid physique was attacked from within by a malignant disease, and in 1879 she died at the height of her reputation.

It would not be a well-rounded portrait of Therese were I to hold back any of the evidence, especially that presented by her contemporary, Emily Soldene. Describing the German diva, the opéra bouffe star wrote: "The great singer's corsets were stiff, laced dreadfully tight, and audibly creaked." No wonder some contemporary wags referred to her as "Old Ironsides."

VIII

Maria Piccolomini

Whose voice captured Europe and lost America

THE doors of the Cardigan Theatre at Turin had closed after the evening's performance, but no one went home. The audience milled around the portico waiting for their heroine, the star of the opera, Maria Piccolomini. Finally she emerged, the little diva with the sweet lyric voice, and climbed into her carriage. Then the hot-blooded youths, according to custom, started to unhitch her horses from the carriage so they themselves could pull their idol through the streets. Other stars had been pleased enough with this demonstration, but Maria was another pattern of a woman.

With eyes flashing and cheeks flushed with anger she cried out for them to leave her carriage as it was, that she preferred to have it drawn by horses rather than by donkeys, and that they ought to know better than to put themselves in the place of beasts, as Italy had higher and nobler duties for its sons: "Keep your strength for Italy—our country needs all your energies!" And this was long before Mussolini rallied his citizens to the "nobler" ideal of bombing unarmed natives. The young Italians ignored the diva's commands, so Maria stepped down from the carriage, re-entered the theater and left by a secret exit. Of course, stage folks have footed it from theaters before, but it was because of low finances rather than outraged dignity.

Maria Piccolomini was born at Siena in 1834 and while still a small child was recognized as a singer of great promise. Immediately her voice was entrusted to Romani, the leading professional coach of his day, and she was ready for her debut in *Lucrezia Borgia* when she was only a few months past her sixteenth birthday.

For an opera singer she labored under one great disadvantage—her figure was far below average height but she compensated for her small presence by her grace and the liveliness of her expression, by her sweet soprano voice and the dramatic flair with which she interpreted her roles. In brief, she measured up vocally rather than physically. Following her debut in 1852 as Lucrezia, she sang the opera to delighted audiences for twenty successive nights. Hers was the technique of coloratura singing and many years after her death a critic bitterly complained: "The break-neck vocal ability of the strings of pearl,—canary bird style of warbling came on with Piccolomini in the '50's and has thriven to the detriment of other styles since."

From Piccolomini to Lily Pons, the audiences of every decade have loved to hear the vocal gymnastics of a perfectly pitched coloratura soprano. It is certainly true that such virtuosity is not to be confused with an aesthetic performance, but the public enjoys hearing exquisitely clear, limpid notes faultlessly following one another, just as it enjoys seeing a juggler keep ten gilded balls in the air simultaneously.

For Maria struggle was no part of her early career. Her ancestry was ancient and illustrious, and this accident of noble birth combined with the family's opulence assisted her in getting for her own those parts for which her sweet light voice was best suited. Of all the roles she sang in Turin, that of *La Traviata,* the adaptation of "The Lady of the Camellias" made the greatest sensation, with Maria in *Figlia del Reggimenti* second in popularity.

Four years Piccolomini toured Italy, remaining a full season in each important musical center. Florence, Rome, Palermo and Verona were all held spellbound by the young artiste who, brought up in the sheltered home of her father, knew no passion and no vice, and yet with consummate artistry and deep feeling could express so hauntingly the profound emotions of the dying courtesan, Camille. But then, haven't there also been actresses who brilliantly characterized Lucrezia Borgia without having previously poisoned anyone?

Italy was not big enough to demand a permanent priority on the talents of the little Maria. English tourists to Rome and Florence brought home enthusiastic reports of the new prima donna and as Lumley, the manager, expressed it, "Maria Piccolomini was booked at last for the Majesty's Theatre" in London. On Saturday, May 24, 1856, the tiny star of high lineage and vocal voltage, made her debut in Verdi's *La Traviata,* the first production of that opera on the Anglo-Italian boards. The *London Times* was greatly taken by her performance, and after praising the sprightliness of the Bacchanalian song in the second act, the critic wrote that Maria became an object of real solicitude as the opera progressed. "The shriek of agony with which she takes leave of *Arturo* makes the stalls seriously uncomfortable, and when she reappears with very pallid cheeks, and her pulmonary complaint has been aggravated by mental distress, the case is grievous indeed." The *London Spectator* had to admit that the weakness and helplessness feigned by Maria caught the audience's sympathy to a far greater degree than the performance of Jenny Lind. As a matter of record, at the close of the opera she was called before the curtain thirty times—or maybe forty; what are ten encores more or less among friends?

After two years of continual triumph in England, Maria Piccolomini gave her farewell performance in the gigantic Crystal Palace at Sydenham and had no difficulty whatsoever in filling it. Reading many contemporary reviews, we receive the impression that her success was due more to her fine gift for dramatic acting rather than her voice, although the latter was a pure soprano sfogato, "clear, penetrating and yet extremely sweet." Nowhere do we read of its beauty, always its sweetness; nowhere do we read of its power, only its purity. When she sang Adina in *L'Elixir d'amore* in July, 1857, to a great ovation, it was because the music of that opera is light and facile, making no great demand on vocal power. "It requires sweetness, spirit, grace and expression"—four fields in which Piccolomini excelled.

When *L'Elixir d'amore* was produced, the *London Illustrated News* bewailed the fact that it would not have the same success as *La Traviata;* first, because it was no novelty, Malibran had introduced it and it had been sung steadily ever since, but secondly because "it is so full of simple, genuine melody welded to so natural a tale . . . that the multitude would prefer *Traviata* to *Elixir* just as they would prefer bad champagne to first-class claret. They can recognize effervescence, but are unable to detect flavor."

Like Lind, Piccolomini was warmly generous with her public and when Mlle. Poinsot could not appear in *Les Huguenots* because of a "severe indisposition," Maria consented to give *La Figlia del Reggimenti* without the necessary rehearsal. The fad for Piccolomini in London followed the pattern of Jenny Lind. It was an "influence" as well as an enthusiasm, and everything that was novel, graceful or charming took Maria's name, whether it was a race horse or a cigar, and the lovely lady's picture appeared on the title pages of all the waltzes, polkas and quadrilles of the period. Barrel-organists ground out the arias from *La Traviata* which the Italian cantatrice had made famous, and portraits of Piccolomini peered out of all the music-shop windows. One diplomat, when asked whom he liked better, Patti or Piccolomini, shrewdly answered "both."

Then the little diva fulfilled an engagement in America for the manager, Bernard Ullman, and the happy picture changed completely. Her choice of entrepreneur was an unfortunate one. Ullman was often in-

MARIA

PICCOLOMINI

For One Night Only Positively.

First and Only Appearance of

PICCOLOMINI !

The public are respectfully informed that M'LLE PICCOLOMINI will give ONE GRAND CONCERT in TROY,

On Tuesday Evening, Feb 15, 1859,

Commencing at 8 o'clock,

Being Positively the ONLY PERFORMANCE she can give in this City.

SIG. MUZIO, - - - - Conductor.

PROGRAMME: PART FIRST.

1—ROMANCE ......SIG. MAGGIOROTTI ......Mercadante

2—GRACE! GRACE! Robert le Diable ......M'LLE GHIONI ......Meyerbeer

3—DRINKING SONG, La Traviata ......M'LLE PICCOLOMINI and SIG. LORINI. ......Verdi

4—FANTASIA FOR VIOLIN ......MR. WOLLENHAUPT ......

5—ROMANZA—Spirto Gentil, La Favorita ......SIG. LORINI ......Donizetti

6—DUETT—Nozze de Figaro ......M'LLE PICCOLOMINI and M'LLE GHIONI. ......Mozart

PART SECOND.

7—LARGO AL FACTOTUM—Barber of Seville ......SIG. MAGGIOROTTI ......Rossini

8—THE CELEBRATED PICCOLOMINI WALTZ, [Composed expressly for M'lle Piccolomini by] ......M'LLE PICCOLOMINI. ......Sig. Muzio

9—SERENADE FROM DON PASQUALE ......SIG. LORINI ......Donizetti

10—FANTASIA FOR VIOLIN—"The Swallows," ......MR. WOLLENHAUPT ......Balfe

11—ARIA FROM LA ZINGARA, ...M'LLE GHIONI ......Donizetti

12—DUETT ......M'LLE PICCOLOMINI and SIG. MAGGIOROTTI.

CONDUCTOR - - - - SIG. MUZIO.

Price of Reserved Seats, $1,50.

ADMISSION in the Evening at the Door, $1 00, with the privilege of occupying such Seats as may not be previously secured.

ACADEMY OF MUSIC CONCERT BOOK, expressly prepared for M'lle Piccolomini's Concerts, containing the correct translation of all the pieces sung in their Concerts.

BEAUTIFUL MINIATURE PHOTOGRAPHS of M'LLE PICCOLOMINI, taken from life. For Sale at the Music Stores and at the Concert Room. Price 25 Cents.

PICCOLOMINI CARTOON

WITH BRIGNOLI

hot water with the press for giving them stories without a trace of fact, which they were forced to retract in later editorials. Henry C. Lahee said of him: "He had developed a remarkable talent for advertising and for organizing combinations and schemes without any regard for the truth; that he not merely dallied, but actually wrestled with it, and left it gasping for breath." As a sample of Ullman's methods, it may be mentioned that Piccolomini was announced as a lineal descendant of Charlemagne, and great-granddaughter of Max Piccolomini, the hero of Schiller's *Tragedy of Wallenstein*.

Poor little Maria! If her voice had been as magnificent as her publicized ancestry, America might have forgiven her manager's exaggerated claims. Ullman need not have gone to quite such flights of imaginative folly, for there was nothing at all the matter with Piccolomini's actual family tree. He did not at all need to graft new branches upon it. Her ancestors were nobles of Tuscany, two of whom occupied the Papal chair under the names of Pius II and Pius III. One of her cousins was the well-known Cardinal Piccolomini, and Ullman made a serious mistake by incorporating Charlemagne into the picture.

Even before hearing her, the public became deeply skeptical, and then, when they did hear her and discovered that while she was more petite, prettier, more full of coquetry and allure than any of the opera singers whom they had previously known, she actually had little of what Professor Odell calls "vocal authority," their rage was complete. The *Tribune* was particularly vitriolic. They persisted in contrasting the managerships of P. T. Barnum and Ullman, the respective voices of Jenny Lind and Maria Piccolomini, to the detriment of the latter.

The Spirit of the Times, on November 16, 1858, summed up American public opinion in a most unpleasant manner, not hesitating to stoop to anti-Catholicism, just as other sheets in discussing Ullman did not hesitate to raise racial issues. The whole affair was so acrimonious and sordid that only a great genius such as Adelina Patti could possibly have overcome the bad publicity.

"We are sorry for Piccolomini. From all that we hear she seems to be a very nice little body—a good daughter and sister, and a most pious observer of the formularies of her religion—but something more than all of this is needed to establish the reputation of a prima donna. We want VOICE, Voice, Voice, and with voice, one a little more cultivated than an averagely circumstanced American woman acquires at an average boarding school."

There is no question but that this scathing criticism was thoroughly unfair. Certainly the audiences of London and Italy were not untutored in music appreciation. There is a possibility, of course, that Maria's voice was affected by the ocean trip and that her first appearances were not as

This Tuesday Evening, November 23rd,

Will be presented, for the first time in America, Mozart's celebrated Opera, in four acts, of

LE NOZZE DI FIGARO

(The Marriage of Figaro.)

CHARACTERS:

Susannah.......................................Mlle. Piccolomini
The Countess.......................................Mme. Ghioni
Cherubino.......................................Mme. Berkel
Marcelline.......................................Mme. Morra
Figaro.......................................Herr Formes
The Count.......................................Signor Florenza
Bartolo.......................................Signor Weinlich
Antonio.......................................Signor Muller
Don Basilio.......................................Mr. Perring
Don Curzio.......................................Signor Barratini

CONDUCTOR.......................................CARL ANSCHUTZ
LEADER.......................................THEO. THOMAS
STAGE MANAGER.......................................AMATI DUBREUL

Doors open at a quarter past Seven ; to commence at Eight o'clock.

To-morrow Wednesday, Nov. 24th,

Second and last night of

LE NOZZE DI FIGARO

THE PICCOLOMINI OPERA LIBRETTO.

An elegant edition of the Opera Libretto containing the original Italian, with a correct English translation as performed by

MLLE. PICCOLOMINI

at Her Majesty's Theatre, London, and at the Academy of Music, New York, has been expressly published for **THE PERFORMANCES OF MLLE. PICCOLOMINI**

THE PICCOLOMINI OPERA LIBRETTO

contains also a biographical sketch and portrait of **MLLE. PICCOLOMINI** and **SIX PAGES OF MUSIC,** containing the Gems of the Opera, expressly arranged for this edition,

PRICE 25 CENTS.

For sale at the Academy of Music and the regular ticket offices.

satisfactory as they might have been, but the main reason why she fell afoul of public opinion was the unfortunate character of Ullman, whose extreme unpopularity was voiced in an article appearing in *Music and Drama:* "The official flavor of Mr. Ullman has developed into a prevailing perfume of a most unpleasant nature. It leaves a bad odor in the nostrils of the community at large—worse still, some of his Barnumisms have reflected on the name and fame of poor Piccolomini—and she, dear, conceited and fascinating little impostor, is made the tool of her unscrupulous manager.

"We object to the storm of popular indignation being allowed to burst on pretty Piccolomini's head. Let the lightning of the press and public wither Ullman, but she is too good to be thus sacrificed. The great mistake made by the *Courier des Etats Unis* to their treatment of opera at the Academy of Music was in not discriminating in their just wrath and censure between the manager and the star. In their eagerness to strike at Ullman, they have cruelly wounded Piccolomini, which was a needless, ungallant thing to do."

The director of the Academy did his level best to ruin her prospects further by attempting to hold a ticket auction as Barnum had been wont to do with Jenny Lind when Americans were clamoring to hear her. But as far as Piccolomini was concerned, instead of clamoring prospective bidders were as quiet as clams and far from paying hundreds for each ticket, three dollars was the highest premium bid and from then the fall in price was quick and sudden to twenty-five cents. To make matters even more humiliating for the little prima donna, only thirteen bidders were present in all. Candidly, her auction was a devil's auction, because it certainly played hell with her prestige.

In spite of all these incredibly nasty drawbacks, Piccolomini's American audiences were not totally blind to her charms and her fine flair for dramatic acting. She really succeeded in persuading one part of her audience at least, that there could be satisfactory opera singers who were not vocal marvels, but whose personal talents compensated for lack of voice. Maria was but the first of the long line of these stars which was to follow and she suffered for it.

The next year found the diva back in London, filled with relief at leaving behind her such a blighting memory, and when the Marquis Gartoni della Forgia asked her hand in marriage Maria Piccolomini gratefully accepted, and left the turbulent stage far behind, happy in the thought that Hymen would make her forget Ullman.

IX

Parepa-Rosa

Who loved to imitate the Scotch bagpipes

THERE is a musical anecdote which tells how a deaf man who never in his life had heard a sound was taken to one of Mlle. Euphrosyne Parepa's concerts and miraculously heard one of "The Incomparable's" flutelike high notes. Be that as it may, Parepa-Rosa, as she later came to be known, had one of the world's most magnificent voices. The day that General Grant honored the Boston Jubilee with his presence in 1869, the diva rose to sing. Surrounded by a choral group of ten thousand voices and facing sixty thousand in her audience, she turned deathly pale and for one hideous moment it seemed as though she would be unable to sing. But Parepa recovered herself rapidly and sang "Let the Bright Seraphim" from *Samson and Delilah* as it never had been sung before. Her remarkably clear ringing voice penetrated every part of the huge auditorium and someone said that her voice was five hundred feet long and three hundred feet wide—the size of the building.

Even if her voice did not measure to such limitless proportions, her girth very nearly did. Fortunately for her, in those days, there was no "corporation" tax. Had telephone booths been known in Parepa's day, it is doubtful if she could have squeezed into one, and when a woman can't squeeze into a telephone booth "there's no use talking." In the *Marriage of Figaro*, there is a scene where she was obliged to hide. The audience, fond as they were of her, always laughed when Parepa, so generously upholstered, went dutifully unseen by her thin little sweetheart.

When she married her manager, Carl Rosa, an excellent director and conductor, she paid no attention to the weight differential between them although it was enormous. Carl was the smallest of men. Fortunately she fell for him—not on him. He had a large capacity for argumentation. Once when he disagreed with his wife over a trivial matter and stormed at her, Parepa looked at him calmly and said, "Carl, don't you contradict me; if you persist, I will pick you up and set you on the mantelpiece." Carl gave in. Have you ever seen a Victorian mantelpiece? He no doubt preferred defeat to being perched between a stuffed owl and a glass bell protecting a bunch of waxed flowers.

That Parepa-Rosa could sing was no great surprise. Her mother was Elizabeth Seguin, the sister of the celebrated basso, Mr. Edmund Seguin. Parepa's mother had a beautiful voice of her own, was a true artiste and more completely devoted to her profession than she was to her nobleman husband, Demetrius Parepa. Quick to recognize her daughter's extraordinary ability, she trained her immediately for the operatic stage. In 1856, at the age of sixteen, Parepa made her debut—at the Opera House on the island of Malta. The scouts heard and appreciated her and she was immediately engaged for Naples. Two years later, the astute Mr. Gye had her under contract for the Royal National Opera in London where she made her English debut in Herold's forgotten opera *Zampa*.

In an interview for the press the massive, good-natured, jolly young singer said, "My life makes an Arab of me, a female troubadour, a singing vagabond, but when I am rich enough I shall marry some good man for love, build me a home and fill my house with little children, all my own. I love little children. Do you know that *Norma* nearly breaks my heart? They tell me that I am too young to sing in *Norma*, that only those who have been mothers and sorrowed deeply know anything about that wonderful opera . . . I do not sorrow. I have been brokenhearted, and I know the wretchedness of an unhappy wife: but God is good. He permits me to forget and I feel now when I am singing as if there were no such thing as years, and no coldness in age. I am wild with hope tonight. Don't you see it in my face?"

The sorrow of which she spoke may have been the death of her first husband, Captain Carrol, in 1863, only sixteen months after their marriage. The wretchedness to which she referred no doubt had something to do with the several thousand dollars' worth of debts which were her only heritage, and which she repaid from the proceeds of her American tour.

In the same interview she announced with her customary directness the qualifications to be had by Husband No. 2: "My next husband must be a devotee of music, and enjoy it as intensely as I do. When a man loves me truly, and is possessed of that one sentiment in common with me, he may be rich or poor, a giant or a pigmy, an Apollo or a Caliban, I shall marry him all the same, and be happy with him . . ."

NATIONAL PEACE JUBILEE.

GRAND

Sacred Concert,

AT THE

COLISEUM,

On Sunday Evening, June 20th, 1869.

THE GREAT JUBILEE CHORUS,

ORCHESTRA OF 250 MUSICIANS,

With the assistance of

MAD. PAREPA ROSA,

MISS ADELAIDE PHILLIPPS,

AND

OLE BULL.

Programme.

PART I.

1 Jubel Overture.......... Weber

2 Gloria, from "Twelfth Mass.".......... Mozart

3 Aria. "Let the bright seraphim," from the Oratorio of "Samson." Handel

Sung by Madame PAREPA ROSA.
(Trumpet Obligato by Mr ARBUCKLE.)

4 Inflammatus. From "Stabat Mater.".......... Rossini

5 American Hymn.......... Keller

6 "Thanks be to God." From "Elijah.".......... Mendelssohn

PART II.

1 Overture, "Tannhaüser.".......... Wagner

2 "See the conquering hero comes." From "Judas Maccabæus." Handel

3 Aria. "Lascia chia piangia".......... Handel

Sung by Miss ADELAIDE PHILLIPPS

4 Choral. "Judgment Hymn.".......... Martin Luther

5 Fantasie on Mozart's "La ci darem.".......... Ole Bull

(Violin Solo without accompaniment.)
Performed by OLE BULL.

6 "He watching over Israel." From "Elijah.".......... Mendelssohn

7 "Lift thine eyes." Trio from "Elijah.".......... Mendelssohn

Sung by Madame PAREPA ROSA, Miss ANNA S. WHITTEN and Miss ADELAIDE PHILLIPPS.

8 "Hallelujah Chorus." From "Messiah.".......... Handel

Conductors. - - - Carl Zerrahn, Julius Eichberg and P. S. Gilmore
Organists. - - - - - - - - - J. H. Willcox and J. B. Sharland

Doors open at 6. Concert to commence at 8 o'clock precisely.

A. M. LUNT, Printer, 112 Washington Street, Boston.

MME. PAREPA-ROSA
Famous singer in oratorio, concert and opera

Carl Rosa filled the bill, even to being a pigmy. Parepa never minded looking like a beautiful young giantess as she stood by his side, any more than he minded being dwarfed by her height and her breadth. At the famous Liederkranz Ball the year of their marriage, they were beautifully burlesqued. An immensely tall Teuton dressed as a bride with a lady's wig, white satin robes, lace veil and flowers walked about with a small boy, dressed meticulously in the full dress of a gentleman fitted to his size. The tall veiled bride led the little man about by one hand while in the husband's other hand a small ladder was carried. Every so often, when he wished to converse with his bride, the groom would tug at her draperies or pull at her hand until she was made to understand that an interview was desired. The ladder was placed against her well-fortified breast, and the little husband ran up until his face was on the same level as his companion's.

The beauty of the burleque was that the Rosas were at the Liederkranz Ball and had every opportunity of seeing the hilarious tableau for themselves. Carl Rosa, who might have justifiably felt hurt, smiled "very pleasantly" according to an eyewitness, while Parepa laughed like a child until tears rolled down her dimpled cheeks. One of her favorite ditties was an old nursery rhyme which she used to sing in a sweet-voiced undertone:

> I've got a little husband, no bigger than my thumb,
> I'll put him in a pint cup and there I'll make him drum.

Of all the singers written about, none had the same human quality of friendliness that Parepa felt. She was ready to take the whole world to her bosom. It was ample enough. Perhaps it was her sense of humor that gave her such a mellow attitude toward life and toward art. Unlike Malibran, who burst into tears when her rival sang, or Minnie Hauk, who hated Calvé for her triumph in *Carmen* years after she herself had stopped singing, Parepa never felt the slightest jealousy.

"We cannot have too much music, nor too many songs," she said. "An artist is an example and everybody should be glad to hear of a new one. By and by I am going to find that home that I have dreamed about, and all those children, and I don't want to leave a great silent space where I have been so long."

Opera was not Parepa's only field of musical endeavor. Like Therese Tietjens, she sang everything and everywhere. Her ballad singing had the true natural ring and won her great popularity among plain people. Whether she sang the light, brittle tour de force, "The Nightingale's Trill," or the sonorous declamations of Handel's oratorios, she was equally successful. Parepa's oratorio method was as nearly perfect as one could wish for. She herself was strongly motivated by religion, and reverence was an integral part of her renditions. No demands made by the composer were too exacting for the flexibility or compass of her voice, and no demands made by her audiences for encores and more encores were ever ignored by Parepa.

Parepa and Carl Rosa formed their own concert company of about one hundred persons, and their presentations made history because of their insistence on perfect ensemble work. Parepa's own voice with its range of two and a half octaves did much to make the project a success.

After the curtain went down on the stage of the Grand Opera one night, and Parepa-Rosa stepped into the street to go to her waiting carriage, a small boy looked up at her and said, "Would me Lady, please?" He held in his hand one white lily which he was giving her as the token of his deep admiration. The boy was known as "Little Elfin" in the neighborhood where he played violin for pennies from passers-by.

Parepa was touched. "You heard me sing?"

"Me Lady, I hid under the stairs, and oh, Me Lady, I could die."

No applause ever received by the diva could have equaled this boy's appreciation. "Meet me here tomorrow night," she said.

The next night was Parepa-Rosa's last appearance of the season. The Grand Opera was filled to the doors and when she appeared for her last song, the curtains swept back and she walked forward with all her customary majesty. To the amazement of the audience, a small boy stood next to her with a violin and as she sang he accompanied her with the soft, sweet strains of his instrument. After the first hush of surprise, the whole audience burst into rapturous applause, sensing in the dramatic tableau the sentimentality that never failed to move the people who lived in the nineteenth century. Little Elfin and Big Parepa shared the honors of the evening.

From 1869 to 1872, her company successfully toured the United States and were acclaimed the most satisfactory of all the English opera troupes. Carl was a superior conductor and the performances went off with all the éclat one would expect from a group of artists that was more like a big, happy family than the usual knock-down and drag-out fight between singer, director and manager. During these four years, many of the more important operas were produced in English for the first time, among them *Les Huguenots, Oberon* and *Fidelio*. The sounds coming from the cars in which the Rosa Opera Company traveled astonished the other voyagers because Parepa's favorite trick was to imitate the weird music of the Scotch bagpipe with her voice carrying the melody, and the others droning the harmony.

Female members of her audience wondered for years at the strange place Parepa wore a bracelet, above her elbow. The golden band concealed a deep and particularly ugly vaccination scar. As the diva grew

WAITING.

ASPETTANDO.

Poetry by ELLEN H. FLAGG.

Moderato con espressione.

mf

quasi recitativo.

The stars shine on his path - way, The trees bend back the
L'astro bril - la in suo cam - mi - no E l'ol - mo om

affretto. *rall* *sf*

quietamente.

leaves, To guide him to the mead - ow, A - mong the gold - en
bro - so al pra - to l'ad - du - ce Fra le do - ra - te

tranquillo.

senza porto.

sheaves, Where stand I, longing, lov - ing, And list -'ning, as I wait,
messi E so - lo a te pen - so E at - ten - do il tuo ve - nir

f *mf* *p* *tranquillo.*

This song is published in sheet form, 1-2 a tone lower.

older and stouter, the band refused to expand and it would have been a costly business to buy gold enough to encircle so enormous an arm, so she substituted, when wearing short sleeves, a garter effect made of ribbons or a trail of artificial flowers, both of which frilly additions were not too becoming on so massive a person. One night, speaking of the scar to an American girl who sat in her dressing room, Parepa bewailed her misfortune. In a moment, her admirer took one of the candles off the dressing table, and holding it above the diva's arm, let one drop of the melted wax fall upon the scar. A flesh-tinted powder followed this surprising operation and completed the camouflage. Parepa was enormously grateful—as only she could be—and her make-up box thereafter always contained a bit of wax candle.

The man whom I knew who also knew Parepa-Rosa was my old friend Dehnhoff, of the music firm of Spear and Dehnhoff, located in 1872 at 717 Broadway where he published almost all of the two hundred or more compositions written by one of America's most prolific classical song composers, Harrison Millard. Parepa-Rosa was a great admirer of Millard's music, and whenever she was able, she sang "When the Tide Comes In," "Waiting," "Dear Little Heart," "Speak, Oh Speak to Me Again," and "Ave Maria," the only one destined to a degree of musical immortality. In order to stimulate the sale of Millard's music, she kindly suggested his works to other concert singers, one of whom, at least, Salvatti, followed her example.

There is a Lincoln anecdote about Harrison Millard and the patriotic song "Viva La America." As a volunteer from Massachusetts, the composer entered the army in 1863 and while on the way South, his regiment from Boston was reviewed by the President and his son, Robert. The band played "Viva La America" and Lincoln found it so inspiring that he asked them to repeat the number and the name of its composer. The Colonel told him that the air was written by one of the men in his regiment. Lincoln asked that he be presented to the young man and having met him, gave him a card saying, "Call me when the War is over and after you are discharged show me this paper." The result of the encounter was that Millard found himself in a berth in the New York City Custom House when peace was declared, and was only dislodged from it in 1892 when President Cleveland's second term ousted him.

Millard's job never interfered with his music. We can imagine him now, perched on a high stool in the Custom House, tickling his nose with one end of his quill pen while he scratched down musical notes with the other. He was completely impartial, writing Masses for the Catholic Church one week and Sacred Solos and Quartettes for the Protestants the next. But no matter what he wrote, Parepa-Rosa never ceased being an admirer of his really fine musical works.

On July 15, 1868, the first Parepa-Rosa concert on the Pacific Coast was given at Platt's Hall on Montgomery Street in San Francisco under the managerial aegis of De Vivo who had assured Parepa that she would take home "a very big bag of gold" and become the idol of the music-starved California audiences who had heard no one comparable to herself with the exception of Mme. Anna Bishop.

De Vivo was correct. At the close of her aria from Verdi's *Ernani*, the prima donna received an ovation and a dozen curtain calls. She followed Grand Opera with the stark and moving simplicity of two old English ballads and the audience went wild with enthusiasm quieting only when she reappeared to sing the old-time "Five O'clock in the Morning" which she popularized. The press was unanimous in stating that she was the greatest singer who had ever visited them. Parepa rewarded the Far Westerners with twenty-four opera nights for the month of August, and as Lucia di Lammermoor in the mad scene, her voice performed so brilliantly on the staccato passages, the runs and chromatic scales, that she surpassed the triumph of her concert debut. *Norma* also proved to be enormously popular and far better suited to the matronliness of her figure. The season netted Parepa $30,000 in gold, which she exchanged for about $50,000 in greenbacks, and all this on an original investment of $6,000.

Parepa was a social as well as an artistic success, attending parties at William C. Ralston's country estate at Palo Alto, where the aristocrats of the Golden Gate city toasted her in champagne, and when her benefit was played, showed their concrete appreciation by presenting her with diamond rings, bracelets, and even a brick made of silver and gold.

Ralston, president of the California Bank, was one of the commercial pillars of San Francisco and financed among many other enterprises the California Theatre, Palace Hotel, Grand Hotel, San Francisco Sugar Refinery, Mission Woolen Mills, etc. Probably he overextended himself, which, combined with a mining and commercial panic in 1875, compelled his bank to close its doors on August 26th of that year. Ralston was forced to resign the presidency, an audit showing that the bank's funds were almost depleted. He went to North Beach for his usual daily swim and later his dead body was found floating in the water. His friends said he had died of a stroke, his enemies claimed he had committed suicide. Some time later, at a local variety theater, the Adelphi, a play was produced called *Hunted to Death*, based on his allegedly having been double-crossed by his financial associates. It created quite a stir, as it showed them up in none too favorable a light.

De Vivo's next plan was to have Parepa-Rosa sing in the forbidden Mormon Temple at Salt Lake City, an enormous auditorium, seating 20,000 persons instead of the 2,000 able to get into the Mormon Theatre.

ADA PHILLIPS

BRIGNOLI
Famous tenor — appeared with Mme. Rosa

PAREPA-ROSA

When appealed to, Brigham Young was adamant. "No," replied the old Mormon, "that temple we use for our Church services and nothing else." De Vivo appealed to him many times, even braving the surprise of twenty-two wives all neatly encircled by a ten-foot wall, and who no doubt considered him a "harem-scarem" sort of fellow. But his powers of persuasion had no effect on Brigham. It was difficult to be satisfied with the theater after entertaining thoughts of the Temple and its possible gate receipts. But Brigham would not even relent to the extent of allowing Parepa to sing a program strictly confined to sacred music, so the disappointed diva appeared in the theater. Her manager's disappointment, however, was minimized when, after excellent publicity, the concert grossed $3,400.

It was not too long afterwards that the Patriarch changed his attitude and allowed Patti, Nilsson and Gerster to sing in the Temple itself.

Parepa followed her Western trip with a tour of one hundred and fifty concerts which included one at the Brooklyn Academy of Music with receipts totaling $2,700, the largest ever taken at that house except when the distinguished tragedienne, Ristori, played *Elizabeth, Queen of England* to a $3,650 house. While Parepa herself was the main attraction, Jules Levy, the concert virtuoso, appeared on the same program and was exceedingly popular. De Vivo engaged him by cabling England and offering him $1,000 a month.

In Baltimore, illness caused Parepa's withdrawal for many months, during which time Miss Adelaide Phillips replaced her. De Vivo told a dramatic editor that Parepa had exclamatory rheumatism. "You mean inflammatory rheumatism," corrected the latter, "exclamatory means to holler out." "Indeed," replied De Vivo, "and that's what she's doing all the time." On her recovery, Parepa gave two oratorio nights in Chicago which were artistically and financially the crowning success of the season. Parepa-Rosa was immediately hailed as the greatest oratorio singer ever heard in this country. This second concert tour, beginning in Chicago on December 4, 1868, and ending in that same city the first week of June, 1869, gave the Rosa a clear profit of $89,000.

At the close of the season in Chicago, she contracted with C. D. Hess of the Crosby Opera House to organize the Parepa Rosa English Opera Company for the season of 1869-70.

Carl Rosa was to furnish the entire company of the best available artists to support Parepa-Rosa and all scores, orchestral parts of the operas, costumes of the principal artists and half of the railroad fares, in return for 55 per cent of the gross receipts.

C. D. Hess was to supply all the principal theaters with gas, fire, scenery and all employees, advertising, printing programs and posting, distributing, transportation of scenery and baggage, transportation of the company in omnibuses or carriages from stations to hotels and back, chorus and orchestra, telegrams and all other expenses concerning the performances, besides half of the railroad fares. For this, C. D. Hess was to receive 45 per cent of the gross receipts and 45 per cent of the profits from the sale of librettos.

The advent of Parepa-Rosa in San Francisco was the beginning of a new musical era in California and opened the way for other celebrities. A year later Brignoli's Grand Concert Company played there, and the great violinist, Mme. Camilla Urso, and her company were there at the same time.

When Signor Brignoli was touring with the Parepa Rosa Concert Company, they were nearing the town where they were to appear. Brignoli invited my old friend, James W. Morrissey, the treasurer of the company, to dine with him. They all stood up as they came in sight of the depot. The train gave a lurch and Brignoli fell flat on his face. He cried: "I am killed! I am killed!" Gradually he dragged himself to a standing position near the door to which he clung with his left hand while he convulsively grasped at his chest with his right hand. He wasn't even bruised, but regardless of the fact whether every bone in his body might have been broken, he sang the prison solo from *Il Trovatore* in his usual exquisite style, exclaiming as he finished: "Thank God, my voice is still there! Come on, Morrissey, let us go and dine."

They tell a very pathetic story about Brignoli, who was certainly one of the most popular tenors of his time. When Clara Louise Kellogg was a struggling young singer, Brignoli was kind and helpful to her. Later, at Saratoga, when Kellogg was a successful prima donna and the tenor was on the downgrade, she practically ignored him when they met, even refusing to let him appear with her at a concert which would have given the old fellow a substantial sum of money.

Real friends came to Brignoli's rescue when he was dying in New York, at the Everett House. It was too late to save him, but his last days were spent in comfort. At the end, his mind wandered back to the time of his early triumphs and he passed away singing one of his favorite airs.

In 1875, Ilma Di Murska visited California and in January, 1880, Carlotta Patti and her Grand Concert Company; in 1882 the Nilsson Grand Concert Company under the management of Henry E. Abbey; in 1884 La Diva Patti with Colonel Mapleson's Grand Opera Company, and Gerster; and the year after came Patti, Fursch-Madi and Emma Nevada. The following year the Theodore Thomas Symphony Concert Company with Materna, Fursch-Madi appeared there. The Abbey, Schoeffel and Grau Opera Company, with Patti, Scalchi, Albani, Nordica, Tamagno, visited San Francisco in 1889-90.

The Campanini Concert Company, the largest organization on the road at the time, went to California in 1889, and in 1889, also, the Albani

VIVA L'AMERICA

HOME OF THE FREE.

EDITION IN ORIGINAL KEY B FLAT

EDITION IN KEY OF

NATIONAL SONG

BY

. MILLAR

NEW YORK

PUBLISHED BY FIRTH POND & CO 547 BROADWAY

O DITSON & Co

H KLEBER & BRO

C Y FONDA.

P P WERLEIN

HARRISON MILLARD'S VIVA L'AMERI

Song that attracted Lincoln

VIVA L'AMERICA, HOME OF THE FREE

H. MILLARD.

Concert Company. The Ristori Italian Dramatic Company went there in 1875 and in 1885 and the Salvini Dramatic Company in 1886.

In 1884, the Papenheim German Opera Company was billed under Mme. Fabri's direction, producing for the first time Wagner's *Lohengrin*.

Wieniawski and Wilhelmj, the celebrated violinists, also visited California in the seventies, and Joseffy, the great pianist, in 1885. In later years Paderewski, Ysaye, Thomson and others visited the Golden Gate.

It is to the credit of the San Francisco public that they patronized all these great artists liberally forty, fifty, sixty and seventy years ago. The city has been paradoxically described as "built on hills" but the people were strictly "on the level." San Franciscans were specially proud of the Tivoli, opened early in 1879 on Eddy Street. It was a concert hall, featuring a ladies' orchestra, and a 25-cent admission check entitled you to liquid refreshment to that amount. But the idea did not take very well, and by midsummer the proprietors, Kreling Brothers, were ready to "yield the ghost." As a final straw they produced *Pinafore* and from then on, the Tivoli's prosperity was assured. Tivoli enjoys the distinction of having the world's longest run of stock opera, twenty-seven years, up to the big fire of 1906. Among famous stars who have appeared there were Luisa Tetrazzini, Enrico Campobello, Alice Nielsen, Helene Dingeon, Gracie Plaisted, etc.—not bad for a "25 and 50¢ gate."

About 1870 the talented tenor Thomas Whiffen signed to appear with the English Opera Troupe, headed by Parepa-Rosa. Two or three years previously he had married Miss Dalby, later the talented Mrs. Thomas Whiffen. There was no chance for his young wife in the same company, so she rejoined the troupe of the well-known singer and impersonator, William Horace Lingard, and his wife, the beautiful Alice Dunning Lingard. Mrs. Whiffen accompanied Lingard in such famous popular songs introduced by him as "Captain Jinks of the Horse Marines" and "Walking Down Broadway."

As the Whiffens were very much in love with each other, the separate engagements in their young married life caused both many heartaches. The nearest they came together that season was when the Parepa-Rosa company played Cincinnati and Lingard, St. Louis. Whiffen, however, managed to have the Parepa-Rosa repertoire so arranged that he could get away over the weekend and surprise his wife. Taking the train, he got into St. Louis, but the Mississippi lay between them and the river was frozen, so no ferryboats ran. Tom, knowing how limited his stay must be, walked to the bank of the river. It seemed hopeless. The broken ice stretched for miles. If it were a sweetheart, well, perhaps, but a wife—well, the natives just laughed. He ought to be glad the river was between them. An idea struck Tom. Perhaps he got it from Eliza crossing on the ice. There was a lumberyard on the bank of the river. He bought a big plank and threw it across a cake of ice. The ice wobbled but held, and balancing himself Tom crept out. By throwing it to another floe, by slipping, crawling, sometimes dropping into water up to his waist, he reached the opposite bank and ran to the hotel. And thus he proved that although he may have been "all wet" as a traveler, he certainly wasn't as a husband.

It was ironic that the deep yearning for children which Parepa-Rosa expressed all through her life should have been the cause of her death. Back from an Egyptian trip, she was only too happy to find herself in London waiting for the birth of the child who so constantly filled her thoughts. Her physician suggested that she should not plan too much on the future. On Christmas Eve, Parepa passed the evening singing the music of Elsa in *Lohengrin*, which her husband had arranged to produce at Drury Lane in March. The next day she was taken ill. After the birth of her dead child, it seemed that she was doing well and would recover. Carl Rosa rejoined his opera company, which was touring the provinces, convinced that his wife would soon be as well as ever. Suddenly her symptoms became very unfavorable and he rushed back to London just in time to be at her bedside when she died in delirium, on January 21st, calling out for her baby.

X

Christine Nilsson

Who was born to plow fields and lived to sing operas

IN AUGUST of 1843 on a small farm called Snugge in the Province of Smaland, Sweden, a farmer's daughter was born. She was baptized Kristina but everyone called her "Stina" and no one paid too much attention to her because she was the youngest of seven children. Her father, the third generation to till the soil for the wealthy landowner, had finally to sell his interest in the farm, and move his family. Thus he learned to his disillusionment the difference between a sharecropper and a cropsharer. As Mother Kristina Katarina sat in the kitchen weeping for the rooftree which she was forced to leave behind her, little Stina climbed into her lap and whispered consolingly, "Don't cry, mother, when I grow up, I'll earn money and we'll all come back to Snugge." And not too many years later, Christine Nilsson, hailed as the "Second Swedish Nightingale," earned enough money in Paris to buy Snugge back for her family.

In spite of her family's poverty, Stina enjoyed a carefree childhood in the beautiful countryside. With six older brothers and sisters to share the chores, very few fell to the lot of the baby who spent most of her time vying with boys in their most active games. Stina climbed trees with the same ease with which later she ascended scales, and she could turn a succession of cart wheels that would have been the pride of an adagio dancer. Kristina did not escape unharmed from all these physical pyrotechnics. A heavy wooden shoe somehow came forcibly in contact with her nose as she romped in the barn one day, and because of this accident her left profile and her right profile were facial contradictions. Then too, during a wood-chopping contest—obviously Stina was no airy, fairy Lillian—the tomboy became incensed because her masculine competitor was beating her, and she ran over to stop him. The lad's ax inadvertently fell on her left hand almost severing her little finger. Although they could not afford a doctor, her father so bandaged it that it healed well leaving only a small scar. Years later a noted Continental critic told her that she had the most beautiful hands he had ever seen. Stina was always outspoken. "These hands," she said, with one of her most bewitching smiles, "which you are good enough to admire, have done a lot of work in their time. You must remember that they are peasant's hands and were made to handle a plow. I have never forgotten; I have never been ashamed of it. And," she added characteristically, "money that comes from tilling the soil is never in danger of soiling the till."

One more scar on Kristina's body was a constant reminder of her peasant origin. On her right foot she carried a white line where the flesh had finally healed after the barefoot child had stepped upon a newly sharpened scythe. Stina had been on her way to feed the pigs, holding an apronful of scraps before her so that she did not see the bright glint of the blade half hidden in the grass. However, as her stage work never included a barefoot dance, the audience was none the wiser.

It is perhaps amazing to think that this young girl ever found herself musically. How did she finally emerge from the pigsty and the corncrib to become a fabulous prima donna? Stina's older brother, Karl, was the proud possessor of a violin, a treasure which none of the other children was allowed to touch, not because the violin was intrinsically a valuable one, but because Karl played it at village dances, weddings and funerals earning a little money to augment the family income.

Kristina, however, paid no attention to the prohibitions. When Karl was away working in the field, she climbed upon a chair, and took down the fiddle. She loved to sing and it was not long before she had taught herself how to play tunes. When her mother upbraided her for not being able to handle soup ladles and paring knives as well as she handled the violin bow, Stina smiled and answered, "But I'm not going to grow up to be a farm maid."

The first real tragedy of the farm child's life was when Karl left home to work elsewhere and took his beloved fiddle along. From that moment on, her one ambition was to earn enough money to buy one of her own. In those days the main road was often cursed by a series of gates which had to be opened before the coaches and carriages could pass through. To save themselves from getting down from the driver's seat, the travelers would toss down coins to the children who were waiting at the gates to open them. Here Stina often waited and fought with the boys, scrambling in the dust for the "gate-coin." Whatever fell to her lot she saved and finally had enough to buy her beloved instrument.

From then on, she played, as Karl had done, for country dances, but she gave added value, by singing as she played. Her father, who was a member of the church choir, encouraged all of her musical impulses to the best of his ability, because it seemed obvious to him that his children would earn a far better living with their talents than he had been able to wrest from the soil.

Stina's appreciative audience began to grow larger. It was at the country fairs that she found more and more people willing to pay to hear her play her violin and sing. Her program included sentimental love songs, folk songs, and topical ballads. One of the favorites which she had often to repeat was a ditty beginning with the following tortured syntax, "A heaven, a heaven, my heart you are."

At one of these fairs, Stina met her first impresario, though one would never have guessed it to look at him. Karl Kruse was a hurdy-gurdy man with a dancing bear at the end of a rope, but he was astute enough to recognize in Kristina a distinct asset to his act, and they joined forces. After a few performances together, it was obvious that the bear would no longer be needed, and poor Bruin would have been obliged to apply to the WPA had it existed in those days.

In July, 1857, a great summer fair was held at Ljungby, sixty kilometers from Stina's home. She and her mother walked the entire distance. The gathering was a large one. The farmers came from near and far to exchange and sell livestock, and farm produce, and to drink Swedish wine. When they could no longer pronounce "Ljungby" they knew they had enough. Their wives came to sell dairy products and exhibit their handicraft and needlework, and to buy necessities and little luxuries from the traveling merchants. Friends and relatives, separated for long months, came to meet each other again, and after the haymaking, everyone came to have a good, riotous time.

Stina was just fourteen when she stood before these good people at Ljungby and enchanted them by playing her fiddle and singing at the same time. And how she could sing! Her voice followed the violin notes all the way up the scale until it sounded like a series of exquisite bird calls, so clear and sweet and penetrating that they seemed scarcely human. She stood on a stone stairway leading into one of the houses facing the village square as she sang, and below her on the cobblestones stood the town apothecary, amazed at the voice of this untrained girl. He promptly invited her to the inn where his friend, Judge Tornerhjelm, could hear her and decide for himself whether this girl was a great musical "find." He did not think twice but invited Stina to his estate by the sea and Mlle. Walerius, also known as the Baroness von Leuhausen, was retained as her teacher. The young girl was so innocent and untutored that her education actually began in the Judge's home. Asked when she was born, Stina answered, "When the rye was ripe." She learned very rapidly, for she

CHRISTINE NILSSON
Second Swedish nightingale

proved to be natively intelligent, musically gifted and energetic enough to study long hours without losing her ability to concentrate. One Victorian biographer remarked in his typically nineteenth century fashion: "The uncut diamond soon began to sparkle." Although Kristina was lonesome for her family and the gaiety of the life to which she was accustomed, she did not demur when her father came to sign the permit which allowed the Judge to be responsible for the young girl's education. Almost from the beginning, Stina felt within herself the way she was destined to tread.

In 1860, a new singer, Christina Nilsson, made her debut in the Salon de la Croix in Stockholm. The Queen, the Dowager Queen, Prince Oscar and his Duchess, and Princess Eugenie were all in the distinguished audience. Our little Stina sang an aria from *The Marriage of Figaro* and the Cavatina from the opera *Robert Le Diable*. The press was not too enthusiastic, for the critics thought her sponsors had arranged too difficult a program for the young singer who was not quite ready for it. These critics did not in the least dampen Stina's ardor. If she needed more training, the obvious thing to do was to get it and Paris was the place. First she studied under M. Masnet and then under M. Wartel, the highest priced instructor in the world at that time. For four years she worked in his studio. She was often nervous when rehearsing and while going over her parts, Kristina would tear her handkerchiefs to shreds and even rip off the trimmings on her dresses. But nobody ever saw the singer nervous in public. At this period the young artiste had not yet decided whether her voice and talent were suitable for opera but one evening she heard Mme. Miolan-Carvalho, the coloratura soprano, sing in *La Reine Topaze*, by Gounod, at the Théâtre Lyrique, and was inspired to attempt the operatic stage. Wartel, who had hoped for this, was full of enthusiasm for her decision and he took her to see Rossini and Meyerbeer. In tryouts, her voice ranged with ease and perfection three and one-eighth octaves, from F to G, from alto to soprano, which made her, if I may coin the word, a sort of Sop-ralto. The three men judged her ready to make her operatic debut.

Kristina's first contract with the Théâtre Lyrique was for three years. Her salary for the first year was to be 2,000 francs, for the second 2,500, and for the third 3,000.

Finally then, at the age of twenty-one, Christine Nilsson made her debut on October 27, 1864, as Violetta in *La Traviata*. The press agents gave her age as eighteen, and she made a distinctly good impression on that night's audience, which included the Emperor and Empress.

Christine's first great triumph was in the role of the Queen of Night in Mozart's opera, *The Magic Flute*. This part was written for an exceptional voice and Nilsson had it. She was immediately able to sing the miraculous aria in Act III as it was originally written with its strenuous staccato passages. She sang it without any feeling of strain, and the ovation was so tremendous that she was forced to sing it twice at the première. This was but the beginning of a series of successes. Paris adored her and the critics now called her "a true daughter of the North, a sister of Jenny Lind."

On a vacation to Sweden in the summer of 1866, the only time Stina sang was in the little village church of her home parish.

When she returned to Paris, the managers of the Théâtre Lyrique, in recognition of her popularity, scrapped the old contract and raised her salary to 50,000 francs per year. One of the first parts she sang on her return was the title role in Flotow's *Martha*. Patti had sung the part in Italian the previous winter, which gave the Parisians no opportunity to compare the two prima donnas. One diplomatic critic said that each one was supreme and no comparison as to excellence was possible, since their interpretations were utterly different. Flotow himself was not so hesitant. Christine delighted him. "No artist," said he, "with the exception of Jenny Lind, pleased me as much as Miss Nilsson." In 1866, the artiste added three new roles to her repertoire: Elvira in *Don Juan*, Myrrha in *Sardanapalus*, and a part in *The Corn Flowers*. Jules Cohen, the forgotten composer of the latter, carefully inserted a waltz staccato passage, remembering the success of *The Magic Flute*. But not even this concession to opportunism saved his opera from oblivion.

On May 6, 1867, London applauded Nilsson's Violetta as warmly as Paris had, and here the diva found Patti as a rival, well-established for several seasons. Christine heard that Adelina was getting £200 a night at Covent Garden and insisted on being paid the same amount at Her Majesty's Theatre. Colonel Mapleson, who did not yet know whether the second Swedish Nightingale would draw as well as the first, was hesitant about so high a salary, but she insisted, and having no alternative, he was forced to consent. Then Patti refused to sing for only £200 because Nilsson, unknown to London, was receiving that amount. Gye, her manager, in a panic, hit upon a compromise and Adelina, who was always sharp where money was concerned, agreed to take 200 guineas instead. There was no real jealousy between the two singers because they were both sensible enough to see that the city could provide enough honor, glamour and gold for both of them.

Unlike her temperamental contemporary at Covent Garden, Christine had none of the willful caprice associated with the creative genius. She was, in truth, the people's artist, and her affection for humankind was deeply rooted in her own past. She was summoned to Windsor Castle to sing for Queen Victoria on the same day that she had already promised to sing for the poor girls at a convent. Without hesitation, she declined the royal invitation, explaining that she would not disappoint the children who were eagerly expecting her. Victoria, another unaffected genius, arranged the next available date, when she complimented Christine highly and presented her with a ruby and diamond bracelet.

Every three years England celebrated a Handel Memorial with a concert in the Crystal Palace. While in London, Christine sang with an orchestra and chorus of four thousand. Thirty thousand people heard her sing two arias from *Judas Maccabeus*, particularly excited by the coloratura rendition. Nilsson returned to Paris in the spring of 1869 to give a benefit concert for her native Sweden, the failure of whose crops had caused widespread famine. After singing, Christine personally went through the audience, making the collection and 9,000 francs went back to alleviate the suffering in her homeland. Nilsson's farewell performance in Paris before leaving for America earned 20,000 francs, of which the Emperor had donated one thousand. The net went to the Music and Dramatic Benefit Fund.

Before Christine left France, she created a role that is certainly worth mentioning. The Paris Grand Opera planned the premiere of Ambroise Thomas's new opera based on Shakespeare's *Hamlet*. Only one singer in Paris was considered as "made" for the part of Ophelia. The sensation of this opus, which has since slipped into obscurity, was the coloratura aria in the mad scene—a staccato song not composed by Thomas. A few days before the premiere, Christine had heard a group of her countrywomen sing an old Swedish folk song, "Neckens Polska," in Paris. She was charmed by its strange beauty. Nilsson in collaboration with her director had it inserted in the mad scene and it was an instantaneous hit.

At seven in the morning of the day that the S.S. *Cuba* was scheduled to arrive at her dock at ten, many people were crowding the pier. It was 1870 and the anxious crowd was awaiting Christine Nilsson's first visit to America. My old chemistry teacher, Professor Doremus, of the College of the City of New York, together with Max Strakosch, the manager who brought her to these shores, and a deputation from the Philharmonic Society, constituted her committee of welcome. Max had lured her to the New World with a reported salary of $1,500 a performance, and the plan seemed to be to treat her handsomely.

So far as we know, Nilsson was the only song bird in whose honor a real parade was given. The evening of her arrival it started from Germania Hall on Third Avenue, New York, and was an impressive sight. Twelve police officers marching abreast formed the first line followed by eight torchbearers. The torches in this case were paper lanterns mounted on three-foot poles. Next came the American and Swedish flags, a band known as Dodsworth's Music Corps, and eight more torchbearers. The Swedish flag had another inning but this time it was flanked by two white and gold standards, one bearing the name of Jenny Lind, the other that

FASHIONABLE OLD STEINWAY HALL
Where Nilsson made her American debut in 1870

of Christine Nilsson. Eight more torchbearers cast the proper amount of effulgence on the flags of various singing societies while eight others lit up a chorus of Scandinavians with their director. The American, Swedish, Danish and Norwegian flags properly illuminated followed along, as did the august "President of the Committee and attending Callers." Any gloom that these dignitaries might have shed was dispelled by eight more torchbearers, and the enthusiastic marchers with six hundred more colored lanterns.

The parade marched up Third Avenue to 14th Street, over to Fourth Avenue and ending at the Professor's home where Stina was the guest of honor. The torchbearers formed a great circle, within which stood the musicians and singers. Nilsson graciously appeared at an upstairs window amidst the cheers of the serenaders; when the cheering subsided, she thanked them all for coming and said this occasion would become one of her fondest memories. And so it did because quite unconsciously, while playing Swedish folk songs, the musicians chose the first tune which little Stina had ever played on her violin. At one o'clock the serenaders filed past the first-floor balcony while the prima donna waved good night to them, after which for aught we know they extinguished their torches and "lit up" themselves.

Although this Juliette scene was actually her first appearance before the American public, it was a silent one and on September 19, 1870, Christine made her American debut at fashionable Steinway Hall then on 14th Street between Union Square and Third Avenue. Almost three thousand persons jammed the auditorium, having paid three and four dollars a seat. Vieuxtemps, the violinist, shared the program with Nilsson and opened the concert. He received politely impatient applause. No one had come to hear him. Everyone was waiting for the successor to Jenny Lind. Finally Christine came before the curtain, dressed in heavy white satin trimmed in valenciennes lace, looking like a bride. In her hair which, according to the current fashion, resembled a bird's nest, she had pinned a diamond hummingbird and a diamond butterfly poised in a diamond flower.

The Concert Program was printed on elegant linen stock which had been scented with a new perfume called "Nilsson Bouquet."

The critics hailed her as the brilliant singer she was, and she started on tour. Outside New York, Nilsson sang one hundred and twenty concerts in twenty-three cities. With the money she earned, she bought houses in New York, Boston and Chicago and gave a thousand dollars to the victims of the Chicago fire. In 1872, at the end of one of her great tours, she was reported to have earned $250,000 and her managers only $50,000 less.

During one of these tours she and my old friend Max Maretzek were traveling by train from Cincinnati to Buffalo. Max had a Gargantuan appetite and he had brought along a big sausage and a loaf of rye bread

Nilsson suddenly sniffed the air and asked, "Are you eating sausage again, Max?" She turned around and he quickly stuffed what was left in his coat pocket. The diva, momentarily forgetting her life on the farm, scolded him for eating such "common" food.

Then the unexpected happened. An accident delayed the train for several hours and the prima donna was getting hungry. Her hearty appetite was crying out to be fed. She looked around and discovered Max fast asleep. She tiptoed over and was about to steal the offending sausage when Max woke up and she was forced to confess: "I know you have some left. Be a good fellow and let me have it."

While touring in the Middle West, the plight of the yellow fever sufferers in New Orleans was called to Christine's attention. At the close of the week, she offered to stay over Sunday and give a Sacred Concert for their benefit, with the entire proceeds to be given to the fund. Her generosity was acclaimed and the house was jammed with people who were only too delighted to have an additional and unexpected opportunity to enjoy her voice again, especially as she promised a wide variety of selections from her repertoire—a sort of refined, classic musical smörgasbord, as it were. Admission was free but the singer announced through the papers that she personally would circulate through the audience collecting from each listener whatever he or she could afford to give, as she had done on behalf of her own countrymen during the Swedish famine some years before. At the intermission, after a wild ovation, she came down the aisles carrying a silver basket, and accompanied by two gentlemen with larger wicker baskets into which she poured the offerings as her smaller one became brimful. She ascended the balcony and even the gallery, disseminating her smiles and her charm and gathering in the cash. Her plan was a great success, the proceeds exceeded $5,000. But there was a behind-the-scenes story that afternoon which was even more interesting than Christine's success as a money raiser.

In the nineteenth century, no member of the Methodist Church was allowed to attend either the theater or opera. A wealthy and well-known manufacturer, a pillar and financial supporter of Methodism in the community, was present at the concert and with two or three other prominent citizens made a little speech from the stage.

When this broke in the newspapers, the Elders of his church made a strong protest concerning what they termed "the scandal" of their fellow member attending the Opera House. A great schism ensued. Some claimed that since all the selections were sacred, the concert could not be considered a theatrical enterprise, but his Elders prevailed and demanded that the offender be expelled for his lapse from duty. The guilty man sent in his resignation with that of his entire family, a loss that dealt the church treasury a solar plexus blow from which it never recovered.

Then came Nilsson's first farewell to America, a concert held in the Academy of Music. She gave the first act from *La Traviata*, the second act from *Lucia di Lammermoor*, and Ophelia's death scene from *Hamlet*. Professor Doremus gave her a private farewell party, presenting her as a parting gift with a banjo inlaid with silver and gold. Christine had so enjoyed the Negroes' banjo playing in the deep South that she had learned the instrument herself and loved to play upon it the songs of Stephen Foster. Auguste Rouzaud, a young Frenchman, had followed Nilsson to America. Thirty-six years old, very good-looking, the press announced that he was the diva's fiancé. Together they made a trip to Niagara Falls, the honeymooner's paradise, and to Saratoga Spa. What the American reporters failed to find out, the French journalists did. Rouzaud was born in the tropics, on the Isle de Bourbon, and was Creole.

After her return to England, Christine married Auguste on July 27, 1872, in Westminster Abbey, London. Sweden's Minister to England gave her away and England's Crown Princess presented her with a diamond bracelet. The bridal gown designed by Worth of Paris was reported to have cost a thousand francs. After the ceremony, a Member of Parliament, Sir Cavendish Bentinck, gave a luncheon for the wedding party and everyone begged Nilsson to sing. Christine smiled but refused to sing any arias from her opera repertoire, or any songs from her concert programs, on her wedding day. Instead she took up her American banjo and accompanied herself as she sang the plantation songs of long, long ago which she claimed "warmed her heart."

Stina's marriage had an extremely good influence on her singing although the critics did not give M. Rouzaud credit for the change. One London paper observed: "Miss Nilsson has nothing to learn from the Americans. But appearing before American audiences seems to have developed the dramatic side of her talent, for now she plays with a passion and a fire which we were unaccustomed to note in her before. Her voice is still incomparable, while her singing is just as perfect and eloquent as before, it now seems—judging from the applause by the public—to have gained in its power to charm an audience."

All this sounds like the happy ending of an up-from-slavery story with a Cinderella twist: born in poverty, adopted, in this instance by a fairy godfather, trained to be a great singer, triumphant in Europe and America, and happily wedded in the famous old Abbey to the man of her choice. But Nilsson's tale was far from ended. The next chapter was to be written in Russia. The Imperial Opera of St. Petersburg signed a contract with Christine, paying her 200,000 francs for a four months' and ten days' engagement.

Nilsson chose for her debut the part of Ophelia in *Hamlet*. Patti, who had been heard on the same stage previously, caused the walls of the

Mme. Nilsson's Songs

- Now Was I Wrong? — 4
- Old Folks at Home. — 4
- Let Me Dream Again. — 4
- Ave Maria! Gounod — 4
- Angel's Serenade. Braga — 6
- Jewel Song. Faust — 4
- Egyptian Lullaby. Pratt — Slumber Song. — 4
- Angels Ever Bright & Fair. Handel. — 4
- Mignon's Song. Thomas. — "Hast thou seen the land?" — 5
- Love Smiles No More. Swedish Song — Nilsson's Favorite. — 4
- Calling the Cows. — "Kulla Kulla." — 4
- The Ball. Swedish Song — "Come my little maiden." — 4
- Dalecalian March. Swedish Air — Courage, Honor, &c. — 4

THE QUEEN OF SONG.

BOSTON.
Published by OLIVER DITSON & CO. 451 Washington St.

NEW YORK. C.H. DITSON & CO. — SAVANNAH GA. LUDDEN & BATES. — BALTIMORE MD. OTTO SUTRO. — CINCINNATI. GEO.D.NEWHALL & CO. — SAN FRANCISCO. SHERMAN CLAY & CO. — PHILA. J. E. DITSON & CO.

CHICAGO. LYON & HEALY. — J.H. BUFFORD'S SONS LITH. BOSTON & NEW YORK. — ST LOUIS. J.L. PETERS.

opera house to shake with thunderous applause, but Christine was not so received, possibly because the advance publicity had been inadequate. But as the opera proceeded, and Stina's exquisite voice filled the far reaches of the auditorium, the audience thawed, and by the third act, responded to her great talent with an ovation that even surpassed that which they had tendered Adelina. Because of the emotional reaction of the Slavic people, Nilsson found it necessary to advertise in the papers, asking her patrons not to prolong the performance by too much applause and too many curtain calls.

Musical St. Petersburg was, after Christine's première, divided into two warring camps composed of those who preferred Patti and those who preferred Nilsson. In February of 1873, the two camps had an opportunity to "fight it out" with applause when the two singers finally appeared on the same concert program for the Assembly of Nobles. Theatrical history does not record which of the ladies was given top billing. Christine, with her superior sympathy and understanding of the national character of her audience, wisely chose to sing "Liuba Henja" (Love Me)—a simple Russian melody which she interpreted so beautifully and sang so naturally that the audience went wild. Poor Patti could not cope with that stroke of genius.

On March 1, 1873, Nilsson sang her farewell performance in Russia as Marguerite in Faust. In the garden scene in Act II, Marguerite opens the jewel box which Faust has placed before her cottage. Usually filled with garish copies of gems in paste, Christine was amazed to discover this time that it contained farewell presents from her admirers including the Czar and Czarina—a magnificent set of emerald and diamond jewels.

Remembering Christine's tomboy youth, we are able to believe the story of how Stina went bear hunting while in Russia. With unerring aim, the prima donna shot a charging bear square in the chest and he fell dead in the snow. The hunters had the enormous animal stuffed and sent it to Christine's home in London, where he became a familiar figure in the entrance hall, standing on his hind legs and holding a silver salver for visiting cards in his great paws.

In 1882, Christine's husband died, a great tragedy for the singer. With half of the money she earned, he had speculated. While the diva herself did not at all care what became of her fortune, Auguste, in whose family there was a streak of insanity, suffered a mental relapse from the worry. He imagined himself a stock or a bond going up, up, up and in order to realize this wish fulfillment graphically, he started climbing the tallest trees in the garden. But soon he sank into a coma, and passed away.

Five years later Christine remarried. Her new husband was Count Miranda, a Spanish diplomat and leading figure in Parisian society. The following year, Christine bade her adoring public farewell forever from an

English concert stage. She left while her voice was perfection, at the zenith of her career. No pathetic performance of an aging prima donna ever marred her reputation. But four years after her retirement she traveled all the way from Madrid to London to sing a duet from *La Traviata* with Sims Reeves in his farewell benefit concert in Royal Albert Hall. He was the English tenor who had appeared with Emily Soldene at her debut. Now, old and penniless, he was still Nilsson's friend and, never breaking a promise once made, she journeyed all that distance to make certain that his benefit would be a success.

The very last time Christine appeared before an audience was for charity at Menton on the Riviera in 1893. The 50-year-old singer played violin at that time, choosing, with her usual flair for the dramatic, an old Swedish favorite beginning "Fourteen years I believe that I was . . ." which in its English version is known as "Time went by and I turned seventeen." On her far-flung journeys over the globe, Nilsson never ceased to remember and long for her Sweden. She went back home a few times. On one occasion, several people were trampled to death in a riot which started in a public square in Stockholm when Nilsson sang from a hotel balcony with her usual generosity. Christine, who was always buying homes, and a feeling of security with them, possibly because she experienced the tragedy of being dispossessed in her early youth, acquired a little country estate near her birthplace, called Vik, meaning cove or bay, and here in 1922 little Stina passed away.

XI

Adelina Patti

Who refused to sing without $5,000 in cash

TWO opera singers appeared in Madrid on the night of February 9, 1843. The tenor was Salvatore Patti from Sicily. The soprano was his wife, Caterina, of Roman and Venetian forebears. The opera was *Norma*. Although she knew she was about to give birth to a child, and the stork was parked virtually behind the scenes, Caterina completed her performance. At two o'clock on the following afternoon, a child was born, a little daughter who was christened Adela Juana Maria Patti, to be known to the whole world as Adelina Patti. The Pattis brought their child to New York, together with their other children and Caterina's children by her first husband.

In 1850, my friend of later days, Max Maretzek, lived next door to the Patti family in East 10th Street and he became particularly fond of Adelina and she of him. On her way home from school or coming back from play in the afternoons, Adelina and her youngest sister would stop in at the famous impresario's office in the Astor Place Opera House. On May 10, 1849, this had been the scene of the Astor Place Riots against MacCready, an English actor, in retaliation for an alleged slight accorded the American actor, Edwin Forrest, in London, some time before. Thirty-four persons were killed in these riots, in spite of the militia.

At Maretzek's request, Adelina would sing the aria from *Ernani* or the Swedish songs made famous by Jenny Lind. As soon as she opened her mouth, and that glorious voice poured out, the office would be crowded with people, the halls jammed, and, thankful for the rare opportunity, others stopped on the street to hear what they could through the open window. A child prodigy always creates amazement in the listener, but with Adelina it was something more. The people who heard her recognized immediately that here was a voice that was not just a wonderful possession for one as young as she, but that it would have been a priceless gift for any adult.

Then Max, overcome with appreciation if not with generosity, would give Adelina half a dollar and she and her sister would dash to the nearest candy store to spend their all on sweets.

Maretzek's relationship to the Pattis was not just that of a neighbor. Mme. Barili-Patti sang *Norma* at the Boston Athenaeum with his opera company. This production was very much a family affair for Amalia Patti sang Adalgisa and little Adelina appeared as one of Norma's children. During rehearsals, Adelina insisted on singing along with her mother and sister during the duet of "Mirao Norma." In spite of continual scoldings, she did not seem able to restrain her overwhelming desire to accompany the music with her voice, until her angry mother took her over her knee and gave her a sound parental spanking before the entire company. Max laughed remembering the incident. "Then she received a spanking for singing, and later she received five thousand dollars!"

It was Mapleson who paid her this enormous nightly fee at the peak of her triumph, and she never accepted less up to and including her final appearance in London when she was sixty-five years old. It was always paid her in advance, and under no circumstances would she wait until the end of the performance. Mapleson once remarked, "How can such a sweet voice turn so sour when it comes to business matters." In his book *Forty-Odd Years in the Literary Workshop*, James L. Ford reports a conversation he once had with an Italian named Buchignani, who kept a cafe on Third Avenue near 15th Street, much frequented by singers and musicians of the Academy of Music. He claimed that after Ettore Barili, Patti's half brother, had died in poverty, she was asked to help bury him. With a shrug of her shoulders, she is said to have replied, "When he had money why didn't he save it," and refused to lend any aid. At a contemporary period, another half brother was employed as a dishwasher at Riccadonna's Union Square restaurant.

An important epoch in Adelina's career was the spring of 1850 when she was seven and Max Maretzek arranged a charity concert at Tripler's Hall and invited her to appear. The parents, their friends, and Maurice Strakosch who was married to Amalia, Adelina's elder sister, smiled tolerantly as the little girl came on and climbed a table so that the audience could see her. A few critics were there, covering the concert as routine work.

Adelina knew the aria "Casta diva," which Norma sings in Bellini's opera and which her mother had sung the night before Adelina's birth. She had heard her mother sing it while working around the house. Adelina

ADELINA PATTI
Famous diva of opera

MAX MARETZEK
Famous impresario, discovered Patti

MME. ADELINA PATTI'S CONCERTS.

HENRY E. ABBEY, Director.

MADAME ADELINA PATTI.

SIGNOR ERNESTO NICOLINI, TENORE. SIGNOR AUGUSTO PINTO, BASSO.

SIGNOR FEDERICO SALVATI, BARITONO. SIGNOR A. GORNO, PIANISTA.

MLLE. THERESE CASTELLAN, VIOLONISTE.

GRAND ORCHESTRA, SIGNOR F. D'AURIA, CONDUCTOR.

HAVERLY'S CHICAGO THEATRE

Thursday Evening, January 5, 1882, at 8.15 Precisely.

PROGRAMME.

PART THE FIRST.

1. OVERTURE—*Euryanthe*, . . . GRAND ORCHESTRA. . . . WEBER
2. ROMANZA—"Ah! non avea più lagrime" (*Maria di Rudenz*), . . . Mr. LEVILLY. . . . DONIZETTI
3. GRAND SCENA ED ARIA—"Bel raggio" (*Semiramide*), . . . Mme. ADELINA PATTI. . . . ROSSINI
4. ARIA—"Il mio tesoro" (*D. Giovanni*), . . . Signor NICOLINI. . . . MOZART
5. ROMANZA—"O casto fior" (*Re di Lahore*), . . . Signor SALVATI. . . . MASSENET
6. SONG—"She Wore a Wreath of Roses," . . . Mme. ADELINA PATTI. . . . JOSEPH P. KNIGHT
7. SCENE DE BALLET—Pour Violon avec Orchestre, . . . Mlle. T. CASTELLAN. . . . DE BERIOT

Accompanist, . . . Signor GORNO.

PART THE SECOND.

Third Act from **FAUST** Gounod's Opera,

In Costumes and with Scenery, with the following Cast:

MARGHERITA, . . . MME. ADELINA PATTI

MARTA, . . . SIGNORA BETTINI

SIEBEL, . . . SIGNORA DINSONI

MEPHISTOPHELE, . . . SIGNOR PINTO

AND

FAUST, . . . Signor NICOLINI

Conductor, . . . Signor D'AURIA.

Last Concert, Saturday Matinee, January 7th, at 2 o'clock.

FOURTH ACT, "TROVATORE."

Steinway & Sons' celebrated Pianos used at all Adelina Patti Concerts.

Distinguished Honors and Awards decreed to Steinway & Sons, New York: Two Medals for the Highest degree of Excellence in all their pianos and for the best pianoforte material, the Highest Award at Centennial Exhibition, Philadelphia, 1876. The first of the Grand Gold Medals of Honor at the Exposition Universelle, Paris, 1867. Grand Testimonial Medal and Membership from Société des Beaux Arts, Paris, 1867. First Prize Medal at Great International Exhibition, London, 1862. Decree of Membership from Royal Academies of Fine Arts at Berlin and Stockholm. Grand Honorary Gold Medal and Decoration from H. M. Charles XV. of Sweden.

was a born singer, a marvelous imitator, the quickest "study" in the history of the musical stage. At the close of "Casta diva" even her relatives were astonished at her magnificent rendition and there was a storm of applause from the audience. As an encore she sang the Rondo from *La Sonnambula* and Eckert's enormously difficult "Echo Song" which Jenny Lind used to introduce as her program *piece de resistance*. No one had taught Adelina the song—she had merely picked it up with her sensitive musical ear. The critics pushed their way through the crowd that surrounded the little girl and eagerly questioned her parents. Next day, the papers said that "Little Miss Patti" was the most astounding real prodigy ever to appear in America. Adelina's lame sister, Carlotta, who was supposed to have the only voice among the children worth training, was bitterly jealous, but she lived to have her own concert triumphs and to win one superlative crown: her voice was the highest soprano ever known, extending as it did to G sharp in alto. What an item that would have been for Ripley.

Adelina's brother-in-law was quick to see the gold mine Max Maretzek had unearthed for him in the bosom of his own family, and from that time on Maurice Strakosch became her manager, coach, personal representative and impresario. Taking Amalie as his spouse was the luckiest thing he ever did. He had discovered that marrying melody was sometimes quite as profitable as marrying money.

On May 5, 1852, Adelina made what appears to have been her professional debut in Metropolitan Hall. The critic of the *New York Albion* wrote: "The interest of this concert was further sustained by the performance of the wonderful child, Signorina A. Patti, whose extraordinary execution evoked more than one shower of bouquets and furores of applause. The development of precocious powers are too often unattended by a fulfilment of their promise in maturity, but if the exquisite ear which she shows, particularly in the exactness of her repeat in the 'Echo Song,' and the facility with which she masters some of the chief difficulties of the Italian style, be sustained during some ten or twelve years' study, great things may be expected. . . ." Thus did this anonymous and verbose critic correctly estimate Adelina's career and I can imagine how often in later years he must have bragged to his cronies about being the first critic to call serious attention to her miraculous voice. Perhaps he was the original "I told you so."

"Little Miss Patti" toured with Strakosch as manager, sometimes appearing alone, but more often giving joint concerts with other artists, at first with Gottschalk, the pianist, then with Ole Bull, the famous Norwegian violinist. For several years, they toured most of the states, Canada, Mexico and Cuba. Wherever they went, they met with unqualified success. Adelina's share of the net earnings was $20,000, most of which her father invested in a house in the country.

— ASTOR PLACE OPERA HOUSE AND RIOT

me of the McCready (English) — Forrest (American) rivalry

(Insert) — EDWIN FORREST

(Bottom) — INTERIOR ASTOR PLACE OPERA HOUSE

At this period in her life, Adelina remained unspoiled. She matured slowly. Her singing was something that she loved but it came so easily to her that her chief pleasure was not, as one might expect, applause, but her dolls. Once in Cincinnati, Strakosch promised Adelina a certain kind of doll which she particularly desired and then forgot to buy it for her. The concert hall was crowded, the audience was impatient for the artiste to appear. In the wings, Strakosch found Adelina weeping with disappointment. She said through her tears that she would not go on without the new doll. He pleaded with her but he was wasting eloquence and time. There was only one way to solve the problem. He went out and bought the doll and the audience waited. Adelina was all smiles when Strakosch returned. She went on the stage and sang like a little angel, while the new doll sat propped up in a chair in the wings watching her.

I can fully appreciate this incident. Excepting as to some of the details, the same thing happened in our home when my grand-daughter as a child, cried, almost heartbroken, for a doll she called her "Wah! Wah!"

Next to dolls, Adelina liked champagne best. When most young ladies her age were drinking cocoa, she was allowed to sip the sparkling wine that made her voice tingle. One night, while she was touring with Ole Bull, they sat down to dinner and Adelina demanded a glass of her favorite champagne. The Norwegian was horrified and refused to give her any. She slapped his face, and thus his objection to giving her champagne caused real pain. These anecdotes will, in part, reveal the headstrong, self-indulgent child who developed into one of our greatest opera stars.

It was at the close of this tour that Strakosch decided that his young protégée must study for the operatic stage. After a few more concerts, "Little Miss Patti" went into retirement.

Then, in her seventeenth year, on the memorable evening of November 24, 1859, Adelina Patti took the city by storm when she sang her first operatic part, the title role in *Lucia di Lammermoor* at the old Academy of Music in New York. Her weekly salary was only a hundred dollars. The critics were ecstatic in their praise and the newspapers, with their usual disregard for factual accuracy, called her a New York girl. For many years her public believed this to be true and Patti never denied the story and it was, of course, almost true. She had arrived in New York as a baby and she had received both education and training there.

King Edward, then Prince of Wales, visited this country in 1860 under the pseudonym of "Lord Renfrew." He missed Patti in New York, and in Philadelphia he expressed a desire to hear her. Ullman and Strakosch immediately brought their company to Philadelphia where they gave a special command performance at the Academy of Music on October 10, 1860. Adelina sang *Martha* and the delighted Prince went behind the scenes—a favorite custom of his in later years—to thank the young prima

OPERATIC IMPRESARIO

CELEBRITIES

COL. J. H. MAPLESON

MAURICE GRAU

HENRY E. ABBEY

Des services reçus l'on doit se souvenir,
Et la reconnaißance est un juste salaire
Qui dans un coeur bien né ne doit jamais
finir

Amalia Patti Strakosch

N.Y. 4 Février 1860

MAURICE STRAKOSCH

Husband of Amalia Patti — manager of Adelina Patti

AMALIA PATTI STRAKOSCH

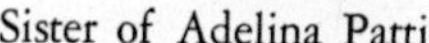

Sister of Adelina Patti

AN INCIDENT

MANY there are to-day who can recall the night, in the early 80's, at the Academy of Music, New York, when a new coloratura singer stepped into fame almost unheralded in the middle of a Mapleson opera season. Grand opera up to that night had been a serious problem for the doughty old colonel, and it was said that the sheriff was "on the doorstep" on the very evening when Etelka Gerster, the Hungarian soprano, carried the audience off its feet and set it literally crazy by her sensational vocalization. That audience was so enthralled by the marvelous voice and methods of execution of Gerster that it is a truth—many forgot they were in an opera house.

That night saved Mapleson, for, at Gerster's second appearance, as *Amina* in "Sonnambula," every seat in the house was sold before the doors were opened, and this was not an ordinary achievement in the period whereof I write. Gerster became the rage and for three years her name was one to conjure with. The fame that had come to her in a night was so distinctly unusual and emphatic that the history of grand opera in this country cannot record any similar achievement to this day. Others have come, been heard and conquered, but no triumph so sensational as Gerster's has ever been witnessed by an American audience.

The career of Etelka Gerster received its impetus from a New York audience, and, sad to relate, that same career ended as suddenly as it began, also before a New York audience, a decade later.

After Gerster left this country, having amassed a large fortune through three years of constant success, little was heard of her save that she was singing abroad. Rumor had it that her voice was not what it had been, and American impresarios were reluctant to accord to the diva the $1,250 a night she demanded for a concert tour. Nevertheless that intrepid Yankee, Henry E. Abbey, despite the rumors he had heard, engaged Gerster for a sixty-concert season in 1892-3 at her own terms.

At length announcement was made of the opening concert at the Metropolitan Opera House. The public had heard the rumors, but Abbey's confidence in the diva was shared by all. The opera house was sold out, a galaxy of well-known singers was secured to surround the star. In all the years that I have attended musical events I never observed an audience so full of anticipation as that gathering that had come to pay homage to the greatest living coloratura singer.

Finally Gerster appeared for the first number in the opening part of the program. Such an ovation not even Patti had ever received. Gerster did not appear the least nervous, and before she sang her first note, if there were any in the audience doubtful as to her vocal condition, her self-possession in the face of that tumultuous welcome would have restored their confidence.

It was truly the same Gerster who had come ten years before and conquered in a night. There she stood before the welcoming audience that had paid fabulous prices to hear her sing. The tension was something awful, for with the first notes was to be determined whether rumor had lied. But, alas!

Gerster was voiceless!

How she did try to coax those trills and roulades from that wonderful throat!

But we will drop the curtain here. Gerster's career had ended that night, for she never again recovered her voice, and that audience of three thousand music lovers went slowly from the opera house the saddest assemblage I have ever seen. Many were in tears, for had not their favorite singer failed almost in the same manner as she had triumphed at her début ten years before?

ETELKA GERSTER

OLE BULL
Started as a minstrel — famous violin virtuoso in later years

donna. The sad aftermath of this story is that nobody, not even Patti, received a dollar for singing as the receipts were attached by the stockholders of the New York Academy of Music. Perhaps this was the experience that later caused Adelina to insist upon payment before every performance.

In the spring of 1861 Maretzek arranged with Maurice Strakosch, Patti's brother-in-law and manager, to present an opera company in Mexico, headed by the young prima donna. He was carrying out his plans when Strakosch and Adelina's father decided to take the girl to London. Maretzek received a telegram saying that Patti was afraid to go to Mexico as she had heard that that country was full of highway robbers. Meanwhile, Patti, Strakosch and Signor Patti were on their way to London when Maretzek received a telegram telling him the truth and ending hopefully: "Adelina and her Papa send you their best regards." Maretzek was stranded in Mexico City, with an opera company on his hands but no leading prima donna. He saved the situation by giving operas new to Mexicans with his best remaining singers and by producing a Mexican opera composed by a member of his orchestra and appealing to the patriotism of opera lovers to support a native production, and last but not least by making roller skating popular.

The skating scene in *Le Prophète* was a sensational success. Maretzek believed he could make roller skating the rage. He remembered Niblo's advice some years before to start a rink and forget the opera, and to a certain extent acted upon it. A roller skating club was started, and similar clubs were formed in all classes of society. The new sport caught on like wildfire. Each club in rotation asked for and paid for the privilege of displaying their skill in the skating scene in *Le Prophète* to their friends. The opera house was crowded while the novelty lasted. "And thus," said Maretzek, "the Gran Teatro Nacional became a well-paying skating hall with a performance of Meyerbeer's masterpiece thrown in as an added entertainment for the same price of admission." Those in the audience who essayed to put on roller skates for the first time, contributed what perhaps might be called a diverting "floor show."

It was delightful and most encouraging to achieve fame in New York, but American audiences were still naïve—this country was merely "the provinces" when compared with sophisticated Europe. London was the city to be conquered next. Because of her excellent notices, all the concert halls bid for Mlle. Patti and Covent Garden won the honor of presenting Adelina to her first British audience. She received £32 10s. a performance. On the night of May 14, 1861, she appeared as Amina in Bellini's *La Sonnambula*. Her performance was the most brilliantly successful debut ever recorded in the history of the lyric stage. The phenomenal supremacy she achieved that night she never lost. Charles Dickens wrote of her: "The new singer, in her early girlhood, is already a perfect artist, one who is to set Europe on fire."

The summer after her English debut, she commanded 500 guineas for three concerts at Birmingham. At one of these performances, the conductor received a note from a member of the audience, telling him how deeply impressed she was by the beauty of Patti's voice and her singing technique. The conductor passed Jenny Lind's note to Adelina Patti.

The prima donna sang Marguerite in Germany, Spain and France, and always in Italian. During these early years of triumph, Adelina had no private life. Her manager guarded her jealously. If she fell in love, he was careful to see that she rapidly fell out of it again. Suitors were methodically discouraged. But Strakosch failed in his self-imposed task of guardian of Adelina's virtue in Paris. The diva loved Paris and the Second Empire loved Patti. Empress Eugénie, who had a genius for matchmaking, was anxious to find a husband for her favorite opera star; and after painstaking machinations, finally persuaded Adelina that she was in love with the Emperor's equerry, the Marquis de Caux, whom she married in London in 1868.

The made match was never a success. The couple separated after nine years. The Marquis would have had to be the Angel Gabriel to please the temperamental Adelina and he was certainly not that. The great emotional satisfactions of married life were not to be hers at the moment, but as a compensation, Adelina had the world at her feet. Her operatic triumphs were increasing, and her terms along with them. *Punch* printed a quatrain remarking:

> Patti, Patti cake, Fronchi mon!
> So do I, messiers, come orte as I can.
> Roulez et tournez et marques "with care"
> Et pasez au publique a ten dollars a chair.

All the lighter roles were hers, for she was a born comedienne and her incomparable voice dominated the stage. Rosina in *The Barber of Seville* was her favorite role. "I like the *Barbiere* best of all my operas. I love the comedy and the constant fun. I can laugh and feel joyous all the time. Birds always sing best when they feel happy. I revel in the 'Lesson' scene. I can do what I please there, and it always amuses me to introduce music written after Rossini wrote the opera." The highest praise she ever received was when Sarah Bernhardt, the greatest of Camilles, wept over Adelina's operatic Camille in *La Traviata*.

Before she divorced the Marquis, in 1885, Patti had met Ernest Nicolini, the French tenor, who was to be her "first real love." As the Victorians so gently expressed it—she "united her fortunes with his." They sang together in England, in Europe and America, much to the sorrow of the critics who found his voice far inferior to hers. When resting, they lived in a castle in

Wales, Craig-y-Nos, Rock of Night. In spite of the fact that she was obliged to part with half her fortune to be rid of the Marquis, she could live in luxury. New York was paying her $5,000 a performance, and the wealthy patrons of the Argentine gave even more for the privilege of hearing her sing.

Ever since she had been a small child, Adelina had admired and loved the talents of Jenny Lind. It was only in after years that she learned that Jenny herself reciprocated this admiration. Once, early in the eighties, Mme. Lind-Goldschmidt went to hear Patti at Covent Garden. She was accompanied by Sir Arthur Sullivan who, when he next met Adelina, asked her if she would like to know what Jenny Lind had said about her. "I would indeed," she replied.

"Well," said Sir Arthur, "she made this remark: 'There is only one Niagara, and there is only one Patti.' "

When the rivalry between Patti and Etelka Gerster was at its height, the reporters learned that General Crittenden, Governor of Missouri, had kissed Adelina. In an interview she laughed and said, "I had just finished singing 'Home, Sweet Home' when a nice looking old gentleman, who introduced himself as Governor Crittenden, began congratulating me. 'Madame Patti,' he said, 'I may never see you again,' and before I knew it he was kissing me. When a gentleman, and a nice old gentleman too, and a Governor of a great State, kisses one so quickly that one has not time to object, what can one do?"

The reporters went to Etelka Gerster and asked her if she had heard about the Patti kiss. "I have heard that Governor Crittenden kissed Patti before she had time to object," Gerster replied, "but I can't understand why the incident has created so much talk. There is nothing wrong in a man kissing a woman old enough to be his mother." At another time when Gerster was in the audience, and an enthusiastic auditor anticipated that Patti would sing tonight as she never had before, Gerster's satiric comment was, "That means she will sing on the key." There were "cats" then as now.

In January, 1884, Colonel Mapleson took her opera company from Boston to Montreal. He had paid for the train in advance and thought that the price included Adelina's private car. When the train arrived at Montreal, a railroad official appeared and asked for an additional $300, as a special charge for Patti's own car. Mapleson did not have the amount with him and he was unable to get it until the box office at the opera house opened. The official refused to trust the impresario and ordered the car shunted to a distant part of the yards and placed under guard. Patti, meanwhile, was sleeping in the car, blissfully unaware that she had been seized for debt. The Colonel was frantic and, after a Keystone Chase, finally located the opera house treasurer, got the money and raced back to the railroad to free his star from "protective custody." For the railroad official, may it be added it was fortunate for him that Adelina slept throughout the argument.

In 1886, she became Adelina Patti-Nicolini and was truly happy with her newly legalized position. She was both Queen of Song and Queen of Opera and in love with love. She looked wonderfully young, and her beauty defied the passage of time. For twelve years, between engagements, she played at being Lady Bountiful in Wales, in the grounds of the castle.

Then Nicolini fell ill and no doctor was able to cure him. He died in 1898 and Patti seemed heartbroken. There was, however, within Adelina a passion for life and an unending zest for experience, and to the astonishment of her friends, within the year, she announced her engagement to Baron Rolf Cederström, a Swedish doctor whom she married on January 9, 1899, when she was nearly fifty-six, but looked no older than her husband, who was in his thirties.

The doctor was not the romantic lover she craved. He was more of a keeper. His eye was on her fortune and he frowned on the lavish entertainments she so enjoyed giving. He alienated her friends and berated her extravagance. To him a guest was merely a person who ate without paying, nor could he understand the need of serving caviar at fifteen dollars a pound, when Swedish anchovies at two dollars a keg would do just as well.

It was soon evident, however, that people and excitement were the tonic that kept Patti young. When she found herself without them, she began to lose her glorious health. She sang her last opera at Covent Garden in 1898, but her ultimate farewell as a concert singer was not given until 1906 at Albert Hall. America said farewell to her in 1903, long after she should have retired gracefully. It was remarked that Cederström urged her to make the trip, for while "it was painful, rather than pleasurable" there was no question about its being profitable. She went home with fifty thousand additional pounds. How Patti preserved her voice through so many trying years is no great secret. She never abused her vocal cords. If she did not feel well, she would not sing. And if the opera was one which she knew well, she refused to attend rehearsals. On the days when she was to sing, she remained as completely relaxed as possible—not even reading because of the possible effect it might have on her nerves.

Finck said that Bauermeister, the modest little soprano who was at Covent Garden and at the Metropolitan under Maurice Grau, gave still another reason why Adelina preserved her voice intact for so many years. "At Covent Garden," she said, "in the ensembles at the end of an act, when the chorus and orchestra were crashing at once, Mme. Patti did not sing the prima donna's top notes. It was always the good Bauermeister's mission to sing those top notes instead and the audiences were none the wiser." In other words, Patti started the fashion that was later to flourish in the moving-picture industry—she hired a "ghost singer," a vocal "stand-in."

Only once again was the public allowed to hear her voice. In 1914, to aid the Red Cross, she appeared before the footlights of Albert Hall and sang "Home, Sweet Home" in her own unforgettable manner with what the critics said was "her magical charm of old."

Adelina Patti died at her castle in Wales and left the shrewd doctor her estate of several millions which he promptly transferred to his native land. Her stage costumes, operatic scores and personal treasures can all be found in the Museum at Stockholm, which is scarcely the place for them. New York, London, Paris or Berlin—any of the scenes of her greatest triumphs should have fallen heir to this collection. Her magnificent, almost priceless jewels disappeared. Apparently they were converted into Swedish investments.

It would be useless for me to attempt an appraisal of Adelina Patti's gifts, particularly since she herself once summed them up as follows: "I know that although they call me Queen of Song, it is not because I am the greatest singer, but because there are many gifts in the same person in me. I am not beautiful, but I pass for pretty; that's one. I am tolerably graceful; that's two. I am a good dresser; that's three. I have a way with me that's piquant; that's four. I like my public; that's five, for my public likes me and I never tire of pleasing them. I have a good voice; that's six. I know how to sing very well, my way; that's seven. I always know my music; that gives comfort to the audience, and may count as eight. I act fairly well the roles I sing; that's nine. What more could one want in a singer?"

On the thirty-fifth anniversary of Patti's first appearance an elaborate public dinner was planned, but several prominent women refused to come on account of the scandal caused by her divorce from the Marquis de Caux and her elopement with Nicolini. A stag party was arranged instead to be held in the ballroom of the Hotel Brunswick.

Seventy of the best-known men in New York were received by Patti in the ballroom, where she sat like a queen. She was in splendid humor and was enjoying the affair. At the dinner Maretzek told stories about the diva. He related how she refused to sing at Tripler's Hall, when she was a little girl, unless he would buy her a pound of candy. Max agreed, if she would give a kiss in return. With a laugh Patti sprang to her feet at the anniversary party and said: "Max, I kissed you for a box of candy then; now I'll give you a kiss for nothing."

XII

Carlotta Patti

Whose phenomenal voice reached G sharp above the high C and embraced 2½ octaves

GUY WESTMORE CARRYL helped to immortalize at least one great singer for the present generation in his fable of the Fox and the Raven. The raven, sitting high on a tree, was holding a particularly succulent piece of cheese in his beak which the fox coveted. With his usual slyness, the animal laid a plot. He would douse the bird with flattery about her voice, and the raven, overcome with pride, would open her beak to sing and the cheese would fall into the fox's mouth. There was one comparison which the fox had to employ if he were to impress the raven. He looked up.

"Sweet fowl," he said
"You're more than merely natty,
I hear you sing to beat the band
And Adelina Patti.
Pray render with your liquid tongue
A bit from 'Gotterdämmerung.' "

No poet, however, not even a versifier, ever immortalized Adelina's sister, Carlotta. The present generation has never heard of Carlotta. They not only do not know that Adelina had a sister but they are totally ignorant of the fact that she was for many years the leading woman concert singer in Europe as well as America. While time has completely overshadowed Carlotta's reputation, it had added to Adelina's. But during their lifetimes, there was actually no personal tragedy of one sister's triumphs breaking the heart of the other. When Adelina swept opera audiences off their feet, Carlotta thrilled the concert-goers.

Like her sister, Carlotta, who came first, was born in the wings of the musical stage. It really had the stork worried, because on the stage door was a sign reading, "Positively no admittance behind the scenes." But he was no doubt a resourceful bird because history reports that in 1840 the prima donna Signora Patti, while fulfilling an engagement at the Pegola Theatre in Florence, gave birth to Carlotta, a little girl of many talents. Before her voice was discovered, she was skilled as a painter, and when music finally became her field, she selected the pianoforte as her instrument, not yet realizing that she had been endowed by nature with a thrilling instrument all her own. When the Patti clan moved en masse to America to sing Italian opera in New York, Carlotta immediately studied under Henri Herz, who incidentally was the first concert star to appear in San Francisco in 1850, tickets costing six dollars.

It was during this period that another sister married Signor Scola, professor of music, and teacher to both Adelina and Carlotta. Signora Scola, shortly after her marriage, exhibited symptoms of consumption and it fell to Carlotta to go with her as nurse to South America whose climate the inept medicos of that era felt would be helpful. There Carlotta's sister wasted away before her eyes and when she returned it was alone, an experience for the young person that sobered her high spirits and saddened her expression.

Carlotta found on her return that the widower was busy training her younger sister's voice, and to take her own mind off her loss, she, too, decided to study voice under the master, never dreaming that the training would disclose a vocal apparatus which became famous as "the highest soprano ever known."

By 1861, Ullman, the impresario, heard her voice at her first professional engagement in New York, and immediately decided that it was of a caliber fine enough to be heard at the Grand Concerts of the New York Academy of Music. This for Carlotta was an auspicious beginning. Just as today a successful concert at Carnegie Hall is all that is needed to start off a new voice or a new instrumentalist on a tour of the States, at that time the Academy of Music was the measure of a singer's ability. Once accepted by the critics as belonging to that revered company of artists who appeared year after year at the Academy, Carlotta had no difficulty whatsoever in making a tour of the chief cities in the United States, each one of which acclaimed her.

In the midst of her concert tour, the Abolitionist movement came to its logical conclusion: the South, unwilling to sacrifice its landed property privileges where human beings were considered part of that property, seceded from the Union, and the President went to war to preserve national unity. The news from the battlefront, with the ever-lengthening lists of the dead and wounded, completely absorbed public interest. No invention

MAURICE GRAU AND MAX STRAKOSCH
Caricature — Stockholders' Action

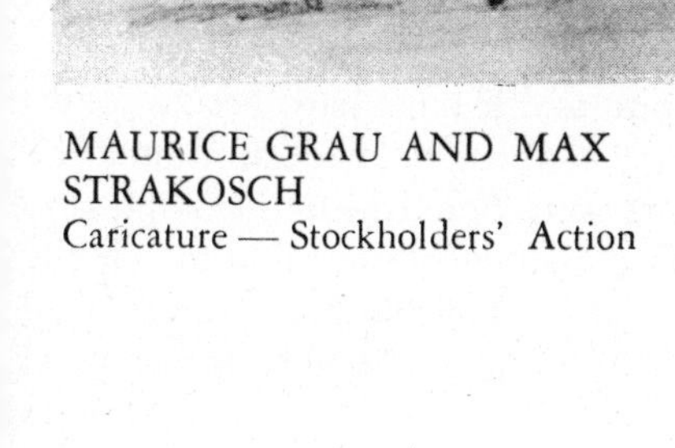

CARLOTTA PATTI
Just missed being as famous as Adelina

of the impresarios could catch the fancy of a nation torn with civil strife. In New York the dramatic stage, as well as the musical, languished without its customary support from the people. The managers of the Opera House were particularly distraught, unable to devise any novelty that might catch the fancy of the war-absorbed people.

Suddenly someone suggested that if the concert favorite, Carlotta Patti, could be persuaded to appear in opera for the first time, the size of their audience would be assured. Carlotta herself did not rejoice in this decision, flattering as it was. She had always been reluctant to appear as a dramatic actress because, following an accident in her early youth, one leg was slightly abnormal in development and she walked unevenly. Had Carlotta not felt indebted to the managers for their support of her debut years, she probably would never have consented to appear because she was hypersensitive about her affliction. The managers themselves did not at all consider this imperfection a drawback. They were convinced that her magnificent voice, her handsome face and the power of her dramatic expression would so delight the public that they would not even be aware of her halting gait.

Carlotta was finally persuaded to appear and it must have been a source of great satisfaction to everyone concerned, when she made an immediate success and proved to be the magnetic attraction which the impresario had predicted. A near-by stationer joked that he wasn't able to sell the Academy of Music box office any more red ink. Carlotta appeared in all the roles previously sung by Adelina, displaying a flexibility in her vocal production that caused a sensation among the amateurs. It is difficult to know just why Carlotta's reputation never equaled that of Adelina. It was probably because she was not wedded to the operatic stage, and returned to concert program for preference, where the greatest popularity could not equal the public encomiums then lavished on stars of the opera. Another factor was undoubtedly her own personality. Carlotta was stately and handsome and a perfect artist but there was something sad about her charm and she possessed neither the vivacity nor the sex appeal of her even more beautiful sister.

By 1863, Covent Garden was clamoring for Carlotta, and in April of that year she made a tour through the appreciative provinces. Before appearing in England, the singer was full of doubts as to whether she could win her European audiences. It was one thing for an artist to establish herself on the Continent and then, at the height of her reputation, deign to appear in America, sweeping all opposition before her; another, to be famous in the United States, and make that single reputation count in the musically supercilious Old World. Advertised as a "sensation," Carlotta was afraid she might be considered sensationally overrated, rather than sensationally talented. In the last analysis, her audience on April 16th was swept off their feet by the sweet larklike notes of her upper register which one critic described as seeming "to descend from some ethereal region." It was the fact that she was a vocal phenomenon which gained her the first plaudits of the crowd, only afterwards did they fully realize her qualifications as an accomplished woman singer. London made her the star of the musical season, and as such she was the honored guest star of the last concert of the New Philharmonic Society. By that time Carlotta's name was magic, and St. James held the largest "assemblage" within its memory.

It was during this same year that Buford, famous American print maker, presented Carlotta's admiring public with a magnificent lithographic portrait of the singer which appeared in all the music-shop windows.

The Royal Italian Opera House, in 1864, was the scene of promenade concerts and the *London Chronicle* on August 13th announced: "As a matter of course, Mlle. Carlotta Patti is the bright particular star."

But Adelina's elder sister never forgot that America gave her her first success and, though she visited almost all parts of the world where a concert could be given, including China, Japan, Burma, Brazil, Chile, Australia and even New Zealand, she constantly returned to America and her country's enthusiastic acclaim. Her apartment in Paris was filled with curiosities and objects of art which she had collected in her travels, and it gave the impression of being an overcrowded museum rather than a human habitation. In 1872, Ullman began a remarkable concert series at old Steinway Hall. Evidently his unwise management of little Maria Piccolomini twenty years before had been a lesson. At any rate, he did nothing to compromise Carlotta's career. Her father was still Signor Patti, a member of the first Italian Opera Troupe, and everyone remembered him, so Ullman did not indulge in any flights of imagination about her parentage or ancestry.

With Carlotta as an additional attraction, Strakosch's company included Signor Mario, the leading tenor of the day, the favorite of both Paris and London. In 1854 he had visited the States under Mr. Hackett's management with his wife Giulia Grisi, and was more than partly responsible for the series of triumphant performances known as the "Great Grisi Season." Then he was at the height of his career and the Academy of Music resounded with the best male voice ever to ring in its hallowed rafters. Home-grown Annie Louise Cary, mezzo-soprano and contralto, and Teresa Carreño, pianist, were both presented by Strakosch.

Carlotta, who had not been home since 1869, was in magnificent voice and scored an immense success. Her audiences swooned with delight at everything from the mad scene from *Lucia* to the simple "Coming Through the Rye." Poor Mario was merely tolerated because of his former successes. His voice had lost most of its tonal purity and all of its sweetness, retaining only its magnificent mezzo quality, superior to that of any tenor except perhaps Brignoli.

Seven years later, when Carlotta was thirty-nine, she married Ernest Demunck, the violoncellist, and continued to sing in concerts to the delight of all her followers.

In case you are still bothered about the raven and the canny fox who used Adelina's name, we think it only fair to present the denouement. With such high praise ringing in his ears:

> In flattery completely doused,
> He gave the "Jewel Song" from *Faust*.
> But gravitation's law, of course,
> As Isaac Newton showed it,
> Exerted in the cheese its force,
> And elsewhere soon bestowed it.

The name of Carlotta Patti may not have spanned the decades with the same ease as her sister's but that, certainly, was not her fault, although it is our loss. In her declining years, she was wont to dwell on the shortcomings of her heart and lungs. And thus she gravitated from vocal concerts to organ recitals.

XIII

Pauline Lucca

Who was warned to "modify some of her business" in Faust

BORN of Italian-Irish parents in Vienna on April 25, 1841, Pauline Lucca developed into a magnificent singer and a fascinating woman. When she was only fifteen, her voice attracted attention as she sang at the Karlskirche in Vienna. Soon the astute music lovers of that city were flocking to church, not, alas, to pay attention to the divine services, or the texts which Lucca sang, but to listen with rapt, aesthetic attention to the exquisite voice that dominated the choir. From church, it was but a short step to the Vienna Opera House, where Lucca began modestly enough in the chorus to get her training. But the chorus master, the musical director and the manager of the opera himself soon realized that in Pauline they had acquired a voice and a personality destined to bring all three of them the reflected glory of developing a new operatic star.

As a beginning, Lucca was allowed to try the solo passages of the Bridesmaids' Chorus in *Der Freischütz* and she sang them with so much art and charm that the same people who had suddenly found piety so satisfying now gave up churchgoing and turned to the opera house where *Die Freischütz* suddenly became very popular, and a minor ovation took place with alarming regularity after the solo passages, sparingly meted out to the Bridesmaid, who had died into silence. The manager of the Vienna Opera was no fool, he understood that he had under his protective wing a prima donna, but he had not been quick enough to offer Lucca a contract so that she might have begun her career as a diva in the City of Song.

The small town of Olmütz had already signed Pauline to sing leading parts, and it was there that Lucca displayed much of her talent and gave some strong indications of her temperament. Things were not easy for

Lucca in the small Austrian town. There she was, an inexperienced prima donna, surrounded by strongly entrenched colleagues who had been singing for years without any competition from a young musical upstart fresh from sophisticated Vienna. The old singers fought with Lucca at every opportunity, and the culmination of one argument was an insult delivered by the seniors' star. Lucca insisted upon an apology. When it was not forthcoming, Lucca threatened to leave the theater and the company.

The manager pointed out that if she left his company, it would be a breach of contract which would seriously jeopardize her career with other operatic managers, and threatened to fine her if she should attempt anything of the kind.

Lucca then gave some indication of the audacity for which she later became famous. She forestalled the breach of contract action by turning to the commander of the garrison at Olmütz, accusing herself of breach of contract, and demanding that he arrest her immediately, a duty under the existing police regulations. Since the story of the argument and the insult, as well as news of the attitude of the theater leader, had already become common talk throughout the city, the commander, in order to prevent further trouble, as he thought, foolishly took Lucca into protective custody at the citadel.

This was just what Lucca's friends had desired. They immediately raised a hue and cry, and started an organized campaign to free Lucca not only from the citadel but from the contract. Finally, in desperation, the permission was granted and she was allowed to leave Olmütz with her engagement largely unfulfilled.

The anticlimax shook the small town. After Lucca had successfully made her departure, it slowly occurred to the principals of the drama that the young diva had actually engineered the whole episode, argument and all, because she had already signed a contract for the Prague Opera and was desperate to find a means of legally securing her freedom from Olmütz.

In Prague, her performance of Valentine in *Les Huguenots* aroused the greatest enthusiasm and Meyerbeer, who heard her, was so delighted therewith that he desired to be presented to her. Entering her dressing room, he rushed up and planted two large appreciative kisses, one on each cheek, much to Lucca's surprise and embarrassment. Perhaps she even wondered what sort of medals he was going to pin on her to back up that sort of salutation. After all, she had not the slightest notion of the stranger's identity. By the next day, however, she had learned several things about Meyerbeer, the most important being that he was the reason for the new contract which was promptly offered her to appear in Berlin for the season that was to begin in eight months. Meyerbeer could not wait to hear her sing in his *L'Africaine*. "This is my Selika," he had cried out when first he saw and heard Lucca. It was not, however, till 1865 that she sang this

PAULINE LUCCA AND CHANCELLOR BISMARCK
The suppressed picture that started a scandal (taken at Ischl, in 1865)

PAULINE LUCCA

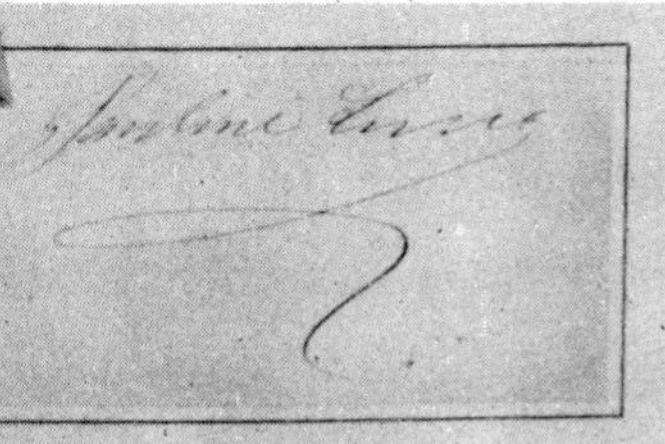

role and made it her greatest triumph. When Meyerbeer first met her, she had been unable to sing in French and therefore could not then delight him with the fulfillment of seeing her as the star of his favorite opera.

Lucca had a great deal of fun in Berlin, as she did wherever she went She became friendly with Bismarck and a few years later persuaded him to be photographed with her. The innocent photograph made a sensation It was copied and sold all over the Continent for many years. Scandal had coupled their names for a long time, and although in the eyes of the public he was "the Iron Chancellor," he was plain everyday putty to Pauline She was accused of having published this picture in a spirit of revenge Hermann Klein, a most devoted biographer, wrote that, during the Franco Prussian War, Pauline coaxed Bismarck into giving her a special pass to visit the German Army at the front. Herr Klein in a burst of under statement declared "her curious adventures near Metz aroused consider able talk at this time." Bismarck adherents publicly demonstrated agains the diva, who was not the type of woman to suffer in silence. One night when called before the curtain by her usual enthusiastic applause, Lucca stepped to the footlights and looked her audience in the eye. She then abused them in choice Viennese patois for insulting a woman and said she would never sing in Berlin again. Some accused a rival prima donna, Fra Mallinger, and the "Wagnerites" for starting the trouble.

Pauline's particular genius was to set tongues wagging about her. While *Les Huguenots* met with London's approval in 1863, the Victorian audi ences frowned heavily upon her portrayal of Marguerite to Mario's Faus and Faure's Mephistopheles just one year later. They complained tha Lucca's Marguerite was "a very forward minx" and they questioned th "propriety" of the scene in the garden. These were probably self-constitute custodians of public morals, and the forerunners of our own Comstock They called her Marguerite "too knowing" and "an absolute little devil. Gye, who was managing Covent Garden at the time, asked her to "modif some of her business" in *Faust*, which merely acted as a signal for Lucc to blow up. She would play it her way or not at all. In the midst of th argument she pleaded ill-health and fled back to Berlin, where folks wer more realistic about sex.

This time, Adelina Patti was her rival. Lucca and Patti were the sam age and vied with each other in many cities other than Berlin. Mme Marchesi, hearing them both in Vienna, wrote from her experience as celebrated vocal teacher: "This was a rare treat, for every evening one ha the choice between Patti, with her extraordinarily beautiful voice an delightful method, and Lucca, with her marvelous dramatic talent. Th former excited the greatest admiration and carried us quite away with th charm of her singing; but the latter appealed to the feelings of her aud nces and in great dramatic moments would take our hearts by storm. t was a thousand pities that Lucca's natural and remarkable talent should ot have been properly cultivated. The wonderful progress she subsequently nade in her singing was mainly due to the excellent example of Italian ngers before her. She was the best *Carmen* I ever saw."

The director of the Berlin Opera found himself, after engaging Patti, a strange position. He possessed in his company two beautiful and dmirable singers, but while he paid Lucca one thousand francs a month, atti was to receive one thousand francs a night. For purely commercial easons, he was anxious for Lucca to eclipse Patti. At the time he was otoriously behindhand with salaries. When asked why she was content to ccept a thousand francs a month when Patti was getting a thousand ancs a night, Lucca replied promptly, "I get mine." In spite of the stage valry, the two singers were good friends, in so far as we are able to judge oday. The only place where Lucca was able to replace Patti completely as inside the tummies of German populace. Pauline's eyes were extraordiarily beautiful, very large and gray-blue in color. They became so famous at some enterprising bakers in the sixties introduced to the public a new ake called "Lucca Augen." It became an instantaneous success, and today, nless Hitler does not like them, "Lucca Augen" are sold in all good akeries, candy shops and cafés, and are as well-known and popular as Schiller Locken."

In 1872, Lucca came to America to sing in Max Maretzek's opera company. She and Clara Louise Kellogg were co-stars. Selika was the role in hich Lucca made her debut and the crowded house was enchanted with er velvetlike mezzo-soprano voice and spirited acting. New Yorkers were ot the least bit shocked at her Marguerite; in fact, they preferred her to ilsson in the Church Scene because of her dramatic ardor. If Kellogg as jealous of Lucca's success in the role which she herself often sang, e gave no sign of it, and had her artistic revenge in *Mignon* when, as ilina, she sang the "Polonaise" so brilliantly that her ovation eclipsed that the star.

It is always difficult to be impartial in judging vocal merit when a diva s also the priceless gift of charm and dramatic talent. The *New York imes*, writing of Lucca as Zerlina, claimed that she "abounds in grace, arkle and coquetry. She rivets the eyes of her public as much as she arms their ears, for her by-play is full of piquancy and suggestive expreson and her mobile and handsome face is a study that always rewards amination."

In the tradition of singers, Lucca married twice, the first time Baron n Rahden, the second time Baron von Wallhofen, while she was touring merica. Pauline herself laughed at the titles. "It appears to be the fate all prima donnas to marry a title and to work harder than ever afterwards. Look at all of us past and present,—always the same thing ove and over again. I married a Baron, then Adelina Patti married a Marquis,– that was a step higher,—so," she added, laughing, "I thought two Baron ought to be equal to one Marquis."

Lucca was a perfect terror with a contract. When, in 1874, she wa scheduled to return to America she could not do so because the govern ment of Cuba would not allow her to leave until the forty operatic pe formances she agreed to give with di Murska, Vizzoni and others had bee presented. As a matter of fact, it was difficult for her to select a refug from the courts in 1874. Germany was filled with subpoenas for contemp of court; Paris, London and Vienna all were waiting breathlessly for th appearance of the diva—the public to hear her sing, her former manage to levy fines on her for breach of contract. Lausanne, Switzerland, seeme the safest place for her second honeymoon and there she went. But i 1876 Mr. Gye of the Royal Italian Opera, Covent Garden, who ha obtained a verdict of $16,000 against Lucca, waived his claim to have he back in London, singing for him again. It definitely established the fac that he was a glutton for punishment and also proved that the reputatio of Lucca's charms was not exaggerated.

From 1874 through 1889, Pauline appeared each season as leading singe at the Viennese Opera. In 1876 she visited Brussels. The next year foun her in Russia. From 1882 to 1884, she again pleased her English audienc and finally she was forced to retire. Lucca spent her later years in teachin ambitious young women to sing, just as if there wasn't enough sufferin in this world already. "Inspire yourself with the situation," she begged pupil who was training for a tragic role. "Put yourself in the poor woman place. If you were deserted by a lover whom you adored, what woul you do?"

"I would look for another" was the unexpected answer.

Pauline Lucca laughed and laughed. It was certainly what she also woul have done.

XIV

Clara Louise Kellogg

Who, when one year old, carried a tune perfectly

PICTURE, if you are able, a large Negro mammy with a little, 10-month-old girl on her knee. So far there is nothing unusual in the sight of a baby girl with her nurse, but the nurse is humming n the rich contralto voice of her race, and the baby is singing too. At ten nonths a little girl can be expected to imitate a sound or two, but this hild, known to the world as Clara Louise Kellogg, by the time she was a ear old, could sing along with her mammy in perfect tune.

> Hey, Jim along,—Jim along Josy;
> Hey, Jim along,—Jim along, Joe!

Years later, Clara attempted to account for this inborn talent of hers hat flowered so richly: "In some people the need for music and the ower to make it are just as instinctive as they are in birds—what effects have achieved and what success I have found must be laid to this big, iving fact. Music was in me and it had to find expression . . . From my arliest days my love for music showed itself in my constant attempts to ing and my deep attention when anyone performed on any instrument, ven when I was so little I could not reach the keyboard on the piano, ven on tip-toe."

Born in Sumterville, South Carolina, when her father was principal of umter Academy, a scholarly import from New England, her youth was a horoughly musical one. "Mama played the organ, Papa played the flute." nd Clara sang. We can easily imagine Sunday evening in the front arlor with the musical Kellogg family grouped around the organ in the ight of flickering candles.

In 1856, the family moved to New York and it was there that Clara received the beginning of her musical education. Colonel Henry G. Stebbins, a wealthy businessman and one of the leading directors of the Academy of Music, the Metropolitan's predecessor as the home of opera was her first "angel." He was responsible not only for her musical education but also for her debut when she was ready for it. In 1861, she sang for her first audience at an evening party given by Mr. Edward Cooper and that same year she made her formal debut as Gilda in Verdi's *Rigoletto* at the Academy of Music. She managed to learn French but never could master German, important though it was for the career of a singer. She would have sympathized with H. C. Bunner, who composed the amusing couplet:

> Goethe wrote in the German tongue,
> He must have learned it very young.

Because of this language difficulty, when she sang Senta in *The Flying Dutchman*, she had permission to sing it in English. Senta was created by Clara in this country, and she was very proud of having this honor Elsa also met with her approval, but, though she loved the music of Wagner passionately, she realized that Isolde was beyond her capabilities "The heavier parts such as Isolde, I should hardly care to sing." Her favorite opera was *Faust*, probably because she helped to popularize it in America

"The first time I played Marguerite, the audience gaped with amazement. The first hour or two no sign was made whether of approval or otherwise. Finally they awoke to the beauty of it, and at the end there were thunders of applause. It had been a success. So often was this experience repeated that I grew to prefer Marguerite to any other part."

And it was Marguerite which she elected to sing at her debut in London at Her Majesty's Theatre in November of 1867. For an American singer to dare European audiences was a brave move indeed, and Clara more than rose to the occasion. She was a credit to her country and there was no critic who could deny it, and this at a time when the prejudice against everything and everybody American in the musical world was acute, not just abroad where our people were considered aesthetic barbarians, but even in our own country where the dilettantes followed the European vogue without deviation. Clara's success in London was all the more remarkable when we realize that she appeared at the exact time when the greatest galaxy of singers were all behind footlights at the same time Adelina Patti, Therese Tietjens, Nilsson and Parepa-Rosa were her rival and yet Clara Louise Kellogg, with her very plain name and her American background, held her own with all of them. She had the rare distinction of being the first American prima donna of any standing who went to Europe and "made good." It is encouraging to remember that she di

CLARA LOUISE KELLOGG

not adopt any strange-sounding name to help her get on in the world, although it would certainly have been difficult to Italianize "Kellogg," although equally difficult perhaps to Americanize Piccolomini. One enthusiast wrote:

"She appears to possess every requirement, physical and mental, for the full delineation of the character [Marguerite], unquestionably one of the most engaging in the entire repertory of the modern lyric drama and her voice is a legitimate soprano of extremely agreeable quality, flexible, as was shown by her facile delivery of the well known apostrophe to the jewels . . . Always in tune, Miss Kellogg has a voice indeed that leaves little to be wished for, and she proves by the use of it that her studies have always been assiduous and on the right path. She is in fact, though so young, a thoroughly accomplished singer."

The next year, Clara began the season as Violetta in *La Traviata*. The Prince and Princess of Wales were present and led the ovation which followed Clara's inspired singing. For the first time in his life, the Prince at that period went behind scenes to shake hands and congratulate the young cantatrice, an honor he claimed never before paid by him to any singer.

The 1870's found Clara back in America touring the country. On the day of a concert scheduled in Utica, Clara was invited to visit the State Lunatic Asylum where she sang to the more quiet patients, much to their delight. Enchanted with the way in which they reacted to the charm of her voice, she begged to be allowed to sing to the more dangerous cases. "Let me sing to the mad people," she pleaded. The superintendent agreed and led her to the wards where the more violent cases were kept. The noise was deafening as she entered, enough to discourage the most intrepid artist. But Clara began to sing, and as the bell-like notes filled the room, a spell seemed to be cast over the patients. The hubbub subsided and the upturned faces turned towards Clara were full of hope and even content. When the song stopped, they crowded around her. "She must be an angel," one said. Another, perhaps to register his enthusiasm, cryptically remarked, "She should be here all the time." At any event, it was the forerunner of a fact later on established as therapeutically sound, of the beneficent effects of music upon the mentally deranged.

After the asylum concert the superintendent escorted Clara around the grounds. He stopped before one of the inmates named Sam, and taking a dime and a nickel from his pocket, placed them in the palm of his hand and told Sam to take his choice. Sam took the nickel. Clara, puzzled, tried the same stunt. Again Sam picked up the nickel. So she said to Sam, "When somebody offers you a nickel and a dime, why do you always take the nickel?" "Because," replied Sam, "if I took the dime, folks would quit offering it."

KELLOGG = VALSE.

English words by **ARTHUR MATTHISON.** Musica di **ARDITI.**

con grazia e ben marcato.
p
When those fair......... ru - by por......... tals un - close,
Quan - do schiu........ di il tuo lab......... bro gen - til
p
rit.........
ten.
When love's song........ from thy lips ten - der - ly flows, ah then!
A so........ a............ ri pa - ro............. le d'a - mor ah, si!
ten.
pp
rit.........
a tempo.
Thou dost seem....... Goddess Flo - ra in - deed, Who
Sem - bri a Flo - - ra la De....... a d'A - pril Che
p a tempo.
cres.
f
rit.
with flow - 'rets a - dorns ev - 'ry valley and mead.
la ter - - ra la - ter ra fe - con - da di fior;
brillante.
p
mf
rit.
tempo.
cres.
7308

Even if Clara's own voice had not brought her deserved fame, the fact that she discovered and developed the wonderful voice of Emma Abbott would always redound to her credit.

Emma's father, who gave music lessons in Peoria—and precious little he got for them—once traveled all the way to Chicago to hear a great opera star. When he returned, he described to little Emma how this beautiful lady had stood on the stage and sung while the crowd cheered and threw bouquets at her. Emma was thrilled. "But, papa," she asked, "was the stage going? If so, I should think she would have been afraid of falling off." In those days, a stage was only a stagecoach to the little girl.

When only twelve Emma realized that her help was needed to eke out the family income, so she took her guitar and the voice she had been born with and went out on the streets to sing and play. Once she gave a concert all her own and made ten dollars, a fortune to her in those days of starvation. When Peoria did not seem to appreciate her gifts, she literally took to the road, pawning what small things she owned when the public turned a deaf ear to her music. When they could have heard her for nothing, they passed by, when it cost many dollars to hear her, they could not hear her often enough.

When things were very bad, she cut off her long hair and sold it for switches, and once even was forced to part with her beloved instrument. Her courage and determination never failed her. When Parepa-Rosa was to appear in New York City, Emma sang her way from Illinois to New York to hear her, only to be disappointed by the diva's illness. In 1870 in Toledo, poverty not only stared her in the face, it positively looked cross-eyed at her. In fact, things looked so black to the young girl that for a brief moment she thought of suicide, but playing her guitar revived her love of music and of life itself.

Then luck changed. At the Russell House, Detroit, after singing, playing and taking up a collection, a lady with a gentle voice said to her: "My dear, I want to ask you why you are doing this thing? Don't your relatives know that you have a voice—a beautiful voice? You've astonished me this evening. With training you can rise far above this. Under the right instruction you can become a great singer, a prima donna . . . You are thin and pale . . . You are having a hard time, I know."

After hearing Emma's pathetic history, the lady said: "I can't let you go on like this. You must come to New York. We shall find a way to have that voice developed. My name is Kellogg . . . Clara Louise Kellogg. Will you come?"

The rest of the story has become history—how Miss Kellogg became Emma's best friend and adviser, never failing to give her an introduction when one was needed, or money if that were required—opening with the key of her own success the portals of the world of music and society for the younger girl.

One night, through an invitation obtained for her by Clara, Emma Abbott was to make her appearance at the home of August Belmont. A wet and windy night meant nothing to Emma, who had tramped the countryside in all kinds of weather, and she walked to the Belmont mansion. Not until the butler's horrified glance took in the mud-splashed hem of her dress, and then swept up to the limp wet feather in her hat, did Emma realize that she presented a rather striking contrast to the beautifully gowned women who crowded the salon. The tittering might have grown in volume had not Clara stepped forward and put her protégée at her ease, and when she sang, the audience could not help but admire; after her exquisite voice was still, the applause shook the crystal candelabra.

One of her most attentive listeners that night was Horace Greeley, editor of the *New York Tribune*, who, enchanted at his first meeting her, remained a lifelong and devoted friend. It was through his influence that Emma became soprano in Dr. Chapin's Church, and it was he who was chiefly instrumental in raising the money needed to send the young girl to Europe for further vocal study.

Once in Paris, Emma worked so indefatigably that she strained her voice and awoke one day to find it had vanished. Months passed and Emma had all but given up hope when she returned to her guitar for comfort, and later explained:

"One morning when Paris was sparkling in mellow sunlight and birds were pouring out melodies, the voice in the guitar seemed to rise in exultant notes, and as easily and as gently as a baby opens its eyes from sleep, I began to sing—to sing, mind you! and as well as ever. I laughed; I cried; I danced about the room. Winter had passed; Spring had come; my hopes were again in blossom!"

The Baroness Solomon de Rothschild lent Emma several thousand francs to continue her studying because the proud little singer would not again approach Clara or the friends in New York who had helped her get started.

Then, quite suddenly, Clara's protégée was ready for her debut and my friend, J. W. Morrissey, managed her for five years. A genius at publicity, Jimmy succeeded in placing her before the public as one of America's leading stage and concert stars.

When Emma played the lead in *Paul and Virginia*, she implanted so fervent a kiss on Paul as the climax of the third act, that the operagoers of Louisville who witnessed the première, gasped at her audacity. One of the married auditors is said to have remarked to his wife, "Why can't you kiss like that?" She complained about it to a local newspaper publisher,

EMMA ABBOTT

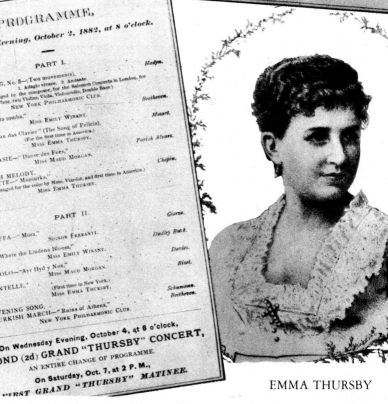

CHICKERING HALL

The "Thursby" Grand Concer[t]

Mr. MAURICE STRAKOSCH very respectfully announces the first appear[ance of]

MISS EMMA THURSBY

(Since her return from her brilliant triumphs in Europe) in

THREE GRAND "THURSBY" CONCERTS,

Monday Ev'g, Oct. 2d, Wednesday Ev'g, Oct. 4th

AT EIGHT O'CLOCK, AND

Saturday Matinee, Oct. 7th, at 2 o'clock.

MISS EMMA THURSBY

WILL BE ASSISTED BY

MISS EMILY WINANT, MISS MAUD MORGAN

SIGNOR PIETRO FERRANTI,

AND

THE NEW YORK PHILHARMONIC CLUB,

COMPRISING THE FOLLOWING ARTISTS:

RICHARD ARNOLD,	Violin.	EUGENE WEINER,	Flute
EMIL GRAMM,	Viola.	REINHARDT RICHTER,	Violin.
CHARLES WERNER,	Violoncello.	LUDWIG E. MANOLY,	Double Bass.

PRICES:—Admission Tickets, $1.00. Reserved Seats, 50c. Extra.

Seats can be had at CHICKERING HALL; also at SCHUBERTH'S, BRENTANO'S, POND'S, and at 111 Broadway.

THE CHICKERING PIANO USED AT THE THURSBY CONCERTS.

[D]OORS OPEN AT 7:15 O'CLOCK. CONCERT COMMENCES AT 8.

PROGRAMME,

For Monday Evening, October 2, 1882, at 8 o'clock.

PART I.

1. SYMPHONY IN G, No. 3—(Two movements), *Hadyn.*
   1. Adagio vivace. 2. Andante.
   (Expressly arranged by the composer, for the Salomon Concerts in London, for Flute, two Violins, Viola, Violoncello, Double Bass.)
   NEW YORK PHILHARMONIC CLUB.
2. ARIA—"In questa tomba," *Beethoven.*
   MISS EMILY WINANT.
3. SONG, "Phillis an das Clavier" (The Song of Felicia), *Mozart.*
   (For the first time in America.)
   MISS EMMA THURSBY.
4. HARP FANTASIE—"Danse des Fees," *Parish Alvars.*
   MISS MAUD MORGAN.
5. { *a.* SWEDISH MELODY, { *b.* COQUETTE—"Mazourka," *Chopin.*
   (Arranged for the voice by Mme. Viardot, and first time in America.)
   MISS EMMA THURSBY.

PART II.

1. ARIA BUFFA—"Mora," *Giorza.*
   SIGNOR FERRANTI.
2. SONG—"Where the Lindens Bloom," *Dudley Buck.*
   MISS EMILY WINANT.
3. HARP SOLO—"Ayr Hyd y Nos," *Davies.*
   MISS MAUD MORGAN.
4. "TARANTELLE," *Bizet.*
   (First time in New York.)
   MISS EMMA THURSBY.
5. { *a.* EVENING SONG, *Schumann.* { *b.* TURKISH MARCH—"Ruins of Athens," *Beethoven.*
   NEW YORK PHILHARMONIC CLUB.

On Wednesday Evening, October 4, at 8 o'clock,

SECOND (2d) GRAND "THURSBY" CONCERT,

AN ENTIRE CHANGE OF PROGRAMME.

On Saturday, Oct. 7, at 2 P. M.,

FIRST GRAND "THURSBY" MATINEE.

EMMA THURSBY

Colonel Watterson, who editorialized in next day's *Courier-Journal* as follows: "Was it right? Was it proper? What was Emma Abbott, who stood for the best on the stage, thinking of?"

Emma was frightened at the public reaction and was perfectly willing to leave out the embrace but Morrissey would not hear of it. "You know it's all right. We know it's all right! Evil to them who evil think."

Now that decades have flown by, it is all right to investigate unemotionally the component parts of the notorious "Emma Abbott kiss." Although through opera glasses it seemed like a real and enthusiastic salute, the cold fact is that it was the imitation of a kiss. Emma simply pressed her lips to a dimple on the chin of the tenor and the nineteenth century trembled. As the years have advanced both ladies still live in the memories of the concertgoers: Clara through her vocalization and Emma through her osculation. The "Emma Abbott kiss" is spoken of to this day.

In 1872, Clara Louise Kellogg was back in London at the Drury Lane and then she returned to the United States to appear in Italian opera. Finally, following the example of Parepa-Rosa, she organized her own English Opera Company with over one hundred artists. *Il Trovatore, Faust, Carmen,* and *The Bohemian Girl* were the four operas they produced at Colonel Sinn's Park Theatre in Brooklyn, and then started off on one of those endless tours through the States which proved that Americans in the eighties were far more willing to support good music than our public of today. Even the *Boston Herald* acclaimed her return, stating that it was one of the most notable events of the season. The critic particularly liked the wonderful "trill" which Clara executed in *Il Trovatore,* and the exquisite skill with which she sang the "Polonaise" in *Mignon.* And then he could not resist saying with pardonable national pride, that Miss Kellogg could attempt music which Mme. Lucca did not dare to try.

When the diva was no longer young, she sang more frequently in concerts, and less often in grand opera. In 1887 she married Carl Strakosch, the nephew of the two famous entrepreneurs, Max and Maurice, and built a home called Elpstone near New Hartford, Connecticut, where they retired to hunt, shoot, raise horses and dogs and flowers. Whether Clara liked her life or retirement is open to question. We cannot help but remember Rostand's play. "What is your life?" they asked Chanticleer. "My song." "What is your song?" "My life," he answered.

XV

Minnie Hauk

Who was Bizet's ideal Carmen

WITH Europe giving birth to most of the famous song birds, it is a pleasure to write about Minnie Hauk, who was born in the United States on November 16, 1852, of German-American parentage. Although born in New York, her family settled with her in Leavenworth, Kansas, because of her mother's health. It is difficult to perceive why anyone should choose Leavenworth as a residence unless it be an involuntary action influenced by the dictum of a federal judge. Minnie's early life was made constantly precarious by a series of wars, inundations, hurricanes and attacks from the Indians, who in the fifties still provided Kansans with ample excuses to erect stockades and tote around double-barreled shotguns. And to make matters still worse, Kansas voted itself dry—not that this had any appreciable effect on the flow of alcoholic beverages. It is recorded that a tourist once asked a Leavenworth policeman where he could get a drink. Pointing to the Y.M.C.A. Building, the minion of the law replied, "That is the only place where you can't get it." When the Hauks had become sufficiently fed up with all these residential handicaps, they moved to New Orleans which offered a far different sort of existence for those who could afford it. Known as the city of good foods, it was also, judging by the number of duels fought in that era, the home of good feuds. Beautiful women and gentlemen with gold-headed canes were provided with rich viands and exotic beverages by the Creole slave labor of the era—not to mention their entire living which was underwritten by the plantation laborers.

The Hauks had every right to expect a different kind of life in the more civilized and more decadent New Orleans, but with their usual talent for moving right in with the hornets, they found themselves in the pearl of the Gulf cities at the time it was being besieged by the Northern troops. Cotton presses were going up in smoke and ships were flaming along with the wharves where they rode at anchor. The Union soldiers were busy doing at least half the things of which they were later accused by our Southern colonels.

Little Minnie did not worry too much about these world-shaking events. She walked through the plantations at the edge of the city, climbing trees to get nearer to the birds whose songs she tried to imitate, and stopped at the slave quarters to listen to the Negro melodies, to learn them and to practice on their favorite instrument, the banjo, as Christine Nilsson did at the height of her fame. Minnie loved the theater from the very beginning and when she was still a small child she organized theatrical performances among her playmates. She worked up such a reputation for this that when a benefit was planned for the "Widows and Orphans of the Wars," Minnie was invited to sing although she was then not more than twelve years old.

Having tried her voice in the South, her roving parents came back to New York which was, then as now, the musical center of America, and Minnie immediately began serious study under Signor Errani. Leonard Jerome of Madison Square placed his private theater at her disposal and she made several operatic appearances there, notably as Amina in *La Sonnambula*. These tentative debuts were so successful that Mlle. Hauk—the Mlle. was a concession to the public with their passion for imported talent—made her first public appearance in the same role at the Old Academy of Music in Brooklyn. Later she returned to Manhattan for a debut there at the Winter Garden as Proscovia in *L'Etoile du Nord* with Clara Louise Kellogg.

The next year, reversing the customary procedure, Mlle. Hauk sailed from west to east to appear before her first English audience at the Italian Opera House in London in November. She chose to appear as Amina and her beautiful voice combined with her great dramatic ability won her the public and also the favor of the Royal Family. It was her misfortune, however, to have had most of her troubles with her fellow singers, managers and others of European nationality who deeply resented the young American's rapid ascent to stardom, when, as everyone of culture claimed, only low comedians could be produced by the provincial States. Much recrimination resulted, both polite and otherwise. But when they realized that Minnie could give as good as she received, they decided to "lay off Macduff" and at least a veneer of outward amity was established.

From the very beginning of her career, it was obvious that Minnie could act. The posturing and facial gymnastics which passed for acting on the lyric stage became outmoded as soon as Minnie proved that a singer could demonstrate the same intelligent, emotional portrayals as a great actress. Because of her outstanding gifts in the dramatic field, she received many offers to appear on the speaking stage, the only diva of her century who was so honored. Quite naturally, she declined them all, and continued to combine both her talents to the utter delight of her audience.

After her first appearance in Europe, Minnie sang one season each at the Italian Opera House in Paris, Moscow, St. Petersburg, then three years at the Imperial Opera in Vienna, two years in Berlin, one winter season in Brussels and Budapest, and four spring seasons at Her Majesty's in London. Her Viennese sojourn was a happy and successful one. She occupied the position of leading soprano, and when Berlin demanded her, she filled the same capacity there.

In March, 1876, while Mlle. Hauk was filling an engagement at the Hungarian Theatre at Budapest, Richard Wagner went to see the young diva who was creating such a sensation in that city and whose fame had already reached him in Germany. That evening, Hans Richter was the conductor, the skilled musician with whom Minnie studied Elsa in *Lohengrin* and Senta in *The Flying Dutchman.* In honor of Wagner, both these operas were given during his visit.

Minnie Hauk sang these two roles, for the first time in Italian, as the German language was not allowed at the National Opera House. After the performance of *Lohengrin,* Wagner said he had never seen a better Elsa, an opinion in which Hans Richter and all the other musical critics who witnessed the performance concurred. Richter afterwards declared, in the presence of Mme. Mallinger, Director Herbeck and others, that she was the best Elsa on the stage. Minnie took the greatest pains with her costumes as well as her vocal delivery. Before she undertook to sing Elsa, Professor Campenhausen, then celebrated as the head of the Duesseldorf School of Painting, made the sketches for the gowns she was to wear, faithfully portraying the original ducal costumes.

When Minnie Hauk sang Senta on a subsequent occasion, Wagner jumped up in his box and exclaimed: "Thank goodness there is an artiste who knows how to act and sing according to the symphonic intentions of the author."

It was in Berlin that Minnie's sonorous and full voice was considered the most exquisite interpreter of the school of music which Weber had founded. During this period Berlin was contending with Vienna for the intellectual and artistic leadership of all Europe, and in order to win the diva's favor and her continual presence, an honor was bestowed upon her which Adelina Patti, who also received her musical training in America, was permitted to share. Both ladies were given the rank and title of "Imperial German Chamber Singer." Although in this day and age, with

MINNIE HAUK
Greatest single inspiration
to American singing

COMSTOCK'S OPERA HOUSE.

FRIDAY EVENING, NOVEMBER 17, 1882.

FIRST APPEARANCE IN COLUMBUS OF Mme.

Minnie Hauk,

—WITH THE—

STRAKOSCH ENGLISH OPERA COMPANY,

PRODUCING BIZET'S CHARMING OPERA.

CARMEN

MINNIE HAUK, in her world renowned rendition of (in which role she has been recognized by the press and public of both hemispheres as the unrivaled exponent and creator.)	CARMEN
LETITIA FRITCH, (her first appearance in Opera,) as	Michaela
MISS VINCENT	Prasquita
MISS SEYMOUR as	Mercedes
MR. TRAVERNER as	Don Jose
MR. GEO. SWEET as (The Toreador)	Escamillo
MR. HOGAN as	Remendado
MR. JUERGENS as	Don Cairo
MR. SEAMONS as	Morales
MR. LEONI as	Zuniga

Mme. MINNIE HAUK will introduce, in Second Act, a Spanish Song, "MANDOLINATA."

Chorus and Orchestra under the Direction of MR. DENOVELLIS.

The Piano used by the STRAKOSCH ENGLISH OPERA COMPANY has been kindly furnished by MR. T. H. SCHNEIDER.

THE CARMEN OPERA LIBRETTO (the only correct edition with English words,) for sale at the Door. Price 25 Cents

Journal Print

MINNIE HAUK as *CARMEN*

Teuton "culture" being what it is, that would not be considered a rank and title but just a rank title.

Brussels clamored to hear Mlle. Hauk. A committee of prominent Belgian citizens invited her to appear at the celebrated Théâtre de la Mounaie, one of the leading opera houses in Europe. Honored by Emperors and Princes, her brow bedecked with laurels, she went to Brussels to add more triumphs to her already spectacular career. The Grand Conservertoire Royal de Music, conferred upon her a gold medal struck expressly for her.

As if in thanks for the generous treatment which she received from the Belgians, on January 2, 1878, she created the celebrated dramatic role of Carmen, the cigarette girl. The King and Queen were present, as well as the leading music critics of London and Paris, and the sensation this most popular opera made at its opening foreshadowed the immortal quality of its leading role. Oh, to be a good Carmen—that is the prayer of every opera singer who loves to act as well as sing. What an opportunity to love, hate and die all in one blissfully musical evening.

On returning to England and Her Majesty's, she sang Violetta in *La Traviata*, Marguerite in *Faust*, Mignon and Katharina in *The Taming of the Shrew* which she created. Although her singing of Wagner's music was perfection itself, it was as an interpreter of Bizet's music that she became most famous. That composer eulogized her as the ideal conception of his Carmen. At the time she sang, Minnie's repertoire was the largest of any opera singer in the world, and she was capable of singing in Italian, French, English, German, and even Hungarian.

The next year she came home to reward her own countrymen by singing where they could hear and see her. But Minnie herself could, at this time, barely see them. Her eyes were failing and while the public was never advised of this affliction, she sang for years able only to see the cloudy outlines of objects. Many years later a well-known low comedian, though totally blind, insisted on carrying on as a monologist. For over a year audiences never suspected his affliction, as he flatly refused to permit press agents to use same for advertising purposes.

When Minnie Hauk was twenty-nine, she married Baron Ernst von Hesse-Wartegg, an explorer and the author of many books about Asia and the Orient. When finally her eyesight became too dim to continue her career she traveled extensively with her husband and finally settled at Lucerne, where journalists often visited her and wrote about her in lengthy interviews.

In November of 1912, a most unusual error was perpetrated in the New York papers. Minnie Hauk's death was reported. It was a case for Mark Twain who certainly could have put into her very alive mouth his famous words, "The report of my death has been grossly exaggerated."

The Baron von Hesse-Wartegg was obliged to cable from Lucerne that he had been receiving all manner of wires commiserating with him on his loss, and of telegraphic money orders from all over America to buy flowers for the sad interment. The Baron added that he failed to understand the object of all this grief and sympathy for he had lost none of his family, Minnie Hauk herself being in excellent health. Of course, he admitted, it was all very flattering.

Minnie was certainly far from deceased. She was alive enough when Calvé made her sensational tour as Carmen, to be wild with jealousy of the younger woman, and it was not until seventeen years after the false report that she actually passed away at seventy-seven, almost totally blind. Her last years were not financially comfortable and as late as 1924 Geraldine Farrar, in gratitude to the woman who had created Carmen, the role Farrar was to make her own particular property at the Metropolitan Opera House, headed a committee to obtain funds with which to make the aging diva's last years more tolerable. It was found then that many people believed her to have been dead for many years, having read the original notice but having missed the subsequent retraction.

It would be wrong to underestimate in any way the importance of Minnie Hauk to the development of our native talent in a period when it was much neglected. Oscar Thompson believes that she was the greatest single inspiration to American singing that this country ever produced. From prairie child to prima donna—Minnie Hauk was the embodiment of the American Success Story.

PART THREE

I

Lola Montez

First glamour girl of the forties

ON THE evening of June 3, 1843, Her Majesty's Theatre, London, held a capacity audience. Royalty were present. The King of Hanover, the Dowager Queen, the Duchess of Kent, and the Duke and Duchess of Cambridge were suitably installed in the boxes with many members of the House of Lords. *The Barber of Seville* was being played, but the unusual excitement in the house was due to the debut of an entr'acte dancer billed as "Donna Lola Montez of the Teatro Real, Seville, for the first time on any English Stage."

The curtains parted revealing a Moorish setting flanked by a pair of Moorish handmaidens. The curtained back entrance was slowly drawn and Lola appeared while the house rocked with applause. "How magnificently Spanish!" The appreciative whisper could be heard throughout the house. The luscious woman before them was tall, full-breasted, with jet-black hair and enormous black eyes of flashing brilliancy. Her full passionate lips were smiling with an inner excitement and she gave an immediate impression of great beauty combined with great magnetism. The sound of castanets and the rhythms of a Spanish dance began in the orchestra, while on the stage Lola's limbs began to undulate with voluptuous dips and sensuous movements. The beatific expressions on the faces of several members of Parliament indicated that they "endorsed the motion." The house was enchanted with the dance "El Olano." One critic wrote: "Lithe and graceful as a young fawn, every movement that she made seemed instinct with melody. Her dark eyes were blazing and flashing with excitement. Her feet, legs and ankles were almost faultless. As she swept around the stage, her slender waist swayed to the music and her graceful neck and head bent with it, like a flower that bends with the impulse given to its stem by the wind."

For ten ecstatic minutes the audience remained enraptured, when suddenly from the right omnibus box came the loud and surprised exclamation: "Why, it's Betty James!" Lord Ravetagh, a rebuffed suitor, had recognized the woman and the fraud perpetrated on the public. While others applauded, he hissed, and his friends, taking their cue from him, added to the sibilant comment. The hissing grew louder and more insistent.

The body of the audience, knowing nothing about the matter, concluded that the beautiful dancer did not know her business and began to hiss also. The curtain came down and Lola's brief career as a dancer in England was over.

But who was Betty James and how did she become Lola Montez? How did an Irishwoman become a Spanish dancer?

In 1824 in Limerick, a little girl with a long name was born to a 20-year-old captain in the King's Own Scottish Borders and a beautiful Irish girl of fifteen who boasted as one of her ancestors, Count Montalvo, a Spanish grandee of Moorish blood. The baby was baptized Marie Dolores Elisa Rosenna Gilbert. She was called Dolores, the diminutive of which is Lola. When only four her father was sent to India with his young family and he died there before his exquisite child was seven. Mrs. Gilbert promptly married his best friend, John Craigie of the Bengal Army.

The charming child Lola was growing competitively too beautiful for her young mother, who decided that Lola was being spoiled in Calcutta, and sent her at the age of eight on a four months' trip back to London to be raised in the home of Sir Jasper Nichols, relatives of her stepfather. When in 1837, Mrs. Craigie followed her daughter to England, she found Lola at Bath, already causing a minor sensation with her really overwhelming beauty of face and body. Mama made some rapid calculations, and after a period of affection and shopping, told her daughter that she had been affianced to Sir Abraham Lumley, a distinguished gentleman of seventy with plenty of money, who was anxiously waiting her return to India to marry him. Lola was told that he had given his promise, to which she naïvely responded, "At seventy, what can a man promise?" And right there Lola gave one of her earliest performances of temperament. She stormed and raved at her mother for the picture bride tactics of her not overfond parent. She flatly refused Sir Abraham but her mother only smiled and wrote the hopeful fiancé that his bride-to-be was not only beautiful but high-spirited. These events taking place in the early nineteenth century, it never occurred to Mrs. Craigie that a daughter could deviate from Mama's wishes, so she was more than startled when Lola chose the obvious way out of a distasteful engagement by eloping with the nearest gentlemen, a handsome but rattlebrained person named Thomas James.

"This dismal life," Lola complained in later years, "weighed on me to such an extent, that I should have assuredly done something desperate if my husband just then had not been ordered to return to India." The boat ride down proved that James could consume far more porter than the average Britisher, and that Lola's beauty was more magnetic than ever. Her first season in gay Calcutta was anything but boring since she became, overnight, the reigning beauty.

The Honorable Emily Eden, sister of the Viceroy, Lord Ashland, wrote about Lola in her diaries: "Simla is much moved just now by the arrival of a Mrs. James who has been talked of as the great beauty of the year. . . . She is very pretty and a good little thing apparently. They are very poor, and she is young and lively and if she falls into bad habits, she would soon laugh herself out of foolish scrapes. At present the husband and wife appear very fond of each other, but a girl who marries at fifteen hardly knows what she likes."

Emily Eden was an astute prophet. When the viceregal party departed from Karnal, Lola moped at the quiet and could not get on with James, so she returned to the lesser of two evils—her mother's home at Calcutta. But the welcome she received caused Lola to remark, "You make me feel so unnecessary." Mama lost no time in suggesting that Lola return to England. There never could be enough ocean between them. On the voyage back a certain Mr. Lennox cheered up Lola so successfully that when she returned to England, her husband sued her for divorce accusing her of misconduct with the gentleman aboard the good ship *Larkins* and subsequently at the Imperial Hotel, Covent Garden. The Court, satisfied with the proofs submitted, issued the decree and both lover and husband vanished from Lola's life.

It was then, left alone in London in the 1840's, that this hopeful beginning of an adventuress decided to become a dancer. For four months she studied under a Spanish professor and then went to Madrid to learn more about the art. While there she assumed the name of "Montez" which she kept for the rest of her life, passing herself off as a Spaniard, partly for professional reasons and partly to conceal her identity as the divorced wife of Captain James.

After Lord Ravetagh had so bitterly broken up what would have been a great professional triumph of Lola, she wrote to the *Era* on June 21st, protesting against the report that she had long been known in London as a disreputable character. She positively asserted that she was a native of Seville and had never before been in London. With this overwhelming whopper she tried to piece together the ruins of her shattered career. Perhaps a less ambitious woman would have abandoned public life after such an inauspicious beginning, but Lola knew well what had prompted the hissing—a spurned lord is seldom a generous creature—and while she was not foolhardy enough to try a comeback in London, she had the whole Continent from which to choose. She decided to begin at Brussels, and without any well-formulated plans, she set out for that city. She reached there both friendless and penniless, and was reduced to street singing to keep herself from starvation. Even in those days she was said to have the carriage of a duchess and the wit of a pothouse lady.

However, Lola never had to worry for any length of time. While there was a man left in the world, she was perfectly sure of being able to get along. One such gentleman picked her up in Brussels and took her with him to Warsaw. As a traveling companion, Lola was a magnificent addition to any entourage. At twenty-six, she was more beautiful than ever. Even her critics and detractors, too numerous to mention, reluctantly admitted that hers was an almost magical loveliness. Sparkling vivacity and a strong personality, not without intellectual attributes, were characteristics to which no one could be indifferent for any length of time. Had Lola to depend on her ability to dance, she would never have been heard of again, but when she was on the stage, the audience saw her, not as a great technician, but as a beautiful woman, embodying all the charms for which the average man longs. She was a wish-fulfillment dream come true.

When Lola at last was engaged and appeared at the theater in Warsaw, she was again hissed by two or three people evidently under instruction of some secret party. The next night the same thing occurred. The third night Lola rushed down to the footlights and declared that she had discovered that these hisses were planned by the director of the theater, because she had refused certain gifts from an old roue prince, who controlled the stock of the theater and was accustomed to receive certain liberties from its stars as dividends.

A shower of applause from the audience greeted this bold statement. Here was a pretty mess. An immense crowd of Polish men who hated both the Prince and the director, escorted her to her hotel. She found herself a heroine without the least intending it. In a moment of rage, she had done what in Boston is known as "spilling the beans"; in brief, she had told the truth about two powerfully influential but unprincipled men without stopping to count the cost, and had succeeded in setting the whole city of Warsaw by the ears.

The French Consul gallantly came forward and claimed Lola as a French subject, thereby saving her from immediate arrest but a peremptory order stated that she must quit Warsaw immediately.

After a brief sojourn in Russia, Lola went to Dresden in 1844 and there she met the great composer, Franz Liszt. This was the kind of man to whom the dancer could submit most willingly. She was always one of these erotic women who could become more easily excited by a man's mental attributes or talents than by any physical advantages he might possess. In all her subsequent relations, her sensuous craving to be loved by persons of strong character and prominence made the theme of her amours. On the other hand, in Lola, Liszt met his temperamental match. Both artists were actuated by a contempt and haughty intolerance of those who claimed attention because of the accident of birth alone. The furor created by Lola's appearance at the theater in Dresden among the men was as great as that caused by Liszt's among the women. This one amatory episode Lola treats with unusual reserve in her memoirs. She mentions meeting the distinguished composer and describes the reception accorded him. About their personal relationship she had nothing to say, and yet at the time, the rumor echoed from country to country that Liszt was held enchanted by the "Andalusian."

Lola's first appearance in Paris was not very successful. On March 30, 1844, she appeared before the footlights. The Parisians recognized her surpassing beauty but saw little that was not meretricious in her dancing. Immediately sensing the critical mood of the audience, Lola made a characteristic bid for their favor. Her satin shoe slipped off accidentally on purpose. She threw it with one of her superb gestures into the boxes, where it was pounced upon and brandished as a precious relic by a noted gentleman of fashion. In later years Charmion caught the idea by tossing garters from a trapeze.

Lola's maneuver seems to have succeeded for the *Constitutionnel* next morning found it necessary to warn young dancers against the dangers of fictitious applause. Théophile Gautier was less gallant. He spoke of Lola sarcastically: "The only thing Andalusian about Lola Montez is that she possesses a magnificent pair of black eyes;—she babbles Spanish very indifferently; French hardly at all and English passably *(sic!)* which is her country."

As at Her Majesty's in London, so was it at the Paris Opera—Lola's first appearance was her last.

Early in March, 1845, Lola, despite her failure at the Opera, obtained an engagement at the Porte Saint-Martin Théâtre for the musical comedy *La Micheau Bois.* Rather disappointed at her failure to turn out continuous triumphs, she announced to a friend: "The moment I get a nice sum of money, I am going to try to hook a prince." With her beauty and figure, she certainly had the right kind of bait.

Lola was now more than ever an abnormally ambitious woman, eager to play a leading part in the world's great affairs. She was possessed of her personal courage and of charms such as would have earned the Legion of Honor for any man. She feared nothing. Although her intellect and natural faculties were stunted and checked under the early Victorian system of education, her contact with so many gifted and great men had developed her worldly outlook.

While hers was no artistic triumph in Paris, Lola was very happy indeed in the company with which she found herself. The literary lights of Louis Philippe's reign were her great admirers, excepting, of course, Gautier. Alexandre Dumas pére literally threw his large bulk at her exquisite feet. Méry worshiped her and Claudin called her an enchantress. "There was about her," he wrote, "something provoking and voluptuous which drew you. Her skin was white, her wavy hair like the tendrils of a woodbine, her eyes tameless and wild, her mouth like a budding pomegranate." All of which probably sounded much less fatuous in its original French.

With this comforting adulation it was Dujarrier whom she loved. He was a young man of twenty-nine, editor of *La Presse*, and skilled in political economy. He understood politics and taught Lola as much about government as she taught him about love. Although she loved him dearly, Lola, in arranging their approaching wedding trip through Spain, invited both Dumas and Méry to go with them. Who but Lola could have conceived the idea of going on a honeymoon with two "spares"? Before the marriage could take place, however, the man of strong convictions was killed, victim of a journalistic duel. This was Lola's only happy, although sad love affair. All the others ended disastrously.

Ambition in Lola thrived and revived as sentiment waned. She turned her eyes toward Germany, with its 36 sovereigns. No matter where she went, she knew that she could hardly fail to encounter a prince. She traveled about from watering place to watering place; from Wiesbaden to Hamburg; from Hamburg to Baden-Baden. It was rumored that at the latter resort, the Prince of Orange was among her admirers. She also met Puissant Prince Henry of Reuss, who promptly fell in love with her.

At the Court of Reuss she suffered the agonies of boredom. The etiquette was strict and the deference exacted by Prince Henry was as compelling as though he had been the Emperor. In his small territory he wielded an absolute power of pettiness.

Lola soon showed her impatience. She infringed on His Highness's prerogative by chastising his servants. The indulgent Prince could still overlook this, but when Henry one morning beheld her walking straight across his favorite flower beds intentionally to provoke him, he could stand it no longer. It evidently made a difference which of his beds she transgressed. With his own august hand, he wrote and signed an order expelling Lola Montez from the principality, yea, verily, ruling her off the "turf."

Aimlessly, the Venus of her generation journeyed south toward Munich. The Court Theatre at Munich bore a very high reputation throughout Europe and seemed to Lola the proper place to display her charms and

MADAME
LOLA MONTEZ
(COUNTESS OF LANDSFELD)
Will give her Lecture, entitled
JOHN BULL AT HOME
AT
MOZART HALL,
663 BROADWAY,
Thursday Evening, Dec. 15, 1859,

Containing some pleasant gossip, in which many things are said,

MORE IN LAUGHTER THAN IN ANGER.

It is believed that this is one of the most original and sparkling lectures that has been given by the brilliant and facetious Countess of Landsfeld; while her pictures of English life are humorous and amusing, they are, at the same time, free from every taint of ill nature and abuse.

THEMES OF THE LECTURE:

THEME I.

THE COMIC SIDE OF ENGLISH CHARACTER.

To laugh at national follies is not abuse. The folly of abusing America to the English or the English to America. Laughable national portraits. The real origin of the Yankee character. The reason why English writers on America and its institutions have made such ridiculous mistakes. A challenge to Mr. Dickens and Mr. Thackeray on their great spittoon question. Tit-for-tat. A very delicate question of national cleanliness and decency logically settled in favor of America.

ENGLISH AND A

The traits which the Englis
English origin. Characteristi
form of government fashions c
A demonstration that free inst
as the mighty struggle throug
elements of which the English
John Bull. What has made
mirror, in which the English

To be had a

Doors open at Sev

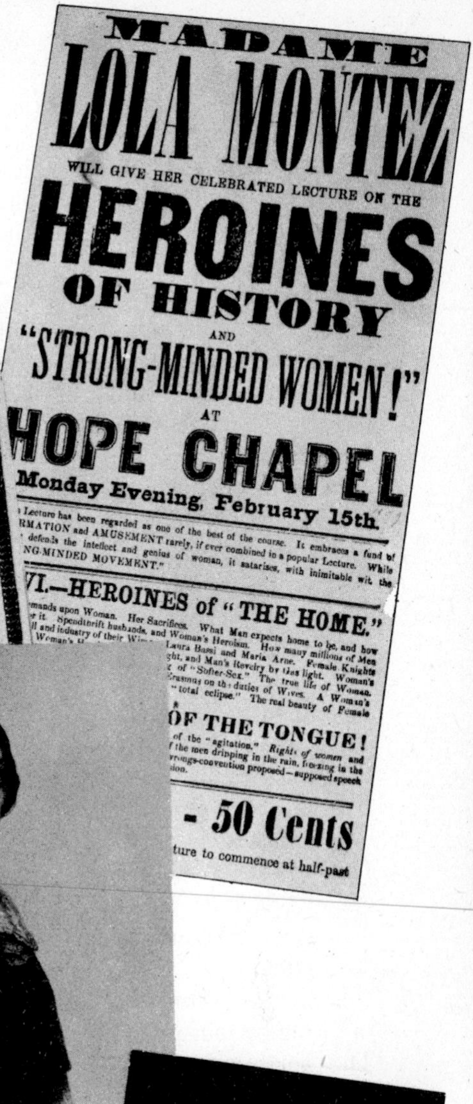

MADAME
LOLA MONTEZ
WILL GIVE HER CELEBRATED LECTURE ON THE
HEROINES OF HISTORY
AND
"STRONG-MINDED WOMEN!"
AT
HOPE CHAPEL
Monday Evening, February 15th.

Lecture has been regarded as one of the best of the course. It embraces a fund of
RMATION and AMUSEMENT rarely, if ever combined in a popular Lecture. While
defends the intellect and genius of woman, it satarises, with inimitable wit, the
NG-MINDED MOVEMENT."

VI.—HEROINES of "THE HOME."

mands upon Woman. Her Sacrifices. What Man expects home to be, and how
r it. Spendthrift husbands, and Woman's Heroism. How many millions of Men
ll and industry of their Wi Laura Bassi and Maria Arne. Female Knights
Woman's ght, and Man's Revelry by this light. Woman's
of "Softer-Sex." The true life of Woman.
Erasmus on the duties of Wives. A Woman's
"total eclipse." The real beauty of Female

OF THE TONGUE!

of the "agitation." Rights of women and
f the men dripping in the rain, freezing in the
wrongs-convention proposed—supposed speech
sion.

- 50 Cents

ture to commence at half-past

LOLA MONTEZ

GYPSY ROSE LEE
Bernhardt of the striptease

accomplishments. She sought an audience with Ludwig the Bavarian prince, then sixty-one years old. He was not disposed to grant it.

Weary of waiting in the anteroom, and expecting a refusal, she coolly followed an aide-de-camp into the royal presence. She stood before the astonished King, dazzlingly beautiful. To a passionate admirer of loveliness like Ludwig, her beauty was an all-sufficient excuse for her audacity. After collecting his faculties and listening to her petition, the King commanded her to appear at the Court Theatre. Two days later the King said to one of his ministers: "I know not how, but I am bewitched."

She was selected to teach the King Spanish and Lola did not refuse the offer. It was not to be expected that the public or the King's clerical advisers would accept a platonic view of Lola's presence at Court. Whatever the cause, antagonism to beautiful Lola soon manifested itself among the King's advisers.

Meanwhile Ludwig introduced her to his ministers as his "best friend." The Jesuits immediately circulated the report that she was his mistress, which may or may not have been true. Few rumors about Lola were ever unfounded in fact.

King Ludwig was delighted with Lola and experienced a rebirth of interest in his kingdom and the ruling of it, during which he freely asked and took advice of the "foreign adventuress" as Baron Pechman, Chief of the Munich Police, was wont to call Lola. When the police chief suggested at a later date that there might possibly be, in the kingdom, other more highly trained advisers, Ludwig went into a rage and exclaimed "Begone!" (It is nice to know, isn't it, that someone actually did use that word once.) "Begone! You will find the country of Landshut purer," which was merely a subtle way of telling the impudent fellow that he was being given "the gate."

Finally on February 11, 1847, a remarkable document was presented to the King by four ministers refusing to grant naturalization to Lola Montez. The signatures made Ludwig laugh, but not the contents:

Von Abel
Von Gimpenberg
Von Siensheim
Von Schrenk

What elegant names they would have been for Van Heusen collars. Indignation got the better of amusement and Ludwig asked von Abel whether it was the only copy in existence. Von Abel rashly said, "Yes," but a few days later, the *Augsburg Zeitung* published the document for all the world to read. In deep anger the King gave von Abel twenty-four hours to reconsider his decision. Von Abel, feeling the public was with him, refused to budge and the King promptly dismissed him and all colleagues from office. The same evening at Lola's reception, Ludwig told Lola what he had done and then gave forth one of his remarkable declamatory utterances: "I will not give Lola up," he declared. "I will not give up that noble, princely being." And then he delivered himself of a bit of reminiscent oratory: "My kingdom for Lola."

Ludwig's action during this incident impressed the rest of the cabinet with the deep sincerity of his regard for Montez, so the naturalization was consented to. Shortly afterwards, she was raised to the peerage with the title of Countess Landesfeld. She has also been called the Countess of Landsberg, a pardonable error since there was a Landsberg but there was never a Landesfeld. Lola was further granted an annuity of twenty thousand florins and with the money which had been left her by Dujarrier she was now wealthy. Among other gifts from Ludwig, she received the freehold of the Royal Court Theatre and actually, under her title, maintained feudal rights over two thousand souls. Those who opposed her were promptly designated as "heels." The cream on the tart was when she was made Canoness of the Order of St. Theresa. In her most extravagant moments, it is doubtful whether Lola ever expected to be associated even remotely with a saint. Metzger, the architect, built her a jewel of a palace in the Bauernstrasse where the great galleries are located. Lola's portrait painted by royal command graced the Gallery of Beauties and Ludwig often stood before it as though worshiping at a shrine.

Lola then began to dabble in politics seriously. She was a republican and had visions of becoming a perpetual president herself. She was also a Protestant, which was not the healthiest thing to be in Munich. The Catholic Corps of students started an innocent-looking parade. The parade swelled into a dangerous mob which had as their objective the doors of Lola's little palace and the *femme fatale* behind them. Lola, with her usual instinct for dramatic entrances, did not fly out the back door as one might have expected, but appeared on the front steps to address the angry people. Some of the students arranged themselves as a bodyguard for her and Ludwig peered out of a window watching the brawl.

In a few days the King's anger made itself felt when he ordered the closing of the university and banished all alien students, their leave-taking to begin within twenty-four hours. Then the opposition rose, led by the boardinghouse proprietresses. A thousand times twenty-five marks a month —"with breakfast"—was in danger of departing. Suddenly, with their modest revenue in jeopardy, all of Munich realized at once that the bewitched King and his wicked favorite had to be taught a lesson. They were. A weak and apologetic Ludwig himself signed Lola's banishment papers. Such is life. One day seated on her throne, and next day thrown on her seat.

After she left, the people of Munich expressed their long-accumulated hatred by wrecking her property. With a flair for the theatrical, Lola returned in disguise to try to see Ludwig again, but she was deported. This time it took. She was not, alas, as effective a creature as Magda Lupescu. In the last analysis she could not hold her man.

Switzerland next fell heir to Lola's charms; then London, where she remarried and was indicted for bigamy. In Paris, she fortunately met an American entrepreneur, Edward Willis, who made her an offer to cross the ocean, a project which filled her with delight. Lola's thirst for adventure never deserted her. A few major setbacks like the one at Munich never discouraged her, they merely whetted her appetite for more successful adventures.

When Lola arrived in New York harbor in 1851, the American reporters were reborn. Lola was the best copy imaginable. The *New York Tribune* told its readers on December 6th:

"She has a face of great beauty, and a pair of black Spanish eyes, which flash fire when she speaks. She has black hair, with curls in ringlets by the sides of her face. Her nose is of pure Grecian cast, while her cheek bones are high and give a Moorish appearance to her countenance. She said 'many bad things had been said about her' by the American press, and yet she is not the woman she has been represented to be. If she were, she believes her admirers would be still more numerous. She expressed herself as fearful she will not be properly considered in New York, but hopes that a discriminating public will judge her after they have seen her and not before."

On the 27th of December, 1851, she appeared at the Broadway Theatre in the title role of *Betley, the Tyrolean,* a musical comedy part written especially for her. It was expected she would be a great attraction and seats were put up at public auction on the previous Saturday, but the piece was withdrawn on January 19, 1852, public curiosity having been satisfied.

She next secured an engagement at the Walnut Street Theatre, Philadelphia. In May she went back to New York, appearing at the Broadway Theatre in a dramatized version of her career in Munich, written by C. P. T. Ware. The piece ran five nights only. Even during these brief runs, and though the box office tariff in New York did not exceed one dollar in those days, Lola amassed a considerable sum of money.

She now hit upon a somewhat original scheme, which quickly enriched her purse. She organized a reception to which anyone paying one dollar was admitted to shake her by the hand and gaze upon the splendor of her beauty. They could also converse with her in English, Spanish, French and German, provided they were so gifted.

From New York, Lola went to New Orleans, which was swarming at that period with persons either going to or coming home from the Mecca of gold seekers: California. Although the first rush was over, thousands of fortune hunters went every month to see whether they could not wring a Republican's ransom from a handful of gravel. Lola became infected with the fever of avarice and the whole adventure appealed to her zest for continuous excitement. She sailed for San Francisco from the Gulf. The trip was long and tiresome, but Lola was never one to allow a voyage to bore her. Patrick Purdy Hull, owner and editor of the *San Francisco Whig*, and a tall, likable, roughneck politician, became her lover, and after their arrival in the Golden Gate city, her husband, their vows being spoken at the Mission Dolores on July 1, 1853. Lola subsequently asserted that she made Hull her spouse because he was the best story teller she had ever known. When at the marriage service he declared that he would cherish her until death, he may not have told his best story, but it certainly was his biggest one, for they parted soon afterwards, although probably more through Lola's wishes than his own. Perhaps it was characteristic of her that, although a stranger in a strange land, she had been able to garner all the leading citizens to be present at her wedding ceremony.

Soon after her arrival, she opened at the American Theatre and drew large audiences that came more out of curiosity than to have their hunger for distinguished acting appeased. She made a tremendous hit with her Spider Dance, which gained its voluptuous appeal from Lola endeavoring to shake countless India-rubber spiders from off her very tight-fitting costume. It was an exhibition of sensuousness that Gypsy Rose Lee would have given her right arm to have originated. California in those days had not only its army of gold seekers, but also a horde of moral busybodies who insisted that she put entirely too much sin into her sinuosity. Her San Francisco engagement concluded, she next toured the rough mining camps. Meanwhile Lola had taken up with a Herr Doktor Adler, but before she had time to "give him the go-by," he accidentally shot himself while hunting. Feeling that she had had enough of the grand passion, she retired to Grass Valley, in the Sierra Nevada Mountains. Accustomed as she had been to the luxuries of a king's palace, Lola settled down to a most primitive life. In 1854, a reporter from the *San Francisco Herald* looked her up. He described her as "living a quiet and apparently cosy life, surrounded by her pet birds, dogs, goats, sheep, hens and turkeys; and her pony, a favorite and a constant companion in all her mountain rambles."

One day, Lola's home was caught in a forest fire and went up in smoke. Accordingly, she sailed from California to Australia in 1855. Tooning of the Victoria Theatre in Sydney engaged her to appear as a dramatic star in an opus enticingly titled *Lola Montez in Bavaria*. The theater was jammed. The next week she appeared in the *Orphan of Russia*, another thriller which she herself had translated from the French. But as in most cases, her audiences merely came to see what she looked like as they would go to the zoo to see a newly imported Himalayan goat, and Lola was not a good enough actress to create a steady following for herself, so the second week in September she went to tap the curiosity of the citizens of Melbourne.

On her way there, she had a dispute with a member of her company, a woman who did not hesitate to issue a writ of attachment against her. The sheriff boarded the steamer to arrest Lola. Lola, in turn, sent word from her cabin that she was willing to be taken ashore, but that she thought it only fair to tell him that she was quite naked and intended to remain so. The sheriff afterwards apologetically explained to a friend that he could hardly be expected to enter her cabin under prevailing conditions. Seeing a look of incredulity on his friend's face, the sheriff inquired what he would have done under the circumstances, to which the latter replied, "The same as you, you—liar."

Melbourne was reminiscent of California, being at the height of its own gold rush. The population of the Port Philip district had grown in five years from 75,000 to 364,000. In Geelong, Australia, Lola fell ill, but when she recovered she went out to the gold fields with some of the toughest and most desperate men in the Antipodes. If she was still looking for excitement, she got it in the town of Ballarat. When Lola arrived, the editor of the local newspaper gave her a write-up which put the worst possible construction upon the episodes of Lola's past life. Several days later, he was rash enough to appear at the United States Hotel where the Irish actress was staying. Lola heard he was downstairs, and armed with a riding whip, she laid it across his back lustily till bystanders rescued the newspaperman. At the theater that night, she received an ovation for the bold way in which she had protected her good name, though it was difficult to see why she wished to do it when she, at the same time, devoted so much energy and passion to giving herself a bad one. But as Lola later explained in an interview, "I never claimed to be famous. Notorious I have always been."

The year 1856 found Lola back in France, vociferously denying newspaper reports that the actor Mancleve had committed suicide on her account by throwing himself from the Pic du Midi. The romantic interval over, Lola made a trek back to America and appeared at the Green Street Theatre, Albany, in 1857. Subsequently, this famous old playhouse was run as a variety theater by Fred Levantine, an equilibrist whose name in later years became F. F. Proctor, as a partner of B. F. Keith.

Whatever else one could say about Lola Montez, she had always approached life most realistically, so it was a surprise to many when she became a deep believer in spiritualism. She gave a series of unsuccessful lectures on this subject at "Hope Chapel," 720 Broadway, in New York

City. The reporters thought they were pretty funny although they were meant to be most serious. In an emotional orgy of sympathy with the masses, Lola showered her earnings on the poor and the physically handicapped until her purse grew so light that she determined to recross the Atlantic to see what she could do about replenishing it.

On November 23, 1858, the American Steamship *Pacific* landed at Galway, and Lola Montez, who had left Ireland twenty years before as the bride of Thomas James, returned home. She appeared in Dublin, billed more as a public curiosity than as an actress. Women flocked to see what it was that had attracted so many prominent men, and her Irish tour promised to be profitable.

When the *Freeman* referred in an article to her relations with Dujarrier and the King of Bavaria, she sat down at her desk and immediately wrote a letter to the newspapers defending her character. She said that her relationship with both men had been highly proper. To Dujarrier she had been engaged, to Ludwig she was merely a friend and adviser. She blamed the rumors on Austrian intrigue at the Munich Court and threw in a few voluntary criticisms of the influence of the Jesuits. In Ireland this was not the most politic thing to do, so at the New Year she crossed to Manchester and showed herself off to the public at so much a view in Sheffield, Worcester, Bristol and Bath. This lecture tour was a great success even though she was forced to contend with a powerful counter attraction in the person of Phineas T. Barnum himself. While her houses were crowded, the public was disappointed. Lola was neither as young nor as beautiful as she had been and, of course, could not demonstrate her personal allure on a lecture platform. If she had come out and laid about her with a whip and then done a strip tease, her popularity would never have waned. Later, burlesque would have claimed her.

At last she arrived in London to lecture in St. James Hall. The *Era* gives a good description of how she appeared to her audiences in 1859:

"Following closely upon the heels of Mr. Barnum, Madame Lola Montez, parenthetically putting forth her more aristocratic title of Countess Landesfeld, commenced on Thursday evening, April 7, 1859, the first of a series of lectures. If any felt that they were about to behold a formidable looking woman of Amazonian audacity, and palpably strong-wristed as well as strong-minded, their disappointment must have been grievous.

"Lola Montez, who made a graceful and impressive obeisance to those who gave her so cordial a reception, appeared simply as a good-looking young lady, in the bloom of womanhood, clad in a plain black dress.

"She had an easy, unrestrained manner of talking, earnestly and distinctly. There was the slightest touch of a foreign accent, that might belong to any language from Irish to Bavarian. The subject discussed by the fair lecturer was the distinction between the English and the American character. There was no attempt on her part to weave into the subject threads of personal interest; no mention of any incident that had happened to her. A more inoffensive entertainment could hardly be imagined. Whatever the disquisitions of the Countess may be, there is no doubt that many will go to hear them, for the sake of the peculiar celebrity of the lecturer."

During this entire tour a fundamental change took place in Lola's character. The love which she had once lavished on men of flesh and blood she now lavished on the worship of an unseen God. Unable to affix a mortal crown to her head while on earth, she shifted her ambition and worked towards winning a heavenly crown in the hereafter. The spiritual diary which she kept at this time is revealing. "Lord have mercy on the weary wanderer, Oh give me a meek and lowly heart." Lola was really too young for remorse. She was only forty-one. In a few months the fortune she had earned during her tours had been entirely dissipated, and Lola was so full of religion and self-reproach that she could no longer organize her remarkable versatility to continue making a livelihood.

In 1860, Lola was back in New York, actually threatened with poverty, when she met an old school friend of hers who was now married to a Mr. Buchanan, florist. The couple were not only religious but generous and they provided for Lola without question. All she did for them was to change from Methodism to become a member of the less emotional Episcopalian Church. She passed much of her time in deep retirement reading and studying the Bible, and doing rescue work. She realized that consumption had begun, and very little was left of her opulent beauty. Only her great and brilliant eyes remained the same. She went to Whiter Shores in 1861 after a fitful lifespan of forty-three years. Her writings combine *The Arts of Beauty* and *Lectures*, which were published in 1858 and contain an autobiography. She was buried in Greenwood Cemetery and a tablet erected to her memory.

II

Adah Isaacs Menken

The naked lady in pink tights

ADAH ISAACS MENKEN—not a beautiful name, certainly, but one which became a synonym for everything that was glamorous and exciting in nineteenth century theatrical America. I like to think that this fabulous woman and I some time in our very different lives sat beneath the same roof somewhere in New York City, she at the end of her career and I a very young man indeed. It might have been in Pfaff's Restaurant, or the National Theatre, or the "Naish," as we called it on the Bowery when my friend, Mike Heuman, later of Terrace Garden, managed it, or at the famous "Old Bowery" Theatre where Menken also played and where I spent the happiest days of my hoodlum boyhood. Every two bits that I could collect in those days was spent at the Old Bowery, but there were not enough of them, alas, to keep me in the continuous state of ecstasy which I craved.

My own dad told me about Menken and her prize-fighter lover and husband, Heenan, the "Benicia Boy" who fought Sayres, the English champion, to a draw in the days when boxing gloves were unknown and men hit out with their bare fists and stood up until they fell down with no time limits to the bouts. I have also read so much about him since that I sometimes feel as though we had met, especially when he battled Morrisey in Troy, my home town. Dad, who settled there in 1850, and later cast his first ballot for Abe Lincoln, was a great lover of sports, and saw Heenan fight, and told me of the beautiful Menken who had eloped with Booth. Someone told Dad this story. There is absolutely no one to vouch for it.

When Adah played opposite Edwin Booth, they were a magnetic double attraction. The theater was always packed, and the excitement ran high. Both women and men were satisfied with what the editors raved about as "their God-given genius." During one engagement, Booth and Adah agreed, at its termination, to leave the city together, and make it appear an elopement. They carried through the publicity stunt and the headlines obligingly read: "Elopement: the Pretty Jewess and the Son of Genius." When the bubble burst, the public chuckled and said that it was Booth's love of a good joke. Personally, if I, in the actor's place, found myself beginning even a staged elopement with so fascinating a woman, I would probably have completed it.

Adah's own story must speak for her. What her effect on the public was may be judged by the titles bestowed on her by her lovers, friends, poets, authors, editors, husbands and men of genius: "The Menken," "Cleopatra in a Crinoline," "La Belle Menken," "The Royal Bengal Tiger," "The Fiery Centauress," and the most famous of all, "The Naked Lady." The last one enabled "The Menken" to prove that even if unadorned, she was by no means unadored. Fulsome adjectives gushed also from enthusiastic pens. She was beautiful, glamorous and ambitious, were a few of the many.

What did this woman do that her name was constantly on the lips of men and women alike, and continuously appeared in print? She was a true poetess. In her famous book of poems, *Infelicia*, several depicted her own life struggles and disappointments in the Supreme Passion. She was an actress even if no Rachel. *Mazeppa* was her star role, she was its first and best exponent and Menken and Mazeppa became almost synonymous. In London, Cora Pearl attempted the part, and in America Fanny Louise Buckingham and Fannie Herring, the Bowery's sensational favorites followed in Adah's footsteps, but trailed far behind.

Never having seen the Menken in this role, I did see the others at Harry Miner's Theatre where Ike Rose passed me in so that I could watch breathlessly while the buxom beauty dashed up the high runway half nude, lashed to the back of a "white fiery steed of Tartary," conscripted from some near-by livery stable. Of Buckingham and Herring, it was the former who was the favorite. One night at the Chestnut Street Theatre in Quaker Philadelphia, a deputy sheriff sat waiting in a box for the end of the performance which he had no desire to miss before arresting her for outraging public decency, as a Quaker City Comstock put it. Miss Buckingham made a rapid decision, remained on the horse's back and drove the nag through the lobby of the theater and out onto the street to freedom before the police officer knew what had happened.

Mazeppa alone could not have made Menken. She was a great beauty, her head with its short wavy curls reminiscent of Lord Byron's. To describe her brilliant eyes, her alluring smile, her seductive figure after so many years would but palely counterfeit in words, the warm, exquisite creature who was Adah. Her capriciousness was part of her charm, her waywardness delighted all those who led prosaic lives. Someone said of her, that she married after each matinee. Compared, however, with certain moving-picture stars and society matrons of today, La Menken was a novice, a mere amateur.

And now, I give you who have the misfortune of never having been able to see this captivating woman, a picture of her life, and to Adah, herself, a toast in the nineteenth century style: sparkling champagne from her own satin slipper.

Adah was born in New Orleans. Like Minerva sprung from the head of Jove, or more like Venus ascending from the sea, this beautiful woman's parents were long a mystery. Adah took great pride and ingenuity in beclouding the facts of her birth and for many years it was anyone's guess how the actress came into the world. From time to time, with alarming speed, she changed fathers. James McCord, Richard Irving Spencer, Ricardo La Fuertes and James Campbell all vied for the honor. Her mother also had a chameleon quality. She alternated between a Creole and a Jewess of Franco-Spanish descent. While there was a distinct pleasure in not quite knowing all about the parentage of a woman about whose own person everyone knew, the Age of Realism is upon us and John S. Kendall made a scholarly study in 1938 to determine the identity of her parents. Mr. Kendall was motivated by curiosity. Why, he asked himself, should such a cloud, and a rosy cloud at that, obscure Adah's identity? Was it done to conceal facts of which the actress had no reason to be proud, facts which might act as a deterrent to one pursuing a theatrical career? Or was it merely Adah's immense capacity for fabrication at work? Her fibs were Munchausen in character. Her education was a haphazard one of self-help, and yet La Menken stated several times without blushing that she had translated the *Iliad* from Greek into French at the age of twelve.

Another whopper which she repeated frequently was that Indians had captured her in Texas, that she spent weeks in captivity and escaped under conditions so romantic and adventurous that the most lurid dime novel could not equal them. Adah recalled every detail of this adventure except the time when it happened. She could never quite make up her mind whether she dealt with the aborigines just before or just after her first marriage.

When Mr. Kendall looked up birth records in New Orleans, he discovered in church records that her father was Auguste Theodore, a "free man of color," and her mother was a Creole. This explains very easily why Adah avoided telling the truth about her origin and why she should have invented fantastic tales about her ancestry. It would also explain why she never returned to New Orleans after her marriage, since in Louisiana there was a law prohibiting a person of Negro blood from uniting in marriage with a white person.

ADAH ISAACS MENKEN

ADAH ISAACS MENKEN
Taken in the spring of 1867 at the height of her fame

Adah's mixed racial heritage might also have been the cause of her dark beauty which made her known as a Jewess, a faith she embraced only after marrying Mr. Menken. Her temperament, volatility and genius all could have been the result of such mixed racial strains.

There is only one document about her whole life that is positively dependable: her marriage certificate. Adah was legally married, but the facts and figures on the document might well have been the figments of her elastic imagination. Ada Bertha Theodore she called herself and gave the date of her birth as June 15, 1835.

Adah as a child learned to dance with her sister Josephine, and the two young girls became a part of the ballet at the French Opera House in New Orleans. Even at that age, Adah was full of piquancy and coquetry with the result that she became a great favorite. It was here that she adopted her first pseudonym, "Bertha Theodore." Languages in New Orleans were an essential. With rapidity, Adah mastered French and Spanish, speaking them both with fluid ease which in later years only served to confuse those amateur historians who attempted to fix her evanescent nationality.

From New Orleans to Havana was a natural step in the right theatrical direction. Adah danced through a very successful engagement at the Tacon Teatro in that second Paris, and emerged with one of her gratuitous titles, "Queen of the Plaza." In 1853 she found herself in Texas doing amateur theatricals, and three years later she married her first husband, Alexander Isaac Menken. It was a good marriage from any standpoint. Menken was a handsome musician, the son of a Cincinnati merchant. His parents' objections melted away when they met the lovely lady of his choice, and they were delighted to discover that she added to her natural endowments certain desirable cultivations such as knowledge of language, and a talent for painting and versification. They became great friends and it was to their credit that in later years when Adah was open to severe criticism for her moral laxity, no word of censure came from her parents-in-law.

Adah, the name by which we know "La Belle Menken," was taken by her at the same time as she embraced the Jewish faith when she married Mr. Menken. Before that, she was Adelaide. Celia Logan was present when young Menken presented his bride to his mother: "Never shall I forget the hush which fell, even upon the children, as the pair paused for a moment at the door, as if to ask permission to enter. Adah Menken must at that time have been one of the most peerless beauties that ever dazzled human eyes, while Isaac himself was a remarkably handsome man."

This seemingly auspicious and even decorative beginning to a marriage did not fare very well. Like most men of his racial origin, Menken wanted family life and children. Adah could not, on the other hand, give up her love of the footlights and attempted to arouse the same excitement in him by making him her manager. Managers, however, do not come in for the applause and adulation, so to Mr. Menken the project was profitless and a dreary grind. Then, too, other difficulties arose. Adah's beauty acted as a magnet to men who showered her with unsolicited attention. This irked Alexander, but their final flare-up, and the reason for their separation, was the argument that raged over the actress's smoking. In the fifties, women did not smoke. To Mr. Menken the habit seemed vulgar; to Mrs. Menken, it was a good reason to get angry, and besides she liked cigarettes. So a combination of jealousy and criticism parted the couple who began life together in such dewy-eyed rapture, and Mr. Menken went his way no longer contributing to the support of his wife.

Adah, in telling of her dramatic debut, described her opening in *Fazio* in the role of Bianca, once played by the magnificent tragedienne, Ristori, and also by Matilda Heron, whose daughter Bijou married Henry Miller, the father of Gilbert. This was merely one of her imaginative fancies, calculated to steal her rival's thunder. Charlotte Crompton had appeared as Bianca after Adah had left the company, and it was her success which Adah so casually adapted for herself. New Orleans had seen La Menken on May 30, 1858, as Lady Freelove in *A Wife's First Lesson,* then in *A Day in Paris,* a small-sized tour de force in which the busy lady took six separate parts. She added "songs and dances" to her acting in *The Maid of Munster* and *The Unprotected Female.* Why she bothered borrowing Charlotte's laurels, is difficult to see, because through J. S. Charles' management, the company did very nicely indeed until the terrible riots broke out in New Orleans in connection with the municipal election. On June 5th, Charles was forced to close the theater, and when three days later, he opened again, Adah was no longer with him, but Charlotte was. Apparently Adah had been frightened by the street fighting and preferred not to continue her engagement.

Odell, mentioning Menken's early theatrical career, wrote: "No one, I suppose, could foresee her later international fame, her dragging in her train, hearts of poets as well as those of gilded youths." The *Tribune* suggested that what she wanted was "taming down" and that her talent "is like the gold in quartz veins—all in the rough; and so must undergo the refining process of intelligent and critical audiences." Everyone, however, agreed that she had a "dashing style" and was full of promise. One confused newspaper critic, in reviewing her performance in *Mazeppa,* stated he would have to see her in other parts before he could determine which was her "line"; although, based on what he had already witnessed, he felt certain that it wouldn't be "the clothes line."

On the 3rd of April, 1859, Adah entered her second matrimonial venture, this time with John C. Heenan, the prizefighter. She had met him in

ASTLEY'S

LESSEE -Nov.-7.-1864 MR. E. T. SMITH.

☞ UNPRECEDENTED SUCCESS OF MISS ADAH ISAACS

MENKEN

AS MAZEPPA!

Which will be Performed every Evening until further notice.

ROADWAY THEATRE

Corner of Broadway and Broome St.

EORGE WOOD.........................MANAGER
. T. Collins.........................*Acting Manager*

Third Week of the Engagement of

MISS ADAH ISAACS

MENKEN

LAST NIGHTS

Of MISS MENKEN in her World-Renowned Speciality of MAZEPPA, which, although attracting Crowded Houses, must give place to the pre-arranged determination of the Manager to present this

Celebrated Artiste

In another character, in which she has attained a Far-famed Popularity.

EVERY EVENING,

Commencing at Eight o'Clock, and

SATURDAY, MATINEE,

Commencing at half-past 1 o'Clock, the Grand Equestrian Spectacle, in three Acts, entitled

MAZEPPA

OR THE

Wild Horse of Tartary.

MAZEPPA, under the assumed name of CASSIMIR ....MISS ADAH ISAACS MENKEN

WILD HORSE OF TARTARY, by the Champion Steed ....BLACK BESS

POLES.

The Castellan of Laurinski..................Mr. H. Jordan
Premislaus, Count of Palestine..................Mr. F. J. Evans
Rudzloff, Chamberlain..................Mr. T. L. Donnelly
Drolinsko.........Mr. E. H. Eberle | Sentinel..................Mr. Atkins
Officer.........Mr. J. D. Bilby | Meja..................Mr. Harris
Olinsko, the Castellan's daughter..................Miss J. Tyson
Agatha, Olinska's nurse..................Mrs. G. F. Tyrell
Zemilla..................Mrs. J. G. Saville
Pages, Knights, Guards, Heralds, Banner Bearers, Ladies in-Waiting, Domestics, &c..................Company

TARTARS.

Abder Khan, King of Tartary..................Mr. H. Rainer
Thamar, a conspiring chieftain..................Mr. J. G. Saville
Zemba.........Mr. W. H. Carpenter | Second Elder..........Mr. G. George
First Elder.........Mr. Briggs | Conspirator..........Mr. Hudson
Koskar.........} Shepherds {.........Mr. J. W Goodman
Kadas.........} Shepherds {.........Mr. W. H. Beekman
Oneiza..................Miss Saidee Cole
First Shepherdess..................Miss C. Troy
Second Shepherdess..................Miss Hampton
Chieftains, Warriors, Priests, Shepherds, Shepherdesses, &c,..Company

---

Broadway Theatre

Corner of BROADWAY and BROOME STREET.

STAGE MANAGER..................G. H. GILBERT
Machinist.........Levi Gurnsey | Leader of Orchestra..H. Eckhart
Prompter.........J. D. Bilby | Properties.......W. G. Peterson

"Bring forth the horse." The horse was brought;
In truth he was a noble steed,
A tartar of the Ukraine breed,
Who looked as though the speed of thought
Were in his limbs; but he was wild,
Wild as the wild deer, and untaught,
With spur and bridle undefiled;
'Twas but a day he had been caught,
And snorting with erected mane,
And struggling fiercely but in vain;
In the full roam of wrath and dread.
To me the desert born was led;
They bound me on—that menial throng—
Upon his back with many a thong;
They loosed him with a sudden lash;
Away! away! and on we dash;
Torrents less rabid and less rash.

(Byron's Mazeppa.)

Synopsis of Scenery and Incidents.

Act 1.—Scene 1st. Castle Laurinski by Moonlight. Appearance of Cassimir and Olinska. The Lover's Vows. Grand Procession! Arrival of Count Premislaus to claim Olinska's hand. Despair and jealousy of Cassimir. Attempt on the life of Premislaus. Dreadful doom of Cassimir. The Wild Horse.

Act 2.—Tartar Landscape. The Wild Horse appears at full speed. Terror of the Shepherds. Chorus and Tartar Dance. Arrival of Thamar, the conspiring Chief. His determination to possess the Tartarian Crown. The Shepherd Monarch. Rescue of Cassimir from the back of the exhausted steed. He is recognized as the long lost Mazeppa. Tartar tent. Attempt of Thamar on the life of Abder Khan. Sudden interposition of Mazeppa. Grand Sword Combat. Defeat of Thamar. Recognition of Mazeppa as King of Tartary.

Act 3.—Despair of Olinska. Her resolve to join her lover in the tomb. Arrival of Mazeppa in disguise. His proof of Olinska's affection. Garden of Laurinski. Preparations for the Nuptials. Interruption. Cassimir, Mazeppa, one, now King of Tartary. Defeat of the Poles, and Tableau. Union of the Lovers.

NEW SCENERY..................By R. GRAIN

Notwithstanding the Enormous Expenses of this Engagement, the

PRICES of ADMISSION

Will remain at their

PRESENT LOW STANDARD RATES!

ADMISSION, Family Circle..................50 CENTS
Reserved Seats, Dress Circle and Parquette..................75 Cents
Orchestra Chairs..................$1.00
Private Boxes..................$10.00

☞ Box office open from 8 to 6 o'Clock daily, when places may be secured for either Evening or Matinee of the Engagement, and patrons abroad may procure tickets with reserved seats, by forwarding the specified date and amount in current funds, addressed to G. T. Collins, Broadway Theatre.

NO EXTRA CHARGE FOR BOOKING.

EVENING—Doors open at 7¼. Begins at 8 o'Clock.
MATINEE—Doors open at 12½. Begins at 1½ o'Clock

POSITIVELY NO FREE LIST

DURING MISS MENKEN'S ENGAGEMENT

the office of the *New York Clipper*, probably introduced by Ed James, connected with its sporting department, and her staunch admirer. At any event, Adah fell in love with Heenan's obvious masculinity. No one could have suited her less. Broke himself, he displayed a rare talent for spending her money as rapidly as she earned it, and for entertainment he beat up his darling Adah after dinner. While he was still in the courting mood, he had taught Menken some of the technique of defense, and during these family fisticuffs, Mrs. Heenan often held her own. Adah was too beautiful and too bright a woman to put up with such a bellicose mate, so they separated after a few months and she won her divorce in 1862. Heenan, who failed as a husband, did not do badly in the ring. Sayres, International Champion, met him in England, was knocked down twenty times in over two hours of fighting (thirty-seven rounds), but to save the day and their heavy wagers, the Britishers leapt into the ring when it looked as though the favorite would be knocked out in a matter of moments, and called the fight a "draw."

Before leaving Adah forever, Heenan had given her the only thing of which he was capable: a pregnancy. To add to her troubles, the papers discovered and widely heralded the fact that Adah in her guileless fashion had neglected to divorce Menken before she took on Heenan. Immediately the public took sides. The prudes blamed it all on Adah's wickedness, the enchanted admirers claimed that such a young, unsophisticated creature could not be held responsible, that obviously her husband should have attended to such important legal details and that she had every right to assume that he had done so. As soon as the scandal broke, Mr. Menken did what was expected of him, and immediately freed Adah, but not, of course, in time to legalize her unborn child. Fortunately for all concerned, the baby did not survive its birth.

Frank Queen, editor of the *New York Clipper*, then proved himself a devoted friend and champion by publishing an article which did much to reinstate her in the good opinion of theater audiences:

"The short time Adah Menken has been before the public, no actress has been more talked about, vilified and misrepresented.

"Systematic efforts seem to have been made by certain persons to injure her in the estimation of the public, and thus deprive her of the means of earning an honest living in the profession she has adopted.

"She came to the city almost friendless, with nothing to rely upon but her own energetic spirit.

"The association of her name with that of John C. Heenan has made her the target for almost every newspaper scribbler in the country, who has severally married her to Tom Thumb, James Buchanan and the King of the Cannibal Islands. She has at times been compelled to answer these calumnies, but her letters have been altered to suit the purpose of the

JOHN C. HEENAN, American Champion
Menken's second husband

ADAH ISAACS MENKEN WITH HER BABY

The child of James Paul Barkley, her fourth and last husband. George Sand was godmother.

TOM SAYERS

Champion of England and his Trophies

editors, the real intent and meaning of the writer being perverted, and herself wilfully misrepresented in every possible way. We trust that the scribblers have got to the end of their tether and that they will hereafter assist (as they have hitherto endeavored to retard) in her efforts to support herself in a legitimate calling."

That Frank Queen was not only a staunch friend, but an influential one, was proved by the effect of his article, excerpts of which were widely republished. It was his natural influence as editor of such a popular, leading sheet as the *Clipper* that secured for her the engagement at the old Bowery, and it was his suggestion that she bill herself as Mrs. John C. Heenan to commercialize her husband's coming international fight.

Life was not easy for Adah. Disillusioned by her love affairs, humiliated by the public charge of bigamy, heartbroken at the loss of her baby, impoverished between engagements, there was nothing "radiant" about Menken at this period of her life. Heenan, his pockets bulging with gold earned by giving boxing exhibitions all over England, returned to America and repudiated Adah completely. He even claimed that he had never married her.

Adah never lacked pluck. She kept on trying. At one time she gave readings from Shakespeare at Hope Chapel where Lola Montez had lectured before her, and at Clinton Hall on Eighth Street, she lectured on the "Age of Irrepressibles." During these difficult days, she lived in a furnished room on Third Avenue near 14th Street, hoping against hope that something "big" would turn up. She even played "Bones" in a minstrel show to make ends meet, and appeared on the stage giving truly great impersonations of Edwin Booth and the tragedienne, Charlotte Cushman. She even appeared in variety with Blondin, the hero of Niagara Falls, who crossed the whirlpool on a tightrope. But Blondin was too smart to allow Adah on the rope with him, because he realized that he would never be able to "walk the strait and narrow" once he came under her influence.

When Montez died, Adah fancied there was a likeness between them, and she unsuccessfully attempted to act in a play based on the beautiful courtezan's life. She tried *Lady Teazle* and failed also.

Finally, her old adviser and director, James Murdock, suggested that Adah forget her aspirations to become a second Rachel or Ristori, and try *Mazeppa*, so perfectly suited to her boyish face and admirable figure. Up to that time, a male equestrian was traditionally required to ride the fiery untamed steed. Sometimes even a stage dummy was attached to the horse, to carry out the illusion, but never had a woman of flesh and blood, and a beautiful one at that, appeared strapped to the stallion.

Murdock agreed that a female Mazeppa of divine form was sure to capture the imagination of the public and create a sensation. He dwelt on the beauty of her head and bosom, he thought in terms of her exquisite legs liberally shown and cleverly advertised.

Convinced that Murdock had hit upon something intriguing, Adah approached the well-known manager of stage attractions, Captain John P. Smith, with the idea.

Menken's engagement in *Mazeppa* by Captain Smith proved a bonanza and was the turning point in her life. All her future reputation, all her later literary contacts sprang directly or indirectly from her association with this greatly criticized drama, that enjoyed a vogue all through the sixties, seventies and eighties and was a Bowery favorite even as late as the nineties. As to Menken's first appearance at rehearsals, Captain Smith said:

"I found her nervous and anxious, full of trepidation, as she dressed or rather undressed for the part. I assured her there was no danger and that she had only to hold on like grim death, and the mare 'Belle Beauty' would do the rest."

The Captain was, however, too sanguine in his expectations. The mare, who had been trained to a specific routine, was upset by changes made by Adah. Nervous and fidgety, as the mare ran up the inclined runway, her foot slipped and she plunged off, falling with a terrible crash to the stage below with Menken strapped to her back. Smith was terrified. He was certain that his star had been killed. "We lifted Menken, pale as a ghost, nearly lifeless, the blood streaming from her beautiful shoulder. Then with the help of the tackle, we raised 'Belle Beauty.' "

After both woman and mare had recovered from their fall, rehearsals were resumed and the mare successfully carried the beauty on her back up the steep runway, built like a spiral so that everyone in the audience would have a long view of so much alluring charm.

The curtain for the first performance of *Mazeppa* was finally raised at Smith's Green Street Theatre, Albany, on June 7, 1861, where a few years before, Lola Montez had also appeared.

Lincoln was about to march troops against Virginia, a seceding state. The approach of war was felt by everyone. People were on edge, under high tension, and relaxation at the theater was the only outlet for their pent-up feelings, especially when such a sensation as *Mazeppa* was promised.

The performance was every bit as sensational as Murdock had prophesied. The smart set and the prudes alike actually believed they were looking at a woman in the nude. The flesh-colored tights worn by Adah were completely unknown in 1861, and the audiences thought they were gazing on bare skin. Their imaginations had been inflamed by the publicity and soon the plaudits of the public and the mouth-to-mouth advertising of the daring performances crowded the theater.

Off stage Menken's behavior at this time was a model of virtue. Success made her contented and happy and she overflowed with a desire to do kindnesses for others, so that she was praised on all sides for her liberal charities.

Menken's fame had preceded her to California, and thus, due arrangements having been made with Manager Tom Maguire, she made her appearance at Maguire's Opera House, San Francisco, on August 24, 1863, and was received with wild acclaim. San Francisco had quite a Bohemian colony at this time, and recognizing in her a kindred spirit, she was made one of them. There she met the pick and flower of the Coast's literati, including Bret Harte, Ina Coolbrith, Adah Clare and Charles Stoddard. This was no doubt the reason for prolonging her stay. She also found time to contribute to the *Golden Era*, a famous San Francisco literary weekly of early days, many of the poems which subsequently appeared in her volume *Infelicia*.

Perhaps, however, the true state of Adah's feelings at this time can be best determined by a letter she wrote to Ed James about her life and associates in California:

> Dear Ed:
>
> . . . If you have a sister, never permit her to marry a "gentleman." I am in tears. I have not been in bed all night. . . . All the sports like me. During my last week I gave a complimentary benefit to St. Francis Hook and Ladder Co. They presented me with a beautiful fire belt and serenaded me with the finest band in the State and finished up with "Three Cheers for Adah."

California newspaper scribes were on the whole kind to "The Menken," but a plethoric scrapbook does not always indicate a bulging pocketbook. And thus, on her return to New York, she was hard put for even life's necessities. She lived in a cheap room and was even compelled to accept an engagement at the Canterbury Melodeon, 663 Broadway, where Dave Braham, later father-in-law of Ned Harrigan of Harrigan and Hart, was leader of the orchestra. Dave wrote the melodies to four hundred of Harrigan and Hart's famous songs.

But America was beginning to look rather small to Adah, remembering what an international flavor had been bestowed on Lola Montez because of her travels.

In 1863 Astley's Amphitheatre in London offered to present the Adorable Menken in *Mazeppa*. It was a great opportunity for "The Naked Lady." The English manager offered her half the receipts, the cost of grooms and an equestrian director, the stage box, ample undressing rooms and a complete company.

While rehearsing in London, Adah was subjected to some harsh criticisms; so, like Lola before her, she sat down to write the editor who maligned her:

"In your *Leader* last week in *The Morale of American Art,* you associate my name with what an American Journal terms 'The Naked Drama' and express the hope that Mr. E. T. Smith will not degrade Astley's by an exhibit of indecency. As I am about to appear at that establishment, such an observation is calculated to do me serious injury, and I am sure you will allow me a few words of explanation, as you confess you know nothing of the actress or her piece. To begin with the play is *Mazeppa* and I impersonate the hero, but my costume, or rather want of costume, as might be inferred, is not in the least indelicate and in no way more open to invidious comment than the dress worn by Cerito Rosati, or even the grotesque garbs employed by ladies of the London stage.

"I have long been a student of sculpture and my attitudes selected from the works of Canova, present a classicality which has been invariably recognized by the foremost of American critics.

"I may add that my performance of *Mazeppa* had a most prosperous career in America and as is usual in such cases, my success created a host of imitators and some of these ladies, I hear, have adopted a style of drapery inconsistent with delicacy and good taste.

"*Mazeppa,* like any other specialty, is easily vulgarized. Let *La Sylphide* be scantily dressed, or ungracefully acted, by an indifferent artist and what will be more offensive.

"The critics found no fault with Mrs. Charles Kean's embodiment of Don, and the young ladies who exhibit their well-formed limbs in the Haymarket or the Strand burlesques (notable in such parts as Cupid or Ixion) are not accused of indelicacy.

"At any rate, do me the favor as a stranger to suspend your opinion of my representation, and after you witness it, I am quite willing to abide your criticism.

"Yours very truly,
"Adah Isaacs Menken"

Whether the editor changed his mind after seeing the performance, we do not know, but we know what Mark Lemon thought because he published his reactions in *Punch:*

> Here's half the town,—if bills be true,
> To Astley's nightly thronging,
> To see "The Menken" throw aside
> All to her sex belonging.
> Stripping off woman's modesty,
> With woman's outward trappings,
> A bare-backed jade on bare-backed steed,
> In Cartlich's old strapping.

Cartlich played Mazeppa in London in 1831.

The *London Review* remarked that Adah looked like "Lady Godiva in a shift" and added that "of course, respectable people go to see the spectacle and not her figure." Charles Dickens, in a letter, described how he attempted to get in to see "this heroine" one night and was obliged to turn away from the box office because the house was completely sold out, even for him. Adah did very well indeed financially. In London at this time she was earning $1,500 a week, while later, in America, she earned $500 for a single performance. Only opera stars had been able to command such salaries. Edmund Kean never earned nearly so much, nor did all the famous English tragedians including MacCready, who would have been satisfied to earn in a week what The Menken earned in a night.

Naturally, Adah's performance was meat for the gossipmongers. Her reputation was torn into shreds so small that they would not even serve as a costume for Mazeppa. Adah tried to combat this by being the soul of generosity. Everything she earned above her living expenses went to destitute families and actors and actresses down on their luck. Writing about Adah after her death, the *Boston Courier* said: "No one cared less for money, and had her income been a thousand dollars a minute, she would have been poor at the end of an hour."

Heenan, filled with hope at Adah's prosperity, came courting her again, but she, consumed with a desire for revenge, kept him guessing and finally made it clear to him that she was not at all interested. When, in a burst of enthusiasm, she married Robert H. Newell, a writer of children's books under the pseudonym of "Orpheus Kerr" no one could imagine what the fiery woman saw in the kindly gentleman, and after the briefest time, she also could not see what had attracted her, and Husband III was divorced in 1865.

The next year, Adah began thinking of New York, but whether to augment her career or to follow Mr. Barkley, destined to be her fourth mate, we have no means of knowing. Manager Wood of the Broadway Theatre was intensely interested by some sugar-coated articles which appeared in the press through the good offices of some of her close friends, and Adah bluffed him into giving her a contract at her own lavish terms. The opening was an enormous success. At thirty-one, Adah was still a dashing beauty. Horace Greeley was kind enough to criticize her nudity in the *New York Tribune* which helped to swell the box-office receipts. Mr. Wood in a blurb, came to her rescue:

"Miss Adah dresses the part very prettily and displays a leg, or rather two legs, in silk fleshings of such delicate proportions that they would have made a Saint Anthony lift his eyes from the prayer book. To see Miss Adah in the matured beauty of her womanhood, costumed as she is costumed, is worth the price of admission alone."

When Menken reached California, she was worshiped by the Poet of the West, Joaquin Miller. Artemus Ward also courted and proposed to her. All men seemed fond of her, either attracted by her physical charms or intrigued by her gift for making verses. The Rev. Dr. Wise of Cincinnati, father of Dr. Stephen Wise, taught her German after she was already proficient in Latin, French, Spanish and Hebrew. Adah told so many fairy stories about her talents that the author keeps thinking as he reports these intellectual wonders, "How do you know,—vas you dere, Charlie?"

The poet, Charles Warren Stoddard, was most eloquent in her praise. He wrote that every curve of her limbs was like a line in a Persian love story, and that she was a vision of celestial harmony made manifest in the flesh. Under her picture, he inscribed:

> Wild was her look, wild was her air,
> Back from her shoulders streamed her hair,
> Her looks that wont her brow to shade,
> Started erectly from her head.
> Her figure seems to rise more high.
> From her pale lips, a frantic cry
> Rang sharply through the moon's pale light,
> And life to her was sudden night.

But La Belle Menken had never been to Paris, so to her it was as if she had never been truly admired, or her talent tested. Gautier and Zola were both present when she made her debut at the Gaïté on December 31, 1866, and both were enchanted along with the rest of the populace. She received the greatest ovation ever accorded an American, and was obliged to take nine curtain calls at the end of the performance. Théophile Gautier, who had been a harsh critic of Adah's predecessor, Lola Montez, wrote warmly: "A beautiful and elegant woman, svelte and admirably proportioned, who mimes with rare intelligence."

The French equivalent for "Standing Room Only" was displayed night after night. A French Winchell of that period whispered: "Her astonishing beauty and charm has turned all masculine heads, and her throng of lovers, among whom can be counted the most illustrious Bohemians of Paris, excite the jealousy and envy of her own sex."

The glamour that was Menken's attracted Hippolyte de Villemessant, the great Paris journalist who owned *Le Figaro*, and many other magazines. He gave orders to gather every scrap of Menken news and created literary and art receptions for her. Through these she received unparalleled publicity, and met every notable in Paris. At one performance alone Napoleon III, the King of Greece, the Duke of Edinburgh and the Prince Imperial were all in attendance. Her close advisers in Paris were Charles Dickens, Charles Reade and the tragedian, Charles Fechter, who coached her in dramatics. In all of Paris only one other performer could claim a like popularity, and that was Hortense Schneider of the Opéra Bouffe.

ADAH ISAACS MENKEN ON DUMAS' KNEE

The suppressed photograph that scandalized Paris

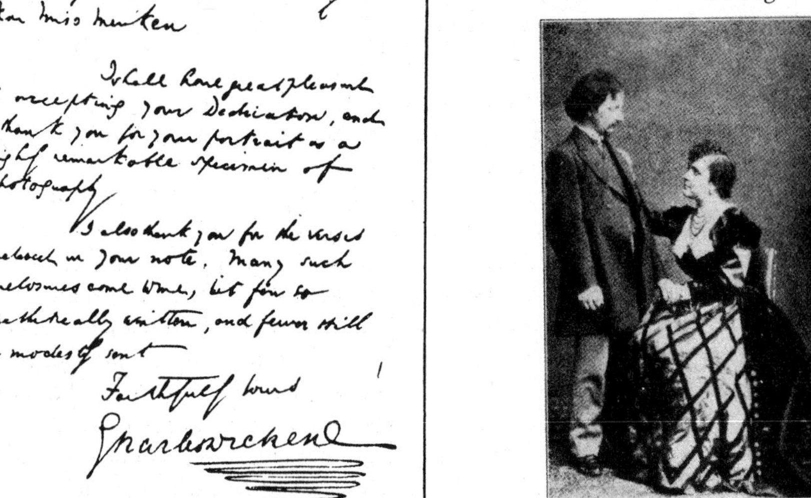

Gad's Hill Place,
Higham by Rochester, Kent.

Monday Twenty First October 1867

Dear Miss Menken

I shall have great pleasure in accepting your Dedication, and I thank you for your portrait as a highly remarkable specimen of Photography.

I also thank you for the verses enclosed in your note. Many such enclosures come to me, but few so pathetically written, and fewer still so modestly sent.

Faithfully Yours

Charles Dickens

ADAH ISAACS MENK
WITH SWINBURN

More sinned against
sinning

LETTER FROM DICKENS

The letter in which he accepted the dedication of the actresses's book of poems

One evening in February, Alexandre Dumas, fat, and with a shock of white curly hair, went to the theater to see Menken. The sequel was foreordained. The great writer who had been turned down by Rachel a quarter of a century before was now looked upon with favor by Adah who was only half his age. They were inseparable. Adah was delighted with his sophisticated reminiscences and flattered that a man of talent was courting her. All through her short and stormy life, she had a penchant for literary figures. An effective actress, she broke her heart because she was not equally effective as a poetess. Bernard Falk suspected that Adah was consumed with a desire for immortality, and, unwilling to chance it on *Mazeppa* alone, felt that her association with great men of letters would assure her a niche in the Hall of Fame. Obviously, she was correct. Here we are, in 1943, still writing about this extraordinary woman.

Unfortunately for the reputation of both Dumas and Menken—not that either had much left—they indulged in the rather indiscreet pastime of having some intimate but presumably private photographs taken. The unexpected publication of these by the mercenary photographer caused such a scandal that even Alexandre Dumas fils was shocked at his father. He remonstrated mildly and received the following note:

"My dear Alexandre:

"Despite my advancing years I have found a Marguerite to whom I can play the part of Armand Duval."

The tactful roué referred, of course, to his son's play, *La Dame aux Camellias.*

When the photographer, pleased with the sensation and the money he was making refused to stop the sale of the pictures, Dumas took the matter to court, and succeeded in having the prints withdrawn and the negatives destroyed.

In August, Menken returned to England to look after the long-delayed publication of her poems. When there she revived her salons for literary personages. Dickens, Reade, Swinburne, Rossetti, Tom Hood, all came to call and remained to admire. Before she met Swinburne, Rossetti suggested that she go to call on him instead of having the trouble to describe the poet to Adah. Banteringly, he challenged her to stay the night. The wager between them was ten pounds. Menken stayed the night, but returned the ten pounds Rossetti sent her. She became Swinburne's mistress more because she hoped he could do something for her verse than because she loved the poet, drunkard that he was and idol of the undergraduates. The morning after the first night, she lost no time in broaching the subject nearest her heart. Swinburne laughed. "My darling, a woman with such beautiful legs need not bother about poetry." Taking stock of her relations with Swinburne, Adah concluded she had gone from verse to worse.

In 1868, Adah's health began to fail although she was only thirty-seven. She worried constantly about the delays in publishing the poems she set such store by, and flooded the publishers with letters begging them to complete arrangements. Menken was a little less radiant when she returned to Paris to play *The Pirates of Savannah.* After two rehearsals, she collapsed. The medical men who had been treating her for inflammatory rheumatism discovered too late that she had an infected abscess on her left side. Menken fully realized her plight, and wrote bravely to a friend:

"I am lost to art and life. Yet when all is said and done, have I not at my age tasted more of life than most women who live to be a hundred? It is fair, then, that I should go where old people go."

Attended by a Jewish rabbi, faithful to the last to her adopted religion, Menken passed away in the arms of her maid, and was buried in Père-Lachaise.

In her last sickness, Dumas never came near her. Dickens was in London. Swinburne was very busy drinking himself silly, although he had admired and gone over the proofs of *Infelicia* that she never lived to see in print.

One of the French papers, which had made ribald fun of the actress during her lifetime, was touched by the circumstances of her death. F. C. Hiley translated the quatrain:

Ungrateful animals, mankind!
Walking his riders hearse behind,
Mourner in chief her horse appears,
But where are all her Cavaliers?

Miscellaneous Reference List

THE FAVORABLE RECEPTION and earnest appreciation accorded to the numerous reference lists in the writer's previous work, *They All Sang* (From Tony Pastor to Rudy Vallee), has been the incentive which has induced him to compile further not only additional lists of the 90's—but also of the 80's—70's—60's and earlier decades. The task has been interesting, but not easy, and almost never-ending.

However, many well-known public figures and other private and professional individuals appear to have found a distinct value and use for the reference lists in the earlier book. This is shown by letters in possession of the writer from newspapermen, magazine writers, authors, public librarians, directors of radio studios, record makers, film directors and officials, orchestras, singers, concert and stage stars, etc. This being the case, they will all surely find many new values in the addenda to music and songs, and in the many new interesting items in the lists covering the periods mentioned above.

If, through use of these lists, the writer can in any way foster Americana by aiding future research, or if he can perhaps revive and restore to a music-loving world old songs and ballads, gradually disappearing, and give renewed credit to those who created these beautiful works, his reward for a tireless effort will be more than ample. This will be especially so, if he can instill in ambitious young singers and in mature artists a serious desire to emulate the world-famous singers of other days, and if it will also, in these troublesome times, encourage old-time song collecting, for this reason:

Old-time song collecting is now one of the most intriguing and fascinating of hobbies. It has everything to commend it. It is a delightfully instructive, interesting and profitable hobby. It is the ideal avocation for anyone with a love for barter, and a liberal education for art lovers. It is a perfect type of Americana, depicting every decade, invention and event. It runs the gamut of American life, wars and history. It introduces you to outstanding personalities, and the passing moods, fashions and cycles of days past and present. It combines entertainment with knowledge. A man of modest means becomes a real collector with opportunities for research and treasure hunts.

Many old-time songs are embellished with artistic lithographs and engravings. Pictures and music go together and a good frontispiece to good old music has an added charm. Charles Dickens' subjects are in demand and a rare title page was even executed by Whistler and commands big sums.

Dr. Rosenbach, famous collector of rare books, tells in his *Book Hunter's Holiday* of the thrills and adventures of hunting up a rare book. That's a fine viewpoint for the man of means. No less exciting than hunting rare books or big game is the hunt for rare old music to the man of modest means. Dr. Rosenbach employs the phrases "intrinsic and never-flagging interest," "real living excitement," "stirring adventures," "personal association which adds to the mysterious lure," "the thrill of obsession," "the scent of the hunter," "by some sixth sense you know it must exist somewhere," "watchfulness, patience and courage are required to be successful" and "the fair sex cannot be excluded from the game."

It is amazing how these very expressive thoughts apply as fully to the game of hunting up old music as to rare books. This alone should entice thousands to take up this latest of all enjoyable hobbies.

Just as with Currier and Ives, or genuine antiques, old-time music, as rare Americana, is jumping in value more and more every year. It is common knowledge how the rarer Stephen Foster songs are eagerly sought for by thousands, spurred on by the well-advertised premium prices of hundreds of dollars, offered by the Foster Foundation in Indianapolis, so admirably presided over by that estimable philanthropist, Josiah Kirby Lilly.

Coming up strongly in value are the rare early Negro and minstrel songs of James G. Bland and others. Included among many other song rarities are *Dickens* items, *Lincoln* and Abolition, *Jennie Lind, Malibran, Christine Nilsson* and other famous singers, *Washington* and *Presidents* of the United States, *American Revolution, Early Indian, Civil War,* early editions of "*Hot Time*" (Spanish War), "*Over There*" (First World War), *New York* items and *Temperance* items, early editions *Gilbert and Sullivan* and *English Ballads, Historical* items and items of *Invention,* early copies "*Star-Spangled Banner,*" "*America,*" "*Yankee Doodle,*" "*Columbia,*" and other *Patriotic* tunes. Also old-time American "*Pop*" writers like *Paul Dresser, Danks, Root, Work, Cooper, Harrison Millard,* etc.

Many of Harrigan and Hart's famous song successes, from their famous comedy dramas depicting life in lower New York in the 80's and 90's, are also collectors' items and bring better prices every year.

EXCERPTS FROM *MUSICAL HISTORICAL CAVALCADE*

(Through the Courtesy of the Compiler, Julius Mattfield, with additions by the author.)

1814 Star-Spangled Banner
Words—Francis Scott Key
Music from Anacreon in Heaven

1820 Love Letter
Composed and sung by Mr. Braham in "Family Quarrels"

1824 Hunters of Kentucky
By S. Woodworth

1829 From Greenland's Icy Mountains
Words—Bishop
Music—Lowell Mason

1830 Old Oaken Bucket
Poem—Samuel Woodworth
Music—Old Scotch Air

Buy a Broom
Sung by Mme. Vestris

1831 Mary's Lamb
Words—Sarah Josepha Hale
Music—Dr. Lowell Mason

1834 Bird at Sea
Mrs. Hemans

1837 Brave Old Oak
Words—H. F. Chorley
Music—E. T. Loder

1841 My Mother's Bible
Music—Henry Russell

Tea in the Arbour
By J. Beuler

1842 Stars Their Early Vigils Keep
Written and sung by Dr. Oliver Wendell Holmes
Music—James G. Maeder

1845 Handsome Man
John Frances, Esq.

They Don't Propose
John Frances, Esq.

Blue Juanita
By Mrs. M. D. Sullivan

1850 Cheer, Boys, Cheer
Words—Chas. Mackay
Music—Henry Russell

I've Left my Snow-Clad Hills
Jenny Lind

Jenny Lind's Bird Song
Jenny Lind

Ossian's Serenade
Jenny Lind

Salut à la France
La Fille du Regiment

Zeekel and Huldy
Words—Hosea Bigelow (James Russell Lowell)
Music—J. J. Hutchinson

Five Pound Polka
Composed by Stephen Glover

1852 A Little More Cider
By Austin Hart

1852 Do They Miss Me at Home
Words and Music—S. M. Grannis

Ever of Thee
Words—Geo. Linley
Music—Foley Hall

Lilly Dale
Words and Music—H. S. Thompson

Massa's in the Cold, Cold Ground
Stephen Collins Foster

The Rock Beside the Sea
Words—Chas. Crozat Converse
Music (Not Known)

The Young Folks at Home
Words—Frank Spencer
Music—Miss Hattie Livingston (Composed for Woods Minstrels)

NOTE: In 1852 Harriet Beecher Stowe's "Uncle Tom's Cabin" was published. Sales eventually mounted to hundreds of thousands. Flotow's opera "Martha" was performed in the United States.

1853 The Hazel Dell
Words and Music by Wurzel (Geo. Fred. Root)

My Old Kentucky Home, Good Night
Stephen Collins Foster

Goodbye Farewell
Music—J. R. Thomas

1854 My Last Cigar
J. M. Hubbard

Hard Times Come Again No More
Stephen Collins Foster

Jeanie with the Light Brown Hair
Stephen Collins Foster

The Monastery Bells
Music by Louis Alfred Lefeburne Wety

Poet and Peasant Overture
Music by Franz von Suppe

There's Music in the Air
Hymn for S.A.T.B., with piano accompaniment
Words—Frances Jane Crosby (Mrs. Alexander Van Alstyne)
Music—Geo. Frederick Root

1854 What Is Home Without a Mother
Words and Music by Alice Hawthorne
(Pseudonym of Septimus Winner)
Willie, We Have Missed You
Words and Music—Stephen Collins Foster

1855 Dearest Spot on Earth Is Home
By Wrighton
Come Where My Love Lies Dreaming
Part Song for S.A.T.B.
Words and music by Stephen Collins Foster
Listen to the Mocking Bird
Words and Music by Alice Hawthorne
(Septimus Winner)
Melody in F (Piano Solo)
Music by Anton Rubinstein
Rosalie, the Prairie Flower
Words and Music—Wurzel
(Geo. Frederick Root)
Star of the Evening
Words and Melody by James M. Sayle
Arranged by Henry Tucker
The Sword of Bunker Hill
Words—William Ross Wallace
Music—Bernard Covert
Twinkling Stars Are Laughing Love
Words and Music by John Ordway
NOTE: *Il Trovatore* had its première at the Academy of Music.

1856 The Arrow and the Song
Words—Henry W. Longfellow
Music—William Michael Balfe
The Cottage by the Sea
Words and Music—John Rogers Thomas
Darling Little Nellie Gray
Words and Music—Benj. Russell Hanby
Hark, I Hear an Angel Sing
Words—W. C. B.
Music—R. G. Shrival
Kathleen Mavourneen
Words and Music—Fred. Nicholls Crouch

1856 The Last Hope (Piano Solo)
Music — Louis Moreau Gottschalk
Old Friends and Old Times
Words—Charles Swain
Music—John Rogers Thomas
Root Hog or Die
Words and Music—Richard J. McGowan (?)
Stars of the Summer Night
Part Song, for T.T.B.B.
Words—Henry W. Longfellow
Music—Isaac Baker Woodbury
(Usually published anonymously)
Quilting Party
Words—Frances Kyle
Music—J. Fletcher

1857 Come Into the Garden, Maud
Words—Alfred Lord Tennyson
Music—Wm. Michael Balfe
Flee as a Bird
Mrs. Mary S. B. Danna
Arranged by Geo. Frederick Root
Jingle Bells or the One Horse Open Sleigh
Words and Music—J. S. Pierpont
Little White Cottage
Words by M. S. Pike
Melody—J. S. Pike
Arranged by J. S. Pierpont
My Grandma's Advice
Words and Music—*M* (?)
Arranged by Edward Kanski
The Village Blacksmith
Words—Henry W. Longfellow
Music—Willoughby Hunter Weiss
NOTE: Italian opera is now played regularly in Philadelphia, after the opening of Academy of Music with Grand Ball. Bryant's Minstrels were organized in New York.

1858 Bonny Eloise, the Belle of Mohawk Vale
Words—Geo. W. Ellicott
Music—John Rogers Thomas

1858 Christmas Song
(Original French Title, "Cantique de Noël")
Author of French words unknown
English Words—John Sullivan Dwight
Music—Adolphe Adam
Published earlier in Paris; first sung at Midnight Mass, Christmas Eve, 1847.
La Prière D'Une Vierge
English title—"A Maiden's Prayer"
Piano Solo—Music by Thecla Baderzenska
Thou Art So Near and Yet So Far
Original German Title, "Mir nah und doch so fern"
Words and Music—Alexander Reichardt
Warbling at Eve (Piano Solo)
Music—Henry Brinly Richards

1859 Let Me Kiss Him for His Mother
John P. Ordway
Jingle Bells
J. Pierpont
Il Bacio (known as the Kiss Waltz)
Composed for Mme. Piccolomini
The Louisiana Lowlands
Words and Music Anonymous
NOTE: Adelina Patti made her debut at the Academy of Music, New York. As a child star, she had appeared at Niblo's Garden in 1851.

1860 Annie Lisle
Words and Music—H. S. Thompson
Dixie Land
Words and Music—Daniel Decatur Emmett
Arranged by W. S. Hobbs
Old Black Joe
Words and Music—Stephen Collins Foster
Rock Me to Sleep, Mother
Words—Florence Percy
Music—Ernest Leslie

1860 Sweet Spirit, Hear My Prayer
Music—William Vincent Wallace
Words—Edward Fitzbak
'Tis But a Little Faded Flower
Words—Fred'k Enoch
Music—John Rogers Thomas
Alice, Where Art Thou
Words—Wellington Gurnsey
Music—Joseph Ascher
Balm of Gilead
Arranged by H. T. Bryant, Boston
Cavatina—Op. 157, for Violin and Piano
Music—Joachim Raff
Down by the River I Stray
Music—J. R. Thomas
Gideon's Band
Arranged by Chas. R. Dodward
Kittie Wells
Charles E. Atherton
Maryland, My Maryland
Words—James Ryder Randall
Music—German Folk Song: O Tannenbaum, O Tannenbaum
Arranged by C. E. Baltimore
Missouri (A Voice from the South)
Composed and Sung by Harry Macarthy (The Arkansas Comedian)
Ole Shady (The Song of the Contraband)
Words and Music—Benjamin Russell Hanby
The Vacant Chair (or, We Shall Meet But We Shall Miss Him)
Words—H. S. Washburn
Music—Geo. Frederick Root
The Volunteer
Composed and Sung by Harry Macarthy
Won't You Tell Me Why, Robin
Words and Music—Claribel—Pseudonym of Mrs. Charles C. Barnard, nee Charlotte Alington

1862 Drummer Boy of Shiloh
Will S. Hays

1862 Battle Hymn of the Republic
Julia Ward Howe (Written in 1861)
Music: Glory, Glory Hallelujah, ascribed to William Steffe, but published anonymously
The Bonnie Blue Flag
Song of the Confederate States during the Civil War
Words—Mrs. Annie Chambers-Ketchum
Music—Henry Macarthy
NOTE: This was a very famous song—it read thus:
"We are a band of brothers,
Native to our soil,
Fighting for our property,
We've gained by honest toil," etc.
Evangeline
Words and Music—Wm. Shakespeare Hays
Grafted Into the Army
Words and Music—Henry Clay Work
Killarney
Words—Edmund Falcolner
Music—Wm. Michael Balfe
Kingdom Coming
Words and Music—Henry Clay Work
We Are Coming Father Abraham, 300,000 More
Words and Music—Stephen C. Foster
We've a Million in the Field
Words and Music—Stephen C. Foster

1863 Babylon Is Fallen
Words and Music—Henry Clay Work
The Battle Cry of Freedom
Words and Music—George Frederick Root
Folks That Put on Airs
Words and Music—W. H. Coulston
Just Before the Battle, Mother
Words and Music—George Frederick Root
Weeping, Sad and Lonely (or, "When This Cruel War Is Over")
Words—Charles Carroll Sawyer
Music—Henry Tucker
When Johnny Comes Marching Home
Words and Music—Louis Lambert
(Pseudonym of Patrick Sarsfield Gilmore)
NOTE: This was a famous Confederate song. "Johnny" means "Johnny Reb." (About this time over 1,000 were killed in New York City draft riots.)

1864 All Quiet Along the Potomac Tonight
Words—Lamar Fontaine
Music—John Hill Hewett, Richmond
Beautiful Dreamer
Words and Music—Stephen Collins Foster
The Dying Poet (Piano Solo)
Music by Seven Octaves (Pseudonym of Louis Moreau Gottschalk)
Take Back the Heart You Gave
Words and Music—Claribel
(Mrs. Charles C. Barnard, nee Charlotte Alington)
Tenting on the Old Camp Ground
Words and Music—Walter Kittredge
Tramp, Tramp, Tramp
Words and Music—George Frederick Root
Wake Nicodemus
Words and Music—Henry Clay Work
The War Is Over, Mary
Words—George Cooper
Music—John Rogers Thomas
Work for the Night Is Coming (Hymn)
Words—Annie L. Walker
Music—Lowell Mason
NOTE: Adah Isaacs Menken, the California actress, sailed for London, where she made her debut as Mazeppa. She died in Paris in 1868.

1865 Arkansas Traveller
Author Unknown
Beautiful Isle of the Sea
Words—George Cooper
Music—John Rogers Thomas
Beware
Words—Henry W. Longfellow
Music—Charles Moulton
Carry Me Back to Tennessee (or, Ellie Rhee)
By Sep Winner
The Little Brown Church
Words and Music—William S. Pitts
Marching Through Georgia
Words and Music—Henry Clay Work
Nicodemus Johnson
Words (?)
Music—J. B. Murphy
The past year was a marked social season. It is estimated that in New York alone 600 *balls* took place.

1866 Write Me a Letter from Home
Will S. Hays
When You and I Were Young, Maggie
Words—George W. Johnson
Music—J. A. Butterfield
NOTE: *The Black Crook* was the dramatic hit, running 474 performances which, with periodic revivals, eventually brought a grand total of 773.
NOTE: Mr. Howard Paul, at the Arch Street Theatre in Philadelphia, first danced the can-can in a piece called "Ripples on the Lake."
Belle Mahone
J. H. McNaughton

1867 Angel's Serenade
Original Italian title, "La Serenata"
English words—Henry Millard
Music—Gaetano Braga
Beautiful Bird Sing On
Words and Music—T. H. Howe
Blue Danube
Original German title, "An der schoenen blauen Donau"

1867 Waltz—Music—Johann Strauss
First performed in Vienna February 13, 1867
The Bridge
Words—H. W. Longfellow
Music—Lady Carew
Croquet
Words—C. H. Webb
Music—John Rogers Thomas
Waiting
Words—E. H. Flagg
Music—Harrison Millard
We Are Marching to Zion (Hymn)
Words—Isaac Watts
Music—Rev. Robert Lowery
NOTE: In 1867, "Under the Gaslight" was produced at the New York Theatre, New York.

1868 Captain Jinks of the Horse Marines
Words—William Horace Lingard
Music—T. Macloglin
The song was introduced in America, by the Lingard Comedy Company, from London, where it had been sung by them.
Chant Sans Paroles (No. 3 in "Souvenir de Hapsal" Op. 2)
Piano Solo
Music—Peter Tschaikowsky
The Man on the Flying Trapeze
Words—George Leybourne
Music—Alfred Lee
Sung by Johnny Allen
Her Bright Smile Haunts Me Still
Words—J. E. Carpenter
Music—W. T. Wrighton
Lullaby
Original German Title "Wiegenlied" (No. 4 in "Fuenf Lieder" Op. 49)
German words from "Des Knaben Wunderhorn" (2nd verse by George Scherer)
English words—Mrs. Natalia MacFarren
Music—Johannes Brahms
Tales from the Vienna Woods
Original German Title "Ge-

1868 schichten aus dem Wienerwald"
Waltz—Music—Johann Strauss
First performed in Vienna, June 9, 1868

Whispering Hope
(Duet for Soprano and Alto)
Words and Music—Alice Hawthorne (Septimus Winner)

Sweet Bye and Bye
Words—S. Fillmore Bennett

Ten Little Injuns
By Septimus Winner

NOTE: *Humpty Dumpty* was the dramatic hit of the year, running 483 performances and later going through periodic revivals. G. L. Fox played his role 1,128 times.

NOTE: Barnum's Museum burned in New York, and in the same city the elevated lines were undergoing tests.

1869 Birds of the Night
Words—Lionel H. Lewin
Music—Sir Arthur Sullivan

Light Cavalry Overture
Original German Title "Leichte Kavallerie"
Orchestral Composition—Music—Franz von Suppe

The Little Brown Jug
Words and Music—R. A. Eastburn (Pseudonym of J. E. Winner)

Near the Cross (Jesus Keep Me Near the Cross)
Hymn—Words—Frances Jane Crosby (Mrs. Alexander Van Alstyne)
Music—William Howard Doane

Shoo Fly—Don't Bodder Me
Words—Billy Reeves
Sung by Cool Burgess

Sweet Genevieve
Words—George Cooper
Music—Henry Cooper

Up in a Balloon
By Leybourne

Wine, Woman and Song
Original German Title, "Wein, Weib und Gesang"

1869 Waltz—Music—Johann Strauss—Op. 333
First performed in Vienna, February 2, 1869.

NOTE: Hanlon Bros. put on the American market a bicycle—a wooden affair—they had experimented with in their act.

NOTE: James Gordon Bennett, *New York Herald*, dispatched Stanley to Africa to find the explorer, David Livingstone. High financial transactions, plus the flashiness of the newly found wealth has caused various writers to label the period now in progress as "The Gilded Age" and "The Great Barbecue."

1870 Heathen Chinee
Words—Bret Harte
Music—F. B. Boote

Looking Back
Words—Louisa Gray
Music—Sir Arthur Sullivan

Pass Me Not, O Gentle Saviour
Hymn—Words—Frances Jane Crosby (Mrs. Alexander Van Alstyne)
Music—William Howard Doane

Rescue the Perishing (Hymn)
Words—Frances Jane Crosby (Mrs. Alexander Van Alstyne)
Music—William Howard Doane

NOTE: The steamboat *Robert E. Lee* paddled from New Orleans to St. Louis in 3 days, 18 hours and 14 minutes, for a record. Following the boom in railroads, the United States found itself with 49,168 miles of roadbed. Opera houses, music halls and theaters were opening right and left, with even the smallest towns boasting of at least one of these ornamental, begilded structures. The South began to challenge traditional New England as a cotton textile center. "Frou Frou" was playing at the Fifth Avenue Theatre, New York. In order to squeeze into the new tight-skirted fashions,

1870 some belles had to tie their knees together.

1871 Beware
Part Song for A.T.T.B.
(Also for S.A.T.B.)
Words—H. W. Longfellow
Music—John Liptrot Hatton
Good-bye Liza Jane
Arranged by Eddie Fox
The Little Old Log Cabin in the Lane
Music—William Shakespeare Hays
Mollie Darling
Words and Music—William Shakespeare Hays
Onward, Christian Soldiers
Words—Sabine Baring Gould
Music—Sir Arthur Sullivan
(Published as a supplement to the *Musical Times*, London, December, 1871)
Reuben, Reuben, I've Been Thinking
Words—Harry Birch
Music—Wm. Gooch
The Sea Hath Its Pearls
Words—Henry W. Longfellow
Translated from the German of Heinrich Heine
Music—Charles Gounod
Something for Jesus (Hymn)
Words—S. D. Phelps
Music—Rev. Robert Lowry
(Published by the Bigelow & Main Corp., 1871. *Main* used to be the man at head of the M. E. Pub. Co.—They published the Methodist Christian Advocate)
Susan Jane
Words and Music—William Shakespeare Hays

NOTE: Mrs. O'Leary's famed cow kicked over a lantern in her stall and started the Chicago conflagration, and an estimated $200,000,000 destruction resulted.

For feminine learning Smith College was founded. P. T. Barnum's "Greatest Show on Earth," the traveling circus and menagerie, got under way.

1872 The Angel and the Child
Words—Henry W. Longfellow
Music—Virginia Gabriel
Come, Ye Faithful, Raise the Strain (Hymn Tune)
St. Kevin
Words—John Mason Neale, from the Greek of "St. John of Damascus"—8th Century
Music—Sir Arthur Sullivan
I Need Thee Every Hour (Hymn)
Words—Annie S. Hawks
Music—Rev. Robert Lowry
Oh, Sam
Words and Music—William Shakespeare Hays
Polish Dance (Piano Solo)
Original German Title "Polnischer National Tanz"
Music by Xaver Scharwenka, Op. 3, No. 1

NOTE: The current aspirations of United States society were exemplified by Ward McAllister, social leader, who organized the "Patriarchs"—25 names deemed by him as fit to create and lead New York society.

Herr Johann Strauss, the celebrated composer, made his debut at the Academy of Music, New York. A fire in Boston wiped out over 700 buildings and caused close to $1,000,000 property damage.

Col. James Fisk, Jr., "The King of Wall Street," was shot and killed by Edward S. Stokes.

1873 Eilleen Allanna
Words—E. S. Marble
Music—Jas. Rogers Thomas
Good Night, Good Night Beloved
Part song for S.A.T.B.
Words—H. W. Longfellow
Music—Ciro Pinsuti
Good Sweet Ham
Words and Music—Henry Hart
Arranged by James E. Stewart

1873 The Mulligan Guard
Words—Edward Harrigan
Music—Dave Braham
Silver Threads Among the Gold
Words—Eben E. Rexford
Music—Hart Pease Danks
Wiener Blut (Waltz)
Music—Johann Strauss, Op. 354
NOTE: Banks were failing throughout the nation, resulting in a panic on the stock exchange.
Henry Clay Frick began consolidating his vast coke-manufacturing business.

1874 Alabama Blossoms
Words and Music—Frank Dumont
Arranged by James E. Stewart
Barbara Frietchie
Words—John G. Whittier
Music—Elizabeth Solman
Patrick's Day Parade
Words—Edward Harrigan
Music—Dave Braham
The Skidmore Guard
Words—Edward Harrigan
Music—Dave Braham
Trabling Back to Georgia
Words—Arthur W. French
Music—Charles D. Blake
NOTE: Agitation against the evils of alcohol caused in this year the founding of the National Woman's Christian Temperance Union.
In New York City "Boss" William M. Tweed (Tammany) was convicted of fraud in the amount of about $6,000,000 and sent to prison, where, after an escape and capture, he died in 1878.
A kidnaping made the front pages, when the infant Charley Ross was stolen from his home in Germantown, Pa., and disappeared forever; this *disappearance forever* has, however, been disputed, and several men who claimed to be the original kidnaped Charley Ross turned up,

1874 but were never believed.
Five years of secondary postwar depression commenced—the No. 15 depression since 1790.

1875 All the Way My Saviour Leads Me (Hymn)
Words—Frances Jane Crosby (Mrs. Alexander Van Alstyne)
Music—Rev. Robert Lowry
Angel Gabriel
Words (?)
Music—James E. Stewart
Angels Meet Me at the Cross Roads
Words and Music—William Shakespeare Hays
Fully Persuaded (Hymn)
Words—Rev. J. Atchison
Music—William F. Sherwin
Let Me Dream Again
Words—B. C. Stevenson
Music—Sir Arthur Sullivan
When the Tide Comes In
Music—Harrison Millard
NOTE: Delmonico's and, soon, Sherry's were the fashionable New York restaurants and rendezvous. The chaperone was a fashion feature. Banjos were popular musical instruments, as also were guitars and, later, mandolins.
The first Kentucky Derby was run and won by the horse Aristides.
Variety Theaters, from which vaudeville developed a decade later, were opening everywhere.

1876 Grandfather's Clock
Words and Music—Henry Clay Work
I'll Take You Home Again, Kathleen
Words and Music—Thomas W. Westendorf
It Is Well with My Soul (Hymn)
Words—H. C. Spofford
Music—Paul P. Bliss
My Dearest Heart
Words (?)
Music—Sir Arthur Sullivan

1876 The Ninety and Nine (Hymn)
Words—E. C. Clephane
Music—Ira D. Sankey
NOTE: When I was a young man the most famous hymn singers of the day were Dwight L. Moody and Ira D. Sankey (Moody & Sankey). Like Rodeheaver used to be with Billy Sunday, they were associated with the great evangelist, DeWitt C. Talmadge. The Tilton-Henry Ward Beecher scandal, both eminent churchmen, pastors and preachers, became the sensation of the times.
Rose of Killarney
Words—George Cooper
Music—John Rogers Thomas
See That My Grave's Kept Green
Written, composed and sung by Gus Williams
Trusting Jesus, That Is All (Hymn)
Words—E. P. Stites
Music—Ira Davis Sankey
NOTE: Princeton University held an intercollegiate convention, with Columbia, Harvard and Yale (at Springfield) from which modern football developed in which the touchdown is the deciding factor.
Colorado joined the Union.
Sitting Bull's Sioux Indian warriors, massacred General Custer and 276 soldiers.
Bell and Gray invented the telephone.
In Philadelphia the Centennial World's Fair opened to the tune of a march composed by Richard Wagner.

1877 Early in de Mornin'
Words and Music—William Shakespeare Hays
Hiding in Thee (Hymn)
Words—William O. Cushing
Music—Ira David Sankey
The Lost Chord
Words—Adelaide Proctor
Music—Sir Arthur Sullivan

1877 Roll Out—Heave Dat Cotton
Words and Music—William Shakespeare Hays
Where Is My Wandering Boy Tonight (Hymn)
Music—Rev. Robert Lowry
NOTE: Railroad strikes swept the nation (virtually every major line) in a labor battle after 10% wage cuts. Federal troops were called out—property damage ran into millions.
In the Pennsylvania coal region a number of "Molly Maguires" were hanged for various murders. The "Maguires" was a secret organization purporting to keep up the wage standards, as well as to keep the foreign element out of the coal labor market, and their activities had for years terrorized the community.
Mme. Modjeska, celebrated tragedienne, made her American debut at the California Theatre in San Francisco.
Humor entered the magazine field as an editorial formula, with *Puck*. Eventually Hearst bought *Puck* and even now uses the name on the first page of his "Comic Weekly." Edison heard "Mary Had a Little Lamb" on his first phonograph.

1878 Carry Me Back to Ole Virginny
Words and Music—James A. Bland
Come Where the Lillies Bloom
Will L. Thompson
Emmett's Lullaby
(Fritz Our Cousin German)
Words and Music—Joseph K. Emmett
A Flower from Mother's Grave
Words and Music—Harry Kennedy
Old Wooden Rocker
By Harrison Millard

1878 Saviour, Breathe an Evening Blessing (Hymn)
Words—J. Edmeston
Music—George Coles Stebbens
Skidmore Fancy Ball
Words—Edward Harrigan
Music—Dave Braham
Sweet Mary Ann, or Such an Education Has My Mary Ann
Words—Edward Harrigan
Music—Dave Braham
Where Was Moses When the Light Went Out
Music arranged by Max Reinor
NOTE: Yellow fever was a scourge during this year. (Over 10,000 died in Memphis, Tenn.)
Tidewater Oil began piping oil over the Alleghenies instead of shipping in barrels.
Bizet's opera "Carmen" had its initial United States performance, at the Academy of Music, New York, with Minnie Hauk in the title role.

1879 The Babies on Our Block
Words—Edward Harrigan
Music—Dave Braham
In the Morning by the Bright Light
Words and Music—James A. Bland
NOTE: News of Edison's invention of incandescent lamps caused such a rush of curiosity seekers to Menlo Park, New Jersey, that the Pennsylvania Railway had to put on extra trains.
George B. Selden applied for a patent on a vehicle powered with an internal combustion engine. It was granted in 1895.
Theaters continued opening everywhere.
Gilbert and Sullivan's "H.M.S. Pinafore" was playing simultaneously in big cities.
Dion Boucicault, the successful and prolific playwright, had "Contempt of Court" on the boards at Wallack's. His biggest success was "The Shaugran."

1880 Cradle's Empty, Baby's Gone
Words and Music—Harry Kennedy
The Five Cent Shave
Words and Music—Thomas Cannon
The Full Moon Union
(The Mulligan Guard's Surprise)
Words—Edward Harrigan
Music—Dave Braham
Funiculi Funicula
(Song in Neapolitan dialect)
Music—Luiga Denza
De Golden Wedding
Words and Music—James A. Bland
Hide Thou Me (Hymn)
Words—Frances Jane Crosby
Music—Rev. Robert Lowry
Locked Out After Nine
(The Mulligan Guard's Picnic)
Words—Edward Harrigan
Music—Dave Braham
The Mulligan Braves
(The Mulligan Guard's Nominee)
Words—Edward Harrigan
Music—Dave Braham
Never Take the Horseshoe from the Door (Mulligan Guards)
Words—Edward Harrigan
Music—Dave Braham
The Skidmore Masquerade
Words—Edward Harrigan
Music—Dave Braham
Songs My Mother Taught Me
German Title "Als die alte Mutter" (No. 4 in "Zigeunermelodien," Op. 55)
German words—Adolph Heyduk
English words—Mrs. Natalia MacFarren
Music—Anton Dvořák
Why Did They Dig Ma's Grave So Deep
Words and Music—Joseph P. Skelly
NOTE: Highlights of the era now coming into bloom included the banjo, mandolin, guitar, family album, horsehair furniture, the *parlor*, which later developed

1880 into the *drawing room*, the bicycle, and (still) the *chaperone*.

Nearly 15% of all women, 10 or over, were gainfully employed.

Per million United States population, there were now 894 manicurists, barbers and hairdressers.

Public-school teachers were now composed of 57.2% women.

United States population crossed the 50,000,000 mark.

First Salvation Army drive was launched.

Hebe, an elephant in the Cooper and Bailey show, gave birth to the first elephant born in captivity in this country.

At 116th Street and Broadway a bullfight was staged, but the venture was later dropped for want of customers.

Sarah Bernhardt, the great French tragedienne, arrived in America, appearing at Booth's Theatre, New York, in "Adrienne Lecouvreur."

After Lilly Langtry, the famous beauty, had donned a kilted skirt and jersey to show off her figure, the feminine world at large tried to duplicate her. Tailor-made clothes for women were something new and fashionable.

1881 Goodbye
Words—G. T. Whyte-Melville
Music—Francesco Paolo Tosti

I Am Coming (Hymn)
Words—Helen R. Young
Music—Ira D. Sankey

Paddy Duffy's Cart
Words—Edward Harrigan
Music—Dave Braham

Tell It Out Among the Nations That the Lord Is King (Hymn)
By Frances Ridley Havergal
Arranged by Ira D. Sankey

NOTE: Tony Pastor started his theater and when he launched his new venture, *Variety* was the prevalent entertainment.

1881 Pastor was one of its leading exponents. Later he turned it into *Vaudeville*, after B. F. Keith originated what he termed "polite vaudeville."

President Garfield was assassinated by Charles Guiteau.

American Red Cross was founded with Clara Barton in charge.

Negro education received a stimulus through Booker T. Washington by the founding of Tuskegee Institute.

Edwin Booth reappeared on the American stage, after an English engagement.

1882 I Never Drink Behind the Bar
Words—Edward Harrigan
Music—Dave Braham

I'll Be Ready When the Great Day Comes
Words and Music—James S. Putnam

The Market on Saturday Night
Words—Edward Harrigan
Music—Dave Braham

McNally's Row of Flats
Words—Edward Harrigan
Music—Dave Braham

When the Clock in the Tower Strikes Twelve
Words—Edward Harrigan
Music—Dave Braham

NOTE: Lilly Langtry made her debut in America, at Wallack's, as Hester Grazebrook in "An Unequal Match."

Jumbo, the elephant, arrived from England and was promptly exhibited by P. T. Barnum.

First Edison electric lighting station was opened on Pearl Street.

"East Lynne" (with Ada Gray) was a popular play.

1883 Marguerite
Words and Music—C. A. White

My Dad's Dinner Pail
Words—Edward Harrigan
Music—Dave Braham

1883 Strolling on the Brooklyn Bridge
Words—George Cooper
Music—Joseph P. Skelly
When the Mists Have Rolled Away (Hymn)
Words—Annie Herbert
Music—Ira D. Sankey
NOTE: Brooklyn Bridge opened.
The novel of the year was "The Bread Winners."
The *Ladies' Home Journal* was founded.
Buffalo Bill (Col. Wm. F. Cody) launched his Wild West show.
Joseph Pulitzer bought the *New York World* from Jay Gould. (Or rather, Gould and Joseph Pulitzer together owned *The World*. Joseph Pulitzer bought out Gould.)

1884 Always Take Mother's Advice
Words and Music—Jennie Lindsay
Listen to My Tale of Woe
Words—Eugene Field
Music—Hubbard T. Smith
Plum Pudding
Words—Edward Harrigan
Music—Dave Braham
The Sea Hath Its Pearls
Part Song for S.A.T.B.
Henry W. Longfellow
Translated from the German of Heinrich Heine
White Wings
Words and Music—Banks Winter (Well-known minstrel and father of Winona Winter)
NOTE: Electric trolley car was invented.
L. E. Waterman in this year and Paul E. Wirt, in 1885, worked out the fountain pen.
Mark Twain's "Adventures of Huckleberry Finn" appeared in print.

1885 At the Cross (Hymn)
Words—Isaac Watts
Music—R. E. Hudson

1885 The Gum Tree Canoe
Words—S. S. Steele
Music—A. F. Winnemore
Poverty's Tears Ebb and Flow
Words—Edward Harrigan
Music—Dave Braham
Remember, Boy, You're Irish
Words and Music—William J. Scanlan
Still as the Night
Original German title "Still wie die Nacht"
German words traditional
English words—Mrs. John P. Morgan
Music—Karl Bohm
NOTE: Mergenthaler invented the linotype.
Cable cars appeared in New York.

1886 At Midnight on My Pillow Lying (Erminie)
Words—Claxon Bellamy and Harry Paulton
Music—Edward Jacobowski
Darkest the Hour (Erminie)
Words—Claxon Bellamy and Harry Paulton
Music—Edward Jacobowski
Dear Mother in Dreams I See Her (Erminie)
Words and Music—Claxon Bellamy and Harry Paulton
Forever with the Lord
Words—W. James Montgomery
Music—Charles Gounod
The Gladiator March
Music—John Philip Sousa
The Letter That Never Came
Words and Music—Paul Dresser
Maggie, the Cows Are in the Clover
Words and Music—Al. W. Filson
Never Take No for an Answer
Words and Music—W. F. Mitchell
A Soldier's Life (Erminie)
Words—Claxon Bellamy and Harry Paulton
Music—Edward Jacobowski

1886 What the Dickie Birds Say (Erminie)
Words—Claxon Bellamy and Harry Paulton
Music—Edward Jacobowski
NOTE: Statue of Liberty unveiled.
Peace signed with the Apache Indians.
Anarchist riots in Chicago (Haymarket) resulted in several deaths, followed by convictions and hangings.
Earthquake killed 40 in Charleston, S. C.

1887 Come, Oh Come to Me (Hymn)
Words—Mrs. James G. Johnson
Music—James McGranahan
I Will Sing the Wondrous Story (Hymn)
Words—F. W. Rawley
Music—Peter Bilhorn
If the Waters Could Speak as They Flow
Words and Music—Charles Graham
If You Love Me, Darling, Tell Me with Your Eyes
Words—Samuel Minturn Peck
Music—Hubbard T. Peck
The Outcast Unknown
Words and Music—Paul Dresser
Rock-a-Bye Baby
Words and Music—Effie I. Canning
The Song That Reached My Heart
Words and Music—Julian Jordan
The Swan
Original French Title "Le Cygne"
Music by Camille Saint-Saëns
Though Your Sins Be as Scarlet (Hymn)
Words—Frances Jane Crosby (Mrs. Alexander Van Alstyne)
Music—Howard Doane
Wait Till the Tide Comes In
Words—George Propheter
Music—Gussie L. Davis
NOTE: The Indians became United States citizens via the Dawes Act

1887 and were allotted land in individual holdings.
Elsie Hoffman, the actress, made her American debut.
Plays of the season were "Pa," "Dr. Jekyll and Mr. Hyde," "C.O.D.," "The Wife," by David Belasco and H. C. De-Mille, and "A Hole in the Ground" produced by Charlie Hoyt.

1888 Menuet (No. 1 in "Humoresque de Concert" Op. 14 Book 1)
Piano Solo
Music—Ignace Paderewski
The Mottoes Framed Upon the Wall
Words—William Devere
Music—W. S. Mullaly
Oh, That We Two Were Maying
No. 8 in the Collection—Sketch Book, Op. 2
Words—Charles Kingsley
Music—Ethelbert Nevin
The Convict and the Bird
Words and Music—Paul Dresser
Drill, Ye Tarriers, Drill
Published by Frank Harding
L'Internationale
Original French Words by Eugene Pottier
Music—Pierre Degeyter
Se Saran Rose
Italian Words by Pietro Mazzini
Music—Luigi Arditi
Semper Fidelis (March)
John Philip Sousa
The Whistling Coon
Words and Music—Sam Devere
With All Her Faults I Love Her Still
Words and Music—Monroe H. Rosenfeld
NOTE: The first bona fide golf course in the United States was started at Yonkers, N. Y. It was called St. Andrews and boasted a six-hole course.
De Wolf Hopper recited "Casey at the Bat" for the first time in Wallack's Theatre, New York.

1888 E. H. Sothern launched his career as a star, under Daniel Frohman, in a play called "The Highest Bidder."

1889 Down Went McGinty
Words and Music—Joseph Flynn
Little Girl, Don't Cry
Poem—James Whitcomb Riley
Music—Edward Campion
Oh, Promise Me
(Afterwards introduced in "Robin Hood")
Words—W. Clement Scott
Music—Reginald DeKoven
Playmates
Words and Music—Harry Dacre
The Thunderer (March)
John Philip Sousa

NOTE: The *London Times* is and has been for a long time known as "The Thunderer."

The Washington Post (March)
John Philip Sousa

NOTE: John L. Sullivan beat the late Jake Kilrain in the last bare-knuckle championship prize fight in the United States (75 rounds).

In May steady rains burst the reservoir above Johnstown, Pa., sending down a flood that wiped out 2,000 lives.

The Royal Order of Moose was founded.

Marie Wainwright appeared in New York for the first time in "Twelfth Night."

Richard Mansfield gave a new rendition of "Richard III."

1889 Baldwin Bros. advertised "double balloon ascensions, with parachute descents."

Eastman Kodak Co. in *Scribner's* advertised the Kodak as a simple, snapshooting device, thereby launching the great and profitable vogue of amateur photography.

MISCELLANEOUS

Still, Still with Thee
Words—Harriet Beecher Stowe
Music—J. S. Fearis
Chiming Bells of Long Ago
Written by George Cooper
Music—C. F. Shattuck
Lorena
Music—J. P. Webster
Hutchinson, Get Off the Track
Jesse Hutchinson, Jr.
Buy a Broom
Sung by Mme. Vestris
All Quiet Along the Potomac Tonight
Words—Lamar Fontaine
Music—J. H. Hewitt
Chieftain's Daughter
Henry Russell
Little Maude
Music—J. P. Webster
I Buckle to My Slender Side
Poetry—William Cullen Bryant
Music—E. Ives, Jr.
Annabel Lee
Poem—Edgar Allan Poe
Music—E. F. Falconnet

The Roll of Honor

The following veterans honored their profession in a career on the stage or in kindred fields of entertainment for about forty and, in many cases, fifty years or more.

Whether a star of the greatest magnitude and fame—a supporting actor or actress—a strolling player—a performer in opera, stock, legitimate, variety, vaudeville, circus—midget or clown—singer or dancer, minstrel or monologist, or what have you—why should it matter? Why make any distinction, remembering the old adage—"All men are equal, on and under the turf?" What a joy for me to remember these veterans, many but recently passed on, and who will soon be forgotten by their public. Not necessarily only the stars of the theater, but the plodders, who often in the face of reverses stuck to their profession for decades.

I consider myself extremely fortunate either to have witnessed performances by or to have met or known a goodly number of the following players and personalities, the majority of whom have gone—a few of whom are still with us.

The big point at issue is that countless thousands of the great amusement-loving public enjoyed while they were with us, or still enjoy in some fashion, either through reading or through reminiscing, the splendid efforts of the gifted personalities herein listed. It was with a spirit of deep reverence that I compiled, with much research, these unforgettable names, many septuagenarians or octogenarians, others who lived but a few years less..

Each one of them handed over the footlights for decades, or entertained in his own way, an eager public, with laughs, thrills, or tears of emotion. "The actor in his time plays many parts." They cannot in the nature of things all be successes. "The play's the thing," and he or she must have, in the course of a long experience, struck a good average; otherwise none would hardly have endured for half a century or more in a very trying profession.

If my "honor list" serves to bring back pleasant memories to any of the thousands who witnessed and enjoyed some of their efforts to amuse, I shall consider myself well repaid for all the work of compiling this list. I am of the minority that realizes the great strain an actor or actress is under in trying to put over a part. Often, in unavoidable failure, my sympathies have gone out to those who frequently, despite great handicaps, earnestly tried to give the audience the best in them.

CHARLES S. ABBE (73)*

Actor. Started at the Boston Museum. Was with Edwin Booth and Charles Frohman. Played with Maude Adams, Annie Russell, Alfred Lunt, etc. Fifty years on stage.

WINTHROP AMES (66)

Famous producer and theater owner. Built Little and Booth Theatres, N. Y. Produced "The Pigeon," "Old English," "Escape," "Beggar on Horseback." Staged modern and classical plays. Connected with theater 40 years.

GEORGE BACKUS (81)

Actor, on the stage over 40 years. Played with Kate Claxton in "The Two Orphans." Was a member of the original "Down East Company."

Originally a banker, he was persuaded by James O'Neill, father of Eugene, to accept a part in "The Celebrated Case," which opened in 1892. He was the author of several plays and also appeared in films.

ANGELO BADA (65)

Operatic tenor. Sang tenor roles at Metropolitan Opera House more than three decades. The dean of the Met's personnel, in point of continuous service. He was brought to this country from La Scala, Milan, by the late Giulio Gatti-Casazza when the impresario became director in 1908.

Bada made his New York debut in "Aïda" and eventually achieved a repertoire of over 150 operas.

He specialized in dramatic characterizations, and although he sang chiefly Italian roles, he often appeared in French and German operas.

REGINALD BARLOW (76)

Veteran actor, over 60 years in show business. The Barlow of the old-time minstrel troupe of Barlow, Wilson, Primrose and West was the father of Reginald Barlow, an actor distinguished by a long and varied career on stage and screen.

At the age of 9 Reginald appeared in his father's minstrel company and in the early years of his career, the programs of such standard stage successes as "Monbars," "Sign of the Cross," "Monte Cristo," "Silver King" and the musical success "Madcap Princess" carried his name in important roles.

After serving as a colonel in World War I, he played in "Old Lady 31," "Blood Money" and many other productions. Later he turned to the screen and appeared in "Washington Serenade," "Witness Vanishes" and other films.

The Colonel on horseback was a striking Broadway figure in the exciting days of the Actors' Equity strike.

*A number following the name indicates age at death.

HATTIE DELARO BARNES (81)

Comic opera singer, on the stage nearly 40 years. Former singer and comedienne, she made her debut in comic opera in 1881. Her last appearance was in Cohan and Harris' "A Tailor-Made Man" in 1918.

Hattie Delaro, as she was known at the time, played in support of Lillian Russell in "Dorothy" at the Standard Theatre, New York. Early in her stage career she played in various Gilbert and Sullivan operas. She also fulfilled singing engagements at the Tivoli Opera House in San Francisco. In 1885 she played Pitti-Sing in the original production of the "Mikado" at the Hollis Street Theatre, Boston.

In the same production Richard Mansfield played "Koko," and many Savoyards who have seen many Kokos since claim that this distinguished star of later years stood out as one of the best Kokos of them all.

Hattie Delaro also appeared in "Mam'selle Awkins," "Around the World in Eighty Days" and "The Man in the Moon."

SIR JAMES MATTHEW BARRIE (77)

Famous playwright and novelist. Wrote "Peter Pan," "The Little Minister," "Admirable Crichton," "What Every Woman Knows." Connected with theater 40 years.

ETHEL BARRYMORE

Dramatic actress, 40 years on the stage and still a current star success. Of the famous Barrymore trio of stage stars, John, Lionel and Ethel. She is the daughter of a famous actor of the 90's, Maurice Barrymore, and a niece of John Drew, her mother having been Georgiana Drew.

Born in Philadelphia in 1878, her first appearance was at the Empire Theatre, New York, in 1895 in "That Independent Young Person," Maude Adams and John Drew also being in the cast.

She distinguished herself as a member of the Empire Theatre Stock Company in "Secret Service," both in America and in London. While there, she was engaged by Henry Irving to play several important roles and in "Peter the Great," particularly, she was acclaimed by the English critics and press.

Her first appearance as a star was in "Captain Jinks" under the management of Charles Frohman in 1900. "Cousin Kate," "Sunday," "A Doll's House," Barrie's "Alice Sit-by-the-Fire," "The Twelve Pound Look," "Declasse," White Oaks," "The Silver Box" and many other plays brought a personal triumph to Miss Barrymore. She recently created an outstanding characterization in the New York success, "The Corn Is Green."

JOHN BARRYMORE (60)

Internationally known stage, screen and radio star, on the stage and in films about 40 years. Son of the celebrated actor Maurice Barrymore, he came of a theatrical family dating back to the eighteenth century. His mother Georgie Drew was the daughter of an Irish actor of pre-Civil War days, and her mother was Louisa Lane, the daughter of Thomas Frederick Lane, English actor. Thus there was handed down to John, as well as to all the Barrymores and to all the Drews, a stage inheritance and family tradition that showed in their acting hereditary traits of genius.

John Barrymore made his stage debut in 1903 in "Magda" which soon brought him engagements on Broadway and in London with William Collier in "The Dictator." Other early successes were in "Are You a Mason?" and "Half a Husband," both comedy roles. In 1916 he successfully essayed serious parts, the critics declaring that his portrayal of Falder in Galworthy's "Justice" was both "artistic and self-effacing." Du Maurier's "Peter Ibbetson," Shakespeare's "Richard III" and "Hamlet" soon followed.

He appeared on Broadway as Hamlet 101 times, breaking the record of Edwin Booth. However, Barrymore's portrayal of the Melancholy Dane, while it evoked great praise even in London, did not approach the intellectual diction and mature acting genius of Booth, America's greatest tragedian in the part.

In Benelli's "The Jest" it seemed to his audiences that John Barrymore had almost reached the height of his acting career. From this superb characterization, the peak of his triumph on the legitimate stage, to the ribald buffooneries of some of Barrymore's last continuity on the radio, he truly fell from the sublime to the ridiculous, a painful episode to his numerous followers and admirers.

John and his equally famous brother, Lionel, were cast together in the films "Arsène Lupin," "Grand Hotel" and "Dinner at Eight," all outstanding dual triumphs for the brothers. In "Rasputin," their famous sister, Ethel, was also in the cast.

His escapades inspired the plays "The Royal Family" and "My Dear Children," both a real delight to large audiences of playgoers.

As to John Barrymore's career on and off the stage, this youngest member of the royal family of the theater became not only one of the greatest male stars, but he earned to the very last the reputation of being one of the most whimsical personalities in the long family tree, quite in line with the Barrymore tradition.

John Barrymore married four times, each venture ending unsuccessfully. His first wife was Katherine Harris; his second, Mrs. Leonard M. Thomas, the former Blanche Oelrichs, who wrote under the name Michael Strange; the third, Dolores Costello, screen star; and the fourth a stage-struck girl who had written him a fan letter, Elaine Jacobs, who changed her name to Elaine Barrie "because it was like Barrymore."

His obits in five and six columns of the *New York Times* and *New York Herald Tribune* of May 30th, 1942, contain numerous criticisms and incidents in his many-sided career. Also a quite complete list of his many successful plays and films.

No doubt entire volumes already have or will in time be devoted to this unique and great American stage personality. The simple mission here is to include him as one of the greatest in our "Roll of Honor" for his 40 years of service in plays and films, leaving it to others more ably to chronicle in full for posterity John Barrymore's theatrical genius and achievements.

LIONEL BARRYMORE

Famous American stage and film actor, 50 years in show business and still going strong (in 1943). Following is an excerpt from an article by Edward Lawrence:

"During an interview with Mr. Barrymore, a casual mention of Ethel and John Barrymore mellowed his voice and he caressed the names like a benediction. The three Barrymores were the sons and daughters of Maurice Barrymore and Georgiana Drew Barrymore. None of them cared a hoot for acting, Lionel and

John with ambitions to be artists, and Ethel a concert pianist. Twice Lionel fought bitterly against the theatre as a career, but eventually he was forced into the theatre.

"Mr. Barrymore talks fondly of himself as a youngster watching his godmother, Helena Modjeska, do scenes with his father; performances of his uncle John Drew and his grandmother's 'Mrs. Malaprop,' and Joseph Jefferson, who he says 'was damned good at anything he played.' . . .

"To adequately cover Lionel Barrymore's 50 years as an actor would require a book. His first bona fide professional appearance took place on Christmas night 1893 in 'The Rivals.' He was 15 and that year his mother died.

"Of the rest Mr. Barrymore had little to say. Everybody knew, he insisted, about 'Peter Ibbetson,' 'The Jest' and 'The Copperhead.' He intends to make pictures as long as he is wanted.

"He was waiting (at the time of the interview) for Director Victor Fleming to discuss a role in MGM's 'A Guy Named Joe,' with Spencer Tracy and Irene Dunne. It was something to tide him over between his numerous 'Dr. Gillespie' films."

BLANCHE BATES (69)

Noted actress, nearly 40 years on stage. In the Belasco days she was one of the leading stars on the American stage. Her first appearance was in the city in which she died, San Francisco. It was just a small part in a local production.

It was in such starring roles as "The Girl of the Golden West," "Madame Butterfly" (Cho-Cho-San), Belasco's "Darling of the Gods" (Yo-San), "Under Two Flags" (Cigarette), that this fine actress made the hits of her career in the early 90's. The parts she created not only were the result of painstaking study and serious hard work, but they contributed much to the general success and long runs of the plays, and won for her general acclaim in all the principal theaters of the United States. She was the wife of George Creel.

ALICE BELMORE (73)

Leading actress of the English and American stage; had a stage career of 40 years. Mrs. Alice Belmore Cliffe supported such sterling English actors as Sir Henry Irving, Sir Charles Wyndham and Wilson Barrett. She appeared with the latter in "Claudian."

When Mr. Barrett's English Company came to America, at the turn of the century, she played important roles in several English successes. In "Sir Anthony" by Haddon Chambers, she achieved her first American success.

Other appearances here were in "Androcles and the Lion," "Hay Fever," "Paddy the Next Best Thing," "Michael and Mary," "Windows," and recently in Katharine Cornell's revival of "Doctor's Dilemma" and Chekhov's "Three Sisters."

Alice Belmore entered the profession when still a very young girl.

LAURA BENNETT (79)

Veteran actress. Widow of John A. Shields (minstrel known as Harry Woodson). Appeared in revival of "The Black Crook" in the 70's. Supported Lillian Russell at Tony Pastor's Theatre. Appeared in "Social Whirl," "Song and Dance Man," "Seven Keys to Baldpate." She was 60 years on the stage.

J. HARRY BENRIMO (67)

Playwright and actor, connected with plays and the theater for 35 years. He wrote one of the classics of the American theater, "The Yellow Jacket," in collaboration with Geo. C. Hazleton, Jr. The original production in 1912 was followed by frequent revivals, and productions in England and other countries invariably met with a warm reception.

Another successful play which Mr. Benrimo wrote with Harrison Rhodes was brought to the stage in 1917. In stock at the old Alcazar in San Francisco, the city of his birth, and in other stock companies, Benrimo played every male part in "Hamlet," except the star part, and every male role in "Romeo and Juliet."

After his debut in London and New York in the Chinese play gem "The First Born," Benrimo joined the Charles Frohman Stock Company, and for many years he was a distinctive figure in the history of the American theater.

The list of his engagements is a long one. He supported such celebrated stars as Modjeska, James O'Neill, Odette Tyler, Mrs. Leslie Carter, Rose Stahl, Henry Miller. He appeared in the Belasco days in "Darling of the Gods," "Girl of the Golden West" and "Rose of the Rancho."

Always a bon vivant and immaculate in his appearance and attire, he was a colorful figure. Meeting with him on occasions, as I did, one could not but be impressed with his showmanship and keen knowledge of the glory of the theater of other days.

VALERIE BERGERE (71)

Played in musical comedy stock, vaudeville, screen and stage productions for 43 years.

ANNIE MACK BERLEIN (85)

Actress. With Edwin Booth in "Hamlet" and "Romeo and Juliet." Supported Joseph Jefferson. Supported Ellen Terry, John Barrymore and Lotta. On stage 40 years.

BEN BERNIE (52)

Stage, Radio, Screen Entertainer, and Dance Orchestra Director. His moniker of the "Old Maestro" was as well known as his own name. It will always be remembered by millions of his radio fans and an army of his close friends from coast to coast, during a career of over 35 years in show business, vaudeville, on the screen and over radio, which made him one of America's highest paid entertainers. His trademark, "Bernie and all the lads" and his sign-off, "Au revoir, a fond cheerio, a bit of toodle-oo, God bless you and pleasant dreams," will likewise live in the memory of hosts of his admirers who were entertained by his programs over the air.

After his recent passing, Charlie Mack said near the finish of a tribute to Ben: "What a guy!" Abel Green, the well-known editor of *Variety*, headed a paragraph of his personal obit with the simple but very expressive and all-embracing words, "A nice guy."

Jack Pulaski, an authority on sports and who ought to know, said: "Ben went for plenty at the dice table and at the track, but his bridge was on a par with tournament players." My own guess is that the sport of kings gave Ben the best thrills of his life, as an outlet for his sporty and plenty emotional nature. As one of the kings of show business, he had every right to indulge himself, knowing as he did that he could afford it and still be helpful and generous to many of the profession, who were down on their luck.

Georgie Jessel's closing lines, at the Coast's farewell to Bernie, have been called a tender tribute "from one minstrel to another." What the profession really thought of Bernie is recorded in Danton Walker's column. He was told by Bernie's stage partner, Phil Baker, that "Ben was one actor whom other actors liked. I couldn't pay him a higher tribute."

To the almost unprecedented sentiment displayed by those who knew him well, I add my humble bit, keeping it in the mood of Broadway that Bernie loved. The expressions used in tribute to him—"a nice guy," "a grand guy," "what a guy" fit the colorful personality of the "Maestro" perfectly. It is my great privilege to add from many years of personal experience that "Ben Bernie was above all a regular guy."

He is survived by his widow, Dorothy; a son, Private Jason, and a brother, Herman, who was his manager.

GEORGE L. BICKEL (78)

Veteran stage and film comic, more than 50 years on the stage. Began his career as a circus clown. In the 90's he formed the comedy team of Bickel and Watson, later Bickel, Watson and Wrothe. They were in the early Ziegfeld "Follies" and White's "Scandals." He was a versatile comedian, having played black-face, Irish comedy and Dutch comic.

He was also a clown with the old Sells and Forepaugh circus and with the Donaldson and Gregory circus in the 90's.

He starred in "Me, Him and I" for three years, and later made comedies for the Edison and Fox Film Companies.

JULES BLEDSOE (44)

Noted Negro baritone and composer, Bachelor of Music, concert singer over 25 years. He was connected with several opera companies and about ten years ago he appeared in his famous role of Emperor Jones in New York City.

Bledsoe had sung this role some time previously in Amsterdam, Rotterdam and The Hague with marked success. He sang Amonasro in "Aïda" and was heard also in other well-known operas, and in many recitals in American concert halls, as well as on radio from coast to coast.

The high spot of his career was his long engagement with "Show Boat," in which his wonderful rendition of "Ol' Man River" with his trained and powerful baritone voice never failed to win for him the enthusiastic applause of his audience.

Charlie Winninger, who played Capt'n Andy in the same show, declared that "Mr. Bledsoe was one of the really great artists of the Negro race."

Bledsoe played the piano and could sing in five or six different languages.

One of his favorite songs was "The Kaddish of my Ancestry," in which this talented Negro artist had studied with great care not only the English words and the melody but also the perfect pronunciation and intonation of excerpts of the ancient Hebrew prayer that run through the song.

Mr. Bledsoe's own compositions included "Does Ah Love You" and a song dedicated to President Roosevelt.

WM. BOAG (72)

Veteran actor-manager; 25 years with David Warfield and 30 years stage manager with David Belasco.

JESSIE BOND (89)

Pioneer Savoyard, on the stage nearly 40 years. She was the last but one of the first Gilbert and Sullivan Company, the only surviving member of that historical English group being Durward Lely of Glasgow.

Miss Bond appeared as a child pianist when she was eight. In 1862 she appeared as a vocalist first at St. George's Hall, Liverpool, later at St. James Hall and Crystal Palace, London.

She studied under Manuel Garcia and made her stage debut as Hebe in the first production "H.M.S. Pinafore" at the Opera Comique Theatre on May 25th, 1878. In the United States, Miss Bond played the same part at the Fifth Avenue Theatre in 1879, also Edith in "Pirates of Penzance."

Among the many subsequent roles played by Miss Bond during her years with the Savoy Company, were "Iolanthe," Melissa in "Princess Ida," Constance in "The Sorcerer," Pitti-Sing in "Mikado," Mad Margaret in "Ruddigore," Phoebe Meryll in "Yeoman of the Guard," Tessa in "The Gondoliers," Chinna Loofah in "Nautch Girl."

She also appeared in several Gilbert and Sullivan revivals and left the stage when she was 46 to marry Lewis Ransome after he had patiently waited for twelve years.

JAMES M. BRADFORD (89)

Actor. Associated with Edwin Booth, Lawrence Barrett, John McCullough. Served with Union forces during Civil War. In theater 50 years.

ALICE BRADY (46)

Actress, over 30 years in the theater. One of the loveliest and most versatile of our American actresses. Her father, the well-known manager and theater veteran, Wm. A. Brady, co-starred her with her stepmother, Grace George.

Alice Brady played in 32 silent movies and in sound; she won the Motion Picture Academy reward in 1938 for her fine performance of Mrs. O'Leary in "Old Chicago."

Whether in gay and infectious comedy, which seemed her forte, or in dramatic parts like O'Neill's "Mourning Becomes Electra," she was equally at home.

She started her career as Marie Rose in memory of her mother, a singer and dancer, Rose Marie Denee.

JOHN P. BRAWN

Stage, screen and radio actor, more than 50 years before the public. Beginning as a boy whistler in Niblo's Garden, Mr. Brawn graduated to Charlie Hoyt's "Trip to Chinatown" Company. Old-timers will remember the whistling waiter, in that very amusing and successful comedy. Mr. Brawn played the part, and scored a real hit in it, for five seasons.

Later he went to England and in the London production of George Ade's "The College Widow," he proved to be a valuable comedy adjunct to the cast.

Turning to motion pictures, his "Dream of a Rarebit Fiend" was a highly entertaining bit of trick photography, and it has earned a permanent place in the historical collection of the New York Museum of Modern Art.

EDMUND BREESE (64)

Actor. Played Shylock to Mme. Rhea's Portia. Supported James O'Neill in "Monte Cristo." Also Otis Skinner and Ada Rehan in "Taming of the Shrew." On stage 40 years.

JOSEPH D. BRENNEN (81)

Noted character actor, more than four decades on the stage. Theater audiences from coast to coast had hissed him in Otis Skinner's production of "Uncle Tom's Cabin" when he portrayed Simon Legree. Hisses to him, however, meant merely the applause of an audience, for his well-acted characterization of the villain in Harriet Beecher Stowe's immortal masterpiece.

Mr. Brennen became widely known in later years by linking himself with the productions of leading managers David Belasco, David Warfield, William Gillette, and other outstanding notables of the theater. He was with Warfield in "The Return of Peter Grimm."

His father had been a police inspector and comptroller of New York, where the actor was born. While sheriff, the father in 1871 had served the warrant for the arrest of "Boss" Tweed in the cleanup of the Tammany graft ring.

Mr. Brennen began his stage career in 1886 and appeared as recently as 1930, nearly 50 years after his first performance.

CHARLES BURNHAM (85)

Veteran manager. Staged the first American production of "The Mikado." Almost 60 years' activity in theatricals.

Mr. Burnham started as an usher in Daly's Little Theatre in 24th Street, New York City. Later at the famous Daly's Theatre on Broadway, Mr. Burnham was promoted to the box office. He toured the company with the Daly troupe on its fall and spring tours. He managed successively Bijou Heron, Pike's Opera House, Cincinnati, John D. Stetson's Theatre and the J. K. Emmet (Fritz) Company.

After a term as treasurer of the Standard Theatre, New York, he became manager of Wallack's second theater, 30th Street and Broadway, where he was interested in such successes as "The Squaw Man," "The County Chairman" and "Alias Jimmy Valentine."

MRS. PATRICK CAMPBELL (75)

Famous actress, with a stage career of 50 years. Six packed columns in *Who's Who of the Theatre* are required merely to list her performances in America and Great Britain. She was an actress of great talent, who worked as hard and as often as any great figure of her time.

Like many great artists, Mrs. Campbell was very temperamental, and her manager, George Tyler, seemed to enjoy these spells, for he said of her, "You laughed instead of trying to strangle her." Her whims and wit brought her many columns of newspaper notice. One episode related to her lighting a cigarette at the Plaza Hotel. She was asked by a shocked management to put it out, because in 1907 ladies did not smoke in public and the hotel catered especially to ladies.

In 1902 she insisted that 42nd Street in front of the Republic Theatre be spread with tanbark, because she had complained that the noise outside was spoiling her performance in "Magda." She also gained a great deal of publicity by winning $22,000 in one afternoon at a women's bridge party.

She was married to Patrick Campbell and when he died, she took to the stage, more from financial necessity than by choice of a career. She joined a dramatic club in 1886 and soon was engaged by Ben Greet touring with that and other theatrical companies mostly in Shakespearean roles.

Her London engagements soon brought her the smashing success in the title role of Pinero's "The Second Mrs. Tanqueray" in 1893. Later she played with Beerbohm Tree in "John O' Dreams" and with John Hare in "The Notorious Mrs. Ebbsmith." She played Juliet opposite Forbes-Robertson and then came her American engagement in 1901, under the management of Liebler & Co. After another American tour, she returned to England and joined Sarah Bernhardt in a performance of "Pelleas and Melisande."

In 1922 she published *My Life and Some Letters*, including some written by George Bernard Shaw when she was ill. The letters were a sensation.

She always played Shaw's "Pygmalion" with a last line "happy ending," which she had herself written, although he never agreed to it.

In 1914 she became the wife of George Cornwallis West.

Mrs. Campbell made several motion pictures, and her last visit to the United States was in 1938.

JAMES CAREW (62)

Veteran actor (England and America). Married Ellen Terry. Appeared with her in many successes. 40 years in the theater.

RICHARD CARLE (69)

Veteran character actor and comedian, about 50 years on the stage. Richard Carle was a versatile, clever entertainer. Ever since the 90's he appeared as a monologist, a song-and-dance man, a musical comedy comedian and singer, a writer of songs and theatrical sketches and a film actor.

Thousands who visited the theaters in the old days enjoyed his comic songs or stage antics in such vehicles as "The Country Sport," "Lady Slavey," "Excelsior Jr.," "Round of Pleasure," "Mam'selle Awkins." Perhaps they saw him in musical plays to which he contributed a part of the lyrics and libretto as for instance, "The Tenderfoot," "The Storks," "The Mayor of Tokyo" and "Spring Chicken," the latter his greatest success. His best-known songs were "I Picked a Lemon in the Garden of Love," "I Fell in Love with Polly" and "Peculiar Julia."

He appeared in shows with such prominent players as Edna May and Marie Cahill and in films with Marlene Dietrich, Claudette Colbert and many others.

MRS. LESLIE CARTER (75)

Famous actress and star, born in Louisville, Ky. Appeared in "Ugly Duckling," "Heart of Maryland," "Za-Za," "Du Barry," "Andrea," etc., under David Belasco's management. 40 years on stage.

Under Mr. Belasco's tutelage, she played in Audran's musical comedy "Miss

Helyett," which ran for two years. In "The Heart of Maryland" she became even a greater popular favorite, as the piece scored a run of 145 performances. In "Za-Za," by Belasco, which Rejane played in Paris, Mrs. Carter was hailed by the American press as an outstanding actress and by some critics as the American Bernhardt. "Du Barry," also written by Belasco, was even more phenomenal in box-office receipts and she showed in this perhaps more talent as an emotional actress than in any other stage vehicle.

After a sensational break with Belasco the manager, who had seen in her many possibilities of undeveloped talent, she appeared under the management of Charles Dillingham and finally with her own company, but her popularity strangely waned and she gradually faded out of the Broadway limelight.

FEODOR CHALIAPIN (65)

Celebrated Russian basso. Famous as "Boris Godounoff," "Ivan the Terrible," "Mephistopheles," etc. Forty years on the stage.

BLANCHE CHAPMAN (90)

Celebrated actress, over 70 years in the theater. She came from a theatrical family, which traced its start back to 1733, four generations connected with theatricals.

Mrs. Blanche Chapman Ford was the widow of Henry Clay Ford, manager of Ford's Theatre, Washington, where Abraham Lincoln was assassinated. She made her debut as a child in "Mr. and Mrs. Peter White." Mrs. Ford fell heir to the armchair Lincoln was sitting in the fateful night he was shot.

Mrs. Ford had appeared with Edwin Booth, Edwin Forrest, Joseph Jefferson, Dion Boucicault and others. She had appeared in more than 100 light operas. As a singer she was the first actress to be seen in the role of Josephine in "H.M.S. Pinafore" when that operetta made its American debut.

ALEXANDER CLARK (66)

A very droll and versatile comedian. First appearance in "Pinafore." Supported Lillian Russell, Willie Collier, Fay Templeton, etc. On stage 40 years.

H. COOPER CLIFFE (76)

Veteran Shakespearean actor. Debut with D'Oyley Carte, 1879. Supported Henry Irving, Mrs. Fiske, Laurette Taylor, etc. Appeared on the stage 57 years.

E. E. CLIVE (60)

British actor, on the stage and in films about 40 years. Was a master of the various dialects of the British Isles. During Frohman's occupancy of his London Theatre, Clive appeared for a time under his management. Clive managed the Copley Theatre in Boston and also produced plays in Los Angeles.

His British characters in films stood out and are well-remembered in "Bull-dog Drummond," "Lloyds of London," "Night Must Fall," "Charlie Chan in London," "Captain Blood," "Cain and Mabel," and many others.

ROSE COGHLAN (Mrs. John T. Sullivan)

Veteran actress, 40 years on the stage. Her father was Francis Coghlan, a publisher of Continental guides, and a friend of Charles Dickens. Her brother was Charles Coghlan, the well-known actor. As a child she appeared as one of the witches in Macbeth. After engagements with Adelaide Neilson and J. L. Toole, E. A. Sothern brought her to America in 1871 when she appeared in Wilkie Collins' "Woman in White." She then played a season with Lydia Thompson's English Burlesque at Wallack's in 1873. Her important successes later in Shakespearean parts and in drama and comedy were Viola in "Twelfth Night," Queen in "Hamlet," "East Lynne," "Scrap of Paper," "Moths," "Silver King," "School for Scandal," "A Woman of No Importance," etc., etc.

GEO. M. COHAN (64)

Distinguished American song writer, manager, actor, producer and playwright; over 50 years in the theater.

I knew Geo. M. Cohan when! In my book of the 90's, *They All Sang* (From Tony Pastor to Rudy Vallee) it was my great privilege to devote several pages to pictures of George himself and of the Four Cohans and also to some personal anecdotes of our association in the 90's.

After Mr. Cohan's recent passing, long and exhaustive articles on this fine veteran actor appeared in the entire press of the country. These obits are so convincing and accessible to everybody that a brief review of a few of the highlights of Mr. Cohan's career is all that is necessary for me to give him his place high up in this Roll of Honor of the veterans of the theater and its allied amusements.

George M. Cohan was one of America's best-known theatrical figures. As a writer of many songs, star of many memorable stage productions, and as an all-round showman, his versatility and his prolific powers to write and produce seemed almost uncanny.

In the early days of his song-writing career, after he had written "I Guess I'll Have to Telegraph My Baby" and "Venus My Shining Star," I often met Georgie in front of his publishers, Spaulding & Gray. They were at 29 E. 20th St., while our publishing emporium (consisting then of a room and bedroom) was at No. 45 E. 20th, just down the street.

In those days George occasionally indulged in champagne suppers for breakfast. One morning George said, "Would you like to know, Ed, how I write my songs, or rather how I don't write them? I go to bed—while I am sound asleep, the spirit moves me—I get up, take pencil and paper in hand. The spirit moves me again, and I write and write, line after line, and presto soon my song is finished."

I never forgot those words or the Cohanesque manner in which he expressed himself many times to me, whether it was a cordial invitation to "bust in on a feller" or being backstage on a winter's night to join him in a hot toddy. I often wondered, when he seemed for a period to be getting ahead slowly the hard way, whether his friendly "moving spirit" had deserted him.

Then when he came into his own once again, he forged ahead with lightning speed until he reached the peak of his Broadway financial and professional success. I could not but think that this song-and-dance man, who could write the libretto, lyrics and melodies of scores of musical plays, play the star parts, select the cast, direct and produce the book, the songs and the dances of the play and manage his shows, was in his own right a superman. Otherwise the "moving spirit" to which he so seriously credited his success was certainly on the scene again, prompting and rewarding him for the many good deeds to "down-and-outers" that George M. Cohan was said to have performed.

After his passing, as already mentioned, the dailies all over the United States carried full pages or columns of George M. Cohan's tremendously active life. At this time, therefore, most of the theatergoers and of the public interested are familiar with the details of his eventful career. For those who may have missed the newspaper accounts of his passing, I feel that I should briefly review a few high spots in the life of the most colorful figure in his line of work that the American theater ever knew or perhaps will ever see again.

The old-time variety act of the Four Cohans—Jerry, his father; Helen, his mother; Josephine, his sister; and Georgie himself—was a sensation in the early 90's and deservedly so. As a character, singing and dancing top-line act, they were unexcelled and in a class by themselves, the nearest approach being possibly the Four Mortons of the same period. The Morton Family also were headliners, fine dancers and clever exponents of the comedy characters of the Emerald Isle.

The Four Cohans toured the country for a number of years, appeared at Tony Pastor's, where I saw them often, and in 1893 were booked as the big attraction at Keith's old Union Square Theatre. During his variety and vaudeville days Cohan had written for others and for the family use over 150 skits. For the Four Cohans, George wrote the very successful sketches "The Governor's Son" and "Running for Office." Both of these were extended into a full evening's performance as musical plays.

George followed with "Little Johnny Jones," a solid hit on the legitimate stage, which ran for several years. By this time he was a full-fledged and talented song writer as his numbers in "Little Johnny Jones" proved. His tunes had a distinctive lilt and he insisted on speed in connection with them, so they never dragged during a performance, and the public carried them away through their catchy appeal. One song success followed after another. The long list includes such favorites as "Give My Regards to Broadway," "So Long, Mary," "Always Leave Them Laughing When You Say Goodbye," "Mary Is a Grand Old Name," "I'm a Yankee Doodle Dandy," "You're a Grand Old Flag," "Then I'd Be Satisfied with Life," "Popularity," "When We Are Married" and finally his immortal war tune "Over There."

In the early part of the century, Cohan began his unparalleled career with his partner, Sam Harris (Cohan and Harris). These managers produced a long series of successful plays including "Broadway Jones," "Get-Rich-Quick Wallingford," "Seven Keys to Baldpate," "The Yankee Prince," "Little Johnny Jones," "The Song and Dance Man," "Little Millionaire," "The Tavern," "The Merry Malones," "The American Idea," "Tailor-Made Man," "Geo. Washington Jr.," "Officer 666" and many others.

At the Knickerbocker bar after the first performance of the "Officer 666" show, George said to me, "What do you think, Ed? When I wrote it, I thought it was a cock-eyed melodrama. As you saw tonight, it turned out to be a big laughing comedy hit. Sam didn't want any part of it after the rehearsals, so I bought out his end."

Many years ago at an Actors Fund Fair, a unique satin quilt was raffled off. It was won by a fellow Friar and close friend of George's. It was the vogue in those days to present printed satin programs in various colors to each lady in the audience on the 100th performance of a successful play. The quilt consisted of a great variety of these satin programs sewed together and shaped into a bed quilt. The four tassels, one at each corner, were taken from the first horses used in Barnum's Circus.

George M. Cohan was a great admirer of his friend's prize quilt, because of its quaintness, and the rarity of the old satin theater programs used in such profusion. On the occasion of George's birthday on the 4th of July, a dinner was tendered to him by a number of his friends and the owner of the prized quilt presented it to Cohan.

Another Friar in a very warm speech made the presentation, touching on the great genius shown by George M. Cohan in the theater. Among other things, he pronounced him "the greatest producer in the world." At this, the original owner of the quilt broke in with, "You're wrong! The greatest producer in the world is Jerry Cohan—father and producer of George M."

In 1937 Cohan showed his versatility as an actor, by a very creditable impersonation of President Roosevelt in the Sam Harris production "I'd Rather Be Right." When Cohan was given the gold Congressional Medal of Honor in recognition of his great patriotic song, "Over There," President Roosevelt, who made the presentation, greeted him with a handshake and referring to his impersonation remarked, "Well, how's my double?"

In the Theatre Guild show, Eugene O'Neill's "Ah, Wilderness," Cohan played for the long run of this play an important character part which proved one of the major successes of his career.

Cohan's first marriage was to Ethel Levey, a prominent performer of the 90's and still living. Their daughter, Georgette Cohan, also survives. Later he married Agnes Nolan, and the result of that union was two daughters, Mary and Helen, and a son, George M. Cohan, Jr.

This master showman, who reached the peak of his popularity the hard way, after many bitter battles and disappointments, this writer of both words and music of many song hits that stirred human hearts, this playwright, producer and manager of many plays, passed away November 5, 1942. His demise little more than a year after the death of his business associate, Sam H. Harris, dropped the curtain on one of the most famous managerial duos in the history of American theatricals.

NANETTE COMSTOCK (68)

Actress, in the theater about 35 years. Miss Comstock appeared in many favorite comedies in the later 80's, including "Charley's Aunt," "Bootle's Baby" and Hoyt's "Hole in the Ground." About the same period she essayed parts in the well-known dramas "Mavourneen" and "Shenandoah."

In the late 90's she toured with Otis Skinner in "The Liars" and several other plays in his repertoire. She also appeared with such outstanding public favorites as Wilton Lackaye and John Mason. Important engagements in her career were with the productions "Lion and the Mouse," "Lover's Lane," "The Diplomat," "The Virginian," "The Altar of Friendship," "Caught in the Rain" and "The Crisis."

She was an Albany girl, and a stage favorite in England as well as in her own country, having appeared in London on three trips over.

CHARLES EMERSON COOK (71)

Critic, press agent, writer and librettist, 50 years connected with theatricals. Was for many years an associate and aide to the late David Belasco. He worked his way through Harvard by writing reviews and interviews for the *Boston Herald*. After 15 years with Belasco, Mr. Cook started on his own as a stage director and producer. His best work was "Red Feather," a Ziegfeld Production, in which Grace Von Studdiford starred. The musical score throughout, one of the most musicianly and melodic in many years, was composed by Reginald De Koven. Inspired by this score, Charles Emerson Cook, wedded to it in lyrical form one gem after the other, matching the many varied and rare tempos including madrigals with perfect meters. These lyrics were issued later by public request in separate and artistic form.

Mr. Cook was general press agent and business manager for H. H. Frazee for a period of years during which "No! No! Nanette" and other successes ran under the Frazee banner. For nine years Mr. Cook managed summer stock at Martha's Vineyard. He was a founder of the Friars Club.

JOE COOK (52)

Comedian, retired from the stage after 35 years. A madcap comedian, amazingly versatile, and one who entertained millions with his ever-changing acts of fun in every phase of the show world.

He was born in Evansville, Ind., in 1890 and crashed the New York stage when about 17 with a combination of pure nerve and comedy.

His rise in vaudeville for 15 years was rapid and continuous. Musical comedy managers, among them Raymond Hitchcock and Earl Carroll, soon hired him for the legitimate, and his appearances in "Hitchy Koo," "Vanities," "Fine and Dandy," "Hold Your Horses" and "Rain or Shine" were a succession of successes through the years. One of his great laughing skits was "The Saga of the Four Hawaiians."

A son, Joe Cook, Jr., promises to carry on the stage traditions of his father, as an eccentric bicyclist, comedian and dancer.

MADGE CARR COOK (77)

Actress. Mother of Eleanor Robson. Created title part in "Mrs. Wiggs of the Cabbage Patch." On stage 50 years.

T. C. COOKE (64)

Shakespearean player, manager and producer, on stage 44 years. Thomas Coffin Cooke made his debut in Louisville, Ky., in 1895 in "Young Mrs. Winthrop." His first Broadway appearance was as Quince in "Midsummer Night's Dream" in 1906. It was also Annie Russell's first appearance in a Shakespearean role.

Mr. Cooke was associated for 25 years with Wagenhals and Kemper; for a long period as their stage manager. He supported such stars as Louis James, Frederick Warde, Helena Modjeska and Kathryn Kidder. He played with Laurette Taylor, Wm. Hodge, and was with the all-star cast in "She Stoops to Conquer." He also directed stock for five years. In Shakespearean roles he played Osric in "Hamlet," Ross in "Macbeth," and Camillo in "The Winter's Tale." He also appeared for three years as Joe Brooks in "Paid in Full."

Mr. Cooke had done considerable radio work with "The Goldbergs" and "Easy Aces" program and had made radio appearances with Helen Menken.

FRAZER COULTER (88)

Actor. Appeared in "The School for Scandal." Also supported Lawrence Barrett, Fanny Davenport, William Crane, Richard Mansfield. Connected with the stage 40 years.

LAURA HOPE CREWS (62)

Veteran stage and screen comedienne, 58 years in theater and films. A back stage baby, she made her debut in San Francisco when only four years old in "Bootle's Baby." Two years later she toured in "Editha's Burglar." Her salary was $7.50 per week.

In 1901 she made her New York debut and starred in such productions as "The Great Divide" and "Mr. Pim Passes." Later she became leading lady for the outstanding actor of the time, Henry Miller.

Miss Crews could handle any type of part and she was recognized not only as a versatile character actress of skill and charm, but she distinguished herself also as an accomplished comedienne. Shortly before her passing, illness compelled her to give up a leading part in "Arsenic and Old Lace." In the Pulitzer Prize play by Sidney Howard, entitled "The Silver Cord," she played the serious role of the Selfish Mother. Later she was selected for the screen version of the same play.

She had successfully portrayed many roles in old-time stock companies: Alcazar Stock Company, San Francisco (1898), H. V. Donnelly Stock Company, New York (1900). With the latter she made a hit in "The Girl I Left Behind Me." Among other successful parts we recall her appearances in "What Happened to Jones," "Ranson's Folly," "Merely Mary Ann," "Peter Ibbetson" and many others. She was best remembered by her movie audiences as Aunt Pity-Pat in "Gone With the Wind," and in "The Man Who Came to Dinner."

EDWARD HAROLD CROSBY (75)

Dramatic critic and author. Author of "Catspaw," "Hour of Reckoning," "The Taking of Helen," etc. Critic of *Boston Post* for 44 years.

FRANK CRUMIT (54)

Musical comedy, radio and phonograph artist, singing and entertaining over 30 years. With a repertoire of many thousands of songs, it is little wonder that Frank Crumit was a universal favorite with the masses and with all his associates. He was chosen Shepherd of the Lambs at their club in 1935.

About 30 years ago he entered vaudeville. His act depended upon his breezy personality and informal talk over the footlights and also his singing voice to his own accompaniment on the ukulele. He was always careful to have a good selection of songs, some of them his own compositions.

In the early days of the phonograph industry, the field was a specialized one in which an old-time coterie of phonograph artists prevailed. When the change of policy came many years later and the recording companies selected certain vaudeville stars, Frank Crumit eventually got in his inning with a home-run hit, "The Gay Caballero," which is said to have topped two million records. Those were the days when other famous vaudevillians like Nora Bayes made the ecords of "Shine On, Harvest Moon" and Eddie Leonard "Ida, Sweet As Apple Cider." Several of Crumit's records were right up in sales with the leaders.

Frank Crumit made his appearance in 1918 in "Betty Be Good" and later n the "Greenwich Village Follies," "No, No, Nanette," "Queen High" and other musical comedies. In several of these Miss Julia Sanderson was an imporant member of the cast. In 1927 the couple were married. One year later Mr. Crumit and Miss Sanderson embarked on a highly successful radio career. rom the start, each broadcasting program brought them increasing popularity, or thousands of listeners enjoyed more and more the good-natured personality f Mr. Crumit and the tinkling laugh and ever-pleasing quality of Miss Sanderon's voice.

Together for 16 years, they formed an ideal combination in "The Battle of he Sexes" and other broadcasts, until Mr. Crumit's death broke the partnerip and took to another world one of the two aptly-termed "Sweethearts of e Air."

CHARLES DALTON (77)

Veteran actor, on stage 57 years. Played many classic and modern roles in oth England and America. Died at his home in Stamford, Conn., in June, 1942

Charles Dalton was an Englishman by birth, and first studied singing with s uncle Edwin Holland, a well-known singer.

While witnessing a performance of Edwin Booth, the theatrical fire entered s veins, and inspired by the great actor, his ambition turned to the stage. His but occurred in 1883 on a tour with Alice Lingard, known in America as lice Dunning. Dalton's London debut was in my English friend, Clement ott's "Sister Mary." The same writer was also the author of "Oh, Promise e," for which famous song Reginald De Koven wrote the melody.

Dalton's first appearance on the American stage was in "The Prodigal aughter" in 1893. Returning to London, he played an entire season with rbes-Robertson in François Coppee's "For the Crown." He also supported ga Nethersole as Don José in "Carmen."

In 1896 Dalton visited America again to play for a solid five years. He played ince Dimitri in "Resurrection" and Brandon in "When Knighthood Was in ower." In 1904 he was leading man with Nance O'Neil, appearing with her "Macbeth," and in 1907 he joined James O'Neill's Company.

His memorable roles include parts in "Mid-Channel," 1910; "Trelawny of e Wells," 1911; "Case of Becky," 1911; "Kismet," 1914. He also appeared th Ethel Barrymore in "Drifted Apart" and toured as Taffy in "Trilby" th Phyllis Neilson-Terry.

In 1916 he played Duke of Buckingham in "Henry VIII" with Sir Herbert erbohm Tree. In 1919-1920 he was old Bill in "The Better Ole"; in 1921 iggs in "Three Live Ghosts"; in 1921, Antonon in "A Hundred Years Old"; nathan Wild in "Children of Darkness."

At various times he had also appeared with Forbes-Robertson, Blanche Walsh d Maxine Elliott. Also with Helen Hayes in "Mary of Scotland"; with tharine Cornell as Capulet in "Romeo and Juliet." His last engagement s with Maurice Evans' revival of "Richard II" in 1940, having previously peared with Mr. Evans in "Henry IV" and "Romeo and Juliet."

WILLIAM DANFORTH (73)

Actor and comedian, on the stage over 60 years. Made his stage debut as Dick Deadeye in Gilbert and Sullivan's "Pinafore" 62 years ago when a lad of 11. The older theatergoers who remember him in a round of Gilbert and Sullivan works including "Mikado," "Ruddigore," "Pirates of Penzance" and other Gilbertian gems, will miss one of the most famous comedians of light opera of all time.

William Danforth also appeared in Reginald De Koven's great American opera "Robin Hood" being at the time a member of the Bostonians, together with De Wolf Hopper.

He appeared in more than 100 productions, in America and in London. "Wang," "Idol's Eye," "Bluebeard," "Yankee Consul," "Girl from Montmartre," "Adele," "Floradora" are but a few out of many in which his notable character delineations helped to make theatrical history.

In "Pinafore" he played at one time or another almost all the male characters and one female character, including Dick Deadeye, Captain Corcoran, Sir Joseph Porter, and Little Buttercup.

At 15, he sang the bass part in "Fatinitza" with the Boston Juvenile Opera Co. He was closely associated with another favorite American comedian, Frank Daniels, in such successes as "Ameer," "Half a King," Monks of Malabar," "Wizard of the Nile," "Miss Simplicity," "Miss Hook of Holland."

He further played an important role in De Koven's important opera "Happyland" in which De Wolf Hopper starred. It was in the Gilbert and Sullivan shows, however, that the unique talents and unctuous humor shone, especially in "The Mikado," which he is said to have performed more times than anyone else in the world.

He gave 5,000 Gilbert and Sullivan performances and knew his roles so well that he needed no rehearsals. He was almost as well-known in his perfect type "father" and "king" roles as in Gilbert and Sullivan characters. His "comic heavy" brigand and "pirate" chief delineations were likewise outstanding.

JEFFERSON D'ANGELIS (74)

Comic opera comedian. In "Variety" theaters in 1874. Later principa comedian New York Casino Co. and one of the three foremost comic opera comedians, De Wolf Hopper, Digby Bell and D'Angelis. Was with Lillian Russell and Della Fox. 60 years on the stage.

MRS. WM. DAVENE (81)

Circus acrobat, queen of the big top, over 50 years in circus and theater Mrs. Davene traveled with her parents, also circus acrobats, and made her firs appearance when only 7 years old, touring Europe in circus and vaudeville She spent 4 years with the Rentz circus, and then performed with other unit throughout South America. While with the Robbins circus, she met Bill Davene, English aerialist. Under their billing Mlle. Lotta and Billy Davene (her husband) they gave a request show to President Harrison and were presented to Queen Victoria and the Sultan of Turkey.

ROBERT H. ("BOB") DAVIS (73)

Veteran editor, author, dramatist, reporter and photographer, connected with journalism, drama and photography about 50 years. Everybody's pal and friend (mine included) passed on, when Bob Davis, the roving reporter, made his earthly exit recently.

According to the *New York Tribune*, he had covered more than 300,000 miles on his job. His column "Bob Davis Recalls" appeared in the *New York Sun* for years and Davis built up a lasting reputation as the editor of *Munsey's Magazine* and others.

His discovery of writing talent brought into the limelight of public favor such fine writers as O. Henry, Mary Roberts Rinehart, Fannie Hurst, Zane Grey, George Jean Nathan, Octavus Roy Cohen, Dorothy Canfield, Ben Ames Williams, Sophie Kerr, James Oliver Curwood, and a host of others.

Bob Davis was a singularly sympathetic and encouraging man, and he took great pains, even at the very first interview, to give you his confidence and his friendship and he made you feel welcome and at home in his presence. Even with chance acquaintances, he did not wait for their call. Instead he often, to cultivate a new friendship, would call first himself, if the occasion warranted, and this in spite of his tremendously busy editorial hours and duties.

Mr. Davis took surprisingly artistic photographs of many celebrities he interviewed at home and abroad, and of many persons among his large coterie of friends. These efforts met with so much distinction that an exhibition of his selected works was held at the American Art Galleries and attracted much public attention. A published collection of his portraits is titled *Man Makes His Own Mask*.

Mr. Davis not only introduced first the works of O. Henry and placed him under contract, but inspired and encouraged him in many ways.

The many books which Mr. Davis wrote included a biography of O. Henry, in collaboration with Arthur B. Maurice. Mr. Davis also wrote a number of plays. The Associated Press elected him an honorary life member of the organization.

He was born in Nebraska in 1869, a son of the Rev. George Ransome Davis and Silvia Nicholls Davis. In 1890 he married Madge Lee Hutchinson of New York, who usually accompanied him on his many trips to almost all the countries of the world.

CHARLES TURNER DAZEY (85)

Playwright. Wrote "Rusticana" and "In Old Kentucky." Connected with stage 40 years.

CLIFFORD DEMPSEY (73)

First appearance with Olga Nethersole, 1882. More than 59 years on stage.

HENRY E. DIXEY (84)

One of America's foremost stage stars in the 80's and 90's; a stage career covering 58 years. The recent death of Henry E. Dixey marks the passing of one of America's foremost stage personalities. From the age of nine, when he made his theatrical debut in a melodrama in Boston, until 1929, he played in almost every branch of the theater, appearing in comedy, drama, farce, comic opera and vaudeville.

In 1884 he took the title role in "Adonis," which played at the Bijou Theatre, where it had a run of 619 performances, the record up to that time. In 1886 he played the part at the Gaiety Theatre, London, his first European appearance. It was in this play, his greatest, that he gave his memorable imitation of Sir Henry Irving. After returning from London he toured the United States in "Adonis" until 1889, when he returned to the New York stage in "The Seven Ages" at the Standard Theatre.

Following his debut in Boston in "Under the Gaslight," he played seven parts in "Evangeline." In this he also played the forepart of a heifer, making it eight roles in all. Thenceforth his talents became recognized, and almost every season found him as a star in a Broadway production. Among his early plays were "The Corsair," "Hiawatha," "Horrors," "Robinson Crusoe," "Cinderella," "The Sorcerer" and "H.M.S. Pinafore."

Dixey was a strikingly handsome actor, an expert dancer, and he retained his dancing agility in his later years. In 1928, at 68, he took over the leading role in "The Merry Malones." His last Broadway stage appearance was in 1929 in "The Beaux' Stratagem."

During the Gay 90's there was a long-standing feud between Dixey and the late Wilton Lackaye. Each was a star in his own right, each was handsome, and there was no secret that jealousy was the cause of their frequent clashes.

In 1899 Dixey made what was considered his most noteworthy success since "Adonis" as David Garrick in Stuart Robson's "Oliver Goldsmith." In 1900 he played in "The Burgomaster" and in 1901 returned to the London stage in "The Whirl of the Town." He returned to New York in 1902 to appear in "A Modern Magdalen," and the next year toured in "Over a Welsh Rarebit" and "Facing the Music."

At the Empire Theatre here in 1904 he appeared in "Little Mary." Later in the same year he was seen in "The Art of Acting" and in 1905 he made a notable hit as Lieutenant Robert Warburton in "The Man on the Box" at the Madison Square Theatre. He later toured in that piece for some time.

He made a vaudeville tour in a sketch called "David Garrick" in 1907 and appeared the next year in New York as Papa Lebonard in the play of that name. In the same year he played the title role in "The Devil" and appeared in "Mary Jane's Pa." He toured in the latter show in 1909 and appeared in New York in 1910 as Mr. Buttles in the play of that name. In the same year he appeared also in "The Naked Truth" and in 1911 had a leading role in "Bought and Paid For." He next appeared in "Becky Sharp" with Mrs. Fiske at the Lyceum in New York, and a little later, also with her, in "Mrs. Bumpstead-Leigh." Then came his reappearance as Sir Joseph Porter in a "Pinafore" revival.

Dixey made a fortune in his profession, but his wealth was dissipated and for the last 10 years of his life he found the going hard. He went to Atlantic City 10 years ago and he lived there in a modest hotel.

Among other famous roles were Pierre Niklas in "Gypsy Love," Madison Atwood in "Room 44," Malvolio in "Twelfth Night," Long John Silver in "Treasure Island," O'Neill in "The Deluge," Ali Baba in "Chu Chin Chow," Brandon Sullivan in "The Outrageous Mrs. Palmer," Fag in "The Rivals," Sir Benjamin Backbite in "The School for Scandal," Diggory in "She Stoops to Conquer," and Picard in "The Two Orphans."

MALCOLM DOUGLAS (60)

Veteran actor, on stage 36 years. Malcolm Douglas in his time played many parts. In 1899 he made his debut in Richard Mansfield's "Cyrano de Bergerac" at the Hollis Street Theatre, Boston. He barnstormed with Mansfield's Company in "Beau Brummel," "Jekyll and Hyde," "Prince Karl," "Arms and the Man," "Henry V" and "Parisian Romance." In 1899 he made his New York debut also in "Cyrano de Bergerac." Under the Henry B. Harris management he played in "The Lion and the Mouse" and "The Talker."

When Mrs. Fiske starred in "Mrs. Bumpstead-Leigh," he played several parts in the original production. Then followed ten years of appearances, from 1912 to 1922 in "Information, Please," "The Pawn," "Discovering America," "The Fight," etc.

Among important roles he was cast in "This Thing Called Love," "Spread Eagle," "Young Blood" and other plays. His recent appearances were in "Cross Roads," "Dinner at Eight" and "Five Star Final." In the last two, his performances earned critical approval.

MAJOR DOYLE (70)

Midget and actor for 50 years. He was 3 feet 5 inches tall.

JOHN DREW (73)

Veteran actor and son of the famous American actor and actress, Mr. and Mrs. John Drew. Young Drew made his first appearance in 1873 at a benefit for his sister Georgiana. The best account of his lifework on the stage of over 40 years is told in his own memoirs *My Years on the Stage* published by Dutton. Excerpts from the foreword written by Booth Tarkington speak of him as follows:

"What he has played most congenially, and with the manliest humor of his time have been the roles of gentlemen. . . . Here was the nature of the man always present in his acting; and I think it has been because of that and because of his humor—his own distinctive humor—that he has charmed the best American public throughout so many fortunate years. John Drew has been an actual feature of the best American life ever since his youth—indeed he is one of its institutions; and there is a long gratitude due him."

VIRGINIA EARLE (62)

Actress and singer. Musical comedy star of the 90's in the United States and Australia. Debut at 12 in juvenile "Mikado." Nearly 50 years on stage.

ROBERT EDESON

Veteran actor and film artist; son of a well-known comedian, George R. Edeson. Played in "Incog." Edeson was with Charles Hoyt's Co. and the Empire Stock. With the latter he appeared in "The Masqueraders," "Under the Red Robe," "The Little Minister" and other successes. He starred in "Soldiers of Fortune," "Ranson's Folly" and "Strongheart." About 30 years on stage.

EFFIE ELLSLER (87)

Old-time actress, connected with the stage 65 years. Born of theatrical parents, Effie Ellsler was on the stage from childhood until she was about 80.

Her mother had played Portia to Edwin Booth's Shylock. She first played Little Eva in "Uncle Tom's Cabin," until her father, the well-known manager, John A. Ellsler, a partner of Joseph Jefferson, gave her selected parts with his stock company.

In 1880 she was a sensation in the title role of Steele Mackaye's "Hazel Kirke," at the Madison Square Theatre, which ran nearly 500 performances, a record at the time. Later Miss Ellsler joined the Union Square Theatre Company, appearing in Buchanan's "Storm Beaten" and Bartley Campbell's "Separation."

She toured the country several seasons in a great hit "Woman against Woman." Her other parts were in "Camille," "Woman of the Nile" and "Barbara Frietchie." She also played character parts in the pictures "The Whole Town's Talking" and "Daddy Longlegs." Effie Ellsler's husband, Frank Weston, was her leading man for many years.

EDWARD EMERY (77)

Of an old English theatrical family. Was with Wilson Barrett, Charles Hawtrey, and Sir Charles Wyndham. Supported Mrs. Fiske, Ethel Barrymore, Margaret Anglin. Father of Edward Emery, Jr. Nearly 50 years on stage.

WM. H. EVARTS (73)

Character actor, 52 years in the theater. Made his debut at 13 in the well-known thriller "The Octoroon," at the old Globe Theatre, Boston.

Evarts' comedy parts and character roles embraced more than 2,000 delineations during his career. Recently he presented dramatic sketches with his wife Ethel over the air.

BARNEY FAGAN (87)

Famous minstrel, song-and-dance man and song writer. Over 50 years in show business.

SYDNEY FAIRBROTHER (66)

Versatile actress, famous for Cockney roles, on stage 51 years. An English actress well known on the British stage, she came to this country with the Kendals in the 90's. She made her first appearance at the Haymarket Theatre, London, in 1889.

Miss Sydney Fairbrother appeared during her career in a score of plays including "David Copperfield" and "Tulip Time." Her manager, Sydney Carroll, wrote of her "with her quaint and whimsical personality, her gift for converting sheer oddity into fascination, epitomizes in her manner and mien all that is worth-while in Cockney fun and character. The grand comic spirit that used to be part and parcel of London life, but which seems to be rapidly disappearing, as the noise, smells and impatience of modern city existence increase, is hers still to command." Among the British pictures seen in New York in which Miss Fairbrother appeared were "Brewster's Millions," "Nell Gwyn" and "Chu Chin Chow."

WILLIAM FAVERSHAM (72)

Famous actor and greatest matinee idol of his day, 50 years on the stage. Mr. Faversham ran away from home to become an actor. *Who's Who in the Theatre* requires three columns to list all the parts he played. His first appearance was in "Swiss Cottage" in London in 1886. His last role was with "Lord and Lady Algy" in 1932. He was an outstanding success in everything. He essayed parts in "A Doll's House," "Hamlet" and plays by Shaw, but he always loved Shakespeare best. Headline writers once called him "the hero of a thousand matinees." He was the youngest of 11 sons and after meeting the famous English actress Marie De Dray, he determined to become an actor, and Carlotta Le Clerq, once a famous actress, taught him dramatic art.

Young Faversham once walked out of rehearsals after being engaged by Henry Irving because he felt that the part was not important enough. He acted "Leo" in Rider Haggard's "She," at old Niblo's Garden. Daniel Frohman placed him under contract and once lent him to Minnie Maddern.

He was in such successes as "Prince and the Pauper" and "All the Comforts of Home." The critics first warmed up to him when he took the role of the Titled Libertine in Bronson Howard's "Aristocracy." He was second to Henry Miller in "Masqueraders" and "Sowing the Wind." He became leading man of the famous Empire Stock Co. in 1896 and appeared in many popular roles. He scored a notable success in "Under the Red Robe" and the "Squaw Man." The latter ran for three seasons in New York and on the road.

He acted Romeo to the Juliet of Maude Adams. At one time he formed his own company and revived "Julius Caesar," "Othello" and "Romeo and Juliet." His last appearances on the stage after a period in films were in 1931 when he was with Fritz Leiber in dramas for the Chicago Shakespearean Company.

Miss Julie Opp, a charming and capable actress, supported Mr. Faversham in Shakespearean repertoire and later became his wife.

One of Faversham's sons was a survivor on the torpedoed *Zam Zam* recently.

GEORGE D. FAWCETT (77)

Veteran star and character actor. Played with Salvini, Nat Goodwin, Maude Adams. Fifty years on stage and in films.

DEXTER FELLOWES (66)

Dean of circus press agents and with the circus for nearly 50 years.

FRANK FERGUSON (74)

Actor, playwright, dramatic critic. Played in light opera. Wrote 41 one-act plays. Forty years on stage.

WM. J. FERGUSON (85)

A fine actor of many parts for 60 years. He was the last survivor of the company playing Ford's Theatre, Washington, D. C., the night Lincoln was shot. Supported Richard Mansfield and many famous stars. He appeared with three outstanding stars of the 70's in their favorite plays: John T. Raymond in "Colonel Sellers" and Mr. and Mrs. W. J. Florence in "The Mighty Dollar."

Among a long list of roles, successfully played by Mr. Ferguson, the best remembered were in such plays as "Hazel Kirke," "The Fatal Card," "The

Girl from Maxim's," "Brixton Burglary," "A Modern Magdalen," "Romeo and Juliet" with Eleanor Robson and Kyrle Bellew, "Secret of Polichinelle," "Walls of Jericho" with James J. Hackett and "The Love Letter" with Virginia Harned.

LEW FIELDS (74)

Theatrical manager and famous comedian, 60 years on the stage. One of the most famous comedy teams in the history of the American theater, Weber and Fields, was broken up in July, 1941, by the death of the noted comedian Lew Fields.

When the boys were 8 years old, they had already rehearsed and routined a comedy act. This developed in later years into a series of German-dialect comedy sketches so universally famous and popular that a score of their ludicrous and side-splitting broken "English as she is speakded" lines became almost household words. Their best lines were repeated outside of the theater to hosts of friends by patrons of Weber and Fields' fashionable music hall, where the brightest stars of the stage scintillated wit and travesty nightly to packed houses for years.

These stars included such celebrities as Lillian Russell, Dave Warfield, Pete Dailey, Ross and Fenton, John T. Kelly, Sam Bernard, Louis Mann, William Collier, De Wolf Hopper, Frankie Bailey, Bessie McCoy and others, besides Weber and Fields themselves, forming no doubt the greatest record-breaking aggregation of high-salaried stage artists ever gathered together in a Music Hall Company.

An excerpt from an editorial in the *New York Times* recently under the heading "Lew Fields" eulogizes him and his partner, Joe Weber, with a pen picture so truthfully portrayed that as a friend of both the boys on and off the stage for over 40 years, I could not but be impressed with the accuracy with which it sums up much of their united career in these lines:

"Lew was long and Joe Weber was short. They grew up together as if by agreement and for comic effect. . . . Lew and Joe may be said to have learned to act before they felt steady on their legs. Their fun was simpler and heartier than ours.

"You would be bored to read the book of their once famous game of pool or burlesque bank—one finds in some of their scenes such properties as a cigar in the mouth of a bust, and a pig in a canary's cage—those derby hats, like shallow little shells, that tuft of chin beard, those checked suits audible afar were irresistible.

"In their burlesque plays they did finer work and may be said to have anticipated the revue. In the town of their time, their theatre,—was it our first little theatre?—was an institution, a temple of drollery, a place where it was 'right' to go, a sight and sound of New York. 'Weber and Fields' was a landmark. One could name at least a dozen accomplished actors and actresses who were in the companies of this famous pair. They have been a part of New York . . ."

As a producer, Lew Fields put over such Broadway musical successes as "It Happened in Nordland," "The Girl Behind the Counter," "Old Dutch," "The Sun Dodgers" and "The Midnight Sons."

Weber and Fields celebrated their golden jubilee in 1932.

HARRISON G. FISKE (81)

Famous manager, journalist and critic, connected with dramatic criticism, journalism and theatrical management over 50 years. The recent passing of Mr. Fiske removes one of the last great stalwarts in the line of old-time American theatrical managers among such distinguished company as Augustin Daly, Charles Frohman, Daniel Frohman, David Belasco, Klaw and Erlanger, Florenz Ziegfeld, and Morris Gest.

His earlier career as a distinguished dramatic critic and journalist is too well-described in theatrical annals to require repetition here. His work and writings in the *New York Dramatic Mirror*, beginning as a young man of 21, cover an era of many years, in which his facile pen, scholarly knowledge and intuition and fearless criticism enabled the *Dramatic Mirror* to occupy as a chronicle the same foremost position in connection with the legitimate stage that its contemporary the *New York Clipper* occupied in general theatrical news and sports. For about 20 years after the 90's, he took a leading part in the fight against the then formidable theatrical syndicate and trust that practically controlled the leading theaters and bookings in the United States.

Mr. Fiske married the eminent star Minnie Maddern, whom he learned to know as a child actress of 12.

He produced, directed and managed many of Mrs. Fiske's successful plays. These included "Ghosts" and several others by Ibsen. Under his direction notable dramatic roles such as Tess of the D'Urbervilles, Becky Sharp, Salvation Nell and Mary of Magdala were created by Mrs. Fiske and brought her laurels as an inspired actress of unusual genius.

Mr. Fiske was the author of several plays including "Sara Crewe," and his record of productions on the American stage numbered nearly 150.

CISSY FITZGERALD (68)

Star of musicals, was before the public 40 years. Mrs. Cissy Tucker (Cissy Fitzgerald), the original "Gayety Girl" in the United States, appeared under the management of George Edwardes in London and Charles Frohman in America. She was said to be the first woman to appear in motion-picture plays. In the "talkies" she played roles in "The Masqueraders," "Ladies of the Night" and "Laugh, Clown, Laugh." Her billing in musical comedy was "See Cissy Wink!"

MICHEL FOKINE (62)

"Father of the Modern Ballet," famous dancer and founder of the modern dance about 40 years ago. Fokine revolutionized the traditional movements of the ballet, with its pink tights and short ballet skirt. He based his modern ideas of dance on beautiful movements true to life, artistic and emotional.

For the immortal dancer Anna Pavlowa, he created her pièce de résistance "The Dying Swan" which she danced to the "Pavlowa Gavotte" based on the melody of Paul Lincké's famous composition "The Glow Worm."

Michel Fokine and his wife and dancing partner, Vera Fokine, surrounded themselves with a company of the world's most famous dancers, including not only Pavlowa but also Karsavina, Nijinski, Mordkin, Bolm and others. Their first great success was in Paris, under impresario Serge Diaghileff, a tremendous engagement, and the real start of the sensational history of the modern ballet.

An engagement in London followed and soon the enterprising manager Morris Gest brought Fokine to America to stage the dances for Gest's production "Aphrodite."

Becoming an American citizen, he created an "American Ballet," but his greatest fame in this country rested on his creation of the "Ballet Russe," which received tumultuous applause at every performance in seasonal appearances from 1919 to about 1934.

His better known dance creations were "Fire Bird," "Petruchka," "Don Juan," "Le Coq d'Or," "Spectre de la Rosa" and "Prince Igor." He also revived "Les Sylphides" and "Carnaval" and was commissioned to create new ballets based on Offenbach's "La Belle Hélène" and "Bluebeard."

He was head of the Michel Fokine and Vera Fokine Ballet from 1925 until the year of his death in 1942.

JAMES FORBES (66)

Playwright-actor and dramatic critic. Wrote "Chorus Lady," "Travelling Salesman," "Famous Mrs. Fair." Associated with stage 50 years.

SIR JOHNSTON FORBES-ROBERTSON (84)

Famous manager, actor and star. Debut 1874 in "Mary Stuart." Toured with Ellen Terry. Played leads with Henry Irving, Mary Anderson, Modjeska. Famous success in "As You Like It," "Passing of Third Floor Back," etc. Married Gertrude Elliott. Appeared on stage over 40 years.

Forbes-Robertson made a very successful American tour. He played Buckingham to Henry Irving's Henry VIII. The chief success of his career was his impersonation of Hamlet. He appeared with Mrs. Patrick Campbell in "Magda," "Macbeth" and "Pelleas and Melisande." In 1906-07 he toured again in America in Bernard Shaw's comedy-drama "Caesar and Cleopatra."

He was the son of John Forbes-Robertson, art critic and journalist, and he himself had studied painting and had been admitted as a student at the Royal Academy School of Art, London. His inclination, however, was toward the stage, and he became one of England's foremost actors.

ARTHUR FORREST (74)

Actor. Was with the elder Mrs. John Drew. Also with Mme. Januschek, Richard Mansfield, Kate Claxton, Lester Wallack, etc. Over 40 years in the theater.

ALEXANDER FRANK (73)

Began career under Sir Henry Irving. Played with Olga Nethersole, Richard Mansfield, Henry Miller, Ethel Barrymore, Mrs. Leslie Carter, James K. Hackett, etc. Nearly 50 years on stage.

NAHAN FRANKO

Over 40 years before the public. Veteran violinist and soloist. Concert master and first violin at Metropolitan Opera House.

CHARLES FROHMAN (55)

Internationally famous theatrical manager, 38 years in theatricals. C.F., as he was affectionately called by his intimates, was born in Sandusky, Ohio, June 17,

1860; he died on the high seas the day the *Lusitania* was torpedoed on that awful Black Friday, May 7, 1915, when 1,346 persons perished.

At the age of 17 Charles Frohman organized a minstrel company. He was the whole works—manager, treasurer, ticket seller, prompter and interlocutor of the little show to which the admission was one cent. Shortly after he became treasurer of Hooley's Theatre in Brooklyn and later of Haverly's Minstrels.

Work was the only play Charles Frohman knew and it was sheer vitality and energy economically expended that made him the proprietor and manager of a dozen first-class theaters in New York and eight in London, and 13 touring companies in the United Kingdom.

Through the bookings of the great theatrical syndicate of which Charley Frohman and Abe Erlanger were the moving spirits, Frohman did more than his share in the direction and control of hundreds of theaters in the United States, starting with Bronson Howard's play "Shenandoah" in 1887. Frohman followed this success with many others too numerous to mention here, including "Men and Women," "Wilkinson's Widows," "Gloriana" and "Jane." Soon his world-famous slogan "Charles Frohman Presents" graced the theatrical notices in the press and on the billboards, announcing 50 or more separate organizations headed by practically all the great stars in the theatrical firmament of that period.

Thus in their time, among many others, came Maude Adams in "The Little Minister," "Peter Pan," "What Every Woman Knows" and "L'Aiglon"; John Drew in "Masked Ball," "Second in Command," "Butterflies," "A Marriage of Convenience," "The Liar," "Richard Carvel," "My Wife," "The Mummy and the Humming Bird," "His House in Order" and "The Duke of Killicrankie"; Ethel Barrymore in "Captain Jinks," "A Scrap of Paper," "Cousin Kate Sunday," "A Doll's House" and Henry Miller in "The Only Way."

But my mission here is merely to outline a few of his activities. Volumes could be written about C.F. and his numerous production experiences covering the four decades of his theatrical life. In London, Paris, Berlin and Vienna, Charles Frohman's reputation was the open-sesame to the doors of Barrie, Pinero, Rostand, Dumas, Bronson Howard, Augustus Thomas and all the famous playwrights of the period. They gave him practically first choice of all their new works. This was also true of the owners of the leading theaters in New York and London and they reserved for Frohman shows their very best bookings.

As for his dealings with his stars and with the army of players and employees who came in contact with Mr. Frohman in the conduct of his numerous enterprises, it has often been pointed out in the public press that he stood head and shoulders above many of his contemporaries with these unique traits. He was a legitimate businessman and treated men and women of the stage in a businesslike manner. He never signed a contract with those who were under his management. His word was better than many a man's contract. He never had a lawsuit with an actor. He never thrust himself into the limelight for applause. He dignified the business of producing and of managing theaters by his clean and respectable policies.

From a London viewpoint, John Savoy said that he did not think that any English actor-managers were as popular as Charles Frohman or more genuinely beloved by actors; that he did more than any other man to bring the English and American stage together to create international good-fellowship and to further the cause of dramatic art on both sides of the Atlantic. The French authors lauded Mr. Frohman with these words, among many: "Charles Frohman had many claims on the friendship of our Society. It can never forget that for more than a quarter of a century he was the most active workman, the most useful propagator of French dramatic genius on the other side of the ocean. All the authors whom success caressed with his wing, thanks to him, saw their works made known to the immense American public."

Sir James M. Barrie, in the *London Daily Mail,* called him "The man who never broke his word" and also expressed this thought, among others: "He was very dogged. I had only one quarrel with him, but it lasted all of the 16 years I knew him. He wanted me to be a playwright and I wanted to be a novelist. All those years I fought him on that. He always won, but not because of his doggedness—only because he was so lovable that one had to do as he wanted. He also threatened, if I stopped, to reproduce the old plays and print my name in large electric letters over the entrance to the theatre. His innumerable companies were as children to him. He chided them as children, soothed them, and forgave them, and certainly loved them as children. He exulted in those who became great names in that world and gave them beautiful toys to play with."

No two men in the profession probably were ever more intimate in spirit than Charles Frohman and David Belasco. The latter recalled, at the time of Frohman's passing, when he and "Charley" were ambitious, dreaming boys, rooming together, walking the streets while the city slept—sometimes clear to the Battery—eating their nightly tea and pie in a pastry shop, planning, always planning, to become great men. And then he recalled his comrade at the zenith of his career, when he "controlled more theatres, had more authors under contract, had assembled more stars than any 20 other men in the world," but who was still the same simple little man, the cheery-hearted boy whom he had known —from whom in his opinion Barrie conceived his Peter Pan—the boy "who never grew up."

A few lines of the estimate of Charles Frohman by Paul M. Potter, playwright, stated in the *New York Herald:* "Work and worry would have killed Charles Frohman if the submarine had spared him. His work was his life. For years he had never slept naturally. At all hours of the night, on the Dillingham Farm, through the intervening door, left expressly open, he would be shouting inquiries about our opinion of Ethel Barrymore's new part or Julia Sanderson's new song. His mind was never at rest."

My old friend, Roland Burke Hennessy, the editor of various dramatic journals, knew Charles Frohman since his cubhood days as a reporter. He said of him: "Mr. Frohman had the brain of a genius, the method of a man who does things, and the heart of a child. He loved the simple things. He never played to the galleries. If he went into a public restaurant he ate the things that he liked, rather than the things that were fashionable. He wore clothes that were comfortable, he spoke words that were kindly and expressed thoughts that were good. To talk a few minutes with him was to be convinced of his bigness of mind, his smallness of vanity and his kindliness of intent and action."

In a line from a letter to E. H. Sothern and his wife, Miss Julia Marlowe, written to them by Mr. Frohman before he went to his death on board the *Lusitania,* Mr. Frohman said: "When you think of the number of stars I have managed, a mere submarine makes me laugh."

Soon thereafter came C.F.'s final curtain speech, as related by Miss Rita Jolivet, who was among the last to speak to Charles Frohman on the deck of the *Lusitania* as the boat was about to sink. Miss Jolivet, who was saved, said that Mr. Frohman was perfectly calm and remarked just before the end came: "Why fear death? It is the most beautiful adventure that life gives us."

The following lines convey only in part Augustus Thomas' beautiful eulogy over the remains of Charles Frohman:

"He learned greatly from the world in which we count him one of Nature's noblemen. He learned equally from the mimic world, of which he was an emperor. The history of dramatic enterprise holds no other name so potent, and his monument is the fact that for a generation he used his great power cleanly, wholesomely, optimistically, inspiringly. In a field dependent upon notice, he never bartered self-respect for notoriety. The salacious, the morbid, the demoralizing, were banished by his mere arrival, and this was so not only in the theatre, but in any private group of which he was a member. He was by character one of the strong, and just to be with him was to be decent."

DANIEL FROHMAN (89)

Dean of theatrical managers and president of the Actors' Fund for many years. In 1893 he fathered a bill allowing stage children to appear, with the consent of the Mayor. Frohman never tired of telling of the amazingly low salaries which the stage stars demanded in other days, and which he paid them. William Gillette was glad to get $50; Maude Adams, $35; Margaret Anglin, $40; Henry Miller, $60; and his stage manager, David Belasco, $35. Frohman could also tell some interesting stories of the early great American dramatic stage stars, including Charlotte Cushman, Charles Thorne, Mary Anderson, Clara Morris—all names that illumined the stage of olden days with big letters.

Mr. Frohman managed the Fifth Avenue Theatre in 1877, and from 1879 to 1885 was manager of the Madison Square Theatre, producing such successful plays as "Hazel Kirke," "Esmeralda," "The Rajah" and "May Blossom," in which Georgia Cayvan made her first appearance. His famous stock company at the Lyceum Theatre on Fourth Avenue near 23rd Street embraced, in addition to Miss Cayvan, Effie Shannon, Katherine Florence, Mrs. Walcott, Mrs. Whiffen, Henry Miller, W. J. LeMoyne, Nelson Wheatcroft, Eugene Ormond and William Faversham. It was at Mr. Frohman's New Lyceum that such stars as E. H. Sothern, William Gillette, Mrs. G. H. Gilbert, Sir Charles Wyndham, Ethel Barrymore and many others appeared. The Kendals also came to this country under Daniel Frohman's management.

EDDIE GARVIE (73)

Veteran character actor, minstrel and comedian. Started in 1885 with "In Old Kentucky" Co. Played with Walter Hampden. On the stage 50 years.

MORRIS GEST (61)

Noted showman and producer, a Broadway stage celebrity over 40 years. The life of this, one of America's foremost showmen, has been written up since his passing by the leading press of the country. Anything more than a mere reference to his theatrical fame would seem repetition, especially as the theater-going public at large was closely informed through the years of his wonderful achievements in the American theater. He was a real authority on the finer arts of the stage.

In my previous book, *They All Sang*, I was very glad to devote several pages to the life of "Morrie," as we who knew him intimately since his boyhood learned to call him.

All I can add here is that, despite his eccentricities in later life due to illness,

Morris Gest deserves to be ranked among the rather limited list of real geniuses presiding over American theaters and productions—a worthy name among such shining examples as Augustin Daly, Charles and Daniel Frohman, David Belasco, Imre Kiralfy and Ziegfeld.

The mention of a few of Morris Gest's costly and extraordinary spectacles and productions should carry this conviction home to any well-informed theater-goer as he recalls "The Miracle," "The Chauve Souris," "Chu Chin Chow," "Aphrodite," "The Wanderer," "Mecca," "Afgar," "The Wonder Bar," the original productions of the "Russian Ballet," the Moscow Art Theatre and the theatrical tour of Mme. Duse.

JOHN GILBERT

Noted veteran actor, 60 years on stage. He was a member of the famous Boston Theatre Co.

ETIENNE GIRARDOT (83)

Character actor, 66 years in the theater and films. Girardot originated the part and played the Aunt in "Charley's Aunt" for six years, being selected for the role by the author Brandon Thomas. He studied painting but his success in amateur theatricals induced him to go on the stage. At 17, he made his first professional appearance and at 25 he achieved his first London success in "The Yellow Dwarf."

Girardot's great versatility is shown by the fact that in Shakespearean roles in 1884-1886 he often played as many as fifteen different parts in a week, and one night acted eight separate characters. He played Antonio to Ellen Terry's Beatrice in "Much Ado About Nothing."

He toured with Mr. and Mrs. Bancroft. When he came to the United States after his success abroad to resume his part here in "Charley's Aunt," he made this country his permanent home. He appeared in "Miranda of the Balcony" with Mrs. Fiske and with William Collier in "The Diplomat." Also in "Becky Sharp" and "Lysistrata." In pictures he played in "Clive of India," "The Whole Town's Talking," "The Fire-Brand," "Curly Top" with Shirley Temple, "In Old Kentucky," and "The Story of Vernon and Irene Castle."

JOHN GOLDEN

Author, song writer, producer of more than 125 productions, including "Lightnin'," "Seventh Heaven" and "The First Year." Made his theatrical debut more than 50 years ago. With us still and a prominent manager.

HOWARD GOULD (74)

Actor. Appeared in "Prisoner of Zenda," "Witching Hour," "Madame X," etc. On stage over 40 years.

SIDNEY GRANT

Actor, 50 years on stage.

CLAY M. GREENE (83)

Playwright and actor. Wrote "Wang," "Sharps & Flats," "M'liss." Connected with theater over 40 years.

FRED GRIFFITHS (Frederic George Delaney) (84)

Circus, vaudeville and pantomime artist. Of the Griffiths Brothers team first with Joe Griffiths in Barnum's Circus until the latter's death in 1901, and later still as the Griffiths Brothers, when Fred Jr. replaced him. After a period as a pantomimist Fred appeared throughout Europe and in the United States in circus and vaudeville. In their brother act, he introduced for years the performing horse "Pogo," featured everywhere. The act was included in the Royal Command performance at the London Coliseum. In 1921 a banquet was tendered to him after 60 years in show business.

LEONARD GROVER (94)

Playwright and oldest manager. Was producer of "Black Crook." Discovered Billy Emerson, famous minstrel and greatest song-and-dance man of his day. Grover was the author of "Our Boarding House," "Cad the Tomboy" (starring Carrie Swain). Connected with the theater over 60 years.

GEORGE R. GUY (86)

Veteran minstrel and manager, 65 years in minstrelsy. Guy, Jr., learned the art of dancing and burnt cork minstrelsy from his father George R. Guy, Sr., an expert Negro minstrel during the Civil War.

George, Jr., first appeared in Newark in 1863 in a song-and-dance minstrel specialty, and thereafter through his entire career he remained a minstrel performer.

In 1864 he was joined by his brother and as a team they appeared with Hooley's Minstrels in Brooklyn and at Tony Pastor's, then at 201 Broadway. They also appeared with Barnum's Circus. Soon a tour of the British Isles and Canada followed with the famous Christy minstrels, headed by George Christy, the original introducer of minstrelsy in Philadelphia.

After the father had taught the art of blackface comedy and dancing to five of his brothers, George R. Guy formed with them the famous constellation known as the "Guy Brothers Mighty Minstrels."

At the peak of this troupe's success the company numbered thirty-eight persons and traveled in its own Pullman car. Each of the six boys—Willie, Guy, Charles, Edwin, Arthur and Albert—could sing, dance, and play tambos, banjos and bones.

They could perform numerous acrobatic feats, and they doubled in brass band and orchestra. George could do a somersault and a split without missing a single step of the dance he was performing.

Guy Brothers Mighty Minstrels was a success from the start in the face of the spreading demand for minstrels all over the country, and the competition of such famous minstrel trade-marks as George H. Primrose, Lew Dockstader, Al G. Fields, San Francisco Minstrels, Carncross and Dixie, Simmons and Slocum, Billy Emerson and other powerful box-office drawing names.

JANE HADING (81)

Famous French actress, former favorite of Comédie-Française and Paris Boulevard theaters for nearly three decades. She was born in Marseilles and developed considerable talent in music, winning first prize at the Conservatory there. She made an early appearance in "La Fille de Madame Angot," "La Petite

Marie," "L'Oeil Creve" and other opéra bouffe and musical successes. She later became famous for her roles in "L'Adventurière," "Les Effrontes," and other Comédie-Française plays.

Miss Hading inherited her talent as an actress from her father, one of the great French melodramatic actors of his time. She enjoyed the distinction of being the first woman ever to implant kisses on the lips of her stage partner in her part in Marcel Prevost's "Les Demi-Vierges."

ROBERT T. HAINES (75)

Noted actor, stage director, playwright and producer, 40 years before the footlights. During his stage career, Mr. Haines supported many famous actresses of the American stage, notably Minnie Maddern Fiske, Blanche Bates, Nazimova, Grace George, Olga Nethersole and Frances Starr.

In the "Palace of the King" Mr. Haines made his first New York hit as John of Austria, supporting Viola Allen, one of the top-ranking stars of the period. He also produced and managed sketches for Pauline Lord, Mary Boland, Jacob Ben Ami and Grant Mitchell. In recent years he appeared in many pictures and was on the radio.

IRA HARDS

Actor-director. Debut in 1893 with Charles Frohman Co. Staged "Dracula," "Jarnegan," "Bishop Misbehaves" and other successes. Connected 40 years with the stage.

OTIS HARLAN

Leading comedian in Charles Hoyt's farces for many years, including "Hole in the Ground," "Brass Monkey," "Texas Steer," "Black Sheep," "Stranger in New York," "Night and a Day." He also appeared in "Vanderbilt Cup," "Little Puck," etc. Also many years in films. Over 40 years on the stage.

SAM HARRIS (69)

Successful Broadway theatrical manager, connected with the theater over 60 years. Was a three-time Pulitzer Prize winner with his productions: 1923, "Ice Bound"; 1932, "Of Thee I Sing"; 1937, "You Can't Take It with You."

The American public knew that the Sam Harris name sponsoring a production made it worth seeing. His string of successes included "Rain," "Captain Applejack," "Cradle Snatchers," "Six-Cylinder Love," "Nervous Wreck," "Seven Keys to Baldpate," "Get-Rich-Quick Wallingford," "It Pays to Advertise," "Little Johnny Jones," "Dinner at Eight," "Jubilee," "Man Who Came to Dinner," "Lady in the Dark," "Music Box Revue," "The Spider," "As Thousands Cheer," "The Jazz Singer" and many others.

In the days of Harry Miner's Bowery, Sam Harris, a product of the Bowery himself and born near that thoroughfare, managed pugilists, among them, Terry McGovern, featherweight champion of the world in 1900. He was at one time a member of the producing firm of Sullivan, Harris and Woods, and later closely associated with George M. Cohan and recently with George S. Kaufman and Moss Hart.

His judgment of a play and its details was wise and almost uncanny, and his great percentage of successes bespoke his genius as an old-time and yet marvelously shrewd and up-to-date showman.

ANNIE HART

The original "Bowery" girl. Is still going in her 50th year on stage. Was with "Show Boat."

FRANK HATCH (74)

Connected with the stage about 55 years. California actor, manager and later stage director with William A. Brady productions, in New York and London. He staged "Life," "Lover's Lane," "Uncle Tom's Cabin," "Foxy Grandpa," "Divorçons," etc.

H. DUDLEY HAWLEY (62)

Actor, on American stage 46 years. Made his debut Proctor's 23rd Street Theatre. Was with Richard Mansfield, Nat Goodwin, and some years in Proctor's Fifth Avenue and 125th Street Stock Companies, where he portrayed more than 600 roles. In "Common Clay," he created role of Artie Oakley and played a run of 108 weeks. Also a run of 96 weeks in "Up in Mabel's Room." Also appeared with Mrs. Fiske, Helen Menken, and in many other productions. In his last engagement he played the Doctor in the Clifton Webb Co. of "The Man Who Came to Dinner."

MAX HIRSCHFELD (80)

Musical conductor, arranger and pianist, conductor of grand opera, light opera and musical comedy. Received his musical education in Europe, and as a youth he studied under Kiel, Scharwenka and Moszkowski. He came to America in the early 80's. Some time after his arrival he conducted grand opera at the Tivoli in San Francisco for over ten years. After coming to New York, his greatest successes were in connection with the Victor Herbert operas, Hirschfeld not only rehearsed the music, but conducted practically every Herbert light opera, excepting upon the opening performances or special occasions when Victor himself conducted.

He also conducted the earlier musical comedies of Jerome Kern, and many musical shows of such distinguished American managers as Florenz Ziegfeld and Charles Frohman.

He toured the country as the musical conductor for Schumann-Heink and Fritzie Scheff.

JOSEF HOFMANN

Recently celebrated his golden anniversary as piano virtuoso (50 years). Still active.

DE WOLF HOPPER (77)

Star comedian. Star of "Wang," "El Capitan" and Gilbert and Sullivan operas. Married Edna Wallace, Nella Bergen and four others. Famous for "Casey at the Bat." On stage 57 years.

William De Wolf Hopper was born in New York in 1858. He was descended from the well-known colonial De Wolf family on his mother's side. She was Miss Rosalie De Wolf and traced her genealogy back to the eleventh century, the founder of the family being known as "Olof the sharp-eyed."

De Wolf Hopper studied law for a short time, acted in amateur performances and toured in "Our Boys," having organized his own company. The next venture he managed was "One Hundred Wives," in which I saw him at the Old Windsor Theatre on the Bowery for the first time. After the stranding of this company, he played with Ed Harrigan in "The Blackbird." After engagements in "Hazel Kirke" and "May Blossom," he struck his real forte as a singing comedian of great talent in such comic opera successes as "Black Hussar," "Fledermaus," "Lady or the Tiger," "Boccaccio," "Fatinitza," "Begum," "Panjandrum," "Dr. Syntax," "Mr. Pickwick" and Reginald De Koven's "Happyland." Mr. Hopper also played Falstaff in "The Merry Wives of Windsor" and David in an all-star production of "The Rivals."

WM. INGERSOLL (74)

Actor. Supported Margaret Mather, Nat Goodwin, Mrs. Fiske, Wm. Gillette, etc. On stage 55 years.

FLORA IRWIN

Both May and Flora Irwin were on the stage 50 years. Tony Pastor first presented May and Flora Irwin (The Irwin Sisters) at his theater, 585 Broadway in 1875. At about this time at Pastor's, Nat Goodwin, Evans and Hoey, Lillian Russell and Francis Wilson all appeared on Pastor's Variety bills. The writer saw them all and remembers them well. Flo Irwin married Senator Thomas F. Grady of New York.

JOE JACKSON (69)

Noted comedian and tramp cyclist, over 50 years on the stage. Joseph Francis Jiranek, known to the stage as Joe Jackson, was a comedian beloved by young and old. For more than 40 years he made audiences of thousands laugh with the act which distinguished him throughout the world—his tramp bicycle act.

It was all accomplished by facial expression, pantomimic action, and acrobatic skill. One look at his bedraggled getup, his battered hat and his enormous boots, the worst-looking pair he could find after searching innumerable ash cans, was enough to start off any audience into convulsions.

Like Charlie Chaplin in his earlier career, Jackson never spoke a word. It was all comic pantomime. His moon face, and almost indescribable costume, in a setto with a policeman, his joyful riding stunts on a discarded bike, until it fell to pieces on the stage bit by bit—his chasing all over the stage a loose shirt cuff that bothered him, and dozens of other pantomimic gestures evoked roars of laughter. There was little necessity to change the act. It was always sure-fire and the same belly laughs came at the same spots in his comic routine, night after night, year after year.

Joe Jackson's act was internationally known—he had traveled in America, Europe, Asia and the East Indies, and the Queen of England had enjoyed his performances on several occasions.

He was born in Austria, but became an American citizen many years ago. In his earlier career he was a racing bicyclist and trick rider appearing at Crystal Palace, London, and many leading theaters. He was also the world's champion bicycle polo player.

His last engagement about a year ago in 1942 was at the Roxy, New York, and after taking five encores, he dropped dead on the stage, his last words being "they're still applauding." His wish was "to die in his stage harness" and, as Brooks Atkinson aptly put it, "He died with his boots on."

A son, Joe Jackson, Jr., will probably carry on the act, having been taught the routine by his famous father.

ELLIS JEFFREYS (74)

British actress, stage and screen star over 50 years. Was born in Colombo, Ceylon, in 1868. Her first appearance was in the chorus of Gilbert and Sullivan's "Yeomen of the Guard" in 1889. From the chorus she graduated to light opera and finally rose to the peak of her career in comedy.

Miss Jeffreys played in almost 100 stage productions and many films in the 50 years she appeared before the British and American public. Her first tour in this country in 1895 in "The Notorious Mrs. Ebbsmith" was so successful that she repeated her American visit several times. She sang the leading role in "La Cigale" during its run in London and was best known by her prominent roles in "Sweet Lavender," "Fringe of Society," "The Wedding March," "The Vagabond King," "The Headless Man," "Elixir of Youth," "The Prince Consort" and "She Stoops to Conquer."

In 1930 she was attracted by British movies and had several important parts. She was christened Minnie Gertrude Ellis Jeffries and was the wife of Herbert Sleath, producer.

DEWITT C. JENNINGS (65)

Actor. Was with James O'Neill. Appeared in "Mutiny on the Bounty." Over 40 years on stage.

BERTHA KALICH (64)

Actress and tragedienne in "Marta of the Lowlands," "Monna Vanna," "Magda," "Kreutzer Sonata" and "Riddle Woman." On stage 40 years.

DAME MADGE KENDAL (86)

Actress. Played Little Eva in "Uncle Tom's Cabin." Rosalind to Mr. Kendal's Orlando. Was with E. A. Sothern in "Our American Cousin." On stage about 50 years. She was born in Cleethorpes, Lincolnshire, in 1849, being the daughter of Mr. and Mrs. J. W. Robertson (both well known on the stage), and the sister of T. W. Robertson, the author of "Caste," "School" and "Ours." She played children's parts for a long time and later in 1865 made her debut as Ophelia in "Hamlet."

She came into prominence in "A Hero of Romance" at the Haymarket, London, remaining at that theater for seven years, creating principal parts in W. S. Gilbert's "Pygmalion and Galatea," "The Palace of Truth," "Broken Hearts" and "The Wicked World." At the Prince of Wales Theatre in 1876, she triumphed as Lady Orman in "Peril" and as Dora in "Diplomacy."

The great fame of the Kendals (Mr. and Mrs.) began with their partnership with John Hare and together they managed the St. James Theatre from 1877 to 1888, producing many successful plays. In 1889 the Kendals toured the United States and Canada under the direction of the late Daniel Frohman. The American tour was phenomenally successful and was repeated for five years thereafter.

SAM (MORTON) KENNEDY (79)

On the stage 48 years. What old-timer does not remember Sam Morton of the Four Mortons? Surely, if anyone patronized variety or vaudeville or musical comedy, they must have seen and enjoyed this famous top-line family act.

Sam was a character show by himself. Kittie, his wife, won recognition as one of the best fancy step and jig dancers in the business, and their children, Clara and Paul and, later, Martha and Joe, helped to round out the Four Mortons. They never failed to bring down the house by their clever singing, dancing and comedy. In earlier years, Sam and Kittie Morton appeared as stars of Irish dramas on the order of "Ivy Leaf."

The Four Mortons troupe disbanded after the death of the mother, Kittie Morton, in 1927. Sam Morton's last engagement under the management of Eddie Dowling was in the "Sidewalks of New York" in 1931.

KATHRYN KIDDER (71)

Veteran actress. Wife of Dr. Louis Anspacher. Created Rachel McCreery in "Held by the Enemy" and Dearest in "Little Lord Fauntleroy." Toured with Louis James and Frederick Warde, playing in "Winter's Tale," "Macbeth," "The Rivals," "School for Scandal," "Midsummer Night's Dream," etc. She was on the stage 50 years.

FRANK KINGDON (72)

Actor. Was with Richard Mansfield, Sothern and Marlowe, etc. On stage 40 years.

GERTRUDE SILVER KINGSTON (68)

Actress. With Henry Irving and Beerbohm Tree. American debut in "Captain Brassbound's Conversion." Associated with stage 50 years.

MARC KLAW (78)

Producer. One of the firm of Klaw & Erlanger. Organized the big theatrical syndicate Klaw & Erlanger, Frohman, Nixon & Zimmerman, and Al Hayman. Controlled many stars and Klaw & Erlanger theaters. Connected with theatricals about 50 years.

MATT H. KUSSELL (74)

Actor, manager and producer. Pioneer in the tabloid musical comedy field. His first girl act played the Keith and Western vaudeville circuits. In show business 40 years.

WILTON LACKAYE

Noted veteran character player and actor of many parts. Famous for his original impersonation of Svengali in "Trilby." Almost completed 50 years on the stage.

ERNEST LAWFORD (70)

Actor, with a fine career of over 50 years on the stage. This noted character actor, a prime favorite with English and American audiences for many decades, was the original Charley in "Charley's Aunt."

An Oxford man, he also studied to be a barrister in England, but the stage fortunately won him over. He first appeared in 1890 with the celebrated beauty Lilly Langtry in "As You Like It," but he had previously barnstormed with a "blood-and-thunder" group about Yorkshire.

In a few years he was enjoying an enviable reputation in his profession. Even when he was appearing between spells of illness 49 years later (in 1939) he maintained a high place for himself and never lost even in old age the prestige he had attained in his stage work. While he was with the Ben Greet Company, Mr. Lawford appeared in "Everyman," "School for Scandal," "She Stoops to Conquer" and other old English comedies. He also played in the original production of Oscar Wilde's "A Woman of No Importance." He spent four seasons in the famous Drury Lane productions and played an important part in Charles Frohman's American production of "Peter Pan" with Maude Adams, after which he appeared for fourteen seasons under the Frohman banner.

In the modern-dress "Hamlet" in 1925 the *New York Times* reviewer appraised his performance of Polonius as follows: "Playing that part in formal and informal dress of today, with monocle and closely trimmed beard, Mr. Lawford achieves a splendid character portrait, fatuous, supercilious, plausible to the extreme, yielding nothing to the usual conception of a doddering old fool fit only for the stage." At one time Mr. Lawford also appeared as the Lord Chancellor in "Iolanthe."

M. B. ("MIKE") LEAVITT

Famous veteran manager, producer, minstrel and globe trotter for 50 years—1859 to 1909. Best-informed man in old-time theatricals of every description that I ever met.

GEORGE W. LEDERER (76)

Veteran actor, producer and manager. Started in "Naiad Queen," 1873. Produced "Floradora," "Belle of New York," "Lady Slavey," "Wild Rose," "Passing Show," "Merry Whirl," "In Gay New York," "Rounders." Connected with the stage 57 years.

NATE LEIPZIG (66)

Prestidigitator. President of the Society of Magicians. Performed in 1907 before Prince and Princess of Wales and entire Royal Family at a command performance in Buckingham Palace with King and Queen of Denmark as guests of honor. Performed for Empress Eugénie and the King and Queen of Spain. Master of sleight of hand with cards and coins for 40 years.

EDDIE LEONARD (65)

Veteran of minstrelsy and vaudeville, 45 years on the stage. The passing of Eddie Leonard in July, 1941, took from the American stage not only a minstrel and a vaudevillian who was for decade after decade one of the theater public's greatest idols, but a real trouper and performer from the days of the old minstrel guard to the end of his career.

Off the stage Eddie, as I knew him for perhaps 40 years, was a quaint character, good-natured and smiling, enthusiastic about his stage work and the songs he had written: "Ida, Sweet as Apple Cider," "Roly Boly Eyes," "I Want to Go Back to the Land of Cotton," "Molasses Candy," "Oh! Didn't it Rain,"

"Eddie Leonard's Mandy," "Oh What Eyes," "Don't You Never Tell a Lie," "When We Were Twenty-One," "Lovely Day in June," "I Wish I Was Some Little Girlie's Beau," etc. He also popularized "I'm Goin' to Live Anyhow Till I Die" and "Lit'l Gal."

Eddie Leonard had perhaps more imitators than any other vaudeville favorite, but none approached him in his inimitable rendition of the songs which made him famous. He was the original creator of his drawn-out style of singing, which Alexander Woollcott so aptly described in his review of a show at the Knickerbocker Theatre in 1919. He said: "It presented Eddie Leonard singing, 'Ida' again. Eddie Leonard going back to his old favorite 'Ro-boly,—Bo-boly-ah-ah-ah-ah-eyes,' Eddie Leonard dancing softly and easily his wonderful steps." Leonard was the author of his autobiography *What a Life.*

Eddie Leonard's wife, Mabel Russell, a former professional, was his dresser and constant companion on and off the stage. Eddie was always compelled to take many bows and encores, far more than most performers, and to ease his singing voice Mabel invariably stood in the wings administering cups of lemon and honey after each song.

Eddie was one of the best "hoofers" in minstrelsy and he never spared his many routines of dancing steps when the audience demanded them. In consequence, with his white satin suit and white topper and his frilled white shirt and black face he usually reached his dressing room after his act exhausted and a mass of perspiration. But faithful Mabel was there waiting and in a few moments the trousers and sleeves were blown up and stuffed with tissue paper and hung out to air, ready and dry for the next performance.

Mabel Russell had been previously married to Chris Bruno, son of Gus Bruno of Johnson and Bruno, one of the most famous song-and-dance teams of their day. Later she was one of the team of Bruno and Russell. In 1907, after the death of Bruno, Eddie spotted Mabel at a matinee and their love romance lasted 34 years, until his passing.

Eddie Leonard for 15 years was one of the star performers with the Primrose and West Company, the top minstrel show of its time. He trouped also with Haverlys and other well-known minstrel aggregations and at one time with his own company. He was born in Richmond, Va., and as a youngster was known as Dots Toney. At 15 he hopped a freight train with a young Negro dancer, and they secured their first engagement in a Washington cabaret. Both made their mark later in the entertainment field—Leonard as a standard top-line attraction for almost 45 years, while the other still graces the stage as the foremost Negro dancer of his time, Bill Robinson.

RICHIE LING (70)

Fifty years on stage. Prominent in many Broadway successes. Leading man with Lillian Russell, Fritzie Scheff and Christie MacDonald. First sang "Good Old Summer Time" in "The Defender" in 1902.

EDWARD LOCKTON (64)

Composer, wrote songs and ballads 52 years. Mr. Lockton wrote 2,300 songs of which his "Because" and "Until" sold 3,000,000 copies. Other famous compositions were "Where My Caravan Rested," "Tommy Lad" and "Shipmates of Mine."

His most popular song was "While the Great Dawn Is Shining," written on duty in a sentry box outside Buckingham Palace during the World War.

CISSIE LOFTUS (67)

Noted mimic and dramatic actress; was an outstanding figure in the theatrical world for half a century. Marie Cecelia Loftus was a daughter of the Variety team Ben and Marie Loftus.

At the age of 15 she persuaded the stage manager of a Belfast theater to let her do an imitation. When she opened for a full week in London her salary was $25, but she was such a sensation that this was soon increased to $1,000 and more.

When Mme. Modjeska came into great prominence, Miss Loftus was a member of her company.

As a leading woman for E. H. Sothern, and in leading roles for Daniel Frohman, she was so successful that Sir Henry Irving engaged her as Ellen Terry's successor, and in 1903 she played Marguerite in "Faust" at the Lyceum in London. She was the Ophelia in Sothern's "Hamlet" and Lady Catherine in "If I Were King" written by Justin H. M'Carthy, her first husband.

Who's Who in the Theatre mentions a page and a half of plays Cissie Loftus appeared in. They include almost every kind of a theatrical production. One of her greatest stage triumphs was as Peter Pan in James Barrie's play. She also appeared in several motion-picture roles in 1913 and succeeding years. Her famous imitations were of Harry Lauder, Mrs. Fiske, Nora Bayes, Irene Franklin and practically all the great show people of her day.

COLIE LORELLA (74)

Comedy acrobat; had top billing for 50 years. It is my best impression that the late Colie Lorella was one of the original 3 Lorellas comedy demon acrobats described in my chapter written around "The Black Crook." In any case, in the newspaper accounts of his passing Mr. Lorella is credited as entering the theatrical profession an acrobatic dancer and as being starred at Niblo's Garden, New York, where "The Black Crook" was produced.

At one time he toured Europe with the Barnum & Bailey Circus. He headlined in vaudeville houses for many years here and abroad. In 1920 Mr. Lorella appeared in a musical comedy on Broadway in which Fred Stone was starred.

FRANK LOSEE (81)

Famous actor, stage and screen. Trained with Amaranth Society, Brooklyn. Member of Union Square and Hooley's Theatre Stock Co. Played leads in many companies. Appeared in pictures with Mary Pickford, Marguerite Clark and Pauline Frederick. On stage 50 years.

MONTAGUE LOVE (62)

Veteran stage and screen actor, 40 years on stage. His theatrical activities cover about four decades, starting with touring England in the American play, "The Lion and the Mouse." Since then, in America, he has appeared with Arnold Daly in a series of Shaw plays and in productions of "Husband and Wife" and "The Net." Film appearances include: "Mark of Zorro," "Northwest Mounted Police," "All This, and Heaven Too," "The Sea Hawk" and "Tennessee Johnson."

HELEN (ROBB) LOWELL (71)

Stage and screen actress. Debut with children's "Pinafore" Company. Then adult role "Iolanthe." Created Dearest in "Little Lord Fauntleroy," also appeared in "Show Off." On the stage, 50 years.

ISADORE LUCKSTONE (80)

Pianist, composer, noted accompanist for Caruso, Kreisler, Nordica, and a teacher of voice for nearly half a century. Mr. Luckstone made his professional debut at the age of 15. Soon a leader of a male quartet, at 18 he toured with Joseph Jefferson as orchestra director.

In 1883, 1884 and later in the 80's, he toured with the celebrated violinist Camilla Urso, and made a world tour with Reményi as accompanist to this well-known violinist.

Returning to the United States, he accompanied the great mezzo-soprano Sofia Scalchi, also del Puente, and such stars of Metropolitan Opera fame, as Melba and Sembrich.

He was professor of Education, and former head of the Voice Department at the N. Y. University School of Education.

STANLEY LUPINO (48)

Famous international comedian, 40 years in theatricals. Lupino is a name connected with the English stage since the seventeenth century. Stanley Lupino made his first appearance when a boy of six in the character of a monkey in "King Klondyke."

He appeared with Elsie Janis in "Hello, America." In 1910 he appeared in "Dick Whittington" and in 1914 his brother Barry Lupino cast him for a role in "Sleeping Beauty." During the next eight years he was featured, starred or co-starred in many plays. In his youth he took up prize-fighting for a while and later acrobatics, touring with the Albert and Edmunds troupe of acrobats and also with Ernie Luck and his brother and other vaudeville units.

Stanley Lupino was very versatile in his talents. He wrote songs, the novel *Crazy Days*, and another book *From Stocks to Stars*. In 1926-27 he appeared on Broadway in "Naughty Riquette" and "The Nightingale," after which he returned to England to appear in "So This Is Love" and many other attractions.

WILLIAM MELBOURNE MacDOWELL (84)

Noted actor, matinee idol of the 90's, over 50 years on the stage and in films. "Melbourne" MacDowell made his professional debut in 1877, as the sheriff's officer in "Road to Ruin" with the famous Boston Museum Stock Company, using his full name which he later shortened.

After three years with this company, Mr. MacDowell's reputation as an actor was established, and his rise was rapid. In Montreal, the important part of the Duke in "The Duke's Motto" brought him much acclaim. After Chicago and road engagements, he came to New York, and for 51 weeks played Squire Rodney in "Hazel Kirke" with the Madison Square Stock Company.

In 1884, five years before he married the famous American beauty and actress Fanny Davenport, he was engaged by her for the role of Jean de Siberoux in Victorien Sardou's famous play, "Fedora."

Next he appeared in "Held by the Enemy" for 58 weeks, after which he succeeded Robert Mantell as Loris Ipanoff in "Fedora" with Miss Davenport.

In 1888, still with Miss Davenport, he supported this famous star in the first American production of Sardou's "La Tosca." Mr. MacDowell created the role of Mario, and later played Baron Scarpia in the same production for three years. After that he played Marc Antony to Miss Davenport's Cleopatra. At about this time, Miss Davenport became his wife, and after her death ten years later, Mr. MacDowell continued on the New York stage, finally entering motion pictures.

BURR McINTOSH (79)

Actor, author, poet and photographer, on the stage more than 50 years. Known on the lecture platform as "The Cheerful Philosopher," Burr McIntosh lived a long and useful life, devoted to the arts. At the turn of the century, well known as a prominent actor, he created the part of Taffy in "Trilby." I remember well his characterization, which stood out in the play strongly in splendid support of the fine performances of Wilton Lackaye and others in the principal parts.

Burr McIntosh (christened William) used the former as his stage name. He appeared in the Augustus Thomas successes "Arizona" and "Mizzoura." He made his theatrical debut in 1885 in Bartley Campbell's "Paquita." At that time in the golden era of stage and night life, when the performances of such fine dramatic figures as Edwin Booth, Lawrence Barrett and Modjeska electrified American audiences, Burr McIntosh's name and fame began to appear in print and he soon gained more and more public recognition.

In 1898 he was sent to Cuba by *Leslie's Weekly* to cover with camera and pen the siege of Santiago. He contracted yellow fever, but recovered. In 1905, while ex-President Taft was Secretary of War, Burr McIntosh was appointed official photographer of Taft's trip to the Philippines. In 1909 he toured the United States in "The Gentleman from Mississippi." During the First World War, McIntosh made highly effective patriotic speeches and entertained our boys in army camps in France and Germany.

He attended Princeton and Lafayette colleges and at the 50th reunion of the latter in 1934, there were, as the only survivors, Burr McIntosh and General Peyton C. March, the pitcher and catcher of the varsity baseball team. In 1910 his serious and attractive work in photography took him to California, where he organized his own picture company.

His many active and varied activities included the writing of a book about his Spanish-American War experiences and the publication of *Burr McIntosh's Magazine* of which I prize several presentation copies. The magazine was too artistic for general public sale. His sister, Nancy McIntosh, a talented actress, appeared in Shakespearean productions at Daly's Theatre and also in "Meg Merrilies."

JIM McINTYRE and GEORGE HEATH

Veteran minstrels and black-face comedians. A famous team and best of its kind ever in the business. First artists to introduce buck and wing dancing. In the sketch, "The Georgia Minstrels," they were a tremendous laughing hit, season after season. Klaw and Erlanger put them out on the road in "The Ham Tree," under their management for several seasons. Appeared before the footlights over 40 years.

LIDA McMILLAN (71)

Actress, almost 50 years on the stage. Mrs. Snow (Lida McMillan) made her first appearance in "Lost in New York" in 1889. Later she appeared with the Dearborn Stock Company in Chicago in Stuart Robson's "Comedy of Errors," in "The Henrietta," "The Tavern," "She Stoops to Conquer" and "The Straight Road." She played parts, and she also supported Hattie Williams in Charles Frohman's "Fluffy Ruffles." Mrs. Snow appeared with Walter Huston in "Elmer the Great" and as recently as 1938 in "Prologue to Glory."

ANDREW MACK

Veteran Irish star and song writer, about 40 years on the stage. Starred in "Myles Aroon" and "Arrah-na-pogue." Wrote the song hit, "Heart of My Heart."

BILL (WM. H.) MACK (81)

Vaudeville comedian and dancer, 60 years on the stage. Appeared as a song-and-dance man in "The Black Crook," "Evangeline" and other old musical plays and was a real old New Yorker. In A. Baldwin ("Baldy") Sloane's musical comedy, "The Gingerbread Man," he played under the management of John Cort. Born and bred in the old Chelsea district of New York, he went on the stage as a boy, teaming up with his brother.

Bill Mack's real name was McIlvaine, and the act adopted the professional moniker of Wade and Mack, appearing together for several seasons. Mack appeared later quite regularly on the Keith circuit and at one time sponsored his own show "Town Topics." One of the most lucrative periods of his stage career was spent in a very successful comedy skit written by my friend Ren Shields, entitled "High Life in Jail." Both Ren Shields and Mack appeared in this famous vaudeville sketch for seven consecutive years. Ren Shields was the writer of the perennial song hit, "Good Old Summer Time."

CHARLES MACK (MURRAY & MACK) (73)

Vaudeville trouper for 50 years. With Barnum's Circus at 14. Entertained soldiers in Europe during the World War.

JAMES B. MACKIE (GRIMESY ME BOY)

Over 50 years on stage. Started in old-time variety with Henry E. Dixey; then Mackie & Geyser; later in Hoyt's "Bunch of Keys." His greatest success, star for years in "Grimes' Cellar Door."

JACK MANGEAN (71)

Veteran acrobat, managed the troupe for more than 50 years. Was the originator of many acrobatic tricks. He had toured the world, appearing in circuses, fairs and vaudeville. He founded and managed the famous Mangean Troupe which bore his name. His right name was John T. Regan.

DAVE MARION (73)

Producer and actor. Was with Weber and Fields and Gus Hill. Originated the character of "Snuffy the Cabman." In show business 58 years. Writer of

"Only One Girl in the World for Me," "It's Not What You Were, It's What You Are Today" and other popular songs.

JULIA MARLOWE

Leading star and actress, connected with the American stage over 40 years. One of the finest actresses I ever saw. Wife of E. H. Sothern, one of the best actors of his time. Miss Marlowe starred with Sothern in Shakespearean and many other famous plays. In his fine work, *Julia Marlowe, Her Life and Art*, Charles Edward Russell gives one an excellent idea of this remarkable actress, right at the beginning of his "Introductory Note," by saying:

"On the authority of calculations projected in 1924, Julia Marlowe had then acted in the Shakespearian drama a greater number of times than any other and had drawn to that drama a larger total audience than any other player had ever addressed in it. Novitiate and all, her career in her art had spanned 40 years."

Born in Caldbeck, England, and christened Sarah Frances Frost, her family, through the workings of fate and in self-exile, left England for America, dropped the name of Frost, and the star, who later reached the peak of her fame as Julia Marlowe, became known in her new home near Kansas City as Fanny Brough.

In the year of the Centennial, 1876, and as a child of 11, she joined one of the many children's "Pinafore" troupes, displaying such talent that she was soon playing Sir Joseph Porter. Shortly thereafter she organized a children's company, playing "Uncle Tom's Cabin," essaying the part of "Uncle Tom" herself. On one-night stands in "The Chimes of Normandy," Fanny Brough appeared as Suzanne, later in "The Little Duke," and while still in her teens, as one of Rip's children in Robert McWade's "Rip Van Winkle." At 18, after observing the work of the noted stars Booth and Barrett, Mary Anderson, Joe Jefferson, Fanny Davenport and others, and with her ambition fired by their great portrayals of Shakespearean characters, and with an enthusiasm, initiative and joy for expression far beyond her years, she started in the legitimate at the bottom of the ladder, observing and learning and blessed with a retentive memory.

It required a whole volume like Charles Edward Russell's to follow through the later successful years of Julia Marlowe's eventful stage career, in which as Parthenia in "Ingomar," Pauline ("Lady of Lyons"), Juliet, Viola, Galatea, Rosalind, Julia ("The Hunchback"), Katharine ("Taming of the Shrew"), Mary Tudor ("When Knighthood Was in Flower"), and many others, she epitomized and earned Mr. Russell's great tribute mentioned above.

TULLY MARSHALL (78)

Well-known character actor, on stage and screen 57 years. Was born William Phillips, in Nevada City, California, in 1864, and was aiming at a legal career until he took a course in dramatic literature at Santa Clara University. Starting his stage work in a stock company in San Francisco, he shifted to New York in 1887 to play tragic and comic roles in the company headed by Helena Modjeska. He played all types of parts on the stage, on Broadway and on the road for more than 40 years and at one time doubled as producer and actor in "The Builders" at the Astor Theatre, New York.

Entering pictures in 1916, Marshall played a character role in "Intolerance," but his high spot as a film actor was his playing of the old frontiersman in "The Covered Wagon." Some of his other parts in silent films were played in "The Merry Widow," "He Who Gets Slapped," "Redskin" and "Alias Jimmy Valentine." After the advent of talking pictures he worked in every major studio in a wide variety of roles. Among his recent pictures were "This Gun for Hire" and "Moontide." His last was "Behind Prison Bars," still to be released.

GEORGE T. MEECH (75)

Actor, on American stage over 40 years. Usually cast in supporting roles, he played in "Sherlock Holmes," "The Squaw Man," "Mrs. Wiggs of the Cabbage Patch." He started in his theatrical career at 14, in Chicago, where he was born. From 1905 to 1915 his greatest successes were while playing in "The Marriage Market," "Resurrection" and "Deep Purple."

BERYL MERCER (57)

Noted stage and screen character actress. In the theater all her life. Made her debut at 4 in "East Lynne." Played with Herbert Beerbohm Tree. Appeared in "Lights of London," "Midsummer Night's Dream," "Schulamite," "Pygmalion." Appeared in many film successes. On the stage over 50 years.

THEODORE A. METZ (88)

Composer and musical director, composed "Hot Time in the Old Town," connected with theatricals over 50 years. The story of how "Hot Time" was written has been told many times, and these are my old friend, Metz' own words about it in 1930: "Fifty years ago, I was the leader of the band of McIntyre and Heath's Minstrels. One day while on tour, we passed through a small place in Mississippi called 'Old Town.' A building was on fire. McIntyre remarked, 'There'll be a Hot Time in the Old Town Tonight.' The idea of the melody flashed into my mind, as I unconsciously repeated his words, 'There'll be a hot time in the old town tonight,' and it was no trouble for me to complete it, as soon as some of the words were accepted by singers of the troupe."

In popularity for parades and celebrations of every description, "Hot Time" has never been equaled or supplanted by any other tune, in everyday life, in the movies or on the stage. Its rousing rhythm and melody was the first and the most lasting of jazz ideas. It inspired Teddy Roosevelt's Rough Riders to go over the top in the Spanish-American War and it became the only famous and outstanding melody identified with that war. Theodore Roosevelt, after he became President, greeted old Metz in Chicago by saying, "I'm proud to shake the hand of the man who wrote the song that stirred the nation."

Metz was the composer of many other compositions, among them, "President Roosevelt March," in honor of President Franklin D. Roosevelt. He was also credited in the 90's with having as musical director picked out on his fiddle part of the melody of "Sweet Marie."

DODSON LOMAX MITCHELL (71)

Veteran actor and playwright. Debut in "Fanchon the Cricket" with his famous aunt, Maggie Mitchell. Thirteen seasons with Julia Marlowe. Supported Arnold Daly, John Drew, Nazimova, George M. Cohan and others. On the stage 53 years.

FRANK MONROE (73)

Actor. Debut in "East Lynne." Played in "Virginian," "Checkers," "Cheating Cheaters," "Sag Harbor," "Alias Jimmy Valentine." Forty years on stage.

HARRY MONTAGUE

Versatile actor and author and America's foremost producer of burlesque shows, over 45 years on the stage. Was a singer of topical songs at Tony Pastor's, Globe Theatre, and Parisian Varieties, New York, in the 70's. Developed a flair for writing burlesques and Frenchy afterpieces and remained in that field. In "gold rush" days, he played a year at Ed Chase's Palace Theatre, Denver, and nearly two years at the Bella Union Theatre, San Francisco; and for five years was stage manager for the well-remembered Sam T. Jack's Theatre in Chicago. Montague had an almost inexhaustible supply of opening acts and afterpieces. His wife was a talented seriocomic, Carrie Duncan, who with her younger sister, Sophie, established the original Duncan Sisters and appeared with him on the same bill. For his productions, Montague always chose good box-office titles, among them being "The Bashful Venus," "The Bridal Chamber," "Don't Do It, Tom," "A Bachelor's Bedroom," "The Female Beauty," "The Mormons," "Out All Night," and "Jack the Ripper."

HOWARD PRIESTLEY MORRISON (66)

Actor, director. Debut in "Fate," 1894. Produced "Smilin' Through," "Challenge of Youth," "The Barker," "Fascinating Widow," etc. Connected 50 years with the theater.

JAMES J. MORTON (76)

Minstrel, vaudeville actor and monologist, 40 years on the stage.

MAURICE MOSCOVICH (68)

Veteran stage and screen character actor, over 50 years on the stage. Was a favorite performer on the Yiddish stage where he began his career. He acted in five languages, and at the age of 48 made his English-speaking debut with success here and in London. He had toured the world including Europe, America, South America, Canada, Africa and Australia. He had acted Shakespearean and other roles since 1885. He had also appeared in films, with Shirley Temple, Sonja Henie and others for four years.

Moscovich first acted at the age of 14 in Odessa. His first appearance in America was in Jacob Adler's Company in 1893. In 1908 he appeared at the Pavilion Theatre in London. In England his first English role was "Shylock" in 1919, and in this and other plays he scored a hit and rose to stardom. In New York in 1930 he played the title role in "Josef Suss" from the novel "Power." His favorite role was Iago.

FRANK MOULAN (63)

Well-known comedian and singer. Famous Gilbert and Sullivan repertory artist. Scored success in "Sultan of Zulu." Over 40 years on stage.

LOUISE MULDENER (84)

Actress. Supported many stars. Played Juliet to Edwin Booth's Romeo. Was with Joe Jefferson, Mary Anderson, Marie Wainwright, Walker Whiteside, Henry E. Dixey and Salvini. Forty years on the stage.

IDA MULLE (75)

Light opera star. Little Buttercup in "Pinafore" when 9 years old. Created many light opera roles. In theatricals 50 years.

JAMES S. MURRAY (77)

Character actor. Was with the Wm. T. Carlton Opera Co. in 1893. Was in dramatic and musical stock. Appeared in "Naughty Marietta," "Student Prince," etc. Brother of J. K. Murray, Irish vocalist and comedian. Connected with stage 40 years.

ARTHUR NELSON (73)

Acrobat, performed under the big (circus) top over 40 years. Was the head of the famous circus act, "The Flying Nelsons," the First Family of the circus, and a feature for 40 years with the Barnum and Bailey and Ringling Brothers Circus.

P. T. Barnum brought this son of a famous English acrobat to America in 1880. As his children grew up, each was taught the flying acrobatic routine until in time, about 15 years ago with the Ringling Circus, the act included 9 members of the family—the parents, six daughters and a son. One daughter is still a member of the Ringling Circus, another married the owner of the Cole Brothers Circus, and her sister is a member of the same organization. The other surviving members of "The Flying Nelsons" have left circus life.

MME. EMMA NEVADA (81)

Operatic soprano. Famous California singer, before the public about 40 years. One of the world's most popular operatic sopranos in the 80's and 90's. Tiny of stature, her voice and beauty charmed audiences at the old Academy of Music and the Metropolitan Opera House.

Emma Nevada first appeared at age of 3, when, wrapped in the American flag, she stood on a table and sang our national anthem. At 5, an audience of gold miners showered her with gold pieces at a concert. She was born in Nevada City, California, this accounting for her adopted stage name.

Colonel Mapleson engaged her for Her Majesty's Theatre, London, and she debuted there in 1880 as Amina in "La Sonnambula." Verdi heard her in Genoa and engaged her for La Scala. At the Opéra-Comique, Paris, she appeared in "La Perle du Brésil."

In 1885 the *New York Times* said of her appearance at the Academy of Music, in Gounod's "Mireille": "Mlle. Nevada sang with feeling, skill and brilliancy. Her rendering of a gracefully written and ornate air from 'La Perle du Brésil' by Félicien David introduced in the first act of Gounod's opera was facile and correct, and a brief but sparkling Cadenza quite carried away the listeners."

When Mme. Nevada was 16, she toured the United States with Patti, appearing with her in many operas on alternate nights. Mackenzie's "Rose of Sharon," composed for her, was sung by Mme. Nevada in Covent Garden, London, in 1891.

EDNA MAY OLIVER

Brilliant character comedienne, over 40 years in theater and films. Was born in 1883 and was a descendant of John Quincy Adams. She was one of the most versatile actresses on the American stage and screen. In her childhood her study of voice culture and her experience in amateur theatricals started her career in light opera in 1900. Having also studied piano, she toured as pianist with a ladies' orchestra. It was, however, her long experience with stock companies that developed her genius and brought her to the attention of Broadway audiences in a smash hit, "Oh, Boy."

It was also in "Show Boat" that the familiar long face of Edna May Oliver convulsed her audiences in the character of Patty Ann Hawkes. Soon thereafter Hollywood called her for comedy parts in the films "Little Women," "Alice In Wonderland," "Romeo and Juliet," "Cimarron," "David Copperfield," "Tale of Two Cities" and many others in which she established her reputation as the best character actress on the American stage.

FREDERIC ORMONDE (70)

Veteran Shakespearean actor, appeared with Beerbohm Tree. On the stage 50 years.

ADELINE PATTI

The Diva of Grand Opera, 56 years before the public. (Detailed story on pages 182-197.)

FREDERICK (DODGE) PAULDING (78)

Famous actor and author. First child born in military reservation at West Point. Debut in London at 15 with Henry Irving in "Lyon's Mail." Played Hamlet 400 times before he was 20. Member of Jefferson-Florence Co. On the stage 40 years.

CORSE PAYTON (65)

Actor and producer. "World's best bad actor." Originated the 10-20-30 scale of prices. Produced over 300 plays. Over 40 years on stage.

FANNY ADDISON PITT (93)

Actress. With Margaret Anglin, John Drew, E. H. Sothern, Ethel Barrymore. On stage 45 years.

TYRONE POWER (62)

Noted character actor and stage manager (father of Tyrone Power of film and stage fame). His own father, Harold Power, was long connected with theatricals in London. His grandfather, Tyrone Power, was a well-known Irish comedian in the 30's.

Tyrone Power made his debut in "The Private Secretary" in 1886. He played with Mme. Januschek. For 10 years he appeared under the management of Augustin Daly. Mr Power later starred in Australia, and appeared with Henry

Irving in London. One of his outstanding successes was as Judas Iscariot in Mrs. Fiske's "Mary of Magdala." He was next starred by Charles Frohman in "Ulysses." He also appeared with Mrs. Leslie Carter under the management of Belasco, and he was also leading man with Henrietta Crosman in "The Christian Pilgrim." On the stage about 30 years.

JAMES T. ("JIMMY") POWERS (80)

American legitimate comedian. At one time in his career, James Thomas Powers, a stage veteran of 55 years, was considered the funniest man the American stage had ever known. He ad-libbed naturally with telling effect, increasing the number of laughs with original lines of his own, whenever he felt he could do so judiciously and with advantage to his part and the action of the play.

Powers was a light opera singer and matinee idol playing the best theaters. He first appeared in 1878 as a song-and-dance man at a minor theater in Long Branch. Later he was one of the team of Johnson and Powers, appearing in variety theaters. He appeared in stock as a comedian in these early days at Aberle's stock theater and beer garden on 8th Street, New York, where Jake Aberle's daughter, Lena Aberle, was the singing star of the company.

Powers made his debut in the legitimate in 1880 at the Park Theatre, Boston, in "Fun in a Photograph Gallery," and made his first New York appearance at the Bijou Theatre in the same play. Subsequently he toured this country for several years in "Evangeline" and made his London debut in 1883 with Willie Edouin in "A Bunch of Keys," "Little Red Riding Hood," and the pantomime "Dick Whittington." He also established himself there as a fine comedian in Gilbert and Sullivan's "Mikado" and "Yeomen of the Guard" and in "Geisha," parts he successfully portrayed later in the United States.

Upon Powers' return to this country, he became a recognized star as a result of his successful performances in "The Tin Soldier" and "Nadjy." From that time on, Jimmy Powers' reputation as a finished, delightful comedian became an integral part of American stage history. Beginning in 1891 he played the role of Dick Dasher in "A Straight Tip" for four years, a record at the time.

In 1897 Powers probably started the rise to the peak of his career by becoming a member of the famous Augustin Daly Musical Comedy Company and was this famous company's leading comedian until 1902. One of his most memorable roles during this period was Wun-hi in the "Geisha," which ran over three years and was revived in 1931 with Powers playing the same part. He was also seen as Bob Acres, his most famous role, in the all-star revival of "The Rivals." Powers also essayed successfully roles in Shakespearean plays. Mr. Powers also played in "Erminie," "Circus Girl" and "San Toy." His last stage appearance was in 1935 in George M. Cohan's "Seven Keys to Baldpate." Four years later during his retirement he wrote his own biography, *Twinkle Little Star.* Powers was a leading member of the Players Club and for years, almost to the time of his passing, he walked from his home in the Ansonia Hotel to the clubhouse in Gramercy Park. His widow, the former Rachel Booth, noted as an actress, appeared in many plays with her husband.

E. D. PRICE (86)

Press agent and manager. Was with John McCullough, Ziegfeld, Klaw & Erlanger. Advance agent for 50 years.

ARTHUR PRYOR (71)

Noted bandmaster conducted bands for 50 years. My friend of long standing, Arthur Pryor, was not only a distinguished bandmaster, but a skilled trombonist, and a composer of 250 martial airs and several light operas. He soon won a place in John Philip Sousa's famous band and later formed his own organization calling it "Pryor's Band," just as his father before him, Samuel Pryor, had organized the original "Pryor's Band."

Arthur Pryor conducted a band in Denver for the first time when he was 21 years old. His own band came into existence in 1903 and for many years a friendly rivalry existed between Sousa and the newly formed Pryor band. This band toured all the large American cities and Europe and then settled down for a 30-year career as the big annual attraction on the Boardwalk at Asbury Park where millions enjoyed his concerts. His best-known compositions are "The Whistler and His Dog," "Queen Titania," "On the Jersey Shore" and "American Legion March." He also broadcast in recent years for nationally known sponsors and programs.

MAX REINHARDT (70)

Noted theatrical producer and director. Reinhardt spent approximately 50 years in the theater. When only 19, he played old men's characters in the leading theater of Germany.

He distinguished himself in Ibsen's "Ghosts," also in Gorky's "Lower Depths" and other plays of the period. He created hundreds of characteristic gestures and his was a mighty and forceful accentuation. By acting one part after another at rehearsals, he imbued other actors with the spirit of their parts, so as to carry out the thoughts and meaning of the authors' lines and the accompanying music.

His management of the chorus was original and intensely striking. Actors always realized the advantage of his instructions and they surpassed themselves under his direction with a fire which they did not know they possessed.

It was not very many years before he became the director of the theater in which he had appeared in his youth.

Although he was Viennese, his spectacular stage settings were done in Salzburg and Berlin. When the Nazi plague settled on Germany and other countries, he lost his Berlin theater, his chateau in Salzburg and all his property in Austria.

Arriving in this country, he produced "Midsummer Night's Dream" for the Hollywood Bowl. He also directed in the United States "The Eternal Road" and an English version of Strauss' "Fledermaus," known here as "Rosalinda." At the Century Theatre some years ago he staged "The Miracle" for Morris Gest.

In a production of Offenbach's "Tales of Hoffman," he employed 1,000 people. This master of stage direction, one of the greatest craftsmen in its history, did everything on a similarly large scale, including the building of a colossal temple of the people's art called "Theatre of the Five Thousand."

Louis Nizer—in a great tribute to this master builder and director—in reviewing much of Reinhardt's famous work while he was still living, called him the "Edison of the theater" because he had invented and developed stage devices now universally used in the theatrical world. He introduced the revolving stage, the adaptable proscenium, the runway, the stage apron, the turntable, telescope flooring and apparatus for creating horizon, cloud and scores of other lighting, scenic and sound effects. In short, his resourceful ideas amazed the world.

He discovered and developed Schildkraut, Lubitsch and many others and he had produced almost 500 plays, including plays by Shakespeare and Shaw.

FANNY RICE (77)

Famous singer in operettas. Sang in "Erminie," "Nadjy" and other New York Casino successes. On stage 50 years.

WM. E. RITCHIE (71)

First tramp bicyclist in vaudeville; a performer for 45 years. Developed trick bicycle riding as a child and in his early youth started on the stage. He was on the same bill as Will Rogers and was teamed in several productions with W. C. Fields, the latter doing his famous juggling act, while Ritchie convulsed the audience with his comic tramp bicycle specialty. The team's greatest success was in "Gay New York" at the Casino Theatre, 39th Street and Broadway, from 1897 to 1898.

Mr. Ritchie toured with his wife, "The World's Tiniest Bicyclist," for many years and appeared before the royal families of Europe. Florenz Ziegfeld engaged the Ritchies for his Follies of 1917. In his 70th year, Mr. Ritchie appeared at Christmas time at the Fall River Casino.

FLORENCE ROBERTS (79)

Stage star. Stage and film career covered 60 years. Made her debut in the "Hoop of Gold" at the age of 19 in Brooklyn. Her Broadway appearances in "Za-Za" and "Camille" were under the direction of David Belasco.

She appeared in more than 500 plays and 100 pictures, taking up films after a long and successful stage career, which included stock engagements of 15 years in Philadelphia, long engagements in Boston, and three world tours. Her films included "Babes in Toyland," "Emile Zola," "The Storm," "Les Misérables," "Big Business," "Nobody's Baby." Her recent successes were as the mother in "Jones Family," a role she played in 17 films of that series.

BILL ROBINSON

Celebrated Negro dancer and comedian. Recently celebrated his golden jubilee after 50 years on the stage. Still with us and going strong.

MARGARET A. ROBINSON (73)

Actress, in stock and stage performances over 40 years. Although born in Ontario, Miss Robinson passed all the years of her stage career in the States. She made her debut in Minneapolis at the age of 15, in a stock company production of "Dr. Jekyll and Mr. Hyde." Later in New York, she appeared in many plays including "The Governor of Kentucky" with Wm. H. Crane, "Under Two Flags" with Blanche Bates, and "The Rivals" with Sol Smith Russell. She acted in stock in various key cities, and toured with Charles Frohman's company in "Shenandoah."

MAY ROBSON (78)

Grand veteran of stage and films, associated with the theater for over 50 years. Miss Robson was born in Australia, the name of her parents being Robison, her father being an officer in the British navy. A typographical error in leaving out the I changed her name to Robson. As a girl she ran away from home, and a few years later found her a widow in New York almost penniless. After a scant living painting china and menu cards, she turned in desperation to the stage. Without experience she played a small part in "Hoops of Gold."

It was in 1883 that Miss Robson thus made her first professional appearance on any stage. From that time, for over 40 years, there was hardly a theater in the United States that Miss Robson did not appear in, and she made American stage history in many parts and plays, that built up for her a fine reputation in her chosen profession.

In her climb to stardom, she supported such stars as Leo Dietrichstein, William Faversham, Arnold Daly, Sir Guy Standing, and William Gillette. She starred in "The Rejuvenation of Aunt Mary," and this proved easily her greatest stage triumph. She played other successful parts in "Jim the Penman," "Lord and Lady Algy," "Importance of Being Earnest," "Are You a Mason," "Dorothy Vernon." Her character roles in the films "Reunion in Vienna," "Red Headed Woman" and "Strange Interlude" will long be remembered.

Her other successful picture parts were in "Dinner at Eight," "Anna Karenina," "The White Sister," "Lady for a Day," "The Texan."

She was married when still in her teens to a young inventor, Mr. E. H. Gore. After his death she married a New York physician, Dr. Augustus H. Brown.

Miss Robson and another character actress, Marie Dressler, were warm friends and the resting place of one adjoins that of the other in California.

BENJAMIN F. ROEDER (77)

Called "Old Ben Roeder." General manager for David Belasco. His connection with the Belasco productions and theaters lasted over a period of 40 years.

JOHN R. ROGERS (92)

Press agent. Agent for Minnie Palmer whom he married and starred in "My Sweetheart." Connected with theater 70 years.

PAT ROONEY II

Son of the original Pat Rooney, who was the greatest Irish comic and dancer of his day. Pat Rooney II, a vaudevillian, father of Pat Rooney III, recently celebrated his 50th year on the stage and is still trouping.

MARY RORKE (80)

On the stage 65 years. "Grand old lady of the British stage." Played with many famous stars: Charles Wyndham, Richard Mansfield, Forbes-Robertson, Henry Irving and others. Entered films in 1913.

EDWARD E. ROSE

Celebrated playwright. Dramatized romantic novels: "Janice Meredith," "Richard Carvel," "Alice of Old Vincennes," "Gentleman from Indiana," "David Harum." Connected with stage over 40 years.

I. S. ("IKE") ROSE

Covered 50 years of showmanship. Ike Rose's career is long and interesting, as press agent, manager and showman. He traveled with Jem Mace, the famous

English champion fighter. He also took Herbert Slade the Maori and John L. Sullivan across the country. He met Gus Hill and became his advance man. He was with all Gus Hill's shows which included Weber and Fields, Montgomery and Stone, Rogers Brothers, Lottie Gilson, Billy Carter and Al Reeves.

Ike married and toured with the beautiful Australian dancer, Saharet (painted by von Kaulbach, the court painter, who made the portrait of Bismarck). He represented *Billboard* and managed among others this long list of famous dancing stars: Ruth St. Denis, Cleo de Merode, Mata Hari, Loie Fuller, Isadora Duncan and Maude Allen. He was the first to obtain $1,000 a week for Houdini. He put Billie Burke (Mrs. Ziegfeld) into the business. She was then traveling with her father, Billy Burke, a clown in Forepaugh's Circus. Ike Rose was one of the greatest showmen in Europe for 25 years. He also managed the grown-together freak twin girls and many companies of midgets. He was an internationally known showman and globe trotter and traveled nearly 1,000,000 miles. We were close friends over 40 years, and he was as "regular" as they come.

MORITZ ROSENTHAL

Before the public 50 years. The famous pianist recently celebrated his golden anniversary and still appears.

THOMAS W. ROSS

Over 40 years in the theater. Actor whose experience in stock included several years at the old Park Theatre in Brooklyn, when Henrietta Crosman was its leading lady in the 90's. Recently played in "Our Town."

ANNIE RUSSELL (72)

Actress. First appearance in New York in the chorus and soon as Josephine in "Pinafore." Played in "Hazel Kirke." Starred by Daniel Frohman in "Esmeralda." Played in "Gilded Fool" and "David Garrick." On stage nearly 40 years. This famous actress was born in Liverpool, England, in 1864. She made her first Canadian appearance in "Miss Moulton," with Rose Eytinge, at the Academy of Music, Montreal. Later as the Little Boy in "Rip Van Winkle" and Eva in "Uncle Tom's Cabin."

"Esmeralda," by Frances Hodgson Burnett, was a big success for Miss Russell. She played it 350 times at the Madison Square Theatre, New York, and 1,000 times in all. She was lost to the stage through illness from 1889 to 1894. Fully recovered, she made her reappearance under the management of Charles Frohman at Wallack's, New York, in Sydney Grundy's "New Woman." She also appeared with Nat Goodwin in "David Garrick," "Ambition" and "In Mizzoura," Bret Harte's "Sue" and Sol Smith Russell's "Bachelor's Romance." She was highly praised in London, returning to New York to star in "Miss Hobbs," "Girl and the Judge" and "Mice and Men." In 1905 she played the title role in Shaw's "Major Barbara."

EPES W. ("CHIC") SARGENT (66)

Dramatic critic. Was on the staff of *Variety* from its inception for 40 years.

GEORGE A. SCHILLER (80)

On stage over 60 years. Supported E. H. Sothern. Was with Mrs. John Drew's company, afterward with productions of E. E. Rice. Played parts in "Belle of

New York," "Corsair," "Passing Show," "Madame Sherry," "Hold Your Horses," etc.

MIKE SCOTT

Has been in theaters 50 years, dancing all alone, all over the world (as he puts it).

ANTONIO SCOTTI (70)

Famous baritone opera star. With Metropolitan Opera Company 33 years. On operatic stage about 40 years. His singing was pure art.

MARCELLA SEMBRICH

One of the most famous of the prima donnas of any generation was Mme. Marcella Sembrich. She was born in Galicia in February, 1858. Her father, who was a musician, taught her when a child to play the violin and piano, and as a child she played solos in public. She entered the Conservatory at Lemberg under direction of Professor Wilhelm Stengel, and then went to Vienna for further musical study. She was 16 before her vocal gifts were discovered. Then she went to study with Lamperti at Milan, and made a brilliant debut in 1877 at the Royal Theatre, Athens, as Lucia. The same year she married Professor Stengel. She first came to the United States in 1883 under Henry E. Abbey's management.

When Henry E. Kreybiel first heard Sembrich, he wrote that "her voice awakened echoes of Mme. Patti's organ, but has warmer life blood in it." Sembrich studied Patti's method and mastered much of it in the three seasons she sang with her at Covent Garden, but she just missed the rich, full Italian warmth of the diva. This fact Sembrich graciously recognized when she said: "There is no one in the world to be compared with Patti; nor do I think there has ever been a singer exactly like her. We have all had to work hard to accomplish the things that she did with ridiculous ease." What a generous, modest confession of one great artist to another in a profession noted for running the gamut in petty jealousies, deadly rivalries, calumnies and claques.

In 1880 Sembrich's fame as a *coloratura* soprano had preceded her to London. The critic of the *Standard* wrote: "Mme. Sembrich's debut as Lucia created something in the nature of a *furore* and next morning the advent of a great artist was announced by the critics . . . Her second appearance was as successful as her first. She won her way also into the regard of audiences by her marvelously brilliant singing as the Queen in 'Les Huguenots.' "

Klein said: "These praises and predictions were to be amply verified in her next four seasons . . . Sembrich's voice at this period was singularly entrancing. I was immensely struck with the vibrant quality and bell-like purity of her tone, her impeccable intonation, and the faultless accuracy of her scales. She had a perfect control, and the masterful ease and facility of her execution was displayed over a compass extending to the F in *alt*."

Klein further said: "It was as a Mozart singer that she appealed most of all, for she combined in herself all the superlative gifts that go to the making of that rare phenomenon. Nor would the ordinary spectator ever have guessed how greatly her outward calmness belied her. She was, she confessed, 'a bundle of nerves,' and was so short-sighted, that without her lorgnette she could not distinguish people or objects a couple of yards in front of her. How she managed on the stage, she hardly knew, but apparently the difficulty made no difference to her art."

In the *New York Tribune* Krehbiel wrote: "Mme. Sembrich is a lovely singer, lovely of person, of address, of voice; and her artistic acquirements in the limited field in which Donizetti's opera called them into activity, at least, are of the highest rank. Her style is exquisite and plainly the outgrowth of a thoroughly musical nature. It unites some of the highest elements of art. Such reposefulness of manner, such smoothness and facility in execution, such perfect balance of tone and refinement of expression can be found only in one richly endowed with deep musical feeling and ripe artistic intelligence. She carries her voice wondrously well, throughout a wide register, and from her lowest note to her highest, there is the same quality of tone. It is a voice of fine texture too; it has a velvety softness, yet is brilliant; and though not magnetic in the same degree as the voices of other singers still before the public, it has a fine, sympathetic vein."

At the benefit to Henry E. Abbey at the Metropolitan Opera House in New York, Mme. Sembrich appeared as singer, pianist and violinist, playing the De Beriot Concerto, No. 7, which she had studied with my friend Ovide Musin; played it on his own Maggini violin, which he lent her for the occasion and played it exceedingly well. This benefit netted over $26,000 to Abbey.

At her funeral in 1935 more than 3,500 people thronged into St. Patrick's Cathedral for the impressive service. The operatic and musical world and the stage, as well as many of the patrons of the celebrated horseshoe circle of boxholders at the Metropolitan Opera House, were present to pay a last tribute to this peerless artist and glorious songbird. Seven automobiles were required to carry the flowers. Barring possibly Patti and Melba, Sembrich was my favorite of all singers I have ever heard.

WILLIAM SEYMOUR (82)

Actor and director. Father of May Davenport Seymour, director of the theatrical division, Museum of the City of New York. Played with John Wilkes Booth in 1864. Also with Edwin Booth, Lawrence Barrett, Charlotte Cushman and Joseph Jefferson. Famous as stage director for Charles Frohman. In the theater over 50 years.

OTIS SKINNER (83)

Distinguished actor-writer and producer. A great figure on the American stage for 60 years. Having written his own life story, *Footlights and Spotlights*, one can only repeat a little of what is already well-known of the brilliant histrionic career of Otis Skinner. After witnessing many of his performances, particularly his Shakespearean roles, I have always carried away the thought that only in rare and notable instances such as performances of Henry Irving, Edwin Booth, and Lawrence Barrett have I ever seen and enjoyed a more finished actor.

With the amazing record of 325 parts, including 16 in the plays of Shakespeare, and an experience which included years in stock and the direction of over 30 plays, it is little wonder that Mr. Skinner enjoyed an international reputation not only in every leading city of the United States, but likewise in every foreign capital.

The best stage successes of Edwin Booth, Modjeska, Ada Rehan, Maude Adams, Mrs. Fiske and Henrietta Crosman were illumined by the fine acting and perfect diction of Otis Skinner. On his own, his triumphal "Kismet," an Oriental play by Edward Knoblauch, placed him on an American stage pedestal. In his 60 years before the footlights, he ran the gamut of stage impersonations, playing everything from an elderly Negro in "Woodleigh," a bit in Kiralfy's "Enchantment," and the star part of "Uncle Tom's Cabin," to many of the immortal roles of the Bard of Avon, playing each with intelligence and distinction.

His versatility in adapting himself to many-sided characterizations is easily apparent, in mentioning a few of the best remembered out of the many hundreds he essayed, including "Kismet," "Honor of the Family," "Mister Antonio," "Cock of the Walk," "Richelieu," "Fool's Revenge," "Macbeth," "Merry Wives of Windsor," "Much Ado About Nothing," "Hamlet," "Merchant of Venice," "Taming of the Shrew," "Ruy Blas" and "Richard III." Also many of the Augustin Daly comedy successes.

Mr. Skinner was born in Cambridge, Mass., in 1858, the son of a Universalist clergyman. He was the father of the well-known actress and monologist Cornelia Otis Skinner, recently starring in the play "Theatre." Mr. Skinner was the dean of the American stage and was at the time of his death in 1942 vice-president of the Players.

JOHN C. SLAVIN (71)

Musical comedy comedian, 61 years on the stage. In the 90's and the early 1900's Slavin was a well-known comedian. At the age of 10 he started with the San Francisco minstrels. Later he toured the vaudeville theaters, becoming famous under the team name of Walton and Slavin.

Slavin appeared in many of the Broadway musical successes, among them "Belle of New York," "The Fortune Teller," "His Honor the Mayor," "Little Nemo," "The Country Girl" and "In Gay New York." He was in the original "Jack and the Beanstalk" and played comedy roles with the Lillian Russell Opera Company.

C. AUBREY SMITH (80)

Veteran Stage and Screen Actor. Fifty-one years in the theater in 1943 and still a universal favorite with the great picture-going public. A versatile character artist of wide experience and a shining example of the Shakespearean truism that "an actor in his time plays many parts."

EDGAR (McPHAIL) SMITH (80)

Librettist and actor. Wrote or adapted more than 150 musical plays or comedies, including "Spider and the Fly," "Grand Vizier," "Merry World," etc. Connected with the theater over 40 years.

HARRY B. SMITH (58)

Famous librettist and lyric writer for 40 years. Wrote 300 musical plays, 6,000 songs. Collaborated with Reginald De Koven in "Robin Hood" and with Victor Herbert in "Fortune Teller," "Serenade," etc. Also with John Philip Sousa and Jerome Kern. Connected with stage about 40 years.

Also wrote "The Algerian," "Billionaire," "Casino Girl," "Crystal Slipper," "Doll Girl," "Don Quixote," "Ziegfeld Follies 1907-08-09-10-12," "Foxy Quiller," "Half-a-King," "Highwayman," "Lilac Domino," "Madcap Princess,"

"Miss Innocence," "Maid Marian," "Modest Suzanne," "The Office Boy," "Rob Roy," "The Rounders," "The Siren," "Spring Maid," "The Strollers," "Wild Rose," "Winsome Winnie," "Wizard of the Nile," etc., etc.

MRS. SOL SMITH

Over 50 years on the stage. America's oldest actress.

WINCHELL SMITH (61)

Actor, producer, playwright. Produced "Lightnin'," "Turn to the Right," "Brewster's Millions," "Polly of the Circus," "Fortune Hunter," "Vinegar Tree," etc. Forty years in theatricals.

E. H. (EDWIN HUGH) SOTHERN (74)

Famous actor, second son of Edward A. Sothern, famous English actor, also early American actor at the Boston Museum. Later under the management of Daniel Frohman, 1885 to 1896. First wife, Virginia Harned. Starred in "Romeo and Juliet." Later Sothern married Julia Marlowe. The famous couple, Sothern and Marlowe, occupied a foremost position in American theatrical annals. E. H. Sothern was 50 years on the stage. He was born in New Orleans, La., and was educated in England. His father was opposed to a stage career for him and wished him to become a painter.

The stage was in the younger Sothern's blood, however, and in September, 1879, he made his first appearance at the Broadway Theatre, New York, playing the cabman in "Sam" and utterly collapsing with fright when he met his father on the stage. Later he appeared at the Boston Museum in small parts and in low comedy roles with the John McCullough Company.

In 1881, after his father's death, Mr. Sothern toured in England with his elder brother, Lytton Sothern, after which, returning to America, he went through a period of poverty. Soon, however, under the management of Charles Frohman, Daniel Frohman and in support of Estelle Clayton and Helen Dauvray in "Mona," "Peg Woffington," "Love Chase," "Editha's Burglar" and "Lord Chumley," his stage fame and fortune were at last established.

Success after success followed in "Captain Letterblair," "Maister of Woodborro," "Prisoner of Zenda," "Enemy to the King," "Adventure of Lady Ursula," "King's Musketeer," "Lady of Lyons," Hauptmann's "Sunken Bell" and others. The peak of his stage fame was reached in a series of Shakespearean roles with his wife, Julia Marlowe—which made them public idols in the American theater over a long period of years.

HELEN STRICKLAND (75)

Actress. Played in "Bachelor's Baby," "Dark Victory," "Macbeth," etc. Prominent on stage 60 years.

MAURICE SULLIVAN (75)

Actor and stage director, over 50 years in theatricals. Mr. Sullivan was with the well-known star Nellie McHenry of the Saulsbury Troubadour Co. about 1894.

He also appeared with Roger Bros. Company and in Klaw & Erlanger's "Oh,

Oh Delphine." Other productions in which Mr. Sullivan played were "When Johnnie Comes Marching Home" and "Apple Blossoms."

Until about ten years ago he was connected with vaudeville and stock companies in various cities of the United States.

ANNE SUTHERLAND (75)

Well-known actress, on stage 60 years. A real old trouper in every sense of the old school, she finished an active stage career not long ago. She had played with many of the great stars and in numerous noted productions.

She made her stage debut in Chicago in 1870 at the age of 13 as Little Buttercup in "Pinafore." From the moment that she appeared in this famous Gilbert and Sullivan operetta, she devoted her life to her stage art for many decades excepting for a few parts in radio dramas about 1940. As a trouper, she was equally well-known in the smaller cities of this country as in New York, Chicago, Boston and other large theatrical centers. She credited Joseph Jefferson as her greatest teacher and inspiration for acting and often related incidents of her numerous engagements with such leading producers and managers, as Charles and Daniel Frohman, David Belasco, Henry Miller, Nat Goodwin and Al Woods.

In an interview she told of her childhood visit to an uncle in Edinburgh, which brought her the opportunity to meet and know well Thomas Carlyle and Robert Browning.

One of her last big New York successes was her appearance in the original production of "Craig's Wife." She recounted that her role in "London Calling" represented her 1,249th acting role. We remember her best in "More Than Queen," "Susan Lenox," "White Horse Tavern," "Cheating Cheaters," "Arms and the Man," "Mrs. Erskine's Devotion," "Deep Purple," and Shaw's "You Never Can Tell."

FRANK TANNEHILL, JR.

Connected with the stage over 50 years. Actor, lyricist, manager, playwright. He came from stage stock. He was the son of Frank Tannehill, a widely known actor and manager. His mother was a well-known actress. Frank Tannehill, Jr., was a poet, raconteur, and sportsman. His best-known songs were "Believe" and "Maybe," with music by George Rosey.

MARIE TEMPEST (78)

Eminent stage star, on the stage over 55 years. In her first 15 years in the theater she essayed everything from grand to comic opera, including the title role in "Carmen," Mabel in "Pirates of Penzance" and leading parts in other Gilbert and Sullivan productions. At the height of her success in London, she came and took New York by storm in the 90's and delighted her audiences in soprano roles, rivaling in popularity Lillian Russell, the American favorite of that period.

She studied music under the same famous tutor as Jenny Lind, Manuel Garcia. The stage-struck music student made her debut in 1885 in "Boccaccio." In the title role of Cellier's opera "Dorothy," she appeared in nearly a thousand performances of this outstanding success. In an American-Canadian tour in 1890-1892 she played in "The Red Hussar," followed by "Bohemian Girl," "Fencing Master" and "Algerian," a series of stage successes. Under the management of George Edwardes in London, she met equal favor in "The Artist's

Model," which ran for 100 performances. Her popularity never waned even in straight comedy and "Nell Gwynn" by Anthony Hope again met public favor.

English and American critics were loud in their praises of "Dame Marie," as Miss Tempest was fondly called in later years. In 1925, when she came back with a success by Noel Coward, "Hay Fever," his glowing criticism of her artistry struck the mark when he said of her: "When she steps on the stage, a certain magic occurs, and this magic is in itself unexplainable, and belongs only to the very great." Marie Tempest (formerly Marie Susan Etherington) was born in London in 1864. She was married first to A. E. Izard, later to Cosmo Stuart, and her last husband was her manager, W. Graham Browne.

During the Silver Jubilee of King George V and Queen Mary, Miss Tempest was honored by their presence at a testimonial matinee at which over £5,000 was raised to endow the Marie Tempest Ward at St. George's Hospital for the benefit of actors and actresses.

FAY TEMPLETON (74)

Actress and "star of the nineties," over 60 years on the stage. Favorite of the musical comedy stage and popularizer of songs like "Rosey, You Are My Posey" at Weber and Fields, she made her stage debut at age of 3 (1868) and in 1933 she appeared in Jerome Kern's "Roberta."

Her parents, John and Alice Vane Templeton, operated the Templeton Opera Company which constantly traveled on the road, so the child was virtually born on the stage. At 3 she sang the hit of the day, "Up in a Balloon," in an old-fashioned Southern theater lit by smoky oil lamps, and she was a sensation. At 8 she was playing "Puck" and at 15 she eloped with the minstrel Billy West (Primrose and West). E. E. Rice's famous extravaganza "Evangeline" afforded her the first real hit of her career in the part of Gabrielle at the 14th Street Theatre in 1885.

After divorcing Billy West, she married Howell Osborn (King of the Dudes) who left her $100,000 at his death, and later she married William Patterson, who died in 1932.

At the height of their popularity, she joined Weber and Fields at their Music Hall. In 1905 she reached the crowning point of her career, the role of Mary in George M. Cohan's "Forty-Five Minutes From Broadway." In 1907, after 38 years on the stage, she announced she would retire. Her final performance jammed the Grand Opera House and led to almost hysterical cries for "Speech! Speech!" She came back, however, playing Buttercup in Gilbert and Sullivan's "Pinafore," and "Roberta." An excerpt from a *New York Times* editorial after her passing reads: "Fay Templeton thrived on Gilbert & Sullivan Opera and in her time played both 'Ralph Rackstraw' and 'Buttercup' in 'Pinafore.' "

They say there never was a better Buttercup. But she was making theatrical history back in the forgotten days of "Rip Van Winkle" and "The Two Orphans." What is best and most urbane in the lighter side of the theater for 63 years is woven into the story of Fay Templeton.

FRED TERRY (69)

Actor. First appearance Haymarket Theatre, London, at 15. Played in "Sweet Nell of Old Drury" with his wife, Julia Neilson. Was in "Scarlet Pimpernel" and many Shakespearean plays. In theater 50 years.

JAMES ("JIM") THORNTON (76)

On the stage 57 years. Veteran song writer and monologist. Writer of "My Sweetheart's the Man in the Moon," "Sweet Sixteen," "It Don't Seem Like the Same Old Smile," "Streets of Cairo," "Going for a Pardon," "On the Benches in the Park."

J. RANKEN TOWSE (88)

Dramatic critic. Critic of *New York Evening Post* for 54 years. Wrote *Sixty Years in the Theatre.*

WM. TURNER (81)

Veteran of the films, connected with stage and screen 54 years. Known for his character work playing doorman on the stage, the veteran Wm. Turner had also appeared in films with Tallulah Bankhead and Ruth Chatterton. In 1883 he appeared with Geo. C. Boniface (the 1st) in "The Streets of New York." He also played leading roles in "David Harum" and "Alias Jimmy Valentine." He alternated between stage and films and for many years was a member of the Albee Stock Company.

VIOLET VANBRUGH (75)

Celebrated British actress, over 50 years on the stage. Was not only one of the greatest Shakespearean actresses of England, but she was equally famous in the United States, touring for years with the Kendals and appearing with the foremost American companies.

In her own country Miss Vanbrugh had played practically every important woman's part in Shakespeare. Her first part at 19 was in "Faust and Loose," an old comedy. She toured the provinces with a stock company and soon established herself as one of London's favorite players. Her New York debut was in 1889 at the Fifth Avenue Theatre in "A Scrap of Paper." Later she appeared under Augustin Daly's auspices in such successes as "Twelfth Night," "School for Scandal" and "Love in Tandem."

One of her famous engagements in London was with Henry Irving at the Lyceum appearing as Anne Boleyn in "Henry VIII." As understudy to Ellen Terry she was engaged for Irving's productions of "King Lear" and "Becket." In 1910 she joined Beerbohm Tree's Company at His Majesty's Theatre, making a great hit as Queen Katharine in "Henry VIII." In recent years she appeared with her daughter Prudence in "Merry Wives of Windsor" and other plays.

Excelling in Shakespearean parts, she appeared in 1905 by command of King Edward, at Windsor Castle, as Portia in "Merchant of Venice." Her last performance in 1937 was as Mistress Ford in "Merry Wives of Windsor." She also acted in several films.

QUEENIE VASSAR

Actress. At one time married to Harry Kernell, a favorite comedian on the variety stage. She was 50 years in theatricals and is now living in retirement on the Coast.

BAYARD VEILLER (74)

Well-known American playwright, interested in theatricals the greater part of 60 years. He once claimed that he was a Gilbert and Sullivan fan almost from the time when as a boy of 10 he witnessed a performance of "Patience."

Mr. Veiller wrote "Within the Law," one of the most successful plays of its period. Two of his other successful plays were "The Trial of Mary Dugan" and "Thirteenth Chair." The former was adapted for pictures under Mr. Veiller's personal supervision, and "The Trial of Mary Dugan" duplicated its New York hit in London. He married his leading lady in this show, Margaret Wycherly, and his second wife was a lady writing under the name of Martin Vale, who collaborated with him on some of his later plays.

THOMAS WALKER (WHIMSICAL WALKER)

Veteran circus clown for 50 years with Barnum and Bailey's Circus.

FREDERICK B. WARDE (83)

Famous actor, tragedian and lecturer. Contemporary of Edwin Booth, Lawrence Barrett, Louis James and Thomas Keene, in the 80's and 90's. On stage over 40 years.

BILLY ("BEEF TRUST") WATSON

Manager and comedian, 50 years of stage activity, principally in connection with burlesque.

JOHNNY WATSON (98)

Circus rider, dog trainer, vaudeville artist, 92 years before the public of Great Britain. The oldest vaudeville actor in Great Britain died December 28, 1942, at the age of 98, a little while before he was booked to appear in a "Mother Goose" pantomime.

From the age of 6 until he was 30 he followed the career of a circus rider, but when his legs were broken he was forced to quit. For 60 years thereafter he trouped Great Britain and the Dominions as a dog trainer, and then took up vaudeville. His prize performance was given before the Prince of Wales (later King Edward), several foreign kings, and two prime ministers, William Gladstone and Benjamin Disraeli.

During the First World War, when he was 70, he tried to enlist, but the recruiting officer after his physical turned him down. Then to the amazement of the officer, Johnny made his exit from the room while turning half a dozen back somersaults.

PERCY WEADON (FRANK PRESTON) (79)

Producer and press agent. Was with J. A. McCaull, Bartley Campbell, Steele Mackaye. Co-producer of "Chocolate Soldier." General manager for Belasco, Savage, Klaw and Erlanger and Shubert. Connected with theatricals nearly 50 years.

JOSEPH M. (JOE) WEBER (74)

Of the noted team of comedians Weber & Fields, on the American stage over 50 years. In my earlier book *They All Sang* I included two of my oldest stage friends, Joe Weber and Lew Fields, who were then alive. I referred to Joe on seven different pages and to Weber & Fields on four additional pages. There is little that I can add to the tribute I paid to them at that time. I knew them well and therefore still feel the urge to add my bit to their only too well known stage careers.

Since the recent passing of Joe Weber and his pal and partner, Lew Fields the leading papers of the country have epitomized their lives, as the creators of a new form of entertainment, as the class of all Dutch comedians of their time, as the enterprising producers at tremendous cost of the famous "Weberfields" satirical Broadway burlesques with the most expensive casts ever assembled on any stage in connection with this new form of entertainment.

To gather together and to employ in one happy family such stage stars as Lillian Russell, David Warfield, Fay Templeton, Pete Dailey, Henry E. Dixey, Ross & Fenton, Sam Bernard, John T. Kelly, Louis Mann, Ethel Levey, De Wolf Hopper, Marie Dressler, Willie Collier, Bessie McCoy, Frankie Bailey, and the Music Hall Beauty Chorus was of itself an accomplishment never dreamed of before in the annals of the American stage. To have almost continuously in a career of half of a century made countless millions laugh, with clean, even if largely slapstick fun was also to their credit. To have built up through their business acumen and enterprise the following and devotion of a clientele that never missed a Weber & Fields show, and often paid substantial premiums for opening nights, can only be compared as a chronicle of success with the faithful following of the Savoyards, according to Weber's obit in the *New York Times.*

I could add an entire chapter about the personal side of the boys, if I chose to do so, from their early days in show business on the Bowery, when our close coterie of friends included Gus Hill, Ike Rose, Harry Miner, Roger Brothers (Gus & Max), Maude Raymond, Estelle Wellington, Gus Williams, Tony Pastor, Pat Rooney I, Maggie Cline, Sam Bernard and a host of other celebrities in the good old "variety" days.

That they both managed in their careers worthy musical productions by Victor Herbert and also various other forms of stage plays was proof of their versatility in showmanship and their grasp of the public theatrical pulse.

L. LAWRENCE WEBER (68)

In the theater 55 years. Veteran producing manager. He was engaged in show business in a wide range of activities—acrobat, circus clown, jockey, minstrel, sports promoter, theater owner, show and film producer. His productions included "Little Jessie James," "Moonlight," "The Love Call," etc. Lawrence Weber was a nephew of Joe Weber (Weber & Fields), and associated with him in many of his successful stage ventures was the well-known producer and lyricist Wm. B. Friedlander.

MRS. THOMAS WHIFFEN (91)

Actress. One of the first Buttercups in "Pinafore." With the Daniel Frohman Company in "Charity Ball." Also in "Trelawny of the Wells." On stage 63 years.

WALKER WHITESIDE (73)

Noted actor, on stage nearly 50 years. Earned his earlier stage reputation as a Shakespearean actor. When a young man in his twenties he appeared in New York at the Union Square Theatre as Hamlet. Some years earlier he had earned the sobriquet of the "Boy Tragedian" and had played in "Shylock," "Othello," "King Lear" and "Richard III."

For many years after his debut in New York he toured the country in Shakespearean repertoire, building up a public following, which stood him in good stead as a successful road star for many years. When Liebler produced Zangwill's famous comedy-drama "The Melting Pot," Whiteside was engaged as the star. The play ran 268 times in New York and almost as many performances in London. The other outstanding successful plays in which he starred were "Mr. Wu" and "Typhoon," the former one of his many characterizations of Orientals.

FRANCIS WILSON (81)

Farce and comic opera star comedian, author and lecturer. Played in "Erminie," singing Cadeaux for 1,256 performances. In comic opera for 30 years. Connected with theatricals about 40 years. A grand comedian and closely identified with the history of the Players Club.

FRANK J. WILSTACH (68)

Manager and author with De Wolf Hopper, Sothern and Marlowe, Viola Allen, William Faversham, Mrs. Leslie Carter, etc. In theatricals 40 years.

BANKS WINTER (81)

Minstrel, song writer and singer, father of Winona Winter. Connected with shows 40 years. Author of the popular song, "White Wings."

ALEXANDER WOOLLCOTT (56)

Internationally known critic, author and lecturer, in the public eye over 3 years. Began his schooling in Philadelphia, completing postgraduate work a Columbia University in 1913. The following year he became dramatic critic of the *New York Times*, remaining in that post until 1922, when he switched to the *New York Herald*. From 1925 to 1928 he was on the staff of the *New York World*.

As a drama critic for the New York dailies, Woollcott's reviews of Broadway shows were penetrating, witty and frequently devastating, and in 1916 the Shuberts became so angered by one of his reviews that they banned him from all their theaters. He sued to be readmitted, but the courts ruled against him Later the Shuberts lifted the ban.

He was in uniform during World War I for two years, one year of which he was on the editorial council of *The Stars and Stripes*, doughboy newspaper He was a member of Theta Delta Chi.

As an author he produced such works as *Mrs. Fiske—Her Views on Acting Actors and the Problems of the Stage* in 1917; *The Command Is Forward* in 1919; *Shouts and Murmurs* and *Mr. Dickens Goes to the Play* in 1923 *Enchanted Aisles* in 1924; *The Story of Irving Berlin* in 1925; *Going to Piece* in 1928; *While Rome Burns* in 1934; *The Woollcott Reader* in 1935, an *Woollcott's Second Reader* in 1937. He was also a contributor to numerou periodicals on various subjects.

With George S. Kaufman he wrote "The Channel Road" in 1929 and "Th Dark Tower" in 1933, both of which enjoyed satisfactory runs on Broadway

As an actor he appeared as Harold Sigrift in "Brief Moment" at the Belasc Theatre, New York, in 1931. In 1938 he took the part of Binkie in "Wine c Choice" at the New York Guild Theatre. His most recent appearance on th stage was as Sheridan Whiteside in "The Man Who Came to Dinner."

Radio claimed him as its Town Crier on American networks and for th British Broadcasting System from 1929 to 1940.

Woollcott was unmarried and his home was in Bomoseen, Vt.

HUNTLEY WRIGHT (71)

Musical comedy artist, on stage 48 years. Wright came from a large and distinguished English stage family. He was carried on the stage as an infant by his father, the late Frederic Wright, actor and manager. His mother, Jessie F. Wright, was a well-known English actress, as was also his sister, Miss Haidee Wright. Three other members of his family connected with the theater were Fred, Bertie and Marie Wright.

Huntley Wright made his debut at the Theatre Royal, Edinburgh, in 1887 in the play "False Lights." He toured South Africa under the management of George Edwardes. In London he appeared under Charles Frohman's management in "The Mountain Climber." At the Criterion Theatre in New York in 1907, he played in the successful musical comedy "The Dairy Maids." The list of productions in which he portrayed important parts in both the Old and the New World would easily total more than fifty. He appeared on the stage continuously until the World War in 1914, and after enlisting he rose to the rank of captain. Among the roles he essayed were Vernier in the "Miracle at Verdun," Calicot in "Madame Pompadour," Sandy Bishop in "Too Young to Marry," and Scotty in "Give Me a Ring."

MAY YOHE (77)

Veteran stage and vaudeville actress. Appeared in "The Crystal Prince" in 1887. Vaudeville favorite in New York, London and Paris. Married Lord Francis Hope and owned "Hope" diamond. Married Captain Putnam Bradley Strong, son of Mayor Strong of New York. Nearly 50 years on stage.

OSWALD YORKE

Actor, before the curtain 58 years. Was well-known in both America and Great Britain as a leading player in support of stars. He made his first appearance in Benson's touring stock company in 1884. In 1889 he made his debut at the Strand Theatre, London. He toured the United States with the famous English star, E. S. Willard, and also with John Drew and Maude Adams. At one time he was a member of the Empire Stock Company, under the management of Charles Frohman.

In 1905 he created the part of Bill Walker in Shaw's "Major Barbara" at the Court Theatre, London. In "The Affairs of Anatol," produced by Winthrop Ames, Mr. Yorke played Max, and later in "Treasure Island" he was the Black Dog. His other prominent roles were in "Lost Horizon," "Lady in the Case," "The Whirlwind," "Social Register" and "Barchester Towers." He also directed classic English comedies.

In First World War he took charge of entertainments for American soldiers in France.

J. ARTHUR YOUNG (63)

Character Actor. A career of 45 years on the stage and in films and radio. Mr. Young was favorably received in "Ben Hur," "Smiling Through," "Yellow Jacket," "East Is West," "Lost Horizon," "The Male Animal" and many other successful plays.

Early in his career he was connected with stock companies in Philadelphia, Washington, Detroit and Denver where, as is usually the case with a capable actor, this valuable training stood him in good stead in his later Broadway engagements.

He had also appeared recently in various motion pictures and in several New York and Hollywood radio programs.

35 YEARS OR MORE IN SHOW BUSINESS

THE FOLLOWING ACTORS and show people are still active, or were recently, in some field of entertainment, after a stage career of 35 years or more, and are therefore deserving of honorable mention:

George Arliss
Henry Armetta
Lionel Atwill
Ethel Barrymore
Lionel Barrymore
Jean Bedini
Joe E. Brown
Eddie Cantor
Leo Carrillo
Joseph Cawthorn
William Collier
Charlie Dale
Louise Dresser
Gus Edwards
W. C. Fields
Claude Gillingwater
Dan Healy
Lew Hearn
Joseph E. Howard
Willie & Eugene Howard
Walter Huston
Roger Imhof
Elsie Janis
Al Jolson
Buster Keaton
James Kirkwood
Grace La Rue
Sir Harry Lauder
Victor Moore
Polly Moran
Tom Patricola
B. A. Rolfe
Julia Sanderson
Al Shean
George Sidney
Alison Skipworth
Joe Smith
Fred Stone
Julius Tannen
Herman Timberg
Watson Sisters
Chas. Winninger

Never-to-be-Forgotten Singers, Writers and Their Songs

MUSICAL PROGRAMS: "The Black Crook" and "Evangeline"

RARE MUSICAL REPERTOIRES: Jenny Lind, Christine Nilsson and Other Important Operatic and Concert Stars

FEATURED SONGS OF EARLY AMERICAN FAMILY ENTERTAINERS

FAVORITE EARLY AMERICAN MINSTREL SONGS

FAMOUS OLD-TIME BALLADS AND SONGS WHICH SHOULD NEVER DIE

Musical Programs: "The Black Crook" and "Evangeline"

THE BLACK CROOK

Music by G. Operti

The Operti music was written for the first revival of "The Black Crook," produced by Jarrett and Palmer, starting December 12, 1870, and withdrawn April 8, 1871, after 122 performances.

A four-page program in the Public Library for Niblo's Garden for the week ending January 21, 1871, gives the cast and is interesting because Pauline Markham played Stalacta.

The program says: "Overture and ballet music by G. Operti." A page advertisement lists the songs. All this music was copyrighted in 1870 and published by J. L. Peters, at 599 Broadway, nearly opposite Niblo's Garden.

Operti was the Musical Director at Niblo's.

The various numbers in the score are listed herewith:

The Amazon's March (Op. 201)

Chorus:

O Amazons, we proudly march to victory,
With hearts, with hearts so light.
Ah! Yes gay is the soldier's life,
So gallantly to march and fight.
Tramp, tramp, brave and merry.
Our banners waving to the sky, proudly high!
While we go, sound the song, loud the strain prolong!
On the march, on the march,
Long shall our brave watchword be victory, victory!

Mermaid's Song
Arranged by Iglehardt. Picture of Miss Markham on the cover.

I Said to My Love
Ballad. Picture of Miss Markham on the cover.

I Am Waiting for Thee
Ballad. Picture of Miss Markham on the cover.

Danse de Sabot (Wooden Shoe Waltz)

Flower Dance Mazurka

He's Naughty But He's Nice
Ballad. Picture of Miss Prentige on the cover. (This was Fanny Prentige, who played Carline in this revival of "The Black Crook.")

Oh No! Not in These Boots
Ballad. Picture of Miss Prentige on the cover.

Married On Michaelmas Day
Ballad. Picture of Miss Prentige on the cover.

Lotus Waltz

Golden Terrace Galop

Golden Realm Waltz
Written by J. Harmistoun for the first production of "The Black Crook" in 1866.

Fairy Queen March
Written by J. Harmistoun for the first production of "The Black Crook" in 1866.

You Naughty, Naughty Men
Poem by T. Kennick. Music by G. Bickwell. Sung by Miss Millie Caven-

dish in "The Black Crook" at Niblo's Garden.

Ah, Never Deem My Love to Change

I'm Alone

Why Should I Alone Be Dumb?

NOTE: G. Operti also composed all the music for the "Extravaganza of Aladdin," sung by Eliza Weathersby (as Aladdin), including "Angot On the Brain."

EVANGELINE

American Opéra Bouffe

First Production July 27, 1874

Words by J. Cheever Goodwin. Music by E. E. Rice

Complete musical numbers

Opening Chorus

Thinking, Love, of Thee

Bathing (Trio)

She's Saved

Evangeline (Song and dance)

Sammy Smug

Golden Chains (Duet)

A Farmer Lived (Song and chorus)

In Us You See (Soldiers' chorus)

He Says I Must Go (Finale First Act)

Boorioboola Gha (Chorus)

I'm In Lofe Mit a Shveet Leedle Girls (Song and dance)

We Are Off to Seek for Eva (Duet)

Twelve O'Clock and All Is Well (Quartette)

Policeman's Chant

Polimenicho (Song and chorus)

Where Art Thou Now, My Beloved?

Evangeline (Finale Second Act)

Kissing Song

Go Not Happy Day

O Gabriel, My Best Beloved (Song and dance)

Laughing Eyes of Blue (Song and waltz)

Come to Me Quickly, My Darling

A Hundred Years Ago

Sweet the Song of Birds

Power of Gold

Good Night to One and All (Grand Finale)

Rare Musical Repertoires: Jenny Lind, Christine Nilsson and Other Important Operatic and Concert Stars

Sung by JENNY LIND (1820-1887)

I've Left the Snow Clad Hills
Words by George Linley. Music partly by George Linley. Published by William Vanderbeck, 479 Broadway, N. Y. C. (1850). Old colored litho on stone with Jenny Lind portrait on title page.

Stars of Heaven Are Gleaming
Poem by Wrey. Music by Ahlstron. Published by Stephen W. Marsh, Boston (about 1846). A Swedish favorite. Fine old litho of Jenny Lind in costume on frontispiece.

I Dream of My Fatherland
Words by Fredrika Bremer. Adapted to Swedish air by Karl Muller. Published by A. Fiot, Philadelphia (about 1849). ¾ tempo. Beautiful old litho of Jenny Lind on frontispiece.

By the Sad Sea Waves
Music by Jules Benedict. From the opera "Bride of Venice."

O Loving Heart, Trust On
Words by Henry C. Watson. Music by L. M. Gottschalk (1864).

Jenny Lind's Polka
Music by A. Wallenstein

Thy Blessing, Dearest Mother

Farewell, My Fatherland

My Home, My Happy Home

Come, My Lovely Maiden

Sea King's Bride

Oh Lovely, Lovely Maiden
Written by Meyerbeer

Jenny Lind's Celebrated "Bird" Song

Coming Through the Rye

The Dream

Souvenir of Jenny Lind
L-I-N-D-I-A-N-N-A (Jenny Lind's Dream Waltz)

Jenny Lind's Bridal Polka

Alice's Aria
From "Robert le Diable."

Agatha's Prayer
From "Der Freischütz."

Casta Diva
Aria from "Norma."

Song from "Beatrice ve Tenva"

NOTE: Jenny Lind sang an E above high C.

NOTE: At a concert given in New York on May 9, 1851, by Jenny Lind, the program read as follows:

SACRED

The overture for this concert was
"Joseph in Egypt" (MEHUL)

Air—"I Know That My Redeemer Liveth" (HANDEL)
MLLE. JENNY LIND

"Oh, Rest in the Lord" (*Elijah*—MENDELSSOHN)
JENNY LIND

"Oh, Mighty Pens" (*The Creation*—HAYDN)
"Home, Sweet Home"
JENNY LIND

(Conductor M. BENEDICT of an Orchestra of about 100)

OVERTURE—PART II

"Semiramide"—ROSSINI
Two Songs from "Stabat Mater" (ROSSINI)
SIGNOR SALVI

"Hörst du? Nun du"
SIGNOR SALVI
JENNY LIND

"Fantasia on the Pianoforte" (THALBERG)
MR. R. HOFFMAN

"Home, Sweet Home"
From the opera "Clari, or The Maid of Milan" (BISHOP)
MLLE. JENNY LIND

NOTE: The following songs sung by Jenny Lind were all composed by Felix Mendelssohn:

Echo Answers Through the Forest
O Winter, Cruel Winter
Oh, What Means This Strong Emotion
When Through the Piazzetta
Floating Rides a Soft and Balmy Breeze
Song of Spring
First Violet
Greeting
Shepherd's Song
Traveler's Song

NOTE: The following songs sung by Jenny Lind were all composed by Alex Fesca:

Oh, Calm My Heart's Wild Beating
I am But a Lonely Flower
When Flows This Tear
Oh, Might But My Pangs Return to Me
What Lures Thy Step

Sung by MARIA MALIBRAN (1808-1836)

Selections from "Maid of Artois"
Rouse Thee Up, Shepherd Boy
  English words by William Ball.
The Voice That Says "I Love Thee"
The Waterman
Now the Beams of Morning
The Minstrel
The Meeting
  Notturno for two voices.
The Songs of Home
The Drummer
Dearest Come to Me
  Notturno for two voices.
The Bayadere
The Parting Wish
The Goblin of the Lake
  Notturno for two voices.
Come to the Fete

Row, Boys
English words by William Ball.
Oh, Shall We Go A-Sailing?
Music by Michael Balfe.
Chagrin d'Amour
I'll Weep with Thee
Music by Carl Maria von Weber.
Dewdrop (Rondo)
Music by C. E. Horn. Sung by Mme. Malibran and Miss Paton.
Ah! Non Creda
From "La Sonnambula."
Sing Ye to the Lord
Her favorite sacred song.
Duet
From "Tito Andronico."
NOTE: This duet sung with Mme. Allan was the last time Malibran ever sang. The Concert Hall rang with applause as she fainted in the arms of a friend and nine days later she died, on September 23, 1836.

Sung by PASQUALINO BRIGNOLI (1824-1884)

Che La Morte
From "Il Trovatore."
Serenade
From "Don Pasquale."
O Lovely Night (O Vien La Notte)
Barcarolle. Music by Charles Fradell (1856).

Sung by THERESE JOHANNA ALEXANDRA TIETJENS (1831-1877)

Arditi's Waltz Song (Waltz L'Arditi)
Home, Sweet Home
Magic Flute in Alt
Last Rose of Summer
Casta Diva
From "Norma."
Come Per Me Sereno
From "La Sonnambula."
Ronda
From "Linda."

Sung by CARLOTTA PATTI (1840-1889)

Echo Song
Written by Eckert.
Duet
From "Sappho."
Mercadante
Echo
Written by Sontag.
Rondo
From "La Sonnambula."
Inez
From "Bolero."
Nightingale
Written by Muzio.
Carnival of Venice
Music written expressly for Carlotta Patti, by Sir Julius Benedict.
Where the Bee Sucks
Written by Arne.
Within a Mile of Edinboro
Come Back to Erin
Shadow Song Dinorah
In the Gloaming
Written by Harrison.
Coming Through the Rye
Sicilian Vespers (Bolero)
Ave Maria
Written by Gounod.
At Noontide Lady
Written by Arthur Hill.
First Kiss (Un Primo Bacio)
Written for Mme. Patti by E. Marzo. ¾ tempo.
The Magic Flute
Patti appeared as "Queen of the Night."
Amina
Patti appeared as "Luce di Guest."

Marie Roze
Her favorite songs

Good Night, Beloved
Written by Balfe.
There Is a Green Hill
Written by Gounod.
L'Estasi
Written by Arditi. ¾ tempo.
Dormi Pure (Sleep On)
Written by Scuderi.
Flower of the Alps
Written by Weckerlin.
Rose
Written by Spohr.
Away We'd Fly (Ti Rapirei)
Written by Tosti.
Lullaby (La Ninna Nanna)
Written by Profilli.
Chanson du Printemps (Springtime)
Written by Gounod.
Long, Long Ago
Written by Hatton.
Watching and Waiting
Written by Cowen.
Bend of the River
Written by Blumenthal.
Voice by the Cedar Tree
Written by Saint-Saëns.
List to the Voice of Youth (Gavotte)
Written by Massenet.
Beware
Written by Eliot.
Arrow and the Song
Written by Eliot.
If You Loved Me
Written by Denza.
My Poor Heart Is Broken
Written by Yradier.
On Song's Bright Pinions
Written by Mendelssohn.
Absence
Written by Beethoven.
Speak Again, Love
Written by Lotti.
Love Is Like a Bird Rebellious
Written by Carman.
Brightly the Sunlight
Written by Metna.
First Day of Happiness
Written by Auber.
Oh, What Excess of Joy (Le Premier Jour de Bonheur)
Written by Tostian.
While We Wandered
Written by V. Massie. From "Paul and Virginia."
Chanson de L'Abeille (Bee Song)
Written by V. Masse.
Ohe! Mamma (A Dream of Love)
Written by Tosti.
Now Was I Wrong?
Written by Engel.
Face in the Crowd
Written by Engel.
Love, O Come Back
Written by Pease.
He Loves No Love But Me
Written by Mora.
Sunset
Written by Rae.
Queen of Hearts
Written by Mora.

Sung by Emma Abbott (1850-1891)

Guarany
Written by Gomez.
I Know That My Redeemer Liveth
Crispiano E La Comare
Written by Ricci. Duo by Emma Abbott and Ferrari.
Nabuco
Written by Verdi. Grand Aria.
Non Bu Sogno
Marguerite
From "Faust."
Virginia
From "Paul and Virginia."
Bohemian Girl
Fra Diavolo
Martha

Maritana
Lucia Di Lammermoor
Mid Starry Deeps of Splendor
Written by Murio Celli.
Ouvrez (Open the Door) (Bolero)
Written by Dessauer.
Won't You Tell Me Why, Robin?
Written by Claribel.
Last Rose of Summer
Written by Moore.
Let Me Dream Again
Written by Sullivan.

Sung by MME. HENRIETTA SONTAG (1806-1854)

Auld Robin Grey
Home, Sweet Home
Ah, Consolarmi
From "Linda." Duet with Pozzilini.
Selections from Opera "Lindi Di Chamounix"
Come Per Me Sereno
From "La Sonnambula."
Oh, Luce Di
Selections from Opera "Elisir d'amore"
Selections from "La Donna del Lago"
Selections from "Il Barbiere de Siviglia"

Sung by ADELINA PATTI (1843-1919)
Songs and operatic selections
Patti could sing 36 operas in her repertoire

Voi Che Sapete
From "Nozze di Figaro." Aria.
Una Voce Poca Fa
From "The Barber of Seville." Aria.
Ah, Non Giunge
From "La Sonnambula." Aria.
The Mad Scene
From "Lucia di Lammermoor." Aria.
D'Amor Sul Ali Rossee
From "Il Trovatore."
Ah! Forse Lui
From "La Traviata." Aria.
Waltz Song
From "Romeo and Juliet."
The Jewel Song
From "Faust."
The Last Rose of Summer
From "Martha."
Bird Song
From "I Pagliacci."
Micaela's Aria
From "Carmen."
Elsa's Dream
From "Lohengrin."

NOTE: Mme. Patti's favorite operas, according to her own personal selection of those she loved most, were: "Lucia," "Sonnambula," "Traviata," "Il Barbiere" and "Romeo and Juliet." She said: "It requires two first-class artists to sing the latter and they carry the entire opera."

La Serenata
Written by Tosti.

NOTE: Patti added a coda which was not in the published copy. It belonged to a paraphrase of the song written and played by the violinist Simonetti, which Tosti transcribed for her.

Bel Raggio
The Diva (La Diva)
Written by Visetti. ¾ tempo.
Come, My Dearest (Vien Mio Bene)
Written by Giorza. ¾ tempo.
The Butterfly (La Farfalla)
Written by Gelli. ¾ tempo.
Spring Revel (Le Printemps)
Written by Mattei. ¾ tempo.
What Fond Hope (Ah, Che La Speme)
Written by Cohen. ¾ tempo.
The Return (Il Ritorno)
Written by Lucantoni. ¾ tempo.
Coquette (Mazurka)
Written by Chopin.
Echo of Naples (Eco di Napoli) (Tarantelle)
Written by Bevignanni.

Dream of Love (Sogno d'amore)
  Written by Gregh. ¾ tempo.
My Mandolin (Chante Ma Mandoline)
  Written by Hackensollner.
The First Song (Das Erste Lied)
  Written by Gumbert.
Secret Hope (Speme Arcena)
  Written by Patti.
Love's Plaint (Plainte D'Amour) (Mazurka)
  Written by Chopin.
Home, Sweet Home
  Written by Bishop.
Last Rose of Summer
  Written by Thomas Moore.

Sung by MME. MARCELLA SEMBRICH (1858-1935)
Partial Repertory

Dinorah
  (1880). Sung in London.
Lucia
  (1883). Sung at Metropolitan Opera House.
Mignon
  From "La Fille du Regiment."
The Magic Flute
  Sang the roles of Violetta and Gilda.
Barber of Seville
Lucia di Lammermoor
Lohengrin
  Sang the role of Elsa in Italian and German.
Faust
  Sang the role of Marguerite.
Lakmé
  Sang it in Italian, German and French.
Huguenot
  Written by Meyerbeer. Sang the role of the Queen.
Lucia
  Made her debut in this as leading soprano of Metropolitan Opera House.
Lohengrin
La Bohème
Pagliacci
Merry Wives of Windsor
Rigoletto
La Traviata
Martha
Zauberflöte
Puritani
Les Huguenots
Les Pecheurs de Perles
Romeo and Juliet
Don Pasquale
Nozze di Figaro
Sonnambula
Don Giovanni
Manon
The Maiden's Wish
  Written by Chopin.
  Her favorite song. She ended almost every concert with this little Polish mazurka.

NOTE: Mme. Sembrich died January 11, 1935, at her home, 151 Central Park West, N. Y. C., at the age of 76.

Sung by PAULINE LUCCA (1841-1908)

O Sanctissima Vergine
  Written by Gordigiani.
The Violet
  Written by Mozart.

NOTE: During her season at the Boston Opera House in 1873 Pauline Lucca sang:

Les Huguenots
La Favorita
Faust
Fra Diavolo

Sung by Clara Louise Kellogg (1842-1916)

Valse from "Romeo and Juliet"
Written by Gounod.

Duet from "Hamlet"
Written by Ambroise Thomas. Sung by Miss Kellogg and Signor Petrillo.

Voi Che Sapete
Written by Mozart. From "Nozze di Figaro."

The Jewel Song
Written by Gounod. From "Faust."

Ernani Involami
Written by Verdi. From "Ernani"

Miserere
From "Il Trovatore." Duet. Sung by Miss Kellogg and Signor Brignoli.

Polonaise
Written by Thomas. From "Mignon."

Aria
From "Don Giovanni."

Note: In May, 1873, at McVickers Theatre, Chicago, Clara Louise Kellogg and Pauline Lucca sang in Thomas' opera "Mignon."

Mario (1810-1883)
Songs and Operatic Selections

Robert le Diable
Written by Meyerbeer. Sang title role.

If With All Your Hearts
From Oratorio "Elijah."

Don Pasquale
Sang title role.

Les Huguenots

La Favorita
Achieved his highest point as a dramatic singer in this.

Sung by Christine Nilsson (1843-1921)

Spring and Autumn

The Roses

The Ball

Why Do I Weep for Thee?

Auld Robin Grey (Scotch song)

Proposal
Written by M. S. Downes

Grand Aria and Scena—Mad Song
From "Hamlet."

Ophelia's Song
From "Hamlet."

I'm Alone
Written by Benedict.

Angels Ever Bright and Fair
Written by Handel.

Old Folks at Home
Written by Stephen Foster.

I Know That My Redeemer Liveth

Coming Through the Rye

Join the Dance
Words by George Cooper (1874). Polka mazurka.

Let Me Dream Again
Written by Sullivan.

Ah Perfido!
Written by Beethoven.

La Traviata

Martha

Don Giovanni

Il Flauto Magico

Faust

Judas Maccabaeus (Oratorio)

Nozze di Figaro
Sang the role of Cherubino.

Lucia

La Favorita

Scene and Air—Ophelia
Written by Ambroise Thomas. From the opera "Hamlet."

Quartetto
Written by Flotow. From the opera "Martha."

Grand Cavatina of Violetta.
Written by Verdi. From the opera "La Traviata."

Where's the Cold Heart?
Written by Rossini. From "Stabat Mater." Duet for two sopranos.
Gratias
Written by Rossini. From "Messe Solennelle."
Non Tornio (He'll Come No More)
Scena and Rondo Finale—Mad Scene
Written by Donizetti. From the opera "Lucia di Lammermoor."
Duet
Written by Donizetti. From the opera "Don Pasquale." Duet for soprano and baritone.
Romance
Written by Ambroise Thomas. From the opera "Mignon."
Per Valli—Per Boschi (Through Valley —Through Forest)
Written by F. Blangini. Duet.
Si tu savais (Romanza)
Written by Balfe.
Duet
Written by Donizetti. From the opera "La Favorita."
Romanza—La Spia
Written by Arditi.
Ah! Quel Giorno!
Written by Rossini. From "Semiramide."
Ernani Involami (Cavatina)
Written by Verdi. From the opera "Ernani."
Ave Maria
Written by Gounod.
Romanza
Written by Flotow. From the opera "Martha."
No, No, No
Written by Meyerbeer. From "Les Huguenots."
Duet
From "Barber of Seville."
Dunque Io Son
Written by Rossini.
Last Rose of Summer
Words by Moore. Music by Stephenson.
Duet—Zerlina and Don Juan
Written by Mozart.
Ballata
Written by Verdi. From the opera "Ballo In Maschera."
Duetto—Belisario
Sul Campo Della Gloria
Written by Donizetti.
Duettino
Written by Verdi. From "Il Trovatore."
Parigi O Cara (Duet)
Written by Verdi. From the opera "La Traviata."
O Mio Fernando
Written by Donizetti. From "La Favorita."
The King of Thula (Scena and Aria)
Written by Gounod. From the opera "Faust."
Grand Aria
Written by Weber. From the opera "Der Freischütz."
Shepherd Song
Written by Meyerbeer. From "Dinorah."
Duet
Written by Flotow. From the opera "Martha."
Andante and Miserere
Written by Verdi. From the opera "Il Trovatore."
Cavatina—Nobil Signor
Written by Meyerbeer. From the opera "Les Huguenots."
Brindisi
Written by Ambroise Thomas. From "Hamlet."
Grand Aria
Written by Rossini. From "Semiramide."
Ave Maria
Written by Schubert.
Casta Diva
Written by Bellini. From the opera "Norma."
Scene e Rondo
Written by Rossini. From "Italiana In Algeri."
Romanza
Written by Donizetti. From the opera "La Favorita."

Ah! Che la Speme (What Fond Hope)
Written by Jules Cohen.
Cavatina—Una Voce Poco Fa
Written by Rossini. From the opera "Barber of Seville."
Quando Le Sere Al Placido (When at the Silent Evening Hour)
Written by Verdi. From the opera "Luisa Miller."
Canti Ridi Dormi! (Sing, Smile, Slumber)
Written by Charles Gounod.

Sung by Parepa-Rosa (1836-1874)

Isle of Beauty
Written by Thomas H. Bayly.
Fare Thee Well
Written by Thomas H. Bayly.
Five O'Clock in the Morning
Written by Claribel.
My Heart Is Over the Sea
Written by Claribel.
Nightingale's Trill
Written by Ganz.
As I'd Nothing Else to Do
Written by Hatton.
Why Was I Looking Out?
Written by Blumenthal.
I Cannot Sing the Old Songs
Written by Claribel.
Sing, Birdie, Sing
Written by Ganz.
Ave Maria
Written by Gounod.
The Storm
Written by Hullah.
Estasi (Valse)
Written by Arditi.
My Love and I
Danish Whistle
White Lily
Oh, Say Not Woman's Love Is Bought
Written by Joan Whitaker.
Forsaken
Written by Virginia Gabriel.
Parted from Thee
Written by Matzka.
Why Don't You Linger Yet?
Written by Godfrey.
La Parenza (Parepa Waltz)
Written by Vashetti.
O Lovely Blossom (Valse Chansonette)
Sung at the Bateman concerts.

Note: During the Parepa-Rosa seasons, 1862-1872, the following operas were first produced in England:

The Puritan's Daughter
Le Domino Noir
Les Huguenots
Fidelio
Un Ballo in Maschera
The Water Carrier

Emma Thursby (1845-1931)

My friend Max Maretzek, the impresario, who did so much to encourage the fine singers of the 80's and earlier years, said in a published article about Emma Thursby, one of the first American singers to achieve renown in Europe:

"Emma Thursby is the first importation this season and her sparkling note of exquisite flavor and of the purest color will be retailed on draft on the second of October next (1882) at Chickering Hall, under the personal supervision of the well and favorably known importer, Mr. Maurice Strakosch. The spirit in Miss Thursby's voice and its culture are especially adapted for that class of the public who like to enjoy their after-dinner songs in the concert-room in preference to the Opera House.

"Miss Thursby is now rated in the prima donna concert price-list as No. 1, labeled as excelsior and trade-marked with three golden stars. Adelina Patti or Christine Nilsson may also sing in concerts, but their sphere is the (operatic) stage, while Miss Thursby's is the concert-room. The songs and arias which Miss Thursby pours out to her listening customers are of the vintage of the great musical comets, Mozart and Beethoven."

After several years of musical triumphs abroad, Emma Thursby, now established as the "Queen of the concert-room," sang with great success before packed audiences in New York and on tour. Brooklyn, her native city (Williamsburg, to be exact), not to be outdone and proud of her famous daughter, greeted her fittingly in the *Brooklyn Union* as follows:

"A Greeting to Miss Emma Thursby

"Welcome to thy native land, fair songstress from abroad.
Strew flowers in the path of her, whom Europe doth applaud.
O wondrous gift! A voice that melts two continents in one.
All hail to thee, fair cantatrice, thy triumphs have begun.
Thou hast won alien hearts and gained a royal name;
May every year as on it rolls add lustre to thy fame.
Yet though with foreign laurels decked, thy heart can ne'er rescind
Thy love of native land and home, Columbia's Jenny Lind!"

For the benefit of aspiring and finished concert and radio artists and all other human "larks," who are gifted with one of God's greatest blessings alike to the singer and to the listener, a partial list of the amazingly large repertoire of Emma Thursby is here annexed. The main object is to encourage the ambitious and promote the success of a new generation of singers.

Emma Thursby
Her favorite concert selections

Aime Moi
Written by Chopin.
Air
Written by Grétry. From "Le Tableau Parlant."
Air: Pré aux Clercs
Written by Herold.
Amour Que Veux-Tu De Moi
Written by Lulli.
Ave Maria
Written by Gounod.
Bell Song
Written by Delibes. From "Lakmé."
Bird Song
Written by Taubert.
Bonnie Sweet Bessie
Written by Gilbert.
Care Nome
Written by Verdi. From "Rigoletto."
Cavatina
Written by Weber. From "Freischütz."
Cavatina
From "Linda."
Columbia
Written by Patrick S. Gilmore.
Deh Vieni Non Tardar
Written by Mozart.
Det Første Møde
Written by Grieg.
Way Down Upon the Swanee River
Written by Stephen Foster.
Duetino
Written by Boito. From "Mefistofele."
Echo Song
Written by Bishop.
Embarrassment
Written by Abt.
First Aria of the Queen of the Night.
Written by Mozart.
From "Magic Flute."
Gaily I Trill
Written by Sloman.
God Morgen
Written by Grieg.
Good Night and Pleasant Dreams
Written by Wallace.
Greek Song: Ysstou Kosmo
Written by Bourgault-Ducondray.
Heidenröslein
Written by Schubert.
Happy Children
Written by Massenet.
Hark 'Tis the Linnet

Heroes When with Glory Burning
Written by Othniel.
He Shall Feed His Flock
Written by Handel. From "Messiah."
Home, Sweet Home
Words by John H. Payne. Music by Henry R. Bishop.
Hush, Ye Pretty Warmling Choir
Written by Handel.
I Love My Love
Written by Graham.
I Know That My Redeemer Liveth
From "Messiah."
In der Märznacht
Written by Taubert.
Jeg Elslker dig
Written by Grieg.
Jewel Song
Written by Gounod, from "Faust."
La Calandrina (Air 1750)
Written by Nicolo Jomelli.
La Primavera
Written by Torry.
Last Rose of Summer
Le Chant de L'Abeille
Written by Masse.
Le Chant du Misoli
Written by David. From the opera "La Perle du Brésil."
Let the Bright Seraphim
Written by Handel.
Light from Heaven
Written by Gounod.
Lover and the Bird
Written by Guglielmo.
Lullaby
Written by Alfred H. Pease.
Mad Scene
Written by Thomas. From "Hamlet."
Maid of Dundee
Written by Chopin.
Mia Speranza Adorata
Written by Mozart.
Mignon's Lied
Written by Beethoven.
Mira Che Bianca Luna
Written by Rossini.
My Heart Ever Faithful
Written by Bach.
My Mother Bids Me Bind My Hair
Written by Haydn.
Oh, Had I Jubal's Lyre
Written by Handel.
On Croit a Tout Lorsqu'on Aime
Written by Delibes.
Orpheus with His Lute
Written by Sir Arthur Sullivan.
Place Danger Around Me
Written by Othniel.
Polonaise
Written by Thomas. From "Mignon."
Rode's Variations
Salterbes Get
Written by Ole Bull.
Save Me, O Lord
Written by Randegger.
Shadow Song
Written by Meyerbeer.
From "Dinorah."
She Wandered Down the Mountain Side
Written by Frédéric Clay.
Si Vou N'Avez Rien à Me Dire
Written by Mme. de Rothschild.
Solvejg's Song
Written by Grieg.
Song of Victory
Written by Hiller.
Spanish Song
Written by Yuzenga.
Staccato Polka
Written by Mulder.
Star-Spangled Banner
Swallow Song
Written by Sir Herbert Oakley.
Sweet Bird
Written by Handel.
Tarantelle
Written by Bizet.
Terzetto "Vada Si Via Di Qua"
Written by Martini.
Theme and Variations.
Written by Proch.
Thou Seemst to Me a Flower
Written by Rubinstein.
Twickenham Ferry
Follia a Roma
Written by Ricci.
Valse
Written by Gounod. From "Roméo et Juliette."
Venetiansk Serenade
Written by Johan Svendsen.
Violet
Written by Mozart.
With Verdure Clad
Written by Haydn.

Featured Songs of Early American Family Entertainers

Sung by The Baker Family

(John C., George E., Henry F., Jasper A., Sophia M., Emily E.)

Sung by the celebrated New Hampshire family at their concerts in more than half the States of the Union.

Where Can the Soul Find Rest?
Composed and arranged by John C. Baker. Published by Keith's Publishing House, Boston (1845). For solo and chorus in 6/8 tempo.

Songs and Glees Sung by Them in 1845

Happiest Time Is Now
Parting Requiem
Funeral of an Old Fellow
Inebriate's Lament
Hurray for the Sea Boys
Baker's Farewell
Burman Lover
Barber Shop
Little Sailor Boy's Lament
Indian Girl
Sailor's Grave
Mary's Last Words
Mountaineer's Farewell
Gimson Banner
Years Ago
Baker's Quick March

Henry Clay Barnabee (1833-1917)

Henry Clay Barnabee is best remembered as the Sheriff of Nottingham in Smith and De Koven's "Robin Hood." This famous comic opera was produced by the Bostonians, of which Barnabee was one of the organizers. Previously he had helped to organize the once well-known Boston Ideal Opera Company, which was the predecessor of the Bostonians. According to his own story, he began his theatrical career quite modestly.

When a young man, he was employed in a well-known Boston dry goods store, sang in a church quartette and, with other ambitious acquaintances, organized a dramatic club. He had never met his employer, who was supposed to be a somewhat austere person, and was alarmed when he was suddenly summoned to the boss's private office. He feared dismissal and his spirits sank to zero when his employer said that the night before he had witnessed the club's performance. "My wife and family are away," his employer continued, "and I am giving a stag dinner at my home. All the guests will impersonate some special character. Your acting last night proved that you are particularly clever in Yankee dialect parts and I should like you to appear as my Down East country cousin."

Barnabee said that the dinner was a

great success and that, encouraged by the merchant, he branched out as an amateur entertainer in the larger cities of the Eastern states while still maintaining his commercial connections.

Narragante
Written by Randegger. Trio.

Robin Ruff
Written by Russell. Duo. Sung by Mr. Barnabee and Mr. Fessenden.

In Days of Old
Written by Hatton.

I Love Dearly
Written by Kucken. Quartette.

El Toreador
Trio.

Wanted—A Governess
Written by Barry.

Come, My Sweet
Written by Abt. Quartette.

Sung by MME. ANNA BISHOP (1810-1884)

Bank of the Guadalquiver
Written by L. Lavenu (1847). From the opera "Lindi di Chamounix."

That Holy Spot of Early Days

Magic of a Kindly Smile
Music by George F. Root.

The Alabama
Written by Samuel Lover.

The Bowld Sojer Boy
Written by Samuel Lover.

Widow Machree
Written by Samuel Lover.

Gondolier Row
Written by Samuel Lover.

A Life on the Ocean Wave
Written by Henry Russell.

Slowly Wears the Day, Love
Written by Bochsa.

Sung by MME. ANNA BISHOP AND MISS LOUISE BISHOP

Good Night and Happy Dreams
Written by George Cooper and J. R. Thomas. Song or duettimo.

Beggar Girl
English ballad and vocal duet.

I Am the Bayedère (Je Suis la Bayadère)
Arranged by N. C. Bochsa.

Madame Bishop's Celebrated Tambourine Song
Arranged by N. C. Bochsa.

Slowly Wears the Day, Love
Written by N. C. Bochsa.

Sung by HARRY CLIFTON

Auld Lang Syne
Paddle Your Own Canoe
Put Your Shoulder to the Wheel
As Long as the World Goes Round
Carry Me Back to Ole Virginny
Broken Down
Pulling Hard Against the Stream
It Is Better to Laugh Than to Cry
Young Man from the Country

Sung by CATHERINE HAYES (1825-1861)
Songs in her repertory in 1851

Why Do I Weep for Thee?
I Mourn Thee, But I Love No More
Ah! My Child (Ah! Mon Fils)

O! Sing to Me
Written by C. A. Osborne

My Dreams Are Now No More of Thee

Written and sung by The Hutchinson Family
(Judson, Abby, John, Asa)

Excelsior
Poem by Henry Wadsworth Longfellow. Music by Hutchinson Family. Published by Firth Hall and Co. (1843). Musical setting of the famous poem in ¾ tempo. With quaint litho of four portraits of Hutchinson Family.

The Old Granite State
Words by John Hutchinson. Music by Hutchinson Family. Published by Firth Hall and Co. (1843). State ballad in 2/4 tempo.

Songs Written and Sung by Them in 1843

Grave of Bonaparte
Eight Dollars a Day
Written by Jesse Hutchinson, Jr.
Glide On My Light Canoe
Indian's Lament
Cot Where We Were Born
Cape Ann
Vesper Song at Sea
We're A Cutting
Go Call the Doctor
Mother's Bible
Vulture of the Alps
We Were Happy and Free
Soldier's Funeral
Axes to Grind
Our Father's Hearth
Jamie's on the Stormy Sea
Sung by Abby Hutchinson.
Bridge of Sighs.
There's a Good Time Coming
Away Down East
Recollections of Home
Snowstorm
Words by Seba Smith. Music by L. Heath (1843). Arranged by Geo. Herves. "Oh God!" she cried in accents wild, "If I must perish, save my child!"
King Alcohol
Kind Words Can Never Die

Sung by Harmoneons
Songs in their repertory in 1848

Dearest Me
She Sleeps in the Valley
Farewell, Tonight We Part
Mountain Wave
I Forget the Gay, Gay World
Serenade
We Come Again with Song to Greet You
Hunting Glee
We Love Our Dark Blue Sea

Songs in their repertory in 1847

Wild Old Woods
Mother, I Leave Thy Dwelling
I Wish She Was Here
Hark to the Banjo Sound
I Hear Thee Speak
Lone Old Indian
Written by L. V. H. Crosby (1847). Also sung by Washington Euterpeans.

Pauline Markham
Songs in her repertory in 1859

Riding in a Steamboat
From "Sinbad the Sailor."
Cymbal Song
From "Sinbad the Sailor."

Sung by TONY PASTOR (1837-1908)
America's own comic vocalist

Tommy, Make Room for Your Uncle
Great Centennial Show
I've Only Been Down to the Club
My Love, My Dove
Awfully Fly
Yankee Doodle
Not Before Pa, Dear
They All Do It
Hilderbrandt Montrose
One Hundred Years
Bold Fisherman
Juliana Jones
I'm Off to Philadelphia
No Smoking Allowed
Augustus Daisy Beau
Fanny Old Girl
After the Opera
After Me
Beautiful Girls
First She Would and Then She Wouldn't
Governor Pays the Bills
Goodbye Charlie
Down in a Coal Mine
He Said, I Said, You Said
If Ever I Cease to Love
It's Naughty but It's Nice
Kiss Behind the Door
Moet and Chandon
Since They Joined the Gang
Polly, Put the Kettle On
Swell with a Glass in His Eye
Where's Rosanna Gone?
Oh, Nicodemus
Pull Down the Blind
Buckles on Her Shoes
Be Always Up and Doing, Boys
It's Funny When You Feel That Way

Sung by JOHN PENDY
Anglo-American Comique

One More Glass Before We're Parted
Words by Edwin V. Page. Music by Vincent Davies. Published by E. H. Harding. Drinking song success. ¾ tempo.
Tommy, Make Room for Your Uncle
Words and music by T. S. Lonsdale. Published by E. H. Harding. 6/8 tempo.
Forgiven
Words and music by Alex Comstock. Published by Harms (1886). ¾ tempo. Sung by ballad singers.
Be Careful When You Find a Friend
Hold Your Tongue
Give Over, John
Give Me a Grip of Your Hand
Oh George—Beautiful George
Something in the City
A Bird in the Hand
Buckles on Her Shoes
Do You Know Where Nowhere Is?
It's No Use Grumbling
The Loving Cup
Poor But a Gentleman Still
Timothy Tottle
Don't Make a Noise

Sung by RAINER FAMILY
Tyrolese-Alpine Singers—Four Men and a Woman

Alpine Horn
Sailor boys' carol (1841).
Sweetheart
Tyrolese in America
Mountain Maid's Invitation
Matin Bell
Miller's Maid
Free Country
She Sleeps
Oh Dear! I'm So Pleased
Good Night, Little Blossom

Sung by Lydia Thompson

Oh, How Delightful
From "Sinbad the Sailor" (1859).
Pretty Darkie, Don't Say No
From "Sinbad the Sailor" (1859).
Velocipede Song
From "Sinbad the Sailor" (1859).
Come Down, Darling, Do
From "Sinbad the Sailor" (1859).

Sung by Gus Williams
Popular star comique and Dutch comedian

You Never Miss the Water Till the Well Runs Dry
Written by Linn.
That's Where You Make the Mistake
Written by Hunt.
After the Opera's Over
Written by Leybourne.
Down in a Coal Mine
Written by Geoghegan.
Blow Your Own Trumpet
I Should Like To
Written by Solomon.
The Scamp
Written by Hunt.
Billiards and Pool
Written by Clarke.
The Macs and the O's
Written by Steirly.
Knock at the Door Tonight
Can Any One Tell Where Dot Cat Is Gone?
Dot Little German Band
Mygel Snyder's Party
Sweet Louisa
Vats the Brice of Beans, Jake?
Dutch Policeman
Pull Down the Blind
It's Funny When You Feel That Way
Ven My Band Begins to Play
Mother Says I Mustn't
Little Fraud

Sung by Williams and Walker

Bert Williams
(1875-1922)

George Walker
(Died 1911)

Nobody
Words by Alex Rogers. Music by Bert Williams. Pub. Attucks Music Pub. Co. (E. B. Marks) (1905). Comedy song. 4/4 tempo. Sung by Bert Williams.
Somebody Lied
Words and music by Jeff T. Brainen and Evans Lloyd. Adapted by Bert Williams. Pub. Will Rossiter, Chicago (1907). Ragtime comedy song. 2/4 tempo. Sung by Bert Williams in "Bandanna Land."
You're in the Right Church but the Wrong Pew
Words by Cecil Mack (R. C. McPherson). Music by Chris Smith. Pub. R. C. McPherson (then Gotham Attucks) (E. B. Marks) (1908). Ragtime comedy song. Sung by Bert Williams.
My Landlady
Words by F. E. Mierich and James T. Brymn. Music by Bert Williams. Pub. Leo Feist (1912). Ragtime comedy song. 4/4 tempo. Sung by Bert Williams in "Ziegfeld Follies."

Me an' de Minstrel Band
Words by Alex Rogers. Music by James Vaughn. Pub. Gotham Attucks (E. B. Marks) (1904). Ragtime minstrel parade song. Sung by George Walker.

Let It Alone
Words by Alex Rogers. Music by Bert Williams. Pub. Gotham Attucks (E. B. Marks) (1906). Ragtime philosophical song. Sung by Bert Williams.

Evah Dahkey Is a King
Words by Paul Laurence Dunbar and E. P. Morgan. Music by John H. Cook. Pub. John H. Cook (then Harry Von Tilzer) (1902). Production song. Sung by Williams and Walker in "Dahomey."

I Don't Care If Yo' Nebber Comes Back
Words by Raymond A. Brown. Music by Monroe H. Rosenfeld. Pub. E. B. Marks (1897). Ragtime song. Sung by Williams and Walker.

Play That Barber Shop Chord
Words by William Tracey. Music by Lewis F. Muir. Pub. J. Fred Helf Co. (E. B. Marks) (1910). Barber shop ragtime song. Sung by Bert Williams.

Porto Rico
Music by Ford T. Dabney. Pub. Shapiro Bernstein Co. (1910). Instrumental ragtime intermezzo. Danced to by Aida Overton Walker (Mrs. George Walker) in Smart Set Company.

Man in the Moon Might Tell
Words and music by Jessie A. Schipp. Pub. E. B. Marks (1899). Comic song. ¾ tempo. Sung by Williams and Walker.

Medicine Man
Words and music by Bert Williams and George Walker. Pub. E. B. Marks (1899). Comic song. Sung by Williams and Walker.

I Don't Like No Cheap Man
Words and music by Bert Williams and George Walker. Pub. E. B. Marks (1897). Comic song. Sung by Williams and Walker.

I'll Keep a Warm Spot in My Heart for You
Words by James Weldon Johnson. Music by J. Rosamond Johnson. Pub. E. B. Marks (1906). Production song. Sung by Aida Overton Walker (Mrs. George Walker) in "Abyssinia."

Why Don't You Get a Lady of Your Own?
Words and music by Bert Williams and George Walker. Pub. E. B. Marks (1898). Ragtime comedy song. Sung by Williams and Walker.

I'm a Jonah Man
Words and music by Alex Rogers. Pub. M. Witmark and Sons (1913). Ragtime minstrel lament. Sung by Bert Williams.

He's Up Against the Real Thing Now
Words by Edward Furber. Music by Bert Williams. Pub. E. B. Marks (1898). Ragtime comedy song. Sung by Williams and Walker.

Not a Man Came Out the Way He Went In
Words and music by Bert Williams and George Walker. Pub. E. B. Marks (1898). Ragtime comedy song. Sung by Williams and Walker.

It's Nobody's Business but My Own
Words and music by Will E. Skidmore and Marshall Walker. Pub. Skidmore Music Co. (E. B. Marks) (1919). Ragtime "Deacon" song. Sung by Bert Williams in "Ziegfeld's 1919 Follies."

She's Getting More Like the White Folks Every Day
Words and music by Bert Williams and George Walker. Pub. Shapiro, Bernstein and Von Tilzer (1901). Ragtime comedy song. Sung by Williams and Walker.

You Cannot Make Your Shimmy Shake on Tea
Words by Rennold Wolfe and Irving Berlin. Music by Irving Berlin. Pub. Irving Berlin, Inc. (1919). Comedy production number. Sung by Bert Williams in "Ziegfeld Follies 1919."

Miscellaneous Singers and Their Songs

Beauty, Wit and Gold
Words and music by Joseph Philip Knight. Sung by Mme. Vestris.

How Could I Forget You, Darling?
Written by Gianelli. Sung by Kelly and Leon's Minstrels.

Female Auctioneer
Sung by Orphean Family (1850).

Maid of Florence
Sung by Mrs. Seguine in "Zampa" at the Park Theatre, N. Y. C.

Man in the Moon Is Looking, Love
Sung in "Babes in the Wood."

Sweet Annie of the Vale
Music by William J. Wetmore, M.D. Sung by the Alleghanians (1851).

My Grandma's Advice
Sung by the Tremaine Family (1857).

Birds of the Night
Music by Sir Arthur Sullivan. Sung by Annie Louise Cary at the Nilsson concerts.

Favorite Early American Minstrel Songs

Sung by Bryant's Minstrels

Black Brigade
Words and music by Dan D. Emmett. Published by William A. Pond and Co. (1863). Plantation song and dance. 2/4 tempo.

Golden Showers
Words and music by James Maas. Published by William A. Pond and Co. (1871). Musical dialogue and gallop. 2/4 tempo. Sung by Tommy Sulby, Little and Mac, Kearn and Wild, Queen and West, Ashcroft and Morton.

Lanigan's Ball
Words by Tony Pastor. Music by Neil Bryant. Published by William A. Pond and Co. (1863). Popular Irish song. 6/8 tempo. Sung by Dan Bryant.

Little Dan
Words and music by Will S. Hays. Published by J. L. Peters, N. Y. C. (1872). Dedicated to Dan Bryant, Jr.

How Are You, Greenbacks?
Sung by Dan Bryant's Minstrels and Mrs. John Wood.

Sung by Christy's Minstrels
Oldest established minstrel company in the United States

Rosa Lee (or Don't Be Foolish, Joe)
May have been written by Stephen Foster. Published by William Hall and Son (1847). 2/4 tempo. Sung by Ethiopian Serenaders, Christy's Minstrels and others.

Carry Me Back to Ole Virginny
Words and music by James A. Bland. Published by C. Holt, Jr., 156 Fulton Street, N. Y. C. (1848). 6/8 tempo.

Farewell, Ladies
Words and music by E. P. Christy. Published by Jacques and Bro., 385 Broadway, N. Y. C. (1847). 2/4 tempo. Sung by E. P. Christy. Beautiful colored old lithograph. Four minstrel scenes by Sarony and Major.

Zip Coon
Published by Firth and Hall (about 1834). Perhaps the first song of its type. 2/4 tempo. Sung by George W. Dixon. Very quaint old litho of Negro courting his girl while Cupid looks on. Rare old edition, possibly first.

Darling, Do You Love Me Yet?
Words by Arthur French. Music by Edwin Christy. Published by Oliver Ditson, Boston (1878).

A Kind Word
Music by T. Peissoni. Published by Gein and Jackson (1852).

Keemo Kimo
Words by George P. Christy. Music by Woods. Published by William Hall and Son, N. Y. C. (1854). Banjo song. 2/4 tempo.

Mary Blane
Words by F. C. German. Arranged by J. H. Howard. Published by Firth and Hall (1847). Favorite Negro song. 2/4 tempo. Sung by Ethiopian Serenaders at the St. James Theatre, London, and Palma's Opera House in New York, also Christy's Minstrels and Campbell's Minstrels.

Lucy Neal

Darky's Life Is Always Gay

Way Down South in Alabama

I Wish I Was in Old Virginny
Darkies, Our Master's Gone to Town
Stop That Knocking
We'll Have a Little Dance Tonight
Cynthia Sue
Carry Me Back to Ole Virginny
Dandy Broadway Swell
Phantom Chorus
Poor Dinah (Who Stole the Toddy)
Oh! Susanna
Give Me the Gal with the Blue Dress On
Uncle Gabriel
Picayune Butler
Happy Are We Darkies So Gay
Jim Crow (Polka)
Farewell, Ladies
 Composed and sung by E. P. Christy (1847).
My Pretty Yeller Gal
Snow Drop Ann
Lily of the Valley
Cinder's Wedding
My Pretty Virginia Gal
Gone to Alabama
Rosa Dear
Walk in the Parlor

Sung by The Ethiopian Serenaders

Rose of Alabama
Rosa Lee
Mary Blane
 (1857). Written by J. H. Howard. Sung at St. James Theatre, London; also Palma's Opera House, N. Y. C.

Sung by San Francisco Minstrels
At San Francisco Opera House, Broadway and 29th Street, New York City

In Her Little Bed We Laid Her
 Words and music by Dexter Smith, and C. A. White. Sung by Dave Wambold.
My Pretty Red Rose
 Words and music by J. P. Skelly. Sung by Dave Wambold.
Don't Be Angry With Me, Darling
 Words by W. L. Gardner. Music by H. P. Danks (1872). Sung by Dave Wambold.
Are Thy Dreams of Me
 Words by W. H. Stoutenbach. Music by Charles T. French (1876).
Jacob Gets the Mitten
 Words and music by W. Wallace
Gypsy's Dream
 Words and music by Stephen Glover.
My Sweetheart May
 Words and music by M. Watson.
Old Cuckoo Clock
Our Skipper and Our Crew
I Left My Love
In the Long Ago
Everything Gone Up
Cavalier's Farewell
Sailor's Wife

Sung by Billy Emerson

Big Sun Flower
I'll Meet My Love at Four
Sweet Little Mary Ann
Dark and Roguish Eyes
Feller That Looks Like Me
Gustavus Adolphus Green
Melissa
Yours Forever
Sociation Ball
Swim Out for Glory
Bidalia McCann
Pretty as a Picture

Sung by New Orleans Serenaders
(S. Sanford, Nelson Kneass,* Max Zorer, J. H. Collins, G. Swaine, T. Burk, Master Ole Bull,† J. C. Rainer)

Nellie Was a Lady
I Hear the Hoofs (or The Lost Child)
Go Way, Black Man
Thou Art Gone from My Gaze
Rosa Clare
Hither We Came (Pirates' Chorus from "Enchantment")
Katy Dean
New Orleans Serenaders' Polka

*Nelson Kneass, famous minstrel and composer of "Ben Bolt."

† Master Ole Bull, later the famous violin virtuoso.

Sung by The Great Southern Original Sable Harmonists

At the time the best band of singers in the United States
(Messrs. William Roark, W. G. Plummer, J. B. Farrell, Larcher, Bond, J. C. Benson, *Manager*)

Old Uncle Ned
Roaring Ribber
Louisiana Belle
Let's Be Gay
We Are the Sable Harmonists
Lynchburg Town
Vianer's History ob de World
Susanna
Floating Scow of Old Virginny
Hard Times
Picayune Butler
Mary Blane
Lucy Neal
Dandy Jim
Lucy Long
O Sally White
Stop Dat Knocking
De Boatman's Dance

Sung by Virginia Serenaders

At their concerts throughout the United States about 1844

All composed by Dan Meyers, the stage name of J. Richard Meyers (Ole Bull), violinist of the Virginia Serenaders and later the celebrated violin virtuoso

Lucy Neal
Ring Boys Ring
Lubly Fan
Alabama Joe
Peter Gray
From "Carolina." Sung by Cool White.

Whitlock's Collection of Ethiopian Melodies

Sung by William Whitlock at the principal theaters in the United States (1846)

Mary Blane
What's That Knockin' at the Door?
Oh Wake Up In the Morning
In De Wild Raccoon Track
Cudjos Wild Hunt
Dandy Jim from Carolina
De Old Grey Goose
De New York Gals
Get Along Home, My Yaller Gal
Gongem Reaper

Sung by Charles T. White
Celebrated Black Apollo

De Floating Scow (or Carry Me Back to Ole Virginny) (the original)

Mary Blane

Who's Dat Knockin'?

Miscellaneous Minstrel Songs

Open Dem Doors
Words and music by Ned Straight. Published by Mrs. Pauline Lieder (1880). Negro spiritual. Sung by minstrels and church singers.

Oh, Tiny, Play That Traumerei
Words by Henry J. Little. Music by J. E. Andino. Published by Musicians Publishing Co. (1910). Ragtime comedy song. Sung by ragtime singers.

De Swellest Gal in Town
Words and music by Harry Von Tilzer. Published by J. W. Stern and Co. (E. B. Marks) (1897). Sung by the famous minstrel, George H. Primrose.

Sitting on the Golden Fence
Words and music by A. Wiggins. Published by Spear and Denhoff (E. B. Marks) (1884). Jubilee song. Sung by the Memphis Students.

Flirting on the Beach
Words and music by E. M. Hall. Published by White Smith and Co. (1878). Old-time song and dance. Sung by Primrose and West.

Eat, Drink and Be Merry
Words and music by George R. Wilson. Published by Leo Feist (1903). Sung by George Wilson with Primrose Minstrels.

Four Little Curly Headed Darkies
Words and music by J. W. Wheeler. Published by S. W. Blair, Boston (1891). Played by Pat S. Gilmore's Band.

Man on the Flying Trapeze
Words by George Leybourne. Music by Alfred Lee. Published by C. M. Tremaine (E. B. Marks) (1868). Old-time comic waltz song.

Hab Dem Ladders Ready
Words and music by Ned Straight. Published by Mrs. Pauline Lieder (1880). Sung by The Kayes.

Hark! Don't You Hear Dem Bells A-Ringing?
Words by Charlie Reed. Music by J. Carroll. Published by C. D. Blake (1885). 2/4 tempo. Sung by Carroll Johnson of Primrose Minstrels.

How Could I Forget You, Darling?
Words by Arthur French. Music by Maurizio G. Gianetti. Published by Ditson and Co. (1877). Sung by Kelly and Leon's Minstrels.

Golden Chariot
Words and music by Ned Straight. Published by Mrs. Pauline Lieder (1880). Sung by Haverly's, Sanford's and other minstrel companies.

We Never Speak As We Pass By
Arranged by James Carleton. Published by Spear and Denhoff (E. B. Marks) (1882). Old-time waltz ballad.

Boatman's Dance (The first Hi De Ho Song)
Published by George Willig, Philadelphia (1850). 2/4 tempo. Sung by Virginia Minstrels.

White Wings
Words and music by Banks Winter. Published by J. W. Stern and Co. (E. B. Marks) (1884). Official song of Young Women's Christian Association. 6/8 tempo. Sung by Banks Winter and all minstrel singers.

We'll Raise De Roof Tonight
Words by H. G. Wheeler. Music by J. W. Wheeler. Published by Blair and Lyon, Boston (1884). Original planta-

tion melody. 2/4 tempo. Sung by Milt G. Barlow.

De Huckleberry Picnic
Words and music by Frank Dumont. Published by J. F. Perry Co. (1879). 2/4 tempo. Sung by Frank Dumont's Minstrels. Dumont was a famous manager and writer as well as minstrel. Quaint old woodcut on last page of title.

Oh! Dat Watermelon

Shine On

Old Simon, the Hot Corn Man

Little Fraud

Dars But Little Consolation

Dancing On the Green

Do What De Good Book Tells You

Put On Your Gospel Wings

Uncle Jeff's Return

Wouldn't You Like to Know

Den We'll Join De Band

Beautiful Caroline

Sweet Louise

Famous Old-Time Ballads and Songs Which Should Never Die

It has not been an easy task but rather a labor of love, to compile a number of the following pages, with some bits of description of *Ballads, Humorous Songs, Sea Songs, Minstrel Ditties,* War *Songs, Operatic Airs, Concert* and *Encore Songs,* all mainly of the old school.

Some are almost or long forgotten—many out of print and obsolete with their writers and publishers among the great majority that have passed on—some indeed remembered here and there by those who hark back to the songs of childhood, at mother's knee—some few cherished and sung to this very day in concert, film and in the theater—some truly revered by those who listen and attach to a fine old song, just as to a fine old painting or a bit of old lace, a deep, nostalgic thrill of genuine joy, that the passing delight of a music hall or night club swing tune fails to evoke.

I have realized, through personal admiration and an experience of fifty years, the vast and amazing success of many of these songs—the fine wholesome impression they left upon their hearers. I am aware of the fame and credit bestowed upon the authors and composers, whose genius in greater or lesser degree made these rare successes possible. I here and now declare that such splendid effusions deserve to live again, as they lived in the days of their creators, and for many decades later were sung and engraved on the hearts and in the minds of millions in all English-speaking countries—aye, in many cases in all countries of the earth.

The big questions I ask myself are: Do they deserve to disappear—the songs—the singers—the writers? Who among the song-loving public and my thousands of professional friends will in the near future do their bit to restore a few of these marvelous songs to their former favor, or perhaps even greater recognition than ever, as has recently been shown to our famous American song writer, Stephen Foster, by a great, phenomenal revival of many of his best works? I make Foster "tops" of the type of writer I refer to, even though I do not list the titles, preferring to believe that the majority of his never-to-be-forgotten works are already widely known to everybody at all musical.

If I could bring about, in this connection, one thing above all else I might desire, it would be to give to the new generations that recognize the genius of Foster, the almost equal joy they would surely find if they sought out or demanded the musical works of others I have listed. I recommend them as well, to the general perusal of the present-day younger school of song writers, not to put them in competition with the seasoned geniuses of other days, but merely to set a goal for the fittest of their works to strive for and attain. They can gain much by informing themselves in a general way of the wholesome (if a bit old-fashioned) philosophy, sentiment, love interest, pathos, humor, sincerity, love of nature and of country of the old-timers. Their ideas were diversified and original—they scanned their verse perfectly and used the King's English. At least these high standards are something that some of our Johnny-newcomers and even some of the other moderns in the song field can well afford to shoot at and particularly those hacks who persist, while they have the opportunity, in grinding out wishy-washy, namby-pamby, subsidized and commercialized hit-the-list, one-type-boy-and-girl tunes. I must, however, note an advance in the cleverness of rhythms and the intricacies of song rhymes and construction as perfected by such masters as Cole Porter, Larry Hart, Irving Berlin, Oscar Hammerstein II, Harry and Robert B. Smith, Ira Gershwin, Noel Coward, Frank Loesser, Johnny Mercer and perhaps a handful of others.

In melodies, the noted old-time composers, here compiled in lists, excelled most of the moderns, in my humble opinion, with the exception of Herbert, Kern, Gershwin, De Koven, Rodgers, Lehar, Lecuona, Lincke, Stolz, Oscar Straus, Kalman, Kerker, Paul Abraham, Bruno Grant, Leo Fall, Sousa, Friml, MacDowell, Nevin, Carmichael, Ellington, Oley Speaks, Earl Robinson, Erich Korngold, Deems Taylor, Arthur Schwartz, Jaromir Weinberger, Grenet, Quiroga, Longas and a few others, who might well, with a few exceptions, be classed as belonging more to the last of the old school rather than to any recent modern list or influence.

To this same old-time school of excellent lyricists and composers belonged Gilbert and Sullivan, who topped in their operatic field all their colleagues and contemporaries.

I refrain from especially mentioning in the lists the great masters of Grand Opera, whose ever-living works have been desecrated and taken for "swing" and other "pop" purposes—a proceeding every true music lover abhors and decries.

Although not listed either, I gratefully acknowledge here my deep admiration for the great works of those fine masters of music—Albeniz, Debussy, Ravel, Shostakovitch, Dohnanyi, Rachmaninoff, Rimsky-Korsakoff, Prokofieff, Satie, Scriabine, Granados, Villa-Lobos, Sibelius and the other immortals.

There has been no attempt in the lists, or chapters, to present them in their completeness, but rather, as the writer has known, heard or collected the titles or subjects (with due allowance as a busy executive) to compile them in his limited spare time.

What is recorded here may, however, as a reference work prove an incentive for young America and oldsters to collect the Americana of song and stage. As a priceless heritage handed down to them, curiosity alone should induce many to collect now, while there is still to be had much interesting data and some very rare items.

Why not inform yourself of the finest eras of grand opera, extravaganza, comedies, tragedies, pantomime, dance and song?

Get the habit and make it your hobby!

Collect old programs of the best days of the American theater before a success depended upon a "bitch," a few "—— damns" or a "toilet" for comedy or dialogue. Learn to treasure showbills, photos, prints and songs. You'll have a whale of a time hunting them out! You'll spend many a joyful hour, growing younger as you grow older, going over these priceless possessions that bring back sweet melodies and memories of your day or the days of Mother and Dad.

"In the early part of the 19th century," says a writer, "the simplicity of the old form of ballad was fast disappearing. Singers wanted something that would show off their voices more and composers no longer wanted to be kept to the limits of the ballad proper." This statement seems to be borne out in great measure by Edward Fitz Ball in his 35 years of a dramatic author's life.

"Ballad singing," he writes, "is very soon to be exploded, unless some new *Bland* or *Waylett* spring up with a voice capable enough to fascinate English ears by simple and pure melody instead of what very few understand, however much they affect it; that is to say the Grand Scena, the bravura, the brilliantes."

Everybody is familiar with the old lady's anecdote, which explained to Dr. Johnson the difficulties of the scena which she had been executing and the doctor's celebrated blunder: "I wish to goodness, madam, such difficulties were impossible."

"I thought perhaps," goes on Fitz Ball, "to apologize for this digression in favor of ballads and ballad singing, which I am always ready to champion, looking upon their sweet composition as a sort of national air."

Written by Franz Abt (1819-1885)

When the Swallows Homeward Fly
Stay, Gentle Morn, Awhile
Golden Sunshine
Say, My Heart, Why Art Thou Beating?
Adieu to the Woodlands
Wanderer's Dream

Tripping Lightly in the Garden
Sunday, the Soothing Sound of Distant Bells
Over Land or Sea
Thou'lt Give to Me a Tear
Snow Drop
Good Morning
O Ye Tears
Sleep Well, Sweet Angel
Haste, Gentle Zephyr
It Was Not Thus to Be
Would I Were a Warbling Bird
At Darksome Night
The Long, Long, Weary Day
How Can I Leave Thee?
I Think of Thee
'Tis Love Alone
Vanish Not, Oh Lovely Dream
Fly Away, Birdling
Oh Ye Tears! Oh Ye Tears!
With Gladsome Heart
When I Am Near Thee, Marie
Herdman's Mountain Home
Dream No More
In the Eve, There Lies the Heart
Evening

Written by Stephen Adams (1844-1913) (Michael Maybrick)

Blue Alsatian Mountains
Words by Claribel. Published by Louis P. Goulland, Boston (about 1880). ¾ tempo. Sung by concert and Variety artists.

They All Love Jack
Words by F. E. Weatherby. Published by S. T. Gordon and Son (about 1880). Nautical song. 6/8 tempo. Sung by Variety artists.

Mona
Words by F. E. Weatherby. Published by S. T. Gordon and Son (about 1880). Nautical love song. 9/8 tempo. Sung by Variety artists.

The Midshipmite
Words by F. E. Weatherby. Published by W. A. Evans and Bros., Boston. Sea song. Sung by all leading singers.

Tar's Farewell
Pub. Evans and Bro., Boston.

For Pity's Sake
Pub. Evans and Bro., Boston.

The Pilgrim
Pub. Pond and Co., N. Y. C., Semi-sacred song.

The Holy City
Pub. Boosey and Co.; also Chappell, London (1892). With organ acc.

A Warrior Bold
Pub. Saalfield, N. Y. C.

True to the Last
Pub. Evans and Bro., Boston.

Good Company
Children of the City
Awake, My Pet
Castle in the Air
Nancy Lee

Written by Luigi Arditi (1822-1903)

The Kiss (Il Bacio)
Night in Venice
Stirrup Cup
Estasi
L'Orologio (The Clock)
L'Orfanella (Little Orphan)
Ilma (Nouvella Valse)
Night of Love
Parla
The Kellogg Waltz

Written by Michael William Balfe (1808-1870)

Then You'll Remember Me (When Other Lips)
Heart Bowed Down
Oh Take Me to Thy Heart Again
Pirates' Chorus
  From "Enchantment."
I Dreamt That I Dwelt in Marble Halls
Don't Let the Roses Listen
Norah Darling
Power of Love
Oh Would She But Name the Day
Blighted Flower
Come Into the Garden, Maud
  Poem by Alfred Lord Tennyson (1857).
We May Be Happy Yet
  From "Daughter of St. Mark."
'Twas Rank and Fame
  From "Rose of Castile."
Sweetheart
Bliss Forever Past
  From "Puritan's Daughter."
Mary, Don't Forget Me
Day Is Done
  For baritone or contralto.
Excelsior
  Duet for tenor and baritone.
Father Pity (Duet)
  From "Puritan's Daughter."
Killarney
  Words by Edmund Falconer (1862).
In a Merry Zingara
Didst Thou But Know
What Joy and Gladness
  From "Puritan's Daughter."
Beneath a Portal
  From "Talisman."
My Cottage Near Rochelle
Trust Her Not (Duet)
Arrow and Song
  Poem by Henry Wadsworth Longfellow (1856).
The Sailor Sighs

Written by Sir Julius Benedict (1804-1885)
Usually known as Sir Jules Benedict

He Giveth His Beloved Sleep
  Sacred song.
By the Sad Sea Waves
  From "Brides of Venice."
Elly Mavourneen
  From "Lily of Killarney."
Take This Lute
I'm Alone
Rose of Erin
Colleen Bawn
  From "Lily of Killarney."
Cruiskeen Lawn
  From "Lily of Killarney."
The Moon Has Raised the Camp Above
  From "Lily of Killarney."
Bachelor's Life
Rage, Thou Angry Storm
Carnival of Venice

Sir Henry R. Bishop (1786-1855)
And "Home, Sweet Home"

To most musicians the idea that ballads may not be of high musical quality savors of absurdity, for Bishop was a composer of high ability, a great conductor and a holder of a musical chair at Oxford.

Ballads which become "popular" are often judged entirely from a "popular" standpoint. The fact that Bishop was the composer of "Home, Sweet Home," a ballad that has taken a place among the national songs of England and other lands, must be accorded a prominent place in our estimation of Bishop.

It was curious and a little disappointing at the time to the English to find that the author of these universally familiar words was not an Englishman, but an American—John Howard Payne. The song appeared in the opera "Clari, the Maid of Milan." It was first sung by Miss Maria Tree, who was said to have created quite a furor by her rendition of it.

In the published music, the tune is described as a Sicilian air, but there can be no doubt that it is Bishop's own. This has been explained by saying that Bishop was asked to edit a collection of national melodies and having no Sicilian air, wrote "Home, Sweet Home" to fill the spot and dubbed it Sicilian.

Whether this is so or not, it seems quite certain that Bishop was the composer. The song has always been a favorite item in the repertory of many famous singers. Jenny Lind used to sing it frequently as an encore, beginning with her tour under the direction of P. T. Barnum in 1850.

Written by SIR HENRY R. BISHOP

Home, Sweet Home
  Words by John H. Payne
Should He Upbraid
My Pretty Jane
Bid Me Discourse
Sleep, Gentle Lady
Love Has Eyes
Where Art Thou?
Foresters Sound the Cheerful Horn (Male Glee)
Mistletoe Bough
  Sung by Mr. Sinclair, Park Theatre, N. Y. C.
Teach, O Teach Me to Forget
Beggar Girl (Duet)
Am I Not Fondly Thine Own?
Leaf and Fountain
Bloom Is on the Rye
Pilgrim of Love
Smile, Mollie Darling
Home of My Youth
Oh! Firm as Oak
Orpheus With His Lute

Written by JAMES A. BLAND (1854-1911)
Of Sprague's Georgia Minstrels
Most famous Negro song writer of his day

Dancing on the Kitchen Floor
  Published by White Smith and Co., Boston (1880). Sung by the Big Four —Smith, Waldron, Cronin and (Master) Martin.

Oh, Dem Golden Slippers
  Published by Oliver Ditson, Boston, also John F. Perry and Co. (1880). 2/4 tempo. Sung by Lotta in "Musette" and "Zip."

Oh, Dem Golden Slippers
  Transcription for piano introducing "In the Morning by the Bright Light." Arranged by A. E. Warren. Published by John F. Perry and Co. (1880).

In the Morning by the Bright Light
  Published by Oliver Ditson, Boston, also John F. Perry and Co. (1879). Minstrel end song. 2/4 tempo. Sung by Harrigan and Hart.

Way Up Yonder
Published by Oliver Ditson, Boston, also John F. Perry and Co. (1880). Minstrel end song.
In the Evening by the Moonlight
Published by Hitchcock's Music Store, Park Row, N. Y. C. (Later E. B. Marks) (1880). Sung by all famous minstrels. James A. Bland's best-known song.
De Golden Wedding
Published by John F. Perry and Co. (1880). 2/4 tempo. Two quaint old Negro woodcuts on inner title sheet and last page.
Keep Them Golden Gates Wide Open
Pub. Hitchcock, N. Y. C. (1880). Ethiopian song.
Angels Are A'Singing
Pub. Hitchcock, N. Y. C. (1880). Ethiopian song.

Written by Dave Braham (1838-1905)

Braham composed the vast majority of the songs sung by Harrigan and Hart from 1872 to 1894. The lyrics were written by Ned Harrigan, although in some isolated cases Harrigan turned out both lyrics and music. In a few instances another writer supplied the words.

Little Widow Dunn
Pitcher of Beer
Paddy Duffy's Cart
Skidmore Fancy Ball
Babies on Our Block
Slavery Days
Patrick's Day Parade
Never Take the Horse-Shoe from the Door
The Regular Army O!
Mary Kelly's Beau
Isle de Blackwell
Skidmore Guard
Over the Hill to the Poor House
Major Gilfeather
The Widow Nolan's Goat
My Dad's Dinner Pail
Hildebrandt Montrose
Gallant 69th
Mulligan Guard
Malone at the Back of the Bar
Sergeant Hickey of the G.A.R.
Pub. Pond and Co. (1893)
Jim Jam Sailors Superfine
Pub. Pond and Co. (1890)
McNally's Row of Flats
Pub. Pond and Co. (1882).
Market on Saturday Night
Pub. Pond and Co. (1882).
Are You There, Moriarity?
Humorous song.
Boot Black
Bold Hibernian Boys
Emancipation Day
Eily Machree
Flirting in the Twilight
Gliding Down the Stream
Ginger Blues

Written by John Braham (1777-1856)

All's Well (Duet)
From "Thirty Thousand."
Anchor's Weigh'd
Death of Nelson
When Thy Bosom Heaves the Sigh

Harrigan and Hart

Edward (Ned) Harrigan Anthony (Tony) Hart

The plays of Harrigan and Hart, as portrayals of New York local characters and life, have never been equaled. The tremendous vogue of these famous stars lasted about 25 years, beginning early in the seventies. With his first partner, Sam Rickey, Harrigan introduced the sketches "Little Fraud" and "Mulcahey Twins."

From 1876 on, faithful Dave Braham furnished almost all the music for the lyrics written by Ned Harrigan. The songs in which Harrigan and Braham collaborated number about 200. In addition to composing all these numbers, Braham orchestrated all the music for every Harrigan and Hart show until the passing of Ned Harrigan himself. Harrigan and Braham were as indissolubly linked as were the names of Gilbert and Sullivan to the English. This happy combination, which so long enthralled New York, was a family affair, for Harrigan married the daughter of Dave Braham, and Martín Hanley, Harrigan's house manager, was the brother of Dave Braham's wife. When Braham and his orchestra came out to play the overture of the songs sung in each show, he was greeted with an ovation and given a big round of applause at the conclusion of the overture.

The old Theatre Comique on the east side of Broadway at No. 514, almost opposite the Art Union, was the home where Harrigan and Hart first came into prominence. The theater proper was on Crosby Street in a building once used as a synagogue. An entrance was made through to Broadway. The auditorium itself was up a flight of stairs. Sandy Spencer's bar was on the ground floor and drinks were served to the theater patrons, who opened a window and called out their orders.

A consideration of Harrigan's activities will give some idea of what a dynamic character he was and how prolific with his pen. Harrigan himself appeared in every one of the plays at regular night and matinee performances. In addition to authoring and staging all the plays himself in the 25 years of his popularity, he personally supervised the management of four theaters which he built at various periods of his career. Under his direction came countless other matters including rehearsals, casting and the writing not only of the plays, but appropriate song lyrics for each. All this is evidence of an amazing versatility and a capacity for industry unique in American showmanship.

The old Theatre Comique was first opened by Henry Wood with his minstrel troupe in 1862. After various managements, Harrigan and Hart assumed charge in February, 1876. They began with the Fall season of 1876-77 and left in April, 1881, to go to their new house further up at 728 Broadway. This theater, the new Comique, burned down in 1884, after which Harrigan and Hart separated, and from then until about 1894 Ned Harrigan carried on alone at two theaters farther uptown.

Some idea of Ned Harrigan's estimate of Tony Hart is conveyed in the following excerpt from an article published by Harrigan in 1903, describing Tony when he was a mere slip of a lad of about 17 with a very sweet voice and a strikingly handsome face: "Tony was always a great inspiration to me; he proved to be, in my opinion, the best impersonator of women that I ever knew on the stage. I had great trouble at first in persuading him to make the trial of these female characters. His success was tremendous. In Chicago the spectators would hardly believe that it was a boy in the role. Bill Pinkerton, the famous detective, came behind the scenes and studied Tony at close range in his make-up and even then, swore that he was a woman. Tony's right name, by the way, was Anthony Cannon."

The two other theaters constructed during the Harrigan era were:

Harrigan's New Park Theatre, at 35th Street and Broadway. (There was an indoor circus previously at this location. Hyde and Behman reconstructed it and leased it to Harrigan.)

Ned Harrigan's Thirty-Fifth Street Theatre was at 35th Street east of Sixth Avenue (later leased by Richard Mansfield, who renamed it The Garrick).

The following Harrigan excerpts are from *They All Sang*, written by Edward B. Marks. This book, enjoying a wide circulation in many countries, is the acknowledged reference work of the music of the period. It contains mention of over 1,500 songs of the nineties and other decades, including the Harrigan era and everything musically outstanding from the turn of the century to the present.

"Edward Harrigan confined the writing of his plays to city life and the whole town sang, whistled or hummed the song melodies which Dave Braham composed.

"New York was a picturesque city. It was a rich, racy period. It needed a Hogarth to draw it, a Dickens to describe it.

"Ned Harrigan, himself a New York man, born of Irish parentage on Scammel Street in 1845, was a little of both. Harrigan and Hart first captured the town in 'The Mulligan Guards', a series started in the early 70's and later developed by Harrigan into plays. The critics, weary of French and English plays, gave approval. A. C. Wheeler, dramatic critic of the World under the name 'Nym Crinkle' said: 'A new order of local drama exists at the Comique.' Later, William Dean Howells discovered Harrigan and wrote enthusiastic pages about Harrigan's 'showing us the street cleaners, the contractors, the grocery men, the shysters, the politicians, the washerwomen, the servant girls, the truckmen, the policemen, the rising Irishmen and Irishwomen.' He said Harrigan had gone a step further than Negro minstrelsy in the creation of a native art.

"A Harrigan and Hart first night was an event. The Seventh Regiment marched to the Comique, led the applause and encored all the songs.

Annotate the hundreds of Harrigan and Braham songs and you have unforgettable pictures of long since vanished phases of New York City life.

"Many a Wall Street broker and thousands of prominent businessmen all over the United States, who visited New York, were among the millions of young fellows of that period who used to watch the gas footlights go up at the old Comique and who enjoyed every single song, bit of dialogue and the witty aphorisms that came across the footlights.

"Gone are the days, but the memories live in the lyrics. 'The Old Neighborhood,' which paints Cherry Hill in the old days, mentions 'down in the Fourth Ward that I love so dear' and 'I'm not too proud to mingle with the crowd.' 'Union Square' is a description of the old Rialto. 'Paddy Duffy's Cart' depicts the boys perched in the lumber cart on summer evenings singing the old songs. 'The Babies On Our Block' paints pictures still dear to the old-timers.

"Organs were much in vogue in those days. They didn't take up much space and left room for the dancers. The gang gathered around the organ, or around the piano, as the case might be, in that gone-forever period, when songs heard on the stage were popularized in the home."

"Old Lavender" was among the best plays in which Harrigan appeared. There was much pathos in it, as well as humorous philosophy. It required character acting somewhat better than that required for the regular Irish types which he had previously portrayed and which it was natural for Ned Harrigan to play. The cast for the hundredth performance showed Harrigan in the title part (Old Lavender), Johnny Wild as Smoke, Dan Collyer as Dick, M. J. Bradley as Reilly and, of course, Harry Fisher, the German Lockmuller of his other plays, was included in the cast.

The memory of all the members of Harrigan's company will remain evergreen with everyone who ever saw a Harrigan and Hart play. As for Harrigan himself, his fame is indelibly stamped on the stage scroll of genius. His portrayals of characters in his line will never be excelled and he will never be replaced.

A chronological list of the Harrigan and Hart plays follows:

Date	*Plays*	*Theaters*
1872	Ned Harrigan with Sam Rickey and later with Tony Hart	Variety Halls and Theaters
1873	Harrigan and Hart	Variety Halls and Theaters
1874	Harrigan and Hart	Variety Halls and Theaters
1875	Harrigan and Hart	Variety Halls and Theaters
1876	Harrigan and Hart	Variety Halls and Theaters
1877	Harrigan and Hart	Old Theatre Comique—514 Broadway
1878	A Celebrated Hard Case	Old Theatre Comique—514 Broadway
1879	Mulligan Guard Ball	Old Theatre Comique—514 Broadway
1879	Mulligan Guard Surprise	Old Theatre Comique—514 Broadway
1879	Mulligan Guard Christmas	Old Theatre Comique—514 Broadway

Date	Plays	Theaters
1880	Mulligan Guard Chowder	Old Theatre Comique—514 Broadway
1880	Mulligan Guard Picnic	Old Theatre Comique—514 Broadway
1880	Mulligan Guard Nominee	Old Theatre Comique—514 Broadway
1880	Mordecai Lyons	Old Theatre Comique—514 Broadway
1881	Mulligan's Silver Wedding	Old Theatre Comique—514 Broadway
1881	The Major	New Comique Theatre—728 Broadway
1881	Squatter Sovereignty	New Comique Theatre—728 Broadway
1882	The Blackbird	New Comique Theatre—728 Broadway
1882	McSorleys	New Comique Theatre—728 Broadway
1883	The Muddy Day	New Comique Theatre—728 Broadway
1883	Cordelia's Aspirations	New Comique Theatre—728 Broadway
1884	Tribulations	New Comique Theatre—728 Broadway
1884	Investigation	New Comique Theatre—728 Broadway (During the run of this play, the theater burned down)
1884	McAllister's Legacy	New Park Theatre—35th St. and Broadway
1885	Old Lavender	New Park Theatre—35th St. and Broadway
1885	The Grip	New Park Theatre—35th St. and Broadway
1886	The Leather Patch	New Park Theatre—35th St. and Broadway
1886	The O'Regans	New Park Theatre—35th St. and Broadway
1887	Pete	New Park Theatre—35th St. and Broadway
1887	McNooney's Visit	New Park Theatre—35th St. and Broadway
1888	Waddy Googan	New Park Theatre—35th St. and Broadway
1889	Lorgaire	New Park Theatre—35th St. and Broadway
1890	Reilly and the 400	Harrigan's new Thirty-Fifth St. Theatre
1891	The Last of the Hogans	Harrigan's new Thirty-Fifth St. Theatre
1893	The Woolen Stocking	Harrigan's new Thirty-Fifth St. Theatre
1894	Notoriety	Harrigan's new Thirty-Fifth St. Theatre (later The Garrick) East of 6th Ave.

Written by FREDERICK BUCKLEY (1833-1864)

Smile Again
Why Do We Mourn for the Past?
I've Been Roaming O'er the Prairies
Somebody's Courting Somebody
Laughing Jennie
We Are Growing Old Together
Days When We Were Young
Forgive and Forget
My Memory Turns with Fondness
Bid Me Not Forget
Our Union Right or Wrong
I'd Choose to Be a Daisy
Kiss Me, Mother, Ere I Die
Leaf by Leaf the Roses Fall
Softly Falls the Moonlight
Tell Me, Is My Father Coming Home?
Kiss Me Quick and Go
Stolen Kisses Are the Sweetest
I Wait for Thee

Written by DOUGLAS BLAKE

Down Among the Sugar Cane
God Bless the Dear Ones at Home
I'm Waiting for a Letter, Love
I Am Coming, Darling, Coming
Little Mollie Brown
Mother, Is the Old Home Lonely?
Peacefully Dreaming

Written by John Blockley (1800-1882)

Love Not
Many Happy Returns of the Day
The Englishman
Evangeline
Jessie's Dream
List to the Convent Bells

Written by Dudley Buck (1839-1909)

Sunset (Op. 76, No. 4)
Dawn Is Breaking O'er Us
When Evening Shades Are Falling
In the Time of Roses
Quick! We Have but a Second (Drinking song)
Shine Out, Stars
Break, Break, Break
  Poem by Tennyson.
Weary Day at Last Is Closing (Serenade)
When the Heart Is Young
Creole Love's Song
The Golden Legend (Choir cantata)
The Legend of Don Munio (Choir cantata)
The Voyage of Columbus (Choir cantata)
Light of Asia (Choir cantata)
Paul Revere's Ride
  Poem by Longfellow.

Written by George Barker (1812-1876)

Haunted Stream
Why Do Summer Roses Fade?
Dublin Bay
I'm Leaving Thee, My Mother Dear
Marion Moore
Where Are the Friends of My Youth?
White Squall
Irish Emigrant

Written by Charles Blamphin

I'll Meet Thee in the Lane
Would I Were a Bird
Just Touch the Harp Gently
Little Maggie May
My Blue Eyed Nellie
Nellie Carey
When the Corn Is Waving, Annie Dear
Angels Are Waiting for Me
Beautiful Emeline
God Bless the Friends We Love
Little Diamond Dew Drop
Pretty Swallow, Homeward Fly
Smile That Brightens Every Eye
Farewell, Jennie

Written by Thomas Haynes Bayly, Esq. (1797-1839)

I Cannot Dance Tonight
My Son Tom
Old Bachelor
Long Long Ago
Mama, Mama, Why Don't the Men Propose?
Pilot
Song of Gulnare
Oh! Come to Me
Musical Wife
She Wore a Wreath of Roses
  Music by J. P. Knight.
Successful Suitor
  Music by J. P. Knight.
Old Friends and True Friends
  Music by J. P. Knight.
Go and Forget That We Have Met
  Music by J. P. Knight.
Ah! Since You Leave Me

Written by Fred Nicholls Crouch (1808-1896)

Kathleen Mavourneen
Words by Mrs. A. B. Crawford (1839).
Katy Lee
Old Elm Tree
Honest Hearts and Willing Hands
Katie Avourneen
(1856).
Sing to Me, Norah
Would I Were With Thee

Written by J. W. Cherry

Like the Songbirds in Summer
Shells of Ocean
Dear Little Shamrock
Will O' the Wisp
When the Autumn Leaves Are Falling
Beautiful Leaves
Shadow and Sunshine

Written by Fabio Campana (1819-1892)

I Live and Love Thee (I'o Vivo et T'Amo)
Roma (Rome)
Do You Remember? (Te'l Rammenti)
See the Pale Moon (Guarda Che Blanca Luna)
Tell Me Thou Lovest Me (Dimmi Che M'Ami)
Ever United (Sempre Insieme)
Maria e Rizzio (Mary and Rizzio)
We'll Go and Seek (Alla Capanna Andiamo)
Come with Me (Viene Meco)
Florentine Flower Girl
For soprano.
One Smile of Thine
In the Time of Orange Blossoms
Joyous Reapers
Messina (Canzone Siciliana)
Speak to Me
Fortune Teller
Weep Not, O Rose

Written by Claribel (1830-1869)
(Charlotte Barnard)

Come Back to Erin
Maggie's Secret
Take Back the Heart You Gave
(Pub. 1864)
You and I
We'd Better Bide a Wee
Janet's Choice
Five O'Clock in the Morning
I Cannot Sing the Old Songs
Strangers Yet
Won't You Tell Me Why, Robin
Note: This was written under the pseudonym Mrs. Chas. C. Barnard, nee Charlotte Allington.
We Sat by the River, You and I
Children's Voices
Drifting
Blue Eyed Nellie
My Heart Is Over the Sea
Maggie's Welcome
Half Mast High
Lowland Mary
What Need Have I the Truth to Tell
When the Pale Moon
Silver Chimes
Skipper and His Boy
Marion's Song
Old Pink Thorn
There's a Silver Lining to Every Cloud
Song of Love (Canto D'Amore)

To Thee (A Te)
Ever ('Tis True) (Cansone)
When Near to Thee (Accano a Te) (Romanza)
Magic Beauty (Sei Troppo Bella) (Canzonetta)
Beautiful Star (Bell 'Astro) (Elegia)
Sweet Angel (Bell 'Angiolo) (Canzonetta)
Flower Girl of Florence (La Floracha Florentina) (Arietta)
In the Gondola (Una Gita In Gondola)
I Cannot Live Alone (No Posso Vivere Senza Di Te)
From the Depths (Dal Profundo Dell Obilo) (Preghiera)
Never Scorn My Love (Non Ti Scordar Di Me)
'Twas an Angel (Era Un Angelo D'Amore)
O Souvenir (O Souvenir) (Melodic)
Unhappy Maiden (La Penserosa)
I Have Lost Her (L'Ho Perdula)
Ah Why? (Perche?)
Firefly (La Farifella) (Canzonetta)
Twilight Time

Written and sung by Cole and Johnson
(Bob Cole, J. Rosamond Johnson, James Weldon Johnson)

Oh Didn't He Ramble
Words and music by Will Handy (Pseudonym of Cole and Johnson). Published by E. B. Marks (1902). Two-step and march. 6/8 tempo.

Under the Bamboo Tree
Words and music by Bob Cole. Published by E. B. Marks (1902). African production number. Sung by Marie Cahill in "Sally in Our Alley."

Sweetest Gal in Town
Words and music by Cole and Johnson. Published by E. B. Marks (1908). Sung by Cole and Johnson.

Why Don't the Band Play?
Words by James Weldon Johnson and Bob Cole. Music by J. Rosamond Johnson. Published by E. B. Marks (1900). Comedy production song. Sung by May Irwin.

Tell Me, Dusky Maiden
Words by James Weldon Johnson and Bob Cole. Music by J. Rosamond Johnson. Published by Howley, Haviland and Dresser, N. Y. C. (1901). Travesty on Floradora Sextette. 2/4 tempo. From the production "Sleeping Beauty and the Beast."

Save It for Me
Words by Bob Cole. Music by J. Rosamond Johnson. Published by E. B. Marks (1903). Negro comedy song. 2/4 tempo. Sung by Marie Cahill, in "Nancy Brown."

Take Me in Your Arms and Say You Love Me (Come Over Here)
Words and music by J. Rosamond Johnson. Published by B. Feldman, London (1912). 2/4 tempo. Sung by Oscar M. Schwartz and Perie Babti.

Tango Dreams
Music by J. Rosamond Johnson. Published by E. B. Marks (1914). Instrumental Brazilian tango. 2/4 tempo. Danced to by Maurice and Walton.

The Old Flag Never Touched the Ground
Words by James Weldon Johnson and Bob Cole. Music by J. Rosamond Johnson. Published by E. B. Marks (1901). Patriotic song. 4/4 tempo. Sung by Primrose and West's Minstrels.

Roll Dem Cotton Bales
Words by James Weldon Johnson. Music by J. Rosamond Johnson. Published by E. B. Marks (1914). Plantation song. 2/4 tempo. Sung by Trixie McCoy.

Louisiana Lize
Words by Bob Cole. Music by J. Rosamond Johnson. Published by E. B. Marks (1899). Southern love song. Sung by Carroll Johnson.

Maid of Timbuctoo
Words by James Weldon Johnson. Music by Bob Cole. Published by E. B. Marks (1903). African love song. 2/4 tempo. Sung by Lillian Russell.

My Castle on the Nile
Words by James Weldon Johnson and Bob Cole. Music by J. Rosamond Johnson. Published by E. B. Marks (1901). Negro comedy song. 2/4 tempo. Sung by Cole and Johnson.

Nobody's Lookin' But the Owl and the Moon
Words by James Weldon Johnson and Bob Cole. Music by J. Rosamond Johnson. Published by E. B. Marks (1901). Negro love song. 4/4 tempo. From the production "Sleeping Beauty and the Beast."

Can't Think Of Nuthin' In the Wide, Wide World
Words by Bob Cole. Music by J. Rosamond Johnson. Published by E. B. Marks (1900). Negro love song. Sung by Cole and Johnson.

Colored Aristocracy
Words and music by Bob Cole. Published by Brooks and Denton, N. Y. C. (1895). Minstrel song. Sung by Sam Jack's Creoles.

Congo Love Song
Words by James Weldon Johnson. Music by J. Rosamond Johnson. Published by E. B. Marks (1903). African love song. 4/4 tempo. Sung by Marie Cahill in "Nancy Brown."

Everybody But Me
Words by Will James and C. J. Hart. Music by J. Rosamond Johnson. Published by B. Feldman, London (1913). Comedy song. Sung by Charles Hart.

I Hope These Few Lines Will Find You Well
Words by Bob Cole. Music by Billy Johnson. Published by Howley Haviland and Co. (1897). Ragtime song. 2/4 tempo. Sung by Bob Cole.

If You'll Be My Eve
Words by James Weldon Johnson. Music by J. Rosamond Johnson. Published by E. B. Marks (1912). Production song. Sung by Alice Lloyd, in "Little Miss Fix It."

Lazy Moon
Words by Bob Cole. Music by J. Rosamond Johnson. Published by E. B. Marks (1903). Soft shoe dance and song. Sung by George Primrose.

Lift Every Voice and Sing
Words by James Weldon Johnson. Music by J. Rosamond Johnson. Published by E. B. Marks (1900). The celebrated Negro National Anthem. Sung by leading Negro and white soloists and choirs.

The Maiden with the Dreamy Eyes
Words by James Weldon Johnson. Music by Bob Cole. Pub. by E. B. Marks (1901). Sung by Anna Held.

Li'l Gal
Words by Paul Laurence Dunbar. Music by J. Rosamond Johnson. Pub. by E. B. Marks (1917). Concert song. Sung by Paul Robeson.

I'll Keep a Warm Spot in My Heart for You
Words by James Weldon Johnson. Music by J. Rosamond Johnson. Pub. by E. B. Marks (1906). Sung by Aida Overton Walker in "Abyssinia."

Run, Brudder Rabbit, Run!
Words by James Weldon Johnson. Music by J. Rosamond Johnson. Pub. by E. B. Marks (1906). Comic song. From the production "Shoo-Fly Regiment."

The Big Red Shawl
Words by Bob Cole. Music by J. Rosamond Johnson. Pub. by E. B. Marks (1908). Indian production song. From "Red Moon."

The Bleeding Moon
Words by Bob Cole. Music by J. Rosamond Johnson. Pub. by E. B. Marks (1908). Indian production song. From "Red Moon."

Sugar Babe
Words by Bob Cole. Music by J. Rosamond Johnson. Pub. by E. B. Marks (1907). Negro love song. 4/4 tempo.

Fishing
Words by James Weldon Johnson.

Music by J. Rosamond Johnson. Pub. by E. B. Marks (1904). Philosophic production song. Sung by Marie Cahill.

Won't Your Mamma Let You Come Out and Play?
Words by James Weldon Johnson. Music by Bob Cole. Pub. by E. B. Marks (1906). Kid song. 4/4 tempo.

Ain't Dat Scan'lous?
Words by Bob Cole and James Weldon Johnson. Music by J. Rosamond Johnson. Pub. by E. B. Marks (1901). Negro comedy song. 2/4 tempo.

Mississippi River (Keep On Croonin')
Words by Frank Abbott. Music by J. Rosamond Johnson. Pub. by E. B. Marks (1932). Fox trot spiritual. 4/4 tempo.

The Katydid, the Cricket and the Frog
Words by James Weldon Johnson. Music by Bob Cole. Pub. by E. B. Marks (1903). Philosophic production song. Sung by Marie Cahill in "Nancy Brown."

Johnnie Get Your Hair Cut (Short Like Mine)
Words and music by J. Rosamond Johnson and Edward Bennett. Pub. by E. B. Marks (1935). Comedy song. 4/4 tempo.

On Lalawana's Shore
Words by James Weldon Johnson. Music by J. Rosamond Johnson. Pub. by E. B. Marks (1904). South Sea Island love song. From the production "Humpty Dumpty."

Ada, My Sweet Potater!
Words by Charles A. Hunter. Music by Bob Cole and James Reese Europe. Pub. by E. B. Marks (1908). Negro love song. Sung by Aida Overton Walker.

Just an Old Banjo (Without Any Strings)
Words by Bartley Costello. Music by J. Rosamond Johnson and Rudy Vallee. Pub. by E. B. Marks (1934). Sung by Rudy Vallee.

Life Is a Dancing Roman Holiday
Words by Frank Sturgis. Music by J. Rosamond Johnson. Pub. by E. B. Marks (1914). Novelty song. 2/4 tempo.

The Scandinavian Glide
Words by Frank Sturgis. Music by J. Rosamond Johnson. Pub. by E. B. Marks (1913). Novelty song. 2/4 tempo.

Father's Got a Job
Words by Bob Cole and James Weldon Johnson. Music by Bob Cole. Pub. by E. B. Marks (1906). Comedy song. 2/4 tempo.

The Pretty Little Squaw from Utah
Words by Bob Cole. Music by J. Rosamond Johnson. Pub. by E. B. Marks (1904). Indian comedy song. 2/4 tempo. Sung by Marie Cahill.

The Soldier Is the Idol of the Nation
Words by James Weldon Johnson. Music by J. Rosamond Johnson. Pub. by E. B. Marks (1903). Military production song. From the production "Nancy Brown."

On the Road to Monterey
Words and music by Bob Cole. Pub. by E. B. Marks (1908). 2/4 tempo. From the production "Red Moon."

The Pathway of Love
Words by Bob Cole. Music by J. Rosamond Johnson. Pub. by E. B. Marks (1908). ¾ tempo. Sung by Abbie Mitchell in "Red Moon."

Life Is a Game of Checkers
Words by Bob Cole and Charles Hunter. Music by J. Rosamond Johnson. Pub. by E. B. Marks (1908). Philosophic song. ¾ tempo. From the production "Red Moon."

Sambo
Words by Bob Cole. Music by James Reese Europe. Pub. by E. B. Marks (1908). Comedy song. 6/8 tempo. From the production "Red Moon."

I've Lost My Teddy Bear
Words by Bob Cole. Music by Bob Cole and J. Rosamond Johnson. Pub. by E. B. Marks (1908). 4/4 tempo. Sung by Anna Held in "Miss Innocence."

There's Always Something Wrong
Words by Bob Cole. Music by J. Rosa-

mond Johnson. Pub. by E. B. Marks (1907). Negro comedy song. 4/4 tempo. From the production "Shoo-Fly Regiment."

On the Gay Luneta
Words by Bob Cole. Music by James Reese Europe. Pub. by E. B. Marks (1906). 2/4 tempo. From the production "Shoo-Fly Regiment."

Who Do You Love?
Words by Bob Cole. Music by J. Rosamond Johnson. Pub. by E. B. Marks (1906). 2/4 tempo. Sung by Eddie Leonard and also in "Shoo-Fly Regiment."

De Bo'd of Education
Words by James Weldon Johnson. Music by J. Rosamond Johnson. Pub. by E. B. Marks (1906). Negro comedy song. 2/4 tempo. From the production "Shoo-Fly Regiment."

The Ghost of Deacon Brown
Words by James Weldon Johnson. Music by J. Rosamond Johnson. Pub. by E. B. Marks (1906). Negro comedy song. 4/4 tempo. From the production "Shoo-Fly Regiment."

Floating Down the Nile
Words by James Weldon Johnson. Music by J. Rosamond Johnson. Pub. by E. B. Marks (1906). Negro love song. 6/8 tempo. From the production "Shoo-Fly Regiment."

Sambo and Dinah
Words by Bob Cole and James Weldon Johnson. Music by Bob Cole. Pub. by E. B. Marks (1905). Negro love song. 2/4 tempo. From the production "Humpty Dumpty."

Mexico
Words by Bob Cole and James Weldon Johnson. Music by Bob Cole. Pub. by E. B. Marks (1905). 2/4 tempo. From the production "Humpty Dumpty."

The Pussy and the Bow-Wow
Words by James Weldon Johnson. Music by J. Rosamond Johnson. Pub. by E. B. Marks (1904). Novelty song. 2/4 tempo. From the production "Humpty Dumpty."

Man, Man, Man
Words by James Weldon Johnson. Music by Bob Cole. Pub. by E. B. Marks (1904). Philosophic song. 2/4 tempo. From the production "Humpty Dumpty."

The Countess of Alagazam
Words and music by Bob Cole. Pub. by E. B. Marks (1904). Comedy song. 6/8 tempo. Sung by George Primrose.

Two Eyes
Words by James Weldon Johnson. Music by J. Rosamond Johnson. Pub. by E. B. Marks (1903). Love song. 4/4 tempo. From the production "Nancy Brown."

If Adam Hadn't Seen the Apple Tree
Words and music by Bob Cole. Pub. by E. B. Marks (1906). Comedy song. 2/4 tempo. From the production "Shoo-Fly Regiment."

I'll Always Love Old Dixie
Words by James Weldon Johnson. Music by J. Rosamond Johnson. Pub. by E. B. Marks (1906). Southern song. 4/4 tempo. From the production "Shoo-Fly Regiment."

Dem Lovin' Words Sound Mighty Good to Me
Words by James Weldon Johnson. Music by J. Rosamond Johnson. Pub. by E. B. Marks (1905). Negro comedy song. 4/4 tempo.

George Cooper (1820-1909)

George Cooper, song writer and author of "Sweet Genevieve," wrote more than 200 songs, many of which attained popularity. He lived at 2172 Washington Avenue, Bronx, to the ripe old age of 89 years.

Mr. Cooper fought in the Civil War as a private in the 22nd New York Infantry. For a time he studied law in the office of Chester A. Arthur, later President and Vice-President. He was a close friend of Tony Pastor and wrote many songs for artists appearing at Pastor's Theatre, including Lillian Russell during her earlier career. A few of Cooper's song successes were "God Bless the Little Church Around the Corner," "Mother, Kiss Me in My Dreams" and "Beautiful Isle of the Sea." He also wrote lyrics to the musical settings of others. Among these were "Babyland."

His greatest success from the standpoint of sales was "Sweet Genevieve," which song enjoyed a return to popularity before his death. Its revival brought Cooper more money in royalties than when it first appeared.

George Cooper was a contemporary of America's foremost song writer, Stephen Foster, and wrote several lyrics to Foster's melodies.

A List of His Songs

Sweet Genevieve
 Music by Henry Tucker (1869).
There Are Plenty of Fish in the Sea
 Music by Stephen C. Foster.
Little Darling, Don't Be Sad
Angels Rock My Babe to Sleep
Kindly Words and Smiling Faces
 Music by J. R. Thomas.
Save the Sweetest Kiss for Me
Wilt Thou Be True
 Music by Stephen C. Foster.
Goodnight and Happy Dreams
 Sung by Mme. Anna Bishop.
Linger Not, Darling
 Music by J. R. Thomas.
There's Sunlight on the Hills
Keep a Little Corner in Your Heart for Me
Glide On, Fair Barque (O Gondola Gentil)
Remember the Loved Ones at Home
Strolling on the Brooklyn Bridge
Beautiful Isle of the Sea
 Music by J. R. Thomas (1865).
War Is Over, Mary
 Music by J. R. Thomas (1864).
Rose of Killarney
Nature Alone Won Her Heart
 Music by Johann Strauss. Kiss waltz from "The Merry World."
Call Me Your Darling Again
 Music by Joe Skelly.
Sing Me Those Pretty Songs Again
 Music by Joe Skelly.
Dashing Bold Cadets
Joy of Song
I Am Not Angry With You, Dearest
 Music by Henry Tucker.
Jimmie Who Lives in the Dell
 Music by J. R. Thomas.
By the Meadow Brook
 Music by J. R. Thomas.
While the Days Are Going By
Guess
If You've Only Got a Moustache
 Music by Stephen C. Foster.
When the World Is Hushed in Sleep
At the Rising of the Moon
Darling Bessie of the Sea
 Music by J. R. Thomas.
O Whisper That You Love Me, Darling
 Music by C. A. White.
American National Guard
 Sung by Lydia Thompson.
Though Lost Yet Loved
Mid Starry Deeps of Splendor
Linger Not, Darling (Serenade)
Pearl of the Isle
Why So Sad, My Precious Darling?
Little Rosebud Leaves So Fair
Apart

Written by H. P. Danks (1834-1903)
(Hart Pease Danks)

When Silver Threads Are Gold Again
Words by Eben E. Rexford. Published by Charles W. Harris (1875).

Cottage Behind the Hill
Words by B. S. Barrett. Published by Brainerd Sons (1860). 2/4 tempo.

He Wipes the Tear from Every Eye
Published by J. L. Peters, N. Y. C. (1869). Sacred song. 3/4 tempo.

Don't Be Angry With Me, Darling
Words by W. L. Gardner. Published by Charles W. Harris (1872). Minstrel song. Sung by D. S. Wambold of San Francisco Minstrels.

He Kissed Her and She Kissed Him
Words by Samuel N. Mitchell. Published by William A. Pond and Co. (1874). Comic song.

Beautiful Dreams
Words by Ida Scott Taylor. Published by White Smith and Co. (1880). Song with chorus ad lib. Sung by Julia Wilson in the comedy "Joshua Whitcomb."

Silver Threads Among the Gold
Words by Eben E. Rexford. Published by Hamilton S. Gordon (1873). The world famous minstrel song and ballad.

Amber Tresses Tied In Blue
Words by J. F. Mitchell. Published by Hamilton S. Gordon (1873). Minstrel song.

One Bright Hour
Published by W. A. Evans and Bro., Boston (1883). Ballad.

My Beautiful Rose
Published by Richard A. Saalfield (1887). Song and chorus.

When I First Saw My Darling's Face
Published by R. A. Saalfield (1880). Song and chorus.

Why So Sad, My Precious Darling?
Words by George Cooper. Published by Hamilton S. Gordon (1871). Song and chorus.

Let the Angels In
Words by Miss Allen. Published by Hamilton S. Gordon (1867). Song and chorus.

Little Face Above the Spread
Words by Samuel N. Mitchell. Published by Hamilton S, Gordon (1874). Song and chorus.

Angels Guard Thy Little Bed
Words by Samuel N. Mitchell. Published by Hamilton S. Gordon (1875). Song and chorus.

'Tis Sweet to Think of Heaven
Words by Samuel N. Mitchell. Published by Hamilton S. Gordon (1865). Song and chorus.

My Mother's Grave

Songs of the Olden Days

Pity, O Savior

Beautiful as an Angel

Tom, If You Love Me So

Herdsman
Sung by Jenny Lind.

Submission
Sacred soprano song.

Cantata Domino
Sacred quartette.

You Are Always Young to Me

Angels Bore Her Home

Where the Sunbeams Drop Their Gold

Oh Happy Eyes—Look Up In Mine

Sleep, My Dear One

Don't You Think So, Kitty?

It Will Not Do to Tell

Reginald De Koven (1859-1920)

Sterling McKinley, M.A. (Oxon), in his *Development of Light Opera*, said of the above fine musician, conductor and composer:

"Reginald De Koven may certainly lay claim to have been the first American operatic composer of importance. In addition to the 'Canterbury Pilgrims,' he composed another romantic music drama, 'Rip Van Winkle,' which commonly takes rank as of Grand Opera calibre. The libretto was based on the memorable Washington Irving tale of the Catskill Mountains which had already received a successful French setting at the hands of Planquette, according to Hayden Coffin. However, the book of De Koven's version departed considerably from Irving's original tale.

"De Koven came over to England as a young man with his clergyman father and graduated at Oxford. Subsequently he studied music at Stuttgart, Frankfort, Vienna, Paris and Florence. During his Italian sojourn he studied singing under Vanucinni, thereby acquiring that practical knowledge of the human voice, which was so invaluable to him as an operatic composer. On settling down in America he became the most successful light opera composer of his day. In all he was responsible for the music of 19 light operas, in addition to the romantic music dramas referred to above.

"His first was the 'Begum' in 1887, while his outstanding successes were 'Robin Hood' and 'Rob Roy,' together with 'Don Quixote,' 'The Tzigane,' 'The Highwayman,' 'The Student King' and 'Red Feather,' in which Grace Van Studdiford starred. A production took place in London of his light opera 'Maid Marian.' "

A List of His Songs

Oh, Promise Me
Brown October Ale
Armourer's Song
Humorous Ghost
To Call Thee Mine
Lesson in Verse
Prince of Good Fellows
Madrigal
Dreaming, Dreaming (Moon Song)
Charge, Boys, Charge
Robin Redbreast
Give Me Thy Heart, Love (Romanza)
Cupid's Grammar (Duet)
Mimette the Human Mermaid (Romance)
Pretty Maiden (Serenade)
Black Sheep (Pastoral)
Happy Is the Summer Day (Madrigal)
Soldier of Love
How I Love Flowers
Lily and the Moon (Duet)
'Twas the Rose (Waltz Song)
Man! Foolish Man (Trio)
Student King (Song)
Fancy Free
Pretty Tyrolese
My Old Bassoon
Rooster and the Lark
Columbine and Harlequin (Duet)
Wine, Woman and Song (Trio)
In Memory Dear (Duet)
Pray, Pretty Maid (Duet)
Pretty Punchinella
Four Seasons
Gay Lieutenant
Love on a Summer's Day
I Want You for My All Time Girl
Serenade D'Amour
Ariella
Message of the Bells
Spanish Grandee
My Lady Faire
Hammock Love Song
Coo-ee
Prince of Borneo
Creole Days
Boys Will Be Boys
Song of the Sea

Gingerbread Boy
Rose and the Breeze
It's Half Past Kissing Time
My Dear Old Jersey Home
Tale of the High Born Rooster
Tragedy of the Hat
Little Milliner
Rosie Lee
Wanda
Merry Cavalier
Robin Hood (Opera)
Rob Roy (Opera)
The Highwayman (Opera)
The Student King (Opera)
Red Feather (Opera)
Beauty Spot (Opera)
Happyland (Opera)
The Begum (Opera)
The Tzigane (Opera)
Canterbury Pilgrims (Opera)
Rip Van Winkle (Opera)
Don Quixote (Opera)

Written and sung by William R. Dempster (1809-1872)

May Queen
Poem by Alfred Tennyson. Published by Oliver Ditson, Boston (1845). Cantata in three parts. Sung by concert singers.

Lament of the Irish Emigrant
Poem by Mrs. Price Blackwood. Published by George P. Reed, Boston (1843). Irish ballad. ¾ tempo. Sung by William R. Dempster and other concert singers. Eighth edition. Lithographed Irish scene on title page.

When the Night Wind Bewaileth (or Never More, Never More)
Words by Epes Sargent, Esq. Published by Oliver Ditson, Boston (1845). ⅜ tempo.

I'm All Alone, All Alone
Words by Lewis F. Thomas. Published by Oliver Ditson, Boston (1846). Sung by concert singers.

Blind Boy

I Canna Lo'e Him Less

Greenwood Tree

Rainy Day
Poem by Henry Wadsworth Longfellow.

Written by Paul Dresser (1857-1906)

Curse of the Dreamer
Published by Howley Haviland and Co. and Herbert H. Taylor (1899). Descriptive song. 6/8 tempo. Sung by minstrel baritones.

Don't Tell Her That You Love Her
Published by Howley Haviland and Co. (1896). Sob ballad. Sung by vaudeville and minstrel performers.

Her Tears Drifted Out With the Tide
Published by Willis Woodward (E. B. Marks) (1890). Sung by minstrel companies.

Here Lies an Actor
Published by Willis Woodward (E. B. Marks) (1889). ¾ tempo. Sung by old-time Variety artists.

After the Ball
Published by Paul Dresser Publishing Co. (1905). War ballad. Sung by vaudeville artists.

Blue and the Gray
Published by Howley Haviland and Co. (1900). Patriotic ballad. Sung by Frank Ritter, and all vaudeville minstrels.

The Convict and the Bird
Published by Willis Woodward (E. B. Marks) (1888). Sung by vaudeville and minstrel artists.

When You Come Back They'll Wonder Who You Are
Published by Howley Haviland and Co. (1902). War song. 2/4 tempo. Sung by vaudeville artists.

Your Mother Wants You Home, Boy
Published by Howley Haviland and Co. (1904). Mother ballad. Sung by Dick Jose.

In Good Old New York Town
Published by Howley Haviland and Co. (1899). War song. Sung by Lottie Gilson.

Just to See Mother's Face Once Again
Published by Willis Woodward (E. B. Marks) (1891). Mother song. Sung by vaudeville artists.

Just Tell Them That You Saw Me
Published by Howley Haviland and Co. (1895). Sob ballad. Sung by vaudeville and minstrel artists.

My Gal Sal (They Called Her Frivolous Sal)
Published by Paul Dresser Publishing Co. (E. B. Marks) (1905). Famous torch ballad. ¾ tempo. Sung by Louise Dresser.

On the Banks of the Wabash
Published by Howley Haviland and Co. (1899). Famous rural song. ¾ tempo. Sung by vaudeville and minstrel artists.

The Pardon Came Too Late
Published by Willis Woodward (E. B. Marks) (1891). War ballad. Sung by vaudeville and minstrel artists.

Take a Seat, Old Lady
Published by Howley Haviland and Co. (1894). Ballad. Sung by Meyer Cohen.

What a Wonderful World It Would Be
Words by J. S. G. Published by Willis Woodward (E. B. Marks) (1889). Press Prize Topical Song. 6/8 tempo.

Calling to Her Boy Just Once Again
Willis Woodward (E. B. Marks) (1900). Mother song. Sung by Dick Jose.

Every Night There's a Light
Published by Willis Woodward (E. B. Marks) (1898). Mother song. Sung by Dick Jose.

He Fought for the Cause He Thought Was Right
Published by Willis Woodward (E. B. Marks) (1898). War song. Sung by Dick Jose.

I Wonder Where She Is Tonight
Published by Willis Woodward (E. B. Marks) (1899). Tear jerker. Sung by Dick Jose.

I'd Still Believe You're True
Published by Willis Woodward (E. B. Marks) (1900). Ballad. Sung by Charles Kent.

In Dear Old Illinois
Published by Willis Woodward (E. B. Marks) (1902). State song. Sung by Dick Jose.

The Letter That Never Came
Published by Willis Woodward (E. B. Marks) (1886). Tear jerker. Sung by May Howard.

When Mother First Taught Me to Play
Published by Willis Woodward (E. B. Marks) (1892). Mother song. Sung by May Howard.

The Lone Grave
Published by Willis Woodward (E. B. Marks) (1890). Minstrel ballad. Sung by minstrels.

Mister Volunteer
Published by Willis Woodward (E. B. Marks) (1901). War song. Sung by minstrels.

My Sweetheart of Long Ago
Published by Willis Woodward (E. B. Marks) (1891). Ballad. Sung by minstrels.

Outcast Unknown
Published by Willis Woodward (E. B. Marks) (1887). Tear jerker. Sung by Chauncey Olcott.

Rosie, Sweet Rosabel
Published by Willis Woodward (E. B. Marks) (1893). Waltz song. Sung by J. Aldrich Libbey.

The Town Where I Was Born
Published by Willis Woodward (E. B. Marks) (1905). Home song. Sung by minstrels.

Bethlehem
Published by Howley Haviland and Co. (1900). Sacred song. Sung by minstrels.

Written by Dolores (1819-1878)

All Yesterday I Was Spinning
Echoes
Clear and Cool

The Brook
Poem by Tennyson.

Written and sung by OLD DAN DECATUR EMMETT (1815-1904)
Leader of Virginia Minstrels (1843)

I Wish I Was in Dixie
Dixie for the Union
De Boatman's Dance
My Own Aunt Sally
Miss Lucy Long
Old King Crow

Written and sung by J. K. EMMET (1841-1891)

Bells Are Ringing (Emmet's Castle Bells)
  Published by John Church (1879). Bell chime song. ¾ tempo. Sung by J. K. Emmet in "Fritz in Ireland."
Emmet's Lullaby
  Published by John Church (1878). Lullaby and yodel. Sung by J. K. Emmet in "Fritz Our German Cousin."
Kiss Me (or Darling Baby, Come)
  Published by John Church (1882). Lullaby and yodel. ¾ tempo. Sung by J. K. Emmet in "Fritz Among the Gypsies."
I Know What Love Is
  Published by John Church (1879). Love song and yodel. Sung by J. K. Emmet in "Fritz in Ireland."
Sweet Violets
  Published by John Church (1882). Flower song and yodel. 6/8 tempo. Sung by J. K. Emmet in "Fritz Among the Gypsies."
Peek-A-Boo
  Published by John Church (about 1880). Yodel song. Sung by J. K. Emmet.

Written by (MARY ANN) VIRGINIA GABRIEL (1825-1877)

Evangeline (Cantata)
Dreamland (Cantata)
Widows Bewitched (Operetta)
A Rainy Day (Operetta)
Follies of a Night (Operetta)
Cleansing Fires
Yet Once Again (Duet)
Oh Willie Boy, Come Home
Estranged
Forsaken
Only
Ruby
When Sparrows Build
Light in the Window
Only a Face at the Window
Weary
Garden of Roses
Parted
Nightfall at Sea
Skipper and His Boy
Across the Sea
One Two, Buckle My Shoe
Robin's Return
Sad Heart, Take Thy Rest
Ship-Boy's Letter
Whatever Is, Is Best

Written and sung by STEPHEN GLOVER (1812-1870)

Song of Blanche Alpine
  Words by Charles Jeffreys. Published by Firth Pond and Co. Old-time Alpine waltz song.
Home That I Love
  Words by Charles Jeffreys. Published by G. Willeg, Jr., Baltimore (about 1844). ⅜ tempo. Sung by parlor singers.
Queen Victoria's Band March
  Published by Firth and Hall, N.,Y. C. Played by military bands.

True Friends Quadrille
Published by Robert Cocks and Co., London. 6/8 tempo.
Annie O' the Banks O' Dee
Words by Mrs. Crawford. Published by Harding, 228 Bowery, N. Y. C. Scotch ballad. Sung by Walter Field of the Alleghanians.
Good Bye at the Door
Words by J. E. Carpenter. Published by Harding, 228 Bowery, N. Y. C. Minstrel ballad. Sung by W. Dwyer of Bryant's Minstrels.
What Are the Wild Waves Saying?
Published by Harding, 228 Bowery, N. Y. C. Famous duet hit. Sung by Paul and Florence in "Dombey and Son."
Valley of Chamonix
Beautiful Moonlight
Vocal Duet.
Gypsy Countess
Vocal Duet.
Slowly and Softly Music Should Flow
Pub. J. W. Lawton, Philadelphia. Vocal duet.
Curfew Bells
Poem by Henry Wadsworth Longfellow. Pub. R. R. McCargo and Co., Boston.
I Love to Hear My Savior's Voice
Pub. Evans and Bro., Boston. Sacred song.
Forsake Me Not
Pub. Saalfield, N. Y. C. Sacred song.
Two Forest Nymphs
Duet.
Changes of the Bells
Duet.
Faith
Murmuring Sea
In the Starlight
Ruth and Naomi
Blanche and Lisette
Tell Us, Oh! Tell Us
I Love the Merry Sunshine
'Tis Hard to Give the Hand
Who'll Come and Play with Me?
Sister's Faithful Love
Harp and the Willow
Let Us Dance on the Sands
Parting
Smiling Faces
It Is Not Always May
Tell Me Where Do Fairies Dwell
Voice from the Waves
Soprano and contralto duet.
Two Cousins
Duet.
Merry Alpine Maid
Duet.
Dream Is Past
Sung by the famous Miss Poole.
Sunshine and Cloud
Rose of Tralee

Written by W. B. Gray (William B. Glenroy)

Old Jim's Christmas Hymn
Published by W. B. Gray and Co. (now E. B. Marks) (1896). Sung by Will F. Denny.
She Is More to Be Pitied Than Censured
Published by W. B. Gray and Co. (now E. B. Marks) (1898). Old-time sob ballad. ¾ tempo. Sung by Lizzie B. Raymond.
Take Back the Engagement Ring
Music by G. L. Spaulding. Published by Spaulding and Gray (now E. B. Marks) (1894). ¾ tempo.
Where the Chicken Got the Axe
Words by Harry Mayo. Published by M. Witmark and Sons (1892). Comic song.
Church Across the Way
Published by W. B. Gray and Co. (now E. B. Marks) (1894). Semi-sacred ballad.
Clancy's Trotter
Published by W. B. Gray and Co. (now E. B. Marks) (1890). Irish comic song. Sung by William B. Glenroy.
Mother of the Girl I Love
Published by W. B. Gray and Co. (now E. B. Marks) (1897). Mother song. Sung by Raymon Moore.

Louis Moreau Gottschalk (1829-1869)

The best of Gottschalk's works was said by a critic to be his "Grande Tarantella." The critic continued:

"Here we have Gottschalk in his most fascinating vein. If the composition were to be put into the retort of criticism on high art principles, little of real musical value would probably be found, apart from the more volatile parts such as the brilliant pianoforte effects; curious combinations of chords and certain indescribable charm and vivacity in style it certainly possesses.

"We have, however, no desire to subject the piece to such a process. It is commonplace if you will, but full of brilliancy and fascinating effects of rhythm and sonority. It is worked up with spirit from the beginning to the end of the tarantella. There is frenzied hilarity, which is never for a moment lost sight of. It is extremely difficult, in the sense of requiring great strength and power of execution, but even players who are far from being really able to play it can appreciate the consummate skill and ingenuity with which the most sparkling effects are reproduced. The ease with which the fingers adapt themselves to what are apparently the most hand-racking passages is marvelous."

Probably only those who had the good fortune to hear Gottschalk play could vividly call to mind the maddening fascination of his playing and thereby get much enjoyment out of the piece.

The memory of Gottschalk remained with his public for a long period of years, and many preferred to stumble through the pages of his "Tarantella" themselves and by themselves, rather than hear anyone else attempt it.

The "Souvenir de Lima" is an innocent enough mazurka by Gottschalk. It is not wanting in strong marked effects in rhythm, and it also has certain rather queer vagaries.

His old publicity manager DeVivio, who captioned him "Gottschalk the adored," wrote as follows in his recollections of a successful tour of seven months with this wonderful American pianist, Louis Moreau Gottschalk, and the great coloratura singer, Carlotta Patti:

"I regard as a triumph my first season of concerts. There were two reasons. First I had procured the engagement of Carlotta Patti, which resulted in foretelling her artistic and financial success. I had also booked the first long concert route which was satisfactory to the directors, Jacob Grau and Max Strakosch, as well as Gottschalk and Patti, who had been fatigued with long rides from one place to another. Naturally, I was proud of my good work and again naturally in the coming season I expected a higher salary.

"As Grau and Strakosch had been so kind to me, I did not feel inclined to speak of an increase until they mentioned it first. Soon I was invited by Grau and Strakosch to have an Italian dinner with them at a restaurant in

Union Square. They talked of the successful season just ended and praised my advance work highly. In fact, they predicted that in a few years I would become their rival as an impresario. I accepted both the prophecy and the compliments with many thanks, and in fact six years later, I became the manager of the Parepa Rosa concert and Italian and English opera companies, the most successful on record, receiving the highest salary paid to any manager at the time for a period of four years.

"To return, however, to my Italian dinner with Grau and his associate, they soon spoke of the coming season. Grau said to Strakosch:

" 'Dear Max, I think next season we ought to raise DeVivio's salary to $75 per week. He deserves it, not only for his clever work, but for his economy in advertising and printing, arranging with railroads and express companies, as well as hotel managers.'

"Max replied: 'I agree—I am perfectly satisfied with DeVivio's excellent work.'

"Turning to me, they asked: 'Are you satisfied to remain with us?', and of course I accepted with thanks."

All cities were not, however, "a bed of roses," even for this genius. In some, his first concerts lost money persistently until he began to play "show pieces" based on popular tunes, when the tide turned and the box-office receipts grew.

In other Western towns, *Protectionism* seemed to have run riot, as the newspaper editors opposed "invasion" from strange pianists and advised their readers to "patronize only local home talent."

There are two pages about Gottschalk in the *Etude* of June, 1914, together with a photograph titled "The real Gottschalk," 1829-1869. In the article he is referred to as a "prodigy."

A List of His Songs

Little Dutch Garden
For mezzo.
King Can Do No Wrong
My Own Sweetheart
At the Sign of the Three Black Crows
For bass.
Blossom i' His Bonnet
For mezzo.
Where Did You Come From, Baby Dear?
For mezzo.
'Tis Thou Alone
For mezzo.
Old Bell Ringer
For baritone or bass.
So, So, Rock-a-By So
For mezzo.
Jolly Old Monk Like Me
For baritone.
Cupid
For mezzo.
In the Shadow of the Cross
Oh, Loving Heart, Trust On
Last Hope
(1856).
Dying Poet (Pseudonym "Seven Octaves")
(1864).
Souvenir de Lima
Tarentella de Bravera
Jerusalem
Cradle Song

Written by P. D. Guglielmo (1810-1873)

The Lover and the Bird
Emma, for Thee I Languish
Stars Are Glowing
Love and Friendship Still Are Thine
Under the Hazel Tree
My Angel (Angelo Mio)
Oh! If I Were a Swallow
Thou Art Too Lovely
Heart, Whence Thy Joy and Sorrow?
I Live for Thee Only
Ever Faithful (Sempre Fidele)
Give Me That Flower (La Camelia)
La Camelia (Romanza)
Heaven and Thee
Mispah (Sacred song)

Written by J. B. Geoghegan

A Hundred Years Ago
Symphonies and accompaniments by John Blockley. Sung by Herbert B. Williams, Shakespearean clown and jester.

The Waggoner

Down in a Coal Mine
Sung by Gus Williams, America's Dutch comique.

Written by John Guest

Cabin with the Roses at the Door
God Bless the Absent One
Middicome Fair (or Uncle Tom Cobleigh)
Only a Face at the Window
Balm of Gilead (Sacred song)
Christ's Mission (Sacred song)
Widow's Mite (Sacred song)
Gypsy Boy (Sacred song)

Written by Chas. W. Glover (1806-1863)

Do They Think of Me at Home?
Be Watchful and Beware
Bashful Young Man

I Miss Thee, My Mother
Words by Eliza Cook (about 1843).

Jeannette and Jeannot

Written by B. Graham Harvey

I Breathe Once More My Native Air
Home of My Heart
City of Light (A Dream of Bethlehem) (Sacred song)
Until the Day Break (Sacred song)
Battle Prayer (Sacred song)
Shepherd True (I Was Wandering and Weary) (Sacred song)

Crossing the Bar (Sacred song)
Poem by Tennyson.

Written by Will S. Hays (1837-1907)
(William Shakespeare Hays)

My Dear Old Southern Home
Published by J. L. Peters (1871). Minstrel song. 4/4 tempo.

Oh, Give Me a Home in the South
Published by J. L. Peters (1872). 6/8 tempo.

Pretty as a Pink
Music by E. Mack (Introducing the melody of Will S. Hays' "Mary, Oh Come Back to Me"). Published by J. L. Peters (1870). Barcarolle redowa fantasie with variations.

How Much Does the Baby Weigh?
Published by George D. Newhall (1880). ¾ tempo. Sung by Lotta in her play "Bob."

Molly Darling
Published by J. L. Peters (1871). ¾ tempo.

Moon Is Out Tonight, Love
Published by J. L. Peters (1867).

Shamus O'Brien
Published by J. L. Peters (1866). 6/8 tempo.

Susan Jane
Published by J. L. Peters (1871). End song and chorus. Sung by Billy Manning.

Take Me Back Home
Published by J. L. Peters (1866). Ballad. 2/4 tempo.

Never Go Back on Your Friend
Published by J. L. Peters (1871). Old-time philosophical song. 6/8 tempo.

Driven from Home
Published by J. L. Peters (1868). ¾ tempo.

Kiss Me Good Night, Mama (I'll Kneel When You Kneel and I'll Look as You Look)
Published by J. L. Peters (1870). ¾ tempo.

Evangeline
Published by J. L. Peters (1862).

Angels Meet Me at the Cross Roads
Published by J. L. Peters (1875).

Little Old Log Cabin in the Lane
Published by J. L. Peters (1871). Plantation song.

Roll Out—Heave That Cotton
Published by J. L. Peters (1877). Plantation song.

Early in the Morning
Published by J. L. Peters (1877). Plantation song.

Oh, Sam
Published by J. L. Peters (1872). Plantation song.

Down in the Cornfield
Published by J. L. Peters (1871). Plantation song.

Genevieve
Published by J. L. Peters. Ballad.

Take This Letter to My Mother
Published by J. L. Peters. Mother song.

Little Dan
Published by J. L. Peters. Minstrel song.

A Heart That Beats Only for Thee
Belle Bradley
Darling Kate
Goodbye, My Boy—God Bless You!
I'm Sitting by the Window, Love
I'm Still a Friend to You
Jessie Dean
Kiss Me Goodbye, Darling
The Last Sweet Smile You Gave Me
Let Me Kiss the Baby
Beautiful Girl of the South
Caroline
Darling Linnie Dorn
Down by the Deep Sad Sea
Gay Young Clerk
Goodbye, Old Home
Laura Lee
Jessie
Katie McFerran
Kitty Ray
Little Dan
Sung by Dan Bryant's Minstrels.
Mistress Jinks
We Parted by the River Side
You've Been a Friend to Me
My Southern Sunny Home
Nora O'Neal
Prettiest Girl I Know
Write Me a Letter
Old Uncle Ben
Song of the Sewing Machine
I'll Remember You in My Prayers
Angel of My Dreams
Nobody's Darling
Baby's Gone
Goodbye Till I See You Again
Night My Father Died
My Dear Old Sunny Home
Home Beyond the Sky
Summer Bloom Hath Passed Away

CHIEF PRODUCTIONS AND INDIVIDUAL COMPOSITIONS
Composed by Victor Herbert (1859-1924)

Operettas

Naughty Marietta
  Libretto by Rida Johnson Young (1910).
    I'm Falling in Love with Someone
    Ah! Sweet Mystery of Life
    Italian Street Song
Mlle. Modiste
  Libretto by Henry Blossom (1905).
    Kiss Me Again
    I Want What I Want When I Want It
    If I Were on the Stage
The Fortune Teller
  Libretto by Harry B. Smith (1898)
    Gypsy Love Song
    Romany Life
Babes in Toyland
  Libretto by Glen MacDonough (1903).
    Toyland
    I Can't Do That Sum
Eileen
  Libretto by Henry Blossom (1917).
    The Irish Have a Great Day Tonight
    Thine Alone
The Only Girl
  Libretto by Henry Blossom (1914).
    When You're Away
Orange Blossoms
  Libretto by B. G. DeSylva and Fred de Gressac (1922).
    A Kiss in the Dark
    Lonely Nest
The Red Mill
  Libretto by Henry Blossom (1906).
    Because You're You
    Every Day Is Ladies' Day with Me
Dream Girl
  Libretto by Rida Johnson Young (1924).
    My Dream Girl
It Happened in Nordland
  Libretto by Glen MacDonough (1905).
    Absinthe Frappe
Princess Pat
  Libretto by Henry Blossom (1915).
    Neapolitan Love Song
The Ameer
  Libretto by Frederic Ranken and Kirke LaShelle (1899).
    Sweet Clarissa
    Cupid Will Guide
Sweethearts
  Libretto by Harry B. Smith and Fred de Gressac (1913).
    Sweethearts
Wizard of the Nile
  Libretto by Harry B. Smith (1895).
The Serenade
  Libretto by Harry B. Smith (1897).
Angel Face
  Libretto by Harry B. Smith (1913).
    I Might Be Your Once in a While

Operas

Natoma
  Libretto by Joseph D. Redding (1911).
Madeleine
  Libretto by Grant Stewart (1914).

Piano Compositions and Songs

Badinage
Al Fresco (Intermezzo)
Pan Americana (Morceau Characteristique)
March of the Toys
Punchinello (Characteristic)
Mascot of the Troop
Indian Summer

Written by Hamilton Hilliard

Only Mine
Galloping Steed
At the Garden Gate
I Love Thee
Who Knows
Flower's Decision
Something of Paradise
Two Can Play at That

Written by John L. Hatton (1809-1866)

Rainy Day
Poem by Henry Wadsworth Longfellow.
Goodbye, Sweetheart
Nothing Else to Do
To Anthea (Bid Me to Live)
Tom the Tinker
Simon the Cellarer
Revenge
Enchantress
Beacon That Lights Me Home
Gentle Flower, Canst Thou Tell?
Mercy and Forgiveness Too
Goodbye, Sweetheart, Goodbye
Sweet Love, Goodnight to Thee

Written by Annie Fortesque Harrison

In the Gloaming
Spring Is Coming
You're Welcome—Always Welcome
Oh, Whisper What Thou Feelest

Written by Julian Jordan

Song That Reached My Heart
Come to My Heart, My Love
Going to Dreamland
Guide Us, Guard Us
He Holds Me in His Hand
Light of My Life
Only to See the Dear Old Place Again
A Loyal Knight
The Old Home So Far, Far Away
Picture on the Wall
Song I'll Ne'er Forget
Flower Girl
Songs of Long Ago
Song of the Troubadours
That Melody Divine
Thro' the Twilight Gray
I Love But One, I Love But You
Kingdom Everlasting
Heavenly Strain
When You're Away
Beautiful Garden of Song

Written by Joseph Philip Knight (1812-1887)

Rocked in the Cradle of the Deep
Words by Emma Willard.
Beauty, Wit and Gold
Sung by Mme. Vestris.
She Wore a Wreath of Roses
Old Veteran
Beautiful Venice
Briar
Henrietta

Written and sung by Harry Kennedy

I Had Fifteen Dollars in My Inside Pocket
Published by Oliver Ditson, Boston (1885). Irish comedy song. Sung by Pat Rooney.
Flower from Mother's Grave
Published by Frank Harding (E. B. Marks) (1878). Tear jerker.
Cradle's Empty, Baby's Gone
Published by Oliver Ditson, Boston (1880). Tear jerker.
Molly and I and the Baby
Published by Oliver Ditson, Boston (1872). ¾ tempo.
I Owe Ten Dollars to O'Grady
Published by Frank Harding (E. B. Marks) (1885). Irish comedy song.
Say Au Revoir But Not Goodbye
Published by Frank Harding (E. B. Marks) (1893). Sung by Helene Mora.

Written and sung by NELSON KNEASS (Died 1869)
Member of New Orleans Serenaders

Ben Bolt
Published by National Music Co., Chicago. Famous song featured in all productions of "Trilby." 4/4 tempo.

I Hear Dar Hoof Upon de Hill
(or The Lost Child)
Published by Firth Pond and Co. (1849). Ethiopian minstrel song. 6/8 tempo. Sung by the New Orleans Serenaders Operatic Troupe—Nelson Kneass, S. Sandford, Max Zoreg, J. H. Collins, G. Swaine, T. Burk, J. C. Ranier and Master Ole Bull, later famous violin virtuoso. Beautiful old lithographed frontispiece containing portraits of the eight New Orleans Serenaders.

Down in the Shady Dell

Written by CLARE KUMMER
Later, the well-known playwright

Dearie
Published by E. B. Marks (1905). Sung by Sallie Fisher.

Somali Land
Published by E. B. Marks (1904). Sung by Marie Cahill.

My Very Own
Published by E. B. Marks (1906). Sung by Sallie Fisher.

Wilderness
Published by E. B. Marks (1907). Sung by Sallie Fisher.

In the Dingle Dongle Dell
Published by E. B. Marks (1904). Sung by Marie Cahill.

The Summer Land
Published by Gibson Claser and Co. (E. B. Marks) (1901). Sung by concert singers.

I Don't Like You
Published by E. B. Marks (1907).

Somebody's Eyes
Published by E. B. Marks (1916).

Golden Love
Published by E. B. Marks (1921).

Mister Noah
Published by E. B. Marks (1907).

Written by GEORGE ALEXANDER LEE (1802-1851)

Away, Away to the Mountain's Brow
Little Pigs
Hurray for the Bonnet of Blue
Come Where the Aspens Quiver
I Am Dreaming of Thee
The MacGregors' Gathering
God Shall Wipe Away All Tears
(Sacred song)
Meet Me in the Willow Glen
My Mother's Plaintive Song
He Wipes the Tear from Every Eye

Written by GEORGE LINLEY (1798-1865)

Swiss Girl
Long, Long, Weary Day
Katie O'Shane
Farewell, Kathleen
Thou Art Gone from My Gaze
Bonnie New Moon
I Hear the Wee Bird Singing
My Dreams Are Now No More of Thee
Words by L. Lavenue. Pub. (1851). Sung by Augustus Braham at the concerts of Catherine Hayes.

Ever of Thee

Written by Samuel Lover (1797-1868)
Famous not only as an Irish lyric poet, but as the maternal grandfather of Victor Herbert

Low Back'd Car
Published by William Hall and Son (1846). Characteristic Irish song. 6/8 tempo. As given by the author in his Irish evenings.
Bowld Sojer Boy
Published by F. D. Benteen (about 1844). Sung by Mr. Collins and by the author in his Irish evenings.
We Have Lived and Loved Together
Melody from recreations, musicales. Composed and arranged by Henry Hertz. Published by Oliver Ditson, Boston (about 1844). 6/8 tempo. Sung by drawing-room singers.
Mollie Bawn
Published by E. H. Harding. Famous Irish song. ¾ tempo. From the opera "I Paddia Whaccio Il Italia."
When the Sun Sinks to Rest
Music by Charles Jarvis. Published in Lady's Musical Journal (1843). Ballad from "Handy Andy."
Widow Machree
Published by William Hall and Son (about 1850). 6/8 tempo. As given by the author in his Irish evenings.
My Mother Dear
Published by Firth Pond and Co. Sung by Mr. Wilson.
Guard-Ship
Four Leaved Shamrock
Hark to My Lute
Listen
Morning Dream
Yes, She Is a Bright Eyed Thing
Soft On the Ear Falls the Serenade
When Gentle Music Sounding
When First I Over the Mountain Trod
Oh! Watch You Well by Daylight
Slaying the Deer
Flower of Natchez
Warship of Peace
Gondolier Row
Fairy Tempter
Fountain and Flower
How Sweet 'Tis to Return
True Love Can Ne'er Forget
Where Art Thou Roving?
Sweet Jesse Was Young and Simple
Oh Do Not Say I Love Thee Not
Two Birds
There's a Charm in the Past
Sigh Not, Love Not, Doubt Not
'Tis Better Not to Know
Forgive but Don't Forget
Now to Ask and Have
I'm Not Myself at All
Fairy Tell
Live in My Heart and Pay No Rent
Bridge of Sighs
What Will You Do, Love Me?
The Soldier
Barney O'Hea
Birth of Saint Patrick
Hour Before Day
Fairy Boy
Haunted Spring
May Dew
Star of the Desert
Secrets Were Not Made for Thee
Rory O'Moore
Dear Love and Native Land Farewell
Oh Native Music
Trysting Tree
Ask Me Not What I Am Thinking
What Will You Do, Love?

Written by Miss M. Lindsey
(Mrs. J. Worthington Bliss)

The Bridge
Tired
Too Late, Too Late
Far Away
Come Unto Me
Too Late
For mezzo-soprano or soprano.
When the Ship Comes Home
For soprano or mezzo-soprano.
Home They Brought Her Warrior Dead

Written by Sidney Lanier (1842-1881)
Distinguished poet, composer and flutist

A Ballad of Trees and the Master
(or Into the Woods the Master Went)
Various musical settings by H. Alexander Matthews, G. W. Chadwick, John Alden Carpenter and Daniel Protheroe.
Field Larks and Black-Birds
Love That Hath Us in the Net
Danse des Moucherons (Gnat Symphony)
Swamp Robins

Written by Stephen C. Massett (1820-1898)

My Bud in Heaven
Just Twenty Years Ago
Our Good Ship Sails Tonight
Fairest Flower of the Vale
Sunset
Words by Thomas Moore.
Violet Eyes
Sung by Louis Braham.
When the Moon on the Lake Is Beaming
The General, the Sergeant and the Flag

Note: The following is an extract of a letter from Gen. McClellan to Mr. Massett: "Expressing my gratification at the manner in which a true incident has been converted into verse."

In all the remarks Gen. McClellan had made to the Army, the burden of his thought and feeling had been: "Stand by Gen. Burnside—do more for him if possible than you have for me." Massett said: "I must not omit to mention a scene which occurred near Catlet's Station, where a portion of Gen. Sickles' command paid their farewell honors to their favorite chief. The color bearer of a Regiment rushed into the presence of the General and showing his tattered banner, said: 'General, I have carried that flag under you through the whole war and now I want to shake hands with you.' At this the Sergeant burst into tears, when Gen. McClellan replied, taking him by the hand: 'Never let it go, will you!' All who witnessed it were deeply affected by the scene."

Written by Thomas Moore (1779-1852)

Harp That Once Thro' Tara's Halls
Believe Me If All Those Endearing Young Charms
Rich and Rare Were the Gems She Wore
No! Not More Welcome
'Tis the Last Rose of Summer
Come Rest in This Bosom
Come O'er the Sea
Avenging and Bright
Nay, Tell Me Not
We May Roam Thro' This World
How Oft Has the Banshee Cried!
Erin! The Tear and the Smile
When First I Met Thee
Tho' the Last Glimpse of Erin
Drink to Her
Erin! Oh Erin!
Eveleen's Bower
As Slow Our Ship
Minstrel Boy
When He Who Adores Thee
I Saw Thy Form in Youthful Prime
Whene'er I See Those Smiling Eyes
Oft in the Stilly Night
Remember Thee
The Time I've Lost in Wooing
You Remember Ellen

Written by Edward B. Marks

My Mother Was a Lady
(or If Jack Were Only Here)
Music by Joseph W. Stern. Pub. E. B. Marks (1896). Tear jerker. ¾ tempo. Sung by Lottie Gilson at Proctor's 58th Street Theatre and by ballad singers and illustrated song singers all over the world. Over 1,000,000 copies sold.

The Little Lost Child
(A Passing Policeman)
Music by Joseph W. Stern. Pub. E. B. Marks (1894). Old-time ballad and first illustrated song. ¾ tempo. Sung by Lottie Gilson, Primrose and West's Minstrels and all ballad singers. First song publication of E. B. Marks (then known as Joseph W. Stern and Co.). Sales over 1,000,000 copies.

Don't Wear Your Heart on Your Sleeve
Music by Joseph W. Stern. Pub. E. B. Marks (1901). Tear jerker. ¾ tempo. Sung by Lottie Gilson.

The Old Postmaster
Music by Joseph W. Stern. Pub. E. B. Marks (1900). Tear jerker. ¾ tempo.

His Last Thoughts Were of You
Music by Joseph W. Stern. Pub. E. B. Marks (1894). Tear jerker and illustrated ballad success. Sung by Minnie Schult, Lottie Gilson and all illustrated song singers.

Caprice
Music by George Rosey. Pub. E. B. Marks (1895). ¾ tempo. Sung by La Porte Sisters.

Games We Used to Play
Music by Joseph W. Stern. Pub. E. B. Marks (1895). ¾ tempo. Sung by Lottie Gilson.

Won't You Take Me Back to Dixie
Words by Edward B. Marks and Gussie L. Davis. Music by George Rosey. Pub. E. B. Marks (1899). Old-time Southern tear jerker. Sung by Lew Palmer.

Kaddish of My Ancestry
Music by Joseph Cherniavsky. Pub. E. B. Marks (1925). Sacred Jewish song. 6/8 tempo. Sung by Cantor Joseph Rosenblatt.

I Don't Blame You, Tom
(or I Still Love You)
Music by Joseph W. Stern. Pub. E. B. Marks (1897). Old-time ballad. ¾ tempo. Sung by Lottie Gilson.

Break the News to Mother Gently
Music by Will H. Fox. Pub. Frank Harding (E. B. Marks) (1892). Old-time tear jerker. Sung by Minnie Schult and Lottie Gilson.

Sweet Melodies and Memories of Home
Music by Will H. Fox. Pub. Frank Harding (E. B. Marks) (1893). Old-time home song. Sung by Minnie Schult and Lottie Gilson.

Teacher and the Boy
Music by Joseph W. Stern. Pub. E. B. Marks (1895). Sentimental tear jerker. ¾ tempo. Sung by Lottie Gilson.

December and May
Music by William Lorraine. Pub. Frank Harding (E. B. Marks) (1893). ¾ tempo. Sung by Lydia Yeamans. Edward B. Marks' first song hit. Also the first "December and May" song.

No One Ever Loved You More Than I
Music by Joseph W. Stern. Pub. E. B. Marks (1896). Love ballad. ¾ tempo. Sung by minstrels and ballad singers.

My Little Circus Queen
Music by Max S. Witt. Pub. E. B. Marks (1896). Circus song. ¾ tempo. Sung by Bonnie Thornton.

Written by Felix McGlennon

Arrah Go On You're Only Fooling
Pub. T. B. Harms (1896). Irish comedy song. 6/8 tempo.

Comrades
Pub. (1887). Descriptive ballad. Sung by Helene Mora.

He Never Cares to Wander from His Own Fireside
Pub. Frank Tousey (1892). Home song. Sung by Helene Mora.

I've Been to Gay Paree
Words by Tom Conley and H. J. Sayers. Pub. Willis Woodward (E. B. Marks) (1893). French comedy song. 2/4 tempo.

Mr. Captain, Stop the Ship
Words by W. A. Archbold. Pub. Spaulding and Gray (E. B. Marks) (1894). Comedy song. Sung by Lew Dockstader and Lottie Gilson.

I've Worked Eight Hours This Day
Pub. Frank Tousey (1888). Irish comedy song. Sung by May Irwin.

Actions Speak Louder Than Words
Pub. Willis Woodward (E. B. Marks) (1891). Philosophical ballad. Sung by Helene Mora.

And Her Golden Hair Was Hanging Down Her Back
Pub. Frank Tousey (1884). Comedy song. Sung by Lottie Gilson.

I Handed It Over to Reilly
Pub. Frank Tousey (1892). Irish comedy song. Sung by Johnnie Carroll.

Oh, Uncle John
Pub. Frank Tousey (1895). Rube comedy song. Sung by Lottie Gilson.

Oh, What a Difference in the Morning
Pub. Frank Tousey (1891). Comedy song. Sung by Lottie Gilson.

One Touch of Nature Makes the Whole World Kin
Pub. Frank Tousey (1897). Philosophical song. Sung by Helene Mora.

That Is Love
Pub. Frank Tousey (1891). Love song. Sung by Helene Mora.

Written by Harrison Millard (1830-1895)

When the Tide Comes In
Words by H. Ashland Kean. Published by Spear and Denhoff (1873). Sea song.

Long Ago
Words by Dave Martin. Published by Harrison Millard, 152 West 37th Street, N. Y. C. (1878). Sea ballad.

Three Original Christmas Carols: In the Manger Lying—List Our Merry Carol—O Lovely Star
Published by Harrison Millard (1871)

Say Not Farewell (Me Dire Adieu)
Published by Spear and Denhoff (1877). Italian and English words.

Viva L'America (Flag of the Free)
Published by Hamilton S. Gordon (E. B. Marks) (1861). Civil War song.
NOTE: Harrison Millard was a band leader in the Civil War. One day when the troops were on parade and were being reviewed by Abraham Lincoln, Millard's band stopped in front of the reviewing stand and played "Flag of the Free." The President called Mr. Millard to the stand and asked the name of the selection that had just been played. When Millard told him it was a new patriotic song that he had just composed, Mr. Lincoln praised the music most highly.

Knights of Honor
Pub. Saalfield, N. Y. C. (1884).

Nearer, My God, to Thee
Words by Sarah F. Adams. Music by Lowell Mason. Pub. Harrison Millard (1884). Sacred song.

Christ Our Passover
Pub. S. T. Gordon (1865). Easter hymn and quartette.

Waiting
(1867). With violin or flute obligato.

Angel's Serenade (La Serenata)
Words by Henry Millard. Music by Galtans Braga (1867). Italian song.

Longing
Secular song.

Under the Daisies
Secular song.

Millard's Mass in G for Mixed Voices
Millard's Mass in G♭ for Mixed Voices
Millard's Mass in F for Mixed Voices

Millard's Mass in C for Mixed Voices
Vespers in D♭ for Mixed Voices
Silver Threads of Song
School singing book.
Babes in the Wood
Operetta for children.
Jack the Giant Killer
Operetta for children.
Little Red Riding Hood
Operetta for children.
Old Mother Hubbard
Operetta for children.
Easter Anthem in E♭
(Christ Our Passover)
Ave Maria No. 11 in F
(Hear Us, O Father)
Ave Maria No. 11 in E♭
(Hear Us, O Father)
Ave Maria No. 8 in G
(Send Down Thy Blessing)
Ave Maria No. 12 in A♭
Ave Verum No. 1 in F
Ave Verum No. 2 in D♭
(Come, Thou Font)
Ave Verum No. 2 in A♭
(Come, Thou Font)
O Jesu Deus Magne
Quartette for mixed voices.
Jesu Dulcis Memoria
Quartette for mixed voices.
Tantum Ergo in C (Hear Us, Father)
Quartette for mixed voices.
Veni Creator in A♭ (Come, Holy Spirit)
Angeline
After
Be Thou Forever Mine
Before
Bury Me in the Sunshine
Be Thou Ever Faithful
Don't Cry So, Norah
Darling
Ebbing Tide
Fairest of Flowers
Faith and Hope
(Old man's song to his wife)
Words ascribed to Rembrandt Peale, Esq.
Far Above the Daisies
Grand Army Song
Going Home with Willie
Happy Dreams

It Might Have Been
I Love My Home
I'll Be the First to Greet Thee
Johnny McSwattigan
Kiss Me Goodbye
Kiss I Offer
Music by S. Sarmiento.
Long Ago
My Heart I'll Keep for You
My Love! My Own!
Not Yet!
Oh Let Me Dream My Life Away
Pretty Zingerella
Patter of Little Feet
Queen of the Sea (Barcarolle)
Words by Geo. Cooper.
Roman Maiden
Red Robin
Rose at the Window
Return
Sing Me the Old Song
Sing Away, Bird
Smile Once Again
Thou Art Far Away
Teddy McGlyn from Dublin
Toby Valse
Thousand a Year
Under the Daisies
Why Should I Love Thee?
Whippoorwill's Songs
With All My Heart I Love You
Whisper Sweet Words
When the Tide Comes In
Again at Evening
Ave Maria
Solos in F and G.
Ave Verum
Solo.
Benedictus
Bonum Est (It Is a Good Thing)
Benedic: Praise the Lord
Christmas Anthem
(And There Were Shepherds)
Come, Holy Spirit
Deus Misecreatur
Domine Dixit, Laudate and Glorias
Easter Anthem (Christ Our Passover)
Fading, Still Fading
I Heard a Voice (Funeral Anthem)
I Will Arise
Jubilate

Magnificat
Mass in G (Complete)
Oh, Rest in the Lord
O Salutaris
Salve Regina
Te Deums
Venite: O, Come Let Us Sing
Vesper Service (Complete)
Latin and English.
Viene Al Mo Sen (Come to My Heart)
For Soprano and Tenor or Two Sopranos.

Written by J. F. MITCHELL

A Letter from Ireland
Pub. Willis Woodward (E. B. Marks) (1886). Irish song. Sung by Jack Walsh.
Absent Son
Pub. Frank Harding (E. B. Marks) (1885). Old-time mother ballad. 6/8 tempo. Sung by Maggie Cline and Johnnie Carroll.
Never Take No For An Answer
Pub. Willis Woodward (E. B. Marks) (1886). Old-time motto song. Sung by Minnie Schult (Mrs. George V. Hube).
Ship That Carries Me Home
Pub. Willis Woodward (E. B. Marks) (1885). Nautical ballad. Sung by minstrels and Variety singers.
Her Own Boy Jack
Pub. Willis Woodward (E. B. Marks) (1886). Old-time mother song. Sung by F. W. Oakland-Thatcher, Primrose and West's Minstrels.

Written by J. L. MOLLOY (1837-1909)

Little Tin Soldier
Pub. National Music Co., Chicago.
Thursday
(Ah Tomorrow Will Be Friday)
Pub. Oliver Ditson, Boston (1899).
In the Month of Flowers (Belle Amour)
Children's Prayers
Pub. Evans and Bro., Boston.
Only Tonight
Pub. G. Schirmer. English song.
London Bridge
Pub. Saalfield, N. Y. C. English song.
King's Highway
Pub. Saalfield, N. Y. C.
Clochette
Pub. Saalfield, N. Y. C.
Old Lace
Pub. Evans and Bro., Boston (1882).
Cricket on the Hearth
Pub. Hitchcock, N. Y. C.
Punchinello
Pub. Hitchcock, N. Y. C. Songs after Hans Andersen.
Little Maid Milking the Cow
Pub. Hitchcock, N. Y. C.
Vanished Years
Clang of the Wooden Shoon
Pub. Hitchcock, N. Y. C. Baritone song.
Polly
Pub. National Music Co., Chicago.
Flitting Days
Pub. National Music Co., Chicago.
(Oh) How Delightful
Sung by Lydia Thompson at Niblo's Garden.
Love's Old Sweet Song
Words by G. Clifton Bingham. Pub. G. Schirmer. The world-famous "Just a Song at Twilight."
The Dustman
Pub. Evans and Bro., Boston.
Sweet Lavender
Pub. Evans and Bro., Boston.
Thady O'Flynn
Davy Jones
Kerry Dance
Boatswain's Story
Blue Eyes
Claudine
Darby and Joan
First Letter
Three Simple Words

Told in the Twilight
Postillion
Old Street Lamp
Wagon
Vagabond
Only Twenty-One
Ding Dong
Wren and the Hen
Snowflakes
Glover
Beautiful Moonlight
Jamie
Rose Marie

Written by Ethelbert Nevin (1862-1901)

Water Scenes (Among them "Narcissus") (Piano)
The Rosary (Vocal)
A Day in Venice
Mighty Lak' A Rose
Lady Floriane's Dream (Pantomime)
Slumber Song
Three Dances (Piano Duet)
Sketch Book
(Piano compositions and songs)
A Book of Songs
(Piano compositions and songs)
May in Tuscany (Suite for Piano)
In Arcadia (Piano)

Written by John Parry (1810-1879)

A.B.C. (Vocal Duet)
Pub. Sep Winner (1868).
Villikens and His Dinah
Wanted a Governess
Also sung by John Parry.
Last Vow
Tell Me, Gentle Stranger
Flying Dutchman
Goodbye, Sweetheart
Dost Thou Love Me, Sister Ruth?
Nora, the Pride of Kildare

Written by Ciro Pinsuti (1829-1888)

I Remember
When the Swallows Come
The Swallow
Thou Gavest Me a Flower
'Tis I
Angel of My Dreams
Raft
Fly Forth, Oh Gentle Dove
I Heard a Voice
I Love My Love

Written by H. W. Petrie

Davy Jones' Locker
Pub. E. B. Marks (1901). Baritone or bass song. 12/8 tempo.
I Don't Want to Play in Your Yard
Words by Philip Wingate. Pub. Petrie Music Co., Chicago (E. B. Marks) (1894). Famous kid song. ¾ tempo.
Port of Missing Ships
Words by Robert F. Roden. Pub. Haviland (1911). Nautical song. 12/8 tempo.
Sea Gull
Words by Robert F. Roden. Pub. Haviland (1916). Baritone or bass song. 6/4 tempo.
Every Night in My Twilight Dreams
Words by Robert F. Roden. Pub. Haviland (1916). Love ballad. ¾ tempo.

Everyone's in Love With Someone
Words by Arthur Gillespie. Pub. E. B. Marks (1907). 4/4 tempo. Sung by Janet Allen (the first Mrs. Jimmie Walker).

Asleep in the Deep
Words by Arthur J. Lamb. Pub. F. A. Mills (1901). Baritone and bass song. Sung by John P. Rogers.

Only Love Me
Words by George Frederick Lyman. Pub. Brainard Sons (E. B. Marks) (1891). ¾ tempo.

Dreaming of You
Words by Rene Bronner. Pub. Haviland (1910). 12/8 tempo.

You Can't Play in Our Yard Any More
Words by Philip Wingate. Pub. Thiebes Sterlin Co., St. Louis (1894). Kid song.

Thousand Leagues Under the Sea
Words by J. T. Branen. Pub. E. B. Marks (1901). Baritone or bass song. 12/8 tempo.

Where the Susquehanna Flows
Words by Rene Bronner. Pub. E. B. Marks (1905). Home song.

Where the Sunset Turns the Ocean's Blue to Gold
Words by Eva Fern Buckner. Pub. Petrie Music Co., Chicago (E. B. Marks). (1902). Minstrel ballad. 4/4 tempo.

Written by John Read (1833-1920)

Whoa, Emma
Pub. Spear and Denhoff (1877). Very popular comic song. 2/4 tempo.

Johnny Morgan Played the Organ
Pub. White Smith and Co., Boston (about 1878). Sung in "Babes In the Wood."

Down by the Old Mill Stream
Old-time ballad. 2/4 tempo. Not to be confused with the later song of the same title.

Grandmother's Chair
Pub. S. T. Gordon and Son. Descriptive song success.

They All Do It
Pub. E. H. Harding. Comic song. 2/4 tempo. Sung by Tony Pastor.

George F. Root (1820-1895)
(Also wrote under nom de plume C. Friedrich Wurzel)

In a long musical life, as useful as it was successful, Root endeared himself to the nation as a song writer and musician. His specialty was writing war songs of the Civil War period.

He died at his summer cottage at Bailey's Beach, Maine. He was the last of the Elder School of American Composers and was the pupil and associate of Lowell Mason (1792-1872). His associates were a group of self-taught musicians.

As a balladist, he excelled them all. He wrote the songs and expressed the sentiments of the multitude, especially during the conflict between the North and the South. He put into rhyme the sentiments of soldiers, as well as of those who stayed at home.

He lived in Paris from 1850 to 1854. This added to his musical culture and widened his acquaintance with musicians of European fame.

A List of His Songs

There's Music in the Air
Words by Frances J. Crosby. Pub. Root and Cady, Chicago (1857). For mixed quartette.
Comrades Hasten to the Battle
Words by Thomas Monahan. Pub. Henry Tolman Co., Boston (1864). Civil War song. 4/4 tempo.
Rosalie the Prairie Flower
Pub. Russell and Richardson Musical Exchange, Boston (1855). Prairie song.
The Hazel Dell
Pub. (1853). Old-time ballad.
Flee As a Bird
Words by Mrs. Mary B. Dana. Pub. (1857). Ballad.
The Vacant Chair
Words by H. S. Washburn. Pub. (1861). Civil War song.
Tramp, Tramp, Tramp
Pub. (1864). Civil War song.
Battle Cry of Freedom
Pub. (1863). Civil War song.
Poor Robin's Growing Old
Sung by Woods Minstrels.
Annie Lowe
Sung by Woods Minstrels.
On Old Potomac's Shore
Sung by Woods Minstrels.
There's Something to Live For
Words by Richard Realt. Five Points house of industry.
Old Folks Are Gone
Sung by C. P. Christy at Christy's Opera House, N. Y. C.
Swinging, Swinging, All Day Long
Old Josey
They've Sold Me Down the River
Proud World, Goodbye! I'm Going Home
Father John
Glad to Get Home
Honeysuckle Glen
Church Within the Wood
All Together Again
Call 'Em Names, Jeff
De Day ob Liberty's Comin'
Forward, Boys
Wake, Lady, Wake—
We Are Singing to Thee
God Bless Our Brave Young Volunteers
Liberty Bird
Dreaming Ever Dreaming
Old Friends and True Friends
Time of the Heart
Mother Sweet Mother, Why Linger Away?
I Had a Gentle Mother
Hundred Years Ago
Dearest Brother, We Miss Thee
Mary of the Glen
Look on the Bright Side
Gently, Gently Wake the Song
Futures of Memory
Creeper on the Plain
Father's Coming
They Sleep In the Dust
Only Waiting
Sacred Song
Early Lost, Early Saved
Pub. (1852).
Greenwood Bell
Poem by Frances Jane Crosby of the New York Institute for the Blind.
World As It Is
Song or male quartette.

Written by Henry Russell (1812-1900)
(Also known as Harry Russell)

Sailor Boy (or I Am a Merry Sailor Lad)
Words from Philadelphia Saturday Courier. Music by W. C. Peters. Pub. W. C. Peters (1844). Song of the sea.
Some Love to Roam
O'er the Dark Sea Foam
Words by Charles Mackay. Pub. E. Ferrett and Co., Philadelphia (about 1847). Song of the sea. ¾ tempo.
Brave Old Oak
Words by H. F. Chorley, Esq. Pub. E. Ferrett and Co., Philadelphia (about 1847). Song of the oak.

Fine Old English Gentleman
Pub. E. Ferrett and Co., Philadelphia (about 1847). Song of the olden time.

I Love to Dwell in the Bosom's Cell
Pub. E. Ferrett and Co., Philadelphia (about 1847). A lay of hope.

Old Schoolhouse
Words by Park Benjamin, Esq. Pub. by Charles T. Ceslain, 547 Broadway, N. Y. C. (1841). Old school song. 6/8 tempo. Dedicated to Mrs. James Gordon Bennett.

Starlight Waltz
Music by B. F. Leavens. Pub. Oliver Ditson, Boston (1842). Instrumental waltz. 3/8 tempo.

Fairy Bells
Music by Hon. Mrs. Norton. Pub. Firth and Hall (about 1842). Old ballad.

I'm Afloat, I'm Afloat
Words by Eliza Cook. Pub. George P. Reed, Boston (about 1846). 3/4 tempo.

We Have Been Friends Together
Words by Hon. Mrs. Norton. Pub. E. Ferrett and Co., Philadelphia (about 1847). 3/4 tempo.

Orphan Ballad Singers
Pub. E. Ferrett and Co., Philadelphia (about 1847). Old-time tear jerker.

Far Far Upon the Sea
Words by Charles Mackay, LL.D. Pub. by Musical Bouquet Office, London. Nautical song. From "The Emigrant's Progress." Very old edition with engraved photo of the composer.

Robin Ruff
Pub. William A. Pond and Co. (1875). Old-time ballad.

Cheer Boys
Words by Charles Mackay. Pub. Oliver Ditson, Boston. Old-time nautical song.

Spider and the Fly
Pub. W. C. Petrie, Louisville (1844). Famous old-time comic song. Quaint old first edition with engraved frontispiece.

To the West! To the West!
To the Land of the Free
Words by Charles Mackay. Pub. Musical Bouquet Office, London. 3/4 tempo. From "The Emigrant's Progress." Rare old bit of Americana. Illustrated with litho scenes of the pioneer West. Autographed by Henry Russell.

Woodman, Spare That Tree
Words by George P. Morris, Esq. Pub. Firth Pond and Co. (1837). Famous poem and song success. 13th edition. Beautiful old-time litho on frontispiece.

Newfoundland Dog
Words by F. W. N. Bailey, Esq. Pub. James L. Hewitt and Co. and Firth and Hall (1843). 3/4 tempo. Fine old litho on title page of the sea and the dog.

I'll Be No Submissive Wife
Words by Epes Sargent (the Elder). Pub. (1838). Sung by Mr. Seguin and Mr. Russell.

Life on the Ocean Wave
Nautical song.

Our Native Song
Patriotic song.

Fisher Boy
Old-time song.

Sunny Days Will Come Again
Old-time ballad.

Rouse, Brothers, Rouse
Old-time song.

Come, Maidens, Come
Tyrolean song.

My Heart's in the Highlands
Poem by Robert Burns.

Written by Ren Shields

Go Easy, Mabel
Words by Ren Shields, Ed Moran and Will D. Cobb. Music by J. Fred Helf. Pub. Helf and Hager (E. B. Marks) (1909). Slang popular song. 2/4 tempo. Sung by Lew Dockstader.

Take Me Out for a Joy Ride
Music by Kerry Mills. Pub. F. A. Mills (E. B. Marks) (1909). 3/4 tempo. Sung by Ren Shields.

Up in My Balloon
Music by Percy Wenrich. Pub. E. B.

Marks (1908). ¾ tempo. Sung by Rosie Lloyd.

In the Good Old Summer Time
Words by George Evans, the famous minstrel "Honeyboy" Evans. Pub. Howley Haviland (E. B. Marks) (1902). Greatest popular summer hit of all time. ¾ tempo. Sung by "Honeyboy" Evans.

Come Take a Trip in My Airship
Music by George Evans. Pub. Charles K. Harris (now E. B. Marks) (1904). First popular airship song. ¾ tempo. Sung by Ethel Robinson.

They've Won Every Nation's Battles But Their Own
Words and music by Ren Shields, Johnny Nestor and George Christie. Pub. M. Witmark and Sons (1910). Irish novelty march. 2/4 tempo. Sung by Frank Fogerty, the Dublin minstrel.

Waltz Me Around Again, Willie
Words by Will D. Cobb. Pub. F. A. Mills (E. B. Marks) (1906). ¾ tempo. Sung by Ren Shields.

When You Know That Your Girlie Loves You
Music by Harry I. Davis. Pub. E. B. Marks (1909). Girl Song. Sung by Ren Shields.

Down at Lover's Roost
Music by George Abbott. Pub. Howley Haviland and Dresser (E. B. Marks) (1902). Love song. Sung by Ren Shields.

They Were All Doing the Same
Pub. American Advance Music Co. (1902). Comic song. Sung by Ren Shields.

In the Merry Month of June
Words and music by George Evans and Ren Shields. Pub. Whitney Warner Pub. Co. (1903). Summer song. Sung by Ren Shields.

Sunday Morning When the Church Bells Ring
Music by George Evans. Pub. Charles K. Harris (1903). Ballad. Sung by Ren Shields.

Keep Away from Rosie
Music by George Evans. Pub. Charles K. Harris (1903). Boy-and-girl song. Sung by Ren Shields.

You're the Sweetest Flower That Grows in Tennessee
Music by George Evans. Pub. Charles K. Harris (1903). Ballad. Sung by Ren Shields.

If It's Good Enough for Washington It's Good Enough for Me
Music by Percy Wenrich. Pub. Jerome H. Remick (1908). Patriotic song. Sung by Ren Shields.

Don't Forget to Write Me Every Day
Music by George Christie. Pub. M. Witmark and Sons (1908).

The Longest Way 'Round Is the Sweetest Way Home
Music by Kerry Mills. Pub. F. A. Mills (E. B. Marks) (1908). Home song.

Make a Noise Like a Hoop and Roll Away
Music by J. Fred Helf. Pub. Helf and Hager Co. (E. B. Marks) (1908). Comedy song.

Down Where the Watermelon Grows
Music by George Evans. Pub. Jerome H. Remick (1909). Plantation song.

She's the Daughter of a G.A.R.
Pub. F. A. Mills (E. B. Marks) (1903). Patriotic song.

Save a Little Money for a Rainy Day
Music by Maxwell Silver. Pub. F. A. Mills (E. B. Marks) (1907).

Don't Ever Look for It Among the Irish
Music by George Evans. Pub. Charles K. Harris (1903). Irish song.

Stand Up and Let the Lady Sit Down
Music by Maxwell Silver. Pub. F. A. Mills (E. B. Marks) (1903).

Savannah Anna
Music by Maxwell Silver. Pub. F. A. Mills (E. B. Marks) (1906).

Written by Joseph P. Skelly (1853-1895)

Are You Going to the Ball This Evening?
Pub. Frank Harding (E. B. Marks) (1881). Comedy ditty. Sung by Tony Pastor.
Little Nell and I
Pub. Frank Harding (E. B. Marks) (1891). Ballad.
Mother Is the Best Friend After All
Pub. Frank Harding (E. B. Marks) (1883). Mother song.
My Pretty Red Rose
Pub. Frank Harding (E. B. Marks) (1887). Girl song.
Since Nellie Went Away
Pub. Frank Harding (E. B. Marks) (1892). Tear jerker.
That Old Sweetheart of Mine
Pub. Frank Harding (E. B. Marks) (1891). Love song.
Strolling on the Brooklyn Bridge
Words by George Cooper. (1883).
Why Did They Dig Ma's Grave So Deep? (1870).
Call Me Your Darling Again
Words by George Cooper.
Little Church Around the Corner
Words by Joseph P. Skelly and George Cooper. Music by Edwin Christie. Sung by Edwin Christie.
Never More to See Thy Smile
Words by Joseph P. Skelly and George Cooper. Music by Edwin Christie.
I Feel I'm Growing Old
Music by F. N. Crouch.
Dear Mother, I've Come Home to Die
Music by Henry Tucker.
Just Beyond the Other Shore
Music by H. P. Danks.
Fusileers
Comic song.
Old Rustic Bridge by the Mill
Our Servant Girl's Young Man
Farewell
Sweet Long Ago
Why Should We Live as Strangers?
Oh! Ain't You Awful

Written by Johann Strauss (The Elder) (1804-1849)
Father of Johann Strauss of "Blue Danube" fame

Waltzes

The Life a Dance, The Dance a Life
Etincelles
Artists' Ball
Gabriella
Elisabeth
Songs of the Danube
Loreley-Rhein-Klaenge
Aurora
Queen Victoria

Polkas and Marches, etc.

Radetzky March
Sperl Polka
Kathinka Polka
Venetian Galop
Flora Quadrille

Written by Johann Strauss (1825-1899)
(His best-known compositions only)

Waltzes

Beautiful Blue Danube
Tales from the Vienna Woods
Artist's Life
Vienna Blood
Voices of Spring
Vienna Bonbons
Morning Papers
Emperor Waltz
Southern Roses
Wine, Woman and Song
Life Let Us Cherish

Operettas

The Bat
Gypsy Baron
Prince Methusalem
Merry War
Indigo
A Night in Venice
Waldmeister
Pazman (opera)

Polkas and Marches

Perpetuum Mobile
Pizzicato-Polka
Prince Bariatinsky March
Persian March

Written by OSCAR STRAUS (1870-)

Operettas

Waltz Dream
Chocolate Soldier
Last Waltz
Three Waltzes
Marietta
Teresina

Songs

Love's Roundelay
Piccolo
A Husband's Love
Life Is Love and Laughter
Love Cannot Be Bought
A Country Lass and a Courtly Dame
Kissing Time March
Sweetest Maid of All
Lesson in Love
My Hero
The Merry Husband
Only Human
Little Boy in Corduroy
Let's Try Again
Keep Our Love As It Is Today
On the Downtown Side of an Uptown Street
Two People from Vienna
I'm in Love with Emily

RICHARD STAHL

Richard Stahl was a well-known figure in the world of make-believe in the halcyon days of the American Theater in New York when his close associates were Lillian Russell, Lotta, Mme. Nellie Melba, E. E. Rice, Alfred Aarons, Francis Wilson, James T. Powers, Denman Thompson, Julian Mitchell, Charles Hoyt, Frank McKee and Augustin Daly.

Born of a family prominent in military circles and of vast landed estates, Stahl at an early age showed decided musical talent. Although he studied with the famous Theodore Kullock in Europe and received every advantage musically, it was intended for him to follow a military career in the family tradition.

However, as an officer in a crack cavalry regiment, he soon realized that he did not care to remain a part of the arrogant militaristic class to which he was born and, retiring with the rank of reserve lieutenant, he started on a world tour, stopping en route in California, where his father had extensive mining interests.

He made many friends and saw the possibility of a musical career in America. Returning to his homeland, Germany, by way of the Orient and Suez Canal, he made arrangements and received permission to come back later to the United States, where he remained and became an American citizen, marrying the granddaughter of John Supplee, the noted Philadelphia builder and direct descendant of Hance Supplee of Revolutionary War fame.

Stahl quickly achieved prominence when his opera "Said Pasha" had its première at the Tivoli Opera House in San Francisco and first ran for five consecutive years from coast to coast. Word of his triumph was far-reaching and when Nellie Farren and Fred Leslie introduced his music at the London Gaiety Theatre, critics there acclaimed him the "Strauss of America." "Said Pasha" is believed to be the oldest copyrighted work still to be performed and has played from here to the Antipodes. Some years ago Mrs. Stahl signed a contract with Edward B. Marks to represent her interests in this and other operas.

"Said Pasha" was followed by "The Sea King," which had a long run at A. M. Palmer's Theatre before touring America and Europe. In quick succession came the "Lion Tamer," in which Francis Wilson starred for many seasons. After these operettas Mr. Stahl, believing that musical farce was to play a prominent part in the field of entertainment, composed the music for Donnelly and Girard's "Natural Gas" and "The Rainmakers." At Percy Gaunt's death he joined forces with Charles Hoyt when he wrote the music for "A Milk White Flag," "A Black Sheep," "A Contented Woman," "A Stranger In New York" and "A Day and a Night."

At the same time he was writing the music for the presentations at Koster and Bial's and the incidental music to "The Mummy," starring Robert Hilliard and Amelia Bingham, and "Florida Enchantment," Archibald Clavering Gunther's dramatization of his own novel by the same name. He was also associated with Augustin Daly in the production of "Runaway Girl."

In fact, at the time, Richard Stahl was connected in some way with nearly every theatrical production in New York and his sudden death cut short a brilliant career. His wife and daughter Lorraine live on Gramercy Park, within the gates of which a tree was planted in Richard Stahl's memory some years ago by his friends, Otis Harlan, George Lederer, Edward B. Marks and Percy Rockefeller. Lorraine, who is known as Lorraine Sherwood of the radio, is the "Voice of the Port of New York Authority" and the "Voice of the Kearny Works" for Western Electric. She is said to have inherited no small share of her father's gift of melody.

Richard Stahl composed all the music for the musical comedies produced by Charles A. Hoyt and others (in all over 1,000 compositions).

A List of His Songs

Baby's Jingly Journey Through Alphabet Land
Verses by Charles Noel Douglas. Music by Richard Stahl and George Rosey. Sketches by Ray Brown. Pub. E. B. Marks (1899). 26 musical rhymes for children.

James A. Garfield Inauguration March

One Kiss Tells All

Some Things Are Better Left Unsaid
Sung in Hoyt's musical comedy "Black Sheep."

Fin de siecle (The Languid Man)
Sung by Otis Harlan in Hoyt's "Day and a Night."

My Heart Could Forget All the Past
Dedicated to Minnie Maddern Fiske.

Dream of Home
Words by Sir Thomas Moore.

Idol of My Heart
Sung by Melba and Lillian Russell.

Mandolin Serenade
By M. J. Milton (nom de plume of Richard Stahl). Sung by Therese Vaughn in "1492."

Alabama Patrol (Instrumental)

Cupid's Pranks (Instrumental)

A selected list of comic operas, oratorios, songs, hymns and other musical works composed by SIR ARTHUR SEYMOUR SULLIVAN (1842-1900) (Of the immortal team of Gilbert and Sullivan)

The 14 Gilbert and Sullivan Comic Operas

All librettos by Sir William Schwenk Gilbert (1836-1911)

Thespis (or The Gods Grown Old)
Produced at the Gaiety Theatre, London, December 23, 1871.
NOTE: The score of this first joint effort of the famous collaborators was never published.

Trial by Jury
Produced at the New Royalty Theatre, London, March 25, 1875.

The Sorcerer (or The Elixir of Love)
Produced at the Opera Comique, London, November 17, 1877.

H.M.S. Pinafore
(or The Lass That Loved a Sailor)
Produced at the Opera Comique, London, May 25, 1878.

Pirates of Penzance
(or The Slave of Duty)
Produced first at the Royal Bijou Theatre, Paignton, England, December 30, 1879. First American production at the Fifth Avenue Theatre, N. Y. C., December 31, 1879. First London performance at the Opera Comique, April 3, 1880.

Patience (or Bunthorne's Bride)
Produced at the Opera Comique, London, April 23, 1881.

Iolanthe (or The Peer and the Peri)
Produced at the Savoy Theatre, London, November 25, 1882.

Princess Ida (or Castle Adamant)
Produced at the Savoy Theatre, London, January 25, 1884.

The Mikado (or The Town of Titipu)
Produced at the Savoy Theatre, London, March 14, 1885.

Ruddigore (or The Witch's Curse)
Produced at the Savoy Theatre, London, January 22, 1887.

The Yeomen of the Guard
(or The Merryman and His Maid)
Produced at the Savoy Theatre, London, October 3, 1888.

The Gondoliers
(or The King of Barataria)
Produced at the Savoy Theatre, London, December 7, 1889.

Utopia Limited
(or The Flowers of Progress)
Produced at the Savoy Theatre, London, October 7, 1893.

The Grand Duke (or The Statutory Duel)
Produced at the Savoy Theatre, London, March 7, 1896.

Other Comic Operas, Oratorios, Cantatas and Larger Works

The Tempest
Based on Shakespeare's play. First played in Leipzig, Germany, April 11, 1861.

Kenilworth (Masque)
Produced at the Birmingham Festival, England, September 8, 1864.

Cox and Box (Comic Opera)
Libretto by Burnand and Morton. First produced privately in London, April 27, 1867.

The Contrabandista (Comic Opera)
Libretto by F. C. Burnand. Produced at St. George's Hall, London, December 18, 1867.

The Prodigal Son (Oratorio)
Produced at the Worcester Festival, England, September 8, 1869.

On Shore and Sea (Cantata)
Produced at Albert Hall, London, May 1, 1871.

The Merchant of Venice
Incidental music for Shakespeare's play. Produced at the Princess Theatre, Manchester, England, September 19, 1871.

The Light of the World (Oratorio)
Produced at the Birmingham Festival, England, August 27, 1873.

The Merry Wives of Windsor
Incidental music for Shakespeare's play. Produced at the Gaiety Theatre, London, December 19, 1874.

The Zoo (Comic Opera)
Libretto by B. Rowe. Produced at the St. James' Theatre, London, June 5, 1875.

The Martyr of Antioch
(Sacred Musical Drama)
Produced at Leeds Musical Festival, England, October 15, 1880.

The Golden Legend (Cantata)
Produced at Leeds Musical Festival, England, October 16, 1886.

Macbeth
Incidental music for Shakespeare's play. Produced at the Lyceum Theatre, London, October 29, 1888.

Ivanhoe
Romantic opera adapted from Sir Walter Scott. Libretto by Julian Sturgis. Produced at the Cambridge Circus, England, January 31, 1891.

The Foresters
Incidental music. Produced at Daly's Theatre, N. Y. C., March 25, 1892.

Haddon Hall (Comic Opera)
Libretto by Sydney Grundy. Produced at the Savoy Theatre, London, September 24, 1892.

The Chieftain (Comic Opera) (Enlarged version of "The Contrabandista")
Libretto by F. C. Burnand. Produced at the Savoy Theatre, London, December 12, 1894.

King Arthur
Incidental music. Produced at the Lyceum Theatre, London, January 12, 1895.

Victoria and Merrie England (Ballet)
Produced at the Alhambra Theatre, London, May 25, 1897.

The Beauty Stone
(Romantic Musical Drama)
Libretto by Arthur Wing Pinero and Comyns Carr. Produced at the Savoy Theatre, London, May 28, 1898.

The Rose of Persia (Comic Opera)
Libretto by Basil Hood. Produced at the Savoy Theatre, London, November 29, 1899.

The Emerald Isle (Comic Opera)
Music completed by Edward German. Libretto by Basil Hood. Produced posthumously at the Savoy Theatre, London, April 27, 1901.

Songs, Hymns and Anthems

Sing Unto the Lord and Praise His Name (1855)
His first song. Written when Sullivan was 13.

It was a Lover and His Lass (1857)
Orpheus with His Lute (1863)
Willow Song (1863)
Will He Come? (1865)
If Doughty Deeds My Lady Please (1866)
Arabian Love Song (1866)
She Is Not Fair to Outward View (1866)
O Hush Thee, My Babie (1867)
Give (1867)
What Does Little Birdie Say? (1867)
My Love Beyond the Sea (1867)
Marmion Overture (1867)
The Snow Lies White (1868)
Oh Sweet and Fair (1868)
The Mother's Dream (1868)
Rejoice in the Lord (1868)

Sad Memories (1869)
Birds in the Night (1869)
Looking Back (1870)
It Came Upon a Midnight Clear (1871)
Arrangement of traditional air.
Lead, Kindly Light (1871)
Watchman, What of the Night? (1871)
The Way Is Long and Drear (1871)
Onward, Christian Soldiers (1871)
Words by Sabine Waring-Gould.
St. Kevin (1872)
Golden Days (1872)
Once Again (1872)
Little Maid of Arcadee (1872)
Looking Forward (1873)
Sleep, My Love, Sleep (1874)
Let Me Dream Again (1875)
Sweethearts (1875)
Thou'rt Passing Hence (1875)
My Dearest Heart (1876)
Little Darling, Sleep Again (1876)
When Thou Art Near (1877)
Sometimes (1877)
The Lost Chord (1877)
Words by Adelaide Procter.
I Would I Were a King (1878)
A Shadow (1885)
Tears, Idle Tears (1900)

John Rogers Thomas (1829-1896)

John Rogers Thomas was a vocalist of the Civil War period and a writer of ballads.

He was a Welshman. A great many Welsh had settled in Jersey City, N. J., at about that time. In a block of old brownstone buildings in Jersey City, there was one house which was the home of John Rogers Thomas. He was well-known among the Welsh. There were enough Welsh to have preaching in the Welsh tongue.

The familiar songs of the day were: "Day When You Will Forget Me," "Must We Then Meet As Strangers?" (1875), "Our Own Dear Land," "The Owl," "The Gates Ajar," "Eilleen Alanna," "Rose of Killarney" and many others, most of them still reprinted as old favorites.

A List of His Songs

Must We Meet Then As Strangers?
Pub. Oliver Ditson and Co. (1875)
Old Friends and Old Times
Words by Charles Swan. Pub. Oliver Ditson and Co. (1856).
Bonnie Eloise (Belle of Mohawk Trail)
Words by George W. Elliot. Pub. Oliver Ditson and Co. (1858).
'Tis But a Little Faded Flower
Words by Frederick Enoch. Pub. Oliver Ditson and Co. (1860).
Croquet
Words by C. H. Webb. Pub. Oliver Ditson and Co. (1867).
Eilleen Alanna
Words by E. S. Marble. Pub. Oliver Ditson and Co. (1873).
Rose of Killarney
Words by George Cooper. Pub. Oliver Ditson and Co. (1876).
Happy Be Thy Dreams
Pub. William Hall and Son (1859).
No Crown Without a Cross
Words by George Cooper. Sacred song.
Sweet Be Thy Repose
Tenor song.
Voice of the Mountain Land
Contralto or baritone song.
Apart
Words by George Cooper. Sung by Annie Louise Cary at the Nilsson concerts.
There's Sunlight on the Hills
Words by George Cooper. Sung by

Mr. Stanley and the composer. From "Lady in the Mask."
Birds Will Come Again
Words by George Cooper. Sung by Dave Wambold.
Cottage by the Sea
(1856)
That Song of Thine
Pearl of the Isle
Day When You'll Forget Me
Dew Is on the Blossom
Floating Down the Stream
Old Farm House
Moonlit Sea
Before the Days of Sadness
Say a Kind Word, When You Can
Oh! Don't You Remember the Time
Star of My Home
Down by the River Side
All the Year Round
All in the Merry Way
Annie of the Vale
Beautiful Snowdrops
Beautiful Highlands
Don't Forget to Dream of Me
Good Night and Happy Dreams
Little Birdie
Never Deem My Love Can Change
Beautiful Isle of the Sea
Fishes in the Sea (Song of the Flirt)
Dew Is on the Flower (Serenade)

Written by Henry Tucker

Star of the Evening
Words and music by James M. Sayles. Pub. Oliver Ditson, Boston (1855). 6/8 tempo. Arranged by Henry Tucker.
Weeping Sad and Lonely
(When This Cruel War Is Over)
Words by Charles Carroll Sawyer. Pub. Sawyer and Thompson, Brooklyn (1863). Civil War song. Sung by Woods Minstrels, at Woods Museum, Broadway, N. Y. C.
Jennie Is Waiting for Me
Words by George B. Pennock. Pub. E. H. Harding. 6/8 tempo.
Beside the Sweet Shannon
Pub. William A. Pond and Co. (1877).
Sweet Genevieve
Words by George Cooper.
A Tress of Golden Hair
Words by George Cooper.
Happy Memories
Words by Fanny Crosby.
Grey Hill Plaid
Scotch song.
'Tis Evening Brings My Heart to Thee
Willow Spring
Memory Bells
Violets Under the Snow
All in the Mist of the Morning
Don't Forget the Old Folks
Deep in a Bed of Roses
Lost Star of My Home
Nation Mourns Her Honored Son
Girls, Get a Home of Your Own
Let Me Be Ever Near Thee
Sweet Lurline
Golden Pathway in the Sky
All My Dreams Are Full of Thee
Waiting for the Loved One

Written by H. S. Thompson (1857-1920)

Annie Lisle
Lily Dale
O Bury Me in the Sunshine
Willie's on the Dark Blue Sea
Fly Away O'er the Deep
Mavourneen Asthorpe

Written by Joseph Philbrick Webster (1819-1875)

Always of Thee
I Stand on Memory's Golden Shore
Sweet Bye and Bye
Cousin John
Dawning of the Better Day
Johnny Is a Farmer Boy
Neath the Old Elm Tree
Under the Beautiful Stars
The beatitudes (Cantata)
Signed Ring (Sunday School song book)

William Vincent Wallace (1830-1865)

It is interesting to note how the first performance of this famous musician's opera "Maritana" was reviewed in a quaint criticism of the performance at the Drury Lane Theatre in 1846.

The libretto of "Maritana" was by Fitz Ball. The program names Mr. Horncastle, Mr. Borranani, Mrs. Selby, Mr. H. Phillips, Mr. Harrison, Miss Poole and Miss Romer.

The opening scene is a view of Madrid. The chorus in six-eight time then invites Maritana to sing. She complies in a "romanza"—"It Was a Knight of Princely Mien," three-four beginning in A minor—with a quaint bolero accompaniment, and ending in the major. The choral responses to this pretty air are effective. The second romance is again sung by Maritana—"'Tis The Harp in The Air"—and a more charming composition was never performed. It is in E flat, six-eight time, and the harp, like the softest discords of the Aeolian harp, is heard in mild and flowing arpeggios, a gossamer touch of violins, pizzicatos being apparent in the enchanting choral echoes.

The "Angelus," in the evening prayer that follows, is a clever display of choral power and is splendidly scored. A duet then ensues between Don José and Maritana, in which the composer's skill is developed. Don Caesar has a Bacchanalian Cavatina in B flat minor, full of vigorous writing, but requiring much delicacy of execution—the concerted piece in which Don Caesar in protecting Lazarillo, is provoked to do duel, in which the Holy Week is too noisily scored, although the vocal parts are well disposed. A "morceau d'ensemble" that is next entitled "Pretty Gitani Tell Us" is deliciously Spanish in treatment. It is in three-eight time and opens in B minor, terminating in B major with most piquant orchestration. A spirit of stirring finale, with Don Caesar's arrest, winds up the Act.

The Second Act opens in the interior of a fortress, and we cannot eulogize too strongly on Miss Poole's perfect vocalization throughout this Act. The general tenor of the rest of the performance is along lines of excellence as to Mr. Wallace's melodies and instrumentation, the fine performance of the artists and the enthusiastic reception of the opera by the audience.

William Wallace's composition "Villon" was performed for the first time in London, by the New Symphony Orchestra in 1909. The first performance in the United States was at New York in 1910, the year also that "Villon" was published. It is scored for three flutes, interchangeable, with piccolo, two oboes, English horn, two clarinets, two bassoons, four horns, two trumpets, two tenor trombones, bass tuba, kettledrum, triangles, cymbals, tamtam, tambour de provence, harp and the usual strings. It was said that the first time this symphonic poem was played, the composer had attempted to reflect some of the moods which are met with in Villon's poems.

William Wallace was constantly fighting for the development of English music. He was an interesting figure in England's musical life. His works received much attention in New York.

Wallace designed the cover of his "Freebooter's" songs, the character of the "Freebooter" being much on the order of a Teddy Roosevelt "Rough Rider."

Wallace was born in 1830 in Waterford, Ireland. He stands in the foremost rank of English composers. He received his first instructions on the piano from his father, who was a bandmaster.

Wallace lived in New York from 1843 to 1853. He died in Touraine in the Pyrenees, October 12, 1865.

A memorial service for Wallace was held at St. Thomas' Church in New York—D. Morgan, Rector. The musical numbers were: "O Rest in the Lord"—Mendelssohn, "Come Unto Him," George William Warren, Musical Director. There was chanting by St. Thomas' Choir.

Several memorial statues of Wallace exist. One to commemorate him was placed in his native town of Waterford, Ireland.

Although "Maritana" was produced in 1845, it remained as popular as ever for years.

Wallace had an adventurous career, especially in Australia, where he abandoned music for sheep-raising; and also in South America. Before he died in France he had lost all his savings in speculation, leaving his widow and children in poverty.

A List of His Songs

Sleeping I Dreamed Love
Written and adapted to William Vincent Wallace's beautiful romance "Le Rêve" by Mrs. Mary E. Hewitt. Symphonics and accompaniment by John H. Hewitt. Published by William Hall and Son (1844). 6/8 tempo.

Softly, Ye Night Winds (Companion to "Sleeping I Dreamed Love")
Words by Mrs. Mary E. Hewitt. Music by William Vincent Wallace. Published by William Hall and Son (1851). Sung by old-time ballad singers.

Say, My Heart, Can This Be Love
Words by Henry C. Watson. Music by William Vincent Wallace. Published by William Hall and Son (1853). 9/8 tempo.
Sweet Spirit, Hear My Prayer
Words by Fitzbak. Music by William Vincent Wallace. Published by William Hall and Son (1860). From the opera "Lurline."
A Lowly Youth, the Mountain Child
Star of Love
Sainted Mother
There Is a Flower That Bloometh
From "Maritana."
Exile to His Sister
Scenes That Are Brightest
Why Do I Weep for Thee?
Pub. Evans and Bro., Boston.
Cradle Song
Old Friendship's Smile
There Is Darkness on the Mount
Wild Flowers
'Tis Pleasant to Be Young
In Happy Moments (Day by Day)
From "Maritana."
Holy Mother (Guide His Footsteps)
From "Maritana."
Alas! Those Chimes So Sweetly Stealing
Winds That Waft My Sighs to Thee
Bell-Ringer
Yes! Let Me Like a Soldier Die
From "Maritana."
Give Me a Loving Heart
'Tis the Harp in the Air

Written by William Michael Watson (1840-1889)

Haymaking
Pub. National Music Co., Chicago.
The Song for Me
Pub. National Music Co., Chicago.
Landlord, Come Fill the Flowing Bowl
(Three Jolly Post Boys)
All in a Garden Fair
Anchored
Babylon
Boot and Saddle
Caller Herrin'
Gallant Troubadour
King's Champion
Little Birdie Mine
Marche des Pompiers
Mountebank's Song
Powder Monkey
Thy Sentinel Am I
Voices of the Woods
Yellow Roses

Written by H. C. Watson (1846-1911)

Oh Loving Heart, Trust On
Thine Eyes My Love
Happy Tears, Down Falling
Roving, Restless Streamlet

Written by (J.) Michael Watson

Be Thou My Light
Bid Me Return
Down Mississippi Way
Flora Waltz
Jus' You
One Summer's Day
Under the Greenwood Tree
When the World Was Young

Written by C. A. White (1832-1892)

Marguerite
Come, Birdie, Come
Little Em'ly
Put Me in My Little Bed
Little Tottie Chasing Butterflies
Birds You Must Never Tell

Will You Meet Me by the Stile, Annie?
In Her Little Bed We Laid Her
Sung by Dave Wambold of San Francisco Minstrels.
Gone Before
Beyond the Clouds
Unfinished Prayer
Little Snow White Blossoms
Kiss Me and I'll Go to Sleep
Say Goodbye, Yet Not Farewell
Home by the River
When the Leaves Begin to Turn
(1878). ¾ tempo. For soprano.
Lead Us Not Into Temptation
Sadie Ray
Gone in Her Early Beauty
Alone in the World
Cling to Those Who Cling to You
Sleep, Darling, Sleep
Mother, Take Me Home Again
Why Did He Leave Me?
I'm Leaving Thee, Erin
Mimmie, Hear the Bluebirds Sing
Little Church Around the Corner
Father, Pray with Me Tonight
Dora Lane
Little Clo
Trusting
Kissing Sunbeams

Written by HENRY CLAY WORK (1832-1884)

Ring the Bell, Watchman
Pub. Brainerd, Chicago (1865). Bell song. 4/4 tempo. Sung by Old Time Quartette—Weston Hussy's Minstrels.
Kingdom Coming
Pub. Brainerd, Chicago (1862). Plantation song. 2/4 tempo.
Wake Nicodemus
Pub. Brainerd, Chicago (1864). Minstrel slave song.
Song of a Thousand Years
Pub. Brainerd, Chicago (1863). ¾ tempo. Sung by patriotic societies.
Grandfather's Clock
Pub. Brainerd, Chicago (1876). The most popular American song of its day.
Grandfather's Clock
Pub. Willis Woodward (E. B. Marks) (1876). Published with guitar accompaniment.
Grafted into the Army
Pub. Brainerd, Chicago (1862). War song.
Babylon Is Fallen
Pub. Brainerd, Chicago (1863).
Just Before the Battle, Mother.
Pub. Brainerd, Chicago (1863). War ballad.
Marching Through Georgia
Pub. Brainerd, Chicago (1865). War song. One of the most popular Union Army songs during the Civil War.
Kingdom Come (In the Land of Jubilo)
Pub. Brainerd, Chicago (1863). Jubilee minstrel song. Sung by old-time minstrels and revived by Will Rogers in the film "Too Busy to Work."
Agnes by the River
Andy Veto
Brave Boys Are They
Beautiful Rose
Buckskin Bag of Gold
Come Back to the Farm
Come Home, Father
Corporal Schnapps
Crossing the Grand Sierra
Columbia's Guardian Angel
Crying for Bread
Dad's a Millionaire
Days When We Were Young
First Love Dream
God Save the Nation
Girls at Home
Grandfather Told Me So
Grandmother Told Me So
Lillie of the Snow Storm
(Please, Father, Let Us In)
Little Major
Lilly—Willy—Woken
Lost on the Lady Elgin
Little Hallie
Last Grand Camping Ground
Lily Dale
Mystic Veil

Nellie Lost and Found
No Letters from Home
Now Moses!
Our Captain's Last Words
Poor Kitty Pop-Corn (The Soldier's Pet).
Picture on the Wall
Sleeping for the Flag
Sweet Echo Dell
Ship That Never Returns
Song of the Red Men
Sleep, Baby, Sleep
'Tis Finished! (Sing Hallelujah)
Uncle Joe's Hail Columbia
Watching for Pa
Washington and Lincoln
When the Evening Star Went Down

NOTE: The ocean steamer "Evening Star" was lost on the morning of October 3, 1866.

Who Shall Rule This American Nation
We Are Coming, Sister Mary
We'll Go Down Ourselves
Wake the Boys to Search for Nellie

NOTE: In "The Upshot Family"—a quaint little volume he published himself, No. 36 was stricken from the list with this quaint remark: "Though on an unimpeachable subject, he has been stricken from the list."

The public called one of his famous songs "Father, Dear Father, Come Home With Me Now!" (the opening line of the words and music). Work's title read:

"Come to Me, Father"

"'Tis the
Song of little Mary
Standing at the bar-room door
While the shameful midnight revel
Rages wildly as before."

Work would have changed his tune or at least his words if he could only come back and just peep in at some of the fashionable or unfashionable cocktail bars of today. He would probably have called it "Lady, Dear Lady, Come Home with Me Now" or perhaps even "Mother, Dear Mother," etc.

My prediction is that in about five years women will drink more, smoke more and bet more at the track than men.

Other Famous Old-Time Songs and Their Writers

Maid of Athens
Poem by Byron. Music by Henry Robinson Allen.

One Sweetly Solemn Thought (Sacred song)
Written by R. S. Ambrose.

Alice, Where Art Thou?
Written by J. Ascher.

Life's Dream Is O'er
Written by J. Ascher.

Fisherman's Daughter
Written by Samuel Bagnall.

Starry Night for a Ramble
Written by Samuel Bagnall. Sung by J. H. Milburn.

Wait Till the Moonlight Falls
Written by Samuel Bagnall.

Cackle! Cackle! Cackle!
Written by Samuel Bagnall.

Marriage of Mr. Good and Miss Fish
Written by Fred Bailey.

I Had to Whistle for It
Written by Fred Bailey.

Saved from the Storm
Written by Barri.

Shadow of the Cross
Written by Barri.

Measure Your Wants By Your Means
Written by Batchelder.

Enough Is As Good As a Feast
Written by Batchelder.

Forget Me Not
Written by Wm. Strendale Bennett.

Long Is the Night
Written by Wm. Strendale Bennett.

God Remembers When the World Forgets
Written by Carrie Jacobs Bond.

I Love You Truly
Written by Carrie Jacobs Bond.

Just A'wearyin' for You
Written by Carrie Jacobs Bond.

End of a Perfect Day
Written by Carrie Jacobs Bond.
Jolly Smokers
Written by C. S. Bradley.
Going to Church
Written by Geo. H. Briggs.
The Bridge
Written by Lady Carew.
Sally in Our Alley
Written by Carey.
Tommy Dodd
Written by Clarke.
Maid of Dangollen
Written by Clarke.
I'll Sing Thee Songs of Araby
Written by Frédéric Clay.
Sands O' Dee
Written by Frédéric Clay.
She Wandered Down the Mountain Side
Written by Frédéric Clay.
A Scentless Rose
Written by Frank Conway. Sung by Mrs. Zelda Seguin.
Army and Navy
Written by John Cooke, Jr.
When the Old Man Came Home Sober
Written by John Cooke, Jr.
The More We Have, the More We Want
Written by John Cooke, Jr.
Farewell Forever
Written by Coote.
There's a Letter in the Candle
Written by Coote.
Meet Me at the Lane
Written by J. S. Cox.
I Saw Thee But an Hour
Written by B. C. Cross.
Departure
Written by John Dandy.
Here's Jolly Good Luck to Us All
Written by Vincent Davies.
Bay of Biscay
Written by Davy.
Tom Bowling
Written by Dibdin.
Terence's Farewell to Kathleen
Written by Lady Dufferin.
Katy's Letter
Written by Lady Dufferin.
What Was I to Say?
Written by Elliot.
Good Night
Written by James Emerson.
Melody of Love
Written by James Emerson.
Sweet Be Your Dreams
Written by James Emerson.
When We're Together
Written by James Emerson.
Little Eva
Poem by John G. Whittier. Music by Manuel Emilio (1852). Dedicated to Harriet Beecher Stowe, author of "Uncle Tom's Cabin."
Hokie Pokie (Comic trio)
Written by Farnie.
Kiss Me and Whisper Goodnight
Written by Farrar.
His Love Shines Over All
Written by Forbes.
Maiden in the Greenwood
Written by Forbes.
Sing Birdie Sing
Written by Ganz.
When We Went A'Gleaning
Written by Ganz. For soprano or tenor.
On the Rocks of Aberdeen
Written by Gatty.
Oh Fair Dove, Oh Fond Dove
Written by Gatty.
The North Wind
Written by Gatty.
Drink, Drink, Drink
Written by German.
In Sheltered Vale
Written by German.
When Johnny Comes Marching Home
Written by Patrick Sarsfield Gilmore under the pseudonym of Louis Lambert (1863).
I Love My Love
Written by W. H. J. Graham.
One Dear Smile
Written by W. H. J. Graham.
Tears, Idle Tears
Written by W. H. J. Graham.
Farewell
Written by W. H. J. Graham.
Take Back the Sigh
Written by W. H. J. Graham.
I Am Lonely Tonight
Written by Griffin.

I'll Hang My Harp on a Willow Tree
Written by W. Guernsey.
A Soldier and a Man
Written by Gurland.
Darling Nellie Gray
Written by Benj. Russell Hanby (1856)
Ole Shady (Song of the Contraband)
Written by Benj. Russell Hanby (1861).
Good News on Christmas Morning
Written by Francis J. Hatton.
Good Night
Written by Francis J. Hatton.
Goodbye, Sweetheart
Written by Francis J. Hatton.
Fair Daffodils We Weep to See
Poem by Wordsworth. Music by Francis J. Hatton.
Because I Love You, Dear
Written by C. B. Hawley.
My Little Love
Written by C. B. Hawley.
My Mountain Kate
Written by A. H. Hewitt (1852). Sung by Kunkel's Opera Troupe.
When Lubin Sings
Written by Hobbs.
Within a Mile of Edinburgh Town
Written by James Hook.
The Banks of Allan Water
Written by C. E. Horn.
Cherry Ripe
Written by C. E. Horn.
Indian's Dream
Written by Frank Howard (1848).
Come Live with Me
Written by Frank Howard (1848).
Indian's Exile
Written by Frank Howard (1848).
Mary and the Mossy Old Stile
Written by Frank Howard (1848).
'Twas Off the Blue Canaries (or My Last Cigar)
Written by J. M. Hubbard (1848).
Three Fishers
Written by Hullah.
The Storm
Written by Hullah.
Afton Water
Written by A. Hume.
Ah! Could I Teach the Nightingale
Written by Keller.
Away with Vain Excuses
Written by N. O. Lake, M.D. (1851). An original song and catch, adapted to a popular American melody. Dedicated to Miss Olivia Caroline Stockton.
The Cows Are in the Corn
Written by H. Leslie.
Speed on My Bark
Written by H. Leslie.
Four Jolly Smiths
Written by H. Leslie.
Ferryman Dan
Written by Levey.
Gentle Words
Written by Levey.
Hope
Written by Levey.
Love's Garden
Written by Levey.
Toast of Other Days
Written by Levey.
Moët and Chandon
Written by Geo. Leybourne.
I Wish I Was
Written by Geo. Leybourne.
Capt. Jinks of the Horse Marines
Written by Lingard.
You'll Never Miss the Water Till the Well Runs Dry
Written by Harry Linn.
The Diver
Written by E. J. Loder.
The Bells of Shandon
Written by Mahoney.
O Watchman, Tell Us of the Night
Missionary or Christmas hymn by Bowring. Music by Lowell Mason (1830). Sung at the monthly concert, Park Street Church, Boston.
Smile and Kind Words
Written by T. B. Mason.
Belle Mahone
Written by J. H. McNaughton.
Paving the Way
Written by Milburn.
Always Do to Others
Written by Milburn.
Clementine
Written by Percy Montrose.

Robin Adair (La Dame Blanche)
Written by Moran.
Beware
Poem by Henry Wadsworth Longfellow. Music by Chas. Moulton (1865).
Little Robin
Written by Mullaly.
Little Daisy
Written by Mullaly.
Will He Not Come Back Again?
Written by Baroness Nairne.
The Auld Hoose
Written by Baroness Nairne.
The Rowan Tree
Written by Baroness Nairne.
Land O' the Leal
Written by Baroness Nairne.
I'm Weary, Jean
Written by Baroness Nairne.
A Leaf
(I Opened the Leaves of the Book)
Written by W. H. Neidlinger.
Serenade
Written by W. H. Neidlinger.
Mary of Argyle
Written by Nelson.
Rose of Allandale
Written by Nelson.
Oh That We Two Were Maying
Written by Nevin.
Tapping at the Garden Gate
Written by New.
Grasshopper's Waltz
Written by Nolcini (1839). Derived from the motions of the insect whose name it bears.
Fanny Grey
Written by the Hon. Mrs. Norton.
Juanita
Written by the Hon. Mrs. Norton.
Murmur of the Shells
Written by the Hon. Mrs. Norton.
Tell Me, Does a Flower Love?
Written by Operti, composer of "Black Crook" music. For soprano.
Doomed City
Written by Operti. For baritone or contralto.
The Dream of Love Is O'er
Written by Matt O'Reardon.
Wouldn't You Like to Know?
Written by Packer.
Don't Say One Thing and Mean Another
Written by W. Palmer.
Close to the Threshold
Written by Henry C. Parker.
Barney, Take Me Home Again
Written by George W. Persely.
Won't You Buy My Pretty Flowers?
Written by George W. Persely.
Thou Art So Near and Yet So Far
Written by Reichardt.
Love's Request
Written by Reichardt.
Won't You Dance the Polka?
Written by F. Romani.
O Would I Were a Boy Again
Written by F. Romer.
Just Twenty Years Ago
Written by R. B. Sanford.
Douglas, Tender and True
Written by Scott.
Annie Laurie
Words by Lady John Scott. Music by William Douglas.
At Evening the Weary Shall Rest
Written by C. F. Shattuck.
You Have Stolen My Heart
Written by C. F. Shattuck.
Come Sit Thee Down
Written by John Sinclair (1842). Also sung by John Sinclair.
Johnny Sands
Written by John Sinclair.
When the Silver Snow Is Falling
Written by Smart.
Listening on the Hill
Written by Smart.
By the Blue Sea
Written by Smart.
Silver Line
Written by Edward Solomon.
All on Account of Eliza
Written by Fred Solomon.
Flow Gently, Sweet Afton
Poem by Robert Burns. Music by J. E. Spilman (1838).
I'm Lonely No More
Written by Frank Stanley.
Sweet Minnie of the Vale
Written by Frank Stanley.

Jim the Carter Lad
Written by R. R. Steirly.
Harp That Once Thro' Tara's Halls
Words by Thomas Moore. Music by Sir John Stevenson.
Oft in the Stilly Night
Words by Thomas Moore. Music by Sir John Stevenson.
Flow On, Thou Shining River
Written by Sir John Stevenson.
Alabama Blossoms
Written by Frank Dumont. Arranged by James E. Stewart (1874).
Angel Gabriel
Written by James E. Stewart (1875).
Good Sweet Ham
Words and music by Henry Hart. Arranged by J. E. Stewart (1873).
My Heart Is Breaking
Written by A. Templer.
Annie Lisle
Written by H. S. Thompson (1860).
Lily Dale
Written by H. S. Thompson (1860).
Willie's on the Dark Blue Sea
Written by H. S. Thompson (1860).
Ida May
Written by H. S. Thompson (1860).
Gathering Shells
Written by H. S. Thompson (1860).
Consider the Lilies
Written by Topliffe.
Ruth and Naomi
Written by Topliffe.
Dancing in the Barn
Written by Tom Turner (1878). ¾ tempo.
Love Was Once a Little Boy
Written by Wade.
No Sir
Written by A. M. Wakefield. Spanish ballad.
The Lord Is My Shepherd (Sacred song)
Written by Flora Warner.
Dying Volunteer
Written by J. P. Webster (1863).
The Village Blacksmith
Poem by Longfellow. Music by W. H. Weiss.
Shadow of the Cross (Sacred song)
Written by W. West.
Old Church Pew (Sacred song)
Written by W. West.
Hark the Sabbath Bells (Sacred song)
Written by W. West.
I'll Take You Home Again, Kathleen
Written by Westendorf.
Cot Beneath the Hill
Written by W. J. Wetmore (1841).
All's Well
Written by T. Williams.
Larboard Watch (Duet)
Written by T. Williams.
Listen to the Mocking Bird
Written by Septimus Winner under the pseudonym of Alice Hawthorne (1855). Sung by Rose Merrifield.
Ella Rhee
Written by Septimus Winner (1865).
Whispering Hope
Written by Septimus Winner (1868).
What Is Home Without a Mother?
Written by Septimus Winner (1854).
White Wings
Written by Banks Winter.
Sweet Jennie Bell
Written by Banks Winter.
I've Brought Thee an Ivy Leaf
Written by D. Wood.
Bell Brandon
Written by Frances Woolcott (1854). 60th edition.
Her Bright Smile Haunts Me Still
Written by W. T. Wrighton.
Dearest Spot on Earth Is Home
Written by W. T. Wrighton.
Keep On Never Minding
Written by J. Harrington Young.

BEFORE AND AFTER

TRANSITION OF CHURCHES INTO THEATERS—LATER INTO BUSINESS LOFTS

Eighth Street Theatre (Off Fourth Ave.)
Formerly a house of worship

Dewey Theatre—East 14th Street (Near 4th Ave.)
Formerly a church

Hope Chapel—East side of Broadway—Below 14th Street
Became the home of Kelly and Leon's Minstrels

Church of the Messiah—725 Broadway, Cor. Waverly Place—
Near Wanamaker's—
Was altered into a theater

A. Oakey Hall, later Mayor of New York, at an entertainment in this church, recited these prophetic lines

"E'en in some future age
This pulpit may become a stage."

After the performance the minister declared to Mr. Hall: "If your prophecy proves true, I hope the house will be cursed." But in that he greatly erred.

It became a theater under several famous names: New York Theatre, Worrell Sisters' Theatre, Globe, Daly's Fifth Avenue, Harrigan and Hart's New Theatre Comique and, near the end, The Broadway Fight Club, where some of the very biggest bouts in the world of fisticuffs were staged.

FAMOUS SINGERS AND THEIR TEACHERS

Artist's Name	*Teacher*
Emma Eames	Miss Munger, Boston
Frances Alda	Mme. Marchesi and Frank La Forge
Enrico Caruso	Vergine (Italy)
Julia Claussen	Leydstrom, Stockholm
Andreas Dippel	Leoni and Ress
Geraldine Farrar	Emma Thursby, N. Y. Trabadello (Paris)
Mary Garden	Mrs. S. R. Duff
Alma Gluck	Buzzia Peccia—de Reszke—Sembrich
Emilio de Gonzaga	Moderati—Agramonte, N. Y.
Frieda Hempel	Nicklass—Kempner, Berlin
Bernice de Pasquali (Born Boston, successor to Sembrich)	Oscar Saenger, N. Y.
Marcella Sembrich	Lamperti
Schumann-Heink	Mdme. Leclair (Graz)
Henri Scott (Coatesville, Pa.)	Saluger
Emma Thursby	Julius Meyers, Lamperti, Strakosch

A LIST OF NEW YORK CRITICS IN THE 90's

N. Y. *American*	Alan Dale
N. Y. *Times*	Adolph Klauber
N. Y. *Herald*	Edward Ziegler
N. Y. *Press*	James Garrison
N. Y. *World*	Louis V. De Foe
N. Y. *Tribune*	Arthur Warren
N. Y. *Sun*	Lawrence Reamer
N. Y. *Evening Sun*	Acton Davies
N. Y. *Evening World*	Charles Darnton
N. Y. *Evening Globe*	Louis Sherwin
N. Y. *Evening Mail*	Burns Mantle
N. Y. *Evening Post*	J. Rankin Towse
N. Y. *Evening Telegram*	Robert Welch
N. Y. *Evening Journal*	Mr. Weils
N. Y. *Evening Telegraph*	Rennold Wolf

FAMILIES OF ACTORS (HEREDITARY)

Annie Adams
  Maude Adams
Comedian Billy Barry's Children
  Lydia and Bobby Barry
Maurice Barrymore
  Ethel, John and Lionel Barrymore
Junius Brutus Booth (The Elder)
  Edwin Booth
Dion Boucicault
  (Old Actor and Playwright)
  Aubrey Boucicault
James Burke (Circus Clown)
  Billie Burke
Oliver Doud Byron
  Arthur Byron
E. L. Davenport
  Fanny Davenport
Louise Lane Drew
  John, Sidney and Georgiana Drew
Hugh Fay (Barry & Fay)
  Elfie Fay
James K. Hackett (the Elder)
  James K. Hackett
T. M. Hengler (Delehanty & Hengler)
  Hengler Sisters
James A. Herne
  Crystal and Julie
Matilda Heron
  Bijou Heron, wife of Henry Miller
Phil Nash's Daughters
  Mary and Florence Nash
Tyrone Power—1833
  Maurice Power—1848
  Tyrone Power 2nd
  Tyrone Power 3rd
    (Present-day screen star)
Hal Reed
  Wallace Reid
Roland Reed's Daughter
  Florence Reed
Pat Rooney
  Pat Rooney II
  Pat Rooney III
E. A. Sothern
  E. H. Sothern
Fred Stone
  Dorothy Stone
Frank Tannehill (the Elder)
  Frank Tannehill, Jr.
Wallack (the Elder)
  Lester Wallack
Annie Yeamans (Of Harrigan & Hart)
  Jennie Yeamans
  Lydia Yeamans Titus

Great New York Casts: GRAND OPERA

Tristan and Isolde
  All-star Wagner performance. Metropolitan, December 1, 1888. Lehmann, Niemann, Brandt, Fischer, Alvary, Seidl, conductor.
Lucia
  New York debut of Sembrich. Metropolitan, October 24, 1883. Sembrich debut as Lucia, which was her debut in London, also Patti's in New York. Campanini, Kaschmann.
Lucia
  Metropolitan, December 4, 1893. Debut of Melba as Lucia, with Bauermeister, Dufriche, Mastiobuono, Carbone, Renaldini, Vignas.
Huguenots
  Metropolitan, December 26, 1895. Jean and Edouard de Reszke, Nordica, Scalchi, Melba, Bauermeister.
Huguenots
  Metropolitan, February 20, 1899. Six of the world's foremost operatic artists: Jean and Edouard de Reszke, Sembrich, Nordica, Plançon, Maurel.
Faust
  Opening bill of Metropolitan, October 22, 1883. Nilsson, Campanini, Scalchi, del Puente.
Faust
  Metropolitan, February 1, 1892. Jean and Edouard de Reszke, Scalchi, Eames, Bauermeister.
Faust
  Metropolitan, January 4, 1906. Caruso, Eames, Plançon. "*Faust* without a chorus"—The choristers on strike.
Romeo and Juliet
  Metropolitan, December 14, 1891. Jean

and Edouard de Reszke, Eames, Capoul, Bauermeister.

Romeo and Juliet
Metropolitan, January 19, 1894. Jean de Reszke, Melba.

L'Africaine
Metropolitan, January 15, 1892. Jean and Edouard de Reszke, Nordica, Lassalle, Bauermeister.

Lohengrin
Metropolitan, January 1, 1894. Jean and Edouard de Reszke, Eames, Fusch-Madi.

Lohengrin
Metropolitan, November 22, 1895. Jean and Edouard de Reszke, Nordica.

Lohengrin
Metropolitan, January 9, 1899. Jean and Edouard de Reszke, debut of Schumann-Heink.

Cavalleria Rusticana
Metropolitan, November 29, 1893. Calvé's debut as Santuzza. Guercia as Lola, Bauermeister as Lucia, E. Dufriche as Alfio, Vignas as Turiddu.

Carmen
Metropolitan, December 20, 1893. Debut of Calvé as Carmen. Jean de Reszke and Eames.

Meistersinger
Metropolitan, November 30, 1893. Jean and Edouard de Reszke, Eames, Plançon, David Bispham.

Meistersinger
Metropolitan, January 8, 1894. Jean de Reszke, Eames, Bauermeister.

Marriage of Figaro
Metropolitan, January 31, 1894. Eames, Nordica, Edouard de Reszke, Lablanche.

Double bill
Metropolitan, February 9, 1894. Melba as Violetta in *Traviata*, Calvé as Santuzza in *Cavalleria Rusticana*.

Otello
Metropolitan, December 3, 1894. Tamagno as Otello, Victor Maurel as Iago (his first New York appearance in 20 years), Eames as Desdemona.

Falstaff
Metropolitan, February 4, 1895. Maurel in his original role, Eames, Scalchi, Zelie de Lussan.

Tannhauser
Metropolitan, November 20, 1896. Eames, Bauermeister, Plançon, Lassalle.

Siegfried
Metropolitan, December 30, 1896. Jean and Edouard de Reszke, Melba, Bispham.

Götterdämmerung
Metropolitan, January 24, 1899. Jean and Edouard de Reszke, Nordica, Bispham, Schumann-Heink.

Rigoletto
Metropolitan, November 23, 1903. Debut of Caruso, with Sembrich and Scotti.

Aïda
Metropolitan, November 30, 1903. Caruso's second American appearance, with Gadski, Scotti, Plançon.

Tosca
Metropolitan, December 2, 1903. Caruso's third American appearance. Ternina, Helen Mapleson, Scotti, Dufriche, Rossi, Bois, Begue, Cernusco.

Bohème
Metropolitan, December 5, 1903. Caruso's fourth American appearance. Sembrich, Estelle Liebling, Campanini, Journet, Rossi, Dufriche, Masiero, Gili, Fanelli.

Pagliacci
Metropolitan, December 9, 1903. Caruso's fifth American appearance. Sembrich, Scotti, Muhlmann, Reiss.

Elixir of Love
Metropolitan, January 23, 1904. Caruso's sixth American appearance. Sembrich, Bouton, Scotti, Rossi

Special bill
Metropolitan, March 22, 1919. To celebrate the 25th year of Caruso's operatic career. 2nd act of *Elixir of Love*, Caruso as Nemorino. 1st act of *Pagliacci*, Caruso as Canio. Coronation scene *Le Prophète*, Caruso as John of Leyden.

Gioconda
Metropolitan, November 20, 1905. Caruso, with Nordica, Homer, Plançon.

The Jewess
Metropolitan, December 24, 1920. Caruso as Eleazar, his last role. With Ponselle, Orville Harrold, Leon Rothier.

Special bill
Metropolitan, April 27, 1894. 2nd act of *Romeo and Juliet*, with Jean and Edouard de Reszke, Eames, 2nd act of *Carmen*, with Calvé and Lassalle. 3rd act of *Aïda*, with Nordica and Lassalle. 3rd act of *Werther*, with Jean de Reszke, Eames and Arnoldson. The mad scene from *Hamlet*, by Melba. Aria by Scalchi. The Shadow Song by Arnoldson.

Thaïs
Hammerstein's Manhattan Opera House, November 25, 1907. Mary Garden's American debut, with Renaud as Athanaël, Dalmores, Nicias.

Salome
Hammerstein's Manhattan Opera House, January 28, 1909. Mary Garden, Dalmores, Dufranne, Campanini directing.

Tales of Hoffmann
Hammerstein's Manhattan Opera House, November 14, 1907. Renaud, Gilibert.

Louise
Hammerstein's Manhattan Opera House, January 3, 1908. Mary Garden, Dalmores, Gilibert.

Pelleas and Melisande
Hammerstein's Manhattan Opera House, February 19, 1908. Mary Garden, Jean Pirier, Hector Dufranne, Gerville Reache, Arimondi, Crabbe.

Don Giovanni
Metropolitan, November 28, 1883. Nilsson, Sembrich and Fusch-Madi. A trio which rivals the famous London cast, Tietjens, Nilsson and Patti.

COMIC OPERA

The Chocolate Soldier
Adapted by Stanislaus Stange; music by Oscar Straus. First performance, October 4, 1909. Produced by Whitney Opera Co. Principals Ida Brooks, Hunt, Edith Bradford, J. E. Gardner and William Pruette.

The Chocolate Soldier
Revival. Century Theatre, December 12, 1921. Donald Brian, Tessa Kosta, Detmar Poppen, J. H. Duffey, John Dunsmore.

Erminie
Book by Harry Paulton; music by Edward Jakobowski. Casino, May 10, 1886. Francis Wilson as Caddy, W. S. Daboll as Ravvy, Marie Jansen as Javotte; Pauline Hall, Marion Manola, Jennie Weathersby, Max Freeman, A. W. Maflin, Rose Beaudet, Agnes Folsom, Murry Woods, Harry Pepper, Carl Irving.

About Town
New version of Adolf Phillip's Corner Grocer of Avenue A. Dan Daly, David Warfield, Jennie Weathersby, Willis P. Sweatnam, Jacques Kruger.

Erminie
Revival. Broadway Theatre, October 3, 1893. Francis Wilson, William Broderick, Lulu Glaser, Christie McDonald, Jennie Weathersby, Edward P. Temple.

Erminie
Revival. Casino, May 25, 1898. Francis Wilson, Henry E. Dixey, Pauline Hall, Lulu Glaser, Jennie Weathersby, Edward P. Temple, Kate Uart.

Erminie
Revival. Book revised by Marc Connolly. Park Theatre, January 3, 1921. Francis Wilson, De Wolf Hopper, Alexander Clark, Madge Lessing, Jennie Weathersby.

Evangeline
E. E. Rice. Daly's Fifth Avenue, June 4, 1877. Eliza Weatherby as Gabriel, N. C. Goodwin as LeBlanc, Harry Hunter as Lone Fisherman, G. G. Knight as Captain Dietrich, M. C. Daly as Basil, E. S. Tarr as King Booraboola, C. Rosene as Hans Wagner, Percy Vining as Jailor, Richard Golden as Ringbolt, Henry E. Dixey as Redshake, Richard Golden as Policeman, James

Nolan as Poor Indian, Lizzie Harold as Evangeline, Harry Josephs as Catherine, Lizzie Webster as Eulalie, Blanche Green as Queen Booraboola.

Evangeline
Revival. 14th Street Theatre, October 7, 1885. George T. Fortescue, Amelia Summerville, James S. Maffit, Fay Templeton, Josephine Hall, Mollie Fuller, John A. Mackay, Fred Frear, Irene Verona.

Florodora
Owen Hall and Leslie Stuart. Casino, November 10, 1900. Willie Edouin, R. E. Graham, Cyril Scott, May Edouin, Edna Wallace Hopper, Mabel Barrison. The Sextette Girls: Margaret Walker, Vaughn Texsmith, Marie L. Wilson, Marjorie Relyea, Agnes Wayburn, Daisy Greene.

The Fortune Teller
Harry B. Smith and Victor Herbert. Wallack's, September 26, 1898. Alice Neilson, Eugene Cowles, Joe Cawthorn, Richard Golden, Joseph Herbert, Marguerite Sylva, Marcia van Dresser.

1492
R. A. Barnet and Carl Pflueger. Palmer's, May 15, 1894. Richard Harlow, Walter Jones, Mark Smith, Edward M. Favor, Will H. Sloan, John C. Slavin, Hattie Williams.

The Girl from Up There
C. M. S. McLellan and Gus Kerker. Herald Square, January 7, 1901. Edna May, Dave Montgomery, Fred Stone, Virginia Earle, Edna Aug, Otis Harlan, Harry Davenport, Harry Connor, Charles T. Aldrich, Alf C. Wheelan, Lawrence Wheat.

Chu Chin Chow
Book by Oscar Asche. Music by Frederic Norton. Cast: Oscar Asche, James Herbert, Courtice Pounds, J. V. Bryant, Norman Williams, William Holles, Frank Cochrane, Aileen D'Orme, Sydney Fairbrother, Annie Moore, Violet Essex, Lily Brayton.

Winsome Winnie
Book by Frederick Ranken. Music by Gustave Kerker. Cast: Paula Edwards, Dick Temple, Jobyna Howland, W. P. Carleton, Helen Redmond, Isobel Hall, Wm. E. Philip, James E. Sullivan, Mildred Kearney, Daisy Green, Joseph C. Miron, Wm. Corless, Stella Hammerstein, Julia Sanderson, Clara Pitt, Mazie Follette, Mae Hopkins.

A Madcap Princess
Book by Harry B. Smith. Music by Ludwig Englander. Cast: Lulu Glaser, William Pruette, Bertram Wallis, Donald McLaren, Howard Chambers, Frank Reicher, Arthur Barry, Ralph Lewis, Guy B. Hoffman, H. Chambers, Herbert Freer, Maurice Sims, Reginald Barlow, Elsie Thomas, Maud Ream Stover.

The Office Boy
Book by Harry B. Smith. Music by Ludwig Englander. Cast: Frank Daniels, Alfred Hickman, Sydney Toler, Gilbert Clayton, James C. Reany, David Bennett, Laurence Wheat, W. C. Kelly, Leavitt James, Louise Gunning, Eva Tanguay, Violet Hollis.

Moonshine
Book by Edwin Milton Royle and George V. Hobart. Music by Silvio Hein. Cast: Roy Atwell, Dick Temple, Frances Gordon, J. Ward Kett, Leona Anderson, Marie Cahill, Sadie Harris, Wm. Ingersoll, George Beban, Clara Palmer, H. R. Roberts, H. Guy Woodward, Frederic Paulding.

The Gay Hussars
Book by Grant Stewart. Music by Emmerich Kalman. Cast: William E. Bonney, Florence Reed, Anna Bussert, Alonzo Price, Edwin Wilson, Robert Young, Muriel Terry, Bobby North, Frank Russell, W. H. Denny, Ilon Bergere, Pauline Winters, Sophie Witt, Violet Mack, Mabelle Jones.

Sari
Book by C. C. S. Cushing and E. P. Heath. Music by Emmerich Kalman. Cast: Van Rensselaer Wheeler, J. Humbird Duffey, Mizzi Hajos, Eva Ball, Karl Stall, Blanche Duffield, Charles Meakins, Harry Davenport, Wilmuth Merkyl, Eugene Roder, Harry Crapo.

The Mocking Bird
Book by Sydney Rosenfeld. Music by A. Baldwin Sloane. Cast: Roland Carter, Sydney Deane, Robt. Rogers, Mabelle Gilman, Violet Hollis, Frank Doane, Edgar Atchison-Ely, Claude Boyer, Walter C. Shannon, Louise Mackintosh, Maude Alice Kelly, Ivy Moore, Edythe Truran, Jno. F. Parry, Stella Adams, Sarah Osgood.

The Isle of Spice
Book by Allen Lowe and Geo. E. Stoddard. Music by Paul Schindler and Ben M. Jerome. Cast: Dave Lewis, William M. Armstrong, Denman Maley, Toby Lyons, James C. Marlowe, Joseph Allen, Frank Witter, Adrian Bellevue, Cale Middleton, Florence Holbrook, Maud Alice Kelly, Nettie Black, Stella Maury.

The Student King
Book by Frederic Ranken and Stanislaus Stange. Music by Reginald De Koven. Cast: Wm. C. Weedon, Raymond Hitchcock, Gustave von Seyffertitz, Thos. C. Leary, Bertha Bouscher, Dittmar Poppin, Albert Pellaton, Henry Coote, Percy Parsons, Laurence Rea, Lina Abarbanell, Fannie McIntyre, Flavia Arcaro.

The Rose Maid
Book by Harry B. Smith and Robert B. Smith. Music by Bruno Granichstadten. Cast: J. Humbird Duffey, R. E. Graham, Edith Decker, Al Shean, Arthur Laceby, Adrienne Augarde, May Emory, Philip Sheffield, Dorothy Follis, Juliette Dika, Harry Lambart.

Happyland
Book by Frederic Ranken. Music by Reginald De Koven. Cast: De Wolf Hopper, George B. Frothingham, Will Danforth, Joseph Phillips, Frank Casey, John Dunsmuir, Carl Haydn, Marguerite Clark, Ada Deaves.

The Spring Maid
Book by Harry B. Smith and Robert B. Smith. Music by Heinrich Reinhardt. Cast: Christie MacDonald, William Burress, Lawrence Rea, Elgie Bowen, Ralph Erolle, Tom McNaughton, Jessie Bradbury, Charles Meyers, Blanche Sherwood.

Nancy Brown
Book by Frederic Ranken. Music by Henry K. Hadley. Cast: Edwin Stevens, Albert Parr, Harry Brown, Al. Grant, Alfred Hickman, Madison Smith, Marie Cahill, Grace Cameron, Judith Berolde, Jean Newcombe.

The Siren
Book by Harry B. Smith. Music by Leo Fall. Cast: Frank Moulan, Elizabeth Firth, Gilbert Childs, Donald Brian, F. Pope Stamper, Julia Sanderson, Will West, Florence Morrison.

NIGHT LIFE ON OLD BROADWAY (SOME GO BACK 100 YEARS)

Broadway and Ann St. Barnum's American Museum. Edward A. Sothern of "Lord Dundreary" fame, father of our E. H. Sothern, was a lecturer here.

Broadway No. ??. Charlie White's Melodeon Hall (formerly in the Chinese rooms). Minstrels and birth of "variety" shows.

Broadway No. 514. Harrigan & Hart's Theatre Comique.

Broadway at Grand St. Mechanic's Hall. Headquarters Christy Minstrels and later Dan Bryant's Minstrels. Burned down in same year, 1863, as Barnum's New American Museum.

Broadway at Broome St. Wallack's Lyceum Theatre. Opened by John Brougham. Laura Keene first trod the boards here. Matilda Heron played Camille.

Broadway No. 642. Laura Keene's Varieties Theatre (later the Olympic). At the Olympic "Humpty Dumpty" had its phenomenal run, taking in receipts $1,500,000.

Broadway No. 584. Niblo's Garden. Where "The Black Crook" stirred and delightfully shocked all New York.

Broadway No. 585, opposite Niblo's. Metropolitan Theatre (Varieties). Tony Pastor's second theater. First show version of Denman Thompson's "Old Homestead."

Broadway at 13th St. Wallack's (2nd) Theatre "The Star." Mary Anderson, Henry Irving appeared. Mrs. Leslie Carter made her debut here.

Broadway below 14th St. Hope Chapel, Kelly & Leon's Minstrels. Later New York Theatre, Worrell Sisters' Theatre, Globe Theatre.

Broadway at 10th St. Old London Streets. Daly's Fifth Avenue Theatre. Later Harrigan & Hart's New Theatre Comique.

Where Broadway joins Park Row. Park Theatre. The great English actor of distinction—George Frederic Cooke—captured New York here with his "Richard III." His body lies in St. Paul's Chapel under a monument erected by Edmund Kean and restored by E. A. Sothern.

THE BUSIEST MILE ON OLD BROADWAY

The busiest mile at one time (1880-1890) on old Broadway started at No. 1 and ran up to the junction of that thoroughfare and Park Row. The roar of passing traffic was tremendous. Bright yellow buses with landscape pictures rumbled over the paving stones as ironshod hoofs beat their tattoo on them, as a noisy contrast to our smooth macadam and rubber tires.

Every driver was for himself and the devil take the hindmost, as there were no traffic rules. Often the collision of the buses brought a row between drivers over the splintering wood, and the big lane was sometimes bedlam between the curses of drivers and the screams of the narrowly escaping passengers. The stages added to the din. These traveled to the then-distant Greenwich Village, and even 10 miles up into the country to faraway Harlem. The private coaches of the wealthy, the barouches and victorias, added to the jam as the horses threaded in and out.

It was worth your life to cross Fulton Street at Broadway. Then the wise Aldermen created the 6-foot Broadway Squad to escort the ladies at intervals when they stopped the roaring stream of traffic. And did these gallant escorts enjoy it, when pretty women, raising their skirts enough to show their ankles and pantalettes, stood waiting to be escorted to the pavement opposite? Well, I'll say so.

Finally a bridge about 15 feet high was built over Broadway at Fulton Street from curb to curb for people to cross on. It was just about in front of St. Paul's. But even this overpass raised a storm of disapproval. The prevailing highly moral citizens claimed it corrupted youth, as youngsters with advanced ideas got under the bridge to watch the hoop-skirted, petticoated, white-stockinged, tassel-booted ladies as they unwittingly exposed their hidden charms to the eyes of the wicked on their way over the bridge.

It was a zone of gaiety and windows blazed by night all along its length. Buses, stages, carriages jammed the street. A merry throng of theatergoers, spenders and gilded youth.

In winter, sleighs on steel-bound runners largely supplanted wheels and roisterers, and warmed by straw, buffalo robes and good spirits within and without, they sang catchy songs and made the welkin ring.

To old New Yorkers, it was a fascinating, enchanting region and the high-class theaters, minstrel halls, open-air gardens and semi-respectable resorts were all well attended.

There was always plenty to see and hear of the gay side of New York for visitors from other cities or from abroad.

By contrast, this present-day business section is a cold, drab sight at night.

OLD-TIME COLLOQUIALISMS

Mr. Funk, editor of the late lamented *Literary Digest*, professes to love slang, but is annoyed over it when it becomes stale. For instance, he doesn't like "definitely," "OK," "terrific" and "lousy."

Personally, I agree only partially as to the first three. But as for "lousy," I agree a thousand per cent with the distinguished editor. The filthiest, lowest form of insect life is now the all too common expression of commonplace minds. It rarely disgraced polite society or the stage in the admittedly gay, but still rather wholesome nineties. We are usually careful to be grammatically correct. Why not try to be politely proper in our conversation "He's a louse" and "nuts to you" were not exactly common, daily expressions in days gone by, or rather, I should say they were common, *d——d* common, and so considered.

It wasn't particularly edifying in other days to hear "Aw, rats," but that was gold compared to "Aw, nuts" that we hear so often from present-day morons. To those who know its origin, you couldn't very well pass on the slang definition of "nuts" as the fruit of trees, or a state of mind. Even disguised as "nerts," it still is cheap and vulgar. We needn't be hypersensitive, but why do we have to hear constantly in conversation, or when seeking relaxation and clean fun in the theater, have to listen to unpleasant, low-down language. There is nothing so habit-forming as stage vernacular. The street adopts it and society follows.

We can well dispense with "can" and "fanny," used so frequently by our stage comics. They're not even bedroom. They're just plain latrine, and these vulgarities should be permanently relegated to the discard. A misguided sister is referred to as a "broad" or a "push-over." In the yesteryear they called her a "moll," which was easier on the sensibilities, or a "frail," far more expressive and charitable.

If, therefore, these and similar expressions would disappear "they never would be missed," just as the other nuisances in the Gilbertian ditty.

On the other hand, I have reminded myself of the following homely, yet highly expressive colloquialisms which have partly, if not entirely, disappeared. It can do no harm to list them here, for whatever interest they may arouse in those who still remember them, or those who may want to use them in reference to the period in which they were current.

When writing a book, which is to some extent a chronicle not only of songs and of the theater, but of colloquialisms of the past, one should finish it at the earliest possible moment by keeping at it continuously; otherwise you find your ideas and thoughts running parallel with others in books which may happen to get into print ahead of yours.

In presenting this small list, I am aware that it is only a tiny contribution compared to dictionaries of slang compiled by others. I shall, however, religiously refrain from opening the pages of any other books of this type until my own volume is in print.

In so far as the words and phrases collected here are concerned, they were all actually used or heard by many in the period represented.

Cocktail aisle seat—Augustin Daly, manager of Daly's Theatre, always ordered his friends seated down front on the aisle, so they could exit easily for cocktails at intervals

Dirty shirt hider—An English ascot scarf, which covered the shirt front

A lick and a promise—To slur hurriedly over cleaning or dusting a room

"Post" in the gallery—The man with a rattan, who kept the gallery gods orderly and quiet

Your stable is open—Calling attention to a carelessly closed trouser fly

The upper ten and the lower five—The Broadway swell and the Bowery bum.

As crooked as Pearl St.—A comparison between a very irregular New York street and a similarly crooked individual

Histe the rag—Gallery urchin's cry to raise the curtain.

Too utterly utter—A foppish extremist in manners and dress

Wolfed two tickets—Secured with difficulty two theater passes from the management

Fluffy ruffles—A summery female character in Frohman production with white ruffled shirtwaist and short skirt

Candy butchers—A set of hawkers in burlesque houses, who, during intermission, plug their wares in raucous tones and murderous English

Cheese it, the cop—A street urchin's warning call to the gang

Plunk—A silver dollar

Keeley cure—A "gold" or certain standard cure at the Keeley Institute for Inebriates consisted in part of saturating all the victim's food in whisky to the point of nausea, and was successful in many cases, except in the last stage

Chokers—The high standing collars that completely encircled the necks of the dudes of the 90's

To fetch—Was to swim completely submerged underwater from one end of the city's free baths, if possible, to the other without coming up for air

Sam Sawbones—A young medical student

Frozen turnip—A naturally cold individual

Twiggie-vous?—Do you get it? An expression introduced by Bonnie Thornton at Tony Pastor's in an old song

Target company—A local rifle company parading, usually on Thanksgiving

Target carrier—Negro carrying the company's target at the end of the parade

Ragamuffins—Masquerading street youngsters soliciting pennies on Thanksgiving Day

Lah-de-dah—A swell of the 90's, the theme of the popular song:

> "He wears a paper collar
> La-de-dah—Lah-de-dah
> In his pocket not a dollar
> Lah-de-dah—Lah-de-dah"

Paper collar—Used before linen and cheaper

Celluloid collar—A highly combustible collar

Bed house—A red-light district hotel

Raines' law sandwich—Stale cheese and bread—a permanent fixture on side-door saloon tables, to get around the Raines law providing that on Sunday no drinks be served without food

Powder monkeys—Soldiers seated, arms folded, on powder wagons, accompanying the mounted cannon artillery wagons

Pint of suds—Pitcher of beer

Rush the growler—Chasing the can for a pint of "lager," meaning the beer remaining for a period in kegs to age and improve it

Musical mokes—A black-face musical minstrel act, playing various instruments—Bryant and Hoey, Wood and Beasley of the "Varieties," for example

Muzzler—A homosexual

Seriocomic—An old-time soubrette, capable of singing straight tear jerkers and comic ditties

Doubling in brass—Musicians, playing matinees and nights in minstrel show orchestras and parading mornings as a brass band

Sidewalk conversation—A show term for a pair of wisecracking comedians in variety days, doing their act in a street scene in one: Harry and John Kernell, and Nat Haines and Pettingill were well-known examples

Lancashire clog—A form of clog dancing brought over to America from Lancashire, England, in the old days and danced with wooden clogs

Leg-mania—An eccentric dancing turn in close fitting one-piece black tights. The artists, painted up like black demons, twisted their elongated forms and legs into almost unbelievable shapes, high kicked far above their heads, and doubling up their bodies disappeared in ordinary barrels: the Three Lorellas were an outstanding success in this act for years

Whoops, my Gawd—Favorite oath of the Pansies

Chock-ablock—Full to overflowing

Isle de Blackwell—A former New York prison on Blackwell's Island in the East River; now Welfare Island—"Isle de Blackwell" was a favorite song as sung in the Harrigan and Hart days

Mother Mandlebaum—A "fence" or receiver of stolen goods, sometimes referred to as a "Mother Mandlebaum," named after the most notorious fence of her time, occuppying a whole house over 50 years ago at the corner of Clinton and Rivington streets, and using a dry goods store downstairs as a blind

Flewsie—A flighty, impressionistic young bird

Chowder party—An East Side excursion or picnic where clam chowder was served free-for-all between fights

Seddon's Mouse—An old-time prize fighter in the Steve Brodie days, so called because of his diminutive stature

Jersey lightning—A special brand of black-looking whisky, strong enough to tickle the palate of a heavy drinker; Lew Dockstader, the old-time minstrel, had his own special bottle of "Jersey lightning" behind all the well-known bars in New York and on tour

Alcock's porous plasters—A well-advertised patent medicine of the 90's

Brandeth's pills—A well-advertised patent medicine of the 90's

Dr. Munyon's specific—A well-advertised patent medicine of the 90's. (Adorned with the doctor's picture and the index finger, pointing to heaven, a pose much imitated in variety days)

Lydia Pinkham's compound—A well-advertised patent medicine; the original handsome Lydia Pinkham photograph hasn't aged or changed in 50 years

Shandygaff—A favorite drink with old-time sailors: half beer and half ginger ale

Battle Row—A street of rough tenements; in the late 80's, 63rd Street near the East River earned this sobriquet

Peekaboo waist—A minstrel term for a girl's summer shirtwaist with eyelet embroidery

Red-line—A daily public school game—now long passé
Pass-walk—A daily public school game—now long passé
Prisoner's base—A daily public school game—now long passé
Duck-on-a-rock—A daily public school game—now long passé
Horseshoe the mare—A mischievous boys' game, tying an unsuspecting boy's leg to a private house doorbell, so in imitating a kicking mare, he is caught ringing the bell.
Pogo stick—Children's game
Bar the door—Children's game
One-old-cat—A ball game with a limited number of players, each on his own
Moll bruiser—A tough with prize-fighting proclivities
Take-off—In stage parlance, an impersonation—now an airplane start
Galluses—Suspenders
Smash your baggage—A term by Horatio Alger in his *Ragged Dick* or *Ben the Luggage Boy* series
Flophouse—Old-time lodging house, where for a nickel, the Bowery derelicts flopped down on the floor to sleep it off
Man-hacked—A rooster once licked won't fight again—likewise some men
Chinese pigtails—In the 80's and 90's Chinese allowed their hair to grow in braided pigtail fashion. If cut off, they were barred from returning to their native China
Hand-me-down—Discarded secondhand clothing, stocked in dingy shops, where the clerks pulled in the passing customers
Down the bay—Baxter Street, New York, where the old-clothes men flourished and suits could be bought at almost your own price
Shoving the queer—Passing counterfeit money
Macer—A type of burglar
Bracer—Another type
Green goods—Counterfeit greenbacks sold to hayseeds from the country as genuine bills
Picnic drawers—A closely buttoned-in-the-back protective article of feminine wear for outings and picnics
Shift—An old-time article of female dress, politely referred to now as a "step-in"
How's that for high!—An exclamation of satisfaction
I say! He's a bully boy with a glass eye—English for an outstanding person
Penny Bolivar—A large, round, yellow molasses cake sold for a penny
Washington pie—A cheap, unsavory concoction of apples and dough
Scissors—A firecracker, the stem of which, having failed to go off, is bent in half in the shape of a scissors exposing the powder; when lit, it was often the cause of Fourth of July accidents
The Juba—An old-time juvenile asylum for the correction of wayward youths
Bunger—Pregnancy
Galway sluggers—Sideburns worn by the old-time Irishman
All to the mustard—All to the good
Brush the cobwebs away—Make up
Who Struck Billy Patterson?—A minstrel saying derived from an old minstrel sketch
Hokey-pokey—The original street ice cream, forerunner of "Good Humor"
Klabberjas—An intricate old-time card game
Solo—Another intricate old-time card game
Skaat—Another intricate old-time card game
Out on her shape—A fashionable girl, discarding winter apparel for a tight-fitting suit in the "Easter Parade" to show off her figure
Collo—The opposite of a "big shot," a small-timer
Shaving mugs—Patrons used their own individually decorated and lettered shaving mugs
Quarry—A criminal bird, pursued until captured by detectives
Shinplaster—10-, 25-, and 50-cent paper money, after the Civil War
Hungry Henrietta—A dame with an appetite

Plug-ugly—A shabbily dressed man—particularly as to his tile
Dicer—A derby or stiff hat
An Oscar Hammerstein—Applied to a minstrel high hat on parade
Moody and Sankey—A reference to the famous Evangelists
Here's your hat, what's your hurry?—A polite hint to go
Shindig—A liquor party, dance or brawl
Mixed ale party—An Irish party—the beverage, mixed ale
Triggy-traggy—A Mulberry Street expression for making funny
Buskin—Street musician playing and passing the hat
Blue glass—An old-time fad; the blue glass rays in the sun or light were supposed to possess the virtue of healing
Skirt dance—A dance in a pleated, extension skirt—invented by Loie Fuller
Stack o' wheats—An order of wheat cakes in a beanery
Spieler—A smooth waltzer
Chromo—A homely old dame
Sockdolager—A solid blow, or accomplishment
Gin blossom—The reddish effect on the nose from gin, or any excess drinking
Don't anchor here—Office warning to long-winded callers
Lob—A stiff—a horse unbacked by his stable connections, as shown by receding odds
Spuds—Potatoes
Heel—A failure—a man run down
Soiree—An evening dance
Hop—Hotel summer dance
Cracovienne—A dance—now passé
Lancers—A dance—now passé
Waltz quadrille—A dance—now passé
Redowa—A dance—now passé
Varsouvianna—A dance—now passé
Cachucha—A dance—now passé
Mazurka—A dance—now passé
Motto songs—A vogue in the 80's and 90's: "All is not gold that glitters"; "You'll never miss the water till the well runs dry." (Some singers, like Frank Lewis, specialized in this type of song and were called "motto singers")
Google eye—Cross-eye
Shiner—Black and blue eye, usually from a punch
His name was Dennis—Meaning he was a goner
Chase the duck—Rush a can of beer
Accidentally on purpose—Intentionally, but pretending otherwise
Have a smile—Invitation for a drink
Cockeyed wonder—A left-handed compliment
You can like it or lump it—You have no choice
Sloo-boo—Passing something to another with sly or hidden movement
Cops and robbers—A boyish game, which is self-explanatory
Go bung—Go busted
Grecian bend—An old stylish walk, wearing a bustle extending far behind, and carrying a parasol in front, giving the figure an exaggerated bend
Afterpiece—The short sketch that followed the olio in the old variety theaters.
Filopene—Boy-and-girl penalty game with two kernels in a nut, each eats one, and the one that speaks pays a forfeit to the other
Senna manna—A tea of senna leaves and manna, prescribed by country doctors and used generally and successfully in the old days by mothers for almost all children's minor illnesses
Sour sop—Big fruit salad
He's got the needle—Girl-crazy
Toes getting hungry—Socks torn at the toes
She's no Fanny Elssler—Poor dancer
Hoofer—A minstrel dancer
An onion ballad—A tear jerker
Egg—Referring to a man—good or bad
Pug—A prize fighter
Going to the boneyard—Drawing more dominoes, or borrowing in any game
Funny bone—The bone at the bend of the elbow, a tender spot when struck
Hickory-dickory-dock the mouse went up the clock—A children's game with pencil and paper

Full of fun as a shad is of bones—Extra funny
Belly laughs—Loud guffaws
Wall St. angels—Theatrical promoters
Bobby-dazzler—A perfect specimen
On the town—A female on the loose
Codfish aristocracy—Nouveau-riche
Bedroom songs—Suggestive lyrics
Letting down the performance—Slowing up the show
Many a dollar in the back of the book—A memo of debts
Dolly Varden—A certain fashion type
Put an egg in your shoe and beat it—Equal to "23 skiddoo"
Early piety—Sex overindulgence in youth
Black Maria—A black conveyance for transferring prisoners to court or jail
Living high, wide and fancy—Living above one's means
Use her noggin—Use her brains
Making a pitch—A street fakir's glib sales-talk
Hot goose—Tailor's pressing iron
Thunder and biled wax—A mild cuss word
Crows and woodpeckers—Another
Holy mackerel—Exclamation of surprise
Jiminy crickets—Another
Earthen frog—Stone jug
Playing possum—Foxy
A hiding—A flogging
Keep your eye peeled—Look out
Spit on the axles—Grease the old one-horse chaise
Hi! Hi! G'lang—Giddy-ap
Carry-all—Large wagon for six or eight
Son of the "ould sod"—An Irishman
Full of the old scratch—Full of mischief
Consarn his picture—Darn him
Warning young rapscallions—Birch rod punishment in school
Whoa! You son of iniquity—To a fractious horse
I seed you go ker-chunk—Fall in the creek
A tall, stoop-shouldered, ginger-haired son of a Baptist—Cuss name for tyrannical school janitor
Slop bucket—Garbage can
Old nosey—Prying person
Divil a oncet—Irish for not even once
Ninth part of a man—Picayune person
Every mother's son of you—All of you
Goshermichael!—Exclamation of surprise
Mum as oysters—Secretive
Skin the cat—A saying used to make a tired child laugh while pulling a dress over its head
The old eel pot—A slick person
The old rip—Bony old nag
Moseyed around—Hung around
Dresses and finery—Costumes and decorations
Bejabers!—Irish expression
Begorra—Another Irish expression
Hold your horses—Wait a minute
Blarst my bloody eyes—A British expression
A blooming silly ass—Another British expression
Fall guy—Easy mark
Stuffed monkeys—Small pastry filled with jelly
A beetle—A cheap horse—race-track parlance
Beating the music box—Playing the piano after hours
Get a satchel and ice tongs and haul it away—A race-track expression
Wouldn't that keep you waiting?—Make one hesitate
The lad with the loud lingo—Boisterous person
Back to the woods for yours—Back where you started
Pass the cream, please—Introduce me to the peach
All to the good and two to carry—The best ever
Revelry rags—Dressed up to kill
Chewing the fat—Professional for gossip
You're falling away to a ton—Failure to reduce
Shake hands with a caterpillar—A repulsive person
Isch ge bibble—I should worry
Money stealer—Round, feathery, flying particles of pussy willow
Whole shootin' match—The whole works
Stop your shenanigans—Quit teasing
Jawbreakers—Difficult words

Aw! He's too big for his britches—Self-centered, puffed up
A leather medal—A doubtful honor
Yapping—Repeated scolding
Schlong-gongle—A long-legged person
Old man trust is dead—"Bad Pay" killed him (Old corner grocery reminder)
Horses for courses—Some racehorses prefer certain tracks
Dip—A pickpocket
Butt—Tail end of a cigar
Lean horse for a long race—Allusion to a thin girl
Nearer the bone, the sweeter the meat—Another
A short life and a merry one—Reference to short-lived actors
A drunkard's thirst—Dryness in the mouth
Spitting cotton—A gathering of saliva in unusual thirst
Gunboats—Shoes too large in size
"She" has a name—Objection to "she" as an appellation
Pousse café—Varicolored cocktail of the 90's
Forbidden fruit—A cordial at Bustanoby's Beaux Art, New York
Woman's crowning glory (her hair)—Now profanely called "Hollywood shrubbery"
French leave—A hasty exit
He's gone with Barnum—He's passed on
Janes—Gals
Swindle sheet—Employee's expense account
Tom and Jerry—A hot drink in winter
Low tide in the sugar bowl—Applicable just now
Put on your "stovepipe"—High hat
Oyster of the chicken—Dark marrow in chicken breast corners
No sirree Bob—An emphatic no
You're a sight for sore eyes—Equivalent of "Nice to see you"
Boston cooler—Muskmelon with ice-cream filling
Talking through your hat—Useless gesture
All chassez—Movement in old-time square dance
The Reds—Choice seats near stage of a tent show
Peck horn—Alto horn
Slip horn—Slide trombone
Wildcatting a show—Sizing up the town, then booking it
Bladder—A dissipated female trouper
Ten per, and cakes—A "ham" actor's salary
Blood and thunder—Old Bowery dramas
The nut—Overhead expense of a show
Snipe the town—Billing the town
Tanglefoot—Bad whisky
Tackle the calfskin—Play the banjo
My stack of checks was not so strong—Short of cash
See double but you feel single—Feeling high
Fly a kite—Raising money on a note
Finders, keepers—Exclamation of a finder
Ciau-chow—Italian for so long
No soap—No bribe
No dice—No game
What do yer soy?—Tough for What did you say?
In the chips—In the money
In the blue chips—In the big money
Potsy—A hopping game on alternate numbered flagstones
Bilked—Cheated
Silver caster—Old-time family holder for condiments
Pulpit pounder—A minister
Sky pilot—A preacher
Ah, go sell your papers—Run along
Nightcap—Last drink before sleep
He dished you—He fooled you
Knocking down fares—Dishonest car conductors
All wool and a yard wide—A perfect person or object
Some crust—Some cheek
Cruiser—A streetwalker
Chief cook and bottle washer—Kitchen head
Turkey—A barnstorming theatrical troupe hastily organized around Thanksgiving Day
Side wheeler—A lame man
Milkmen's matinee—Variety shows in early Western mining camp theaters ran till four in the morning
Cupping and leeching—A sign in many old-time barbershops. Leeches for draw-

ing human blood were available

Mud hens—During the Comstock mining boom in San Francisco in the 70's, this was the title of females watching the stock ticker

And the villain still pursued her—From the 10-20-30-cent melodramas. Also used in conjunction with advertised articles. "And the villain still pursued her—in a Bay City hat"—etc.

Irish confetti—A brick

First-part ladies—Early variety theaters opened shows with female minstrel first part. After sitting in the ensemble, first-part ladies sold drinks on commission to patrons of the horseshoe circle of boxes

A block off the old chip—A large son with a small father.

Shiver my timbers—A nautical exclamation equal to "blast me"

Tapping the till—The game responsible for cash registers

Getting your walking papers—A notice of discharge

Save the pieces—Greeting the dropping of china or glass

Remove the debris—A sally to the waiter after a lobster feast

Quail on toast—The old-time bird that went with champagne

Three shakes of a lamb's tail—In a moment

Don't snitch—Don't tell

My onion—My watch

Boardinghouse reach—Hands across the dinner table

Lean on your supper—Admonition to a wife strolling after a meal

Put that in your pipe and smoke it—Think it over

FINALLY

I was drunk, pickled, pie-eyed, cock-eyed, bleary-eyed, glassy-eyed, ossified, spiffed, spifflocated, canned, inebriated, intoxicated, potted, plastered, oiled, boiled, half seas over, on a bender, on a toot, on a bat, on a tear, on a binge, tight, full, high, blotto, stewed, lit, embalmed, ginnied, soused, tanked, shicker, gesoffen, happy, fried, passed out, out cold, boozy, besotted, load on, edge on, bun on, liquored, three sheets to the wind, stiff, under the influence, worshiped at the feet of Bacchus, in my cups, I had a tide aboard.

There are 50 others, but space forbids: Besides, it's a good guessing game!

CALLING YESTERDAY

Harking back, so much happened that is different today that, as an interesting contrast, it is well worth referring to for the record. For instance, grapefruit was shipped on the boats to Mobile as ballast. They didn't care for the bitter taste.

In those days, the poor humble game of our fathers and grandfathers was L-O-T-T-O. Today, with variations, it has been transformed into B-I-N-G-O, with its gambling lure that has even caught the churches for charity affairs. What a box-office draw it now has, clothed in its many titles: S-C-R-E-E-N-O — K-E-N-O — B-A-N-K-R-O-L-L — P-U-S-H-O — F-O-R-T-U-N-E, etc.

The humble *pot cheese* of other days is now *cottage cheese* in summer boardinghouses.

Tonsils out is further tortured with the appellation *tonsillectomy*.

The old time *freak museum* is now the *odditorium*.

The old time *dance hall* is now the *danc-e-teria*.

The *old book shop* is now the *readers' museum*.

Appendicitis is bad enough—but now when they take it out they add an extra tail to the worm, and call it an *appendectomy*.

Redcaps adopted for a short period the jawbreaker *United Transportation Service Employees*.

The venerable old *shoemaker* is now a *doctor of shoes*.

The familiar *No Trespassing* is now *Posted*. It takes a Philadelphia lawyer to figure out why.

Confusion is absolute between an *optician* and an *optometrist*.

The pay-off in signs recently read "Rejuvenation Parlor"—a combined barbershop and laundry in the mountains. You went in with your laundry and came out with a haircut—not sure which branch of the business the sign referred to.

The ugly old *waterfall* hairnet of the 80's, used by old maids mainly, is the useful *curl catcher* worn by young ladies.

The office *clerk* or *clark*, as they would call them in "dear old Lunnon," is now the *receptionist*.

The simple *hairdresser* of time immemorial is now the *hair stylist* or the *scalp and hair counselor*. Girls certainly have their troubles with their God-awful hair-do's anyway.

The caption on music of ye olden times, *symphonies and accompaniment by*, in these speedy days is simply *arranged by*.

In the days long past, music was sold in the *music saloon*; today it's over the *music counter*.

The dignified *I beg your pardon* is now the curt, half-time *I'm sorry* and half the time they're not sorry, or even civil.

The *gunshot examiner* is now the *ballistics expert*.

For years we have had *piggie-back* rides. Now we have also *pickaback* planes.

In the days from the roaring 40's up to the 90's, men wore paper collars, paper cuffs and *dickies*, while the women wore *peekaboo* waists.

Powder monkeys sat stiff as statues, with arms folded, on artillery wagons.

But those were the days when cigar stores advertised with a *wooden punch* or a wooden Indian.

A man used to get his *package* in a saloon, or calling on New Year's Day, which took two days—men's day and ladies' day. Now he gets it in a *package* store and takes it home with him.

In the days before "Vitamins A B C D G," "Tomato Juice" and shirt coats for men, and long before the "cellophane" age fortunately covered a multitude of sins, we were satisfied to order our clothes from a good *merchant tailor*. Today you're not au fait if you do not patronize a *clothes stylist*, while milady goes to the *hair stylist* and *beautician*, instead of the *hairdresser*.

If you want to be very "chi-chi" you should patronize only the *flower stylist*, the *gent's stylist*, the *dentisterie*, and the *book-a-zine*.

Even the ancient *forge* evoluted into a *blacksmith* and it's now a *wagoner*. You bowl only in the *bowl-o-drome* and you buy *simulated* instead of imitation pearls.

Calling yesterday, there was "straight" and "place" betting only at the tracks, before Gleason made the first 1-2-3 or "show" book.

The modernists are even tampering with our fixed traditions of racing. A *foul* is no longer a *foul*; it's an *objection*. Of course the prima facie and real occurrence is a *foul* when committed. The *objection* is secondary and follows the foul. However, a foul by any other name sounds just as bad, so let's keep it the old way in baseball.

Before the beardless age, when mustaches, sideburns and Vandykes signified men, the society divorce of nouveau-riche "Mrs. Hyphen-Hyphen" and the "Count of no account," with an eye on her bank account, came under the head of public amusements in the scandal sheets.

Harking back, before *heebie-jeebie* and the *poo-poo-pa-doop*, the haughty *haberdasher* of today was just a *gent's furnishing store* and the *realtor's* sanctum sanctorum was the lowly *real estate office*.

The *bar and grill* or the *drinkery* was just a *saloon*. There were no *drink-o-mats* or *soda-mats*, just *soda fountains*. The green and red liquid-filled globes, that the lights shone through, designated apothecary shops, as familiar as the wooden Indians, that, in all their regalia, pointed out cigar stores.

The *bargain* basements of yesterday in department stores are now *budget departments*, and even *pipe hospitals* are popping up in our modern business life.

Before the days of *Palookas* and *playboys*, young blades who wore "choker collars" and "dirty-shirt hiders" (ascots) were called, in the lexicon of the flaming youth of the 90's, *dudes*. They were just about as tiresome as a train that doesn't go about its business.

Today the humble *undertaker* of old is a *mortician*, while the modern shoe store displays the sign *pedemodes* and the gas station at the corner is a *lubritorium*.

Those were the days when you shaved in a *barbershop* and left your own mug on the shelf. Nowadays you shave in a *tonsorial parlor* and have to take your mug home with you.

In the years before tea bags, we had *ice-cream parlors*—now some are *ice-cream bars*.

In the kerosene age, the good old country meeting place was the old grocery store, which is now being citified into a *farmery*.

The *aquarium* of other days is now slated to be the *oceanarium*. Poor fish!

What simple happy days were those of linen napkins in all restaurants, seven-cent foaming pints in all saloons, and good oyster stews with old-fashioned big oyster crackers and cole slaw—all for two bits.

"Looking back," it is not alone in things trivial that we have progressed. Our scientists have figured out sanitation, air conditioning, shatterproof glass, radio and many marvels of this modern age. They have made the discoveries of "Athenium Agoria," "ultramicroscopes," "artifacts," "inelastic properties of the earth's interior," also "radioactivity," "prehistoric American culture," "geodesy," "seismology" and many other new ologies.

If I may be pardoned for straying a bit off the path of old-time theaters, artists and music in this one chapter, I should like to suggest this: Take time out, Mr. Scientist, and give us practical home escalators that will start and stop by electric buttons and switches, so grandma, mother and dad wouldn't have to climb those stairs 'steen times a day. How much longer they'd remain with us!

Medical science claims it takes 18 times as much energy to climb stairs as to walk a like distance on the surface. A recent news heading read: "Heart ailments responsible for 72% of our 1,450,427 fatalities." "Time Marches On" and a vastly growing host of victims of our national disease march on with it. "Watch your step and save your steps" should be the slogan with mass escalators the solution. We are a nation of stair climbers: stairs at home—stairs in the subways—railroad stations—race tracks—baseball stands—art galleries—libraries and public buildings. Little wonder heart disease is killing off prematurely, high-pressured executives and other folks by the thousands. If, in the general scheme of things, we must lend distance to dignified becolumned public edifices, have your legislators insist on one or two artistic, cute, storm-covered escalators on the side, and 97 out of every 100 will travel up that way. In other words, less carved stone decoration and more public health and comfort. Department stores long ago sensed the burning necessity of escalators for shoppers.

"Looking back" again—one smoker in a family was the general rule in father's day. Now as I enter a commuter's train and hurry through the smoking cars—plural since both sexes indulge in the weed—I'm sorry, girls, but I must conclude this: Any one of you, who can sit in a smoker night and day with men on railroad trips, each of the sexes inhaling the cigar or cigarette breath of the other, till the bad air is thick enough to cut with a knife and strong enough to stick in your clothes a week, well, any girl who can take that is strong enough to open her own car windows and doors. Frankly, I rather like a girl who lights a cigarette at the right time and place. But imagine courting the girl of today in the celluloid-collar days. If she puffed a cigarette and threw her arms around your neck, there would be some combustion!

Don't you love the little cigarette-smoking creature in the telephone booth, who holds a 15-minute conversation, while you impatiently wait outside? She is standing off some persistent youth at the other end, who wants to inveigle her into an immediate date. She spars and fences, smirks and smiles, rattles off beautiful alibis, promising to see him some other night. You frown, and if looks could kill, she would drop dead. Finally it seems she's going to hang up, but catching her second wind, she smiles benignly at you, starting all over again after depositing her fourth nickel. Meanwhile you hang on, listening to the youth in the next booth giving someone a sure-fire tip on a horse for tomorrow, as he blows clouds of smoke, adding to the foul air of the overworked and abused telephone machine.

There ought to be a law against idiotic, unnecessary, long-winded telephone conversations. People who just babble sweet nothings in a public telephone booth should be put in the stocks. They waste breath, exhale superfluous germs, and give those waiting the busy-gong jitters. Many a critical message is sideswiped by a senseless "chin-wag."

FINALE AND CURTAIN

The recent passing of my good friend, Henry Edward Warner, reminds me of one of his poems. Mr. Warner was a veteran newspaperman in Baltimore, connected with the *Baltimore Sun* for many years. He was also the writer of much verse and hundreds of songs, one of his best-known being "I've Got a Pain in My Sawdust," introduced by Kitty Cheatham in 1908. It is with profound respect to his memory that I quote his poem called "Introspection":

The more I think of who I am, and where I am, and what I am,
The more I think the gods must laugh at what a puny spot I am!
An ant, a crawling thing, a tiny moving molecule I am,
And in my most exalted wisdom, what an errant fool I am!
What finite things to infinite, the dents of Earth to sunspots are,
What time is to Eternity, a candle-flicker to a star,
So is my feeble little soul to that great First Intelligence
That brought me here, and in Its time shall turn the glass and send me hence.

What plans I have, what work I do, what mountains I essay to move,
What thoughts I think, what arguments, what things I labor so to prove,
What grandeurs I may dream, and what as grandeur may delight my eyes
Fade into nothingness beside the glory where the sunset lies!
Could I invent a singing bird or guide a river where it flows:
Could I lend color to the sky or perfume to the stately rose?
O foolish man . . . what futile boasts! The mightiest triumph of your span,
Your greatest work stopped long before the plan of infant gods began!
And so the more I think, I see my true proportions in the glass
And stand uncovered, so to let some disillusioning cortege pass;
And so within my heart I hope for courage in the strife and stress,
But needing strength, I'll find it only when I look to humbleness.

INDEX

Index

OCT 22 1947